THEORIES *of* COUNSELING *and* PSYCHOTHERAPY

CONTEMPORARY APPLICATIONS

James Archer Jr.
University of Florida

Christopher J. McCarthy
University of Texas at Austin

PEARSON

Merrill
Prentice Hall

Upper Saddle River, New Jersey
Columbus, Ohio

Library of Congress Cataloging in Publication Data

Archer, James.
    Theories of counseling and psychotheraphy : contemporary applications / James Archer,
Christopher J. McCarthy.
        p. cm.
    Includes bibliographical references and index.
    ISBN 0-13-113803-0
    1. Mental health counseling.   2. Psychotherapy.   I. McCarthy, Christopher J.   II. Title.
    RC466.A73 2007
    616.89'14—dc22   2006008904

Vice President and Executive Publisher: Jeffery W. Johnston
Publisher: Kevin M. Davis
Development Editor: Autumn Crisp Benson
Editorial Assistant: Sarah N. Kenoyer
Production Editor: Mary Harlan
Production Coordinator: GGS Book Services
Design Coordinator: Diane C. Lorenzo
Text Design and Illustrations: GGS Book Services
Cover Design: Candace Rowley
Cover Image: Corbis
Production Manager: Laura Messerly
Director of Marketing: David Gesell
Marketing Manager: Autumn Purdy
Marketing Coordinator: Brian Mounts

This book was set in Berkeley Book by GGS Book Services. It was printed and bound by R. R. Donnelley & Sons
Company. The cover was printed by The Lehigh Press, Inc.

Pearson Education Ltd.   Pearson Education Australia Pty. Limited
Pearson Education Singapore Pte. Ltd.   Pearson Education North Asia Ltd.
Pearson Education Canada, Ltd.   Pearson Educación de Mexico, S.A. de C.V.
Pearson Education–Japan   Pearson Education Malaysia Pte. Ltd.

10 9 8 7 6 5 4 3 2 1
ISBN: 0-13-113803-0

Preface

Welcome to the fascinating and challenging study of counseling theories! This book is designed to introduce you to the major theories so that you can begin the process of deciding which theory or theories work best for you. We hasten to add that for us, and for many counselors and therapists, this is an ongoing process, and certainly not one that can take place as a result of reading and studying one book. We have written this book primarily as a textbook for beginning graduate students in counseling, psychology, social work, psychiatric nursing, and any other counseling-related field. However, it is also appropriate for undergraduate students seeking to learn more about the field of counseling. We do not assume that readers have any previous coursework or experience in the field, and while we review some of the research associated with each theoretical approach to provide a sense of how this is accomplished for each theory, we do realize that some students may not have previous coursework in research methods or statistics. Our intent is to cover the major theories that have shaped the development of the profession and to demonstrate how these ideas translate into therapeutic interventions.

We hope that our discussion of the various theories allows you to see how your own views and attitudes fit with each approach. One of the major developmental tasks for graduate counseling students is developing their own theoretical approach to counseling. Most do not align themselves with a particular orientation until they are well along in their graduate studies, and even then, many describe themselves as "eclectic" or "integrationist." Eclectic therapists generally draw from a range of different theories, depending on the particular needs of their clients, the setting they work in, and a number of other factors. Integrationists are somewhat similar but usually distinguish themselves by a more systematic way of integrating the various counseling approaches than does someone who is simply eclectic. The point here is that there is no magic formula for deciding on a theoretical orientation. Counselors usually arrive at a theoretical orientation gradually through the influence of their studies, instructors, field supervisors, and personal comfort level with the assumptions of each theory. As you learn about each approach, we encourage you to carefully weigh the assumptions of each counseling model against your own values, experiences, and beliefs.

We want to convey our own interest in and enthusiasm for the field. For us, counseling is about finding meaning and purpose, overcoming obstacles in life, and developing innate potential—in other words, it is about what it means to be human. As we write this book, the field of counseling and psychotherapy seems to be at a crossroads. There are questions about how best to use these counseling models with persons from diverse backgrounds, including such factors as gender, ethnicity, nationality, socioeconomic level, disability, religion, and sexual orientation. Additionally, counseling services cost money, and there is the issue of who pays for them. Some insurance carriers that provided generous mental health benefits a few decades ago have begun asking hard questions of counselors, such as how long clients need to be seen and which approaches provide the quickest treatment for a given diagnosis. Schools and colleges, as well as government agencies and private corporations, are increasingly finding it difficult to provide extensive counseling benefits, and many public psychiatric hospitals and community counseling centers have faced severe budget cutbacks in recent years.

These developments have caused many to question the manner in which counseling services are delivered. An implicit assumption of many of the theories reviewed in this book is that individual clients will seek the services of a counselor when they are no longer able to cope with life circumstances, either because of changes in their lives or because of problems in their psychological functioning (or both). But some argue that perhaps counseling services should be oriented toward groups of people, such as small therapy groups, classrooms, or even neighborhoods and communities. Many also suggest that services should be geared more to prevention of human problems than to remediation, following the old adage that "an ounce of prevention is worth a pound of cure." The bottom line is that all of the theories reviewed in this book are subject to continued debate, research, and modification as we seek to adjust to the demands of the modern world.

SUPPLEMENTARY MATERIALS

Video Role Plays DVD

A set of two DVDs entitled *Video Role Plays* is packaged with this text. The DVDs include video clips of counseling sessions in progress and illustrate how techniques and concepts discussed in the text are used in counseling sessions. Following each video clip, the authors discuss the concept or technique used and how this session may affect future sessions. DVD icons appear throughout the text in the margin to direct you to the appropriate video clip on the DVD.

Online *Instructor's Manual and Test Bank*

The *Instructor's Manual and Test Bank* contains personal application questions, learning activities, multiple-choice questions, and essay questions. The personal application questions and learning activities stimulate students' thinking and help them apply the theories in the text to their own experiences. The *Instructor's Manual and Test Bank* is available online on the Instructor Resource Center at **www.prenhall.com**. To access this supplement, go to **www.prenhall.com**, click on the Instructor Support button, and then go to the Download Supplements section. Here you will be able to login or complete a one-time registration for a user name and password.

Companion Website

You can find the Companion Website for this text at **www.prenhall.com/archer**. For each chapter of the book, the Companion Website presents Main Ideas that identify the chapter's central issues, Multiple-Choice and Essay Questions that allow students to self-assess what they have learned, and Additional Resources and Web Links that provide additional books, articles, journals, videos, and Web sites that relate to chapter content.

ACKNOWLEDGMENTS

My part of this book could not have been completed without the generous and loving support of my wife Karen, and the inspiration provided by many years of clients and graduate students. I also want to mention that the love and support of my two sons, Brian and Jeremy, and what I learned from them about parenting and the developmental process has had a profound effect on my understanding of counseling and psychology. My parents, James and Dorothy, instilled in me a sense of perspective and fairness, and a great respect for hard work and the potential that we all have to influence our own destiny. This has strongly influenced my writing and thinking about psychology and counseling. Finally, I want to thank my co-author Chris McCarthy for agreeing to take on this project with me and for his humor and good nature throughout the entire process.

James Archer

I have many to people to thank for their support as I worked on this book. First, my wife Shelley provided unending love, patience, and encouragement throughout. My children Colleen and Sean provided inspiration by being wonderful children and for their good humor and understanding when they asked, "Are you working on that book again?" I am also very thankful to have wonderful role models in my parents Robert and Nancy.

I am indebted to the graduate students who have taken my classes, conducted research with me, and generally made my job so rewarding. It is their passion for the field that inspired me in this project. Two former graduate students were extremely helpful in preparing this book, Anna Dematatis and Mikalea Sebree.

Finally, I want to thank Jim Archer for the opportunity to co-author this book. As with most writing projects, this one has been both more demanding, and much more rewarding, than I could have expected.

Chris McCarthy

We would both like to thank the following reviewers for their helpful comments and suggestions: Tim Davidson, University of Oklahoma; Phyllis Erdman, Washington State University; Kevin A. Fall, Loyola University New Orleans; Jeannine Feldman, San Diego State University; Mary A. Hermann, Mississippi State University; Marcia V. Marinelli, University of Maryland; Constance R. Matthews, Pennsylvania State University; Thomas Scofield, University of Nebraska at Kearney; and Richard E. Watts, Baylor University. We would like to acknowledge Development Editor Autumn Benson and Publisher Kevin Davis for their support throughout.

We are very grateful to Stephanie Sarkis, Natalie Arce Indelicato, and Shauna Springer for their work on the chapters on Psychopharmacology and Feminist Counseling.

Stephanie Sarkis received her doctorate in Counselor Education from the University of Florida, where she is now an adjunct professor teaching the diagnosis and treatment class. Her dissertation on ADHD received an "Outstanding" dissertation award from the American Psychological Association. She is an NCC LMHC and is the author of *10 Simple Solutions for Adult ADD*, published by New Harbinger. Stephanie is the Director of Evaluations and Assessments for Sarkis Clinical Trials and Sarkis Family Psychiatry in Gainesville, Florida. She also maintains a private practice in Gainesville.

Natalie Arce Indelicato is a Visiting Clinical Assistant Professor at the University of Florida Counseling Center. She received her doctorate in Counselor Education from the University of Florida. Her dissertation examined racial differences in the relational health and depressive symptoms of college women. Natalie co-authored an invited chapter on sexual victimization and college students for a compendium on college mental health practice (in press) and has published on topics such as depression in college women and the impact of men's disclosure of their HIV status. She has considerable experience in campus outreach programming related to eating disorders and sexual assault, and teaches a psychoeducational transition to college.

Shauna H. Springer is currently an Intern Counseling Psychology at the University of South Florida. She received her bachelor's degree from Harvard University, her Master's from Iowa State

University, and PhD from the University of Florida, where she received the "Outstanding Counseling Psychology Student Award." She received a McLaughlin dissertation research award for her doctoral dissertation, which involved a review and meta-analysis of over 300 articles focusing on the effects of external stressors on marital satisfaction. Shauna identifies herself as a narrative therapist and has long-term clinical interest in relationship issues, couples counseling, and women's issues, with a particular focus on body image and eating disorders.

About the Authors

James Archer I have been a Counseling Psychologist for over 30 years. As a therapist, I have experience with adolescents, college students, adults, couples, groups, and families. I was a psychologist and director of a large university counseling center. I have also been in private practice and worked as a consultant for a variety of businesses and organizations, including a stint as consulting psychologist for what was then called a boy's reform school. I have also been a professor of counselor education and psychology and taught mostly applied counseling courses for many years. I love teaching counseling theories, and I have always been fascinated by the many different theories and how different students develop their own approaches to counseling. I received a master's degree in Counseling at San Francisco State University and my doctorate in Counseling Psychology from Michigan State University.

My original therapist training was psychodynamic, not classic analytic, but with a strong emphasis on many classic Freudian principles. As behavioral and cognitive approaches were researched and more widely used, I began to focus more on behavior and thinking. Adlerian psychology appealed to me as I became more interested in how thinking affects behavior, and I really liked (and still do) the Adlerian notion that as people grow up, they develop beliefs about themselves and the world that strongly influence how they behave in the present. More recently, I have been teaching a brief therapy course and have been interested in solution-focused and narrative therapy. These approaches, which are called postmodern, reflect many of the humanistic principles in which I have always believed. My ideas about counseling and therapy have evolved and are still changing. I am challenged and learn from each client I see and from each student who takes one of my classes.

Culturally, I have been most influenced by my Italian heritage and a strong family press to get an education, work hard, and be successful. I am a White male and have, of course, been influenced by gender-role socialization, particularly, I think, in terms of responsibility and high achievement. I have been married for 34 years and have two grown children. In my adult life, certainly the most significant influences on me have been related to family. I feel extremely lucky and grateful for a wonderful and long-lasting relationship with my wife and for the chance to raise two boys who have become warm, caring, and socially responsible men.

I am coauthoring this book primarily because I think it is a great challenge to present material about so many counseling theories in a way that is accessible to students and which allows students to understand how each theory works and to somehow experience what it would be like to be a client and a therapist using the particular approach under study. I really enjoy helping students figure out which theories make sense for them and how they will somehow fit together a theory and approach that work for them. I see the study of this book as a starting point on this journey.

Christopher J. McCarthy My career as a psychologist is a bit shorter than that of my coauthor. I've been in the counseling field for about 15 years now, and I've worked as a high school counselor, as a substance abuse counselor, and as a college counselor while I was in graduate school. After receiving my doctorate, I decided to pursue research and teaching as a career, while also maintaining a small private practice. Like Jim, I teach mainly applied courses in counseling and psychology that help me stay current with trends in professional practice.

I was initially trained in object relations theory, which I came to realize did not really fit me well. I tend to be a somewhat practical, results-oriented person, and the object relations approach did not really suit this part of my personality. One approach that I did favor very early in my training was Carl Rogers's client-centered approach. His nondirective, empathic techniques seemed to me to be the very embodiment of what a counselor should be: warm, caring, and supportive.

Another approach that I rely on heavily in my counseling work is cognitive-behavioral therapy (which you will read about in this book). Early on, I was fascinated by how much our daily experiences are shaped by our perceptions—which are not always entirely accurate. As Shakespeare wrote in *Hamlet*, "There is nothing either good or bad, but thinking makes it so." I am also quite interested in so-called postmodern theories such as solution-focused therapy and narrative therapy (which you will also read about in this book). As you can tell, I am constantly refining my approach to counseling by learning what works for me (or doesn't work!) in my own life. And I learn far more from my students and clients than I teach them.

Counseling is primarily concerned with what it means to be a human being, and every day I learn more about what it means to be a husband, a father of two children, a son, a sibling, a teacher, a researcher—the list goes on and on. I agree wholeheartedly with my coauthor that becoming a counselor is as much a personal journey as it is a professional one. Throughout this journey, I have had the privilege of being happily married for 18 years and together raising two wonderful children who are now 18 and 11 years old. My family is not only a source of strength and support for me but also the foundation for the way I view the world and my relationships with other people. I began my training in the early 1990s, at a time when awareness of human diversity in the counseling process was just beginning to be recognized as a necessary component of counseling training. I was challenged in many ways to examine the impact of my own background as an Irish Catholic middle-class American on the way I viewed the world: in my classes and readings, by my clinical supervisors, and, most important, by my work with clients. I have much to celebrate and cherish about my background, but I am also continually working to recognize how best to understand how others view the world and their experiences.

RESEARCH NAVIGATOR:
RESEARCH MADE SIMPLE!

www.researchnavigator.com

Merrill Education is pleased to introduce Research Navigator—a one-stop research solution for students that simplifies and streamlines the entire research process. At www.researchnavigator.com, students will find extensive resources to enhance their understanding of the research process so they can effectively complete research assignments. In addition, Research Navigator has three exclusive databases of credible and reliable source content to help students focus their research efforts and begin the research process.

How Will Research Navigator Enhance Your Course?

- Extensive content helps students understand the research process, including writing, Internet research, and citing sources.
- Step-by-step tutorial guides students through the entire research process from selecting a topic to revising a rough draft.
- Research Writing in the Disciplines section details the differences in research across disciplines.
- Three exclusive databases—EBSCO's ContentSelect Academic Journal Database, *The New York Times* Search by Subject Archive, and "Best of the Web" Link Library—allow students to easily find journal articles and sources.

What's the Cost?

A subscription to Research Navigator is $7.50 but is available at no additional cost when ordered in conjunction with this textbook. To obtain free passcodes for your students, simply contact your local Merrill/Prentice Hall sales representative, and your representative will send you the Evaluating Online Resource Guide, which contains the code to access Research Navigator as well as tips on how to use Research Navigator and how to evaluate research. To preview the value of this website to your students, please go to www.educatorlearningcenter.com and use the Login Name "Research" and the password "Demo."

Brief Contents

CHAPTER 1 Introduction 2

CHAPTER 2 Psychoanalytic and Psychodynamic Theories 20

CHAPTER 3 Adlerian Counseling 64

CHAPTER 4 Person-Centered Counseling 96

CHAPTER 5 Existential Counseling 128

CHAPTER 6 Gestalt Therapy 162

CHAPTER 7 Reality Therapy 194

CHAPTER 8 Behavior Therapy 232

CHAPTER 9 Cognitive Approaches 266

CHAPTER 10 Feminist Therapy 310

CHAPTER 11 Family Systems Approaches 340

CHAPTER 12 Solution-Focused Therapy 384

CHAPTER 13 Narrative Therapy 418

CHAPTER 14 Psychopharmacological (Biological) Approaches 448

CHAPTER 15 Review and Current Trends 470

Contents

CHAPTER 1 Introduction   2

What Do Counseling Theories Have in Common?   3

How Did We Decide Which Theories to Include in This Book?   5

How Are Counseling Theories Evaluated?   6

How Do You Know if a Client Is Ready for Counseling?   7

What About Managed Care?   8

Multicultural and Diversity Issues   9
    Multicultural Models   *11*
    Theory Dimensions and Multicultural Counseling   *12*
    Multicultural Competency Guidelines   *14*
    Counseling with Specific Populations   *15*

Values and Ethical Issues   16
    Ethics Codes   *17*
    Ethical Principles   *17*

Overview of the Chapter Structure   18

CHAPTER 2 Psychoanalytic and Psychodynamic Theories   20

Voices from the Field: Counselor and Client Reactions   20

Historical Background   21
    Historical Context   *21*
    Development of the Theory   *22*

Assumptions and Core Concepts   29
    View of Human Nature   *29*
    Core Concepts   *31*
    The Unconscious   *33*
    Anxiety   *34*
    Defense Mechanisms   *34*
    Psychosexual Stages   *37*
    Summary of Core Concepts and Freud's Model of Personality   *40*

Therapeutic Relationship   41
    Counselor's Role   *41*
    Counselor-Client Relationship   *42*

Assessment, Goals, and Process of Therapy   42
    Assessment   *43*
    Goals   *44*
    Process of Therapy   *45*

Therapeutic Techniques   49
    Interpretation   *49*
    Free Association   *50*
    Dream Analysis   *51*

Multicultural and Diversity Effectiveness   52

Primary Applications   54
   Play Therapy   54
   Group Work   55

Brief Therapy/Managed Care Effectiveness   56

Integrating the Theory with Other Approaches   57

Research   58

Evaluation of Psychoanalysis   60

Questions and Learning Activities   62

CHAPTER 3   Adlerian Counseling   64

Voices from the Field: Counselor and Client Reactions   64

Historical Background   65
   Historical Context   65
   Development of the Theory   66

Assumptions and Core Concepts   67
   View of Human Nature   67
   Core Concepts   67

Therapeutic Relationship   74
   Counselor's Role   74
   Counselor-Client Relationship   74

Assessment, Goals, and Process of Therapy   74
   Assessment   74
   Goals   79
   Process of Therapy   79

Therapeutic Techniques   80
   Encouragement   80
   Setting Tasks   81
   Using Antisuggestion/Paradoxical Intention   81
   Acting As If   81
   Catching One's Self   82
   Using Push Buttons   82
   Avoiding the Tar Baby   83
   Creating Images   83
   Spitting in the Client's Soup   83

Multicultural and Diversity Effectiveness   84

Primary Applications   85
   Family Counseling/Parenting   85
   Children/Adolescents   87
   Group Work   87

Brief Therapy/Managed Care Effectiveness   88

Integrating the Theory with Other Approaches   89

Research   90

Evaluation of Adlerian Counseling   92

Questions and Learning Activities   93

CHAPTER 4   Person-Centered Counseling   96

Voices from the Field: Counselor and Client Reactions   96

Historical Background   97
Historical Context   97
Development of the Theory   98

Assumptions and Core Concepts   100
View of Human Nature   100
Core Concepts   101

Therapeutic Relationship   103
Counselor's Role   103
Counselor-Client Relationship   105

Assessment, Goals, and Process of Therapy   107
Assessment   107
Goals   107
Process of Therapy   108

Therapeutic Techniques   111

Multicultural and Diversity Effectiveness   114

Primary Applications   115
Couples and Family Counseling   115
Working with Children and Adolescents   115
Educational Settings   116
Group Work   117
Counselor Training   118

Brief Therapy/Managed Care Effectiveness   119

Integrating the Theory with Other Approaches   120

Research   121

Evaluation of Person-Centered Counseling   123

Questions and Learning Activities   124

CHAPTER 5   Existential Counseling   128

Voices from the Field: Counselor and Client Reactions   128

Historical Background   129
Historical Context   129
Development of the Theory   130

Assumptions and Core Concepts   133
View of Human Nature   133
Core Concepts   133

Therapeutic Relationship   137
    Counselor's Role   137
    Counselor-Client Relationship   140

Assessment, Goals, and Process of Therapy   141
    Assessment   141
    Goals   145
    Process of Therapy   146

Therapeutic Techniques   149
    Paradoxical Intention   149
    Dereflection   151

Multicultural and Diversity Effectiveness   151

Primary Applications   153
    Medical Patients   153
    Group Counseling   153
    Couples Work   154

Brief Therapy/Managed Care Effectiveness   155

Integrating the Theory with Other Approaches   156

Research   157

Evaluation of Existential Counseling   159

Questions and Learning Activities   160

CHAPTER 6   Gestalt Therapy   162

Voices from the Field: Counselor and Client Reactions   162

Historical Background   163
    Historical Context   163
    Development of the Theory   164

Assumptions and Core Concepts   166
    View of Human Nature   166
    Core Concepts   167

Therapeutic Relationship   173
    Counselor's Role   173
    Counselor-Client Relationship   175

Assessment, Goals, and Process of Therapy   176
    Assessment   176
    Goals   178
    Process of Therapy   178

Therapeutic Techniques   179
    Giving Directives   180
    Staying with the Feeling   181
    Empty Chair   181
    Having Clients Talk to Parts of Themselves   182
    Playing the Projection   183

Multicultural and Diversity Effectiveness   183

Primary Applications   185
  Group Work   185
  Couples Work   186
  Child and Adolescent Counseling   187

Brief Therapy/Managed Care Effectiveness   187

Integrating the Theory with Other Approaches   188

Research   189

Evaluation of Gestalt Therapy   190

Questions and Learning Activities   191

CHAPTER 7   Reality Therapy   194

Voices from the Field: Counselor and Client Reactions   194

Historical Background   195
  Historical Context   195
  Development of the Theory   196

Assumptions and Core Concepts   198
  View of Human Nature   198
  Core Concepts   199

Therapeutic Relationship   203
  Counselor's Role   203
  Counselor-Client Relationship   204

Assessment, Goals, and Process of Therapy   204
  Assessment   204
  Goals   206
  Process of Therapy   207

Therapeutic Techniques   212
  Using Questions   212
  Doing the Unexpected   214
  Using Bibliotherapy   214
  Allowing or Imposing Consequences   214
  Incorporating Physical Activity and Meditation   214
  Using Humor   215
  Listening for Metaphors   215

Multicultural and Diversity Effectiveness   *215*

Primary Applications   *217*
  School Settings   217
  Couples Counseling   220
  Group Counseling   222
  Work Settings   223

Brief Therapy/Managed Care Effectiveness   224

Integrating the Theory with Other Approaches   225

Research   226

Evaluation of Reality Therapy   228

Questions and Learning Activities   229

CHAPTER 8   Behavior Therapy   232

Voices from the Field: Counselor and Client Reactions   232

Historical Background   233
Historical Context   233
Development of the Theory   234

Assumptions and Core Concepts   234
View of Human Nature   234
Core Concepts   235

Therapeutic Relationship   239
Counselor's Role   239
Counselor-Client Relationship   240

Assessment, Goals, and Process of Therapy   240
Assessment   240
Goals   243
Process of Therapy   243

Therapeutic Techniques   244
Systematic Desensitization and Relaxation Methods   244
In Vivo Desensitization   247
Virtual Reality Exposure Therapy   248
Assertiveness Training   248
Self-Management   249
Multimodal Therapy   250

Multicultural and Diversity Effectiveness   252

Primary Applications   253
Children and Adolescents   253
Career Counseling   255
Group Work   256
Other Applications   257

Brief Therapy/Managed Care Effectiveness   258

Integrating the Theory with Other Approaches   258

Research   259

Evaluation of Behavior Therapy   262

Questions and Learning Activities   263

CHAPTER 9   Cognitive Approaches   266

Voices from the Field: Counselor and Client Reactions   266

Historical Background   268
Historical Context   268

Development of REBT   268

Assumptions and Core Concepts: REBT   269
View of Human Nature   269
Core Concepts   271

Therapeutic Relationship: REBT   273
Counselor's Role   273
Counselor-Client Relationship   273

Assessment, Goals, and Process of Therapy: REBT   273
Assessment   273
Goals   275
Process of Therapy   275

Therapeutic Techniques: REBT   276

Development of Cognitive Therapy   278

Assumptions and Core Concepts: Cognitive Therapy   279
View of Human Nature   279
Core Concepts   279

Therapeutic Relationship: Cognitive Therapy   282
Counselor's Role   282
Counselor-Client Relationship   282

Assessment, Goals, and Process of Therapy: Cognitive Therapy   283
Assessment   283
Goals   286
Process of Therapy   287

Therapeutic Techniques: Cognitive Therapy   287
Identifying Automatic Thoughts   288
Using Logical Analysis   288
Avoiding Retribution   289
Decatastrophizing   289
Challenging Maladaptive Assumptions   289
Modifying Cognitions with Behavioral Techniques   290

Integrated Cognitive-Behavioral Techniques   291
Stress Inoculation   291
Constructivist Cognitive-Behavioral Treatment   293
EMDR (Eye Movement Desensitization Reprocessing)   294
Problem Solving Therapy   294
Treatment Protocols   296

Multicultural and Diversity Effectiveness: REBT and
   Cognitive Therapy   297

Primary Applications: REBT and Cognitive Therapy   298
Couples/Family Counseling   298
Children/Adolescents   299
Group Work   300

Brief Therapy/Managed Care Effectiveness: REBT and Cognitive Therapy   302

Integrating the Theory with Other Approaches   302

Research   303

Evaluation of Cognitive Approaches   304

Questions and Learning Activities   306

CHAPTER 10   Feminist Therapy   310

Natalie F. Arce Indelicato and Shauna H. Springer

Voices from the Field: Counselor and Client Reactions   310

Historical Background   311
  Historical Context   311
  Development of the Theory   313

Assumptions and Core Concepts   315
  View of Human Nature   315
  Core Concepts   316

Therapeutic Relationship   318
  Counselor's Role   318
  Counselor-Client Relationship   319

Assessment, Goals, and Process of Therapy   320
  Assessment   320
  Goals   320
  Process of Therapy   321

Therapeutic Techniques   323
  Gender-Role Analysis   324
  Power Analysis   324
  Consciousness-Raising Groups   324
  Assertiveness Training   325
  Reframing and Relabeling   325
  Demystification of Therapy   326

Multicultural and Diversity Effectiveness   327

Primary Applications   328
  Couples and Families   328
  Men   328
  Children and Adolescents   329
  Feminist Groups   330
  Feminist Supervision   330

Brief Therapy/Managed Care Effectiveness   331

Integrating the Theory with Other Approaches   332

Research   333

Evaluation of Feminist Therapy   334

Questions and Learning Activities   335

CHAPTER 11   Family Systems Approaches   340

Voices from the Field: Counselor and Client Reactions   340

Historical Background   342
  Historical Context   342
  Development of the Theory   343

Structural Family Therapy   344
Salvidor Minuchin   344

Assumptions and Core Concepts: Structural Family Therapy   345
View of Human Nature   345
Core Concepts   346

Therapeutic Relationship: Structural Family Therapy   348

Assessment, Goals, and Process of Therapy: Structural
    Family Therapy   348

Therapeutic Techniques: Structural Family Therapy   349
Intensity   349
Enactment   349
Unbalancing   350
Complementarity   350
Reframing   350

Strategic Family Therapy   351
Jay Haley   351

Assumptions and Core Concepts   351
View of Human Nature   351
Core Concepts   352

Therapeutic Relationship: Strategic Family Therapy   354

Assessment, Goals, and Process of Therapy: Strategic
    Family Therapy   354

Therapeutic Techniques: Strategic Family Therapy   354
Directives   354
Paradoxical Interventions   354
Ordeal Directive   357

Intergenerational Family Systems Therapy   357
Murray Bowen   357

Assumptions and Core Concepts: Intergenerational
    Family Systems Therapy   358
View of Human Nature   358
Core Concepts   358

Therapeutic Relationship: Intergenerational Family
    Systems Therapy   361

Assessment, Goals, and Process of Therapy: Intergenerational Family
    Systems Therapy   362

Therapeutic Techniques: Intergenerational Family Systems Therapy   363
Genograms   363
Detriangulation   363
Going Home Again   365

Humanistic Experiential Family Therapy   366
Virginia Satir   366

Assumptions and Core Concepts: Humanistic Experiential
Family Therapy   366
   View of Human Nature   366
   Core Concepts   367

Therapeutic Relationship: Humanistic Existential Family Therapy   368

Assessment, Goals, and Process of Therapy: Humanistic
Existential Family Therapy   368

Therapeutic Techniques: Humanistic Existential Family Therapy   369
   Use of "I" Statements   369
   Family Sculpting   369
   Family Reconstruction   370
   Therapist Touch and Humor   370

Multicultural and Diversity Effectiveness: Family Systems Approaches   371

Primary Applications: Family Systems Approaches   372
   Couples/Marital   372
   Juvenile Offenders and Substance Abuse   373
   Domestic Violence   373
   Eating Disorders   374

Brief Therapy/Managed Care Effectiveness: Family Systems
Approaches   376

Integrating the Theory with Other Approaches   377

Research   378

Evaluation of Family Systems Approaches   380

Questions and Learning Activities   382

CHAPTER 12   Solution-Focused Therapy   384

Voices from the Field: Counselor and Client Reactions   384

Historical Background   385
   Historical Context   385
   Development of the Theory   386

Assumptions and Core Concepts   388
   View of Human Nature   388
   Core Concepts   388

Therapeutic Relationship   390
   Counselor's Role   390
   Counselor-Client Relationship   390

Assessment, Goals, and Process of Therapy   392
   Assessment   392
   Goals   393
   Process of Therapy   393

Therapeutic Techniques   398
   Miracle Questions   398
   Exception-Finding Questions   399

Scaling Questions   400
Coping Questions   400
Breaks   401
Compliments   401
Tasks   402

Multicultural and Diversity Effectiveness   402

Primary Applications   404
Groups   404
Couples   405
School Counseling   406
Involuntary Clients   408

Brief Therapy/Managed Care Effectiveness   409

Integrating the Theory with Other Approaches   409

Research   411

Evaluation of Solution-Focused Therapy   414

Questions and Learning Activities   415

CHAPTER 13   Narrative Therapy   418

Voices from the Field: Counselor and Client Reactions   418

Historical Background   419
Historical Context   419
Development of the Theory   420

Assumptions and Core Concepts   421
View of Human Nature   421
Core Concepts   422

Therapeutic Relationship   425
Counselor's Role   425
Counselor-Client Relationship   427

Assessment, Goals, and Process of Therapy   427
Assessment   427
Goals   428
Process of Therapy   428

Therapeutic Techniques   432
Questions   433
Metaphors   436
Therapeutic Documents   436
Therapeutic Writing   436

Multicultural and Diversity Effectiveness   437

Primary Applications   438
Family Therapy   438
Couples Therapy   440
Counseling Children and Adolescents   441
Group Work   441

Brief Therapy/Managed Care Effectiveness   442

Integrating the Theory with Other Approaches   443

Research   444

Evaluation of Narrative Therapy   445

Questions and Learning Activities   446

CHAPTER 14   Psychopharmacological (Biological) Approaches   448

Stephanie Sarkis and James Archer Jr.

Voices from the Field: Counselor and Client Reactions   448

Historical Background   449
Historical Context   449
Development of Psychopharmacological Approaches   451

Assumptions and Core Concepts   451
View of Human Nature   451
Core Concepts   452
Major Classes of Medications   453

Therapeutic Relationship   456
Counselor's Role   456
Counselor-Client-Physician Relationships   456

Assessment, Goals, and Process of Therapy   457

Therapeutic Techniques   459
Referrals for Medication   459
Educating Patients About Their Medication   461

Multicultural Applications   462

Primary Applications   463
Substance Abuse   463
Schools   463
Criminal Justice   464

Brief Therapy/Managed Care Effectiveness   464

Integrating Psychotropic Medication with Counseling Theories   464

Research   465

Evaluation of Psychopharmacological Approaches   466

Questions and Learning Activities   467

CHAPTER 15   Review and Current Trends   470

Review   471

The Common Factors and Empirically Supported
Treatment Approaches   471

Trends and Issues   482
    Multiculturalism   482
    Integration   483
    Brief Therapy   485
    Managed Care   485
    Psychopharmacology   486
    Computer Applications   487

What Next?   488

References   489

Index   513

Note: Every effort has been made to provide accurate and current Internet information in this book. However, the Internet and information posted on it are constantly changing, so it is inevitable that some of the Internet addresses listed in this textbook will change.

THEORIES *of* COUNSELING *and* PSYCHOTHERAPY

CHAPTER 1

Introduction

As you begin the study of different systems and methods of counseling and psychotherapy, you may be asking yourself these questions: Why should I study all these theories? Will they really help me be a competent professional? Both are excellent questions. However, before we can really discuss the usefulness of theories, we need to think about how to define *theory*. The dictionary gives several definitions: (1) a belief, policy, or procedure proposed or followed as the basis of action; (2) an ideal or hypothetical set of acts, principles, or circumstances; (3) a plausible or scientifically acceptable general principle or body of principles offered to explain phenomena; and (4) a hypothesis assumed for the sake of argument or investigation. One could argue that all of these definitions apply to counseling theories. Certainly, they are used as a basis for action, and their proponents consider them a plausible way to explain phenomena. They often include a set of principles, and many consider them to be rather tentative—that is, sets of ideas in need of investigation.

We think that counseling theories are very useful to the therapist on a personal level. Every counselor should have a reasonably clear idea of why she is doing what she is doing. This has several advantages. First, it gives the therapist confidence. We have heard hundreds of novice therapists say that they have no idea what they are doing. This usually makes them anxious, and this anxiety surely is communicated to their clients. By developing a clear rationale (personal theory) for what you are doing, you gain a sense of professional presence and expertise. Another advantage of having a theory is that it gives the therapist the ability to think through and plan counseling sessions. You cannot conceptualize what you are doing unless you have a clear way of thinking about it. In a similar vein, you cannot talk about what you are doing unless you have a common language to use with other counselors. We caution, however, that developing this sense of direction and personal theory takes some time, study, and hard work.

One important point we want to make may seem contradictory. On the one hand, we believe that counseling theories can be very useful in guiding counseling and therapy, but on the other hand, none of the theories presented here are really empirically or scientifically proven. Some have more research to back them up than others, but not one has really been accepted as scientific fact—like the law of gravity has been, for example. To illustrate this point, Goldfried and Padawer (1982) cited Charles Lamb's "A Dissertation upon Roast Pig." According to Lamb's humorous essay, early humans in China learned to cook pigs for food only after someone accidentally burned down a house with a pig inside it. People ate the charred pig and liked the taste, but they sure did not want to burn down a building to cook a pig for the next meal. So more practical means such as fire pits and ovens were eventually developed.

While ancients in China at least knew that fire was responsible for cooking pigs, in the field of counseling we are not even sure what mechanism is responsible for change. There seems to be something wonderfully healing about the counselor-client relationship, but we are not exactly sure what the key ingredients are, or the best way to use them for therapeutic purposes. This may explain why we still have so many different counseling theories with very different assumptions about the nature of the counseling relationship. Deciding which approach we prefer for a given person, from a given background, with a given problem, working with a given therapist is still difficult. To this day, there is some controversy as to how useful theories really are in the practice of counseling and psychotherapy.

WHAT DO COUNSELING THEORIES HAVE IN COMMON?

Hubble, Duncan, and Miller (1999) present some compelling arguments for a "common factors" approach. They argue that most of what is curative in counseling and therapy can be attributed to factors that are common to all theories of therapy. They suggest, from their review of counseling and psychotherapy outcome studies, that four major factors account for counseling outcome (client change and growth).

First, Hubble et al. say that 40% of the outcome of counseling is really related to factors in the client's life that cause or facilitate change. "As examples of these factors, persistence, faith, a supportive grandmother, membership in a religious community, sense of personal responsibility, a new job, a good day at the track, a crisis successfully managed all may be included (Duncan et al., 1997)" (Hubble et al., 1999, p. 9). In other words, good and bad experiences are a part of everyday life, and if a client happens to experience a "clustering" of good things while in therapy, these can account for 40% of what happens in counseling, no matter what theory is used.

Suggesting that the largest proportion of a client's success in therapy is the result of nontherapy factors may be surprising to you, but most approaches to counseling do not assume that 1 hour in therapy is sufficient to overcome the other 167 hours in a week that clients spend living their lives. In fact, one of the first things that many counselors do is seek to help clients mobilize resources in their lives—important relationships, self-care skills, community resources—that will help the clients benefit as much as possible from counseling.

Hubble et al. (1999) also contend that relationship factors account for 30% of outcome variance. Their definition of *relationship factors*, drawn from the literature, includes a number of factors that are present no matter what the theoretical orientation: "Caring, empathy, warmth, acceptance, mutual affirmation, and encouragement of risk taking and mastery are but a few" (Hubble et al., 1999, p. 9). Relationship factors therefore refer to specific behaviors on the part of the counselor and the client that strengthen their working relationship.

In the 1960s and 1970s, Carl Rogers, the founder of the client-centered school of counseling (which you will study in a later chapter), built much of his approach to counseling on what he called "core conditions" of the therapeutic relationship. In recent years, considerable research has been done on what has been called the "therapeutic alliance" between the counselor and the client. The following components of a therapeutic relationship, listed by Gaston (1990), have been measured by many rating scales: "(a) the client's affective relationship to the therapist, (b) the client's capacity to work purposefully in therapy, (c) the therapist's empathic understanding and involvement, and (d) the client-therapist agreement on the goals and tasks of therapy" (Hubble et al., 1999, p. 35).

The third factor that Hubble et al. (1999) identify that accounts for 15% of outcome is what they call expectancy and placebo effects. This is basically the client's belief that he will get better. You have probably heard of the placebo effect in medicine, where patients improve but not in response to the treatment used. In therapy, a similar phenomenon is thought to occur: If clients have faith in the therapeutic process and in their therapist, they are much more likely to benefit from counseling.

Finally, Hubble et al. (1999) suggest that the model/technique used by the therapist accounts for only 15% of the treatment effect. In their view, then, the specific theory or technique that the therapist uses is the least important factor in explaining counseling outcome.

This "common factors" view of counseling—in which a number of counseling theories are viewed as more or less equal in effectiveness—stands in stark contrast to a more recent movement in psychology in support of what are called "empirically validated treatments." Proponents of this approach assert that counseling and therapy should be treated as a science and that only those treatment approaches that have been proven successful with specific problems should be used by therapists (and paid for by insurance companies).

A group within the American Psychological Association began in the early 1990s to lobby for empirically validated treatments as an eventual standard for therapists (Chambless, 1993). In order for a treatment to be empirically validated, it must be spelled out in some detail. These detailed treatment plans are sometimes called treatment manuals or treatment protocols. We will discuss them in more detail in a later chapter.

By 1996, treatment guidelines had been developed or proposed for eating disorders, major depression, substance abuse, and bipolar affective disorder (American Psychiatric Association, 1996). There are currently treatment protocols being published for a number of disorders. For example, New Harbinger (2002) has protocols, with a manual for counselor and client available on its Web site, for overcoming agoraphobia, anger, depression, generalized anxiety disorder, obsessive and compulsive disorder, post-traumatic stress disorder (PTSD), and specific phobias. These treatment protocols all claim to be empirically validated.

We take a position somewhere in the middle in this controversy. We certainly agree that there are common factors among all theories. For example, it would be difficult to argue that the relationship isn't important in order for a therapist to be successful with any theory. The question, of course, is just how much the relationship contributes to the effect of counseling. There is also no question in our minds that the client's attitude about counseling, her level of hopefulness, plays an important part. We think, however, that the effective use of a theory by a counselor can help increase a client's hopefulness. For example, if the therapist is confident that what she does in counseling is effective, this attitude will be communicated to the client. Or if the therapist talks on the telephone with the client before counseling, as is advocated in some single-session approaches to counseling, the therapist may directly influence the client's perception by telling the client that her problem is one that counseling can help. The theory or approach the therapist takes can certainly play into how this expectancy is built.

It is hard to argue the point that Hubble et al. (1999) make that what the client brings into counseling is very important and helps determine the outcome of counseling. But in our view, the particular theory or technique used may have a decided influence on how the resources the client brings in affect the counseling. Take the example of a client who has a very supportive family and therefore brings that resource into counseling. One therapist—perhaps a family systems therapist—might immediately mobilize that resource to help with therapy. A different therapist with a different theoretical orientation might focus mostly on the negative thoughts and feelings a client has about himself and talk about how these feelings developed in early childhood, not paying much attention to the family resource and not helping the client activate that resource. The point we are trying to make here is that client differences and resources can, indeed, be influenced by the theoretical orientation of the counselor.

HOW DID WE DECIDE WHICH THEORIES TO INCLUDE IN THIS BOOK?

It has been estimated that there are over four hundred different theories of counseling and psychotherapy, and this number seems to be growing rapidly. This growth may be due in part to the increasing interest in and acceptance of counseling and psychotherapy by the general population. The fact that there has been a large increase in the number of therapists in recent years may also help account for the increasing number of theories. For example, Miller, Hubble, and Duncan (1996) report a 275% increase in the number of therapists from the mid-1980s to 1996. Of course, these four hundred theories vary in how well they satisfy the definition of a theory and in how much research evidence supports them.

You might be asking yourself, given the large number of theories available, which therapies counselors and other mental health workers use most frequently. In reality, most counselors and therapists call themselves eclectic. Eclectic therapists draw from a wide range of theories, depending on the particular needs of their clients and a number of other factors. However, even eclectic therapists usually favor certain theories. To be truly eclectic, one would need to be an expert in all different theoretical approaches. Jensen, Bergin, and Greaves (1990), in a study of clinical psychologists, marriage and family therapists, social workers, and psychiatrists, found that 68% identified themselves as eclectic. The therapists in the study indicated that they used an average of 4.4 different theories in their work. Following is a list of the percentages of those surveyed that used particular theories:

Adlerian	12%
Behavioral	49%
Cognitive	54%
Communications	35%
Dynamic	72%
Existential	26%
Gestalt	23%
Humanistic	42%
Religious/transpersonal	17%
Rogerian/person-centered	23%
Sullivanian	16%
Systems (family systems)	48%

Bechtoldt, Norcross, Wycoff, Pokrywa, and Campbell (2001) surveyed 6,000 psychologists regarding their theoretical orientations. 1,389 clinical and counseling psychiatrists were surveyed, with a 23% return rate. The most often listed orientations for Clinical Psychologists were Eclectic/integrative, Cognitive, Behavioral, and Psychodynamic (in that order) and those most often listed for Counseling Psychologists were Eclectic/integrative, Cognitive, Psychodynamic, and Interpersonal.

In reviewing a number of studies like this, two things are apparent. First, the particular profession seems to make a difference in orientation, and second, there are clearly general orientations that appear to be more frequently used. Eclectic, psychodynamic, and cognitive-behavioral approaches seem to generally be the most popular; however, if one surveys marriage and family therapists, the family systems approach will likely be the most popular. It is important to closely examine the categories in these studies. For example, in the Jensen et al. (1990) study, 72% of the therapists indicated that the *dynamic* approach was one of the theories that they used. This term might include classic analysis, the ego psychology approaches, and brief-therapy dynamic approaches.

In selecting theories for this book, we have taken into account the studies that indicate which theories are most often used. We have also included some theories partly because of their historical significance. In the end, we have covered the major theory divisions: psychodynamic, existential-humanistic, cognitive-behavioral, and postmodern-constructivist. As we will discuss later in this chapter, we have also attempted to infuse multicultural applications into our discussion of all the theories. We deliberately did not write a separate chapter on multicultural counseling because we think it must become a part of all counseling practice. We have included a chapter on pharmacology and counseling. This isn't exactly a separate theory, but the use of medication is certainly based on a biological view of behavior, and it is clearly something that counselors and therapists cannot ignore.

HOW ARE COUNSELING THEORIES EVALUATED?

As you might guess, there are several ways to answer this question. Practitioners, who have clients sitting in front of them wanting help, might be expected to choose a specific counseling approach because it works for their clients. If a client suffers from agoraphobia and a behavioral approach involving systematic desensitization helps alleviate her symptoms, we might expect that counselor to continue using that approach with future clients. The clients who seek counseling services also share the "nothing succeeds like success" philosophy, and so do third parties, such as health maintenance organizations (HMOs) and insurance companies who pay for counseling.

However, the fact that one client's symptoms are reduced with a particular counseling approach or technique is not sufficient proof that a counseling modality really works. Too many other variables come into play. As we discussed previously, the counselor-client relationship can be instrumental in success. So a counselor may attribute a client's progress to a given technique that was used, when in reality there is something about their interpersonal relationship that led to the client's progress. Perhaps it was the mere fact that someone took an interest in the client or that the counselor seemed like an expert and therefore inspired confidence and hope in the client.

Questions about which counseling theories work under what conditions are what inspire researchers to systematically investigate the claims made by the various counseling theorists reviewed in this book. However, the methodologies used to evaluate these theories vary widely, making it difficult to compare the relative effectiveness of each approach. For example, the early psychodynamic theorists relied mainly on case studies to demonstrate both the fundamental principles of their approach and its effectiveness. In contrast, behavioral theorists relied on a more scientific, empirical approach.

Since this is an introductory text, we have not focused a great deal on research supporting the different theories. The complexity of researching theories requires a reasonably strong background in research methodology and statistics, and even then sorting out the reliability and validity of different studies is very difficult. Adding to the complexity is the controversy about common factors versus the value of empirical research on specific theories and techniques. As you will see, we have included a brief section on research for each theory, giving you an overall idea of what research has been done, and we have also provided a sample study for each theory. We hope that this will whet your appetite to learn more about the research process and also to take time to read some journal articles about each theory.

In this book, however, we will concentrate on viewing theories mainly through the lens of the therapist. Hopefully, this will allow you to decide how well each theory "fits" you as a therapist. Does it fit with your view of human nature? Is it likely to work with the kind of clients you want to work with and in the kinds of settings where you want to work? Could you see yourself doing and saying the things recommended by the advocates of that approach? In order to do this, we will try to put you "inside" each theory by providing an overview of the central tenets of each theory, how it was developed, how it is practiced today, and how it is applied in a variety of settings.

HOW DO YOU KNOW IF A CLIENT IS READY FOR COUNSELING?

Not all clients who come in for counseling are ready to confront their issues and problems. Some come in because their mother, their husband, their lover, or a judge tells them they need counseling. Typically, these kinds of clients have not been considered to be "good" clients. Counselors sometimes feel frustrated, inadequate, or angry when clients who are not really ready to change show up in their office.

Prochaska and Norcross (2003) describe a model of stages of change that has been researched and was developed initially in the context of smoking cessation studies to deal with the difficult issue of client motivation. Their model of change, called the transtheoretical model, has evolved over time into a complex and comprehensive explanation of client change. The model identifies five stages of change, which we will discuss later in some detail, when we cover motivational counseling. The stages, however, can be applied to any counseling theory.

Clients in the *precontemplation stage* typically don't believe that they have a problem. A woman who is arrested for drunk driving and required to attend counseling by the court may be in this stage. She may think that she just happened to get caught this one time, while in reality she drinks heavily almost every weekend. Or a man who eats compulsively and who is very overweight may "overlook" the weight problem and think that he is just a bit husky.

Clients in the *contemplation stage* know that they have a problem but have not decided to do anything about it. Someone may know, for example, that she has social anxiety and that she just can't communicate with others. But she may continue being isolated and make no effort to do anything about her anxiety.

In the *preparation stage*, clients have made small steps toward change but aren't really making a serious attempt to change their behavior. The woman who is socially anxious, for example, might read a self-help book and half-heartedly try out a few of the suggestions.

In the *action stage*, clients are working very actively on change. They are willing to commit time and energy, and they typically have made progress toward their goals. Our client with social anxiety might be involved actively in therapy and be using some kind of anxiety reduction techniques to decrease her anxiety to the point where her social interactions are improving.

Finally, in the *maintenance stage*, the focus is on continuing progress and on efforts not to fall back into old behaviors and patterns. One very typical example might be lifelong attendance at Alcoholics Anonymous (AA) meetings. Part of the AA philosophy is that a person is an alcoholic for his entire life, even if he is not drinking. So attendance at AA meetings helps him maintain his sobriety.

Using this model of readiness can be very helpful in thinking about counseling theory and practice. After identifying the client's readiness stage, a counselor can focus her efforts on helping the client move into the next stage. The counselor can also help the client set more realistic goals and advise the client on the desirability of therapy at a particular time.

This idea of readiness stages merits consideration when evaluating counseling theories. Do some theories work better at different stages? Do some theories require a greater level of readiness? The time it takes to move through the stages and to be ready for change can vary considerably among individuals, and they may not always move through the stages in a linear fashion. A person may spend an entire lifetime in the contemplation stage or cycling back and forth between the contemplation and preparation stages, always thinking she would like to change but never doing anything about it. On the other hand, some life crisis might drastically change her circumstances and lead her to move quickly to the action stage.

WHAT ABOUT MANAGED CARE?

The term *managed care* refers to attempts to manage health care costs. Before managed care, doctors and therapists typically were able to decide how much treatment a patient needed. Insurance companies typically paid any claims that were submitted by doctors and therapists. However, when the costs of medical and counseling services skyrocketed and when the so-called third-party payers became responsible for most Americans' health care, there was need to "manage" the care to decrease costs.

The health care system today includes government programs such as Medicare and Medicaid, private insurance companies, and health maintenance organizations. As a result of the changes over the past several decades, particularly as HMOs have changed from nonprofit to for-profit entities, counselors are no longer accountable solely to their clients for the effectiveness of treatment. When a client paid his own way, counseling could continue indefinitely, as long as the client and counselor agreed that it was productive. Now increasing accountability has been demanded from counselors providing mental health services through clearly specified psychological diagnoses, well-defined treatment goals, and strict session limits. Managed care has had a very significant impact on how counselors use counseling approaches and theories. If a counselor has only 6 sessions with a client, she might decide on a very different approach from the one she might use if she was allowed to have 20 sessions with the client.

Everyone seems to agree that we must find some way to manage health care costs (and mental health costs are part of this equation), but arguments rage over how to do it. For some counselors and therapists, managed care is the devil incarnate. Many therapists in private practice have experienced enormous problems working in managed care systems. Perhaps the biggest complaint is that decisions about length of treatment have been taken out of the hands of professionals, who are the ones who should really be making these decisions. Shore (1998) argued that managed care is essentially immoral and that a corporate model of health care with a "bottom line" mentality sacrifices quality for profit. Austad (1996), in a book on the ethics of long-term therapy, argued that the previous mental health system was flawed and favored the small percentage of the population who could afford long-term therapy. She also presented data indicating that brief therapy is, in many instances, as effective as long-term therapy and that research demonstrating this has long been ignored. She discussed the dose response theory, supported by research, which proposes that the early sessions of counseling and therapy produce much higher gains than the later sessions. In other words, the initial dose of counseling is much more effective than the later doses. This might lead one to argue that if resources are limited, they should be used for briefer forms of therapy that are more cost effective.

Perhaps as a result of the need for the briefer forms of therapy required by managed care or perhaps because of the application of research findings and better training in brief approaches to counseling, brief therapy has become a very popular and much discussed model of counseling in recent years. Although many of the forms of therapy we will discuss in this book were originally developed without time limits in mind, most have been adapted to provide a briefer approach to counseling. This is not to say that many therapists do not disagree with this emphasis or to say that there are not still therapists who practice therapy for whatever length of time they and the client feel is necessary. These therapists, however, are typically not involved in insurance or managed care situations. They have strictly fee-for-service practices and are used by clients who can afford to pay. Because of the tremendous impact of managed care and the need for brief counseling, we have included adaptations of theories and discussions of how they might work in a managed care environment.

MULTICULTURAL AND DIVERSITY ISSUES

Although we cannot provide an extensive discussion of multicultural theory here, a discussion of several important issues will be helpful as you study how well the different theories work with people from diverse cultures. We define culture broadly, to include any subgroup that has a set of racial, ethnic, or behavioral characteristics (African Americans; Chinese Americans; gay, lesbian, and transgender persons; etc.). In order to understand the importance of avoiding "cultural encapsulation," a counselor must be truly open to seeing the world from different cultural perspectives. To do this, counselors must work to overcome what Sue and Sue (2003) call "ethnocentric monoculturalism." By this, they mean the assumption by counselors and other mental health therapists that there is a kind of universal set of psychological principles that apply across cultures and groups. Sue and Sue identify five specific components of ethnocentric monoculturalism: belief in one's own superiority, the inferiority of others, the power to impose standards, its manifestation in institutions, and the invisible veil. The invisible veil means that this monoculturalism operates largely in the unconscious. In other words, according to Sue and Sue, counselors and other therapists are unaware of their ethnocentric monoculturalism.

For example, take a counselor who is conducting career counseling with Jin, a Chinese American who is 31. As the counseling proceeds, the discussion focuses on the fact that Jin is unhappy with his work as an engineer. He wants to pursue a new career but is very conflicted because his parents think that he should remain an engineer. The counselor, who is a White female of European descent, assesses the situation and concludes that part of the problem is the fact that Jin, hasn't yet become independent from his parents. The counselor concludes that before Jin, can work on career exploration, he needs some personal counseling to help him work on separating more from his parents.

So what is wrong with this picture? The problem is the counselor's unconscious assumption that the developmental theory that she learned in her graduate human development program applies to all people in all cultures. She has failed to take into account Jin's worldview—his way of viewing the world and how people and families should function. In this case, Jin is from a first-generation Chinese family with very different assumptions about the role of parents and their relationship with their children. In order to escape her cultural encapsulation, the counselor needs to learn more about different cultures and give up the idea that Western psychology always applies.

Another example is the case of Duane, an African-American high school student who is being counseled by his guidance counselor, a former English teacher whose heritage is Norwegian. Duane, who has only a C average, has recently realized that he wants to work toward going to college. When he enters the counselor's office, he notices that the counselor has what Duane perceives to be a disapproving reaction to the way he is dressed. This puts Duane on the defensive, and he becomes silent and sullen. After a few minutes, the counselor concludes to himself that Duane is just not interested in academics and that he needs to explore vocational school. In this case, the counselor responded negatively, perhaps unconsciously, to Duane's clothing. This, in turn, made Duane defensive, and the counselor, concluding that his defensiveness was lack of interest, misinterpreted Duane's intentions. Here we see that the counselor is perhaps unaware of his negative reactions to Duane's dress and behavior, which are probably based on the assumption that his particular ideas about dress and behavior are correct.

Although the concept of cultural encapsulation is perhaps more related to counseling practice than counseling theory, we mention it here because even in evaluating the theories in this book, you must work to avoid culturally bound assumptions in order to truly see how the theories might affect diverse groups and cultures. We don't minimize how difficult this task is, and we are confident that nearly all counselors in training will get additional help with this issue and encouragement to learn about themselves in relationship to other cultures and other worldviews. A great deal has been written about ways in which counselors can begin to confront their own "invisible veil" and better understand and accept diverse cultures (Roysircar, Sandu, & Bibbins, 2003;

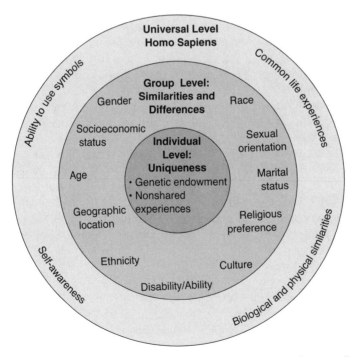

Figure 1.1 A multicultural human identity model. (D. W. Sue and D. Sue, *Counseling the culturally diverse: Theory and practice*, 2003. © Reprinted with permission of John Wiley & Sons, Inc.)

Parker, 1998). Clearly, we do not have the space to address this in depth, but some discussion of these issues will help in the examination of the theories.

Multicultural Models

One valuable tool in evaluating the theories from a multicultural perspective is a model or way of conceptualizing multicultural counseling. We offer a very brief discussion of parts of two models that might be helpful. First is Sue and Sue's (2003) basic model of personal identity. In a sense, this is their view of the areas and dimensions of a person's life that must be considered in effective multicultural counseling (see Figure 1.1).

In this tripartite model, human identity can be examined on three interconnected levels: universal commonalities, group similarities and differences, and individual differences. Note that there are many different groups to which a person may belong. Each of these can be seen as a kind of subculture that has its own unique values and characteristics. A counseling theory that allows or encourages an emphasis on all three of these dimensions has great potential for multicultural counseling. For example, how well does a particular counseling theory work for a 60-year-old, poor, gay, southern, divorced, Hispanic American? How does the theory account for his membership in several different cultures and minority groups? We hope that you will ask yourself these kinds of questions for every theory you study.

Ivey, D'Andrea, Bradford, and Simek-Morgan (2002) provide another model of multicultural counseling. They call it the RESPECTFUL model of counseling and development (p. xvii). Each letter stands for a set of important issues that must be considered in counseling:

R—religious/spiritual history

E—economic class

S—sexual identity

P—psychological maturity

E—ethnic/racial identity

C—chronological/developmental challenges

T—various forms of trauma and threats to well-being

F—family background and history

U—unique physical characteristics

L—location of residence

Each of these areas won't necessarily apply to every client, but a RESPECTFUL approach to counseling means that the counselor will do some level of assessment in each area. For example, Janet, a 45-year-old woman, comes in for counseling and complains of depression. The counselor, in this model, must consider all of the RESPECTFUL factors in counseling this person. By asking about her religious and spiritual background, the counselor learns that Janet has witnessed a number of tragedies in the last several years and her religious faith has been shaken. She comes from a very religious second-generation Italian family. Until recently, she was a devout Catholic herself, but she has not gone to church in several months. She feels very guilty about this, is worried about what her family will think, and is having a real crisis of faith. By exploring this aspect of the client's life, the counselor may have discovered that her depression is largely a result of this religious crisis. Had the counselor ignored this area of her life, she might have assumed that the problem was related to some other more psychologically oriented cause. And this is an example of just one area. Factors in any of these other areas might also have a direct bearing on her depression.

We like this model because of its simplicity and inclusiveness. Again, as you study the theories, ask yourself if the concepts and techniques of the theory allow for a consideration of these issues and an intervention that is appropriate for individual differences in each area. Does rational emotive behavior therapy allow for a consideration of the trauma of racism and oppression? Can person-centered counseling deal with a person who is living on the street?

Theory Dimensions and Multicultural Counseling

Four of the areas that we cover for each counseling theory deserve special attention here because of their relevance to multicultural theory: assessment, process, goals, and counseling relationship. By assessment, we refer to the formal and informal methods a counselor uses to understand and diagnose a client's concerns. The process of counseling refers to the manner in which it is carried out, while the goals of counseling refer to the ultimate outcomes the counselor and client work toward. The counseling relationship, of course, refers to the bond or alliance formed between the counselor and client.

Assessment A great deal of criticism has been leveled at traditional methods of assessment and diagnosis in terms of their application to minority groups. Atkinson (2004) cites a number of different studies showing that African Americans receive different diagnoses than Whites. For example, the studies show that African Americans are more likely to be diagnosed with schizophrenia and less likely to be diagnosed with anxiety disorders. There has been an ongoing debate for years about the disproportionately larger percentage of African-American children in special education classes. Critics have argued that the African-American children are inappropriately assessed as needing special education. Atkinson quotes a report from a 1999 steering committee of the National Institute of Mental Health (NIMH) criticizing the cultural bias of the *Diagnostic and Statistical Manual of Mental Disorders* (DSM), the major psychiatric diagnostic manual:

> The DSM has traditionally concentrated on pathology conceptualized as rooted and fixed in the biological individual. This ignores the way in which many psychiatric problems are not only substantially more prevalent among individuals facing social disadvantage but, in more important ways, constituted by those same economic, family, social, and cultural predicaments. (2004, p. 72)

Assessment, according to multicultural theory, should be based on two concepts: an understanding of the client's worldview and an understanding of the effects of oppression and discrimination by the majority culture. We should note here that formal assessment is not an important aspect of many theories; however, in a practical sense, counselors who use each of the theoretical perspectives are often forced to diagnose because of HMO or insurance company policies. Also, many theories have some form of assessment that fits conceptually with multicultural theory. Pay close attention to how well these assessment methods consider contextual issues like culture, race, and disadvantaged status.

Process The process of counseling can be described as the methods used by the counselor to bring about growth or change. Our underlying question is how effective the theory is in counseling diverse populations and in responding to and recognizing oppression as a factor in counseling. Sue and Sue (2003) focus a great deal on the importance of communication styles between counselor and client in effective multicultural counseling. They discuss several specific factors to consider: proxemics (physical space and distance), kinesis (body movements), paralanguage (aspects of language such as loudness, pauses, hesitation, rate, inflection), and high-low context communication (different meanings of language according to context). They also stress the importance of nonverbal cues and bias in interpretation. One example they cite is the common miscommunication between African Americans and Whites regarding the emotional intensity of communication. They suggest that African-American communication may be intense, emotional, and personal, while Whites may value reasoned, calm discussion, rejecting emotionally laden communication as nonproductive.

We must admit that we are uncomfortable with generalizations like this because of the great variation in styles within these two groups; nonetheless, we certainly believe that counselors should consider their own communication style and how it affects their counseling work with diverse populations. Counselors need to be able to respond appropriately to many different group values and communication styles. You should consider how well each theory allows and encourages a counselor to respond to these diverse values and communication styles.

It is important to note also that different cultures have different kinds of helpers and different ways of seeing helpers. For example, in Native American cultures, ceremonies such as sweat lodges and vision quests are seen as an essential part of holistic healing. Since traditional Native Americans see all things as connected, the concept of harmony has great importance. Counseling theories that take a holistic approach and allow for a more spiritual approach to healing may be more appealing and appropriate with Native American clients. Frey (2003) presents a case study with a Native American boy that incorporates narrative counseling: "Several of the youth's narratives, including those related to family relationships and to his identity development as a Native American, are presented and explored to provide a glimpse into the youth's personal meanings and experiences" (p. 119). D'Andrea (2000) suggests that postmodern, constructivist theories such as narrative counseling, which will be described in a later chapter, fit well with a multicultural perspective.

Goals Another major criticism of traditional counseling theories has been their focus on the individual and on individual change. Many cultures have a more collectivist orientation. As a result, one cannot think about the individual and individual change without considering the family and the social context. Another criticism of traditional counseling theories has to do with the separation of body and mind that seems prevalent in many Western-oriented theories. Continuing with our example of Native American cultures, would individual understanding or behavior change (typical goals of some counseling theories) work with a Native American client whose goal may be to feel a sense of harmony with and spiritual connectedness to the universe (D'Andrea, 2000)?

Another major aspect of multicultural counseling has to do with the sociopolitical nature of counseling work. According to multicultural theory, a counselor must understand that part, and perhaps a very large part, of the difficulties that minority clients present are the result of discrimination and oppression. Take a simple example of Art, a gay male client who works as a waiter. He comes to a counselor because he is depressed. A multiculturally sensitive counselor will immediately consider the possibility that discrimination and homophobia may be essential parts of his problems. In this case, as it turns out, several of the waiters where he works have made snide comments about his dress and the fact that he doesn't walk in a masculine way.

Although Art has dealt with these issues before, the current comments have brought up old feelings of self-doubt and fear of failure. We will raise issues like this as we go through each theory so that you can see how it might work from a multicultural perspective.

Counseling Relationship Although an effective counseling relationship is important in all theories of counseling, it is perhaps even more important in multicultural counseling because of the barriers that arise when client and counselor are from different cultures. How, for example, can a White female counselor really relate to an African-American male client? How can an African-American counselor connect with a first-generation Vietnamese client? There are many barriers, but because there may well be an extra element of mistrust or skepticism on the part of the client, the relationship is even more crucial.

The most obvious barrier to communication between client and counselor is language, and we don't necessarily mean different languages. Different cultures often use very different forms of the same language. A White counselor may have great difficulty understanding some expressions used by an African-American client. Nonverbal communication is also complicated by cultural differences. Eye contact in one culture may mean something quite different in another. The degree of emotional expressiveness may be very different between Asian-American clients and African-American clients. The degree of self-disclosure is another potential barrier. What works in one culture doesn't work in another. We could go on, but our point here is to provide you with some ideas to use when you read the different counseling theories.

We mentioned earlier that in multicultural counseling it is essential for counselors to understand their own biases and to work on getting beyond their own worldview so that they can understand and accept alternate ways of seeing the world. We note here one extension of this notion that multicultural theorists say is essential to effective multicultural counseling. This has to do with self-knowledge about White privilege and how that affects one's understanding of oppressed clients. In this view, White males, the most powerful members of our society, are seen as the most privileged. It follows, then, that it might be most difficult for a White male counselor to really understand the kind of world in which an African-American or Latina woman has grown up.

This notion is too complex to discuss in any detail here, but in general terms, we urge you to consider your own level of privilege and advantage when trying to communicate with someone who has been less privileged. In terms of counseling theory, you will see that two theories tend to accord the notions of oppression and privilege the most credence, feminist therapy and narrative therapy.

Multicultural Competency Guidelines

In 1992 Sue, Arrendondo, and McDavis published an article outlining multicultural competencies and standards in the *Journal of Counseling and Development*. The American Counseling Association (ACA) eventually accepted these standards, and soon thereafter many other counseling-oriented professions published similar guidelines of their own. More recently, Arrendondo, Toporek, Brown, Jones, Locke, Sanchez, and Stadler, working as the American Multicultural Counseling Division (AMCD) Professional Standards and Certification Committee, published a document operarationalizing the competency guidelines. Both of these documents can be accessed on the ACA Web site: www.counseling.org/Content/NavigationMenu/RESOURCES/ MULTICULTURALANDDIVERSITYISSUES/Competencies/Competencies.htm.

These are important documents to the counseling profession. We urge you to examine them closely as they are an important backdrop to studying different counseling theories. The guidelines have three basic sections: awareness of the counselor's own cultural values and biases, awareness of different worldviews, and selection of culturally appropriate strategies for counseling. They discuss attitudes, beliefs, and skills under each subheading.

For example, under awareness of different worldviews, culturally skilled counselors are aware of their own detrimental emotional reactions to other racial and ethnic views, and they are willing to consider their clients' worldviews without being judgmental. In terms of knowledge, culturally skilled counselors understand something about the background and cultural heritage of their culturally different clients and know something about the different models of cultural identity development. They also understand how ethnicity and race affect personality, career choice, psychological problems, and ways of seeking help. And they are aware of issues related to oppression and powerlessness, like poverty and racism. In terms of skills, culturally aware counselors examine the latest research on emotional problems prevalent in particular groups and seek out other experiences that foster their multicultural competencies. They also seek out involvement with people from other ethnic and cultural groups outside of counseling to broaden their understanding of different perspectives in more than an academic sense.

This information on multicultural counseling competencies may not seem directly relevant to the study of counseling theories, but in our views, the process of developing a personal theory through the study of the basic counseling theories should not be seen as a process separate from becoming a culturally sensitive counselor.

Counseling with Specific Populations

Part of what we see as progress in the area of multicultural counseling has been the increasing volume of research and writing about multicultural issues. One segment of this literature describes counseling issues related to specific populations (Atkinson, 2004; Atkinson & Hackett, 2004; Sue & Sue, 2003; Pederson et al., 2002). These resources are extremely helpful in acquainting a counselor with some of the context and issues relevant to a particular culture or group, but they do not necessarily apply to each person in each of these groups. There are considerable variations within groups, just as there are between cultures and groups.

In many instances, clients from different ethnic groups are caught between their traditional culture and the dominant society's culture, and this conflict is often central to the issues brought to counseling. A number of minority identity models have been developed to gauge the degree of identification a person has with his or her race or group. For example, gay, lesbian, and bisexual clients may move from denying their sexual feelings to gradually accepting themselves, with sexual orientation being only one part of a larger identity. When a client like this is in the midst of working through the coming-out process, sexual identity may seem like a very large part of his personhood. Another example might be a middle-class African-American college student who has grown up in the mostly White suburbs. In college, African-American students who identify much more strongly with African-American culture and issues of oppression may confront her. She may begin to develop a different aspect of her African-American identity because of her new peers.

You will need to ask yourself which theories allow for consideration of these types of issues. Few do so directly, but some theories seem to have more room for a kind of multicultural-developmental assessment. The theories that place an emphasis on a clear understanding of a person's individual level of development and how this interacts with the context of his life offer the best opportunity to include these kinds of considerations.

If these issues sound complex, you are right. They require careful consideration and reflection. Perhaps there is really no way to easily fit some of these multicultural concepts into many of the theories we cover. Many consider multicultural counseling to be a "4th force" in counseling, a new approach that has a life and message of its own. As you read these theories, you will be able to wrestle with these questions. Just how well can these very contemporary ideas fit with counseling theories developed in a different time and place and without a particular focus on the role of culture and oppression?

There are many excellent resources to help counselors develop their multicultural awareness, counseling skills, and knowledge of research in the area. We have already mentioned the ACA website. Other sources include Atkinson, *Counseling American minorities*; Atkinson & Hackett, *Counseling diverse populations*; Ivey et al., *Theories of counseling and psychotherapy: A multicultural approach*; Parker, *Consciousness-raising: A primer for multicultural counseling*; Pederson et al., *Counseling across cultures*; Roysicar et al., *Multicultural competencies: A guidebook of practices*; Sue & Sue, *Counseling the culturally diverse: Theory and practice*. (See the References at the back of the book for full citations.)

VALUES AND ETHICAL ISSUES

Before discussing the role of ethics in counseling theories, some clarification of terms is in order. Corey, Corey, and Callanan (2003) suggest that while *values* and *ethics* are used interchangeably, the two terms are not identical. Values pertain to what is *good* and *desirable*, while ethics are moral principles adopted by an individual or group to provide rules for appropriate behavior. For our purposes, values may also be construed as part of the belief system that an individual holds, whereas ethics may be seen as a set of rules sanctioned by a larger group or organization.

Consideration of your own values is important when evaluating the theories covered in this book. Each theory takes a particular stance as to what constitutes mental health, the factors that influence our development, and the best ways to address the concerns that clients bring to counseling. Choosing a counseling theory with which to intervene in a client's life is therefore not an ethically neutral act. The theories that counselors use reveal our values and outlook on the human condition.

As professions develop, standards for proper conduct are usually codified, and Keith-Spiegel and Koocher (1998) have defined the development of ethical codes as moral guides to self-regulation in an attempt to ensure the appropriate use of skills and techniques. Even though counselors may practice using different theoretical orientations, such standards ensure that all clients are served with the same basic standards of care.

While we will not be discussing legal issues in this chapter, it is worth noting that professional ethical codes are also distinct from laws and regulations passed by legislative bodies at the local, state, and federal levels. In many cases, the obligations set forth by ethical codes establish higher standards for professional conduct than the law, which is usually written in terms of what the lowest standards are for professional conduct. However, there are situations where a counselor's professional code of conduct may conflict with the law. For example, counselors must protect their clients' confidentiality, but if the client is involved in a legal proceeding, a judge may order the public release of information about the client. Counselors have various avenues for working through such conflicts, and there are many complex issues to be considered.

Ethics Codes

Standards for professional conduct serve a number of purposes, the most important of which are to provide guidelines for ethical behavior by members of the profession and to educate members of the public who utilize their services (Keith-Spiegel & Koocher, 1998). The American Psychological Association adopted its first code of ethics in 1953, based in part on surveys of its members' most common and difficult ethical challenges, and has revised it four times. Similarly, the American Counseling Association adopted its first code of ethics in 1961 and has since revised its code a number of times.

Practitioners become responsible for a given ethics code when they become members of the professional organization that developed the code. However, there are numerous specialty areas within a broad profession such as counseling, and each may establish its own set of ethical codes. The American Counseling Association, as noted above, has a general set of ethical principles that apply to each of its members, but it also has numerous specialty groups within its organization, such as counselors who specialize in career counseling, group counseling, or school counseling. Because each of these specialty areas entails unique ethical challenges that are not covered in much detail in more general ethics codes, specialty groups often develop their own ethical standards, which supplement the more general standards of the ACA.

For example, group counselors face unique challenges in protecting the confidentiality of their clients, since their personal information is revealed to other group members who are not bound by professional standards protecting their confidentiality. Therefore, the Association for Specialists in Group Work (ASGW), a part of the ACA, has developed specific guidelines to help group leaders handle confidentiality in group settings. Thus, a given counselor may belong to several professional organizations, each with its own set of ethical guidelines that the counselor is responsible for. While these codes usually do not contradict each other, and in fact are designed to help clarify ethical conduct in a specialty area of practice, the counselor is responsibile for being familiar with each.

Ethical Principles

The purpose of this book is to review counseling theories, so, of course, we cannot devote extensive discussion to counseling ethics principles, which deserve their own course (at least) in counseling training. However, two important ethical principles are directly relevant to understanding the theories covered in this book: the notion that clients are entitled to give informed consent for the treatment they receive and the principle that counselors practice only within the boundaries of their competence.

- **Informed consent**—Because of the ambiguities that exist in counseling practice, the varied means that different counselors use, and the importance of considering the client's goals and needs, an essential ethical practice is gaining the informed consent of the client before beginning a counseling intervention. While it is often impossible to fully inform the client about everything that can and does transpire in counseling, it is important to provide general information about the counseling theory or theories a counselor uses and possible risks associated with them, so the client can make an informed decision about whether to participate or not. Therefore, a counselor must not only understand the approach she is using but also be able to communicate enough about it to her clients that they can consent to treatment.

- **Competence**—Counseling, like most other fields, is broad and far-ranging. Counselors must carefully consider whether they have adequate training to use a given intervention and whether they have adequate experience in working with clients from a given background (i.e., age group, ethnic background, etc.). Understanding the counseling theories covered in this book is only the first step in developing the competence to actually put them into practice. Competence is acquired not just through formal coursework but also with ongoing professional development and supervision by a licensed, experienced counselor.

OVERVIEW OF THE CHAPTER STRUCTURE

Now that we have discussed how and why we picked the theories and have given you some basic introductory information, it is time to begin studying the different theories and approaches. In general, we have organized each chapter in the same way. This should provide a kind of model theory for you to examine each. We begin each chapter with comments from counselors and clients for whom the particular theory works or doesn't work; we call it *Voices from the Field: Counselor and Client Reactions*. These are representative comments that we have heard over the years, and we hope they communicate the idea that different theories work for different counselors and for different clients. We don't say that the criticisms in the "Doesn't Work for Me" category are necessarily fair, and we realize that they may be simplistic, but we are trying to communicate the fact that the preferences and perceptions of these theories and their practice vary a great deal.

Next we include a short dialogue and a general description of the approach, as a kind of introduction to the theory. Throughout each chapter, we make extensive use of dialogues between counselors and clients. In some chapters, one or two clients are examined in more detail throughout the chapter, while in other chapters, several different clients are introduced in brief vignettes—depending on which approach works best to illustrate the theory.

We have developed these dialogues to be representative of clients from different backgrounds. The gender of the counselor switches in each chapter—for example, in the chapter on psychoanalysis, the counselor is referred to as "she," while in the following Adlerian chapter, the counselor is referred to as "he."

We offer *Historical Background* information about the context within which the theory was developed and a brief description of the theory development. We then provide the *Assumptions and Core Concepts*. This includes the underlying assumptions as well as the basic tenets and concepts of each theory. Because of the importance of the relationship in counseling, we have included a separate section on the *Therapeutic Relationship* for each theory. After this comes our discussion of how you apply the theory, including *Assessment, Goals, Process, Multicultural and Diversity Effectiveness*, and *Therapeutic Techniques*. In these sections, we have included a number of short counseling segments to help illustrate the concepts involved in each section.

In order to give you an idea of how a particular theory is applied with different populations and in different settings, we cover the *Primary Applications for Each Theory*. Because issues surrounding *Managed Care Effectiveness* are so significant for all mental health practitioners, we also discuss how well the theory works with regard to these issues. Since part of your task will involve *Integrating the Theory with Other Approaches*, each chapter addresses this issue. This part may be a bit confusing because you may be reading about theories that you have not yet studied. We will come back to this issue in the concluding chapter. We think that all mental health counselors and therapists should have some understanding of counseling *Research*. As we have noted before, we don't assume that you necessarily have a background in research methodology and statistics; therefore, we have included only a limited discussion of the research on each theory, along with an example of a typical research study for that theory. Part of your task as a reader and student is an *Evaluation of the Theory* under study. We have included a section listing some of the strengths and weaknesses of each of the theories. We hope that you will get excited about some of these theories and want more information. So we have provided a Web link leading to *Resources (Professional and Self-Help Books, Journals, Web Sites, Videos)* to help you learn more about each theory. Finally, we encourage you to use the *Personal Application Questions and Learning Activities* to get a first-hand feeling for each of the theories.

CHAPTER 2

Psychoanalytic and Psychodynamic Theories

VOICES FROM THE FIELD: COUNSELOR AND CLIENT REACTIONS

Yes, it works for me

Client: I really got a lot out of my work with my counselor. I knew that some difficult things in my background were causing me problems and counseling really helped me understand them better. I've always had a really hard time believing in and standing up for myself. I understand now that the relationship I had with my uncle has a lot to do with how I am today. He and my aunt raised me, so he was like a father to me. It seems strange that even at the age of 47 what happened in my childhood still plays a big role in my life. My uncle was a very rigid and opinionated guy. I was never able to stand up to him, and he ran my life until I moved out on my own. My counselor pointed out that I was being really deferent and always agreeing with what he said, just like I did with my Dad. It was pretty tough to talk about those early years, and it brought up a lot of emotions. But now that I understand things better, I think I can make some changes in my life.

Counselor: It's funny. I never thought I would use Freud's ideas in my counseling, especially since I don't really believe in things like the Oedipus complex. I have found, however, that clients really do play out their relationship problems with the therapist and that you can almost always go back to find out how their current problems are related to experiences in the past. And it is true that the clients are often not really aware of these connections—they really do have defense mechanisms that help them avoid dealing with their issues.

No, it doesn't work for me

Client: Well, I've been in counseling for about four months now, and I'm really not getting anywhere. I still feel really anxious a lot of the time. I already knew that growing up in an abusive family was pretty bad for me, and I can see how always being afraid has led to me being really nervous all the time. But how do I get over it? It doesn't seem like understanding everything helps all that much.

Counselor: I know that there are some modern versions of psychoanalysis that don't necessarily involve years on the couch, but I just can't get into this whole idea of people having these underlying problems that are hidden and need to be pulled out. Sure, some people don't understand their problems, but I think that once they go into counseling, they can learn some problem-solving skills that will help them make change in their life. I'm just not comfortable talking to the client about transference and countertransference. To me, that doesn't seem to have much to do with the specific problems that they bring in.

Roy is a 25-year-old Caucasian male who has been depressed on and off for a number of years. He can't seem to hold a job, although he has a community college degree in X-ray technology. He has been in counseling for a month, and this is his fifth session.

> **Roy:** I don't really think you can help me that much. This whole counseling thing seems like a big waste of time.
>
> **Counselor:** So I guess you are thinking about giving up on it.
>
> **Roy:** Well, I often leave here emotionally exhausted, and I'm just tired of all the effort that doesn't seem to pay off.
>
> **Counselor:** Remember when you told me about your Mom and how she did everything for you, even when you were old enough to do a lot of things for yourself?
>
> **Roy:** Yeah, she was really overprotective.
>
> **Counselor:** And when you did want to be independent, you had a really hard time.
>
> **Roy:** Let's not blame it on my Mom.
>
> **Counselor:** Well, it might sound like that, but I would like you to consider how your wanting to quit therapy and being angry with me for not taking care of you may be similar to what happened between you and your Mom.

Sigmund Freud's theories have profoundly influenced the practice of counseling and therapy for over a century. Although many people think only of classic psychoanalysis, with a patient on the couch, going to therapy frequently for many years (as portrayed in many movies and TV shows), many different theories and approaches have evolved from Freud's theories. In most of them, some of the basic Freudian ideas—like the unconscious, defense mechanisms, and transference—are still seen as important (these terms will be defined and discussed in some detail later in the chapter). In the example above, Roy's psychodynamically oriented therapist is trying to help him link his current feelings and behavior (anger and wanting to leave therapy) to earlier experiences. In very simple terms, the idea is for Roy to understand how his anger and inability to overcome obstacles (therapy, work) are related to his past. The other major goal is for the therapist to help him work through the feelings (anger and fear) and related defense mechanisms (repression of that anger and fear, leading to depression and the inability to persist in the face of obstacles). This occurs within the context of the therapeutic relationship.

HISTORICAL BACKGROUND

Historical Context

Sigmund Freud was one of the most important scientific thinkers of the twentieth century. His theory of a divided mind powered by largely unconscious sexual and aggressive drives resulted from his efforts to understand both the rational and the irrational aspects of human nature. He published one of his most important works, *Three Essays on the Theory of Sexuality*, in 1905. This was about the same time that Albert Einstein published his theories on the nature of light that would transform modern physics and a few decades after the publication of Charles Darwin's *The Origin of Species* in 1859. Each of these revolutionaries changed his respective field, but it was Darwin's ideas about evolution and Freud's theory of the unconscious that were particularly controversial. Western thinkers of the 1800s and early 1900s, who had developed a view of humans as uniquely rationale creatures separate from the animal world, had great difficulty with the idea of humans as somewhat irrational creatures descended from apes.

Although Freud's theories were formed primarily in the late 1800s and early 1900s, the entire twentieth century was the backdrop for the evolution of his ideas into a multitude of different "analytic"-oriented approaches. These different approaches were all influenced by many different contextual factors. Freud developed the original theory in Western Europe during the Victorian era, a time when sexuality was not discussed openly and there was a great emphasis on proper behavior and rigid roles for men and women. Men essentially had absolute control over business, industry, the church, and the home. One must understand this rigidity and the ways in which sexual matters were hidden, at least from public view and discussion, to appreciate how revolutionary Freud's ideas were.

Because there are so many different branches of analytic thought and theory, we cannot discuss the developmental context in much detail; however, three major factors in the twentieth century stand out as influential. First was the immigration of many classically trained analysts to the United States as a result of World Wars I and II. This led to a very strong psychoanalytic movement in the United States—some would say to the exclusion of other approaches for some time.

The second factor was the development of other major forces in psychotherapy, particularly humanistic and behavioral psychology, in the middle of the twentieth century. Humanistic and existential therapists, who advocated a closer, more personal kind of relationship, challenged the idea of a detached analyst conducting an analysis of a client without establishing much emotional contact with the client. Humanistic therapists also were strongly opposed to Freud's basic view of humans as driven by sex and aggression. The behaviorists, seeking more concrete and visible results in counseling, also challenged the psychoanalytic movement and were at least partially responsible for shifting many psychoanalytic therapists toward more focused approaches dealing with specific problems. Both of these influences had an impact on psychoanalytic therapy, moving it toward counseling that involved a face-to-face process that was shorter and perhaps less concerned with psychosexual development and character change.

The third influence was the advent of briefer therapies and managed care at the end of the century. As psychotherapy became more common and acceptable, clients and therapists looked for counseling that took less time and that helped them deal with the increasing stresses and problems associated with the fast pace of modern life. Add to this the fact that health care costs were rising rapidly in the last few decades of the twentieth century, with an associated increase in the cost of counseling and therapy, and you have a strong rationale for briefer and more efficient treatments. Even though modern-day psychodynamic therapists do not necessarily do very brief therapy (1–10 sessions), many have accepted newer psychoanalytic applications that move therapy along more rapidly.

One other interesting note is the way in which psychoanalytic therapy has affected many fields of study outside of psychology. The richness of the theory and its applicability to nearly every human endeavor have attracted attention far beyond the psychotherapeutic community.

Development of the Theory

Freud grew up in a large Jewish family, which placed high value on learning and education. The family moved to Vienna, Austria, when Freud was four years old. He showed great intellectual promise as a child and was an outstanding student. He graduated from the University of Vienna with a medical degree in 1881, and in 1883, he did a residency in neurology and psychiatry.

During his studies, he had become acquainted and collaborated with Josef Breuer, a physiologist and physician. Freud was strongly influenced by one of Breuer's patients, who became known as Ana O. She was suffering from hysteria (temporary paralysis due to psychological factors), and Breuer used hypnosis to successfully treat her. Freud was impressed with these results and went on to study with Charcot, a famous neurologist known for his study of the use of hypnosis to treat hysteria. These experiences, studying how hypnotic suggestion could be used to cure patients with physical symptoms, most certainly influenced his later writing about the unconscious mind.

Although Freud had more interest in academic pursuits, he opened a private practice in 1886 in order to earn enough money to marry and have a family. He learned that a technique called *free association*, having patients lie on a couch and say whatever came into their minds, worked as well as hypnosis in helping patients remember past traumatic events that were caus-ing their current problems. In 1900, he published The *Interpretation of Dreams* (Freud, 1965), a work that presented his ideas on the unconscious mind. In 1901, he published *The Psychopathology of Everyday Life*, hypothesizing that slips of the tongue (Freudian slips) were expressions of the unconscious mind. During this period, he began a self-analysis, examining childhood memories and his childhood hostility toward his father and sexual attraction to his mother. In 1905, when he published his ideas about the importance of childhood sexuality and described the Oedipus complex, childhood sexuality, and the fact that sexuality was such a pow-erful force in personality, he was ostracized for views that were decidedly against Victorian values. In 1902 he became a professor at the University of Vienna and began to gather followers. Soon thereafter he formed the Vienna Psychoanalytical Society, a group of his students and colleagues who met regularly to discuss his theories.

Freud continued to work, develop his theories, and publish prolifically. In 1909, he came to the United States and presented his work at Clark University. This was the beginning of a large and influential psychoanalytic movement in the United States. Freud was diagnosed with jaw can-cer in 1923 and underwent a number of operations and treatments for the rest of his life. The occupying Nazi forces allowed Freud and his family to immigrate to England in 1938, and he died in 1939. Several writers have chronicled Freud's life, the most notable being Ernest Jones (1961).

The impact of Freud's pioneering work on the practice of counseling is unparalleled, and lit-erally hundreds of books have been devoted to it. Many of the counseling models in this book were at least partially inspired by his work or developed in reaction to his ideas. Several impor-tant offshoots of his work were developed by his contemporaries in the Vienna Psychoanalytical Society, such as Alfred Adler, Carl Jung, and Otto Rank, who broke with Freud over fundamen-tal differences in explaining human behavior. Other theorists did not break with Freud but sought to follow in his footsteps, while at the same time refining aspects of the theory, particu-larly the social functions of the personality component Freud labeled the *ego* (to be explained later in this chapter). These theorists go by various labels such as neo-Freudians, self psycholo-gists, and object relations theorists. In terms of contemporary approaches to counseling, Freud's original model of therapy is still referred to as psychoanalysis, while offshoots of his approach such as object relations therapy, which are inspired by Freud's ideas but represent significant departures from Freudian orthodoxy, are typically referred to as psychodynamic theories. We will provide an overview of each of these offshoots of psychoanalysis to show you the many ways in which Freud's work was carried forward to contemporary times.

Freud's Contemporaries: The Vienna Psychoanalytical Society Several members of the Vienna Psychoanalytical Society, while strongly influenced by Freud, developed philosophical differences with him and went on to create their own approaches to counseling. Alfred Adler resigned in 1911 as president of the Society over fundamental differences with Freud about the nature of human motivation. In Chapter 3, we will discuss Adler's individual psychology.

Adler was not the only charter member of the Society to have differences with Freud. Carl Jung, a Swiss physician, was handpicked by Freud to succeed him as leader of the psycho-analytic movement, but Jung followed Adler in resigning as president of the Society in 1913. Whereas Freud attempted to develop a mechanistic theory of personality and therapy based on what was known in his time about human neuroanatomy, Jung was as strongly influenced by religion and philosophy as by medicine. Some of Jung's differences with Freud centered on the nature of the unconscious mind, especially Jung's belief that unconscious processes develop not only from early childhood experiences but also from universal human archetypes.

Jung believed that in addition to a personal unconscious consisting of memories repressed since childhood, humans possess a collective unconscious that is expressed in human culture through art and mythology. Jung noted certain patterns and themes that seemed to transcend specific cultures and historical times, and he theorized that these became part of our collective unconscious. This collective unconscious is inhabited not by actual memories passed down by ancestors but rather by inherited reactions to or impressions of events that humans have encoun-tered over and over throughout history. So along with personal memories, these archetypes become an important component of unconscious life. For example, our reaction to sitting out-side watching a sunset derives partially from our own history of feelings associated with this experience and also from physiological imprints of these reactions passed down genetically through generations of humans watching the sun set (Jung, 1956). Jung developed analytical psychotherapy as a method for bringing both aspects of the unconscious, the personal and the collective, into conscious awareness through methods such as assessment, dream interpretation, and the therapeutic relationship (Jung, 1956).

Otto Rank, another member of Freud's inner circle, found himself ostracized for breaking with major tenets of psychoanalytic thought. Rank came to Freud's attention after he published a book in 1907 attempting to explain art in psychoanalytic terms. Rank served as secretary to the Vienna Psychoanalytical Society, and from 1912 to 1924, he edited the *International Journal of Psychoanalysis*. Rank began to depart from Freud in that he emphasized the mother-child rela-tionship in psychological development, rather than the father-child relationship, and envisioned a less authoritarian role for the therapist. The final nail in the coffin was his publication of *The Trauma of Birth* (1929), in which he emphasized the trauma of birth as the main source for psy-chological symptoms. Freud, who emphasized difficulties in psychosexual development during the first few years of life as the cause of psychopathology, objected strongly to Rank's ideas, and the two parted ways.

Neo-Freudians While ex-Society members such as Adler, Jung, and Rank broke with Freud over major theoretical differences, other theorists sought not to refute Freud but rather to develop neglected aspects of psychoanalytic thought (Monte, 1987). These so-called neo-Freudians included Freud's daughter Anna as well as Eric Fromm, Karen Horney, and Harry Stack Sullivan. While Freud mainly wrote about the vulnerability of the ego to internal psycho-logical wars between the id and superego, the neo-Freudians focused on the adaptive ways in which the ego copes with the demands of the outside world.

Freud's daughter Anna Freud (1971) continued his work, but as a result of her intense study of child development, she began to emphasize the ego as a more dominant force in personality development. The ego, as you will learn, is the integrative part of the psychoanalytic personality structure that focuses on conscious processes and that allows people to balance different parts of themselves as they interact with the world. This was really the beginning of a major shift in analytic thinking. As Wachtel and Messer (1997) put it, "one of the main clinical and theoretical contributions of psychoanalytic ego psychology was to soften and modulate the sweeping claim of Freudian instinct theory that virtually all behavior was energized by, and directly or indirectly, overtly or covertly, in the service of drive gratification" (p. 44). Her student Erik Erikson expanded ego psychology (1950, 1968, 1982; Erikson & Erikson, 1997) and developed a biopsychosocial model of human personality development through the life span, which will be described later in this chapter. As opposed to the classic Freudian emphasis on psychosexual development, Erikson emphasized the importance of the connection between social forces and biology in psychological development. Perhaps the most well known aspect of his theory is the *identity crisis*, part of his adolescent developmental stage.

Karen Horney and Erich Fromm are two other major figures who began as psychoanalysts but came to emphasize social motivations for behavior more than sexual and aggressive impulses. Horney (1942) wrote extensively about the helplessness of infants in early life, which can produce both anxiety and anger toward parental figures, especially if the parents are indifferent to the child's needs. Horney described three unhealthy ways in which a "neurotic personality" deals with the outside world: (1) "moving towards," in which the individual essentially becomes a doormat for other people by giving in to every request; (2) "moving away," by separating oneself from other people and their concerns; and (3) "moving against," by constantly fighting or struggling with others.

While Horney believed that indifferent parents were at the root of neurotic behavior, Fromm (1941) was strongly influenced by the writings of Karl Marx and viewed the larger society, especially industrial capitalism, as the culprit in producing isolation and distress. He was also influenced by existentialism, a brand of philosophy and an approach to counseling we will describe in depth in Chapter 5. Fromm (1976) wrote that the effects of modern consumerism on humans, who have a fundamentally good nature, can be expressed in two modes of being: the having mode, which is consumer oriented, and the being mode, which has to do with the innate qualities of the person but which resists description and categorization.

While Horney and Fromm both recognized social motivations for behavior, Harry Stack Sullivan, another important figure in the development of psychoanalytic thought, theorized that personality actually resides in relationships rather than in the individual (Sullivan, 1953). Sullivan, who received a degree from an unaccredited medical school in 1916, became known for working successfully with male patients hospitalized for schizophrenia. Influenced by both Freud and Jung, he theorized that his patients' disturbances were caused by a split of various personality functions from the conscious control of the ego, thus leading to disorganized speech and thought (Sullivan, 1962). Sullivan's theorizing about the roots of these disorders was also influenced by the work of the famous development psychologist Jean Piaget, who set out a model of how cognitive abilities, particularly in abstract thinking, develop in early childhood and adolescence. Sullivan's complex theory of personality was based on the assumption that views of ourselves are formed primarily in relationships with others and that we learn from early interactions with caregivers how best to manage the anxiety provoked by these relationships.

While Sullivan wrote about an interpersonal therapy based on his ideas in the 1930s, his work did not translate directly into a counseling approach, as did Adlerian counseling and Jungian analysis. However, Gerald Klerman and his wife, Myrna Weissman, developed a more contemporary approach called interpersonal therapy based in part on Sullivan's ideas (Klerman, Weissman, & Rounsville, 1984). A central idea in this short-term structured approach is that working with problematic interpersonal relationships is an important component of treating individuals with depression.

Object Relations Theory   The infusion of Freud's original ideas about psychoanalysis with theories emphasizing social relations led to another type of psychoanalytic theory called object relations therapy. Cashdan (1988) noted that the name for this form of counseling can be confusing: What is an object anyway, and what does it have to do with therapy? The answer is quite straightforward: Objects actually refer to people, and the therapy centers around our relationship with others, whether imagined or real (Cashdan, 1988).

Classic Freudian theory emphasized parent-child relationships as part of the Oedipal stage (characterized by infantile sexual feelings toward a parent and subsequent competition with the mother or father) from ages 3 to 5. Object relations theory emphasized relationships in the first few years of life with other people who become internalized symbolically as "objects" before the traditional Oedipal stage. In other words, starting in the first months of life, infants begin constructing very basic templates of themselves and the outside world (objects) based on their interactions with their primary caregiver, traditionally the mother. The representations of ourselves and other people that we construct in early childhood were theorized to have a powerful impact on our relationships with the outside world, and other people in particular, later in life.

Among the most influential object relations therapists was Melanie Klein (1932), a contemporary of Freud who was among the first to use psychoanalysis with children. This alone made Klein a revolutionary because Freud worked only with adults and their recollections of childhood events. Because children could not engage in the same type of verbal process as adults, Klein pioneered the field of play therapy, in which children's interactions with dolls, toys, and drawings were used for analysis instead of patient-therapist discussions—this will be discussed in more detail in the "Primary Applications" section of this chapter. Klein's play therapy interventions led her to the realization that children devoted far more time to constructing their interpersonal worlds than they did to controlling libidinal drives, as Freud had suggested. These interpersonal worlds were mainly developed through the mother-child relationship, which formed the prototype for subsequent relationships later in life.

Donald Winnicott (1965, 1971, 1975), a British pediatrician, talked about the importance of having a "good enough mother" who provides love and care but also helps the child begin to develop independence. If this occurs, the child develops a "true self" and can become a well-functioning and independent person. If it does not occur, then a "false self" is developed; an adequate independent self with confidence and personal boundaries does not develop. Therapy involves helping the person replace the negative internalized object (self) with a positive object (self).

William Ronald Dodge Fairbairn (1954) is another important figure who is often grouped with Klein and Winnicott as part of the British school of object relations therapy. Fairbairn disagreed with Freud's notion that we are motivated by pleasure seeking or bodily gratification. Instead, he proposed that humans are primarily driven by the need for relationships with others.

Fairbairn described the ideal process of child development as moving from early dependency on caregivers to more mature relationships marked by mutual dependence. In describing how this process unfolds early in life, Fairbairn (1952, 1954) incorporated the notion of splitting, a primitive psychoanalytic defense mechanism in which object representations of others are split into that which is "all good" and that which is "all bad." As with many ideas from object relations theory, this is difficult to describe in brief terms. The gist is that very early in life children are entirely dependent on their primary caregiver but also have to cope with the fact that sometimes she or he disappoints them by being harsh, indifferent, or unavailable. This is extremely threatening to the helpless child and is handled by psychologically constructing both "good object" and "bad object" representations of the caregiver, which get invoked depending on the infant's experience with the relationship at that time. Very strong emotions are attached to both representations: Positive feelings of love and warmth ensue when the good object representation is invoked, while extreme feelings such as rage accompany the bad object representation. If parents continually provide an atmosphere of frustration and rejection, Fairbairn (1954) believed the child might have difficulty moving past this primitive defense when relating to other people in adulthood.

"Splitting" is one of the characteristics of borderline personality disorder described in the *Diagnostic and Statistical Manual of Mental Disorders*. It was exhibited by Glenn Close's character in the movie *Fatal Attraction*. In her early affair with Michael Douglas's character, she was extremely affectionate and kind, but once her philandering partner disappointed her by returning to his wife, she became enraged and violent.

Fairbairn painted the process of psychological development in fairly broad strokes (Cashdan, 1988), but Margaret Mahler (1968), a Viennese pediatrician, provided a more detailed account of the way that relationships with the objects (i.e., people) in our world are central to the formation of identity. Her work with psychotic children led her to study the bonding process between infants and their mothers and to develop a theory of the infant's attempts to establish a separate identity, known as separation-individuation. This unfolds in the first four years of life: The first month of life is marked by an autistic phase in which the infant is not really aware of the outside world. The period from the fifth week of life through the fifth month of life is called the symbiotic phase, in which the infant gradually becomes aware of the caregiver as a separate presence but not yet a separate "object." This is followed by a separation-individuation phase with many subphases, lasting until the third or fourth year of life, in which the child eventually masters various psychological and physical hurdles on the way to establishing an identity. While the theory is too complex to describe in great detail here, one example of a subphase of separation-individuation is *differentiation*, which occurs in the fifth through the tenth months of life. During this time, the infant is increasingly able to discern differences between the mother and strangers. *Stranger anxiety* is a marker for this stage, as the child becomes visibly distressed when left alone with people who are not his mother.

Attachment Theory Siegel (1999) noted that in the middle of the twentieth century, a British psychoanalyst and psychiatrist named John Bowlby used animal behavior research to enrich these traditional analytic views of child development. Bowlby (1969, 1988) believed that infants have a genetic disposition toward forming bonds with caregivers (again, traditionally the mother), which become internalized psychologically as "working models." These working models of attachment are psychological templates for viewing the outside world and relationships with important attachment figures such as parents, peers, and romantic partners. But it all starts with the attachment bond formed with the primary caregiver: A warm and supportive relationship serves as a "secure base" for exploring the outside world (including play and relationships with others), while a cold or inconsistent relationship leads to insecure attachments and a working model of the world and other people as threatening.

Mary Ainsworth (1991), a professor of developmental psychology at the University of Virginia, collaborated with Bowlby in the 1950s and developed a method for assessing children's attachment bonds, called the Infant Strange Situation. In this 20-minute paradigm, the child spends time with her mother, with a stranger, and alone, and the child's reaction to her mother is observed after the child has been separated from her for a few minutes. Aspects of the infant's response to the mother when she returns, including how easily she is soothed and how quickly they return to play, are coded. Securely attached children seek to reconnect with the mother upon her return, are easily soothed, and return to play quickly. Insecurely attached children exhibit a range of different behaviors, such as ignoring the mother and having a hard time being soothed. This finding has been replicated in hundreds of studies, and researchers have also classified children into three distinct types of insecure attachment, which can persist into adulthood (Shaver & Mikulincer, 2005).

Shaver and Mikulincer (2005) noted that increasing evidence is being found for the impact of early childhood relationships on the brain in general and on emotion regulation and interpersonal functioning in particular. They suggested that Freud's mechanistic drive theory was inappropriately rooted in physics (i.e., psychic energy), premature "neurologizing" about the role of neurons in discharging this energy, and speculation about human evolution with respect to sexual and aggressive impulses: "The emphasis now is on mental representations of self and of others, and the importance of close interpersonal relationships and their developmental residues. . . . [T]he links between psychodynamic and neurological impulses have been made less speculative by the advent of neuroscience" (p. 24).

Self Psychology   Another very contemporary application of psychodynamic theory, *self psychology*, was developed by Heinz Kohut (1971, 1977, 1984). He believed that the overriding factor in human development was what might be called a healthy narcissism. In other words, the need for a cohesive sense of self and the related self-esteem is seen as a driving force in personality. According to Wolf (2000), "Self psychology departs significantly from Freudian theory by recognizing the central importance of people's needs for relationships which provide certain types of experiences during growth and development." A person's early experiences and particularly the provision of parental empathy contribute to the development of a healthy and cohesive self. When a strong sense of self is not developed, psychoanalytic therapy involves the creation of a new and more effective self-structure.

Summary of the Development of Psychoanalytic Thought   In our view, analytic theories and thought have developed something like the branches of a tree. There are branches of development going off in many different directions, some connected directly or indirectly to each other and all with some connection to the trunk of the tree, Freudian psychology. The inner limbs of the tree are represented by the neo-Freudians such as Horney, Fromm, and Sullivan, who played early central roles in the development of psychodynamic thought. Westen (1998) noted that many of the therapies that retained Freud's theory of the unconscious but that focused more on interpersonal relationships, rather than the drive of the libido, were termed *psychodynamic* therapies in order to distinguish them from classic psychoanalysis. Therapists who describe themselves as psychodynamic therefore typically view themselves as practicing an updated form of Freud's original form of psychoanalysis.

Other branches of the tree are formed by theorists who departed from Freud but still retained psychoanalytic influences, such as Jung and Adler. Some might even view these offshoots as separate trees altogether that share common ground with psychoanalysis but have developed into distinct and unique counseling approaches (Jungian therapy and Adlerian counseling). While each of these theoretical developments to Freud's theory drew considerable interest, the therapies based on them tended to be lengthy, expensive, and available only to the few who could afford it. Soon a number of theorists were working on various modifications to psychoanalysis designed to create briefer treatments. Some of the outer branches of this Freudian tree are the most recent brief psychodynamic therapies, connected to yet different from earlier versions.

In general, these theorists urged a more focused approach, working on a specific problem or concern in the client's life rather than major personality or character change. These approaches required careful screening to ensure that the patient could tolerate this more focused approach, with more specific goals and some time limitations. Although the approaches were time limited, they were psychoanalytic in the sense that they emphasized the use of the therapeutic relationship to help the client gain insight into and an emotional understanding of how the focal area was related to core inner conflicts. A number of theorists have been involved in this movement, including David Malan (1976, 1979, 2000), James Mann (1973), Habib Davanloo (1978, 1980), Peter Sifneos (1979), and Strupp and Binder (1984). These approaches are probably most popular with therapists using a psychoanalytic framework in the contemporary counseling arena, but a number of more classically oriented analysts still practice longer term and more traditional psychoanalysis, particularly in larger cities with enough clients to support this type of practice.

After we review the basic assumptions and core concepts of classic Freudian psychology and move into the applications sections, we will compare Freud's psychoanalysis to a more contemporary short-term psychodynamic approach. As you can see from the many different branches, psychoanalytic theory is varied and complex, and it is impossible to cover each branch in a survey chapter. By presenting the basics of psychoanalysis and then comparing classic psychoanalysis and short-term psychoanalytic approaches, we provide a broad introduction to this vast area of theory and application. Resources for the various branches of psychoanalytic theory are included in the Web page for this text.

ASSUMPTIONS AND CORE CONCEPTS

View of Human Nature

Freud's theorizing grew out of his clinical work with "hysterics," people suffering from a range of mental disorders that today might be called phobias, instances of intense anxiety without a rational reason, or conversion disorders, physical problems that have psychological roots. Whatever their exact condition, Freud's patients exhibited behaviors that seemed highly irrational in a culture that highly prized restraint and rationality. In seeking to explain such phenomena, it is perhaps not surprising that Freud constructed a view of human nature as constantly in conflict and turmoil.

Freud's (1915) most basic assumption was that human behavior, emotions, and thoughts are determined by innate drives, which he labeled *instincts*. According to Freud, most of our behavior is organized to satisfy these instincts—even activities that seem random or counterproductive. Freud wrote about two basic types of instincts: sex and aggression. He saw both instincts as genetically innate in all human beings, with the sex instinct being the predominant motivator, especially early in life. While Freud originally focused on sex as the primary driving force, he gradually refined his definition of the *sex instinct* to include all of the basic instincts for survival and pleasure, something that later came to be known as the *life instinct*. This included the needs associated with hunger, thirst, and just plain having fun. The carnage of World War I was one of the factors leading Freud (1920) to also hypothesize the presence of a darker side of human nature dictated by instincts for aggression, something he labeled the *death instinct*.

According to Freud, our instincts for both sex and aggression (i.e., life and death) are innate and powerful but ultimately malleable. Instincts are associated with a certain level of pressure directed toward particular objects that will serve to reduce the pressure. In other words, even though our instincts are "hard-wired" into us and cannot be shut off, it is possible to satisfy them in a variety of different ways.

Freud's view of human nature is therefore essentially determined by the necessity to some-how satisfy our instinctual needs in the face of societal restrictions. Our instinctual drives are pri-marily selfish and increase in pressure until met, yet they can be satisfied only in an outside world that preaches self-restraint, ethical conduct, and respect for others. Freud believed that there was a basic structure at work in the human personality to resolve this struggle, involving the id, the ego, and the superego (to be described in more detail later). He talked about these structures of the mind almost as if they were real entities and believed that each had its own "agenda," being constantly in conflict because of limitations placed on the individual by society. Freud recognized the importance of social forces but viewed them mainly as necessary limita-tions on individual drives. Our instincts can never be entirely satiated because the individual is not powerful enough to overcome society's rules and regulations.

In Freud's view, this dilemma created much of the misery that he treated his patients for in psychoanalysis. Freud assumed that the child's early development basically determined her per-sonality. If there were problems later in life, they could be traced back to those early years. He also believed that the inner conflicts between the various components of personality that created prob-lem behaviors were not necessarily within the person's conscious awareness. In fact, Freud assumed that part of one's personality structure was something called the *unconscious*. As you will see later, psychoanalytic therapy is typically accessing some of these unconscious thoughts and feelings. When an unconscious thought slips out without our knowing it, we call it a *Freudian slip*. And according to Freud, there is always a reason behind these slips, somewhere in the psyche.

But what do contemporary psychoanalysts and psychodynamic therapists believe? Do they accept Freud's assumptions? These are hard questions to answer in a general way because, as you saw in our discussion of the evolution of psychoanalytic thought, there are many different streams of development. In an extensive review of the scientific legacy of Sigmund Freud, Westen (1998) noted that psychodynamic theorists today generally adhere to five assumptions about human behavior that originated with Freud. First is the notion of an unconscious mental life, outside of conscious awareness and control. Second is the idea that our various emotional, behavioral, and psychological capacities, which Freud referred to as the id, ego, and superego, operate independently of each other and, at times, conflict. Westen (1998) noted that Freud based this on a simple observation: If a person desires to overcome a symptom, such as binge drinking, and cannot, and there is no biological factor at play, then there is some type of "counter-will" operating, which explains the failure to change the behavior.

A third proposition noted by Westen is that stable patterns of personality begin early in childhood and that experiences early in life have an impact on how people relate to others later in life. Fourth is the notion that mental representations of self and others guide people's relationships with others, an idea clearly seen in the work of object relations theorists. The fifth central tenet of psychodynamic theorists is that personality development involves learning not only to regulate sexual and aggressive instincts but also to move from immature, dependent relationships with others to mature, interdependent relationships. The development of this last proposition owes much to the attention devoted to the ego by Anna Freud and other ego psychologists who followed Freud's work.

Core Concepts

Personality Structure Freud (1923) first explained human personality as a struggle between two separate parts, the id and ego, and later added a third component, the superego. We start life with an id that is the source of all the basic instincts. It operates mostly at an unconscious level and is motivated mainly by the desire to gratify needs and avoid pain and discomfort at all costs. The superego is often equated to what we call the conscience, the part of us that incorporates society's moral values and helps us determine what is right or wrong. It allows us to make moral judgments. Of course, the aims of the id and the superego are often incompatible, and the ego is that part of the personality that has the job of mediating between the id and the superego and rationally deciding how the drives of the id can be satisfied in an acceptable way. This, of course, is not an easy job, and the ego often has to resort to the use of various defense mechanisms, which will be described later, to distort or deny reality in order to serve the needs of both the id and the superego.

Each of these constructs has a role, and if any of them is too strong or too weak, trouble occurs. If a person has internalized unreasonable standards and expectations from his parents, the superego may be too strong and result in anxiety and unhappiness because the ego cannot find a way to satisfy the id's drives for pleasure and for pain avoidance. If a child doesn't incorporate morality and societal standards from his parents, he may be rudderless as an adult, and his ego may be unable to keep him from running afoul of society's standards.

The notions of inner conflict and anxiety are easy to understand from the perspective of the interactions among the id, ego, and superego. As with much of Freudian theory, these concepts have become a part of our language and our thinking. For example, the term *ego strength* is used by many counselors to describe how well a client is able to handle the struggles between what we want to do and what we think we should do. Although, as you will see, some counseling theories don't allow for the existence of hypothetical inner structures, the fact that these ideas are ingrained into our culture means that they are still a part of almost all dynamically oriented therapies. Following is a summary and illustration for each of the ego states.

ID. The id is the source of all psychic energy, and because of it, we start life instinctively seeking to satiate hunger and thirst and to avoid any form of discomfort. The id is ruled by what Freud called the *pleasure principle*, meaning it operates only according to what satisfies instincts, not according to the principles of logic. In the world of the id, which operates mainly at an unconscious level, there is no weighing of what is "reasonable" or considering what is socially acceptable. Of course, as the child develops, these other considerations come into play, but these are the domain of the ego and the superego. The id always operates by seeking pleasure and avoiding pain.

> **Joe Id:** I know I should be out there looking for a job, but it just seems too hard.
> **Counselor:** Well, what seems to get in your way?

> **Joe Id:** Well, I just seem to sit in front of my television and eat most of the day. I'm really up on all the soaps.
>
> **Counselor:** Joe, have you always had a hard time getting things done?
>
> **Joe Id:** Hey, get off my back. I don't feel like looking for a job, OK, and you're not going to make me!

In this example, Joe Id is not motivated to look for a job, which is inconvenient and demands hard work. Instead, it is much easier to sit around all day and watch soap operas. While this may seem appealing to some of us, operating strictly according to the pleasure principle in this case will not serve Joe well in the long run.

EGO. Even though the id is primarily concerned with instinctual gratification, from the example of Joe Id we can see that an id left to its own devices will ultimately prove to be self-destructive. Therefore, Freud believed that as the young child becomes increasingly aware of other people and the need to survive in the outside world, an ego structure of the personality gradually develops out of the primordial cauldron of instincts that is the id. The ego is the reality tester, always attempting to be objective and curb the childlike demands for pleasure pushing out from the id. The ego is the balancer, the part of the personality that organizes and directs.

As opposed to the *pleasure principle*, which rules the id, Freud hypothesized that the ego is governed by the *reality principle*, that which is possible and practical. The ego is therefore tasked with managing what is happening in both the external environment and the internal environment of the individual's instincts. The ego cannot shut off the instinctual energy that flows from the id, but it can manage how best to direct it. The basic problem confronted by the ego is that unmet instincts continue to build until gratified, but the outside world does not always allow for gratification. Anxiety, which we will describe in more detail later in this section, is the main signal to the ego that something in this precarious balancing act is going wrong: Either the id is winning, which will lead to self-destructive behavior, or the superego is taking charge, which will lead to a personality that is overly rigid and perfectionistic.

In order to cope with this anxiety, the ego decides which instinctual drives can be gratified right away, as when we are hungry and find ourselves in a food court at the mall. However, much of the time, instinctual drives cannot be satisfied right away, or at all, so the ego must resort to more creative ways of taming the id's powerful drive. It may be possible, for example, to postpone satisfying certain instincts: If we are very hungry during a long, boring meeting, we might fantasize about what we will eat for lunch until the meeting is over. Other instincts may be impossible to satisfy, such as taking a baseball bat to a neighbor who constantly plays loud music at night. In this case, the ego may be forced to use a *defense mechanism* such as *repression* to deny the instinct.

> **Latisha Ego:** I'm really having a hard time figuring out what to do.
>
> **Counselor:** About what?
>
> **Latisha Ego:** Well, everything. I want to quit my job and move away from here. I really want to try out living in California. I love being near the ocean, but I would be leaving a good job and my relatives would all think I'm crazy.
>
> **Counselor:** So, on the one hand, you want to feel good about where you live, but on the other, you are just afraid to leave a comfortable and good job.
>
> **Latisha Ego:** I just wish I could sort this out and come to some kind of rationale conclusion.

Latisha Ego's desire to find a rational conclusion is an indicator that the reality principle of the ego is in play. She is balancing a move that might give her great pleasure with her current situation, in which she has the approval of others.

SUPEREGO. The superego incorporates the values and standards of parents or caregivers through a process Freud labeled *identification*. Sometimes the superego can be too demanding and require a person to strive for unattainable perfection or morality. The superego is often in conflict with the id, since, according to Freud, the drives of sex and aggression contained within the id are always present and driving us toward their satisfaction. Since society demands that we curb these drives and conform to various laws and norms, the superego must incorporate these standards.

> **Margaret Superego:** I just get so nervous when my boyfriend starts to hint that he wants to have sex.
> **Counselor:** What's going through your mind?
> **Margaret Superego:** I just keep thinking about all those years of my folks telling me how terrible it was to have sex before marriage.
> **Counselor:** So that makes you pretty anxious.
> **Margaret Superego:** Yes! I'm 22 and have been going with Jeff for two years now, and I feel like a prude. I'm just not sure what I want to do.

In our view, it would be unethical for a counselor to tell Margaret what she should do in this particular situation, but it would be important to help her sort through her values and the implications of whatever decision she makes. However, what we see in this scenario is that the force of Margaret's superego is causing so much anxiety, she is having trouble sorting through her own values. She also may have trouble communicating these feelings to her boyfriend.

The Unconscious

The idea that we all have thoughts and feelings that are hidden from our conscious mind is probably the best known part of Freud's theories (Westen, 1998). He believed that a significant part of our memories and the associated feelings is beyond our immediate awareness. This idea probably came from Freud's early work with hypnosis and then free association, where he learned that many parts of the human mind are hidden, yet powerful. Unconscious thoughts and feelings come out in dreams, in slips of the tongue, and in various therapy methods like free association and projective tests. The well-known Rorschach inkblot test is one example of a projective test. A person is shown an inkblot and asked to describe what she sees. Since there is no obvious form, she must project her own thoughts and feelings, and as part of this process, material from the unconscious emerges. Nearly everyone has heard of dream analysis. Freudian dream analysis involves the interpretation of how the symbols and events represent the unconscious mind. As is well known, many of the objects and events have sexual representations in Freudian dream analysis.

Although the material in our unconscious is hidden to us, it still affects our emotions and behavior. In fact, much of psychoanalytic therapy involves helping clients become aware of how their behavior is driven by unconscious drives and emotions. The process of achieving these insights is certainly one of the cornerstones of psychoanalytic therapy. If one can become aware of why she feels and behaves in a certain way and how this is related to unconscious material, typically from her childhood, she has a good chance of eliminating her problem, which also involves more ego strength and control.

Anxiety

Freud (1965) recognized that anxiety was an inevitable consequence of life, starting as early as birth, when the infant is thrust into the outside world, something that was also a central construct for Otto Rank. Early in his theorizing, Freud thought of anxiety mainly as a consequence of dammed-up libidinal energy from the id that has been repressed too long and leaks out from the subconscious. Anxiety is therefore the basic mechanism by which the ego recognizes and attempts to deal with threats to the well-being of the individual. Obviously, not everyone experiences anxiety in quite the same way. Some of Freud's patients found themselves debilitated by it, while others living in the same era seemed to function quite well. While the ego never has an easy go of it in balancing the needs of the id and superego, psychological difficulties are almost always traced back to problems in early childhood development.

Freud (1926) gradually revised his thinking on the nature of anxiety and came to identify three basic types, all of which reside in the ego: reality anxiety, produced by awareness of real threats in our environment; neurotic anxiety, which has to do with the threat of unleashed instinctual drives; and moral anxiety, caused by the concern that one will violate societal rules and expectations. Reality anxiety is healthy in the sense that it makes us aware of potentially real threats in our world, such as a loud noise that comes from the basement in the middle of the night. Neurotic anxiety and moral anxiety, however, come from the threat of the id or the superego's needs overwhelming the personality. Neurotic anxiety is a sign that instinctual drives are becoming too powerful for the ego, while moral anxiety comes from our conscious when our behavior is out of line with our ethical standards. If possible, the ego may be able to deal with this anxiety through rather straightforward methods: For example, neurotic anxiety produced by the id's drive for aggression could satiated by playing soldier with a paintball gun over the weekend; moral anxiety caused by cheating on one's taxes could be alleviated by simply paying the government what is owed. If the ego cannot cope using such straightforward means, it must resort to defense mechanisms to ward off anxiety, which will be discussed next.

Defense Mechanisms

The ego uses various defense mechanisms to help defend against anxiety and keep a person functional. If they are not overused, they serve a useful function and are helpful; however, if they become a repeated way of functioning, then they are problematic. Defense mechanisms tend to help a person avoid painful realities and anxiety, and they are unconscious. Most of them have made it into our popular culture and are often used in everyday language. "You're just rationalizing the fact that you want to spend all that money!" Let's presume that Ralph has his eye on a new suit. He doesn't really need it and he can't afford it, but he is telling his wife that he must look his best at work in order to get promoted. This is not really true and he has enough suits already, but to avoid anxiety and inner conflict, he rationalizes buying it. Too bad for him that his wife recognizes a rationalization when she sees one.

Most of the defense mechanisms seen in therapy are less benign than this one and also harder to uncover. McWilliams (1994) notes that each of us tends to rely on certain defense mechanisms because of at least four factors: (1) our constitutional temperament; (2) the types of stress we experienced in early childhood; (3) the defenses that were modeled, even taught to us, by caregivers or other significant figures early in life; and (4) the types of defense mechanisms that have worked for us in the past. Therefore, with a given in therapy, it would be expected that clients would use the same mechanism for coping over and over, even though it may not be particularly helpful.

McWilliams (1994) distinguished between two basic types of defense mechanisms: primary (or primitive) and higher-order defenses. Both types serve the same basic function of protecting the ego from anxiety. However, higher-order defense mechanisms operate at a more sophisticated level in terms of ego functions than do primary defenses. It is perhaps easiest to understand this distinction in terms of the capacities of the developing ego: very young children, according to Freud, have very little awareness of the outside world or of themselves as distinct from other people. Primitive defenses operate according to the rules of this early stage of development, for example, by ignoring the outside world or simply wishing problems away—sometimes called *magical thinking*. As we grow older, of course, we become more and more aware of the outside world and our separateness from other people: Higher-order defense mechanisms reflect this understanding. In using this type of defense mechanism, the ego may distort reality or focus attention away from that which is unpleasant, but it still operates according to the basic rules of the reality principle. To summarize, primary defense mechanisms show no evidence of the attainment of the reality principle and a lack of awareness of the separateness of people outside of oneself. Higher-order defenses are a more sophisticated way of coping with anxiety that the ego experiences.

Primary Defenses

DENIAL. Denial occurs when a person doesn't allow herself to experience a particular event. Denial is categorized as a primary defense because it involves little thought or introspection, just a reflexive, "this is not happening" way of dealing with an unpleasant event (McWilliams, 1994). Typically, it is a painful or anxiety-provoking event that is just not allowed to come into a person's awareness. Denial can also involve a series of events related to a relationship or general situation. For example, Ted is a 40-year-old man who has been married for 2 years. His wife is overbearing and has emotionally abused him for some time. She is constantly putting him down. His friends have told him not to take this sort of thing on numerous occasions, but he denies that there is any problem. Ted is not able to face the anxiety, guilt, and shame of the situation, so he denies that it exists.

PROJECTION. Projection is a process in which what is inside is misunderstood as coming from the outside (McWilliams, 1994): Thoughts and feelings that we have are attributed to another person. McWilliams notes that in its most benign form, projection can serve as the basis for understanding other people: We use our own thoughts and feelings to attempt to understand the private world of others. However, as a defense mechanism, it involves projecting your own unacceptable impulses and feelings onto another person. It is categorized as a primary defense because it blurs the boundaries between self and others. For example, a client comes in and expresses great concern about his roommate. He says that the roommate seems lonely and isolated and has few friends. He reports that the roommate is very unhappy. It soon comes out that he really doesn't have friends and isn't at all satisfied with his life. He has defended against these feelings by projecting them onto his roommate. Or it may be a more universal kind of projection. A person who feels that everyone is always so angry and hostile may herself be angry and hostile but unable to consciously access those feelings.

DISSOCIATION. McWilliams (1994) noted some trepidation about classifying dissociation as a primitive defense because its use as a defense mechanism is not necessarily indicative of problematic development early in childhood. Any person confronted with a traumatic situation may dissociate by mentally shutting out some awful event and having an out-of-body experience. However, she pointed out that such events themselves are not a normal part of development, and the mind's extreme reaction to such events still warrants the classification of primitive defense. The dissociation associated with severe childhood abuse, sometimes resulting in distinct personality states know as dissociative identity disorder (formerly multiple personality disorder), is an extreme example of the use of dissociation.

Higher-Order Defenses

REPRESSION. Repression involves memories that are pushed out of conscious awareness. As opposed to denial, where the reality of an event is simply not recognized, repressed memories have been consciously evaluated but then deemed too threatening for conscious awareness. Often a person experiences some current anxiety or reaction that is linked to a repressed event, and therapy involves helping him understand the connections between his repression and his current feelings and behavior. For example, Heidi was in an automobile accident as a child when her family was driving through the Rocky Mountains. She was thrown from the car and rolled down a hill. She can't remember the event, although family members have told her about it. But she does know that driving in the mountains makes her very anxious. When she first experienced this anxiety about mountain driving, she didn't realize the connection, but in discussing it with her mom, she was reminded of the accident and then made the connection.

DISPLACEMENT. Displacement involves channeling a particular feeling or frustration to a person, object, or animal, often when one cannot target the real object of frustration. The classic example is the man who is frustrated at work and particularly mad at his boss. He comes home angry and kicks his dog when the dog gets in his way. In addition to animals, spouses, partners, and friends are often the object of displacement. We are reminded of some of the "expressive" therapies popular some decades ago, when clients were encouraged to imagine that couches, pillows, etc., were their mothers, fathers, etc., and beat them with Styrofoam bats. In these approaches, displacement was encouraged to allow a person to feel and express her anger.

SUBLIMATION. Sublimation is the changing of a basic impulse (sex, aggression, fear, etc.) thought by the person to be unacceptable in his societal context into one that is acceptable. For example, a person who feels aggressive may channel that feeling into sports such as football, boxing, and wrestling. Or an individual who has strong, sexual drives and desires that are not acceptable in her culture may express these feelings artistically. Michaelangelo is thought by some to have sublimated homosexual feelings by creating his masterpieces. In one sense, sublimation can be thought of as a particularly effective defense mechanism because it allows an effective expression of unacceptable impulses. On the other hand, it might be seen as a defense that plays into societal oppression because it encourages people not to express their authentic feelings or impulses. It all depends on your basic philosophy: Do our impulses need to be controlled, or do they need to be expressed as part of our self-actualization? You'll see quite a difference as you go through the different theories.

REGRESSION. Regression happens when a person cannot handle a current situation and reverts back to an earlier time when she felt more secure and in control. A child whose parents begin to argue and become estranged may revert back to sucking her thumb. A boy who had become rather independent in his senior year in high school may enter college and feel lost and lonely and begin to call home often and regress back to a state in which he is more dependent on his parents. Regression as a defense is not to be confused with the process of regression used in some therapies to move a person back in time as a way of uncovering repressed memories or encouraging catharsis regarding a past painful event.

REACTION FORMATION. In its simplest form, reaction formation can be understood as a defense in which unacceptable feelings and impulses are turned into their exact opposites. For example, someone who is jealous of an older sibling who has excelled in school might find such feelings threatening and unacceptable. Reaction formation, when used as a defense, would basically entail turning such emotions on their head and expressing nothing but respect and admiration for the sibling. However, reaction formation does not mean that the original feelings of jealousy have gone away, and the person's true feelings are often manifested in some way. For example, the jealous sibling might praise her sibling so often, and in such glowing terms, that the authenticity of these statements becomes suspect to others. Another example might be an athlete who has just lost a big match to a competitor and, when questioned by a reporter, professes nothing but admiration and respect for his opponent.

INTELLECTUALIZATION. Intellectualization refers to an isolation of affect from one's intellect. The person using this defense talks about her feelings in a way that is very isolated and removed. This allows the person to think rationally in situations where her emotionals threaten to overload her intellectual capacities. In an emergency situation, as when one becomes lost in the woods, this defense mechanism can be highly adaptive, allowing one to think through a situation that is highly charged emotionally. However, intellectualization can also be maladaptive, as when problems arise in an intimate relationship and one partner cannot authentically express his feelings to the other when there is conflict.

Psychosexual Stages

Freud believed that personality is shaped by biological drives, which are expressed early in life through preoccupation with specific parts of the body. Each developmental stage involves gratification associated with the function of that part of the body linked with that stage. We have noted that Freud hypothesized instincts for both life (libido) and death (aggression). In his stages of development, he delineated specific parts of the body from which libidinal energy emanated but did not do so for aggressive instincts. Therefore, the stages are known as psychosexual stages of development, although aggressive impulses can come into play in early development as well. The first two stages, the oral and anal stages, revolve around parts of the body associated with the basic functions of life, as the infant derives pleasure from the act of nursing with the mother and later from exerting control over the excretory functions. As the child moves into the phallic, latent, and genital stages, pleasure is expressed less through survival functions and more through a fantasy sexual relationship with the parents.

According to Freud's drive theory of personality, overly frustrating or gratifying the child at each stage can lead to psychological problems later in life. In Freud's terminology, the individual can become *fixated* with the issues of that stage because of this unsuccessful resolution. Early psychoanalytic authors wrote about the "oral" or "anal" as someone who was fixated in that stage and displayed characteristic symptoms of this as an adult. As an adult, someone with an oral personality might depend on smoking for gratification; an anal personality might be overly concerned with cleanliness and order.

Freud was not alone in hypothesizing drives early in life that shape personality, although he certainly received the most notoriety. Some of the stages Freud described (oral, anal, etc.) may seem strange to today's students of psychology, but they are integral to understanding Freud's theory of personality. Much of psychoanalysis can be understood as "unblocking" fixations that occur in one of these stages. Freud's very broad concept of sexuality as a primary driving force and his hypothesis of developmental stages involving sexual development from birth through age 6 have been highly criticized by more contemporary theorists, as has the attendant notion that personality is essentially formed by how a child negotiates these stages up to the age of 6. However, psychodynamic authors still adhere to the notion of basic stages of development and the powerful impact that psychological development early in life can have in adulthood. One of the most noted theorists to revise Freud's theory was Erik Erikson, who developed a stage model that centered on both the psychological and the interpersonal tasks that had to be accomplished to move to the next stage. While his theory was somewhat similar to Freud's in the first 5 or 6 years of life, Erikson extended his theory into adolescence and adulthood, and he focused much less on biological processes than Freud, emphasizing instead the social nature of development.

Freud's Stages Following is a review of Freud's stages of development and the personality problems that could result from unsuccessful resolution of each stage.

ORAL PHASE. This phase extends from birth to 18 months, in which nursing at the mother's breast satisfies the very basic need for food, after which the infant feels full and sleepy. Freud labeled this early part of the oral stage *oral-incorporative* because libidinal gratification comes primarily from the bodily sensations associated with feeding, including those experienced by the mouth, lips, and tongue. As the infant begins teething, the *oral-aggressive* phase appears, in which gratification occurs through biting. Unsuccessful resolution of the oral-aggressive stage can result in a personality that is "biting," i.e., sarcastic and pessimistic. More generally, unsuccessful resolution of the oral phase can lead to problems with trust, love, and relationships later in life. In addition, the adult may seek to satisfy needs for love by accumulating possessions rather than relationships.

ANAL PHASE. This phase occurs from 18 months to about 3 or 4 years, with pleasure coming from holding in and letting go. The anal phase begins as children are introduced to toilet training, a time when their parents come to expect them to hold or let go of bodily waste at the proper times. While Freud did not write extensively about the role of parental behavior in shaping adult personality, he did note that different types of personality issues could arise as a function of how the parents handle the toilet-training experience. Parents who are overly strict in their approach can struggle with the child for power and control, leading the child to express dissatisfaction by defecating at the wrong times. This could lead to what Freud labeled the anal-aggressive personality in adulthood, in which the person is messy and hostile to other people. In contrast, when parents are overly concerned with their child's success in toilet training and lavishly reward the child for progress, the result can be an anal-retentive adult, one who is overly concerned with cleanliness and order and who needs to be productive. Such a person may exhibit the excessive need to control her life and often those of persons close to her.

PHALLIC PHASE. In this stage, which occurs between the ages of 3 and 4, the focus is on genital pleasure. Children begin to experience masturbation pleasure at this age. Also during this stage, the famous (and infamous) Oedipal conflict arises, with boys experiencing castration anxiety and girls an Electra complex. Boys begin to compete with Dad for Mom's sexual affection, and upon realizing that they can't compete with their father, they displace their sexual feelings for mother. During this period, the young boy also experiences castration anxiety, first realizing that unlike girls he has a penis and then fearing that it might be lost. Girls at this stage are still, as are boys, most directed toward their mothers, but when they realize that they don't have a penis and start to experience penis envy, they become more attached to their fathers. Boys and girls who do not successfully negotiate this stage have problems with sexuality and relationships. For example, boys who are treated poorly or ignored by their mothers and overly controlled by their fathers may withdraw from sexual relationships later in life and have lifelong problems with their self-concept. Girls who fail to win their father's approval may become overly feminine in a lifelong attempt to attract him, and other men.

LATENT PHASE. This phase runs from age 6 to puberty, approximately age 12. After the trials and tribulations of the first three stages, this stage is one of relative calm. The sexual drives are latent, and the child is able to focus on tasks such as learning in school, developing social relationships with those of the same age, and acquiring the skills needed to survive in society, such as being responsible about school assignments and household tasks.

GENITAL PHASE. This phase begins at puberty and is a reawakening of sexuality, this time in adult form, with pleasure coming from sexual relationships. Adolescents are severely limited by society in general and parents in particular as to how they can express sexual energy. They are encouraged to begin dating but must find other outlets for libidinal energy such as forming friendships and preparing for a career.

Freud had little to say about the latent or genital stages and nothing to say about development beyond puberty, primarily because he believed that personality was largely formed during the first six years of life. Although Freud has had a profound influence on psychology and on the way we view ourselves, his ideas about these stages and the Oedipal and Electra complexes have had less influence and are largely rejected in modern psychology.

Erikson's Stages In our view, the idea of developmental stages is an interesting and important one, and Erik Erikson (1950, 1968, 1982), one of the later ego psychologists, expanded Freud's ideas into psychosocial stages that have met with far wider acceptance. Erikson's stages also opened up the idea of *adult development*, the notion that people grow and change significantly throughout their lives. Erikson's wife, in a 1997 edition of *The Life Cycle Completed* (Erikson & Erikson, 1997), added several chapters hypothesizing a ninth stage, gerotranscendance. We do not include it because the stage is not described in much detail, although it seems to refer to the very last stages of life, when there is a deepened appreciation of the past and a kind of transcendent appreciation of all things, including death.

Erikson's theory was based on the idea that each stage of human development is characterized by a kind of struggle with two opposing outcomes, one leading to psychological health and one problematic. Following are the stages and a brief explanation of each. Note that the first four stages follow the same time frames as Freud's stages.

INFANCY: TRUST VERSUS MISTRUST (Freud's Oral Stage)—Birth to 18 months. During these crucial first 18 months, the infant learns to either trust or mistrust, depending on how well his basic needs are met. Children who don't develop a sense of trust at this stage typically have problems with trust and relationships later in life.

EARLY CHILDHOOD: AUTONOMY VERSUS SHAME AND DOUBT (Freud's Anal Stage)—18 months to 3 years. In this stage, the child begins to identify as a separate person and struggles to gain some measure of independence. This is influenced by the interaction with parents regarding bowel and bladder control. If a sense of autonomy does not begin to develop, the person may become a dependent and unsure adult.

PRESCHOOL AGE: INITIATIVE VERSUS GUILT (Freud's Phallic Stage)—3 to 6 years. In this stage, the child must learn to be involved socially and to find ways to play and spend time effectively. This is accomplished by developing positive relationships with both parents. If the child is successful, she develops a sense of competence, but if unsuccessful, she may experience guilt and doubt throughout life.

SCHOOL AGE: INDUSTRY VERSUS INFERIORITY (Freud's Latency Stage)—6 to 11 years. During this stage, the child must learn to be industrious and to develop basic academic, social, and motor skills and a sense of gender identity. Feelings of failure, inferiority, and inadequacy may develop if this stage is not successfully negotiated.

ADOLESCENCE: IDENTITY VERSUS ROLE CONFUSION (Freud's Genital Stage)—Teenage years. The notion of identity crisis is perhaps Erikson's most well known contribution. In this stage, the adolescent searches for different aspects of his identity—career, social, sexual, and meaning. Role confusion results if he doesn't find an identity. Teenage experimentation with different lifestyles and rebellion against parental values are a part of this stage.

YOUNG ADULTHOOD: INTIMACY VERSUS ISOLATION—18 years to the early 30s. The developmental task in this stage is to form an intimate relationship with another person. This has typically been when one seeks out a lifetime partner. This stage well illustrates the social aspect of Erikson's stages. Societal expectations for marriage and children are at work, although this is not necessarily the path everyone takes. However, according to the theory, isolation occurs if one does not develop intimate relationships in some way. One strong criticism of this stage has to do with its applicability to females. Critics have noted that women may well follow a different developmental sequence, with the development of intimacy a part of their identity development.

MIDDLE AGE: GENERATIVITY VERSUS STAGNATION—the 30s to the 60s. This is the period when one moves beyond self and family to contribute to society. Individuals must reconcile their early aspirations with their actual accomplishments. Failure to experience a sense of productivity and accomplishment leads to feelings of failure and dissatisfaction.

LATER LIFE: INTEGRITY VERSUS DESPAIR—60 years plus. To gain integrity during this period, one must be able to look back at one's life and feel few regrets, about what was not accomplished in life. Despair comes when a person feels that her life has not been successful and that she made too many wrong choices along the way.

Summary of Core Concepts and Freud's Model of Personality

Freud's psychoanalysis grew out of his attempts to scientifically understand human psychology. Each construct reviewed above fits into a dynamic and interconnected model of personality. Brenner (1974) noted two fundamental hypotheses that are central in this regard: First is the notion of psychic determinism, which means that nothing we do happens by chance. *All behavior*, according to Freud, is determined by sexual and aggressive instincts or drives. These reside in a part of the personality called the id, as well as specific locations in the body, which Freud described in his theory of psychosexual development. At each stage, libidinal energy is associated with a certain part of the body (i.e., oral zone, anal zone, etc.), and over- or underindulgence of these drives was hypothesized to lead to fixation at each stage, which would have repercussions for adult personality.

As part of this development, especially after the first year to 18 months of life, the infant becomes increasingly focused on the outside world, especially the parents, who become a central source of gratification for sexual as well as physiological needs. This increasing focus on the outside world also brings with it an awareness of limits that are set by parents and society at large, and the ego and superego develop to negotiate needs with the outside world and to represent the values of society, respectively. Anxiety plays an important role as a signal to the ego of the danger that the needs of either the id or the superego are about to overwhelm its defenses.

The defense mechanisms used by the ego bring in what Brenner (1974) referred to as Freud's second fundamental hypothesis: that much of our mental life occurs at an unconscious level. We are always attempting to satisfy instinctual drives, but much of our motivation occurs at an unconscious level. This may explain why some behaviors may seem random or disconnected to our conscious minds: The source for these behaviors operates at a nonconscious level. The society around us does not allow for the gratification of all (or even most) of our needs for sex and aggression, but fortunately these needs are malleable: They can be delayed, redirected, or pushed into our unconscious. If the ego is unable to reconcile these needs with the demands of the outside world, psychological symptoms can develop that interfere with the ability to function effectively.

THERAPEUTIC RELATIONSHIP

Counselor's Role

Freud was a physician, and classic psychoanalysis clearly developed from a medical model, with the doctor working to cure the patient. The analyst is the expert and is expected to sort out and interpret the complex system of drives and defenses that are not understood by the client (patient). Although the analyst is the expert, she plays a somewhat passive role at first, allowing the client to present the problem and encouraging her to free associate, to talk freely about whatever is on her mind. This passive approach, characterized in classic analysis by the therapist sitting behind the client, who is on a couch, also allows transference to develop—the client reacts to the therapist as she did to others (namely, her parents) in past relationships. Later in the therapy, the therapist becomes more active, interpreting what she has learned about the client and about the transference to the client. The therapist must also be keenly aware of her own emotional reactions to the client, particularly those reactions that are triggered by the therapist's own past experiences and relationships. This is called *countertransference*.

In more contemporary approaches, such as short-term psychodynamic therapy (to be discussed later in this chapter), the therapist takes a more active role. She may encourage or confront the client early on about defenses the client is using that are counterproductive.

It is fair to say that nearly all of the approaches derived from Freudian psychoanalysis require a therapist who is highly skilled in interpreting therapeutic material and who has considerable insight into her own psychological processes. In classic analysis, the psychoanalyst must undergo extensive analysis herself. For other psychodynamic approaches, it is very likely that the therapist will have had at least some psychotherapy herself. We have observed that therapists drawn to the psychodynamic approaches enjoy the intricacies and the challenge of understanding the client's inner dynamics and of focusing on the interpersonal process. Therapists who do short-term psychodynamic therapy are likely also to be able to challenge clients and tolerate anger and other emotions directed at the therapist.

Counselor-Client Relationship

The relationship between therapist and client, in particular the transference of unconscious feelings from the client to the therapist, plays an important part in the overall process of therapy. This relationship, except in some more recent, interpersonally based psychodynamic approaches, is not always a "real" relationship. This is because the therapist comes to represent people in the client's past life who have been significant—usually the mother or father. In a sense, the therapist, at least for part of the time, doesn't have an authentic or real relationship with the client because she is a stand-in for someone else. Since early connections with parents are crucial, this representation, called *transference*, becomes very important. Of course, transference doesn't occur all the time in the relationship. The therapist also has the role of doctor or expert, particularly when she is interpreting transference and other material to the client. In some more recent psychodynamically oriented therapies, the relationship is seen more as a helping relationship between two people. Interpersonal patterns are important and are observed and discussed, but the nature of the relationship is different (Strupp & Binder, 1984).

ASSESSMENT, GOALS, AND PROCESS OF THERAPY

As noted in our discussion of the different branches of psychoanalysis and psychodynamic therapy, Freud's original ideas have developed in many different directions. In describing assessment, goals, and process, we will focus both on classic psychoanalysis and on an approach called a short-term psychodynamic intervention by Bauer and Kobos (1995). This second approach comes out of the work of Davanloo (1978, 1980) and Malan (1963, 1976, 1979), researchers who developed the first "briefer" approaches, and represents modern attempts to make psychoanalysis briefer and more focused. Malan (1980) wrote the following critique of the classic Freudian approach:

> It needs to be stated categorically that in the early part of this century Freud unwittingly took a wrong turning, which led to disastrous consequences for the future of psychotherapy. This was to react to increasing resistance with increased passivity—eventually adopting the technique of free association on the part of the patient, and the role of "passive sounding board," free-floating attention, and infinite patience on the part of the therapist. The consequences have been strenuously ignored or denied by generations of analysts and dynamic psychotherapists, but are there for all to see. The most obvious effect has been an enormous increase in the duration of treatment—from a few weeks or months to years. (pp. 13–14)

Malan's statement reflects a strong movement in the latter part of the twentieth century away from classic psychoanalysis toward shorter versions. Another of these shorter versions was time-limited dynamic psychotherapy (TLDP) (Levenson, 1995; Strupp & Binder, 1984). It differs from classic analysis and from short-term dynamic intervention in that there is a greater emphasis on the interactive relationship between client and therapist. We note that other important interpersonally based models have been developed, such as the core conflictual relationship theme approach (Luborsky & Crits-Christoph, 1998) and short-term interpersonal psychotherapy (Klerman & Weissman, 1984; Klerman, Weissman & Rounsville, 1995). Although we cannot cover these interpersonal approaches here, we acknowledge their importance and relevance in modern psychodynamic theory.

Assessment

Formal assessment is not a part of classic Freudian psychoanalysis. However, free association, the technique in which the client says whatever comes into his mind, is a kind of assessment in that it begins to open up doors to unconscious material, which can then be analyzed and ultimately connected to current behavior and emotions. In the same way, dream interpretation might be described as assessment because symbols and symbolic events are used to interpret the unconscious. Both free association and dream analysis are also important therapeutic techniques and will be described in more detail in the "Therapeutic Techniques" section of this chapter.

Projective assessment techniques derived from psychoanalytic theories about the unconscious are an important aspect of counseling practice whether or not one subscribes to psychoanalytic theories. As opposed to "objective" assessment techniques like the Weschler Adult Intelligence Scales (WAIS), in which intellectual abilities are assessed in the rather straightforward method of asking the client a question and classifying her answer as correct or incorrect, projective assessment techniques ask the client to respond to ambiguous stimuli in order to gain insight into unconscious processes that shape personality. Perhaps the most famous among these are the Rorschach inkblot test in which the client "projects" her own thoughts and feelings onto pictures of inkblots and thereby releases unconscious material, and the Thematic Apperception Test (TAT), in which the client is shown various drawings of people and is asked to tell a story about each picture.

Scoring and interpreting the results of projective measures such as these is quite complex and cannot be explained in the space we have here. In a nutshell, however, the psychologist administering the test uses the client's reactions to these ambiguous stimuli to make inferences about the unconscious. For example, aggressive instincts that a client might not acknowledge consciously may be revealed in the story that he tells about a TAT card. However, while these assessments developed from psychodynamic ideas, they are usually not a formal component of psychoanalysis. Many psychoanalysts prefer to begin working right away on material gathered from the therapeutic relationship, including the client's behavior in session, rather than "interrupting" this process by administering a formal assessment. Psychologists who may not necessarily be psychodynamically oriented often use projective assessments to better understand the client's personality dynamics before beginning treatment.

Because of the intensive and brief nature of short-term psychodynamic therapy, the client must be able to tolerate intensive and relatively rapid analysis and interpretations of unconscious material. Thus, the therapist must conduct an assessment of the client's suitability for the therapy. Della Selva (1996) describes a kind of trial therapy, where the therapist tries out interpretations to see how the client reacts. She discusses a "spectrum of psychopathology" within which a potential client must be placed. Those with ego fragility and cognitive impairment are not appropriate candidates.

According to Bauer and Kobos (1995), the goal of assessment for this kind of therapy is for the therapist to ascertain whether the client has the capacity to "(1) rapidly enter into a therapeutic alliance, (2) work effectively in an interactional, uncovering treatment, and (3) separate from the therapist once treatment is over with a minimum of distress" (p. 89). They list the selection criteria set out by Malan as requiring the client have

1. Strong motivation for change
2. Area of conflict on which to focus treatment may be delineated

3. Patient responds positively to interpretations based on the emerging focus
4. Patient presents no clear evidence to contraindicate an uncovering treatment (e.g. serious suicide risk, potential psychotic decompensation). (p. 90)

It seems clear that clients must have sufficient ego strength, motivation, a problem focus, and the ability to work with fairly rapid interpretations of unconscious material. The primary way for the therapist to determine this appears to be through an interview in which she determines if the client meets these criteria by testing her ego strength and her ability to work with unconscious material rapidly.

You should note that the term *brief* is relative. In this kind of brief dynamic therapy, we are not talking about only a few sessions. Bloom (1997) reports the average length of Davanloo's therapy is between 10 and 20 sessions, and up to 30 sessions for severe pathology.

Goals

The basic goal of psychoanalysis is "to help the patient achieve a more adaptive compromise between conflicting forces through understanding the nature of the conflicts and dealing with them in a more mature and rational manner" (Arlow, 2005, p. 35). Goals in psychoanalysis can be categorized in two ways, tactical and strategic. The tactical goal is the analysis of an immediate conflict, typically with the analyst (Arlow, 2005). This might occur as a result of some kind of resistance to treatment, for example. Take the case of Jenny, a biracial client who has been in analysis for two years:

Jenny: Sorry I missed the last session. Things just got too hectic at work.
Analyst: Are you sure that's why you missed our session?
Jenny: Yes! I really have been busy.
Analyst: I wonder if it has anything to do with the fact that you left our last session together feeling very angry at your father. That was the first time you had expressed that anger and admitted how badly you thought he treated you.
Jenny: I don't know. . . .I really have been busy, but I was feeling angry at him when I left.
Analyst: And I wonder if you weren't angry at me also.

We can hypothesize here that Jenny is feeling some resistance to treatment because of the anger and pain she must face. The tactical goal here might be for the therapist to help Jenny understand the dynamics of her anger toward the therapist. In this case, the multicultural factors need to be considered also. Since Jenny is biracial, her anger at her father and the therapist might be related to being angry about the way she is treated as a biracial person. Perhaps she blames her father for this. This isn't necessarily the case, but we bring it up to emphasize the importance of looking for cultural factors in any kind of therapy. In psychoanalysis, however, the primary emphasis would typically be on internal conflicts rather than external factors such as cultural influences or oppression.

According to Arlow (2005), "The *strategic goal* [of psychoanalysis] is to elucidate the nature of the unconscious childhood fantasy and to demonstrate the many ways in which it affects the patient's current life" (p. 39). You can see in this case that insight into Jenny's anger and the way it is experienced and defended against can be useful to her. The assumption is that if one gains this insight (intellectually and emotionally), one can better come to grips with inner conflicts and be more effective in life.

The general goal of short-term psychodynamic therapy is not very different from that of classic psychoanalysis, except that there is an underlying assumption that a much briefer and more focused term of therapy will still allow the client to deal with his core conflicts by becoming aware of unconscious attempts to ward off impulses through various defense mechanisms. Bloom (1997) reports that Malan's goals for this therapy were ambitious and that he expected to get at the core conflicts, or at least a significant part of them. Della Selva (1996) describes the goals as a "restructuring" that involves three steps: undoing the regressive defense, redirecting the pathway of impulse and feeling into consciousness, and building the ego so that these feelings and impulses can be experienced directly. Take the example of Larry, a 45-year-old man who is in therapy because he can't seem to maintain effective relationships. He reports that he is always doing the wrong thing and that people get angry with him and don't want to continue relationships.

> **Larry:** Well, it happened again! I thought Jennifer was a good friend, but I forgot her birthday and now she seems angry at me. Why do I always screw up?
>
> **Counselor:** Larry, why does this keep happening to you? Why do so many people get angry at you?
>
> **Larry:** You got me, Doc!
>
> **Counselor:** You know we have talked about how difficult it was in your family when you were growing up and how you always seemed to be left out of things.
>
> **Larry:** Yeah, but what does that have to do with it?
>
> **Counselor:** Well, you must have been pretty angry at your family, and I think you are still angry a lot of the time. Do you think it is possible that you see people as angry at you because you are really so angry inside?
>
> **Larry:** Mmm. . . . I guess it could be. I don't know.
>
> **Counselor:** Remember the times you thought I was angry or disapproving of you, and I really wasn't?

In this scenario, Larry's therapist is trying to get him to confront the regressive defense of projection (projecting his anger onto others) so that he will no longer need to use it as a protection against his own anger. His ego will need to be strong enough to allow him to feel his anger, and this will probably be accomplished by working through the anger he projects onto the therapist, but in reality feels toward his family and himself.

Della Salva (1996) talks about "working through" character change as an overall goal as well as process. We see here, then, the same kind of very broad goal of somehow changing the inner structure of personality, using most of the same language and constructs as Freudian psychoanalysis. The major difference, a revolutionary one at that, is that this can occur much more quickly than with classic psychoanalysis when a much more active and sometimes confrontative therapist moves the whole process along by actively pushing against defenses and resistance.

Process of Therapy

Arlow (2005) describes what is called the *psychoanalytic situation*, a patient lying on a couch looking away from the analyst. This is considered the *technical procedure* for studying the human mind. It is thought to be an ideal situation for analysis because external stimuli are minimized so that the person's inner conflicts and forces can come out. Classic analysis typically requires at least four sessions per week, often for several years, and has four general phases: (1) opening phase, (2) development of transference, (3) working through, and (4) resolution of transference (Arlow, 2005).

In the opening phase, the analyst attempts to learn as much as possible about the patient—without any formal structure. The goal is to create a free-flowing atmosphere in which the client will say whatever comes into her mind. The analyst can then begin to construct a picture of the client's unconscious process and how her unconscious childhood wishes and fantasies are played out in everyday life. In this first phase, the analyst does not typically focus in on the client's primary unconscious conflicts but rather plays a somewhat passive role.

At some point in the analysis, often when the client is beginning to understand some of the major unconscious conflicts related to childhood relationships, usually with her parents, the phenomenon of *transference* occurs. Basically, the client projects feelings about past childhood relationships, usually with her parents, onto the therapist. For example, if the client had a warm and caring father but a very judgmental and critical mother, she will start to see these characteristics in the analyst. The therapist at that point becomes an extremely important person in her life, and she will likely begin to experience the earlier childhood conflicts and fantasies she had with the parental figures. She may begin to work very hard to please the analyst and feel angry and hurt because she feels that she never succeeds. When the transference becomes apparent, the therapist will interpret it to the client and open a discussion of the dynamics involved and related childhood memories. As part of this interpretation, the client will likely come to understand some of the defense mechanisms that she is currently using to defend against these unconscious feelings of anger and hopelessness.

The transference will manifest itself in many different ways, and the interpretation is not a one-time occurrence. Since the therapeutic process is not solely an intellectual exercise, the client *works through* the transference. This happens by experiencing the transference repeatedly and by working to understand its dynamics from both a cognitive and an emotional perspective. The client works through the feelings and emotions related to the unconscious material as she gains more and more understanding of and perspective on her unconscious processes and how they are elicited in therapy through the transference.

Finally, after the client and counselor are convinced that the client understands on an intellectual and an emotional level how the unconscious conflicts brought about by a critical father have played out in her life, the idea of a termination of counseling can be discussed. This itself is a lengthy process that will focus on how the termination of the therapy relationship affects the client. Since the analysis has been years in length and since the analyst has played such a major role in the client's life, a kind of replay of individuation and the giving up of childhood dependence occurs. Also, during this period, the basic transference issues are revisited to ensure that the client has adequately worked through them.

Bloom (1997) quotes Alpert (1992) in summarizing the steps of Davanloo's therapy model (the basis for the short-term dynamic psychotherapy):

1. Therapist inquires into patient's problems.
2. Patient responds to inquiry.
3. Therapist focuses on a problem and labels defenses.
4. Patient experiences discomfort which causes increased resistance.
5. Therapist increases pressure for material and further challenges defenses.

6. Anger is experienced by the patient when his angry impulses become so intense that they break through the defenses erected against them.

7. After the experience of anger, previously unconscious material becomes accessible. (p. 39)

From this description, you can see how the therapist forces the client to respond in a way that helps her break through defenses and get to important unconscious material. You can also see how active and confrontative the therapist can be. Bloom (1997) describes Davanloo's techniques as "remarkably persistent and confrontive" (p. 38). He goes on to report that Davanloo describes his approach as "relentless." Remember that this is a description of Davanloo; other therapists may have different styles and still use this approach.

Davanloo, adopting some concepts from Malan's formulations, developed a model containing two triangles, the *triangle of conflict* and the *triangle of person*, to help explain the dynamics within the client and also within the relationship with the therapist (Bloom, 1997). The triangle of conflict includes impulse, defense, and anxiety. This is the basic analytic model where one's impulses are unacceptable and therefore the internal conflict between the id and the superego creates anxiety and defenses. One leg of the triangle is the impulse, one leg is the defense against the impulse, and one leg is the anxiety experienced from the conflict. One part of psychodynamic work is to strengthen the ego so that it can handle this conflict without the need to unconsciously defend against these impulses, which, in Freudian terms, are related to unresolved issues, often in the Oedipal stage. The triangle of person relates to the person's relationships. One leg is the relationship with the therapist, another is the person's current relationships with others, and the third leg is past relationships, typically with parents.

These triangles are a helpful way of understanding the process of short-term psychodynamic therapy. According to Bauer and Kobos (1995), "The triangle of conflict is used to help the patient explore and understand problematic reactions . . . . The triangle of conflict describes the intrapsychic relationship between repressed and hidden feelings, the anxiety and/or guilt generated as these feelings become conscious (or threaten to do so), and the defenses used to bind the anxiety and avoid awareness and expression of threatening feelings" (p. 224). Examples of both triangles follow.

See DVD

**Chap. 2
Clip 1**

Triangle of Conflict Hector is a 20-year-old male who is half Hispanic and half Italian. He comes to counseling feeling very anxious, with sleep and job performance problems. He is also having a great deal of conflict with his girlfriend. As counseling progresses, the counselor learns that Hector's sexual relationship with his girlfriend is a big part of the problem. She is also very jealous and says that he prefers to spend time with his best friend, Arnie. Hector at first denies any problem, saying that their sex life is fine. Eventually, as the counseling progresses, Hector admits that he isn't really very sexually attracted to his girlfriend and that he has confusing feelings about Arnie. The counselor begins to hypothesize the triangle of conflict shown in Figure 2.1: Hector has repressed sexual feelings for Arnie (leg 1, Impulse); he is anxious and guilty about these feelings, although he is initially not aware of their sexual nature (leg 2, Anxiety); and his initial defense was denial that there was anything wrong with the romantic relationship with his girlfriend (leg 3, Defense).

Triangle of Person At first Hector has a great deal of trouble trusting his counselor, who is male (leg 1 in Figure 2.2). His current relationships with women are conflicted—he has gone out with

Figure 2.1 Hector's triangle of conflict.

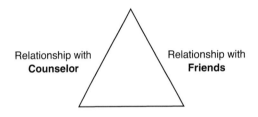

Figure 2.2 Hector's triangle of person.

many women and has made an effort to maintain romantic relationships; he has always had a few very close male friends (leg 2). His relationship with his father has been good on the surface. His father is a "macho" guy who has dominated his mother and who is always kidding Hector about sexual conquests. Hector goes along with this kind of relationship but has never felt close to his father and resents this lack of closeness (leg 3).

An understanding (intellectually and emotionally) of these two triangles is the basis for success in brief psychodynamic therapy. In the above example, Hector begins to realize that he has been defending against his sexual feelings toward his friend and toward males in general, and he gradually lets himself experience the anger, hurt, fear, shame, and all the other emotions related to the situation. At the same time, he works through the mistrustful feelings that he has toward the therapist and begins to understand how his current relationships and feelings have been colored by his past, and probably current, relationship with his father. This is by no means an easy or painless process, and when psychodynamic therapists talk about "short-term" therapy, they do not mean just a few sessions.

From a multicultural perspective, there are many variables to consider in this case. How does Hector's Hispanic background affect his coming to grips with his sexual orientation? What will his future relationship be with his father, other siblings? Can they accept him being gay or bisexual? How will he deal with internal and societal homophobia (fear and hate of homosexuality)? How long will it take him to work through his mistrustful feelings toward the therapist? How will the therapist confront Hector's defenses in a way that will not push him away but will allow him to confront his true feelings? How much time will it take? Is Hector ready developmentally to confront his sexual orientation? Clearly, this case is a challenge for a therapist using a brief psychodynamic approach. Dealing with and working through both triangles and other factors in a limited amount of time will be quite challenging.

THERAPEUTIC TECHNIQUES

Both classical psychoanalysis and short-term dynamic psychotherapy are not really technique oriented. The client-therapist relationship plays a very significant role, as does the process of analyzing material from the client in order to increase the client's intellectual and emotional understanding. However, there are some "techniques" that are a part of this process and that will be discussed in this section: interpretation, free association, and dream analysis. These techniques are really of secondary importance to the therapist's ability to understand and make use of clinical material (i.e., patterns of association in what the client discusses and transference). The assessment methods that we have already mentioned (projective tests) can also be considered techniques because they can play a part of the process. Promoting catharsis for a client, which is a strong expression of emotion often elicited by opening up past memories or by searching an understanding or realization of something painful, might also be called a technique. But in another sense, it is not really a technique, although it does occur during therapy and is often helpful in working through therapy issues. In short-term psychodynamic therapy, a more direct approach, even confrontation, may lead to emotional reactions, and sometimes catharsis occurs rather quickly.

Interpretation

As we noted in the "Process of Therapy" section of this chapter, an important component of psychoanalytic therapy is interpreting the transference relationship between the therapist and client. The psychoanalyst's interpretation offers the patient an explanation for her current symptoms, mainly having to do with unconscious conflicts. However, it is important to note that interpretation is actually a general technique that can be applied to any aspect of the therapeutic relationship: While the transference relationship is a prime candidate, free association and dream analysis also provide important material for interpretation.

Interpretation is the responsibility of the therapist, who is the expert on piecing together clinical material in order to arrive at an understanding of unconscious conflicts that are causing distress for the client. According to Ellman (1991), Freud spoke very clearly about the need for tact on the part of the therapist in offering interpretations: Without a sympathetic attitude toward the client, it would be impossible to achieve positive results in therapy. In other words, the therapist must consider carefully the best time to offer an interpretation and how best to word it. We have seen, however, that in short-term psychodynamic therapy, the therapist is more active, and even confrontational at times. We suspect that this has as much to do with the personality of the counselor as it does with the kind of psychodynamic theory. Nonetheless, it is clear that the briefer forms require quicker and more direct interpretations.

Consider the example of Bernard, a man who, like Hector in the previous example, has a very critical and judgmental father. As counseling progresses, Bernard feels that he just isn't being a good client and that his counselor is bored and unhappy with him.

> **Counselor:** Bernard, I notice that you are here half an hour early for every session and that you keep complimenting me on my office and on how much I am helping you. Yet I sense a lot of anger in your voice.
>
> **Bernard:** Well, I'm only trying to be a good client. What's so wrong about being early?
>
> **Counselor:** Nothing . . . but it seems like you are trying to please me. Is that something like you used to do with your father?
>
> **Bernard:** Yes, I guess that's true. Last time after I left the session, I remembered a time at a family picnic when I was very young. We were playing softball, and my father got very angry because I kept dropping the ball. I just felt so helpless and angry, too. I never could please the SOB.

This is an example of a "gentle confrontation," where the counselor brings up an issue related to possible transference but does it in a nonthreatening way. Perhaps in a different therapeutic situation, a more direct confrontation would be in order. In this particular case, the counselor and client would likely talk about this transference and the related feelings and memories many times as the client worked through his unconscious feelings of worthlessness and the defenses he used to cover them up. According to Arlow (2005), "Analysis of the transference helps the patient understand how one misperceives, misinterprets, and relates to the present in terms of the past" (p. 36).

Free Association

When using the technique of free association, patients tell the therapist everything that comes into their mind without censoring it (Ellman, 1991). Recall that the goal of psychoanalysis and psychodynamic therapies in general is to help the patient deal with unconscious conflicts in a more mature and rational manner. In order to help patients do this, the counselor needs to uncover threatening material that is no longer in the patients' conscious awareness. Free association is an important technique because Freud believed it could be used to identify psychological defenses that patients are using to block ideas or memories that are threatening to them.

In his early work with physician Josef Breuer, Freud relied on hypnosis to uncover unconscious material, but eventually he developed free association as a more effective way of accessing unconscious material. It is expected that at first patients will have a difficult time being spontaneous with associations, which can provide the therapist with important clues about the nature of unconscious resistance.

See DVD

Chap. 2
Clip 2

In the case below, Danielle has come to counseling because she has been experiencing a lot of anxiety, has lost some weight, and is having trouble sleeping. This is also causing a problem at home with her husband Tom and their son.

> **Danielle:** I think this is all related to my new boss. We just don't get along.
>
> **Counselor:** What kinds of things go on?

> **Danielle:** Well, he expects me to be a mind reader. He gives me jobs but doesn't really tell me what he wants. Then he is dissatisfied when I turn the work in.
>
> **Counselor:** What kind of guy is he?
>
> **Danielle:** Well, he's pretty quiet. It's not like he's mean or anything. He is pretty imposing, though.
>
> **Counselor:** Well, let's see if we can better understand some of what is going on with your boss. Please sit back, relax, and tell me the first thing that comes into your mind.
>
> **Danielle:** [Silence] This is weird. I can't think of anything.
>
> **Counselor:** That's OK; it takes some time. Just relax, and tell me anything that comes to you.
>
> **Danielle:** Well . . . for some reason, I am remembering my first date with my husband Tom. He was so nice, such a gentle man . . . and he still is.

The counselor here is using free association to begin the process of unlocking material that may be related to Danielle's problems. This particular memory may not be useful in itself, but it might lead somewhere. Perhaps she will begin to talk about the men in her life and how different Tom is from her father. Maybe she couldn't please her father and always felt anxious around him. Could this situation with her boss be related to that relationship and that anxiety? Has she been defending against feelings of inadequacy all her life? You can see how important the counselor's interpretation is going to be in all this.

Note also that this method might take a long time and contrast it with a more direct method on the part of the therapist (perhaps questions about men in general or about her relationship with the therapist, regarding transference). As an aside, we note here that a feminist critique of this dialogue might point out that there is a great danger that Danielle will be blamed for the conflict. Perhaps her boss is just a very unreasonable, even sexist, person.

Dream Analysis

We wonder what Freud's reaction would be to the enormous interest in dreams that his work has generated for the last century. Freud believed that dreams helped provide a way into the unconscious and that wishes, conflicts, and other material could be uncovered. Dream analysis therefore could be thought of as a specific type of interpretation where the psychoanalyst helps the patient "recover" material from the unconscious by analyzing the dream. Brenner (1974) noted that dreams are a "royal road" to the unconscious mind because nowhere else in one's psychic life are so many unconscious processes revealed so clearly and accessed so readily.

In Freud's view, the dream has two parts, its manifest content and its latent or hidden content (Freud, 1965). The manifest portion of the dream is the content we may (or may not) remember after awakening, such as being on the 50-yard line of a crowded stadium in one's underwear. The latent content of the dream, which exists in the subconscious, can be inferred only by the sensations we experience during the dream and the connections we make to the dream content during waking life (Brenner, 1974). The latent content of the dream stems from repressed sexual and aggressive drives, and the events and images from the manifest content may represent unconscious wishes. We leave it to you to speculate about what unconscious wishes or needs might be expressed in a dream about being in public in one's underwear.

Analysis of dreams was extremely important to Freud in his work on the unconscious and is perhaps one of the more famous techniques in the counseling field. It is often used in classic psychoanalysis, with specific meanings stemming from sexual or aggressive drives assigned to various symbols and metaphors. While some psychoanalytic authors speculated that one could almost create a "dream dictionary" of various manifest dreams images and what they might mean on an unconscious level, this notion has fallen out of favor in more contemporary applications (for a review of sleep and dream research, interested readers are encouraged to consult Ellman & Antrobus, 1991). Rather than discussing Freudian dream analysis, which has few contemporary adherents, we have chosen to focus on a more modern approach used in dream workshops and seminars.

Jeremy Taylor (1992) is a very popular dream interpretation expert and has conducted training workshops around the world. His approach is focused on the exploration and interpretation of dreams and is usually used in groups or workshops in a personal growth context. He believes that only the dreamer can really know for certain what the dream is about, but he does believe that there is a "universal language of metaphors and symbols." He also sees dreams in a very positive light, believing that they are always "in the service of health and wholeness." He cites one example of a woman who had a dream that seemed to her and her dream group to be about some physical problem, even though she was perfectly healthy. Eventually, after she pushed her doctor for a more thorough examination, they discovered that she had an undetected cancer.

Taylor believes that dreams are always related to the social circumstances of the person. During his workshops, people usually share their dreams, and then audience members share their thoughts with the preface "If that were my dream." The idea is that the audience or group members cannot interpret another person's dream, but they can tell what it might mean to them. He also believes that this kind of sharing and participation can be helpful to individuals and that it can help build community.

One of the authors (Archer) participated in one of Taylor's seminars and attests to the fact that members of the audience and those who shared their dreams felt very positive about the experience and believed that they had learned something useful about dreams and about themselves. The multitude of very different reactions to a single dream seemed confusing at times, since audience members had so many different ideas about what each dream meant. This fits, though, with Taylor's notion that dreams can have different meanings and layers.

Dreams and what they mean seem to have fascinated humans for centuries. Freud was certainly the modern "father" of dream interpretation, although some (including Taylor, 1992) credit Carl Jung with more substantial contributions to modern thought about dreams. And as we have seen, a fascination with dreams continues into the twenty-first century as a part of both psychotherapy and our quest for self-understanding and personal growth.

MULTICULTURAL AND DIVERSITY EFFECTIVENESS

Psychoanalytic approaches to counseling have been criticized as not appropriate for or even hostile to minority and female clients from several different perspectives. Sue and Sue (2003) contend that "much of the current therapeutic practice taught in graduate programs derives mainly from clinical experience and research with middle- to upper-class White folks" (p. 9). This is certainly true of psychoanalysis, and most of its derivatives, and since Freudian ideas are part of the basic foundation for much of our thinking about therapy, this appears to be a rather telling criticism. Sue and Sue discuss the incredible complexity involved in understanding the nuances of communication in different cultures. One example that has particular relevance for psychodynamic approaches relates to silence. Psychodynamic therapists, for example, might be tempted to interpret silence in a particular way, but according to Sue and Sue:

> Silence is not always a sign for the listener to take up the conversation. While it may be viewed negatively by many, other cultures interpret the use of silence differently. The British and Arabs use silence for privacy, while the Russians, French, and Spanish read it as agreement among the parties (Hall, 1969, 1976). In Asian culture, silence is traditionally a sign of respect for elders. Furthermore, silence by many Chinese and Japanese is not a floor-yielding signal inviting others to pick up the conversation. Rather, it may indicate a desire to continue speaking after making a particular point. (p. 131)

Affordability is another issue to be considered. Classic psychoanalysis is very costly and is typically affordable only to those with considerable expendable income. Short-term psychodynamic therapy and many other approaches are more affordable but still beyond the reach of those with limited income or no health insurance. This is, of course, true for any counseling, but analytic approaches, even the briefer ones, still involve more sessions than some other therapy approaches.

Perhaps one of the most widely held criticisms has to do with Freud's original concept of male and female roles and development. His concept of penis envy has not particularly endeared him to half the population. Ivey and his colleagues (2002) suggest that "[p]atriarchy and domination are often associated with the psychoanalytic framework" (p. 99). To be fair, we should remember that many of these ideas have not really survived in most of the newer forms of psychoanalytic therapy, although we think it accurate to say that there are still classical psychoanalysts who subscribe to these ideas.

Another aspect of Freudian theory that does not fit well with a multicultural perspective is the emphasis on internal dynamics. Psychodynamic therapies focus on self-insight into individual conflicts and defenses, and external factors such as racism, sexism, and other oppressive forces are not really a part of the therapy. Take the example of Ghalian, an African-American high school student who enters counseling because he has been labeled hostile and aggressive by his teachers and sent to the school counselor. He may appear paranoid, feeling that people are always slighting him and that his teachers feel negatively about him. If the school counselor attempts to interpret these problems as related only to the student's unconscious defenses and inner conflicts, she is missing possible external factors like racism.

From a multicultural/feminist perspective, the expert status of the psychoanalytic therapist allows her to usurp the client's power as she interprets material from the unconscious. This is particularly dangerous because the therapist's values may be imposed on minority clients to whom these values do not apply. Sue and Sue (2003) call this "ethnocentric monoculturalism." On the other hand, one could argue that a modern psychoanalytic therapist, who is highly trained to understand her own reactions during counseling (countertransference), would be able to discern when she is reacting in a racist way or imposing her own cultural values. Also, because it emphasizes insight into the past, the psychoanalytic model might serve as a vehicle to help clients understand how oppressive forces have shaped their thinking about themselves and the world. Ivey et al. (2002) suggest a "focused free association" technique. One step involves having the client free associate about gender, family, and culture. They suggest that this can be an effective adaptation of psychodynamic theory to multicultural issues.

Freud's emphasis on the early psychosexual stages as the major determinants of personality has certainly been questioned. Even the later derivatives, such as short-term psychodynamic therapy, still place considerable emphasis on the early years. This, coupled with the emphasis on insight, makes this approach rather unsuitable for people who have specific problems for which they need advice and consultation. Atkinson and Hackett (2004) put it this way: "Two of the unfortunate legacies that Freud left to mental health professionals are the overemphasis on intrapsychic etiologies for mental health problems and the exclusive reliance on one-to-one psychotherapy for the treatment of psychological disturbances" (p. 4).

PRIMARY APPLICATIONS

Classic psychoanalysis has few applications beyond individual analysis, and we have covered in this chapter what could be considered one of its most important applications: short-term psychodynamic therapy. In this section, we will therefore confine our discussion to two applications that draw heavily on psychodynamic principles: play therapy, which was a part of child psychoanalysis in its early development (Klein, 1932/1975), and group psychotherapy.

Play Therapy

Psychoanalytic theory was the basis for the growth of play therapy. Melanie Klein, working in Berlin, and Anna Freud, working in Vienna, were responsible for this early development. Klein (1932/1975) saw children's play as similar to free association in adults. Content from the child's unconscious mind and developing defenses came out as play unfolded. Esman (1994) cites Klein's classic example of the 3½-year-old boy banging two trucks together head on. The interpretation was that he was thinking about his parents having intercourse. Anna Freud (1927/1974) used her father's basic concepts but focused on the ego and its development. According to Cangelosi (1993), "She was less interested in undoing repressions and much more attentive to the mechanisms that the ego uses to deal with conflicts stemming from id impulses and demands of the superego" (p. 348).

Esman (1994) lists several steps in psychoanalytic play therapy. First, the therapist must establish contact. This is accomplished by using toys as a way of interacting with the child. Bromfield (1999) also emphasized the importance of creating a safe atmosphere and of demonstrating empathy and caring for the child. Next the therapist must conduct the observation. In play therapy, as opposed to psychodynamic work with adults, the therapist must observe the child's play and place it into a meaningful analytic context. Esman sees play as an "ego-mediating mode of behavior, serving a variety of psychological purposes" (p. 14). She points out also that this is not the only place from which the therapist can gain information, and she notes that in the early stages of observation, the therapist should not interpret her hypotheses about psychodynamics but should wait until further information comes out.

The next phase is interpretation. This is where the therapist decides on her interpretation of the child's play behavior and begins to interpret that behavior to the child. This is, of course, considerably more difficult with children, and the language and communication mode must match the child's developmental level. Dependence and strong resistance add to the difficulty.

Esman (1994) provides an example:

> Peter, a six-year-old boy, was engaged in vigorous play with cowboy and Indian figures. The principal "cowboy" was decimating the ranks of the "Indians," flinging them about the room with noisy abandon. To suggest that it appeared that he was expressing his rage against his rigid punitive parents would, at this early stage of treatment, have induced either bland denial or angry resistance. The principal aim of the moment was to connect the action with a named affect—no matter, at that point, whose. Therapeutic tact—and tactics—dictated, then, the comment, "That cowboy sure looks angry at those Indians." "Sure he is," said Peter. "They keep taking his things away from him." (p. 15)

From this, the therapist would work to gradually get more of the child's affect and anger toward his parents out.

Group Work

As is the case with individual therapy, there are many varieties of psychoanalytic group work. The basic Freudian ideas—the unconscious, transference, countertransference, interpretation, insight, defense mechanism, and working through—are all a part of psychoanalytically oriented group counseling, and they are also represented in many other types of group work, sometimes with different labels and combined with other techniques. According to Corey (2004), classic psychoanalytic group work has as its aim the restructuring of personality. "Specifically, psychoanalytic groups reenact the family of origin in a symbolic way via the group so that the historical past of each group member is repeated in the group's presence" (p. 138). Contemporary analytic group approaches have perhaps more modest goals than personality restructuring, but they typically do involve the basic work of connecting the present to past conflicts.

The role of the analytic group therapist varies. By definition, it cannot be as passive as that of the therapist in the early stages of individual classic analysis, where she is a "blank screen" in order to encourage transference and where the client is encouraged to free-associate. The therapist must provide at least some initial structure, although it is not atypical for a group leader to permit long periods of silence, thereby increasing the members' anxiety and tending to force them to confront themselves and their issues.

The group becomes a kind of interpersonal laboratory where members demonstrate their interpersonal styles—resulting in a kind of transference of their core conflicts to the therapist and to other group members. This transference is often made easier because there are a large number of people to remind each member of past relationships. Consider the following example. Paul is a 40-year-old man participating in group counseling for a substance abuse problem. Janet is 22 years old and also in the group. As the group progresses, Janet seems to have an edge in her voice when she talks to Paul; she often disagrees with his comments and seems to have emotions stronger than one would expect when she make these comments:

> **Paul:** I really don't think I can please my wife; she just doesn't give me a chance.
> **Janet:** You keep saying that, Paul, but have you tried very hard?
> **Group Therapist:** Janet, it sounds like you feel annoyed with Paul. Is that right?
> **Janet:** Well, he doesn't seem to be trying that hard.
> **Group Therapist:** But I hear a lot of anger behind your statements. Is that really all directed at Paul?
> **Janet:** Well . . . I don't know. I do feel pretty angry.

Group Therapist: Does Paul remind you of anyone else in your life?
Janet: He is just like my dad. He never follows through on anything.

As you can see, the group therapist is attempting to interpret interpersonal behavior and link it to past conflicts.

The psychoanalytic group leader has a very difficult task. She is performing analysis on the individual group members, while encouraging them to focus on each other and to point out defense mechanisms that they see in other group members. She must come up with hypotheses about the core conflicts and defense systems of each group member and at the same time manage the group. And with 8 to 10 group members, she must also be aware of her own counter-transference reactions and manage them.

The leader is often set up as the parent and the members as her children. Imagine reacting to sibling rivalry and to the anger, disappointment, and manipulation directed at you as a group leader. In contemporary analytic group work, and in other forms of group work, intense emotional demands are made on group leaders. Not only do leaders need to have undergone their own analysis, or at least substantial psychotherapy, but also they need to have experienced group work and have knowledge of group dynamics. In more modern analytically oriented groups, the therapist is more likely to allow herself to react authentically rather than considering her reactions within a transference framework and reacting in a more objective way. Corey (2004), Strupp (1992), and many other modern analytically oriented group therapists have made this point.

The approach to group psychotherapy used by famous psychiatrist and author Irvin Yalom (1995) is a good example of how analytic principles have been incorporated into group psychotherapy. Yalom is primarily known as an existential author, and his views about existential counseling will be described in more detail in that chapter. However, he was also strongly influenced by Freudian ideas and discussed several psychoanalytic therapeutic factors that occur in group psychotherapy, one of which is "the corrective recapitulation of the primary family group." The experience goes beyond insight and is a way for group members to correct earlier negative family experiences that have been causing conflicts and problems in their current life.

Yalom (1995) also talks about the "corrective emotional experience" that promotes interpersonal learning. He suggests that this most often involves one group member expressing anger and rage at another and then learning that this was not a catastrophe and that she and the group could work through the feelings. This, in turn, permits the second group member to try exploring his feelings and relationships in more depth. We mention these aspects of Yalom's approach to group work for two reasons. First, he is perhaps the most prominent writer and theorist on group psychotherapy, and second, his approach demonstrates important psychoanalytic underpinnings. We do hasten to add that other parts of this theory are not analytically oriented. For example, among his other therapeutic factors are the "instillation of hope," altruism, "and imitative behavior," decidedly not psychoanalytic concepts.

BRIEF THERAPY/MANAGED CARE EFFECTIVENESS

Clearly, traditional psychoanalysis is not compatible with a brief therapy/managed care approach. As you have seen, analysis may occur several times per week and can take years. In the past, health insurance companies paid for extended therapy sessions, but in recent years, they have covered fewer and fewer sessions. And as Austad (1997) suggests, there are ethical questions involved in the past practice of providing long-term psychotherapy for a small percentage of the population. As it stands now, only people with considerable financial means can afford classic psychoanalysis.

Short-term psychodynamic therapy is considerably shorter than classic psychoanalysis but may still involve more sessions than are permitted in many insurance and managed care systems. It is difficult to pinpoint a range for the number of sessions, but in discussing different formats for termination, Bauer and Kobos (1995) mention a range for moderately well functioning clients of 10–15 sessions. They also mention the idea of intermittent psychotherapy throughout the life span. They give an example of a patient who receives 6 months of treatment in college and then requires additional treatment later in life to deal with conflicted feelings about a first-born child. However, 6 months of therapy, assuming a weekly meeting, would involve about 25 sessions. In today's health care environment, few managed care or insurance companies will pay for even this many sessions. Many provide only a few sessions—say, 3 to 6—and then require additional justification. You will see as you study the various theories that there are many other approaches that fit better in a brief therapy/managed care environment.

INTEGRATING THE THEORY WITH OTHER APPROACHES

Many of the theories developed after psychoanalysis were a direct result of dissatisfaction with Freud's ideas. Theorists like Alfred Adler, Carl Jung, Albert Ellis, Aaron Beck, Carl Rogers, Fritz Perls, and William Glasser pioneered new theories because they were dissatisfied with psychoanalysis and had ideas of their own about psychotherapy. Some of their theories retain some Freudian ideas, while others are completely incompatible. For example, Ellis's rational emotive behavior therapy and Glasser's reality therapy acknowledge the impact of clients' histories on their current functioning but feel that clients can effect change in their lives without "excavating" the past. Their therapies are present oriented. Beck's cognitive behavior therapy, on the other hand, has some components that fit with some Freudian principles. For example, Beck talks about *schemas*, which are ways of looking at the world that come from the past—not exactly Freudian but at least recognizing the influence of the past. Adler, an early colleague of Freud's, rejected the drive theory and saw people as much more influenced by social forces, but he retained a belief in the importance of the early years. Existential therapists also reject Freudian ideas, but their idea of therapy as an exploration process that is not necessarily problem oriented fits with the classic psychoanalytic view of therapy as a method of gaining insight into one's self. It is rather difficult to integrate psychoanalytic theory in any substantial way with any of these theories, although, as we have pointed out, one can find similarities in some aspects of the theories.

The behavioral approaches are based on a very different view of how people change, yet there have been some successful attempts to integrate them with psychodynamic approaches. It has been our experience that a significant number of counselors use psychodynamic techniques to help clients gain insight and to better understand interpersonal patterns—the idea being that gaining insight into the causes for one's behavior, in terms of early family conflicts and unconscious thoughts and feelings, can free a client up to be better able to pursue behavioral and cognitive changes. As you saw in Chapter 1, most contemporary therapists list themselves as eclectic, using a number of different approaches.

At first glance, it is difficult to see an integration of Freudian ideas with feminist, multicultural, and postmodern theories like solution-focused and narrative therapy, which have very different views of therapy and human nature. However, there have been attempts to integrate feminist and psychodynamic approaches, and in fact, there are feminist psychodynamic therapists, although we doubt many accept the original psychosexual stages. There are also family therapists who incorporate some psychodynamic ideas when working with couples and families. And there are the different branches of analytic theory that, in effect, integrate the original Freudian ideas with their new ideas—object relations, interpersonal, attachment, and short-term psychodynamic theory are but a few of these.

There have been recent attempts to integrate Freudian theory with what we are learning about brain functions and the location of centers of emotion and memory. As these centers are further identified, psychoanalytic theorists will be looking for support for some of Freud's ideas like the existence of an unconscious mind. Many psychodynamic therapists have also integrated the use of psychotropic drugs into their practice, but others argue that drugs can interfere with psychodynamic therapy. For example, deceasing a client's anxiety may help support his defenses and decrease the likelihood that he will face basic conflicts.

RESEARCH

According to Arlow (2005), "No adequate study exists evaluating the results of psychoanalytic therapy. In a general way, this is true of almost all forms of psychotherapy" (p. 39). Perfectly controlled research is particularly difficult with psychoanalysis and psychoanalytic therapies. In fact, the complexity of the therapy and the conceptualization of internal structures and conflicts make empirical research nearly impossible. Much of the early research on Freudian approaches consisted of case studies, typically in-depth analyses of individual cases, usually by the therapist. However, a number of more recent studies have involved major research efforts, following clients for many years. One example is the Menninger Foundation psychoanalytic study begun in 1962 (Galatzer-Levy, Bachrach, Skolnikoff, & Waldron, 2000). For this study, 42 cases were randomly selected, using recorded tapes and psychoanalytically based instruments. A great deal of data was reviewed for each patient, and some were followed for as long as 30 years. The researchers concluded that, overall, psychoanalysis was effective, although a number of the clients did not profit from the analysis. This kind of research, although extensive and systematic, is not considered to be scientific enough by much of the psychological community. However, Steiner (2003) argued that the systematic case study method used in traditional psychoanalytic research fits well with qualitative research, a method that is perhaps gaining ground in counseling and psychology and that can involve an in-depth study using interviews and other methods not dependent on an empirical, scientific model.

Luborsky and colleagues (Luborsky, Crits-Christoph, & Mintz, 1988; Luborsky & Crits-Christoph, 1998) have developed one of the most promising tools for researching and measuring the transference relationship, the core conflictual relationship theme (CCRT) method. According to Luborsky and Crits-Christoph (1998), "After nearly a century of clinical use of Freud's transference concept of a central relationship pattern, the field now has a defined and measured version of this pattern: the CCRT" (p. 12). The CCRT is used to identify a core conflictual relationship pattern by rating client statements about self-other interactions. The measure relies on the clinical judgment of a rater but is quantitative in the sense that there is a rating and category system. Although CCRT identifies a core conflictual relationship pattern, it appears to get at the same pattern that one would expect in a transference relationship. This allows for an objective way to study the relationship of transference to other aspects of psychoanalytic theory. The sample study presented at the end of this section is a description of one such study.

The Missouri Psychoanalytic Counseling Research Project offered another promising approach, focusing on time-limited dynamic therapy, with a variety of process measures. In one study, Patton, Kivlighan, and Multon (1997) used a variety of measures and analysis methods to identify four process factors in short-term psychoanalytic counseling (psychoanalytic technique, working alliance, client resistance, and client transference) and then related them to outcome. The sample was small (16 clients), the therapists were trainees (five doctoral students and one master's student in counseling psychology), and there was no control group, but their use of measurement and analysis represents a creative approach to psychotherapy research in this area. Counselors were trained to provide psychoanalytic counseling according to four major principles taken from Patton and Meara (1992): "(a) helping the client to communicate freely using such techniques as counselor restraint; (b) helping the client to communicate naturally (e.g. beginning the session with current events); (c) using counselor empathy and countertransference to understand and communicate to the client; and (d) promoting client understanding (insight) through techniques such as confrontation and interpretation" (Patton, Kivlighan, & Multon, 1997).

Although we cannot review them here, there are a number of studies examining specific aspects of psychoanalytic theory. Studies on dreams, the unconscious, defense mechanisms, transference, and countertransference have been conducted in a variety of ways. Much research has also been done on psychoanalytic treatment of depression and anxiety. We both agree and disagree with Arlow's (2005) statement that no adequate research has been done on psychoanalytic therapy. Certainly, no double-blind, tightly controlled studies have been possible, but a number of different studies and research projects have shed considerable light on this form of therapy.

SAMPLE RESEARCH: The measurement of the accuracy of interpretations

Goals of the Research

Providing accurate interpretations for clients is an essential component of psychodynamic therapy, and Crits-Christoph, Cooper, and Luborsky (1998) were interested in the accuracy of therapist interpretations and how well they reflected the central or core conflict for the client. In addition, they sought to examine the relationship of accuracy of interpretation to counseling outcomes.

Participants

The participants in the study were 43 patients who participated in the Penn Psychotherapy Project (Luborsky et al., 1988). There were 30 women and 13 men, from 18 to 48 years old. Most were suffering from dysthymic disorder, generalized anxiety disorder, or a variety of personality disorders.

Methods

The CCRT (Core Conflictual Relationship Theme) was used to identify the central conflict theme for each participant. Trained independent judges, who were primarily experienced clinicians, compared the accuracy of therapist interpretations to the CCRT descriptions of a CORE central conflict. The ratings were done from two different early-in-treatment sessions. Two other measures were included in the study: First, a measure of errors in

(continued)

technique was used to assess factors that are inversely related to beneficial treatment, such as failure to focus the session or failure to identify resistance in the client. The authors also included a measure of helping alliance, which assessed the therapeutic bond between the counselor and the client and is noted by the study authors to be a successful predictor of treatment outcome. The relationship of these measures to treatment outcome was then analyzed, using test and interview evaluations for clients when they began therapy and when they terminated treatment.

Results

Crits-Christoph, Cooper, and Luborsky (1998) found the following:

1. The overall level of accuracy of interpretations as measured by the CCRT was low (ranging from 1.49 to 1.81 on a 4-point scale).
2. The accuracy of interpretations was related to outcome measures, as was the helping alliance; in other words, accurate interpretations by the therapist and the formation of a helping bond between counselor and client were related to successful treatment.
3. The errors in technique measure did not show a relationship to therapeutic outcome.

The authors also sought to analyze whether accurate interpretations were related to successful outcome only when the helping alliance was positive, which would be predicted by psychodynamic theory. However, they found that the therapeutic gain from the helping alliance appeared to be independent of the gain from accurate interpretations. The major hypothesis of the study, that accuracy of interpretations is related to outcome, was upheld.

Implications of the research

Because it was correlational in nature, the study did not show cause-and-effect relationships. That is, there is no direct evidence that accurate interpretations caused positive outcome, although the positive correlation between accuracy and outcome tends to support the part of psychoanalytic theory regarding the importance of interpretations in treatment outcome. The nonsignificant relationship between therapist errors and outcome may have been due to the low incidence of errors found in the study: They were not frequent enough to be a strong predictor of outcome. The authors did find it surprising that accurate interpretations predicted outcome even when the therapeutic alliance was not strong; it is generally thought that a strong alliance is necessary for patients to tolerate interpretations. However, because strong alliances were generally found in the study, the lack of variability in this measure could be used, just as with the errors in technique measure, to explain the nonsignificant finding. The authors summarized the main implication of the study as being that if their study was representative of the general field, it would be important for therapists to find ways to improve the accuracy of their interpretations so they could achieve better patient outcomes.

EVALUATION OF PSYCHOANALYSIS

Freud's development of psychoanalysis—and the work of the many researchers and practitioners who followed in his footsteps, broke ranks with him, or refined his ideas—provides much of the context for all of the remaining chapters in this book. In some sense, it all started with Freud.

Clearly, his contemporaries, such as Breuer, had similar ideas about personality and psychopathology, but Freud was the flashpoint: He wrote about his ideas in ways that engaged others, trained and inspired a generation of psychoanalysts, and helped set the stage for the mental health field as we know it today. In evaluating his theory, it is difficult to find a place to start because the impact of his ideas was so profound.

Psychoanalysis has been criticized in a variety of ways, and Westen (1998) makes the following observation: "Many aspects of Freudian theory are indeed out of date, and they should be: Freud died in 1939 and has been slow to undertake further revisions. His critics, however, are equally behind the times, attacking Freudian views of the 1920s as if they continue to have some currency in their original form" (p. 333).

Despite Westen's cautions, Freudian psychoanalysis can be critiqued in a number of areas. First, classic analysis, with several sessions per week, with no initial treatment goals, and lasting years, is clearly a luxury that only a few can afford. As we have noted, this kind of therapy is also incompatible with our current managed care environment. Even the more recent, shorter-term versions, which attempt to develop a specific focus early on, usually take months rather than weeks.

From a multicultural perspective, Freud's theorizing was clearly based in Western European thinking. The emphasis on gaining self-insight and focusing on past conflicts, especially with parents, does not necessarily fit well with clients whose worldviews are more collectivist in nature or whose notions of family emphasize the role of extended family members. For example, the respect and deference given to parents in many Asian cultures and the stronger emphasis on the family and group in African-American cultures don't appear to fit well with Freud's emphasis on the individual and the need to understand internal conflicts via parental transference to the therapist. We hasten to add that this is a criticism of many theories.

However, more contemporary writers have used psychoanalytic principles to understand cultural phenomena. For example, *Long Dark Road* (Ainslie, 2004) is a recently published account of a hate crime that occurred in Texas in 1998, when three men chained James Byrd to the back of a truck and dragged him to his death. In it, Ainslie draws from psychoanalytic ideas while trying to understand how the men could carry out such a monstrous act and how the community was able to hold together despite the national attention and racial conflict the incident provoked.

Freud has also been strongly criticized for the way in which he conceptualized the psychological development of women, with the notion of "penis envy" heading the list. The whole notion of humans as primarily driven by sex and aggression and in need of defenses to become socialized enough to live with each other is certainly in conflict with views of humans as essentially good with natural tendencies toward self-actualization. The role of a distant, emotionally uninvolved therapist has been rejected by most contemporary theorists. Certainly, many modern psychoanalytically oriented counselors and therapists believe in an empathic therapeutic alliance (Strupp, 1992). Another major criticism has been the lack of a concrete focus in the therapy. The use of insight alone has also been criticized as insufficient to produce behavior change. However, this particular judgment is not altogether fair, since the concept of insight includes "working through," which, as you have seen, is a complex and extensive intellectual and emotional process.

While many of his ideas, such as penis envy and the Oedipal complex, have almost become caricatures in modern culture, there is no denying the impact of Freud's ideas in spurring others to take up work in mental health. Those who have carried on his work, including object relations theorists and ego and self psychologists, have continued to refine his ideas and in particular emphasize the social nature of human beings instead of their sexual or aggressive instincts.

Bowlby's attachment theory, for example, mentioned very early in this chapter and drawing from Freudian ideas, has garnered considerable support in a range of different cultures. And modern psychological research into nonconscious aspects of human cognition, neurology, and emotional processes supports many of Freud's ideas about the centrality of unconscious processes, the tendency of the human mind to defend against unpleasant emotions, unconscious motivation, and the continuity of personality from childhood experiences (Westen, 1998).

We think it is safe to say that because Freudian thought dominated psychology for so many years, it has proven to be a very broad target. Many of the criticisms, however, have been directed at classic psychoanalysis and at some of Freud's original ideas. We agree with many of these critiques; however, it is important not to lose sight of the more contemporary applications. The short-term dynamic psychotherapy that we described, although not immune to these criticisms, fits much better with contemporary psychological thinking. As you read through the remaining chapters of this book, you will see that many of the theorists started out as psychoanalysts and developed their theories as a reaction against Freudian ideas. These theories would not have been developed without Freud and the acceptance of his ideas, which popularized the use of talk therapy to treat emotional and physical problems. Freud's impact on the fields of psychology and psychiatry has, indeed, been profound.

Questions and Learning Activities

These questions and activities are designed to stimulate your thinking about this theory and to help you apply some of the ideas to your own life and experience. If possible, you should work with another person or with a small group. Getting others' points of view and sharing your own ideas and perspectives will be invaluable as a way to help you evaluate this theory and its applications.

Discussion Questions

1. What kind of personal reaction do you have when you hear the terms *penis envy* and *castration anxiety?* How will this affect your evaluation of the pros and cons of psychoanalytic therapies?
2. Do you agree with the fundamental Freudian ideas that the basic human instincts are sex and aggression and that we must be socialized to express them in acceptable ways? Why or why not?
3. Do you agree with the idea of an ego, superego, and id? Why or why not?
4. Does Erikson's expansion and modification of the stages of development make sense to you? Why or why not?
5. Have you ever experienced transference in your relationships (behaving or feeling toward a person like you behaved or felt toward one of your parents)?
6. What kinds of people are difficult for you to take? How will this come out countertransference if you are counseling one of these people?
7. What do you think of the idea of a core conflictual relationship theme (CCRT)? Can you identify one for yourself?
8. How would you describe "working through" in psychoanalytic therapy?
9. Do you think that this kind of therapy is possible in only a few sessions? Why or why not?
10. What is your opinion of dream analysis? Do you analyze your own dreams?

11. If you could afford it, would you want to go into analysis for a year, meeting with your analyst a few times per week? Why or why not?
12. Do you believe in the idea of an unconscious mind? Can uncovering unconscious thoughts and feelings help clients in therapy? Why or why not?
13. Do you think that understanding a person's defense mechanisms is helpful?

Defense Mechanisms

- Can you describe the following defense mechanisms in your own words?
- Can you think of a friend or relative who often uses one of the following defense mechanisms? Why do you think he or she does it?
  1. Repression
  2. Denial
  3. Projection
  4. Sublimation
  5. Rationalization
  6. Displacement
  7. Regression

Dream Analysis

Freud believed that patient dreams need to be interpreted and analyzed, recognizing that many events and objects in dreams are related to our innate drives of sex and aggression. Typically, the analyst interprets the dreams and helps the patient understand the meaning. Others' methods of interpretation differ considerably. Jeremy Taylor (discussed in the "Therapeutic Techniques" section) suggests that only the dreamer can really interpret her own dreams. How do you think dreams should be interpreted?

Free Association

How do you think you would respond as a client to free association? Try it. Sit back, let yourself relax, and see what comes into your mind. Write it down and then (with others, if you so choose) see if you can figure out how it relates to life at the present moment.

Personal Defense Mechanisms

According to psychoanalytic theory, defense mechanisms are often useful ways to help keep our id in check. Most people have one or two favorites that they use to deal with life. Can you identify any defense mechanism that you use often? Does it work well for you? Do you think it is a healthy defense?

Companion Website

Now go to the Companion Website at **www.prenhall.com/archer** to assess your understanding of chapter content with multiple-choice and essay questions, and broaden your knowledge with related Web resources and additional print resources.

CHAPTER 3

Adlerian Counseling

VOICES FROM THE FIELD: COUNSELOR AND CLIENT REACTIONS

Yes, it works for me

Client: Hey, that was really interesting. I liked talking about my family and my brothers and sisters. And it was really strange to do those early recollections and try to figure out some things about my childhood. I'm not sure I understand what the counselor was doing, but he seems very warm and interested in me. I guess the idea is for me to figure out how the attitudes I formed as a kid are related to my problems now. I always thought that my problems with people had something to do with the trouble I had in my family. I think I will be able to figure things out, and I hope I can trust people more.

Counselor Trainee: This theory is pretty complex. I'm not sure I totally understand it, but I like the idea that people have a choice and that what they do is for a purpose. I think I buy the idea that feelings and behavior are functional and that it helps to get clients to understand what they are trying to get with their behavior. I think it would take a lot of training to learn how to do a complicated lifestyle analysis, but I do think I can talk to clients about their family and their past and get some idea about how they view themselves and the world. I have a client now who is pretty depressed because she can't help her father and her brother, who are alcoholics. She seems to think that this is her responsibility. I bet she believes that if she is to be a worthwhile person, she has to be able to take care of everyone around her. I think she got this growing up, since she had to take care of the family when her mom left and her dad was drinking so much.

No, it doesn't work for me

Client B: Just what I thought—the only thing missing was a couch! What does all that stuff about my brothers and sisters have to do with the fact that I can never seem to get a promotion at work? Jeez . . . that family constellation questionnaire took forever to fill out, and then we spent two counseling sessions going over it. When are we going to get to my real problems? I understand what the counselor said about figuring out something about how I think about myself, but I want some advice on how to handle things at work. I really don't buy what he was telling me about my using anger. What does that mean anyway?

Counselor Trainee: Here we go again—blame Mom and Dad and your family. I just don't agree with this idea that the early childhood years are so important, and I don't agree with the idea that everything we do is a choice we make in order to achieve some goal. Sometimes people are forced to do things. And how practical is this theory. With managed care, you really don't have time to get into a person's past and do all of this lifestyle stuff. I am doing an internship at a community mental health center, and a lot of our clients don't even come back after the first session, plus we have a limit of six sessions for each client. I wonder if this approach can be done in such a short time? I also have trouble with the idea that people use feelings and behavior to get things. I always thought that you did things because of the reinforcement you get.

Lenny, a 28-year-old high school science teacher, is in counseling because he is depressed about where he is in life. He is disappointed in his career and really doesn't want to be a high school teacher.

> **Counselor:** Lenny, we've talked so much about how you don't like teaching and how depressing it is to face all those kids every day. I was just wondering what you get out of being depressed all the time?
>
> **Lenny:** What do you mean by that? I don't get anything out of being depressed—how could I?
>
> **Counselor:** Well, remember when we talked about the lifestyle questionnaire and we noticed that there was a pattern of your being afraid to try out for a lot of things because your two older brothers were such good athletes and students and you didn't feel that you could compete?
>
> **Lenny:** Yes, but I don't quite get the connection.
>
> **Counselor:** Is it possible that your feeling so depressed about teaching is a way of avoiding the fact that you are just not happy in that career and that you are afraid to "try out" for a different career?

Adlerian psychology is called a psychology of use. The emphasis is on understanding how a client uses his beliefs about life to achieve his goals. For many people in counseling, mistaken beliefs, formulated earlier in life, can create a situation like Lenny's. Part of Lenny's problem is that he has some mistaken beliefs about how to find a place in the world. As you can see, he developed a belief that avoiding "trying out" or competing is the way to avoid anxiety and failure. He now "uses" depression to avoid considering some career choices. The counselor must be able to get into Lenny's frame of reference and private logic about the world in order to understand how he believes he must feel and act in order to achieve his goals.

HISTORICAL BACKGROUND

Historical Context

Alfred Adler developed Adlerian psychology during the late nineteenth and early twentieth centuries. He formed many of his ideas in the stimulating intellectual atmosphere of early-twentieth-century Vienna. As a charter member of Freud's Vienna Circle, a discussion group of doctors and scientists, he was clearly influenced by Freudian ideas and the development of psychoanalytic theory.

A number of historic events occurred that were also part of the context for the development of his theory: the Bolshevik revolution and the rise of Communism, Austria's participation in World War I, and the subsequent hardships after the war. Adler's strong commitment to social reform and social justice was certainly influenced by socialistic ideas. He met his wife, an intellectual and social activist from Russia, when they were both part of a group of socialist students at the University of Vienna. Adler's service in World War I, where he saw for himself the horrific consequences of war, was also probably a factor in his increasing commitment to social reform and his emphasis on social interest as an important aspect of psychological health (Boeree, 2005). There has been speculation that he was also influenced by the location of his early ophthalmology office, which was situated in a lower-class neighborhood next to a circus. His ideas about organ inferiority may have been influenced by his observation of the strengths and weaknesses of patients from the circus (Boeree, 2005).

Development of the Theory

Adler was born in 1870 in Vienna. He was the second of six children and a sickly child. He had rickets, a disease caused by a vitamin deficiency. When Adler was only 3 years old, his younger brother died next to him in bed. Later in life, Adler was run over twice in the street and nearly died of pneumonia. Orgler (1963, p. 16: Mosak & Maniacci, 1999) reports that at one point Adler remembered hearing the doctor tell his father, "Your boy is lost." It seems reasonable to assume that all of these illnesses and the brush with death had a profound impact on Adler's development. Mosak and Maniacci (1999) report that Adler remembered deciding to become a physician when he recovered from his near fatal illness (Adler, 1947). The many illnesses also most certainly influenced his early thinking about the importance of organ inferiority and its effects on personality development.

After a slow start academically (his mathematics teacher at one point recommended that he be apprenticed for a trade), he went on to obtain a medical degree and started a practice in ophthalmology. However, his interest in the social influences and the psychology of his patients led him into the study and practice of psychiatry. Adler's theory is sometimes called *individual psychology* because of his interest in what we now call the "whole person." This part of his thinking was likely influenced by his deep interest in and concern for the social welfare of each individual.

In 1902, Freud invited Adler to join the famous Wednesday evening discussion group, a circle of doctors and scientists interested in Freud's ideas. Adler participated in this group, which became the Vienna Psychoanalytic Society, until 1911 but resigned as president after his disagreements with Freud caused a rift in the Society. Although Adler admired Freud and believed that he had made a great contribution to science, Adler's own ideas developed in a very different direction. Certainly, his own thinking was shaped and stimulated by Freud's revolutionary ideas, but he ultimately rejected the deterministic view of a psyche driven by inner forces. Instead, he placed much more emphasis on the importance of social influences in development and came to believe that humans are goal oriented and that they make choices based on their individual beliefs and how they fit into the world. In 1922, Adler opened a number of child guidance centers in schools in what was probably the first attempt at community mental health. Twenty-eight of these centers were operating in Vienna in 1934 when they were closed by the government during the rise of Nazism (Mosak, 2000).

Seligman (2001) divides Adler's professional development into four periods. The first period was just after he had graduated from medical school and seemed to be searching for a career direction. His early work as an ophthalmologist and a physician was not satisfying, and he became more interested in the mind. The second period, she reports, came during his time in the Vienna Circle, where he felt the strain between his interest in the whole person and healthy emotional development and Freud's theory. The third came when he left the Society and began to further develop his ideas about how people become healthy psychologically. The last stage, according to Seligman, came after his work as a psychiatrist in World War I, when he began to see social interest as more important than the drive to overcome inferiority.

He first came to the United States to lecture in 1926, and foreseeing the growth of Nazism, he moved to New York City, where he remained until his death on a lecture tour in 1938. After his death, the interest in Adler's work declined, largely because of the popularity of Freudian psychoanalysis and the fact that his ideas were in direct opposition to the basic principles of Freud's theory. Many of his students immigrated to the United States and faced strong opposition from Freudian proponents.

Rudolph Dreikurs, a student and colleague of Adler, came to the United States in 1937 and took up the mantle of Adlerian psychology, working hard to revive it. He established the Alfred Adler Institute of Chicago, which became the center of Adlerian psychology for many years. He and his colleagues contributed greatly to the resurgence in the popularity of Adlerian therapy and its applications to couples, families, and education.

ASSUMPTIONS AND CORE CONCEPTS

View of Human Nature

A Person's Perceptions Are Based on His or Her View of Reality Adler believed that we "construct" our reality according to our own way of looking at the world. Mosak and Maniacci (1999, p. 12) quote Adler:

> "I am convinced," Adler [Adler, 1933/1964, p. 19] stated unequivocally, "that a person's behavior springs from this idea . . . because our senses do not receive actual facts, but merely a subjective image of them." Technically speaking, we do not see the world, we apprehend it. Adler [1956, p. 182] spoke of a "schema of apperception [*Apperzeptionshema*]."

This concept has historical and philosophical roots, but Adler can surely be credited with pioneering its application to counseling. This was particularly difficult because the idea ran counter to Freudian notions of an objective psychology with rather specific constructs and ideas about human personality. Mosak and Maniacci (1999) discuss the issue of choice inherent in this kind of constructivist view as a kind of "soft determinism" (p. 18). By this, they mean that all of our choices are limited somewhat by biology and circumstance. They emphasize that we are can always choose how we feel and interpret events, no matter what the circumstances.

Each Person Must Be Viewed as an Individual from a Holistic Perspective Adler suggested that dividing the person up into parts or forces (i.e., id, ego, and superego) was counterproductive because it was mechanistic and missed the individual essence of each person. In his view, understanding the whole person is different than understanding different aspects of his life or personality. This was clearly a rejection of Freudian principles, but it was also an affirmation of the individual's ability to choose and to have a unique perspective on the world.

Human Behavior is Goal Oriented (Teleological) This idea requires a very different way of viewing humans than the idea that behavior is "caused" by some internal or external forces or rewards and punishments. Understanding the causes of behavior is not as important as understanding the goal to which a person is directed. Since we have evolved as social creatures, the most common goal is to belong. For example, a child strives to belong in her family, or a teenager strives to belong to a peer group. As you will see later, understanding and analyzing the way we attempt to reach our goals are at the heart of Adlerian counseling.

Striving for Superiority to Overcome Basic Inferiority is a Normal Part of Life In his earlier work, Adler hypothesized a kind of biological inferiority. He suggested that an individual might strive to overcome particular organ inferiorities and that certain illnesses and weaknesses might be explained by these inferiorities. For example, a person with respiratory difficulties who was never very competitive at running might choose to bulk up through weightlifting to overcome this "inferiority." The concept of organ inferiority later took on a more social and psychological meaning for Adler. He extended the notion of organ inferiority, which usually revolved around a significant physical disability such as those he experienced as a child, to other types of inferiority rooted in the universal experience of coming into the world as small, helpless creatures. Given these humble beginnings, Adler concluded that each of us is constantly striving to overcome our inferiority. This striving, if it is socially directed, can be the impetus for great achievements. Mosak (2000) reports that Adler and others have referred to this central human striving in a number of ways: completion, perfection, superiority, self-realization, self-actualization, competence, and mastery. You can see that these different ideas related to overcoming inferiority greatly broaden the term from Adler's original notion of organ inferiority.

Social Interest and a Positive Involvement in the Community are Hallmarks of a Healthy Personality This basic assumption can be seen in Adler's early life. His development of community family clinics is one example. In his later writings, Adler emphasized this idea of being part of the whole or, in German, the *Gemeinschaftsgefuhl* (Alder, 1933/1964). He believed that social interest was innate but that it needed to be nurtured in a family where cooperation and trust were important values. Social interest and learning to become a productive member of society are important parts of Adlerian therapy.

Core Concepts

Lifestyle The concept of lifestyle is at the heart of Adlerian counseling and therapy. Each individual develops a unique lifestyle, which he then uses throughout life to work toward his goals and to govern his life. Since Adler believed each person had the power and creativity to make choices and govern his own life, this lifestyle or road map for life becomes a profoundly important concept. Adler believed that a person's lifestyle is developed early in life and that it is influenced by both biology and psychosocial factors.

Although Adler talked about organ inferiority and the importance of overcoming these inferiorities, as well as a kind of basic inferiority as a child, Mosak and Maniacci (1999) discuss the importance of the development of the central nervous system in lifestyle development. They suggest that a kind of preverbal learning takes place in terms of how a child sees the world prior to the development of the frontal lobes of the brain between the ages of 5 and 7. As children develop verbal and behavioral ways to negotiate the world, they behave "as if" this early learning was true and develop a more conscious, verbally definable lifestyle. According to Mosak and Maniacci (1999), "They set out to confirm their expectations and apply them in ever increasing wider social fields. Although these are seemingly 'set in stone,' slight modifications continue to occur throughout the life span; however, the core convictions remain constant unless the person has a therapeutic experience" (p. 36). They note that a therapeutic experience can occur from a variety of life experiences, not just from a counseling experience.

Mosak (1954, 2000) divided lifestyle convictions into four areas:

1. The self-concept—the convictions about who I am.
2. The self-ideal (Adler coined this phrase in 1912)—the convictions about what I should be or am obliged to be to have a place.
3. The *Weltbild*, or "picture of the world"—the convictions about the not-self (world, people, nature, and so on) and what the world demands of me.
4. The ethical convictions—the personal "right-wrong" code. (p. 66)

Although a person has emotions related to her lifestyle, this is essentially a cognitive concept. The individual uses this "map" to interpret the world and to interact with it. This is sometimes called a person's *private logic.*

The concept of lifestyle can be very complex. Problems can occur when there are inconsistencies or incongruities in the lifestyle beliefs. The most obvious, perhaps, is an incongruity between the self-ideal and the self-concept. For example, a male client might grow up believing that an ideal man is very good at sports, but he may learn early on that he is not a good athlete. There can also be incongruity between a person's self-concept and her *Weltbild*, her view of the world, when some radical change occurs in her world. A child may be relatively happy and able to operate and grow well in a particular environment, and then his parents get a divorce. Suddenly, his world changes drastically, and at least for a time, there is a great incongruity between his views of himself and of the world. Developmental changes may also create discontinuities. Take, for example, a girl who develops a self-ideal in her early years about her gender identity as a very traditional female. In her family, girls are passive caregivers, are subservient to men, and do not play in rough games. Her self-concept and self-ideal fit well until she enters school and discovers that she is a great athlete, really doesn't like being around girls, and loves to play kickball with the boys.

Family Constellation and Atmosphere Perhaps the most widely known aspect of Adler's work is the influence of birth order; however, these ideas are often misunderstood and misapplied. Birth order is only one aspect of how a person's experience in his family influences his development. The family constellation is important and does have a significant influence on what a child experiences. In general terms, the family and reciprocal relationships with siblings and parents determine how a person finds a place in the family and what he learns about finding a place in the world. In other words, what happens in the family largely determines a person's early lifestyle beliefs.

A multitude of influences can be important and are interrelated with the influence of birth order and sibling relationships. Perhaps paramount are parental attitudes, treatment, and expectations of a child. Related to this are sibling roles and relationships with other relatives living in the household or nearby. Anything that affects the family and the parents has some influence on the children. A child's physical assets, personality, and intelligence also play a role, as do family myths, values, and culture (Nicoll & Hawes, 1985).

Since the birth order can influence lifestyle, let's examine the generalizations developed for each position. We advise caution here because many factors can influence family roles and these descriptions certainly do not always apply. On the other hand, it has been our experience that students and clients often find them to be quite descriptive.

Oldest child. The oldest child is thought to be the most adult and responsible. She is the center of her parents' attention and tends to want to please them. She is often well behaved and a model citizen. If another child comes along, she often experiences considerable discomfort because she has to share what has been her exclusive right to the love and attention of her parents.

Second child. The second child starts out in a kind of competitive mode. He must upset the status quo and compete with the older sibling. He most often finds ways to excel that are different from those of his older sibling. Often he develops a personality that is very different from that of the older sibling. One typical pattern is for the older sibling to feel more comfortable with adults and to have more difficulty being extroverted among peers, while the second child develops very effective social relationships with other children. It is not atypical for the competition between siblings to carry over into adulthood in some fashion.

Middle child. The middle child is said to have the most problems because it is harder to find a place in the family. The oldest child has the advantages of being oldest and most responsible; the youngest often gets the most attention and is able to get away with behavior that the middle child cannot. The middle child feels squeezed, with no identified role as the youngest or the oldest.

Youngest child. The youngest is the pampered one. She needs the most attention for several years and is often able to get what she wants from the parents. Parents are often more relaxed with a second or third child and tend to be a bit more relaxed with rules and regulations. The youngest child may learn to use a kind of helpless attitude to get attention and to manipulate.

Again, we caution against a thoughtless application of these generalizations. In Adler's view, the lifestyle was largely set during the early years of life, when the family influences were greatest. However, some contemporary Adlerian therapists also look to later developmental experiences outside the family as important in shaping the individual's lifestyle. For example, a young woman who realizes that she is sexually attracted to other girls and who ultimately identifies herself as a lesbian may undergo some significant changes in her perceptions about herself and her place in the world. And a man who is passed over for a promotion and fired from his job may change his views about his professional goals and the fairness of the world outside himself. These examples involve fundamental changes to the direction of these persons' lives, and thus their lifestyles, long after early childhood.

When we discuss assessment, you will learn a number of ways to assess lifestyle, but for purposes of understanding the concept, consider some of the questions that need to be answered regarding the family constellation to determine lifestyle:

1. How did the client please his mother and his father?
2. What was his role in the family?
3. What were his relationships with siblings?
4. What important events happened to the family as he was growing up?
5. What was the influence of culture, socioeconomic factors, and other family values and unwritten rules?

Psychology of Use The assumption discussed earlier, that behavior is goal directed and that behavior and emotion are "used" to achieve one's goals, has a very significant influence on the principles of Adlerian counseling. The question of what causes behavior or emotion is essentially replaced by the question of what a person is trying to accomplish by behaving or feeling in a certain way. Another assumption, that human beings are active and creative influencers of their environments, is also important: Motives are directly related to the person's lifestyle and how she believes that she can achieve her goals. This psychology of use principle is really quite different from a cause-and-effect approach to counseling and to human behavior. The following two short counseling excerpts with Janet, a 35-year-old executive in a large bank, demonstrate this difference.

Cause-and-effect approach—Counselor 1

Janet: I'm just at the end of my rope. I feel like I'm on a merry-go-round. . . . I never have time for myself, and when I do, I just feel stressed all the time.

Counselor: That sounds pretty tough. What's your take on why this is all happening?

Janet: I really don't know. I should be happy. I'm very successful at work and I have a great husband and family. I just feel like I'm working so damn hard all the time!

Counselor: Well, it sounds like you are involved in a lot of different things. Would you say that trying to cope with all of these demands might be causing a lot of stress?

Janet: That makes sense . . . maybe I should think about trying to cut back on some of these activities so that I can have some time to myself.

Counselor: Well, that might be a good idea. We can look at your overall time-management picture and also how you cope with the demands on your life.

Psychology of use approach—Counselor 2

See DVD

Chap. 3
Clip 1

Janet: I'm just at the end of my rope. I feel like I'm on a merry-go-round. . . . I never have time for myself, and when I do, I just feel stressed all the time.

Counselor: That sounds pretty tough. What do you get out of being so busy and feeling so stressed?

Janet: What do you mean? I don't get anything except a lot of stress.

Counselor: Yes, but what does this stress do for you? Does it help you keep going and work hard at everything you do?

Janet: Well, in a way. I have always been a high achiever and have felt stressed about doing the best I can do.

Counselor: Would you be willing to take a closer look at some of the beliefs that you have developed that seem to motivate you to make the choices that you make?

We see here a striking difference in the direction that counseling might go in these two segments. Counselor 1 seems to be heading toward a problem-solving approach, hoping to help Janet get better control of her life and figure out ways to change her activities and perhaps learn some ways to relax. In this approach, the basic assumption is that the stress is caused by too many activities. The reasons Janet makes these choices may come out, but they would be seen as part of the causes of her overcommitment.

Counselor 2 moves right into a search for her motives. What does she get out of her current situation and in particular her stress? The underlying assumption is that she has chosen, for some reason, to make the choices that create stress and that, in fact, she is "using" this stress for some purpose. The purpose, as you have guessed, is related to her lifestyle. Somewhere along the way, she has decided that high accomplishments and related stress will help her achieve her goal. In her "private logic," she may believe that in order to be loved and accepted, she must always be on the run and achieving. We can, of course, further speculate that she learned, as a child, that this would bring approval and happiness. You will see later how an assessment of her lifestyle beliefs would be used in counseling.

Mistaken Beliefs   Sometimes people develop distorted lifestyle beliefs as a result of what they have concluded about themselves and the world. In Adlerian terms, these are called *mistaken beliefs*—mistaken because they don't lead to the goals of social connectedness and productivity that Adlerians believe are central to effective psychological functioning. In the previous example, Janet appears to have a mistaken belief that she has to always push herself and create a kind of motivating stress in order to be worthwhile. Mosak (2000, p. 73) lists five kinds of basic mistakes: overgeneralizations, false or impossible goals of "security," misperceptions of life and life's demands, minimization or denial of one's worth, and faulty values. These basic mistakes, when they have become part of a person's lifestyle beliefs, are seen as interfering with that person's healthy growth and development and as being the primary reasons for psychological problems. They are typically examined as part of the lifestyle assessment, which includes an analysis of the family. Mosak reports early attempts by Adler to come up with general themes of mistaken beliefs that are demonstrated by types of lifestyles. As a result of his extensive work on lifestyle types (Mosak, 1959, 1973, 1979), Mosak has identified 14 different general types: getters, controllers, victims, martyrs, drivers, those who need to be superior, inadequate ones, excitement seekers, babies, feeling avoiders, those who need to be good, those who need to be right, those who oppose (aginners), and those who need to be liked (pleasers) (Mosak & Maniacci, 1999, p. 67). These lifestyles all involve clusters of mistaken beliefs that make up certain kinds of lifestyles.

Life Tasks   One's social interests are demonstrated through a series of life tasks. Adlerian counseling usually involves work with a client on accomplishing these life tasks. According to Mosak (2000), Adler originally named three of these: society, work, and sex. The life task of society is to recognize one's interdependence with other members of society. Work is part of a person's contribution to society. He contributes to the overall productivity by his work.

Because of mistaken lifestyle beliefs, clients often have been unable to make progress on the life tasks. Discussion of these tasks might be part of a more extensive therapy involving work to change mistaken lifestyle beliefs that interfere with a variety of life tasks, or it might be part of a briefer focus on a particular life task and how a client is blocked in achieving his life goal in that area. Contemporary versions of Adlerian counseling are not necessarily long term and focused on a lengthy lifestyle analysis and interpretation.

Mosak and Maniacci (1999) provide an extensive discussion of several life tasks and subtasks. They divide the *work task* into six subtasks: (1) occupational choice, (2) occupational preparation, (3) satisfaction, (4) leadership, (5) leisure, and (6) sociovocational issues (relationships with coworkers). It is not difficult to imagine a client in counseling with issues related to any of these six tasks. Take, for example, María, a Mexican-American woman, who is a receptionist in a large dental practice. She has worked at this job since she graduated from a 1-year secretarial course after high school:

> **María:**   I just don't like my job. I'm very good at it, but it has gotten boring and feels like a dead end.
>
> **Counselor:**   So you're not really getting what you want out of a career.

María: That's true. I always thought having a good, steady job was the thing to do, but I just don't even feel like going to work anymore.

Counselor: What do you think this dissatisfaction and boredom means?

María: Well, I don't know. I was pretty happy for the first year of this job, but I don't seem to be going anywhere, and I really don't feel like I am a part of the place.

In this case, the task of counseling might be to work on finding a more rewarding career. Mistaken lifestyle beliefs would be identified first. María may believe that she is not smart enough to handle a more demanding professional career. This could be because when she was growing up, her parents did not encourage her in school. Perhaps related to her cultural background, because of discrimination and limited opportunities for Mexican Americans, her parents may have believed that their daughter could not aspire to a professional career. These limits, then, became part of María's beliefs about her abilities and possibilities early in life. In other words, her "private logic" is a kind of acceptance of a racist-based notion that she is intellectually inferior. This culture-related scenario is only one possibility to be explored. Other possibilities, like being overshadowed by a brilliant older sister, are also possible.

After María gains insight into these mistaken beliefs and is able to have more confidence in her abilities, she may work with the counselor to find a more rewarding career and thereby reach a satisfactory career choice.

The *social task* is divided into two subtasks, belonging and transactions. Belonging involves how an individual finds a way to gain a sense of belonging. An individual might develop mistaken beliefs about how to belong, perhaps by appearing helpless and inadequate, thereby attracting others who want to help. This would be a kind of style of transactions with others that may work for a time but that will eventually create problems. Sometimes ways of belonging that work in a person's family no longer work as they become young adults and attempt to form intimate relationships.

The *sexual task*, according to Mosak and Maniacci (1999), involves sex role definition and identification, sexual development, and sexual behavior. A person must first, as a child, learn to identify sex roles and the differences between societal definitions and expectations of men and women. The boy or girl then begins to see how closely he or she fits the definitions. Those who do not fit well must deal with failing to measure up to these ideals. Later, as sexual development progresses, an individual must come to grips with sexual orientation and sexual behavior.

The *self task* is essentially the task each of us has of deciding how to think and feel about ourselves. It is divided by Mosak and Maniacci (1999) into four categories: survival, body image, opinion, and evaluation. Survival involves how one takes care of oneself physically, body image is how one sees one's body, opinion is what one thinks of oneself, and evaluation is a kind of general good or bad judgment of self.

The *spiritual task* includes the following: relationship to God, religion, relationship to the universe, metaphysical issues, and the meaning of life. The idea of spirituality in counseling has become very popular recently, and counselors have now begun to seriously examine the role of spirituality in counseling (Fukuyama & Sevig, 1999; Sperry, 2003; Tan, 2003). Finally, many of us face the *parenting and family task*. It involves decisions about parenting, marriage, partner relationships, and connections with family members.

Therapists need to understand these tasks of life and how they relate to an individual's connection to the social fabric of society. Such understandings provide a map of how people connect to the world and of their basic motivations in life. In one sense, all problems of living come down to how we negotiate and satisfy these life tasks.

THERAPEUTIC RELATIONSHIP

Counselor's Role

Adlerians do not see the therapist as a doctor who "cures" the patient. Although Adlerian therapists ask for a great deal of information and are involved in interpreting the data they gather, they focus initially on the client as a person and attempt to establish a friendly and genuine relationship. Because the therapist sees the client as a unique individual, with the creative power to change and influence his environment, the counselor has great respect for the client. Adler rejected the traditional distant psychoanalytic approach in favor of more of a relationship of equals. A very important part of the therapy involves the counselor working hard to understand the "private logic" of the client, and this requires a high degree of empathy and understanding. The counselor is also a kind of teacher, helping the client understand more about his mistaken beliefs, where they come from, and how they can be changed. There is a delicate balance to maintain between being an educator and a kind of expert, on the one hand, and respecting the client and maintaining a genuine relationship, on the other.

Counselor-Client Relationship

In order for the relationship and the therapy to work, the client and counselor must cooperate and have mutual goals. The therapist is called on to understand the interpersonal dynamics occurring in the therapy session. Since most clients expect the therapist to behave toward them as others do, the therapist can get a "bird's eye view" of how the client operates in the interpersonal arena. The therapist is also called on to avoid becoming involved in any interpersonal games or manipulation by the client. The client must be willing to trust the therapist and to participate in activities, such as early recollections, where she might feel quite vulnerable. The client must be comfortable with the fact that the Adlerian therapist is both a teacher and a warm, empathetic partner in a journey to uncover and understand issues related to lifestyle assessment that may be painful.

ASSESSMENT, GOALS, AND PROCESS OF THERAPY

Assessment

Assessing lifestyle is a crucial part of Adlerian therapy. A traditional lifestyle assessment may involve an extensive lifestyle questionnaire and interview. The questionnaire might be mailed to a new client or perhaps sent with an e-mail or even completed on an interactive Web site. Eckstein, Baruth, and Mahrer (1992, pp. 43–52) provide a typical set of guidelines for information that needs to be collected in a lifestyle assessment. They include items in the following general categories:

1. **The interviewee's current "way of being in the world."** This includes questions about the client's specific concerns and major stressors and a survey of satisfaction with general life tasks.

2. **Family atmosphere.** A number of specific questions ask about siblings, including their ages and descriptions of their characteristics; comparisons; childhood traumas; family atmosphere; parental expectations of each child; parental relationships; and much more.

3. **Early recollections.** Early recollections are the client's memories of specific incidents in early childhood. It is thought that the client will remember incidents that have particular relevance to his current situation and that provide the counselor with information about how he perceived the world as a child. The idea of these recollections is to provide a window into the client's early life that is not contaminated by the censoring that might take place in direct discussions with the therapist. The client is typically asked questions designed to provide a complete picture of the child's feelings and perceptions at the time. Questions about relationships with parents and siblings are particularly relevant if they are part of the recollection.

Many different formats for the lifestyle analysis have been developed. Stein (2003) provides a 15-question outline for what he calls Adlerian brief therapy. He includes questions such as "What was the behavior of your father and mother towards you?" and "What were your most important personality traits when you were a child?" You can see that these questions are designed, as are those in other lifestyle questionnaires, to help the therapist understand as much as possible about the client's early childhood circumstances and perceptions of her environment.

After the counselor gathers all of this information, he attempts to come up with a formulation of the client's lifestyle. Recall that this consists of the self-concept, the self-ideal, the *Weltbild* (view of the world), and ethical convictions. Perhaps equally as important as the assessment of lifestyle is the fact that the process helps the client begin to gain insight into his mistaken beliefs and how they are limiting his life in the present.

In practice, many counselors use a more limited version of a lifestyle analysis. The reality is that there is often not enough time to do a complete analysis, and in fact, many clients are seen only once or twice. This suggests that counselors might work rather quickly to discover something about a client's lifestyle mistakes in a brief period of time. Following are two examples of a lifestyle analysis. The first example is an abbreviated version of a more traditional assessment that involves the use of an extensive questionnaire and an interview. This kind of assessment might take up the first few counseling sessions. The second example is a much briefer kind of lifestyle analysis, representing what might be used in a brief counseling setting.

Traditional Assessment Herman is a 22-year-old Caucasian graduate student in history.

Herman: That was a very long questionnaire you asked me to fill out. I hope it was worth it.

Counselor: I do appreciate you doing it. I think it will help both of us understand a lot more about how you see the world. I want to spend a few sessions just going over some of the things you put down and asking for some clarification. Is that OK with you?

Herman: Well, if you think it will help . . . you know I am pretty depressed and not doing well in my doctoral program. I really need help.

Counselor: I do understand how tough things are for you, but I need for us to spend some time going over your early experiences in your family. This will help us get a better idea of how to approach the problems you are having now.

Herman: OK . . . I can see that what happened in my family might be affecting me now. Hell . . . I am still having a lot of conflicts with my parents.

Counselor: Let's start out by looking at your lifestyle questionnaire.

LIFESTYLE SUMMARY. After the early counseling sessions with the client, during which the client and counselor go over the lifestyle questionnaire and discuss the contents in considerable detail, a working lifestyle summary can be developed:

1. **Presenting concerns.** Depression, anger at his professors, 50 pounds overweight, very stressed by graduate school. A major focus in terms of life tasks is work—in his case, graduate school. Socially, he is somewhat isolated, although he does interact with other graduate students. He is sexually active with a woman he lives with, but she is also a graduate student, and they have very little time together. He describes their sex life as OK, but he says that he always feels nervous when his partner sees him naked and that this interferes with him really enjoying sex. He says that he has very little time for recreation and relaxation and tends to eat when he is depressed and under stress. When asked about his spiritual life, he laughed and said he had no time to contemplate his navel.

2. **Family atmosphere.** Herman has on ongoing conflict with his parents. When he talks to them on the phone, he usually gets into an argument. He also feels sad and angry that they never acknowledge his academic accomplishments. He has one brother who is 6 years younger. He describes the brother as more "normal" and more relaxed than he is. His parents are not college educated and do not approve of or understand his choice to attend graduate school to study history. They feel that he should do something more practical, that he is wasting his talents. His parents are still together. He describes his father as quiet and distant—he doesn't remember having much contact with him when he was very young. He describes his mother as very high strung. She was hospitalized for depression when he was about 5 or 6. He reports that he remembers feeling different from his parents at a very early age. He was not a typical boy and liked to stay indoors and read books. He remembers his parents always telling him to go outside and play. He says that he always had a hard time pleasing his parents. They always wanted him to be more like a typical boy, and they couldn't understand why he was so interested in books and in drawing. He remembers feeling relieved when his brother was born because his parents stopped paying so much attention to him. He says that his parents watched TV a lot and that the family didn't have much money; they never went on vacations or did fun things together. He doesn't remember a specific childhood trauma but describes himself as an unhappy child until he started school. He loved school and was always able to excel there. He remembers being overweight at a very young age and remembers his mother always telling him that if he would exercise and get outside, he wouldn't be so fat. His parents were very devout Catholics and attended Mass every Sunday. He remembers them taking him to a priest when he was 5 because they were worried

about him being so quiet and not having many friends. He describes his relationship with his younger brother as distant. He reports that his brother gets along better in the family and has always been favored by his parents. A major theme that he remembers, especially when he was younger, was his mother's constant harping at him to lose weight and become more active.

3. **Early recollections.** Herman reported several early recollections; a description of two of them follows:

   - He remembers sitting on the couch with his father, who was reading a book to him. He is not sure of his age but thinks he was about 4. His mother came in and told him to get off the couch and get some exercise. He remembers feeling resentful and angry at his mother because he felt so happy and comfortable with his father reading to him. His father made him go outside and play catch, which he didn't like to do.

   - He remembers a time when he was out playing with the kids in the neighborhood. He says that he was about 6. He thinks it was right when he started first grade. They were going to have a race to see who could run around the block the fastest. He says that he was a fat kid and couldn't run very fast. He decided that he didn't want to compete, but they all laughed at him and called him a fatso. He says that he can still feel the anger and embarrassment as he recalls the incident. He felt like crying but just remembers going to his room to read.

4. **Lifestyle assessment.** As the discussion of his family and his early life experiences developed, Herman was quick to say that he understood that his childhood experiences were related to his problems with eating and with getting angry so easily, but he noted that this had never helped him make any changes. The counselor was careful not to respond to this as resistance but rather suggested that maybe the two of them would be able to figure out how to help him make some positive changes. In terms of lifestyle analysis, the counselor made the following hypotheses with regard to the four elements of lifestyle:

   - *Self-concept:* Herman grew up in a family that didn't seem to value his academic talents, and they still don't. On the one hand, he knows that his academic success is an accomplishment, but this is tempered by his past experience of not fulfilling his parents' expectations. He has a lot of resentment and anger toward his parents, and this seems to be reignited often when he talks with them. He often feels very tentative about himself and very easily threatened. This probably accounts for some some of the conflicts with his professors. He seems to lack the self-confidence to be able to understand that his professors may be wrong and even unfair but that this isn't his fault. He also feels very inadequate physically because he is overweight and is self-conscious about himself sexually.

   - *Self-ideal:* Herman believes that he ought to be a person who pleases his parents. Even though he is 22 years old, he is still hurt every time his parents question his career choice and don't validate his academic accomplishments. His self-ideal is really to be a person who can gain his parents' respect. His self-ideal is also to be slim and muscular and more athletic.

   - *Picture of the world:* Herman often sees the world as unfair. He has always felt judged because he is overweight and because people don't really appreciate "intellectuals." He feels more comfortable in an academic setting as a graduate student but often thinks that he is being unfairly judged by his professors—they don't seem to appreciate how hard he works or what he accomplishes.

- *Ethical convictions:* From the information reported, it is difficult to get much of a picture of Herman's ethical convictions. He seemed to avoid or deny a spiritual part of himself, saying that he didn't have time to contemplate his navel. He does seem to have some strong beliefs that people should be treated fairly. He has a strong perception that he has been treated unfairly by his family and judged as being fat.

5. **Mistaken beliefs:** With these ideas in mind, we can construct some hypotheses about what some of Herman's mistaken beliefs might be:
    1. Since most people are not going to appreciate me and my talents, I need to be wary and fend off any criticism.
    2. I must keep working to get the approval of my parents and others.
    3. I need to compensate for my appearance.

You can see from this abbreviated version of a lifestyle assessment that the assessment itself can be complex and that helping a client change mistaken beliefs that have been an integral part of his life for a long time is no easy task. Remember that the assessment is a process, hopefully with the client fully engaged and working to better understand himself and open to learning more about his lifestyle beliefs. The usually gentle and encouraging manner of Adlerian therapists allows for a great deal of give and take with the counselor.

Brief Lifestyle Assessment Janet is a 35-year-old female who is biracial (African American and Italian): she presents as being anxious and uncertain about some major changes that she is making. She belongs to a health maintenance organization that pays for only the first four outpatient mental health visits, and she can't afford additional visits. She is also moving in about a month, so more visits are not possible.

Janet reports some background information in the first session. Her mother died when she was 6, and she was the oldest of three siblings. She remembers even then feeling the responsibility of taking care of her brothers because she was the oldest. They went to live with her father's parents, who were very old, so growing up she spent much of her time taking care of her brothers and doing all of the household work. As her father's parents got older, she also took care of them. She finished high school and works at the post office as a delivery person. She lived with her father until recently when he died of cancer. She didn't have much of a childhood and had little time for boys or girlfriends. She said that this didn't matter too much, since she didn't have much to offer other people anyway. At school, she had a hard time fitting in because she never knew if she was White or Black. She has been pretty satisfied being isolated, but since her father died, she has decided that she really wants to turn her life around. She has taken a transfer on her job and is moving to a different city where she hopes things will be different.

Since Janet has a limited number of visits, the counselor made some quick hypotheses about her lifestyle beliefs. First, it seemed clear that she had been a caretaker her entire life, always putting others' needs ahead of herself. In a sense, this was her primary identity. When her father died, she lost this role and was at loose ends. She had also avoided social and intimate relationships because she felt useful in her role as caretaker, because she was uncertain of herself as a social being, and because she was confused about her racial identity. Her basic mistakes might be hypothesized as follows:

1. Taking care of others is the way I can be a worthwhile person.
2. I cannot find a place socially as a biracial person.
3. I must avoid socialization because I have little to offer.

The counselor in this case came up with this working hypothesis about Janet in just one session, from a fairly brief discussion of her background. In fact, near the end of the session he shared his hypotheses about her lifestyle mistakes and engaged her in a discussion about her reactions to his interpretations. The danger in this brief analysis is, of course, that the counselor draws his hypotheses prematurely, without having a lot of data to go by.

Goals

The client and counselor work toward the counseling goals—typically to help the client gain insight into his mistaken lifestyle beliefs, develop healthier and more effective beliefs about how to achieve his personal goals, and change behavior patterns based on these mistaken beliefs. From an Adlerian perspective, a person comes to counseling because in some way his attempts to achieve personal goals are not working. The counseling goals will have emotional, behavioral, and cognitive components.

Let's say Martin comes in to counseling because his wife can no longer tolerate his compulsive need to control everything in the household. This control is a result of his experience in a chaotic family, which caused him to decide, as part of his lifestyle beliefs, that he could use control and structure to avoid the pain related to growing up in his out-of-control family. When he comes in, he is angry and depressed and is unable to sleep because of the conflict with his wife. The focus in an Adlerian approach will be to help him realize that controlling his family is not a healthy or effective way to achieve his goals of feeling relaxed and at ease. He will need to change his mistaken belief that control and structure are the best way to achieve his goals. This will involve insight into how he developed these beliefs as a child. He may have used control and structure (lots of activities, control of friends, and locking himself in his room) to avoid his chaotic family and therefore come to believe (mistakenly) that this was the way to avoid pain and anxiety and get along in life. In addition to insight, he will need to work on modifying conditioned ways of behaving related to control.

As we have noted, Adler had clear ideas about what a generally healthy, socially connected life looks like. In defining the basic lifestyle tasks (work, social, sexual, self, spiritual, and parenting and family tasks), Adler sets up an outline for goals for a socially connected and healthy lifestyle. The way in which Martin attempts to accomplish each of these tasks might be affected if he modifies his lifestyle beliefs as a result of counseling.

Process of Therapy

In general, Adlerian therapy includes several phases. We have already discussed the importance of establishing a *relationship* with the client.

Analysis is the next phase. In a sense, the therapist begins to analyze and make hypotheses about the client's lifestyle as soon as counseling begins. This is a kind of process whereby the counselor begins to paint a picture of the client, changing and modifying the picture as more information and impressions emerge. All of this is part of the Adlerian notion that everything the client does, thinks, and feels fits together. The closer the therapist comes to understanding this unique picture, the greater the chance he has of learning the client's private logic.

As we have noted before, the *exploration of lifestyle* is perhaps the heart of Adlerian therapy. We have described this process in some detail earlier, but it is important to understand that it is an information-gathering *and* educational process. The client begins to understand more and more about how his background has shaped his lifestyle as this exploration goes on. As the therapist learns more and more about the client's lifestyle beliefs, he is able to offer interpretations and help the client gain insight into mistaken beliefs.

The stage of *insight* can actually take place at different times in the counseling process. It is most likely to occur as the client explores his lifestyle development and as the therapist helps him gain insight into his goals, his motivation, and how his lifestyle beliefs were formed. Insight is not always or even typically a light bulb suddenly lighting up. It is often a slow process as the client comes to understand how his behavior is related to his mistaken beliefs about how to achieve his goals. Insight is also not a passive process. The knowledge gained must result in positive action.

Reorientation and change are the part of therapy, during which the client is persuaded that he needs to change. This may occur as a result of insights gained through exploration, but it may begin to occur as a result of experience with the therapist or experience outside of therapy. Adlerian counseling is truly a "process," and it is not necessarily linear. These process "steps" don't typically occur in a neat progression. The reorientation phase may be particularly difficult because it requires the client to give up a way of thinking and behaving that, although flawed, may seem safe and secure. Change can feel dangerous and is usually risky.

THERAPEUTIC TECHNIQUES

Adlerian therapy is not a "technique"-oriented approach; however, as part of the process of counseling and helping the client, a number of specific techniques have been described. These are all used to help the client move through the process of insight and understanding of lifestyle beliefs and mistaken apperceptions and to help reorient and persuade the client to change mistaken beliefs and unwanted and unsuccessful behavior.

Encouragement

This is perhaps the most pervasive "technique" that Adlerian therapists use. It takes place throughout therapy and impacts each stage. Initially, a client is typically discouraged, often feeling hopeless. Beginning counseling with a counselor who offers hope, empathy, and understanding can help the client develop hope and a positive expectation of counseling. Encouragement is also particularly important in the reorientation stage, when the client must decide to take a risk and try new ways of thinking and behaving. Sometimes encouragement takes the form of understanding and acknowledging mistaken lifestyle beliefs. Even though these beliefs may be mistaken and creating problems in the person's current life, they may have been useful and protective when first formulated. Take the case of Lauretta, a survivor of sexual abuse by her father.

> **Lauretta:** I know I should learn to trust people. . . . I just keep screwing up relationships. Why do I drive people away?
>
> **Counselor:** I think you know why, don't you?

Lauretta: You're right. . . . I know it's because of what happened to me as a child.

Counselor: You know, even though being guarded is causing you problems now, it sounds to me like it was a pretty good way of dealing with the abuse you suffered as a child. I would say that you showed a lot of strength by finding a way to cope.

Lauretta: . . . I guess that's right, but I don't want to keep on this way!

Setting Tasks

Task setting usually occurs as a way to help the client take a small step toward thinking and behaving in a new and different way. The therapist helps the client set up a plan to try a task that can probably be accomplished successfully. When this occurs in a direct way, it is quite similar to what a behavior therapist might do to help teach a person new behaviors. This is most likely to occur during the reorientation stage as a way of persuading the client that change is possible and desirable. It may also be a way of helping the client change habitual patterns of behavior.

Using Antisuggestion/Paradoxical Intention

In this technique, the client is asked to increase the symptom or problem behavior. For example, a person who feels anxious when he is around strangers would be asked to try to increase his anxiety the next time he is with strangers. Or a person who is so disorganized that she can't get things done would be asked to try to be even sloppier and less organized. The idea behind this approach is that the client will gain a new awareness of the symptom, learn that he or she has some control of the symptom, and decide that it is really something that he or she wants to change.

Acting As If

In this approach, the client is asked to act "as if" he can do something that he thinks he cannot do. In essence, he is asked to suspend his judgment that he can't do something as an experiment. This requires considerable trust in the therapist and willingness to try something new. Take the case of Sandeep. He works in a bank, and because he is an Asian American of Indian descent, his coworkers are always assuming that he knows math and computers well. In reality, he hates computers and is a very verbal and artistic person:

Sandeep: Well, it happened again last week. Somebody just assumed that I could fix her computer. I am really sick of people assuming I'm a computer expert just because I'm Indian. I don't know s--t about computers! It makes me feel depressed about going to work.

Counselor: Hmm. . . . We have talked about this before. These stereotypes really amount to a kind of racism, and I know that these instances hurt you a lot. Do you think that you should report what is going on to the personnel office?

Sandeep: No, definitely not! I like my job and the people I work with. That would really cause more problems.

Counselor: I also know that it is unfair to put the burden on you to respond, . . . but that seems to leave you with the alternative of saying something to your coworkers.

Sandeep: I know, it just isn't fair. But I'm really afraid to say anything.

Counselor: Do you think that the folks at work won't like you if you tell them you don't know anything about computers and that you are offended by their assumptions?

Sandeep: Well, I do think that most of them will understand. I really think they don't realize the assumptions they are making because I'm Indian.

Counselor: Would you be willing to try an experiment?

Sandeep: It depends.

Counselor: Just for one time, with one person, could you act "as if" you were able to tell him that you just don't know much about computers and that you resent his assumptions?

Sandeep: Well, . . . maybe.

Catching One's Self

As a client reaches the stage in Adlerian counseling where she has gained some insight into her lifestyle and how the beliefs that she developed as a child are not necessarily accurate, she typically attempts to avoid actions and feelings that she has habitually used as a way of achieving her goals. Since these behaviors and feelings have been a part of her life for so long, it will probably be difficult to break the pattern. This technique of "catching one's self" is really just teaching a client to watch out for situations where these problem behaviors are likely to occur. For example, Lakisha and her partner Ellen have gone to counseling because Ellen is always deferring to Lakisha and wants her to make all the decisions. Lakisha finds this annoying and feels pressure to always make the right decision.

Counselor: So, Ellen, how did you do this week as far as the decision making?

Ellen: I was able to catch myself and not put another decision on Lakisha.

Counselor: How did you do that?

Ellen: I knew that we didn't have anything to do this weekend, and when I thought about the weekend, I was doing my typical "Well, I wonder what Lakisha wants to do?" Then I realized this is the same old pattern, and I decided that I would suggest something for us to do . . . and I did!

Counselor: Great! You were really able to catch yourself when you tried to put all the decision making on Lakisha! This is a very good first step!

In the counseling with this couple that preceded this session, Ellen had come to realize that one of her mistaken beliefs was that other people were usually smarter and stronger than she was and therefore she could be accepted and loved by always deferring to others.

Using Push Buttons

In this technique, the counselor asks a client to close his eyes and imagine a happy scene where he feels really alive and good about himself. The client is then asked to create a similar scene, but this time it is one in which the client is very unhappy and feels depressed and sad. The point is then made to the client that he can control his thoughts and related feelings. He can push whatever buttons he needs to control thoughts and feelings. This may sound simplistic, and it certainly may not, in itself, convince a client that he has more control; however, it may get him thinking, or it may add to other insights about control that the client is beginning to have.

Avoiding the Tar Baby

In a famous African American Uncle Remus folktale, Brer Fox is fed up with Brer Rabbit being so arrogant and thinking that he is boss of all the animals. Brer Fox creates a "tar baby" from tar and turpentine, disguises it as a person, and hides it where he knows Brer Rabbit will find it. Sure enough, that arrogant Brer Rabbit runs across the tar baby and attempts to interact with him. Since he gets no response, he becomes very annoyed and ultimately expresses his anger by hitting the tar baby. Of course, he gets stuck, and the more he struggles, the more he gets stuck.

Although there have been many interpretations of this fable, the idea here is that to avoid the tar baby, the therapist must control his reactions and not get sucked into attempts at manipulation and control. In a situation where a client, because of faulty beliefs about how to interact with others, behaves badly toward the therapist and attempts to annoy and manipulate him, the therapist must avoid the tar baby by not getting angry at or directive with a client. To do so would only reinforce the client's mistaken beliefs about how the world works and would hamper attempts to form a therapeutic relationship.

Creating Images

As a way of helping clients remember their goals in therapy and how to overcome some of the stumbling blocks, some Adlerian therapists use a clever or humorous image as a way of making a point and giving clients an image to use to overcome difficulties. Mosak (2000) gives an example from a group therapy that illustrates this technique:

> Another patient, fearing sexual impotence, concurred with the therapist's observation that he had never seen an impotent dog. The patient advanced as explanation, "The dog just does what he's supposed to do without worrying about whether he'll be able to perform." The therapist suggested that at his next attempt at sexual intercourse, before he made any advances, he should smile and say inwardly, "Bow Wow." The following week he informed the members of his group, "I bow wowed." (p. 78)

Spitting in the Client's Soup

Sharf describes the derivation of this phrase as a way that children at boarding schools spoiled someone else's food so that they could have it. (2004, p. 137). In Adlerian counseling terms, it means that by a question or comment the counselor changes the meaning of a behavior that the client is using for a particular purpose. He does this in order to "spoil" the problem behavior so that it will no longer "work," thus forcing the client to try a more effective approach.

Take the example of Chumani, a boy who is half Native American and half Irish. He comes from a middle-class family that has not had much contact with his mother's Sioux relatives but that has been more involved with his father's relatives. Chumani is a name that the young man, who was originally named James, has taken as part of an attempt to find his Sioux identity. Chumani is very rebellious; he has dropped out of high school and spends a lot of time in his room drumming and smoking. His parents are both very angry at him.

See DVD

Chap. 3
Clip 2

Chumani: My mom is a real case—she has totally lost her real identity. Both my parents are really ticked off at me for dropping out of school—I don't care, they deserve it!

Counselor: Yes, they have talked to me about you. They say that you are having a hard time.

Chumani: What do they expect?

Counselor: It must be disappointing to you that dropping out of school, spending so much time in your room, and fighting so much with your mom have made it difficult for you to really find out about your Sioux relatives. I would think that would really be interesting to you.

Chumani: Yeah! I would really like to find out more about my early relatives. One of my cousins told me once that we come from a line of chiefs.

The counselor in this example is trying to spit in the client's soup, which in this case is Chumani's rebellious behavior and estrangement from his parents. The counselor is trying to help the client realize that his rebellious behavior is not getting him what he wants by spoiling his rebellious behavior. While Chumani may have a perfect right to be angry with his parents, particularly his mother, his behavior pattern at the moment is not helping him with his goal of learning more about himself as a Sioux.

MULTICULTURAL AND DIVERSITY EFFECTIVENESS

In many respects, Adlerian therapy fits well with the contemporary emphasis on diversity and multicultural context. For example, Adler believed that women experience a kind of "masculine protest" against the restrictions of the feminine role—an idea very different from Freud's notion of penis envy (Mosak, 2000, p. 56). Many of Adler's concepts also fit well with Asian, Native American, and African-American cultural values. The basic respect for a person's beliefs as developed within the context of her experience suggests a respect for different cultural values and contexts. Although Adlerians have not significantly discussed oppression and the effects of an oppressive society on individuals, consideration of culture, racism, and oppression fits naturally into consideration of lifestyles.

The Adlerian emphasis on understanding each client from that person's unique frame of reference encourages the therapist to work hard to understand this frame of reference, and cultural context is an important part of this. Sue and Sue, noted multicultural theorists (2003) provide a definition of development that fits quite well with the Adlerian notion that we each develop unique lifestyle beliefs. They emphasize the importance of the cultural context and the influence that the family, embedded within a culture, has on individual socialization.

One complicating factor when considering the diversity effectiveness of Adlerian therapy is the degree of acculturation a client has experienced. For example, a second-generation Mexican-American 16-year-old may embrace both the family's more traditional Mexican cultural values and the mainstream American teenage cultural values. Because of Adler's emphasis on the development of lifestyle so early in life, later issues of acculturation are not easily dealt with by the traditional lifestyle analysis. The culturally competent Adlerian counselor must understand the complexity of the interaction between the family values learned early on and those imposed by a majority culture later in life. Adler's emphasis on the importance of family as a socializing force does provide a good framework from which to view development.

But what about the differing definitions of family and family values? Culturally competent Adlerian counselors must understand these variations in definitions and roles. In contemporary America, breaking away from the family and developing independence may be the normal course, reflecting a lessened sense of obligation to the family. However, Asian clients, for example, usually emphasize family obligations and the need to honor the family (Sue & Sue, 2003).

In working with African-American clients, the Adlerian counselor may need to take a broader view of who constitutes the family. In many cases, the extended family plays a major role in a child's life, and aunts, uncles, and cousins may figure into the mix of sibling relationships and influences. This can also be true of other cultures (such as Hispanic, Italian, and Greek) where members of the extended family live together or nearby. For example, an African-American boy may grow up living or spending a great deal of time with a cousin who was born two years earlier. It is quite possible that the cousin will take on the role of older sibling.

From a multicultural perspective, some believe that Adlerian theory places too much emphasis on the nuclear family and on its influence on lifestyle beliefs. Jones (1985), for example, and other Afrocentric psychologists argue that racism and oppression, the Afro-American culture, and personal experiences and endowments all significantly influence the development of African Americans.

The Adlerian emphasis on society and the need to contribute to the larger group fits particularly well with Native American cultural values of sharing and cooperation (Sue & Sue, 2003). The Native American idea that the body, mind, and spirit are interconnected in a kind of inseparable unity fits well with Adler's holistic psychology. Psychological complaints of Native Americans might well be related to a sense of imbalance and disharmony. Harmony and spiritual connectedness are often major goals for many Native Americans.

Because Adlerians use a wide variety of techniques as part of the counseling process, the counselor has the option of picking culturally relevant techniques for particular clients. Some studies have suggested that African-American clients prefer action-oriented brief counseling. Sue and Sue (2003) suggest the following for counseling African Americans: "After the therapeutic alliance has been formed, apply problem-solving and time-limited approaches" (p. 308). The techniques of setting task and acting as if might have more appeal because they are specific and concrete, as opposed to the push-button technique, a visualization approach, which seems much more traditionally psychological. And as we have mentioned, brief Adlerian therapy allows for a rather quick assessment of lifestyle beliefs and an action orientation to work on changing ineffective beliefs. But we would caution counselors who use brief therapy to take into account the fact that cultural differences from their client may make getting into that person's frame of reference and interpreting lifestyle beliefs rather difficult in a short time.

PRIMARY APPLICATIONS

Family Counseling/Parenting

One of the best known applications of Adlerian psychology was Dreikurs's work with families and parents. When Dreikurs came to the United States and began to spread the word about Adlerian psychology, he took up Adler's early interest in child guidance clinics and developed a focus on families and parenting. In addition to training and teaching at the institute he founded, Dreikurs and a number of colleagues wrote several very influential self-help books for parents.

The most widely known is *Children: The Challenge* (Dreikurs & Stolz, 1964). Dreikurs and his colleagues also wrote books geared toward the public on parenthood, marriage, children's learning, and many other topics. All of these books emphasize the basic principles of Adlerian psychology and attempt to make them accessible to the general public.

The Systematic Training for Effective Parenting (STEP) program created by Dinkmeyer, Dinkmeyer, and McKay (1997) is a creative, systematic application of Adlerian principles to parent training. Among the major topics covered are how to understand behavior in terms of their children's goals (the four goals of misbehavior being attention, power, revenge, and display of inadequacy), how to understand the purpose of their own emotions and behavior toward their children, how to listen and communicate effectively with their children, how to discipline using natural and logical consequences, and how to conduct family meetings.

Thousands of parents have been involved in this training program and in support groups using the STEP and similar programs. One of the authors (Archer) observed one such weekend support group of several families. One family volunteered to receive counseling on stage by leaders who were not professionals but who had been trained to be leaders in the program and in family counseling. First, the parents were counseled, and then the children were brought in from a play area to give their points of view. The audience was also able to participate after observing all of the sessions. They provided parents with opportunities for feedback and learning about the STEP principles. Variations of this training program have also been used for teachers and other school personnel.

Adlerian approaches have been used in many different family therapy settings. Sherman (1999) provides a very interesting exposition of what he calls *Adlerian systems theory*, an integrated approach. He summarizes the steps of therapy as follows:

1. Elicit the problem as presented by the family, as interpreted by the therapist, and as manifested in a specific pattern of interaction.
2. Join by acknowledging the behavior described and by validating its impact on each member.
3. Assess the direction, purpose, and meaning of the behavior in this system, and formulate and present tentative hypotheses.
4. Look for strengths, positive exceptions, and previously successful solutions.
5. Identify together achievable positive common goals and their possible consequences for the members and others.
6. Overcome obstacles to achievement of the goals by developing new beliefs and meanings, new places and roles, and new knowledge and skills based on increased optimism and empowerment and on increased social feeling.
7. Evaluate the changes by observing, questioning, summarizing, and using before-and-after tests and techniques.
8. Reinforce the changes, and get a commitment to practice the changes and to engage in a follow-up procedure.
9. Terminate in as positive a manner as possible.
10. Follow up the case to evaluate the family's progress and needs. (Copyright © 1999 from *Interventions and Strategies in Counseling and Psychotherapy* by R. Sherman, p. 128. Reproduced by permission of Routledge/Taylor & Francis Group, LLC.)

Sanau-Beckler, Devall, and de la Rosa (2002) discuss the ways in which Adlerian theory can be used to strengthen family resilience for high-risk substance abuse families. They use Walsh's

(1998) idea of three key components of family resilience and suggest strategies for strengthening each component. *Belief*, the first component, can be strengthened by helping the family members find meaning in adversity and by helping them develop more positive attitudes by fostering transcendence and spirituality. *Organizational patterns*, the second component, is strengthened by increasing flexibility, connectedness, and the ability to use social and economic resources. The third component, *communication process*, is strengthened by improving verbal and nonverbal communication, learning to cooperate in problem solving, and developing ways to express emotions more openly (p. 306).

Children/Adolescents

Adlerian principles, related to the importance of social connections and contributions, have been applied in a variety of ways to work with children and adolescents. We mention only a few here. Citing several studies, Schaps (2000) reported that one significant way to counter violence is by building community in schools. An increase in community was causally linked to students' later development of intrinsic academic motivation, concern for others, democratic values, skill and inclination to resolve conflicts equitably, altruistic behavior, intrinsic prosocial motivation, enjoyment of helping others learn, inclusive attitudes toward out-groups, and positive interpersonal behavior.

Adlerian play therapy has been used very successfully with children and adolescents. Kottman (1995) describes several Adlerian applications to play. He covers topics such as building an egalitarian relationship with the child, encouraging, setting limits, understanding the goals of discouraged children, exploring the child's lifestyle, helping the child gain insight, and reorienting/reeducating. He suggests a number of techniques for investigating a child's lifestyle: observing the child-parent interaction; observing the child playing with toys like dolls, animal families, and puppets as a way of acting out family atmospheres; and using art techniques. He uses a kinetic family drawing (KFD) technique adapted from Burns and Kaufman (1970). The instructions are explicit and intended to gather as much information as possible about the family atmosphere: "Draw me a picture of everybody in your family. The picture should show everybody in the family *doing* something" (p. 133). Kottman also suggests having the child draw a symbol for the family and then explain what it means. If the child will not draw, he advises using pictures and photographs of animals to represent the family.

Skill at using play therapy is a must for any therapist working with children or adolescents. As you can see from this sample from Kottman's book, there are many different and creative ways to use Adlerian principles with children and their families. Although children may not be able to verbalize information about the family dynamics and their own lifestyle assumptions, this information is often readily available in less direct ways.

Group Work

Because Adler's theory emphasized the importance of social interest and encouragement, its use in group counseling has been an important application. Dinkmeyer and Sperry (2000) list several foundations of Adlerian group counseling, including the application of basic Adlerian concepts to a group context. For example, group members are encouraged to explore the methods they use to find a place in the group. In general, Adlerian groups focus on helping the group members better understand how they typically try to fit into a social group, and through feedback, they learn about how others see them and how their ways of interacting and achieving their goals may interfere with effective relationships. According to Dinkmeyer and Sperry, the group leader takes an active role. Some of the group leader's tasks include structuring the group, using interaction exercises, encouraging and focusing on assets and positive feedback, and facilitating participation by confronting nonverbal clues.

A variety of groups has been developed using Adlerian principles. The lifestyle group, for example, starts out with each member having 10 minutes to answer the question "Who are you?" The four parts to this group method are (1) presenting yourself to the seminar, (2) sharing responses, (3) drawing your family constellation, and (4) discussing your family constellation. In this group, the emphasis is clearly on helping group members analyze and understand their lifestyle beliefs. Action therapy, developed by O'Connell (1972, 1975), is similar to psychodrama, in which dramatic action scenes are set up with a director and group members who play the parts. The goal is to have members act out different scenarios and then to have for the group help them better understand their goals and motives and their ineffective techniques.

Some group-oriented peer counseling programs in schools have adopted an Adlerian approach to peer counseling. Because a safe environment is developed in which students can receive encouragement from each other and learn new skills, this approach has been very successful. One key to success, which is not that different from most group counseling practices, is to set up a norm of encouragement so that students will give and receive support for engaging in positive social behavior and for trying new and difficult skills. Campbell (2003) reports on one such program in South Florida that focused on promoting student success skills. After a 2-year trial at six different schools, these peer group interventions improved behaviors and academic achievement scores.

BRIEF THERAPY/MANAGED CARE EFFECTIVENESS

As you have seen, although traditional Adlerian therapy and lifestyle analysis can take many sessions, briefer forms have been developed. Consequently, Adlerian therapy can work effectively in a managed care environment. Nicoll (1999) suggests a three-level approach for brief therapy using Adlerian ideas: (1) action and emotion, (2) purpose or function, and (3) rules of interaction. The client's behavior must be understood on all three of these levels, and then an intervention must target the third level. He suggests a four-stage model for this brief therapy, using the acronym BURP (B—behavioral description of the presenting problem, U—underlying rules of interaction assessment, R—reorientation of the client's rules of interaction, and P—prescribing new behavioral rituals) (Nicoll, 1999, p. 22). The U, underlying rules of interaction assessment, appears to be a very abbreviated version of a lifestyle analysis. The amount of time this analysis takes can vary greatly and, as Nicoll points out, can be done as a part of a very brief therapy paradigm. Kopp and Lasky (1999) support the notion that the important parts of lifestyle beliefs and goals can be determined from talking with a client and learning about her behavior patterns, without a lengthy lifestyle analysis. The "brief" version of the lifestyle assessment discussed earlier is an example of this.

Bitter and Nicoll (2000) list 12 "flow stages," which are quite similar to stages in traditional Adlerian therapy, and suggest that clients can go through these stages in varying lengths of time. The flow stages include "data base {information gathered ahead of time} > meeting the person >

the subjective interview > the objective interview > family constellation, the tasks of life, early recollections > disclosing goals and purposes > reorientation/reeducation > encouragement, empowerment > chaos & change, the search for new possibilities > making a difference > terminate interview > stop" (p. 35). Bitter and Nicoll contend that an Adlerian counselor does not "terminate" the relationship; rather, he "terminates" a session. They propose that the more likely scenario is for therapy to be interrupted, with clients coming back sometime later (months, years, etc.). So it would be possible, and even likely, that a client would go through this flow chart in different ways, with different numbers of sessions and time periods between meetings. This method, sometimes called *intermittent counseling*, fits well in a managed care environment.

Although we tend to agree with the notion that Adlerian therapy can be brief, we recognize that the complexity of client problems and experiences does not always allow for a brief approach to Adlerian counseling. We note also that the level of experience of the counselor plays an important role here. An experienced counselor is more likely to be able to understand a client's lifestyle quickly and without a more thorough examination of the family constellation and early recollections. An experienced therapist is also more likely to recognize when this is not possible.

INTEGRATING THE THEORY WITH OTHER APPROACHES

Adler's theory of counseling and psychotherapy fits well with a number of other theories and approaches. Many Adlerians believe that Adler was ahead of his time and that many parts of his theory have been included in more modern approaches to therapy. We tend to agree.

Certainly, the emphasis on a set of lifestyle beliefs as a kind of lens through which to view life is a cognitive concept that can easily be related to the cognitive approaches of Aaron Beck and Albert Ellis. Adler's emphasis on specific techniques for insight and reorientation can easily be integrated into a cognitive-behavioral context. Specific behavioral approaches might be used in the reorientation and change phase. The respect for the client's individual frame of reference and the emphasis on understanding the client's unique way of viewing the world seem quite similar to Rogers's emphasis on a respectful and empathic relationship. These ideas also resonate with existential and postmodern constructivist approaches, and the importance of encouragement certainly fits with a solution-focused approach, where the client's strengths are recognized. The emphasis on choice in Adlerian psychology certainly fits easily with existential ideas about choice and responsibility. Therapy, in many ways, is helping clients learn about and take responsibility for their choices and beliefs as a way of making healthier choices.

Adlerian approaches don't fit well with classical psychoanalysis, although some of the general psychodynamic ideas are compatible. The basic notion that one's past shapes the present is certainly a legacy of Freud. Although Adlerians don't talk about an unconscious, they do assume clients are not completely aware of their own lifestyle beliefs and that therapy helps them "uncover" these beliefs. Adlerian psychology fits better with ego and self-oriented analytic approaches, which emphasize the idea of an early formation of an approach to life. Attachment theory, which emphasizes the early development of a sense of security and attachment, might be seen as a way in which one develops lifestyle beliefs.

Nystul (1999) published one of the few articles specifically discussing an integration of Adlerian therapy with another approach. He proposed a kind of integration with William Glasser's reality therapy that would focus specifically on a problem-solving approach. In the first step of counseling, identifying the client's inefficient approach that is causing him problems, Nystul borrowed some basic questions from Glasser, the founder of reality therapy: What are you doing? Is it working for you? The next step, adding the suffix *-ing* to the problem label (i.e., depression = depressing), helps communicate to the client that he has control over his behavior. He goes on to present a structured problem solving model that includes two important Adlerian concepts, exploring the psychology of use and enhancing the client's motivation.

RESEARCH

Because of Adlerian therapy's complexity and its lack of a structured and specified treatment approach, outcome studies have been difficult to design. Some early outcome studies were conducted (Shlien, Mosak, & Dreikurs, 1962), but they had the same methodological problems as many early counseling theory outcome research studies: questionable outcome measures and difficulty in standardizing the treatment. Unfortunately, there have not been further attempts to develop a body of outcome research on the use of Adlerian psychology in counseling.

Most of the support for Adler's theory has come from the study of particular parts or particular applications of the theory. The most researched aspect of the theory has been Adler's ideas about the effects of birth order on lifestyle and personality. Eckstein (2000) reviewed 151 empirically based studies of birth order and, in general, found considerable support for Adler's descriptions of the oldest, middle, youngest, and only child. Eckstein also quotes a book called *Born to Rebel* (Sulloway, 1996), which is a detailed historical study of scientists involved in radical ideological and technical revolutions throughout history. Sulloway, a professor of the history of science at the Massachusetts Institute of Technology, suggests a "revolutionary personality" that was found in many of the most creative scientists in history who were second or younger siblings.

Some of the more current research has examined birth order using an instrument called the Psychological Birth Order Inventory (PBOI) (Campbell, White, & Stewart, 1991; Stewart & Campbell, 1998). This inventory attempts to identify a person's "perception" of his or her birth order as opposed to the actual birth order. In a recent study, Stewart, Stewart, and Campbell (2001) reported general support for Adler's theory of birth order.

A number of instruments have been developed to study other Adlerian concepts, including scales measuring social interest, lifestyle, and early recollections. By comparing the scores on these measures and by examining the scores of different groups of people, general support has been generated for the existence of the constructs. For example, Gfroerer, Gfroerer, Coleman, & Curlette (2003) examined correlations between the Basic Adlerian Scales for Interpersonal Success—Adult Form (BASIS–A), an inventory of lifestyles, and the PBOI and found that 9 out of 10 scales on the lifestyle measure were related to psychological birth order. They concluded that these correlations further supported Adlerian theory. Stewart et al. (2001) came to similar conclusions from a comparison study.

Although there has been considerable research on many of these measures and attendant comparisons, almost all of it has been published in one journal, *The Journal of Individual Psychology*. This, along with the fact that the instruments used to support the theory are really based on the constructs of the theory, suggests caution in interpreting the results. Watkins and

Guarnaccia (1999) also note that although the BASIS–A has emerged as a major measure of lifestyle, most of the samples come from the Southeast and do not include persons of diverse ethnicities, indicating the need for more diverse samples.

SAMPLE RESEARCH: Teachers' Lifestyles and Perceptions of Student Behavior

Goals of the Research

Kern, Edwards, Flowers, Lambert, and Belangee (1999) conducted an applied research study of teachers' lifestyles and their perceptions of student behavior. The major goal of the study was to see if teachers' lifestyles affected the way they perceived children's behavior.

Participants

Sixty-two teachers and 1,366 students participated in the study. The teachers were almost all Caucasian and female; their median age was 30. The children were drawn from kindergarten through fifth grade classes; they were mainly Caucasian and from middle-class families.

Methods

The researchers gave the teachers an instrument to classify their lifestyles and a behavior checklist to assess their perception of student disruptive behaviors. They used the BASIS–A, a well-known Adlerian lifestyle scale (Kern, Wheeler, & Curlette, 1994), to determine the 62 teachers' lifestyle themes. This scale measures five different lifestyle themes: belonging/social interest, taking charge, going along, wanting recognition, and being cautious. To measure the children's disruptive behavior, they used a behavior checklist and a measure of teacher perceptions of Type A characteristics in children.

Results

The researchers found that the teachers with high belonging/social interest lifestyle scores were less likely to view student behavior as disruptive, while teachers with high taking charge and being cautious lifestyle scores were more likely to see student behavior as disruptive.

Implications of the Research

In discussing the implications of their findings, the researchers suggested that a teacher's knowledge of her lifestyle themes and how these themes might influence her perceptions of students might help her develop more effective ways to deal with students. They concluded that workshops discussing lifestyle scores might be useful for teachers, school counselors, and psychologists. Although this study has many flaws (including a homogeneous group of students, the use of teacher perceptions rather than observed behavior, and an inability to measure many other teacher variables that might be related to their perceptions of disruptive behavior), it is a fair example of applied Adlerian research. While it doesn't provide support for the theory itself, it does suggest ways in which some of the basic concepts can be used in school settings.

EVALUATION OF ADLERIAN COUNSELING

Adlerian theory has a number of strengths and fits well with many contemporary ideas about counseling. The suggestion that each client must be understood within the context of that client's frame of reference is a standard axiom of counseling. It is surprisingly consonant with multicultural theory and postmodern constructivist thinking. Adler's view of clients as having mistaken beliefs, rather than being pathological, and his emphasis on the unity of personality and the whole person are also concepts that appeal to contemporary clients and counselors. There has certainly been some movement in medicine and in psychology toward this kind of holistic, preventive, and growth-oriented approach to physical and psychological health. This perspective allows both counselor and client to view emotional and psychological problems as difficulties that can be overcome and that are not part of some inherent defect. Perhaps one of Adler's greatest contributions is the influence he has had on the development of subsequent counseling theories.

Adler's formulation of lifestyle as a person's beliefs about himself, the world, and his place in it has been criticized as being "common sense," but it has also become the forerunner for cognitive approaches to counseling and therapy. It fits well with our need for briefer approaches to counseling that provide an understandable way for clients to approach their problems. The developmental part of the theory, the idea that one learns these beliefs early in life, is certainly a concept that is well ingrained in our culture. Many clients want to understand how what they learned as children affects their current problems and behaviors. They often like to participate in a lifestyle analysis and gain more insight and self-understanding. Unlike psychoanalysis, though, Adlerian therapy focuses on ways of thinking about the self and the world and on more concrete ways of changing behavior.

The idea that behavior and emotion are goal directed is certainly one of Adler's most interesting and important contributions. Although it is sometimes hard for a client to understand that she is choosing something painful (depression, anxiety), looking at these emotions and behaviors to determine how they are useful offers a very different and often helpful perspective. Even if an extensive lifestyle analysis is not done, a very brief session of counseling can challenge a client to examine her behavior from this new point of view. In this regard, Adlerian counseling has been fairly adaptable to the brief counseling format that is required in today's mental health marketplace. As we have already noted, briefer forms of assessment lifestyle have been developed.

Another great strength of Adlerian counseling has been its application to work with families, children, and schools. Dreikurs's many books interpreting Adlerian principles for the lay public were certainly among the first self-help books available. Also, the STEP educational program for families has helped thousands of parents learn to be better parents. The basic ideas of viewing children's behavior as goal directed and of interpreting negative behavior as unsuccessful ways for children to gain attention and power have enabled many teachers and therapists to work in creative ways with children and families. The adaptation of the theory for preventive and educational purposes is certainly one of its strengths.

There are also disadvantages to an Adlerian approach to counseling. Perhaps the biggest are the breadth of the theory and the fact that Adlerians attempt to incorporate so many different ideas and concepts that are quite difficult to prove empirically. The theory lacks a straightforward organization and structure, and some have criticized the different concepts for being too broad and simplistic. The beginning counselor may find all of the different techniques and concepts difficult to fit together.

Adler's contention that humans can choose their lifestyles and that they can choose to change their lifestyle beliefs seems unrealistic in some situations. Although this optimistic view of change is helpful and encouraging, it may lead counselors to underemphasize the context and the environment. The idea that the major lifestyle beliefs are formed during the first 6 years of life is certainly contestable, and one might argue that later major life events and crises significantly alter our view of ourselves and of the world.

Although it is difficult to fault Adler for not understanding the importance of brain chemistry in pathology, few Adlerians have attempted to integrate psychopharmacological treatments with basic Adlerian theory. Sperry (1999) does discuss the integration of diagnosis using the Diagnostic and Statistical Manual of Mental Disorders and Adlerian psychotherapy and provides a case example suggesting the use of medication as an adjunct to therapy. He elaborates on the idea of integrating Adlerian and biological approaches in a discussion of "biopsychosocial" therapy. Sperry argues that "the biopsychosocial model is a holistic systems perspective for understanding the person and the relationship of the system outside and inside the person that influences both health and illness" (p. 234).

Clearly, Adlerian theory has had a great impact on the development of later theories of counseling and psychotherapy. Although perhaps unacknowledged, his contributions to humanistic-existential psychology, to cognitively based counseling theories, and to family counseling have been particularly noteworthy. And one can even make an argument that Adler's notion of private logic and his understanding that each individual constructs his own reality based on his personal experiences were precursors to postmodern theories of psychotherapy.

Questions and Learning Activities

These questions and activities are designed to stimulate your thinking about this theory and to help you apply some of the ideas to your own life and experience. If possible, you should work with another person or with a small group. Getting others' points of view and sharing your own ideas and perspectives will be invaluable as a way to help you evaluate this theory and its applications.

Discussion Questions

1. Do you believe that a person's lifestyle is set by the time she is 6? Was yours?
2. Do Adler's ideas about birth order make sense to you? Discuss.
3. Can you identify and describe a particular atmosphere in your family when you were growing up?
4. Do you think people use emotions and behaviors to get what they want? Discuss.
5. Are you generally good at "reading" people and getting into their personal frame of reference? Discuss.
6. What do you think of the idea of basic mistakes? How does it fit for you?
7. Do techniques like spitting in the client's soup and using paradoxical intention seem manipulative to you? Why or why not?
8. Do you agree with the authors that Adlerian counseling works well in a multicultural context? Discuss.

9. Can you see yourself using early recollections in counseling? How far back can you remember?

10. What do you think of the lifestyle inventory and the different categories describing lifestyle? Do you think most people fall into several general categories?

11. Do you think that most people are not really aware of their lifestyle beliefs and of the problems that their mistaken beliefs might cause? Can you think of examples?

Learning Activities

Family Atmospheres

With a partner or in a small group, see how many different family atmospheres you can identify. Use your own and also those that you have observed in the families of relatives and friends. Be creative. Make up your own names for the atmospheres that you identify. Discuss how you think these different atmospheres might affect the children growing up in them.

Birth Order

With a partner or in a small group, diagram your place in your family's birth order. Use a line and list the children from oldest to youngest. Make a rough scale so that the distance between siblings is proportionate. Remember to include other children who were in the household. Discuss how well you and your siblings fit Adler's ideas about birth order.

Psychology of Use

With a partner or in a small group, discuss how someone might "use" the following behaviors and emotions: depression, anxiety, reclusiveness, loud aggressive behavior, promiscuity, perfectionism, and avoidance of serious relationships. See if you can come up with examples from your own experience.

Early Recollections

With a partner or in a small group, share one of your earliest recollections—pick something that you can share without distress. See if your partner or other group members can help you "flesh out" the recollection—that is, remember more details and feelings. Don't worry if you can't remember early events. Many people have problems remembering their first years of life.

Methods and Techniques

With a partner or in a small group, try to identify examples of the following techniques—from your own observations or experiences, if possible. You will probably need to review the definitions and examples of these techniques. Your first task will be to make sure that you understand what they mean; then you can think about identifying some examples.

Encouragement

Setting tasks

Using antisuggestion

Using paradoxical intention

Acting as if

Catching one's self

Using push buttons

Avoiding the tar baby

Creating images

Spitting in the client's soup

Lifestyle

Can you identify your own lifestyle in a sentence or two? What are the major motivating factors in your life, and what kind of lifestyle have you developed to help you reach your goals (remember that we are talking not just about career goals but also about interpersonal, philosophical, ethical, and other goals).

Companion Website

Now go to the Companion Web site at www.prenhall.com/archer to assess your understanding of chapter content with multiple-choice and essay questions, and broaden your knowledge with related Web resources and additional print resources.

CHAPTER 4

Person-Centered Counseling

VOICES FROM THE FIELD: COUNSELOR AND CLIENT REACTIONS

Yes, it works for me

Client: I really felt my counselor understood what I was saying. The second I sat down with her, I could tell she really cared about me and understood how I was feeling. I admit at first I felt a little frustrated that she wouldn't give me answers to my problems, but she really hung in there and helped me figure things out for myself. I found myself thinking a lot about our sessions, and I really feel like I learned to trust myself.

Counselor: Finally, I have found an approach that seems to work for me. I thought I would go nuts trying to reflect everything my clients told me, but I realized that if you can understand how they are feeling, and let them know that, you can do a lot of good. It takes a lot of energy to listen that closely, and it's a bit risky to be that open to your own feelings, but I think that's the only way you can really reach others.

No, it doesn't work for me

Client: My counselor was a nice person, and I really feel like she understood what I was going through. But she spent most our time saying "You feel this" or "You feel that." I mean, where does that get us? It seems like all she did was repeat things back to me. Now don't get me wrong—I really felt like she cared about me and wanted to help me. But counseling wasn't at all what I expected. I thought I would have a chance to figure out how my past has gotten me into this situation and to talk about changing my philosophy of life so that I can be a happier person. I think I needed a different kind of therapist.

Counselor: I really don't feel comfortable with person-centered counseling. It seems to me that you don't really offer clients any real help. They expect a counselor to have answers! I thought you went to a counselor to help solve your problems. I admit that I really like helping people get down to the basic feelings underlying their problems, but then what do you do?

María is a Latina college student in her early twenties. She is feeling conflicted about her romantic feelings toward members of the same sex. While this feels right to her, she fears disapproval from her family because it is not in accord with their values and religious beliefs. She has decided to visit her college counseling center.

> **María:** I feel like I've been leading a double life—when I'm away at college, I am pretty open about being a lesbian, but when I'm home, I have to lie and pretend I'm straight.
>
> **Counselor:** You're feeling conflicted because, on the one hand, you don't want to lie about who you are, but on the other hand, you don't want to upset your family.
>
> **María:** Yes, I'm tired of the deception, and I feel it's time to talk to my parents, but how can I know what their reaction will be? What if they disown me? Can you help me?

Counselor: I'll sure do everything I can to help you figure out the right course of action. It sounds like you are very torn right now, wanting to find some way of being honest with your family but also being true to yourself.

Person-centered counseling was developed by Carl Rogers in the middle to latter decades of the twentieth century. This approach is based on a humanistic philosophy that assumes people are inherently growth seeking and naturally capable of leading fulfilling, productive lives. Person-centered counselors seek mainly to help clients resolve difficulties for themselves through the experience of a warm and validating relationship with the counselor.

In the example above, you can see how the counselor focuses on understanding María's concerns and reflecting back to her what she seems to be experiencing and feeling. From the last exchange, we can see that María is understandably seeking concrete suggestions or advice about her concerns from the counselor. But following person-centered principles, the counselor seeks to establish a relationship and help her explore this situation as fully as possible rather than offering advice or suggestions. The guiding assumption here is that María will eventually come to trust her own judgment in making important decisions in her life after experiencing an accepting and warm counseling relationship.

HISTORICAL BACKGROUND

Historical Context

Carl Rogers received his degree in clinical psychology in 1931, and his initial ideas about the nature of counseling emerged from his clinical work with troubled children and their families. Rogers found that with empathy and understanding his clients were capable of making decisions and resolving difficulties in their lives. His approach to counseling was part of a movement by humanistic and existential theorists that came to be known as a "third force" in counseling. These theorists rejected the deterministic view of human nature, expressed by both psychoanalytic and behaviorist theorists, that people are either driven by internal, unconscious forces or shaped by external events. Instead, proponents of this third force viewed people as being innately free, spontaneous, growth seeking, and altruistic (Monte, 1987). Carl Rogers went on to establish a counseling model based on this philosophy: Dysfunctional behaviors, feelings, and thoughts are the result of external forces that interfere with the natural tendency of humans to grow and reach their potential.

Not only was Rogers a pioneer in developing an approach to counseling based on humanistic and existential principles, but also he was extremely influential in shaping counseling as a profession. He was a leader in applying effective principles and techniques for interpersonal communication in order to resolve conflicts among individuals and groups, and he conducted decades of systematic empirical research with colleagues on the therapeutic process. Perhaps most important was the key role he played in spreading the practice of counseling and psychotherapy beyond psychiatry and psychoanalysis to all the helping professions—including psychology, social work, nursing, education, the ministry, and even the public at large (Kirschenbaum & Henderson, 1989). He was the first to use the term *client* in describing the people he worked with, rather than the term *patient*, as is used in medical settings, thus deemphasizing the notion that such persons were sick or ill. Rogers's systematic efforts to understand the counseling process also led to widely (almost universally) accepted methods for training beginning counselors in listening skills, rapport building, and the use of empathy. In the decade prior to his death in 1987, Rogers also sought to apply his person-centered approach on a global level, seeking to reduce conflict and promote understanding among persons from different nationalities, cultures, and religions. He traveled extensively in Europe, Latin America, Russia, and Japan to promote such ideas, and in January 1987, Rogers was nominated for the Nobel Peace Prize by then-Congressman Jim Bates.

Development of the Theory

Carl Rogers was born in a suburb of Chicago in 1902, the fourth of six children. In his book *On Becoming a Person* (Rogers, 1961), Rogers described his upbringing as "marked by close family ties, a very strict and uncompromising religious and ethical atmosphere, and what amounted to a worship of the virtue of hard work" (p. 5). Carl Rogers's father was a successful engineer, and when Rogers was 12 years old, the family moved to a farm west of Chicago. Not surprisingly, Rogers began his undergraduate studies at the University of Wisconsin studying agriculture. However, while a sophomore in college, Rogers attended a conference of student volunteers for evangelical Christian work and decided to revise his career plans to pursue the study of religion and the ministry. The following year, in 1922, he was among 10 students chosen by the World Student Christian Federation to go to China. Rogers described this experience as extremely important in his personal development. During his journey to China, he spent considerable time with fellow students from far more liberal backgrounds than his own, and in meeting citizens of other countries, he came to "realize that sincere and honest people could believe in very divergent religious doctrines" (p. 7). This realization broadened his thinking and led him to revise some of the religious teachings imparted to him by his parents.

In 1924, Rogers married Helen Elliott and began 2 years of graduate study at Union Theological Seminary in New York City. During his time there, he was attracted by courses and lectures on psychology and began to take courses at Teachers College, Columbia University. Eventually, he transferred to Columbia University to study psychology full-time. His ideas about counseling and change are generally viewed as progressing in four stages (Zimring & Raskin, 1992).

Stage 1: Nondirective Counseling (1939–1950) In his first job following graduation, Rogers worked as a child psychologist in the Child Study Department of the Society for Prevention of Cruelty to Children in Rochester, New York, and was deeply immersed in clinical work with children and their families for 12 years. It was here that Rogers formed his beliefs about the proper method for conducting psychotherapy with children and their parents. He was guided by one criterion: "Did it work?" (Rogers, 1961).

Rogers increasingly felt a lack of identification with the field of psychology, which seemed to him fixated at that time on experimental studies with animals that had little to do with human problems. Instead, he felt a closer professional connection to psychiatric social workers, who involved themselves deeply in helping their clients using practical means (Rogers, 1961).

During this time of full-time clinical work, Rogers also managed to publish a book based on his experience: *The Clinical Treatment of the Problem Child* (1939). Its publication soon led to the offer of a full professorship at Ohio State University. In interacting with his students at Ohio State, Rogers came to realize the uniqueness of his approach to counseling, which led him to publish another book, titled *Counseling and Psychotherapy* (1942). In that book, Rogers described a "non-directive" approach, which meant that counselors were urged to avoid giving clients specific suggestions or advice about their concerns.

Rogers (1942) noted several ways in which this nondirective approach differed from the way that counseling was being practiced at that time: (1) It relied on the individual's natural drive toward growth—counseling was more a matter of helping clients realize their potential; (2) great emphasis was placed on clients' feelings rather than on their thoughts; (3) current experiences were valued over past history; and (4) the therapeutic relationship itself was seen as a vehicle for change.

Stage 2: Client-Centered Counseling (1951–1960) The second stage in the progression of Rogers's approach can be marked with the publication of *Client-Centered Therapy* (1951). While Rogers's initial formulation of nondirective counseling emphasized a warm, accepting relationship between the counselor and the client, in *Client-Centered Therapy* he discussed several problems that could emerge when the nondirective approach was misapplied. First, Rogers noted that some counselors, particularly those with little training, took the nondirective approach to mean "anything goes." In other words, the counselor would simply try to listen, stay out of the client's way, and allow the client to figure out his own solutions. Rogers argued that counselors who take such a hands-off approach risk communicating to their clients that they do not care.

A second problem stemmed from Rogers's belief that the therapist's role was to help clients recognize and clarify their feelings. He feared that many practitioners sought to do this using an analytic and sterile approach. Rogers believed that client feelings occur in the context of their life successes, struggles, and hopes for the future, and he deemed it essential that the counselor enter their world as fully as possible, not just to "categorize" their feelings. While nondirective counseling had established the importance of a warm and accepting relationship between the counselor and the client, the publication of *Client-Centered Counseling* emphasized the importance of the counselor understanding the client's internal frame of reference and communicating that understanding to the client.

Stage 3: Emphasis on Experiencing (1961–late 1960s) Carl Rogers's thinking about his approach entered a third phase with the publication of *On Becoming a Person* (1961), in which he emphasized the "experiencing" part of the counseling process. Experiencing refers to awareness of the subjective, internal emotional responses that are triggered when two or more people establish a relationship with each other. Instead of just talking about feelings during the counseling relationship, Rogers believed that feelings should actually be experienced in the moment. For example, if a client describes a particularly painful experience that provokes sadness in the counselor, she should not hesitate to experience such feelings and talk about them with the client. Rogers acknowledged that talking about such private feelings in the moment is often awkward and difficult and entails trust in one's internal experiences (Monte, 1987). Rogers believed that clients in a relationship with an "experiencing" counselor would gradually learn to trust and share their own feelings.

On Becoming a Person represented a significant advance in Rogers's thinking, but its publication coincided with his departure from academic life. While at the University of Wisconsin from 1957 to 1963, Rogers was appointed as a professor in both psychology and psychiatry, and he attempted to integrate training and research in psychology, psychiatry, and social work. He became disillusioned with life in academia, however, and described this time as one of the most of painful in his professional career. At the age of 62, Rogers and his wife moved to California, and he joined the staff of the Western Behavioral Studies Institute (WBSI) in La Jolla, California, which had been founded by Richard Farson, a former student of his at the University of Wisconsin. Later, in 1968, Rogers left the WBSI with several colleagues to start the Center for the Studies of the Person.

Stage 4: The Person-Centered Approach (1970s and 1980s) This fourth stage was marked by Rogers changing the name *client-centered counseling* to the *person-centered approach*. This change reflects the extension of his approach from individual counseling to group work, education, industry, and efforts at promoting world peace. In 1977, Rogers published *Carl Rogers on Personal Power* to describe how his methods could be applied to a broad range of settings and applications.

ASSUMPTIONS AND CORE CONCEPTS

View of Human Nature

Rogers's view of human nature was shaped by his clinical experience and by humanistic and existential theory. Psychoanalytic and behavioral counseling approaches were dominant when he began as a clinician in the 1930s, and Rogers rejected the core assumption of both: that humans do not control their own destinies. Particularly in his clinical work, Rogers saw clients who overcame significant life obstacles such as neglectful families, poverty, and lack of education to make great strides in counseling, and he came to closely identify with the humanists' belief that humans are social, rational, and fully capable of taking charge of their own destiny.

Another important aspect of Rogers's view of human nature comes from the existential theorists' emphasis on phenomenological experience. As you will read in Chapter 5, existentialists such as R. D. Lang (1959) and Rollo May (1961) focused on the importance of individuals making sense of their own existence *as they perceive it* rather than accepting what an outside observer might conclude. Accordingly, assigning labels to the behavior of another—e.g., using diagnostic terms like *depression* and *anxiety*—could potentially be both harmful and useless. Rogers believed that these terms could not only be inaccurate but also contribute to the myth that highly complex behaviors can be reduced to simple terms. Thus, Rogers rejected the notion of labeling the behaviors of others and instead focused on entering the world of the client as fully as possible.

Rogers's view of human nature departed significantly from that of some existential theorists who believed that human misery is caused by awareness of the fundamental concerns of existence—i.e., by the knowledge that life is uncertain and that one day we will die (Lang, 1959). Instead, Rogers believed that the degree of misery a person experiences is related to the discrepancy between what she is and what she is capable of becoming. One of the major goals of person-centered counseling therefore is to lessen this discrepancy by creating a safe and permissive atmosphere where the client is able to get back in touch with her "true" self.

Core Concepts

Self-Actualizing Tendency An important component of Rogers's view of human nature is that we are naturally equipped with what Kurt Goldstein (1939) and Abraham Maslow (1970) labeled a *self-actualizing tendency*, something referred to in the famous Army recruiting slogan "Be all you can be." Rogers embraced the notion that individuals are fundamentally motivated to fulfill their potential to meet basic needs (to eat and drink, to seek shelter and relationships with others), develop greater independence from outside forces, and contribute in a healthy way to the world around them (Meador & Rogers, 1984). He maintained that the evolutionary process has equipped each of us to naturally strive toward the things we want and value, including basic needs for survival, such as air, water, and food, as well as for "higher-order" needs, such as knowledge, beauty, and art. In other words, he believed that the natural order of nature was for living things, including human beings, to continue to develop and grow unless impeded by other living things or the environment.

Organismic Valuing Process Rogers (1942) believed that evolution equipped all humans for self-actualization through the *organismic valuing process*. We are born with the ability to determine what is good for us and what is not: Senses such as taste and smell help us decide what to eat and drink, auditory and visual senses evaluate threats in the environment, and a range of physiological systems keep the body functioning at an optimal level. The important survival mechanisms at work here are obvious very early in life. Anyone who has spent time around infants knows that when it comes to their survival, they are not concerned with other people's opinions, priorities, or attitudes. If they are hungry, they cry until fed, for example. Infants evaluate experiences that maintain their own growth and development and are not swayed by other people's ideas about how they should feel.

Limits to the Self-Actualizing Tendency Rogers (1977) wrote that infants intrinsically know to value that which is growth enhancing, but as we grow and develop, acceptance by and approval of other people gradually gain in importance. The social and cultural context in which we live can both enrich life and block growth. On the one hand, society is critically important to our well-being: We are social creatures, and our very survival, as well as much of the fulfillment and meaning that we derive from life, comes from interactions with other people. However, Rogers also acknowledged the complexity and potential instability of such systems. Well-functioning families can be a source of nurturance and support, while dysfunctional families can inflict serious psychological wounds on children. Healthy cultural institutions can inspire, maintain order, and provide for the well-being of citizens in a society, while ineffective ones can serve to degrade and repress them.

Self and Ideal Self   The *self*, as theorized by Rogers, refers to an organized, consistent set of perceptions and feelings through which we relate to the outside world (Rogers, 1961). Similar to some psychodynamic authors such as Mahler (1968), Rogers believed that early in life infants do not actually have a notion of "self"—in other words, they are not able to distinguish between themselves and the outside world, and they focus only on their own needs. Gradually, as the child matures psychologically, she is able to distinguish her feelings and experiences from those of other people, which has a profound impact on her ability to manage day-to-day interactions with the outside world.

Persons with a healthy sense of self are able not only to recognize and value their feelings as their own (through the organismic valuing process) but also to work with others toward goals that are mutually beneficial. This is an important aspect of development, according to Rogers, because regard for the self (i.e., self-esteem) develops over time as we experience positive regard from others. Rogers (1951) saw this as a rather unique characteristic of human beings, and obviously, parents and other caregivers are an important potential source of positive regard. If such important figures demonstrate positive regard toward the infant unconditionally, the young child experiences self-regard and values her experiences and feelings. If not, she may assign increasing importance to constructing an *ideal self*, which refers to the self-concept the individual would like to possess but does not. The more discrepant the ideal self is from the real self, the more the person is at risk for psychological distress—a state Rogers defined as *incongruence*. In other words, an individual may want to be friendly, likable, and outgoing (ideal self) but may not experience herself that way (perceived self). This discrepancy may develop from interactions with the outside world, as when one is not popular at school or work.

A colleague of Rogers at the University of Chicago, William Stephenson (1953) developed a way to measure a person's experience of the self using what he called a Q-sort. Essentially, a person was provided with as many as 100 cards with written statements describing various aspects of a person's self and was asked to sort them into, for example, nine piles, ranging from "least like me" to "most like me." A sorting task such as this might be conducted to determine how a person experiences herself (perceived self) and what she would most like to become (ideal self). A basic aim of person-centered counseling is to reduce the discrepancy between the ideal self and the "real" self, and the Q-sort method was used by Rogers and his colleagues to research its effectiveness. For example, in a research study, clients could be asked to do a Q-sort prior to beginning counseling and after counseling was over in order to determine if it worked to lower their incongruence.

Conditions of Worth   Rogers saw conditional worth as a key reason that clients were stuck in a state of incongruence—a state of discordance between the person they would like to be and their everyday experience. Incongruence results from the belief that one is worthy only when she meets the expectations of others. Conditions of worth develop when others approve of a person based on what she does rather than on her worth as a person. A discrepancy between the real self and the ideal self develops the more an individual experiences conditions of worth. Her ideal self, based on the approval of others, becomes different from her real self, what she values in herself. Conditions of worth seem inevitable in a modern society, where so much emphasis is placed on achievement.

Rogers (1961) believed that parents would inevitably place conditions of worth on their children as part of the normal socialization process but that this could be balanced by communicating clearly to the children that they are highly valued regardless of what they do. For example, if a child struggles academically in school because she spends most of her time and energy hanging out with friends, the parent might become irritated or upset with the child and scold her. If this happens frequently, the child may experience inner conflict because she wants to please her parent but also to act according to her own wishes and feelings. Conditions of worth put in place a conflict between the self-concept (I want to be a good child) and inner experience (it sure is fun to hang out with my friends rather than study).

The above discussion does not suggest that parents need to indulge their children's every wish or fantasy or risk harming them for life. Even the most dedicated of parents will disappoint their children every now and then, and it is essential that children be socialized to delay gratification and learn to live and work in harmony with other people. The key, however, is the manner in which the parent interacts with the child. If a parent can empathize with the child's feelings ("I know you want to have fun with your friends at school") while still providing direction about appropriate behavior ("but we expect you to play with your friends at recess and not when you are supposed to be listening to the teacher"), the child's inner psychological conflict will be minimized.

THERAPEUTIC RELATIONSHIP

Counselor's Role

The counselor's role in person-centered counseling is nondirective and is distinguished by a number of characteristics unique to this approach. First, nondirective refers to the idea that it is the client who should make decisions about her life, and the counselor should not attempt to influence that outcome by imposing her own preferences and attitudes. Second, as we have noted, it is the person of the counselor, rather than specific techniques, that is thought to be critical to a successful counseling relationship.

The counselor should keep in mind that it is the client's subjective experience that is the focus for counseling—it is not necessary, and in fact could be counterproductive, for the counselor to interpret, diagnose, or direct the counseling process. The therapist's main role therefore is to remove the conditions that restrict the client's awareness and to have an authentic "encounter" with the client; they should meet as fellow human beings, spontaneously, and in the moment. The healing ingredient is the relationship.

In order for a counseling relationship to be therapeutic, Rogers believed the counselor needed the following core conditions.

Unconditional Positive Regard This is the opposite of conditional worth, described in the previous section, and is a central component of the counselor's role in the counseling relationship. It refers to the counselor's ability to see the client as having inherent worth as a human being. The client must feel that whatever she says to the counselor will not cause her to be rejected as a person. This does not mean, however, that the counselor has to endorse every behavior or course of action the client pursues, such as suicide, aggression toward others, or illegal drug use. What it does mean is that the client is seen, at her core, as good and worthy of acceptance as a fellow human being. The counselor must be able to communicate this regard to the client, especially when the client is describing negative emotions or problematic behaviors.

Congruence In the "Core Concepts" section of this chapter, *incongruence* was defined as the discrepancy between one's ideal self and one's real self. Its opposite, congruence, refers to how authentic and genuine the counselor is in the counseling relationship. Rogers believed that for the client to achieve congruence in his own life, the counselor needed to display congruence in the therapeutic relationship, to be real and open to her own feelings and reactions.

In the following example, the counselor is attempting to be genuine while working with an adolescent boy, Hector, who was physically abused:

Hector: I don't see why I should trust you. This is just your job; you don't really care about me. And how can you pretend to know me, anyway? Did your parents ever hit you? You don't know what it feels like!

Counselor: Hector, I hear that you're very upset and that your parents treated you terribly. I don't expect you to trust me right away—I wouldn't trust someone the first time I met her either. And you're right, this is my job—but that doesn't mean I can't also care about you. But we've just met each other, and I suspect it will take some time for us to really get to know each other.

Hector: So you think if you talk to me for a few weeks, then you'll really know what its like to be me?

Counselor: All I can say is that I really want to understand your experiences, and I hope you will help me to understand what you've been going through.

This brief example illustrates that a person-centered counselor would attempt to be as honest as possible in expressing her feelings toward a client. The client in this case, Hector, is extremely mistrustful of adults because of his history of abuse, and the counselor is attempting to be congruent by expressing a willingness to work with Hector but also acknowledging that it is far too early in their relationship for him to trust her.

Empathy Rogers (1959) defined *empathy* as the ability to perceive the internal frame of reference of another person; it is captured by such expressions as "walking in another's shoes" or "crawling into the other person's skin." Rogers was very aware that accurately perceiving another person's world and communicating this empathy were difficult tasks for counselors to do well.

For example, consider the case of Margeurite, a Mexican immigrant to the United States who is experiencing a significant amount of depression because of her isolation from friends and family who still live in her home country. Margeurite is working with a European-American female counselor who was raised in Arizona and currently works there as a counselor. Margeurite describes her concerns this way:

> I moved here to take a job with a big retail company, and I never thought I would feel so isolated. I thought I'd find people here in Arizona who share my culture, and I have, but they're not like my friends and family back in Mexico. I just feel so sad. I can't eat, I can't sleep, and I don't have the energy to do anything.

Can a counselor who may not share Margeurite's experiences or cultural background *really* have empathy for the hardship she is experiencing while living in a different country from friends and family? According to Meador and Rogers (1984), in order to experience empathy for this client, the counselor will have to do more than intellectually understand what the client is saying. They believe that the counselor must "get into the shoes" of the client (p. 163) and not only listen to the client's words but also immerse herself in the client's world. Not only will this counselor need a knowledge of Margeurite and her cultural background, but also she will need to reflect on times in her own life when she felt alone and isolated, which might help her in understanding Margeurite's experience.

In working with Margeurite, an initial attempt to respond with empathy might be "You're feeling lonely and upset because this place is so different and you are cut off from those who mean the most to you." This response includes an attempt to identify some of the feelings that Margeurite is likely experiencing, as well as the context for why she feels that way. Obviously, whether or not the counselor has lived through a similar experience, formulating such a response involves understanding how a person in Margeurite's situation would feel.

Counselor-Client Relationship

Rogers (1961) posed a number of questions for counselors to consider when establishing a relationship with clients, including:

- Can I *be* some way which will be perceived by the other person as trustworthy, as dependable or consistent in some deep sense? (p. 50)
- Can I be expressive enough as a person that what I am will be communicated unambiguously? (p. 51)
- Can I let myself enter fully into the world of his feelings and personal meanings and see these as he does? (p. 53)
- Can I meet this other individual as person who is in the process of becoming, or will I be bound by his past and by my past? (p. 55)

Rogers (1957) articulated six conditions for effective helping, which build on the core conditions for effective helpers identified in the preceding "Counselor's Role" section.

1. *The counselor and client must be in psychological contact.* Rogers believed that the basis for all forms of helping is a warm, therapeutic relationship between the client and the counselor. On one level, this may seem obvious: Of course, helping cannot occur

without a relationship between the counselor and the client. However, Rogers believed that psychological contact entailed much more than simply showing up at the appointed time and listening carefully to a client. According to Rogers, the counselor must be *fully present* in the relationship. In other words, she must be free of distractions and ready to immerse herself in the client's world for as long as the contact is to occur.

2. *The client must be in a state of incongruence.* Incongruence refers to the discrepancy between the real and ideal selves, which were described in the preceding discussion of "core concepts" of Rogers's theory. As was noted there, Rogers believed that each of us is born with an organismic, or innate, valuing process that allows us to determine what kinds of experiences and behaviors will lead us to further growth and development. Unconditional positive regard from others (in this case, the counselor) allows us to continue valuing our own feelings and lessens feelings of incongruence between the real and ideal selves. When we are subjected to terms of conditional worth by others based on what we *do* rather than who we *are*, it forces us to substitute their judgments and feelings for our own. This leads to incongruence between our real self and the ideal self we construct mainly to please others.

3. *The counselor must be congruent in the relationship.* Rogers believed that clients reached a state of incongruence when subjected to terms of conditional worth by other people. The counselor's first job in person-centered counseling is to avoid being incongruent herself. This means that the counselor should be honest and open about sharing her own thoughts and feelings with clients. This does not, however, mean that the counselor is a perfectly congruent person, with her ideal self always in line with her real self. Rogers would be the first to say the counselors are imperfect beings, striving for growth and development just as their clients are.

4. *The counselor must demonstrate unconditional positive regard for the client.* As was described in the "Counselor's Role" section, unconditional positive regard refers to the counselor's ability to see the client (and all people, for that matter) as basically good and worthy. Again, because the client's incongruence is thought to be the result of the conditional regard of others, the counselor must create an environment where the client does not feel judged or devalued. The client needs to feel acceptance from the counselor for his basic personhood and for his feelings. This does not imply that the counselor endorses all of a client's behaviors.

5. *The counselor must experience empathy for the client.* The counselor must be able to enter the client's world and understand, on an emotional level, the feelings and reactions that the client experiences. This does not mean that the therapist must have gone through the exact same experience—only that as a human being she must be able to relate to the client's experiences and feelings.

6. *The client must experience the counselor's unconditional positive regard, congruence, and empathy.* It is not enough for counselors to simply possess these characteristics; they must be experienced by the client. A helping relationship does not exist unless the client actually experiences these conditions from the counselor.

ASSESSMENT, GOALS, AND PROCESS OF THEORY

Assessment

Carl Rogers used formal assessment early in his work with clients but then shifted his focus to developing the therapeutic relationship with the client. According to Rogers, the counselor should be actively engaged in understanding the client's experiences and must constantly be concerned that she is comprehending what the client is saying and demonstrating this awareness back to the client. As we will see in the "Primary Applications" and "Research" sections of this chapter, while Rogers saw a very limited role for assessment in the counseling process, he and his colleagues used such systems extensively for research purposes.

Patterson and Watkins (1982) noted, however, that most counselors use assessment of some type. Patterson (1958) described two components of the person-centered approach that are important when using assessment: (1) Each person has inherent worth that must be respected, and (2) each individual has the right to self-direction in choosing values and goals. If assessment is used in person-centered counseling, it is used for the client's benefit, with the counselor attempting to collect information that will serve the client's goal of self-actualization.

Patterson and Watkins (1982) stated that clients should be given as much information as possible about potential tests to be given and as much freedom as possible in deciding which tests are to be used. When test results are given to the client, the locus of evaluation should remain with the client as much as possible: In other words, an assessment instrument should be avoided if its results can be understood only by the counselor. In person-centered assessment, the client must not be put into the role of being a passive recipient of information. Assessment information provided to the client must therefore be understandable, and all results should be fully disclosed—the counselor should not attempt to withhold unpleasant results. Instead, the counselor and client should both be in agreement about the nature of the information being gathered and the fact that it will be fully disclosed to the client.

Goals

Barrett-Lennard (1998) noted that a wide range of human concerns, including education, the healing of psychic trauma, and personal growth, can be addressed through the person-centered approach. Each topic is addressed through the establishment of an authentic, spontaneous relationship between the counselor/teacher and the client. The goals are established by the client, and while it is presumed that the client will behave differently if counseling is successful, changing behavior is not the focus of the work between the counselor and client. A person who is able to accept her own feelings and develop a healthy sense of self has the potential to develop into what Rogers (1969) called the "fully-functioning person." A fully functioning person will naturally gravitate toward maximizing her own potential and that of the people around her. This creativity may be expressed in any number of different ways, including work, personal relationships, and artistic endeavors such as music or painting.

Rogers did not believe that every person would necessarily reach the goal of becoming a fully functioning person while in counseling. Rather, he spelled out a number of indicators of the degree to which the person was making progress in this direction as a result of her work with a counselor. One important indicator is an increasing openness to one's own experiences, which

Rogers described as the opposite of defensiveness. This entails being able to accept reality, understand one's own feelings and perceptions, and distinguish real feelings and anxieties from those brought on by conditions of worth. In other words, if a person is concerned about some future event, is it because it truly signifies a threat to her well-being, or are feelings of concern caused by the pressure to live up to others' expectations?

Another such indicator is the ability to live in the "here and now." As we noted at the beginning of this chapter, Rogers was influenced by existential theory, particularly the notion that we should live in the present and not the past or future. He did believe that we should learn from our past and prepare for the future, but also that we should be present and experience the here and now and take responsibility for the choices we make in life. Another indicator of progress toward becoming a fully functioning person is an increasing level of organismic valuing, which refers to our ability to trust our own feelings about what works well as a guide toward self-actualization.

Process of Theory

Rogers believed that the establishment of an effective therapeutic relationship at the beginning of counseling would lead the client to reorganize her self-perceptions and be more open to her own feelings and experiences (i.e., her real self). He did not spell out distinct stages of the process and instead wrote about counseling mainly in terms of relationship development with the client. If the counselor displayed the necessary core conditions and was available and open to the client, a relationship would ensue that would have therapeutic benefits to the client.

Other person-centered theorists have attempted to formalize the person-centered approach, at least to a degree. For example, Barrett-Lennard (1998) described several stages of the process of person-centered counseling, which are "each distinct in principle but shading into the next in practice" (p. 106).

In the *entry phase*, the establishment of a safe, trusting, and warm relationship between the counselor and the client is essential. The counselor's openness to the client's experiences, her facilitation of the client's exploration, and her congruence with the client's own perceptions and experiences are vital. According to Barrett-Lennard, advancement through this initial stage of counseling is marked by a number of factors, including the client's acknowledgment of the personal impact of the experiences that have brought her to counseling. In other words, the client will begin to explore not just *what* has happened to cause her distress but also how it has affected her and what she would like to change in her life. She will begin to express her feelings or at least acknowledge that they exist and need to be a focus of counseling. As the client moves beyond simply telling stories about her life, she will begin to treat the counselor as a "real person," as opposed to a remote authority, and acknowledge that being in counseling "matters" (Barrett-Lennard, 1998).

The second stage, *forging a personal working alliance*, involves movement beyond the exploration stage of counseling (Barrett-Lennard, 1998). There are two components, continued development of the client-counselor relationship and movement from "woundedness" to hope. The "client leads the alliance in terms of content issues" (p. 110) and gradually lets go of the notion that the counselor should direct the sessions. Barrett-Lennard saw this as a make-or-break phase of counseling: The "therapist ally needs to come into view for the client in his/her own distinctive likeness as helper-person; and the client likewise needs to become not just a string of feelings and perceptions responded to . . . but an increasingly known whole configured person" (p. 110).

With respect to movement from woundedness to hope, Barrett-Lennard believed that most of us experience psychosocial wounds at one point or another in our lives and that these can flare up again during times of stress. For example, in her past, the client may have experienced diminished self-esteem, feelings of anxiety, or a loss of meaning, and more recent negative events could trigger these feelings again, leaving her without the confidence that something good can come from the counseling effort (Barrett-Lennard, 1998). As therapy progresses, the client hopefully experiences a sense of her burden being lifted and a return to optimism about the future.

After these two initial stages, Barrett-Lennard (1998) noted that the counseling relationship progresses as the client increasingly gains understanding of the discrepancy between her real self and her ideal self. Because of the therapists' unconditional positive regard, the client need not feel defensive about this discrepancy—instead, she can reorganize her experiences, reclaim previous experiences that were once distorted or denied in an attempt to garner acceptance from others (conditional worth), and increasingly reduce the discrepancy between her self as perceived and her ideal self. In so doing, the client will take increasing responsibility for her own life and its direction. She will become more fully aware of her own experiences and feelings and tend to trust her internal experiences more and more in making decisions about her life. As was suggested in the "Goals" section of this chapter, concrete changes in client behaviors are not heavily emphasized, and counseling may be terminated at the point where the client feels capable of continued progress without the assistance of the counseling relationship, even if she has not necessarily reached all of her goals.

Rogers believed that the counselor and client move through these stages primarily because the counselor is able to empathize with, and develop an understanding of, the client through reflection. This involves the counselor paraphrasing what she has heard from the client in her own words, paying particular attention to the feelings the client is expressing. The value of reflection is twofold: First, it allows the counselor to demonstrate to the client that she is listening and understanding what the client has said. Second, the process of reflection allows the client to explore her own thoughts and feelings as they are repeated back to her—in other words, the counselor acts as a sounding board for the client.

Many beginning counselors have reservations about relying on the use of reflections and being nondirective. Counseling students enter the profession to help other people, and many wonder if their clients will really find their reflections to be helpful. They also worry about sounding like they are just parroting back what the client is saying, when what their client really wants is solutions and advice.

To further examine this issue, consider the case of Kevin, a 17-year-old African-American junior in high school, who needs advice about courses to take in his senior year. His parents believe strongly in the value of a "practical education" that will allow him to be financially successful, and they want him to take courses in his last year of high school that will prepare him for college, including honors courses in English and history. Neither of his parents attended college, and both worked very hard to develop their own food services company. After years of long, grueling work building their company, they saved enough money to send Kevin to college. Understandably, they want Kevin to benefit from their own hard work and to be able to earn a good living without having to endure the long hours they did.

Kevin, however, loves electronics and wants to focus on courses that will prepare him to go to technical school or possibly into the military so he can start a career repairing electrical equipment. Kevin is now at a decision point—he needs to register for classes for next year and desperately wants to take classes that will allow him to pursue his passion for electronics. But he knows this will upset his parents because they equate a college degree with financial security. So Kevin has come to see his school counselor to get help making decisions about his classes and communicating with his parents.

See DVD

Chap. 4
Clip 1

A counselor attempting to be directive and "solve" Kevin's problem:

Counselor: So, Kevin, it sounds like you are struggling with a difficult choice here, whether to please yourself or please your parents. Which is more important to you?

Kevin: Well, I want to be happy, you know? I like everything about electronics—it involves math and science, which I like, but it's also about a sense of really doing something important, you know, by fixing things.

Counselor: So it's pretty clear that you should go the trade school route with your classes rather than college preparation. How can you tell your parents about your choice?

Kevin: Well, I think they'll freak out. Look, their lives have not been easy—I can't believe how hard they worked when I was growing up. But they had a dream for me: that I could make it without killing myself like they did. That I could be a college grad and have status. I don't think they ever really felt important.

Counselor: OK, I hear you, but let's talk about the best way to break it to them.

Kevin: Well, in my family, you just don't do that sort of thing—you don't openly question what your parents have in mind for you.

Counselor: But let's say you did, what would they say?

Kevin: Well, I don't know. . . .

While many of the questions asked by the counselor in this example may seem reasonable, it is important to note the effect that this form of interviewing has on the counseling relationship. First, the counselor in this example is more or less in control of the direction that the session takes—she asks the questions and leads the client to specific areas of exploration. Second, the counselor is not establishing a relationship between herself and the client—she seems to be more of an advisor than a counselor. Third, there is the question of whether this counselor is demonstrating respect for Kevin's values and goals. The counselor seems to be pushing Kevin to make a career choice.

Also, urging Kevin to talk to his parents right away may be inappropriate for any number of reasons. For example, Kevin's family may react negatively if Kevin simply announces his career choice—they may expect to be consulted first. Thus, the counselor's suggestion that Kevin make a choice and immediately announce it to his parents could cause conflict in Kevin's family. This could damage the relationship between Kevin and the counselor as well and cause Kevin to question whether the counselor really had the potential for understanding his concerns. Contrast this example with the more nondirective approach a person-centered counselor would use.

See DVD

Chap. 4
Clip 1

A nondirective counselor using reflection with Kevin:

Counselor: Kevin, it sounds like you feel conflicted—on the one hand, you want to pursue classes and a career that you really enjoy, but on the other hand, you don't want to disappoint your parents.

Kevin: Yeah. . . . I really want to get training in electrical repair, and that seems to be what all my friends are doing—they are choosing the courses *they* want.

Counselor: It sounds like a real struggle: Do I go with my own interests, like many of my friends, or go with my parents' wishes?

Kevin: Yeah, and they said they would pay for college, so I feel like I owe them that.

Counselor: You really want to honor their expectations and the hopes they have for you.

Kevin: Yes, but I don't want to be miserable, either.

Counselor: So it seems like uncharted territory in a way—you can't do both things, and it's not clear how you can reconcile what your parents want and what you want for yourself.

Kevin: Yeah, I guess I need to find a way to talk with them. . . .

In the second example, the counselor is letting the client take the lead by reflecting back the client's feelings and thoughts. Eventually, the issue of Kevin talking with his parents still comes up, but in this case, it was his idea, not the counselor's. Rogers believed that an important strength of the nondirective approach is that it gives clients the ability to find their own solutions, and the counselor's role is to assist clients in this exploration without guiding them toward any particular outcome.

THERAPEUTIC TECHNIQUES

Person-centered counseling does not lend itself to the use of specific therapeutic techniques. Rogers thought that a reliance on such prescriptions would detract from the authenticity of the counseling relationship, and he criticized some counseling theories textbooks as inaccurately portraying his approach as a series of techniques (Rogers, 1980).

Although many person-centered counselors downplay the role of the counselor in directing change, Miller and Rollnick (2002) developed an approach called motivational interviewing (MI), which is a brief, directive method for adapting Rogers's principles with clients who are ambivalent about change. They defined MI as a "client-centered, directive method for enhancing intrinsic motivation to change by exploring and resolving ambivalence" (p. 25). According to these authors, "Counsel in a directive, confrontational manner and client resistance goes up. Counsel in a reflective, supportive manner, and resistance goes down while change talk increases" (p. 9). They see this approach as an evolution of the person-centered approach in that the focus is on the person's interests and concerns. However, MI differs from the person-centered approach in focusing on ambivalence about change as a natural human condition.

Recall that Rogers viewed self-actualization as a natural tendency, which could be facilitated by removing obstacles to an individual's growth. Miller and Rollnick built on research by Prochaska, DiClemente, and Norcross (1992) suggesting that clients enter counseling with varying levels of motivation for change and that client-centered techniques alone might not be sufficient to resolve the ambivalence that clients may have toward effecting change in their lives. An important tenet of MI is that it is incorrect to label almost anyone as "unmotivated." Everyone has motivations, but these motivations may not be aligned with the preferences of important people in her life (such as teachers, parents, partners, etc.). A student with lagging performance in school is not necessarily unmotivated, but she may be *more* motivated to play a musical instrument, participate in a sport, or hang out with friends than to study for tests.

Miller and Rollnick pointed out that common wisdom suggests that the best way to motivate people is to punish them: in other words, to threaten them, take away privileges, or invoke consequences. However, they suggested that many clients who come to counseling ambivalent about change are, in fact, already suffering, and further negative consequences may serve only to paralyze them or invoke psychological defenses such as minimizing the impact of their struggles. According to Miller and Rollnick, "People often get stuck, not because they fail to appreciate the down side of their situation, but they feel at least two ways about it. The way out of the forest has to do with exploring and following what the person is experiencing and what, from his or her perspective, truly matters" (2002, p. 12).

Miller and Rollnick noted that MI builds on Rogers's person-centered methods to help clients develop the motivation to change. This approach is grounded in Rogers's belief that counselors need to establish a therapeutic relationship by demonstrating accurate empathy. Since MI is specifically designed to help clients reduce ambivalence about problematic aspects of their lives, it is critical that MI counselors seek to understand their clients' feelings and experiences without judging them.

It is also essential that the MI counselor not "take sides" when a client express conflicting feelings about change. For example, a client who is having trouble with alcohol may express ambivalence about giving it up forever: On the one hand, the client may talk about how much she enjoys having drinks with friends and how alcohol helps her relax when she is tense. On the other hand, she may also feel ashamed of losing control when drinking and regret how much alcohol interferes with her life and overall health. Miller and Rollnick pointed out that many people, including counselors, are tempted to argue for the "stop drinking" side of the client's ambivalence. However, this can have the unintended consequence of forcing the client to defend her feelings and actions when drinking. The more people confront her about drinking, the more she may feel a need to defend her current behavior. Therefore, counselors using MI have to be careful about accepting all aspects of the client's ambivalence.

Another important feature of MI counseling is that while a counselor using MI needs to express empathy, she is not expected to accept people as they are or simply use reflective listening to follow clients down an avenue they happen to discuss. Instead, Miller and Rollnick suggested the counselor should help the client "develop a discrepancy between present behavior and his or her broader goals and values" (2002, p. 38). In other words, the counselor should look for any opportunity to help the client realize how a problematic behavior is getting in the way of what she wants to accomplish in life. Miller and Rollnick pointed out that many people who seek counseling already perceive significant discrepancies between what is happening in their lives and what they want to have happen. However, it is important that the counselor wait until the client states her own reasons for change rather than having them come from the counselor.

Finally, MI counselors need to focus on supporting the self-efficacy of their clients—essentially, this means helping the client maintain a sense of hope and optimism about her potential to effect meaningful change. One of the greatest obstacles the client faces in making changes is a loss of faith in her own abilities or capacities. The counselor's role is therefore to not only give the client the responsibility for making decisions about change but also affirm her ability to do so.

Let's consider two different approaches to working with Frank, who was arrested for driving under the influence of alcohol (DUI) and is attending substance abuse counseling as a condition of probation.

Counselor: Would you like to tell me something about how you got the DUI?

Frank: Well, I was at a wedding and I admit I had too much to drink. But I was driving just fine, and then I had a tire blow out. A cop sees me on the side of the road, and when he came up to help me, he noticed the beer on my breath. So he takes me to the station, gives me a blood alcohol test, and now I'm stuck here. This sucks, if you want to know to the truth.

Counselor: So the whole thing seems unfair and you're pretty ticked off.

Frank: Wouldn't you be mad? I don't have a problem with alcohol. I'm just unlucky that I happened to get a flat tire.

Counselor: Well, it sounds like alcohol has caused you at least one problem . . . getting arrested.

Frank: Yeah, but like I said, I was just unlucky. I didn't kill anybody or anything. I hardly ever get drunk and I never get into fights or anything.

Counselor: So this is the first time that drinking has caused you trouble. It could be a warning sign of more trouble to come if you don't seriously look at your alcohol use.

Frank: Are you kidding? I just told you I don't have a problem, and after this, I might never drink again!

In the example above, the counselor is being directive by pointing out the possibility, based on the arrest for driving under the influence, that the client is at least in the early stages of abusing alcohol. While the counselor's intention may be to point out the obvious and help the client admit this possibility, it is clear that the client is resisting the suggestion. Rather than rolling with resistance, as Miller and Rollnick suggested, the counselor is meeting it head on and forcing her client to argue the other side—that he doesn't have a problem. It is not hard to imagine that the more the counselor presses this point, the more the client might feel compelled to resist it.

Next let's consider how a counselor might use MI with the same client.

See DVD

Chap. 4
Clip 2

Counselor: Would you like to tell me something about how you got the DUI?

Frank: Well, I was at a wedding and I admit I had too much to drink. But I was driving just fine, and then I had a tire blow out. A cop sees me on the side of the road, and when he came up to help me, he noticed the beer on my breath. So he takes me to the station, gives me a blood alcohol test, and now I'm stuck here. This sucks, if you want to know to the truth.

Counselor: So the whole thing seems unfair and you're pretty ticked off.

Frank: Wouldn't you be mad? I don't have a problem with alcohol. I'm just unlucky that I happened to get a flat tire.

Counselor: So drinking usually doesn't get you in trouble, but this time it sure did.

Frank: Yeah, I guess I was just unlucky. I could have just called a cab or something, but I didn't. I thought I was fine.

Counselor: So somehow you missed the warning signs that you were intoxicated, and it's landed you here.

Frank: Yes, and I want to get out of here as soon as possible.

Miller and Rollnick noted that change is facilitated by focusing on the disadvantages of the status quo and the advantages of change. In the previous example, we saw that the client was not open to labeling himself as a substance abuser. However, the counselor in this example is mainly focusing on the undesirable aspects of the client's current situation and, over time, will engage the client in a discussion of the advantages of change. This will hopefully result in greater motivation for change. In this example, the client might be encouraged to identify situations in which he acts irresponsibly after using alcohol, as when he decides to drive after drinking. However, using MI, the counselor would attempt to elicit more discussion of the client's dissatisfaction with his current situation rather than labeling the client or offering advice.

MULTICULTURAL AND DIVERSITY EFFECTIVENESS

Helms and Cook (1999) wrote that the global perspective, cross-cultural harmony, and spiritual connections emphasized by Rogers in the latter stages of his career make it possible to communicate with clients on a deeper level than is possible in psychodynamic and behavioral approaches. Rogers and his associates conducted numerous workshops all over the world, including South Africa and Belfast, Ireland, both sites of intense cultural and religious conflict. They had an undeniable global impact, and human services workers in places such as Japan, Australia, and South America have used elements of person-centered approaches.

In many of his international workshops, Rogers worked to bring groups in conflict together using the person-centered approach. By working to bring these groups into contact with each other, Rogers hoped to facilitate mutual understanding where little existed before. In many cases, he reported significant progress in a matter of days as individuals worked through long group sessions with a person-centered facilitator.

When used in multicultural counseling with individuals and small groups, the person-centered approach offers a number of strengths. Ivey, D'Andrea, Ivey, and Simek-Morgan (2002) cited Lerner's (1992) contention that its positive notion of humans makes the theory appealing to those interested in working with women and persons from diverse cultural backgrounds. Van Kalmthout (1998) pointed out that the person-centered approach can be seen as a system of meaning making—as each person follows the unique path of her life, she is moving away from facades or attempts to please others and toward self-direction, complexity, and openness to experience.

However, person-centered counseling can have significant limitations when working with persons from diverse backgrounds. First, the theory relies heavily on mutual understanding between the client and counselor, which can be difficult to achieve between individuals with significant cultural differences. Second, the emphasis on the *innate* growth potential of individuals can lead to neglect of the powerful influence of culture. Rogers's notion that the environment serves mainly to limit the innate growth-seeking potential may underestimate the importance of social institutions, customs, and values to human progress. Hawlin and Moore (1998) also noted that the person-centered approach runs the risk of colluding with the prevailing power structure if it does not explicitly identify how certain segments of a society can be systematically oppressed. Finally, Ivey et al. (2002) pointed out that the term *person-* or *client-centered* can imply a secular focus on the individual that can obscure the value of this approach for non-middle-class and non-European–North American clients who may seek a collectivist and/or spiritual focus.

In order to address concerns such as these, Glauser and Bozarth (2001) suggested balancing fundamental aspects of the multicultural counseling movement with the person-centered approach. Their concern was that the emphasis on multicultural competency might lead to an overreliance on techniques for understanding the client's cultural background at the expense of an authentic human relationship. For example, they noted that even though the client and counselor may come from different cultural frames of reference, it is essential that both work to understand each other as individuals with unique experiences, as well as members of cultural groups with characteristic attitudes, values, and beliefs. Also, they suggested the importance of understanding extratherapeutic variables that are impacting a client, such as systematic discrimination, from the *client's* perspective, not that of the counselor.

PRIMARY APPLICATIONS

Rogers's core conditions for counseling are so well accepted in counseling practice that it can be difficult to separate what is truly a person-centered intervention from an intervention that incorporates some of its principles but also relies on other counseling theories. Some of the more common applications of person-centered counseling are reviewed next.

Couples and Family Counseling

Rogers did not write directly about marital or couples therapy but did author a book for the general public entitled *Becoming Partners: Marriage and Its Alternatives* (1972). It included interviews with couples that, while not necessarily therapy, were intended to facilitate communication.

Ely, Guerney, and Stover (1973) described a version of person-centered couples counseling called *conjugal therapy*. Each member of the couple practices the roles of speaker and listener on certain topics, and a facilitator is present to help them communicate. In a somewhat different approach to couples work, Esser and Schneider (1990) distinguished between work with couples and partnership therapy, focusing on the relationship itself using person-centered principles. Commonly, the couple's therapist is fully present when working with them to facilitate their effective communication. Programs for families include psychoeducation, in which parents are trained in interpersonal communication skills (Levant, 1983).

Working with Children and Adolescents

Given that Carl Rogers's early clinical work was with children and their families, it is not surprising that his approach is well represented in approaches to working with children and adolescents. The field of child therapy drew heavily from Rogers's work, and Axline directly referenced Rogers's ideas about the counseling process in *Play Therapy* (1947). This approach involves children playing with various objects, such as puppets, dolls, fingerpaint, clay, and sand, as a medium for communication. Axline presented a number of principles for play therapy based on person-centered ideas, including (1) establishment of a warm, friendly relationship between the child and the counselor; (2) acceptance of the child exactly as she or he is; (3) establishment of a permissive atmosphere in which the child is able to freely express feelings; and (4) reflection of the child's feelings so she gains insight.

Erdman et al. (1996) noted that many of Rogers's basic ideas about counseling skills, such as reflecting client feelings, need to be adapted when working with children. They point out that many counselors become frustrated in working with children when they attempt to use basic counseling skills for adults. "It is not uncommon to hear surprise and concern in statements such as 'When I restated what the child said, he asked me why I was repeating what he just said' and questions such as 'What do you do with kids when they just won't talk to you?'" (p. 374).

Erdman, Lampe, and Lampe further pointed out that children often lack abstract reasoning abilities and may not question their thoughts or reasons for doing things. They therefore recommended a number of modifications to person-centered techniques when working with children. First, counselors need to establish an appropriate physical environment. While adults may be capable of sitting in an empty room with two chairs, children need an environment that puts them at ease and offers the opportunity to interact with their environment. Books, toys, and furnishings appropriate for children from various backgrounds (e.g., gender, ethnicity) are therefore essential.

A second important consideration when using a person-centered perspective with children is the need to use listening skills that are appropriate for younger individuals. Reflective listening skills can be far more important than questioning skills early in the relationship with a child, since it is important to understand the child's experiences from her own perspective. When questions are asked, they should be simple and easily understood, such as "Which of your friends do you spend the most time with?" The open-ended questions that person-centered counselors use to promote self-exploration with adults may confuse children. Third, it is also important that the counselor attend to nonverbal cues and be able to understand these cues in terms of the child's cultural background. Asking the child for help when appropriate (e.g., "Please help me understand what you meant when you said. . . .") helps reverse the typical adult-child authoritative positions. Finally, it also important that the counselor refrain from criticizing, blaming, or challenging the child about a problem while she talks about it.

Geertjens and Waaldijik (1998) suggested specific requirements when person-centered counseling is used with adolescents. They noted that to be genuine, therapists should draw on their own experiences as adolescents. For example, the counselor should use her own experiences with her parents, or parental figures, to understand the adolescent's frame of reference and communicate this in language that the adolescent can understand. They also noted that without the demonstration of unconditional positive regard, a therapist working with children and adolescents cannot get far. "Unconditional positive regard will therefore above all aim at the recognition of the uniqueness, the particularity of the single adolescent at this moment of their life" (p. 165). Finally, they noted that empathy is an "ongoing process of checking hypotheses, in which the therapist becomes acquainted with the inner world of the client in cognitive as well as emotional respects" (p. 166).

Educational Settings

Rogers (1989) believed his person-centered approach had many applications to educational settings and detailed a number of qualities that facilitated learning. He saw many teachers as taking on an inauthentic role of "educator" rather than being a real person with specific likes and dislikes. Just as he encouraged counselors to be authentic and real in their interactions with clients, he thought that teachers should do the same with students. He even encouraged teachers to communicate their feelings toward student projects in an authentic manner: "[T]hus, she is a person to her students, not a faceless embodiment of a curriculum requirement nor a sterile tube through which knowledge is passed from one generation to the next" (p. 306, as cited in Kirschenbaum & Henderson, 1989).

Rogers believed that effective teachers demonstrate a caring for and an acceptance of the learner as a separate person with worth in her own right. This type of teacher is able to tolerate the personal feelings that both disturb and promote learning—e.g., the student may be enthusiastic one day, distracted the next. Finally, just as Rogers stressed the importance of using empathy in counseling situations, he also thought that this was an important skill for educators to use with their students.

Group Work

Rogers was a pioneer in group work, and immediately following World War II, he and his associates at the University of Chicago Counseling Center used groups to train counselors intending to work with patients in Veterans Administration hospitals (Rogers, 1970). Rogers believed that the same core conditions important in individual counseling—empathy, acceptance, warmth, congruence, and unconditional positive regard—need to exist in the group, modeled first by the group facilitator (a term Rogers preferred to group leader) and then among the group members as the group developed.

Rogers (1970) described some of the basic stages that typically emerge in encounter groups over time. Groups usually start with an initial awkward "milling around" stage, in which members engage mostly in small talk and discussions are halting and awkward. Inevitably, Rogers believed that some members would begin disclosing personal information, which could lead to ambivalence among other members who are uncertain about whether they want to trust the group. Hopefully, over time, the members' trust in the group will increase, and they will begin to share their feelings in the group and relate more intimate details about their own lives. According to Rogers, an important component of development in the group's life is the extent to which members begin to share information with each other in the group—in other words, the extent to which they begin to take the risk of communicating honestly and openly with each other.

As the group continues to develop, Rogers believed it was important that each member receive feedback from others and in doing so "rapidly acquire[s] a great deal of data as to how he appears to others" (1970, p. 29). Rogers believed that by giving feedback about how they experience each other, the members come closer and closer to what he described as "the basic encounter," in which persons come to know each other and reveal parts of themselves in ways that do not happen in everyday life. He saw this experience as one of the central and change-producing aspects of participation in groups. Rogers believed that eventually such experiences would lead to concrete behavior changes in the group and in the outside world.

Rogers described encounter groups, another approach that he pioneered, in his book *Carl Rogers on Encounter Groups* (1970). The encounter group movement closely paralleled some of the cultural shifts that occurred in the United States in the 1960s and 1970s, including freedom of expression, self-discovery, and the need to get in touch with one's feelings. Encounter groups were somewhat different from the groups described previously in that the emphasis was on personal growth and freedom of expression. According to Rogers, encounter groups lead to "more personal independence, few hidden feelings, more willingness to innovate, more opposition to institutional rigidities" (p. 13). The leaders of such groups might not even be professional counselors. Some of these groups took place in wilderness settings and could consist of continuous, marathon meetings lasting several days.

Lieberman, Yalom, and Miles (1973) conducted one of the most famous studies of the encounter group movement and found that while many members benefited from such experiences, 8% of the participants in the study experienced psychological injury that was still present 6 months after the group ended. Lieberman et al. found that in large measure the effectiveness of the group leaders made the difference in how much members benefited. Specifically, they found that leaders who demonstrated high levels of meaning attribution and empathy had the best outcomes. Meaning attribution was defined in the study as providing explanations, clarification, and a cognitive framework for change in the members, while empathy referred to one of the core conditions of the therapist identified by Rogers. As Yalom put it, "The Rogerian factors of empathy, genuineness, and unconditional positive regard thus seem incomplete; we must add the cognitive function of the leader" (1995, p. 498).

Counselor Training

Elements of the person-centered approach have become an essential component of training in basic counseling skills, sometimes labeled *micro-skills* training because of the emphasis on specific, fundamental skills important to counselor effectiveness. Carkhuff (2000) developed one specific model based on person-centered principles and described two specific components of counselor skills: attending and verbal response. Attending skills refer to the nonverbal behaviors of the counselor. According to Carkhuff, more than half of the communication between counselors and clients takes place nonverbally through posture, eye contact, and tone of voice, for example. Therefore, when we refer to the attending skills of the counselor, we are referring to the nonverbal behaviors that communicate the extent to which the counselor is "attending" to the concerns of the client. Among the nonverbal behaviors that facilitate communication is squaring, in which the counselor is positioned directly in front of the client, adopts an open posture (i.e., she is not crossing her arms or otherwise indicating that she is not receptive to the client), leans in toward the client to communicate interest, and maintains eye contact. In addition to these nonverbal behaviors, Carkhuff described a number of fundamental verbal responses that are essential components of counseling. These include accurately paraphrasing what the client has said and demonstrating empathy by responding to the client's feelings.

Counselor training models like Carkuff's, which emphasize non-verbal and verbal skills, go a step beyond person-centered counseling by concretizing specific skills that counselors need to have when interacting with clients. Rogers was quite concerned that such approaches would turn his authentic model of counseling into a technical endeavor. However, such approaches do maintain his nondirective stance toward counseling by exploring client concerns while avoiding specific suggestions for advice, and they do provide more specific direction for counselors who are attempting to be person centered.

BRIEF THERAPY/MANAGED CARE EFFECTIVENESS

Person-centered principles are widely used in a range of counseling interventions in health care and medical settings. Rogers's methods are not typically classified as a brief form of therapy, but neither did Rogers emphasize a protracted series of meetings between the counselor and the client before the core conditions of therapy could be realized. In other words, person-centered counseling can be described as somewhere in the middle of the continuum of theories presented in this book with respect to its suitability for brief therapy: The emphasis on the counselor-client relationship necessitates that enough sessions occur for a therapeutic bond to be developed, but once that is established, its benefits can be immediately realized.

Rogers's ideas and principles have impacted the health care system itself through patient-centered medicine, an approach first introduced by Balint, Hunt, Joyce, Marinker, and Woodcock (1970) and centered on the idea that patients need to be intricately involved in the treatment process. According to this approach, the doctor should work to understand not only the patient's illness but also her *experience* of the illness (Laine & Davidoff, 1996). In addition, the doctor is encouraged to involve the patient in the details of her diagnosis, the treatment opportunities available, and their various costs and benefits.

According to Stewart et al. (1995), disease is a theoretical construct or abstraction, while illness refers to the patient's illness experience. For example, arthritis is a disease that involves inflammation of a joint, characterized by pain, swelling, stiffness, and redness. However, for any given patient, the illness experience can be quite different in terms of where the arthritis affects her, how much discomfort it causes her, and how much it impairs her life. To understand the illness experience, medical personnel must be able to explore with patients *their* ideas about what is wrong with them; their feelings, especially about being ill; the impact of their problems on their current functioning; and their expectations for what should be done (Stewart et al., 1995). The doctor-patient relationship is the key to this holistic approach to medicine. As doctors get to know their patients better after seeing them time after time for a range of different concerns, they are better able to be helpful in managing subsequent problems.

The patient-centered approach represents something of a departure from Western medicine as it is typically practiced, where the doctor is the authority and primary decision maker (along with third-party payers). However, it has generated considerable support both abroad and in the United States and also provides an increasing opportunity for the involvement of counselors and psychologists in health care settings. Since they have extensive training in the person-centered skills necessary to conduct patient-centered medicine (e.g., rapport building, reflective listening), counselors and psychologists are in a position to play a vital role.

Use of the person-centered approach might be limited in managed care settings due to its avoidance of labels or diagnoses. Rogers believed that such systems were both inadequate for understanding other people and potentially distracting to a counseling relationship. Instead, it is the counselor's job to understand the client as a unique person with strengths and areas for growth that need to be addressed in counseling sessions.

INTEGRATING THE THEORY WITH OTHER APPROACHES

Carl Rogers's core conditions of helping—acceptance, warmth, congruence, and unconditional positive regard—have become widely viewed as essential fundamental counselor skills (Carkhuff, 2000), particularly for establishing a therapeutic bond between the counselor and the client at the outset of counseling (Cheston, 2000). Frank and Frank (1991) suggested that all counseling approaches are variations of time-honored procedures for healing, including an emotionally charged relationship in a healing setting. In his writing, teaching, and practice, Rogers conveyed the importance of this type of relationship between the counselor and client. The nondirective component of Rogers's theory also ensured that it was the client's goals, not those of the counselor, that would get addressed in counseling. The emphasis on understanding the client's internal frame of reference can also be an asset in working with clients from diverse backgrounds.

These characteristics of person-centered counseling allow it to be integrated with other counseling approaches that emphasize the establishment of a therapeutic and respectful relationship between the counselor and the client. For example, Alfred Adler rejected the traditional distant psychoanalytic approach in favor of a relationship of equals. Feminist approaches emphasize the egalitarian nature of the counseling relationship, as do existential approaches. Postmodern approaches such as solution-focused therapy and narrative therapy also posit a relationship between client and counselor that does not place the therapist in a more powerful or authoritative position than the client.

While Fritz Perls was known for being confrontational with clients, and thus very much unlike Rogers, more recent Gestalt therapists have emphasized a phenomenological approach to understanding how their clients organize and understand their world. Such efforts require that a counselor be able to enter the world of the client, which is consistent with Rogers's beliefs about the importance of the counselor demonstrating empathy. William Glasser's reality therapy also emphasized the bond between client and counselor in understanding how clients are meeting their needs.

Integrating Rogers's person-centered approach with counseling approaches that do not emphasize the counselor-client relationship or that call for the counselor to fill a prescriptive role in helping clients change is more problematic. However, as we have mentioned before, it is difficult to find a modern counseling theory that does not recognize the need for some type of rapport between client and counselor. Classic psychoanalysis, with the therapist as a distant figure sitting behind a couch, is one that does not seem to fit well with the person-centered approach; however, contemporary analytic approaches require a therapeutic alliance. Cognitive-behavioral and behavioral approaches, while emphasizing the therapist as more of an expert, also rely on the formation of a relationship of some sort. They do not, however, fit well with the nondirective nature of person-centered counseling.

RESEARCH

While Carl Rogers deemphasized the role of formal assessment in counseling, he believed strongly in the value of empirical research in evaluating the counseling process. Thus, even though he advocated a nontechnical, phenomenological approach to working with clients, he also stood for rigorous empirical evaluation of the counseling process—a rather unique combination. Even critics of the person-centered approach credit Rogers and his colleagues for attempting to evaluate the effectiveness not only of the general person-centered approach but also of specific elements of the counseling process. Rogers and his colleagues were among the first to empirically examine what actually happens in the counseling relationship, using transcriptions of session tapes, observations of counseling sessions, and objective measures based on theoretical components of the person-centered approach.

How does the person-centered approach fare when compared to other systems of counseling? Using the meta-analysis technique reviewed in previous chapters, Smith, Glass, and Miller (1980) were able to quantitatively rank the average "effect" of existing counseling theories based on 475 existing studies. Client-centered therapy was ranked fourteenth among the various theories evaluated, but the overall effectiveness measures of the counseling theories reviewed was so similar that the authors concluded there was little evidence to suggest that one theory of counseling was superior to any other. While other researchers have found that the person-centered approach produces benefits when compared to wait-list or no-treatment groups (Grawe, Donati, & Bernauer, 1998), others have found that it fares less well when compared to behavioral interventions (Weisz, Weiss, Han, Granger, & Morton, 1995).

In addition to the overall effectiveness of the person-centered approach, Rogers's notions of empathy, genuineness, and acceptance were studied for decades using quantitative measures of the constructs he hypothesized to be essential in effective counseling. The efforts of Truax and Carkhuff, two colleagues associated with Rogers at the University of Wisconsin, are especially noteworthy in this regard. They developed a range of rating scales measuring constructs such as accurate empathy, nonpossesive warmth, and concreteness or specificity of expression in interpersonal processes. While Patterson (1985) compiled an integrated summary supporting the importance of these constructs in effective counseling, others have found the evidence less persuasive (Beutler, Crago, & Arezmendi, 1986). Levant and Shlien (1984) pointed out that until the mid-1970s considerable research supported the core conditions of Rogers's theory, but this finding was called into question by researchers outside the client-centered tradition who criticized some of these studies for having faulty designs.

Many studies of person-centered counseling involve researchers listening to segments of tapes from counseling sessions and then rating the behaviors of the counselor and the clients according to the objective rating scale of a given construct (such as warmth or empathy). This approach has been criticized for evaluating only segments of counseling sessions, for incorporating methodological flaws, and for insufficiently considering the subjective reactions of clients in sessions. However, Orlinsky and Howard (1986) conducted an extensive analysis of the literature and found that dimensions such as these were related to positive counseling outcomes for clients.

Overall therefore person-centered counseling has been subjected to considerable empirical investigation, spurred initially by the efforts of Rogers himself and his students. There is considerable support for the proposition that counselors must possess the core conditions of counseling (empathy, congruence, and unconditional positive regard) if counseling is to be effective. However, it less clear that these conditions alone will lead to successful counseling. This, in part, explains why many counselors consider the core conditions to be an important foundation with which to approach counseling—but one that needs to be supplemented with interventions from other counseling models.

SAMPLE RESEARCH: Examination of process variables in counseling

Goals of the Research

Martin, Carkhuff, and Berenson (1966) studied whether counselors in training demonstrated higher levels of the core conditions than close friends. They conducted this study because at the time it was acknowledged that in some ways the process of counseling was similar to what happens in a friend relationship. Martin et al. sought to evaluate whether one type of helper (best available friend or professional counselor) would be rated higher in terms of Rogers's core facilitative conditions for helping.

Participants

Martin et al. conducted this study with six college students who volunteered to be interviewed by both a professional counselor and their "best available friend."

Methods

Martin et al. gave the following instruction to each of the interviewees: "All of us either in the present or during the past year or so have had a number of experiences which have been very difficult for us. If you feel the person whom you will be seeing is helpful, please feel free to discuss these experiences (pp. 356–357)." Each friend and counselor was given the instruction "Simply relate to the person you will see as you ordinarily do in order to be helpful to them" (p. 357). Following each interview, the interviewee filled out a questionnaire with 50 items, 10 for each of the facilitative conditions of helping: empathy, positive regard, genuineness, concreteness or specificity of expression, and the client dimension of self-exploration. Martin et al. tape-recorded all of the interviews, and three 4-minute excerpts from each interview were rated independently by three trained graduate students, using 5-point scales to assess each of the five process variables according to procedures developed by the second author of the study, Carkhuff.

Results

Even though most of the participants in the study had known their designated friends for 1 year or more, the results of this study showed that according to the self-reports of the volunteer interviewees and the ratings made of the tapes by the graduate counseling students, the professional counselors were rated higher on the five facilitative conditions than the best available friends. The only scale for which counselors were not rated as statistically significantly higher was the interviewee's ratings for level of self-exploration.

Implications of the Research

According to Martin et al., the differences in ratings between the two groups were important because the average ratings for the counselors hovered around 3 on the 5-point scale used, while the friends generally scored around 2. Using Carkhuff's scale for helper effectiveness, the level 3 represents a minimum level of facilitative functioning—i.e., the person is at least being minimally helpful and is not doing anything unhelpful. At level 2, the person is generally being helpful only infrequently. Both the self-reports of the interviewee and the ratings of graduate students in counseling suggested that trained counselors are able to demonstrate the core conditions of helping more frequently than are friends.

EVALUATION OF PERSON-CENTERED COUNSELING

One of the main contributions of person-centered counseling to the field is a specification of fundamental counseling skills to be used in a wide range of counseling applications. In his writings, Rogers articulated a philosophy of how the counselor should "be"—open to the experiences of their clients and themselves, nonjudgmental, warm, and accepting, even prizing, of the clients as fellow human beings. These ideas about the personhood of the counselor are so well accepted today they have become part of the popular culture. However, at the time of his writing, Rogers's vision of the role of the counselor was a significant departure from the training of psychoanalytic and behavioral practitioners. Thorne (1992) suggested that "much that was revolutionary in the early years of client-centered therapy is now apparently taken for granted by practitioners of many different therapeutic schools. It is this fact which leads some therapists to believe that person-centered therapy is what everyone does at the outset of a therapeutic relationship before embarking on the *real* therapy which, of course, bears an entirely different brand label" (p. 44).

One of the major criticisms of person-centered counseling is that it offers few prescriptions for problem solving. Clients might be inclined to seek another counselor who will offer more specific suggestions and not place as much responsibility on them. Beginning counselors who use this approach may see it as an effective means for getting to know their clients better at the outset of counseling but as insufficient for "real" change.

Many students training to be counselors face perhaps one of their biggest struggles with the person-centered approach's assumption that counselors have to be nondirective; i.e., they should not offer the client specific advice or direction about what choices to make in life but rather should help the client make decisions for herself. This tension between letting the client choose her own goals and exercising one's judgment about what is best for the client is reflected in professional ethics codes, which mandate that the client's goals for change should be respected but also provide specific conditions under which the counselor must intervene despite a client's wishes (for example, if the client's behavior endangers herself or another person). In any case, many counselors feel like they need to "do something" to help their clients and are uneasy with the notion of providing little or no concrete advice to clients.

The person-centered approach assumes an innate potential for growth in clients. While many counselors might subscribe to this notion generally, those with experience in working with clients who have been exposed to dysfunctional families, trauma, loss, substance abuse, and the like question whether such individuals will be able to overcome such obstacles unless the counselor resorts to techniques and interventions intended to overcome the consequences of such experiences. For example, a client who comes from a family of substance abusers and has had a lifelong addiction to alcohol might, indeed, have innate potential for growth, but this potential could well be masked as long as the addiction persists.

There are those who criticize Rogers's emphasis on the "personhood" of the counselor rather than on specific skills that the counselor will need in working with clients. As we noted earlier in this chapter, authors such as Carkhuff (2000) have developed systematic training models that seek to translate Rogers's general ideas into specific concrete abilities and skills that counselors need to possess—such as attending and responding skills. This criticism of Rogers's approach also seems to be reflected in professional training standards for counselors that define counselor competence in terms of specific training, experiences, and abilities rather than more general personal qualities. A further criticism of this approach is that even well-defined counselor skills based on Rogers's approach are useful for building the counselor-client relationship only early on.

Rogers strongly believed that a helping relationship is one that unlocks the innate human capacity for growth and self-improvement, and it was therefore not necessary for the counselor to use a range of techniques or interventions. Instead, Rogers saw these as potential obstacles to a real and authentic human relationship. Rogers's focus on the therapeutic factors that exist in this relationship spurred considerable research on the process of counseling and could be said to have demystified it considerably. Rogers did not believe that the counselor needed to serve as an expert in this relationship, which is in sharp contrast to other approaches, such as psychodynamic counseling and behavioral therapy, that tend to view the counselor as an expert. This demystification of the role of the counselor helped expand the practice of counseling beyond the exclusive domain of psychiatrists and psychoanalysts to the helping professions, including nursing, social work, counseling, and education. During the latter stages of his career, Rogers came to view his approach as not just a means for counseling but also part of a worldwide movement for peace, justice, and international cooperation.

Questions and Learning Activities

These questions and activities are designed to stimulate your thinking about this theory and to help you apply some of the ideas to your own life and experience. If possible, you should work with another person or with a small group. Getting others' points of view and sharing your own ideas and perspectives will be invaluable as a way to help you evaluate this theory and its applications.

Personal Application Questions

Consider the following questions when you think about using this approach in your own counseling:

1. Do you believe that people inherently strive toward growth if left to their own devices?
2. Can the experience of unconditional positive regard, congruence, and empathy help clients change negative feelings and attitudes?

3. Rogers believed that it is imperative for counselors to be "authentic" in the counseling relationship. Can you see yourself being this open with clients and with yourself?

4. Will you be able to help clients find their own answers and resist offering solutions or advice?

5. Do you think that Rogers's "necessary and sufficient" conditions are all that is necessary for clients to change?

6. How does person-centered counseling seem to fit in the setting or population with which you want to work (school, private practice, agency, teenagers, etc.)?

Learning Activities

Carl Rogers for a Day

One way to test out the effectiveness of the person-centered approach is to intentionally test it in everyday life. Unlike some of the counseling theories presented in this book, this approach can actually be tested in everyday life. Rogers believed that humans naturally respond to persons who demonstrate genuine interest in and concern for them. In order to test this proposition, try "being Carl Rogers" for an hour or two, perhaps on your next trip to the mall. Whenever you encounter another shopper or salesperson, attempt some form of authentic communication with them (remember, you cannot fake being authentic). If a salesperson seems a bit rude or abrupt with you while checking out, try to communicate your awareness of her feelings in a nonconfrontational way, perhaps with a comment like "You seem a bit overwhelmed. I hope it's nothing I did." If she is particularly helpful, acknowledge this as well. The important thing here is to notice the reactions of other people if you take but a moment or two to acknowledge their status as fellow human beings.

Unconditional Positive Regard

Rogers thought it essential that counselors be able to demonstrate acceptance, warmth, and the prizing of clients regardless of their actions or attitudes. Are there certain types of clients for whom you could not demonstrate unconditional positive regard (for example, for a client who had molested a child or battered a spouse)? Counselors have an ethical responsibility to avoid counseling clients for whom they could not work effectively, including clients whose behaviors they find objectionable. Make a list for yourself of personal characteristics or behaviors that, if demonstrated by a client, would make it hard for you to work with her. Discuss your list with another person or a small group.

Identifying Feelings

A key component of person-centered counseling is identifying a client's feelings. One way to practice identifying feelings is by listening to different types of music—jazz, rock, folk, country, etc. For each song, attempt to label the predominant feeling being expressed. This activity should be done in a group if possible so that you can compare the different feelings that the group members express.

Building a Feeling Vocabulary

Although Rogers cautioned against being "analytical" in labeling feelings, many authors of counseling training texts emphasize the importance of having a rich feeling vocabulary—in other words, having a variety of feeling words so that one can be as accurate as possible when responding to the feelings of others. Individually or in a group, make as long a list as you can of all the positive and negative feeling words that you can remember.

The Person-Centered Approach: A Copernican Revolution?

In his book *Carl Rogers on Personal Power* (1977), Rogers described how a social revolution based on person-centered principles might transform society. To counter skeptics, he pointed out that in the past many "knew" the earth was flat before Copernicus and Galileo proved them wrong and that many people "knew" that invisible micro-organisms could not possibly cause human diseases until they were also proven wrong. In this book, he attempted to debunk the "common sense" view that people are not inherently good and growth seeking with contradictory evidence.

Below are several examples of such beliefs, with contrasting arguments from Rogers. For each example, compare the "common sense" statement with that of Rogers. Which position seems correct to you? Discuss your judgments with another person or a small group. Remember, as you discuss each topic, to try to understand each person's point of view *in a nonjudgmental way*.

Example 1:

"Common sense" says: It is hopelessly idealistic to think that the human organism is basically trustworthy.

Rogers's view: Research tends to confirm the notion that people are trustworthy.

Example 2:

"Common sense" says: A family or marriage without a recognized strong authority is doomed to failure.

Rogers's view: Where control is shared, where the facilitative conditions are present, it has been demonstrated that vital, sound, enriching relationships occur.

Example 3:

"Common sense" says: We must assume responsibility for young people, since they are not capable of self-government. It is stupid to think otherwise.

Rogers's view: In a facilitative climate, responsible behavior develops and flowers in young and old alike.

Example 4:

"Common sense" says: Teachers must be in control of their students.

Rogers's view: It has been established that where teachers share their power and trust their students, self-directed learning takes place at a greater rate than in teacher-controlled classrooms.

Example 5:

"Common sense" says: Deep religious feuds and cultural and racial bitterness are hopeless. It is a fantasy to think these factions can be reconciled.

Rogers's view: The fact is that small-scale examples exist in abundance to show that improved communication, a reduction in hostility, and steps toward resolving the tensions are entirely possible and rest on intensive group approaches.

Example 6:

"Common sense" says: It is obvious that in any organization there has to be one boss. Any other idea is preposterous.

Rogers's view: It has been substantiated that leaders who trust organization members, who share and diffuse power, and who maintain open personal communication create better Morale, have more productive organizations, and facilitate the development of new leaders. (Rogers, 1977, pp. 287–290. Reprinted by permission of SLL/Sterling Lord Literistic, Inc. Copyright by Carl R. Rogers.)

Practicing Listening/Empathy Skills

Work with a triad, with one person as listener, one as speaker, and one as feedback giver. Have the speaker describe an event or experience to the listener. The listener's job is just to be a good listener and express understanding of the event or experience and the person's feelings related to the situation. After a few minutes, stop and have the feedback giver provide feedback to the listener about what she saw. Also have the speaker discuss how she reacted to the listener, and in particular if she felt understood. Let each person play each role.

Companion Website

Now go to the Companion Web site at www.prenhall.com/archer to assess your understanding of chapter content with multiple-choice and essay questions, and broaden your knowledge with related Web resources and additional print resources.

CHAPTER 5

Existential Counseling

VOICES FROM THE FIELD: COUNSELOR AND CLIENT REACTIONS

Yes, it works for me

Client: My counselor wasn't exactly what I expected. I heard that counseling involved delving into your past, but he wasn't concerned with that. Instead, he helped me take a look at what I was doing with my life and the choices I am making. At times, he really encouraged me to take responsibility for myself. It was hard at first, but after seeing him several times, I have a much better idea of where I'm going in life.

Counselor: I really like existential counseling because it's not just a set of techniques—we talk about philosophy and what is important in life. I also enjoy being able to be myself in the relationship. I entered the field of counseling to help people grapple with life—the ups, the downs, the successes, and the failures. Existential counseling gives me a way to address those issues in a meaningful way.

No, it doesn't work for me

Client: To be honest, I can't see why anyone would seek out a counselor to talk about existential issues. I mean, isn't that what religion is for? I wanted to learn how to get along with my family better and I hoped for a counselor who could give me advice on how to do that. Instead, he kept asking me what I wanted out of my family relationships and how that related to what I really wanted out of life. He was a really nice person, but he seemed to put everything back on me. I guess I can see what he was trying to do, but couldn't we start with a few useful strategies for managing conflict first?

Counselor: I think that existential philosophy is really interesting, but I don't see how it makes much sense as a basis for counseling. I think people want more concrete help, and very few of my clients want to talk about the meaning of life. Existential counseling might work for philosophy majors, but I don't see it for your everyday client.

Sayid is a 20-year-old international student from Pakistan who is studying engineering at a university in the United States. He has a girlfriend who is European-American and born in the U.S. Sayid has enjoyed studying in the U.S. and as college graduation approaches, he is distraught at the prospect of returning to his home country. At the encouragement of his girlfriend, he has decided to seek help from a mental health counselor.

> **Sayid:** Lately, I find that I cannot sleep more than an hour or two at a time. The thought of going back to Pakistan is upsetting me. I mean, my family is there, and I love them, but I feel like I've started a new life here, and I want to stay.
>
> **Counselor:** I can see that you are very upset. It certainly is not easy to contemplate a change like that. There must be quite a lot to consider in weighing this decision.

Sayid: Well, everyone back home expects me to return. I guess legally I could try to become a citizen, but my family would never accept that. They only sent me to study here, not to renounce my citizenship!

Counselor: I hear that you really feel torn, but I guess when it comes right down to it, you have to make a decision. What do you think would help you make the decision?

Existential counseling is based on a philosophical concern with what it means to be human. Existential counselors do not necessarily engage in philosophical discussions with their clients, but they do attempt to help them find meaning and purpose, take responsibility for their decisions, and come to terms with the finite and fragile nature of life. While not necessarily explicit, it is assumed that existential themes form the backdrop for topics that emerge in counseling. Once existential realities are acknowledged and addressed, this approach assumes that clients will be better able to live in a purposeful way and to cope with their life circumstances. In the example provided above, Sayid is distressed over an important life decision that he has to make. Rather than offering him solutions or techniques for making this decision, the counselor is encouraging him to take responsibility for providing his own answers. Given Sayid's status as an international student, it will also be important to help him examine the complex cultural, legal, and educational factors that may impact his choice.

HISTORICAL BACKGROUND

Historical Context

Existential philosophy is concerned with how human beings find meaning in the face of the sometimes harsh and inescapable realities of life. Existentialism acquired its name from the fundamental notion that "existence precedes essence": We do not define our existence; it defines us.

As a school of philosophy, existentialism is several hundred years old, but its application to counseling is much more recent, dating from the 1940s and 1950s. Existential counseling is not identified with any one theorist but rather emerged from the work of psychologists and psychiatrists in Europe following World War II (May & Yalom, 1984). Its prominence as one of the major counseling models can be attributed to at least two factors. First is the growth of the existential philosophical movement in the early to mid-1900s. During this time, citizens of the Western world faced some of the unpleasant realities of living through the Industrial Revolution and were ready to embrace existential ideas. For example, large factories had sprung up in many Western nations, necessitating the movement of workers from rural to urban areas to fill jobs in construction and on assembly lines. Once there, many found crowded living conditions, long working hours, and the increased isolation of living apart from their original communities. This fundamental shift in how people lived was soon followed by the two World Wars, which together had a profound impact on how people thought about the human condition. Cushman (1990) described life in Western societies following World War II as beset by a "significant absence of community, tradition, and shared meaning" (p. 600). Existential thinkers believed it essential that such realities be acknowledged in order to understand how they impacted the welfare of human beings in modern society.

While these sociocultural factors led to an embrace of existential philosophy, the existential counseling movement was also propelled by disagreements with Freudian psychoanalysis.

van Deurzen (2002) pointed out that existential counseling is the only approach to depart from Freud by replacing psychoanalysis with a system of philosophy rather than psychology. Victor Frankl was a leader in reacting to Freud's deterministic notions about human behavior and replacing it with a belief in humans' ability to free themselves from material surroundings by searching for meaning in life, a form of counseling he labeled logotherapy (logos = meaning; therapeia = healing).

As a philosophical movement, existentialism peaked in popularity in the years following World War II and as an approach to counseling was intertwined with the humanistic "third force" movement in counseling that blossomed in the 1960s and 1970s. Today, however, there are relatively few counselors who identify their primary theoretical orientation as existential. It has generated little in the way of empirical research, mainly because its central tenets reject the notion that humans can be objectively studied. In fact, scholarship of any type on existential therapy has been somewhat scarce in recent years.

Many counselors today still do acknowledge the importance of existential themes in counseling. Further, there appears to be a reawakening concern with the fundamental nature of what it means to be human among many counseling theorists and researchers (McKnight, 1996; Richardson, Fowers, & Guignon, 1999). While such theorists are not necessarily existentialists, they do acknowledge a concern that the enterprise of counseling has become too intertwined with a consumer culture that places material goods and services above meaningful contact with human beings. Therefore, existential focus on what it means to be human continues to retain an important role among the major systems of counseling.

Development of the Theory

Existentialism is both a philosophical movement and an approach to counseling, and we will therefore divide this section into overviews of both. A thorough examination of the development of the existential philosophy movement is outside the scope of this book; our intent is mainly to provide a context for how it has shaped existential counseling.

Existential Philosophy   Many of the individuals credited with advancing the existential movement did not necessarily label themselves as existentialists and included philosophers, playwrights, authors, and leaders of political movements. One who influenced early existential thought was Edmund Husserl (1859–1938), a German philosopher and mathematician who developed phenomenology as an approach to understanding human consciousness. Phenomenology involves studying only that which is available to us in our consciousness rather than through more abstract methods of acquiring knowledge, such as scientific experiments or logical inference. Husserl's ideas had a powerful influence on the existential approach to psychological investigation.

Martin Heidegger (1889–1976), a pupil of Husserl, is generally credited as a leading existential thinker. Heidegger's book *Being and Time* (1962) concerned awareness of *Dasein* (being-in-the-world)—in other words, what it meant to exist. Heidegger believed that humans find themselves in a world of cultural and natural surroundings that can sustain them but that also dominate their existence. It is tempting for individuals to be consumed with everyday details and moment-to-moment living, something that has been labeled the "tyranny of the trivial." Such a preoccupation, Heidegger thought, leads to a mechanistic and unexamined life.

Heidegger also thought that the dread associated with the reality of death sooner or later becomes a source of anxiety no matter how consumed we are with everyday existence. Once confronted, this anxiety can be a prime motivator to lead an authentic and purposeful life, which includes concern for the welfare of others. However, individuals can also choose to cope with this anxiety in an inauthentic way by embracing conformity and conventionality and thus escaping any meaningful analysis of what it means to be human.

Soren Kierkegaard (1813–1855), a Danish religious philosopher and author, is often credited as the first existentialist and, in fact, coined the term *existentialism*. He believed that humans aspire to be like God but must constantly struggle with the temporary nature of life and the material concerns necessary to sustain it. According to Kierkegaard, ultimate religious truth can by found only through individual and personal experience, not through passive acceptance of religious dogma. In contrast, Friederich Nietzsche (1844–1900), a German philosopher who rejected the notions of God and an afterlife, thought that theistic beliefs impair humans' ability to rationally cope with life on earth. Instead, Nietzsche embraced the notion of *life-affirmation* and thought that individuals could realize their potential only by accepting both the rational and the irrational aspects of human nature. Kierkegaard and Nietzsche thus represent two fundamentally different approaches to tackling the question of what makes life meaningful. Kierkegaard represents the theistic existentialists, who believe that meaning in life comes from understanding God, while Nietzsche represents atheistic existentialists, who reject the existence of God and maintain that we must create meaning rather than discover it.

Karl Jaspers (1883–1969), a German psychiatrist and philosopher, contributed to the existential movement by merging basic ideas shared by Kierkegaard and Nietzsche. Jaspers disliked philosophers in academia; he regarded them as too doctrinaire and unwilling to challenge conventional ideas (Kaufman, 1989). Even though he did not subscribe to Kierkegaard's notions of Christianity or Nietzsche's strident opposition to it, he credited both for grappling honestly with fundamental ideas about the nature of existence: in fact, he called them "the original philosophers of the age" (p. 23).

Most prominent among the existentialists was French writer Jean-Paul Sartre (1905–1980), who studied at the University of Freiburg under Husserl and Heidegger. In 1941, while a private in the French army, Sartre was captured and imprisoned in Germany. After 9 months of captivity, he escaped and joined the French Resistance, and these experiences had a profound impact on him. His major work, *Being and Nothingness* (1956), dealt with what he saw as the irrational and absurd nature of humankind, due to the fact that in the world human beings are unnecessary. In his view, humans see themselves as the center of the universe despite the fact that the natural world does not depend on them.

Existential Counseling Existentialists have developed powerful critiques of prevailing notions about the nature of mental illness, as well as an approach to counseling based on existential philosophy. Several important figures have been associated with what is sometimes called the "antipsychiatry movement," led by those who challenged prevailing ideas about how to treat those classified as mentally ill. The "antipsychiatry" label does not really do justice to the complex critiques offered by these individuals: While they held antiestablishment views, they did not necessarily advocate an end to psychiatry. Karl Jaspers, who was introduced in the previous section, questioned the common practice in the early twentieth century of diagnosing mental disorders based on symptoms and instead suggested it was important to understand the function and meaning particular symptoms had for patients. In other words, what is important about a patient's psychosis is not what a patient thinks he sees or hears (the content) but rather the fact that such experiences cannot be accounted for by any outside stimuli.

R. D. Laing (1927–1989), while sometimes labeled a member of the antipsychiatry movement, actually disagreed with Jaspers's premise that mental disorders such as psychoses, for example, were unknowable (i.e., made no sense). Laing noted that while patient symptoms such as hallucinations seemed strange to outside observers, they, in fact, represented valid expressions of that person's experiences that were important for a therapist to understand. Laing credited the work of Gregory Bateson and his colleagues on "double-bind" communications in families, as one example. Bateson suggested that schizophrenic symptoms in family members are in part caused by faulty communication by the parents, which is discussed further in Chapter 11 on family systems therapy. Thomas Szasz, another important figure in this movement, argued that mental illness is a myth: According to Szasz, most of what are regarded as mental disorders are actually failures to adjust to one's environment, and much of the blame should, in fact, be placed on our institutions, not those we label as patients (Szasz, 1960).

Theologian Martin Buber (1878–1965) was an important figure in the establishment of existentialism as an approach to counseling, as he described the nature of existential dialogue; his views will be discussed in the "Therapeutic Relationship" section of this chapter. Victor Frankl (1905–1997), along with Swiss psychiatrists Ludwig Binswager (1881–1966) and Medard Boss (1903–1990), is credited with pioneering existential counseling. Frankl was born in Vienna and was interested in psychology and Freud's psychoanalysis as early as his high school years. Prior to completing medical school in 1930, he organized free service counseling centers in Vienna. After being awarded his medical degree, he practiced in both neurology and psychiatry. His life was changed by his imprisonment, along with his wife and members of his family, in a Nazi concentration camp in 1942. Frankl was the only member of his family to survive this ordeal, along with his sister who had managed to emigrate to Australia.

Frankl attributed his survival of the Nazi death camps to his ability to find meaning, purpose, and hope even in his bleak surroundings. He contracted typhoid fever and was able to sustain himself by attempting to reconstruct a book he was writing, which the Nazis had discovered and destroyed, *The Doctor and the Soul* (1965), on stolen scraps of paper. Once his concentration camp was liberated by Allied forces, Frankl faced the despair wrought by the loss of nearly his entire family. However, he managed to publish *The Doctor and the Soul*, which earned him a teaching appointment at the University of Vienna Medical School. Over the course of just 9 days, he wrote another book that would sell millions of copies worldwide, *Man's Search for Meaning* (1963). This book described his experiences in the concentration camps and introduced logotherapy as a therapeutic approach aimed at helping clients find meaning in life.

Rollo May (1909–1994) is generally credited with bringing existential counseling to the United States. While studying at the Union Theological Seminary, he met Paul Tillich, an existential theologian who profoundly influenced his views. Like Frankl, May faced death when afflicted with tuberculosis; this caused him to spend 3 years in a sanatorium, during which time he studied existential philosophy. He received the first Ph.D. in clinical psychology awarded by Columbia University in 1949, and he went on to teach at many prestigious universities. In 1958, he published *Existence* with Ernest Angel and Henri Ellenberger, which introduced the United States to existential thinking.

Two other important figures in existential counseling are Irvin Yalom and Emmy van Deurzen. Yalom was trained as a psychiatrist and eventually became a professor of psychiatry at Stanford University, where he still works. Yalom published one of the most comprehensive and popularly accepted books on existential counseling titled *Existential Psychotherapy* (1980). In addition, he has written several books about his work with clients that contain existential themes: *Love's Executioner and Other Tales of Psychotherapy* (1989) and *Momma and the Meaning of Life: Tales of Psychotherapy* (1999). Emmy van Deurzen is a counseling psychologist who founded and directs the New School of Psychotherapy and Counselling. She also founded the Society for Existential Analysis and wrote *Everyday Mysteries: Existential Dimensions of Psychotherapy* (1997) and *Existential Counselling and Psychotherapy in Practice* (2002). We refer to this last book frequently in this chapter.

ASSUMPTIONS AND CORE CONCEPTS

View of Human Nature

Existentialists believe that finding meaning in life is the only way to cope with the anxiety brought on by existence. Realizing that we are now alive but will not always be so confronts us with this fundamental question: What is life all about? According to existentialists, we can answer this question only by finding meaning and purpose in life. As was noted earlier, some existentialists sought an answer by turning to religion and spirituality. Kierkegaard and Frankl, for example, assumed that God has a purpose for our lives and that we can resolve existential issues only by finding and fulfilling this purpose. In contrast, atheistic existentialists such as Sartre and Camus did not believe in an afterlife and thought that humans had to *create* meaning instead of finding it in religious pursuits.

Yalom (1980) wrote that existential counselors view awareness of existential concerns as the central source of anxiety for humans, in contrast to Freud's belief that anxiety is caused by unconscious drives. Existentialists also disagree with Freud about the role of defense mechanisms and human health: For Freud, defense mechanisms such as sublimation and denial, used properly, are the only hope that the ego has for taming the wild impulses of the id. Existential counselors view defense mechanisms as ultimately counterproductive. Using defense mechanisms to distract us from the anxiety that naturally follows awareness of our existence robs us of the opportunity to use this anxiety productively to live life to its fullest. Acknowledging the fragility and temporary nature of existence is necessary to fully realize the purpose and direction embedded in our everyday life.

Core Concepts

Ultimate Concerns of Life Yalom (1980) wrote that four "givens of existence" form the ultimate reality on which existential concerns rest. It is these realities that must be confronted in order to lead life in an authentic manner. First, and perhaps most obvious, is the reality that each of us will eventually die. Yalom pointed out that this is a "terrible truth" (p. 8) that is always with us, something that we cannot escape despite the powerful survival instincts we possess. Acknowledgment of this reality is not unique to existentialists: Each of the world's major religions is, of course, concerned with the nature of life and the afterlife, and this reality is also grappled with in philosophy and the arts. However, many existentialists believed that Western culture tends to downplay such realities by promoting youth and consumerism, and existentialism provides a vehicle for understanding how some clients suffer from unhappiness despite having material wealth (Johnathan, 1997).

Concerns about the finite nature of life can be particularly important for clients who themselves are facing severe or terminal illness or have had this happen to those close to them. In these cases, existential counseling focuses on acknowledging the presence of mortality and how this is impacting these clients' lives. However, existential counselors assume that the finality of life is a source of anxiety for all of us, and attempts to push this reality out of awareness interfere with the ability to lead a meaningful life.

The second given of existence is freedom. Yalom (1980) pointed out that freedom is usually thought of as a universal positive in many cultures, but from an existential perspective, it has a "terrifying implication: it means that beneath us there is no ground—nothing, a void, an abyss" (p. 9). Viewing freedom as a source of existential anxiety is likely counterintuitive for citizens of many Western cultures who place an extremely high value on freedom. But existentialists maintain that freedom creates anxiety because it confronts us with both the responsibilities and the uncertainties of the outcomes of our choices. In other words, a person who is free to make choices about his life has no one else to blame but himself for the consequences of his decisions.

As one example of this phenomenon, Barry Schwartz, a professor of social theory at Swarthmore College, wrote about the psychological factors associated with this part of the human condition. In his book *The Paradox of Choice* (2004), Schwartz argued that too much freedom to make choices, at least when it comes to economic transactions, can actually reduce one's happiness. While not an existentialist, Schwartz pointed out that being confronted with dozens of everyday choices, ranging from the mundane (choosing a toothpaste) to the critical (choosing the right health plan), can be quite stressful. Each choice can involve considerable time to research and evaluate one's options, and once a choice is made, one is often faced with lingering doubts about whether the right choice has been made. In a similar fashion, Yalom (1980) argued that living in a world of freedom, where there are no boundaries and where the possibilities are endless, leaves you ultimately responsible for everything about your life. Everything that goes wrong, from suffering a drop in your stock portfolio, to running out of money to pay your bills, to picking out a paint color for your bedroom that looks atrocious, is your responsibility.

The third ultimate concern Yalom (1980) identified is existential isolation, which means that no matter how strong our social networks and community ties are, we are ultimately alone in the world. Undeniably, humans are social creatures: We live in communities large and small, and our very survival depends on our ability to work together. Tension is therefore created by the desire for meaningful connections to other people and the existential fact that we are ultimately alone in the world. We can certainly choose to involve ourselves as much as possible with other people, belong to communities and organizations, and strengthen the bonds that we have with other people. But this does not change the reality that we must confront much of life on our own. Students can study in groups but must usually take tests on their own. At the end of every family reunion or birthday party, everyone must say their good-byes.

Finally, Yalom (1980) identified a fourth concern as meaninglessness. "If we must die, if we constitute our own world, if each is ultimately alone in an indifferent universe, then what meaning does life have"? (p. 9). Yalom is clearly an atheistic existentialist who does not believe in an afterlife, and he perceives this reality as again creating a tension for humans: We are meaning-making creatures living in a universe with no meaning.

Being in the World Binswager (1975) used the term *Dasein*, or being-in-the-world, to describe humans' ability to think about and attach meaning to their experiences. Unlike other living creatures, humans are self-aware, contemplate our place in the world, and think abstractly. We have developed language and culture and, to a large extent (at least in some industrialized nations), tamed much of the natural world in order to feed, clothe, and shelter ourselves. However, the mind that is able to contemplate the future and our role in the world is also able to foresee our own demise. Existentialists believe that this puts us in touch with the ultimate concerns of life that Yalom (1980) described.

Existential counselors have identified four ways of being in the world that are essential to understanding the human condition. These four levels "provide a map of human existence on which an individual's position and trajectory can be plotted and understood" (van Deurzen, 2002, p. 62).

Boss (1963) proposed three such levels, which are usually referred to by their German names. First is the *Umwelt*, or the natural world, which includes all of our physical surroundings. While this level of being in the world is the most "concrete," and in many ways places limitations on us that are a function of our biology, existentialists still believe that we attach our own meanings and interpretations to our physical surroundings (Spinelli, 1989). For example, a person working for a large corporation and inhabiting a cubicle in a downtown office could view his surroundings as exciting and stimulating or as isolating and confining, depending on his interpretation of his surroundings. If he sees himself as a vital part of a prosperous corporation and has a generally positive view of his coworkers in the nearby cubicles, it is very likely that he will view his environment in positive terms. However, if he sees himself as working for a greedy, faceless bureaucracy and his coworkers as scheming backstabbers, he will very likely perceive his environment as hostile.

The second way of being in the world is the *Mitwelt*, that of being with other people in the world. The *Mitwelt* refers to our interactions with other people and includes "the inferences we draw about our race, class, gender, language, culture and the codes of our society" (Johnathan, 1997, p. 138). Just as is the case with the physical world, the *Mitwelt* is subject to our perceptions: We can see others as basically trustworthy or untrustworthy, helpful or hostile, which will affect our interactions with them. The meanings that are generated in the social world can therefore be heavily influenced by culture and by a person's experiences.

The *Eigenwelt* refers to the "own-world," our experience of our own thoughts, perceptions, and feelings. May and Yalom (1984) described this mode of being as the least understood in modern psychology: "It is a grasping of what something in the world . . . means to me" (p. 358). In other words, the *Eigenwelt* refers to our perceptions of ourselves along such dimensions as interests, values, intelligence, motivation, and character. The *Eigenwelt* can profoundly affect how we interact with the other modes of being, such as the *Mitwelt*. For example, if the *Eigenwelt* includes the self-perception that we are capable and assertive, we are likely to view the *Mitwelt*, or social world, as a place where we can interact with others honestly and as equals.

Finally, van Deurzen (2002) suggested a fourth mode of being in the world, the *Uberwelt*, or spiritual dimension. This refers to a "person's connection to the abstract and metaphysical aspects of living" (p. 86). This mode of being can refer to a person's religious beliefs but also includes his personal understanding of the world and his place in it. In other words, the *Uberwelt* "is the domain of experience where people create meaning for themselves and make sense of things" (p. 86).

Authentic Living Awareness in each of the modes of living allows one to lead an authentic life. Authentic living refers to an awareness, and acceptance, of the choices and opportunities available in life. According to van Deurzen (2002), the "experience of increasing vitality and enjoyment in living is the hallmark of authentic life" (p. 45). In contrast, inauthentic living "is characterized by a sense of imposed duty or the experience of discontentment with one's fate" (p. 45). Those unable or unwilling to live an authentic life can feel as if they are robotically going through the motions of daily life without any creativity, spontaneity, or passion.

Existential (normal) and Neurotic Anxiety Existentialists view anxiety as inevitable, given the unpredictable nature of life (Bugental, 1981; May, 1977). Sources of this anxiety include Yalom's (1980) four fundamental concerns of human existence reviewed previously. None of us can be certain about what the future holds, and it is therefore impossible to escape feeling wary and uncertain about what life has in store.

Bugental (1981) maintained that we are accustomed to thinking of anxiety as undesirable but that it is an appropriate response to the situation in which humans find themselves. Existential, or normal, anxiety is the natural result of such awareness. However, neurotic anxiety results when one walls off the unpleasant but natural realities of life. According to Bugental, neurotic anxiety "is always accompanied by some reduction in out total being . . . as we try to maintain security with such an illusion, we are less real in our living and so our anxiety is renewed, thus requiring greater defensive efforts" (p. 25).

Existential anxiety can serve as a productive force for making the most out of life. Common expressions such as "You only go around once in life" and "Seize the day" refer to the finite nature of life and the importance of making the most of the time that we have on earth. May and Yalom (1984) wrote that "normal" existential anxiety has three characteristics. First, it is proportionate to the situation confronted: Excessive amounts of anxiety are not produced by everyday inconveniences such as catching a cold or getting a parking ticket. Second, it does not require repression; in other words, we can come to terms with it intellectually and need not attempt to ignore it. And third, it can be used creatively to identify and confront the reality that has given rise to feelings of anxiety.

Existential anxiety is particularly likely to be triggered by a major life event, such as a death, the loss of a job, divorce, or a life transition. Take the case of Kim, a Vietnamese man who came to the United States during the Vietnam War. He grew up to become as successful businessman and remained very close to his parents. He lost his mother and father in the same year. Although he has a family of his own, he had great trouble getting over the loss and spent considerable time thinking about the past and his life in general. His family worried about him because he was moody and seemed anxious, and they persuaded him to see a counselor.

> **Counselor:** When you made the appointment over the telephone, you said your wife was worried about you; that she said you seemed distant and worried.
>
> **Kim:** I know; I haven't been myself lately. After my Dad died, I just started doing a lot of thinking and wondering about my choices in life. Things are so different for me than they were for my parents.
>
> **Counselor:** I guess losing them has really made you stop and think about your own life.
>
> **Kim:** That's true. I have been giving everything a lot of thought.
>
> **Counselor:** Would you be willing to share some of those thoughts with me? I know that we have pretty different cultural backgrounds, but I will try very hard to understand what is going on for you.

Kim has been experiencing what can be called existential anxiety. Because of a loss, he has begun to reassess his life and is experiencing some of the discomfort and even fear related to a sudden reassessment of life. The counselor gives him no answers or suggestions for change; he just helps Kim explore the questions and ultimately any decisions he might make about change. He is also sensitive to cultural issues and openly recognizes the fact that he can't really understand what it has been like for Kim to come to this country as a refugee.

One does not need all the answers to all of life's mysteries to live a meaningful life. In fact, Bugental (1981) offered the observation that "once we recognize the process nature of human experience and the infinite potentialities of human thinking and discovery, we give up hope of an orderly and completed system of thinking. But having given that up, we are begun upon an intellectual adventure which has within it high excitement and genuine creative potential" (p. 7). In other words, it is the courage and willingness to confront and question existential realities that is important for authentic living.

In contrast, neurotic anxiety stems from an inability or unwillingness to examine the realities of life, and according to May and Yalom (1984), it has three characteristics that are the flip sides of those associated with existential anxiety. First, neurotic anxiety is not appropriate to a given situation. A Hollywood movie star obsessed with appearing young may resort to expensive and dangerous plastic surgery after the appearance of a single wrinkle in his face. Second, it is repressed and not dealt with consciously. Such a movie star would likely not admit to a fear of growing older but might blame Hollywood's obsession with youth as the cause for his anxiety. And third, neurotic anxiety tends to paralyze the person rather than helping him lead a more creative and authentic life. Our Hollywood movie star might find it necessary to have several such surgeries, and thus spend much of his time visiting doctors and recovering from surgery, rather than leading a full life.

Search for Meaning: Existential counseling involves helping clients search for a source of meaning in life in order to transform anxiety caused by the ultimate concerns of life into purposeful and authentic living. Victor Frankl is perhaps best know for translating this important idea into an approach to counseling that he labeled logotherapy. As described earlier in this chapter, Frankl personally confronted, and overcame, extreme hardship and loss as a prisoner in Nazi concentration camps in World War II. He was able to overcome his circumstances by reframing his experience so as to find hope and meaning. Frankl described these experiences in his book *Man's Search for Meaning* (1963), in which he describes both what happened to him and the central tenets of logotherapy. Logotherapy, which will be described in more detail in the "Therapeutic Techniques" section of this chapter, involves first helping a client find meaning and purpose in life and then helping him act on it.

THERAPEUTIC RELATIONSHIP

Counselor's Role

Existential counselors believe that the relationship between the counselor and the client is the primary mechanism of change. The nature of this relationship in existential counseling, including Martin Buber's (1958) notion of the "I-Thou relationship," will be discussed in the following "Counselor-Client Relationship" section. In this section, we will focus on van Deurzen's (2002) description of existential counseling as a philosophical investigation in which the counselor acts in the role of sage or guide. According to Bugental (1981), "Psychotherapy is not the treatment of an illness. It is a philosophical venture" (p. 42).

The counselor's role in existential counseling is therefore both simple and complex. In one respect, the role of the counselor is relatively straightforward: helping clients confront existential realities and find meaning and purpose in life. However, the search for meaning in life is always complex, far-reaching, and never fully resolved.

van Deurzen (2002) wrote that in existential counseling the counselor must address the client's anxiety at the outset of the relationship. In order for the client and the counselor to work on existential concerns, more immediate and practical considerations must be addressed. In other words, from the moment that he meets the counselor, the client will likely experience a range of concerns about the risks and benefits of entering into counseling. One such risk is the vulnerability of sharing his deepest concerns with a total stranger (the counselor): Will this person be able to help me? By seeking help, am I admitting that my life has become uncontrollable? According to van Deurzen (2002), existential counselors must be "sensitive to the ways in which the particular client attempts to alleviate her anxiety [and] needs to provide some evidence of her ability to encompass this and further anxiety" (p. 33). One way to do this is to elaborate on practical matters important in the counseling relationship, such as the frequency, length, duration, and cost of counseling sessions (van Deurzen, 1997).

Existential counselors vary considerably in the techniques and approaches they use. However, the assessment and diagnostic roles of the counselor are deemphasized in favor of the counselor's role as a "mentor in the art of living" (van Deurzen, 2002, p. 25). In other words, the counselor functions more like a sage than a technician or teacher. The existential practitioner must be deeply committed to understanding life without becoming dogmatic or caught up in abstractions.

A brief example may serve to illustrate how an existential counselor might serve as a sage or mentor in life. Tomas is a Mexican-American man in his early twenties who lives in a small community in the southwestern United States. His parents were migrant farmworkers who came to the United States from Mexico when he was very young. Tomas remembers moving back and forth across the country from California to Florida as his parents found various seasonal jobs in orchards and vineyards while he was growing up. Tomas was able to complete his high school education during this time despite the constant moves, and recently his parents found steady work in an Arizona town where they live with Tomas and his three siblings. After getting his high school diploma, Tomas found part-time work in an electronic appliance store and started taking classes at the local community college. He has struggled mightily in his first semester of college and has recently become quite depressed about the prospect of failing out of college and being stuck in what he fears will be a "dead-end job." His faculty advisor was able to help him sort through his academic options, but as he learned of Tomas's feelings of distress and his inability to sleep, she referred him to the campus counseling center.

> **Tomas:** I haven't been able to sleep since I got my midterm grades—two F's and a D. Maybe I should just give up now and try to cut my losses—I don't want to waste my time and money here if I can't cut it. And I don't want to disappoint my family—they worked so hard for so many years so my brothers and sister and I could have a better chance in life.
>
> **Counselor:** Tomas, I think anyone would be upset with getting disappointing grades like that, especially since it's your first semester and you've worked so hard to do

well. I'd like to help you figure out what's happened and what you want to do about it.

Tomas: Well, can you tell me if I belong in college? I mean, you went to graduate school; you can probably do that, right?

Counselor: I can certainly try to help you figure that out for yourself, but it's not really the kind of question that I, or anybody else here, can definitively answer for you. Failing a class is a serious matter, but it sounds like that's not the whole picture. It also seems to me that you're quite concerned about whether your efforts are worth it or not and how this is going to look to your family.

Tomas: I guess that's true—I mean is it worth failing and disappointing my family? I just don't know—you have no idea how many times I've heard about the hardships my parents put up with, what it would mean for them if I were to make it here.

Counselor: Tomas, I can certainly appreciate how important your parents are to you and the concerns you have about doing well in college. One thing I do know is that many students face these same concerns, and each must make very important decisions about how to approach his studies: Is it worth it? What do I have to gain, and what do I have to lose? These are things that we can work on together, but I don't think you'll necessarily find any easy answers—I can only promise I'll support you in trying to figure out answers for yourself.

Tomas's case illustrates how an existential counselor might function in the role of sage. First, the counselor is deeply interested in helping Tomas figure out how to make the best decisions possible about his studies. However, as opposed to someone who uses a more educational or directive counseling approach, he is not in the business of giving advice or providing solutions. Instead, the counselor's role is to help Tomas assume responsibility for his choices and to confront the unacknowledged anxiety that might lie behind his feelings of distress and lack of sleep.

Existential counselors believe that people who attempt only to make life as safe and comfortable as possible will destroy their potential to live creative and fulfilling lives. In the above example, we see that Tomas is now at a point where he is questioning his decision to attend college in the face of some disappointing grades. His decision about whether or not to persist in his studies in the face of this disappointment will likely have a tremendous impact on his life, and it can be assumed that it has placed him in touch with some of the ultimate concerns of life described earlier in this chapter. This might have become a source of anxiety for Tomas, and Tomas's counselor is probably suspecting that rather than acknowledging it, Tomas is at least partly in denial and attempting to place the burden of responsibility for this choice onto the counselor.

We can further see in this example that the counselor is refusing to let Tomas relinquish responsibility for the choices he has to make. The counselor is beginning to suggest that there may be no easy answer to Tomas's concern—he might take the difficult path of trying to raise his grades, or he might choose to at least temporarily leave school. In either case, the counselor's role is to attempt to help Tomas understand and accept the freedom that he has and to apply this knowledge to a fuller understanding of how he wants to lead his life.

A final comment on this case study has to do with Tomas's cultural background, which was not explicitly addressed in this vignette but which likely plays an important role in Tomas's current situation. Some have criticized existential counseling for having an individualistic focus at the heart of its philosophy, which might not be consistent with the views of persons from collectivistic cultures. While we will further explore these criticisms in the "Multicultural and Diversity Effectiveness" section of this chapter, at this point it is important to note that Tomas, as a person from a Mexican-American family, would need a counselor who understood his cultural values. For example, the counselor would need to be open to the possibility that Tomas will not want to work on his individual needs at the expense of his family's approval.

Counselor-Client Relationship

As was noted in the previous section, existential counselors believe that the relationship between the counselor and the client is the primary mechanism of change. In describing the nature of this relationship, existentialists often refer to Martin Buber's (1958) notion of the "I-Thou relationship." Buber believed that we can understand ourselves only in the context of our relationship with the outside world and with other people, an idea that was also important to Gestalt theorists. That is, Buber believed that "I" has meaning only in the context of an I-It or I-Thou relationship. By I-It relationships, Buber meant the instrumental day-to-day interactions with other people and things that keep the world running, such as buying goods and services, making appointments, and generally keeping things running smoothly. While such transactions are necessary, Buber contrasted them with an I-Thou relationship in which the other person is contacted in a truly spontaneous and authentic way.

Existential counselors believe that most of us typically relate to other people at the beginning of a relationship in I-It mode—we treat them as objects in our world rather than other beings. Consider for a moment the way many of us behave during a trip to the grocery store, particularly when we are in a hurry and want to get out as fast as possible. We might rush through the aisles, grabbing what we need and hurrying to the checkout counter. If we are polite, the checkout person will receive a quick hello, but that is probably the extent of our relationship with the person—we treat him pretty much the same way that we treat the objects on the shelf or the credit card machine we use to pay for our purchases.

Existential counselors believe that we treat many of the people in our world as we do the checkout person in the example above: more as "things" in our environment than as authentic, living and breathing people with their own worlds, responsibilities, and lives. This does not necessarily point to a character flaw in human beings but rather underscores much of the human condition: We are alone in the world and sometimes need "special circumstances" for us to overcome our isolation and our tendency to relate to others only on a superficial level. Authenticity therefore is a primary existential value in the counseling relationship. According to Strasser and Strasser (1997), "[T]he true authenticity of human beings is to face and be aware of the temporality of our existence" (p. 27).

Confronting this aloneness by being authentic with others is central to existential counseling. May (1953) wrote that our self-awareness underlies the ability to distinguish between "I" and the world. According to Bugental (1981), this is a paradox that must be dealt with in that "each of us is ultimately alone in relationship to others" (p. 28). Bugental pointed out that a number of terms have been used by existential writers to describe how the relationship between two people slowly becomes more genuine and authentic. *Encounter* refers to the experiencing of two people and whether the relationship can be described in I-It or I-Thou terms. Bugental wrote that "when I meet you and regard you as an object rather than as another subject, I give you status of a thing rather than a be-ing . . . when I meet you and recognize you as another be-ing, this is an 'I-Thou' relationship and is an encounter" (p. 29).

Recognition of the other person as a person in his own right with his own attitudes and experiences is known as *confirmation*. A third term used by Bugental (1981) to describe the relationship between the counselor and the client is *dialogue*, which is the attempt to communicate each individual's shared perspective through shared discourse. Obviously, verbal exchanges are the primary way this happens in counseling, and the process presupposes that the counselor is willing to attempt to understand the client's experiences as openly and honestly as possible. A final term used by Bugental to describe the counseling relationship is *engagement*, which occurs when an individual lets another person matter to him. This could be viewed as a relationship in which I-Thou predominates and in counseling terms could be described as one in which a working alliance is achieved.

ASSESSMENT, GOALS, AND PROCESS OF THERAPY

Assessment

An initial assessment of the client's capacity to enter into an authentic relationship is important in existential counseling, and formal assessment instruments are sometimes used for this purpose. However, diagnostic labels such as those in the *Diagnostic and Statistical Manual of Mental Disorders* (*DSM*) and extended formal assessments typically do not play a central role in existential counseling, since they could detract from the authenticity of the I-Thou relationship and could distract clients from core existential issues by focusing on labels and diagnoses. Further, as was noted in the "Development of the Theory" section of this chapter, existentialists such as Jaspers, Laing, and Szasz have offered powerful critiques of the traditional methods of diagnosing clients. While diagnostic systems such as the *DSM* have been revised to address concerns about the potential harm associated with diagnostic labels, formal diagnoses are still not typically used in existential counseling.

An important assessment goal is to establish how capable the client is of identifying what to him are the core themes he most needs to work on in counseling. Typically, this is conducted as part of the dialogue between counselor and client rather than through formal assessment. Cohn (1997) suggested that when first contacting clients, existential counselors must avoid seeing them as sets of facts and circumstances that can be understood in an objective way. Instead, he pointed to the importance of seeing each encounter between client and counselor as a unique and subjective exchange of ideas and experiences. Then, because any given meeting between a counselor and a client is unique, "there is no client as such. If two therapists meet the same client, it is not the same client" (p. 33). Cohn also advanced the idea that what the client tells the counselor in the context of the therapeutic relationship is unique—he may have told another counselor something different entirely. It then follows that there cannot be an objective assessment of clients: "[T]his would imply an objective situation independent of time, place and the contribution of the assessing therapist" (p. 34).

Some existential counselors do use formal means of assessment to help identify existential issues for clients to work on, as well as to serve as indicators of treatment effectiveness. For example, the Life Attitudes Profile–Revised was developed by Reker (1994) to assess meaning and purpose in life, and Crumbaugh and Henrion (1988) developed the Purpose in Life Test to evaluate individual attitudes about life goals and death. Relatively brief inventories of this type can be used at the outset of counseling to help clients identify which existential concerns are most relevant to them as they begin counseling. In addition, inventories that capture existential themes, or even projective instruments that tap some of the same issues, such as the Thematic Apperception Test (TAT), could be used to evaluate the progress of counseling.

A more widely used means of assessing clients' concerns in existential counseling is the exploration of dreams. Freud pioneered the interpretation of dreams as a method of accessing unconscious material that had been pushed from awareness by his patients. However, existential counselors typically view dreams as vehicles for better understanding the real person rather than as methods of accessing the unconscious (May, 1983). van Deurzen (2002) wrote that "an existential-phenomenological approach to dreams focuses on an individual's expression of their world relations as they appear in the dream" (p. 109). In other words, humans define their existence through their relationship with the outside world, and analysis of dreams is a method of furthering this understanding. In existential dream analysis, phenomena stand for what they are and are not symbolic of something else: "[W]e exist as much in our waking lives as we do in our dreaming states, they are different aspects of the same existence" (van Deurzen, 2002, p. 110).

The fundamental goal of assessment in existential counseling, whether it is accomplished through dialogue between the counselor and the client, formal assessment, or dream analysis, is to understand the pattern of the client's being in the world. As was reviewed earlier in this chapter, existential counselors are concerned with four modes of being in the world: the natural world (*Umwelt*), the social world (*Mitwelt*), the world of the self (*Eigenwelt*), and the spiritual world (*Uberwelt*). Let us return now to the case of Tomas, the Mexican-American man in his early twenties. Recall that Tomas lives in a small community in the southwestern United States and has parents who were migrant farmworkers and who moved often while Tomas was growing up. One assessment goal of Tomas's existential counselor is to try to understand his four modes of being.

Tomas's Natural World (Umwelt)   In working with Tomas, an existential counselor will want to explore his physical health and the impact that his lack of sleep is having on his ability to function at both work and school: How long ago did his sleeping problems start? What kinds of efforts has he made to correct the situation? What is a "normal" amount of sleep for Tomas? van Deurzen (2002) commented that hobbies and leisure activities are examples of positive living in the natural world, and this is another area that might be explored in counseling with Tomas. This might be particularly important in this case because balancing school, work, and other activities might be an issue for Tomas. On a more general level, an existential counselor might explore with Tomas his feelings about the world he lives in: Whom does he live with, and where does he spend much of his day? Does he have a conducive atmosphere in which to pursue his work and studies (i.e., an adequate place to read, access to the library, etc.)? As an example, consider this exchange between Tomas and his counselor.

> **Counselor:** Tomas, we've talked a little about your academic concerns and your difficulty sleeping, and I wonder if we could talk a little more about what you do right before you go to sleep. Now I'm not necessarily a sleep expert—I'm not going to tell you to use a different pillow or drink warm milk before you go to bed—but I am interested in knowing something about your world so we can get to the heart of your concerns.
>
> **Tomas:** What do you mean exactly, like my bedtime routine?
>
> **Counselor:** Well, just generally how you spend your time in the evenings, maybe anything in your routine that has changed lately, that kind of thing.

> **Tomas:** Well, my work schedule has changed quite a bit lately, so sometimes I study right before I go to bed after I get home—I usually lie there for awhile trying to catch up on my reading. I used to go to the library to read when I worked mostly days, but now every other workday is at night.

This information may or may not be important in addressing Tomas's concerns, but it does illustrate that existential counselors are not interested solely in abstract philosophical concerns; how a client actually spends each day is inextricably connected to each of the other modes of being, and just as important to assess. In this case, a recent change in Tomas's work schedule could be profoundly impacting when he is able to study, whom he is able to study with, and his pattern of sleeping.

Tomas's Social World (Mitwelt) Understanding Tomas's social world will necessitate exploration of cultural values that he and his family share and can allow the counselor to gain a greater understanding of how these factors may be impacting his experience. For example, the counselor might explore Tomas's social world in order to better understand what educational values he holds and how his parents influenced their development.

> **Counselor:** Tomas, you mentioned that you haven't been able to sleep since receiving your midterm grades and that you worry about disappointing your family. Could we talk about that a bit more?
>
> **Tomas:** Well, I mean my parents mostly. It took them a long time to get their high school diplomas, but they did it. And they see education as the way to get ahead in America.
>
> **Counselor:** And what about your educational values?
>
> **Tomas:** Well, I certainly know it's important. School was never easy for me, but I grew up around people without a lot of formal education, and it's pretty clear you can't get ahead that way.

Even in this short exchange, we can garner some understanding of Tomas's educational values and how they were influenced by his parents. It will therefore be important to clarify what level of academic performance he considers acceptable and what it will take for him to perform at that level. In addition, the accuracy of his perceptions about his parents' reactions could be examined: Would they really react with disappointment, or would their overriding sentiment be eagerness to help Tomas get on the right track academically?

Tomas's Personal World (Eigenwelt) van Deurzen (2002) described this world as that of a person's relationship with himself—it contains intimacy with the self and other people and everything that is felt to be part of the self. To a certain extent therefore it overlaps with the *Mitwelt*. The inner world includes thoughts, character traits, ideas, aspirations, and people that are identified as one's own, and van Deurzen (2002) asserted that while Western values place a high premium on individualism and an outgoing nature toward others, a rich inner life receives far less attention.

In working with Tomas, a counselor might begin by exploring what he perceives to be his personal strengths: When does he feel most at home and accepted? What does he perceive to be his most outstanding characteristics, and how does he believe these characteristics are manifested in the outside world? What does he perceive to be his accomplishments in the world of work and in the educational setting? It is entirely possible that because of his recent setback in college, he will downplay any strength he has, so it will up to the counselor to explore this dimension as fully as possible.

> **Counselor:** Tomas, I realize you've struggled recently in school, but I wonder what has helped you in the past in school. What are your strengths as a student?
>
> **Tomas:** Well, it's kind of hard to remember now, this year has been such a nightmare so far . . .
>
> **Counselor:** I can certainly understand how upsetting that is for you right now, but what about in high school . . . do you feel like there were areas that came easily to you?
>
> **Tomas:** Well, I guess I was pretty good at math, and I thought about some kind of technical career in college, but I just couldn't see someone like me being an engineer or anything.

Here the counselor is attempting to explore Tomas's private world, particularly his views about himself in the academic world, which is one of the central reasons he sought out counseling. Tomas's last comment, that he was good at math but couldn't see himself as an engineer, may be particularly revealing and provide the counselor with insight into his private universe. Perhaps Tomas's parents did not encourage his interest in technical fields, or he may have been influenced by cultural stereotypes where people in technical fields are mainly portrayed as white males. In any case, this is likely an area that could be a focus for further exploration.

Tomas's Spiritual World (Uberwelt)   While this dimension of being in the world can involve a person's religious beliefs, even those who do not subscribe to formal religious traditions have ideas about themselves, the world, and the afterlife. However, existential counseling is not about advocating a transcendental or mystical experience; it is about making explicit a person's existing views on life.

In Tomas's case, exploration of his views of life could well consist of exploring the meaning he attaches to his work and educational experiences. Clearly, part of his motivation comes from his parents and the sacrifices they have made for him, but it is also reasonable to assume that he has an implicit worldview of what makes life meaningful because he fears being stuck in a "dead-end job."

> **Counselor:** Tomas, one thing you mentioned that seems a concern for you is getting stuck in a dead-end job. Could you tell me more about what you mean by that?
>
> **Tomas:** Well, right now I just work for an hourly wage. Someone controls my schedule, and I don't make enough to buy the things in life I want, like a house. I guess that's part of it.
>
> **Counselor:** So meaningful work would be a job where you call some of the shots and where you earn enough to live comfortably?
>
> **Tomas:** Well, not necessarily a lot of money, but it's about respect. It's about doing something that matters in the world.
>
> **Counselor:** Kind of a sense that you are contributing something?
>
> **Tomas:** Yeah, that's right. I'm not real religious, but I want to be a part of something good.

In this exchange, we see that exploration of Tomas's spiritual world does not necessarily entail exploration of his religious beliefs. His work and schooling are a vital part of his everyday experience and are likely intimately tied to his views on life and meaning whether he acknowledges them or not. This final segment of assessment of the four modes of being also suggests some of the ways that these four modes relate to each other and operate simultaneously in Tomas's world: In the natural world, he confronts a job that may have some unpleasant conditions attached to it, and he is hopeful that his schooling will provide a way out to a better job. His views of what constitutes a better job are shaped in his private world, where his values have been strongly influenced by his parents. He is highly desirous of a job that will earn him respect and enable him to make contributions in the social world. And finally, it is in the spiritual world where many of these ideas come into play, where Tomas has shaped a vision of the role and meaning of work that guides his day-to-day activities.

Goals

Bugental (1981, 1990) believed that authenticity is the central concern of existential therapy and described it as encompassing an awareness of the various modes of living and their interconnectedness, a willingness to confront the fundamental concerns of living, and openly and honestly communicating with others. Bugental (1981) noted that in doing so he was "seeking to characterize an ideal or ultimate condition of authenticity with the recognition that we are always somewhat less than fully authentic" (p. 33). In other words, authenticity is something that the counselor and client aspire to without ever being able to fully realize it.

Authenticity, and an awareness of how one lives in the various modes of being, is inextricably tied to another essential goal of existential counseling, the search for meaning in life. As was noted at the beginning of this chapter, existentialists are united in the belief that finding meaning in life is essential but disagree as to what the exact nature of the search should be. For example, Yalom (1980) wrote about the "problem" of meaning by asserting two contradictory propositions. First, human beings seem to require meaning in life. As Frankl (1978), the founder of logotherapy, wrote, "[M]an is always reaching out for meaning, always setting out on his search for meaning; in other words, what I call the 'will to meaning' is even to be regarded as 'man's primary concern'" (p. 29). The second proposition Yalom (1980) identified, however, is that "there exists no 'meaning', no grand design in the universe, no guidelines for living other than those the individual creates" (p. 423).

For Yalom and other atheistic existentialists, therefore, the central task in finding meaning in life in the face of a random and indifferent universe is to *create* meaning because otherwise it does not exist. Frankl (1967) took a different approach to the second proposition described above by asserting that there is meaning in life and that we must *discover* it rather than creating it. Frankl's logotherapy confronts clients with the need to identify this meaning and the personal responsibility they must take in finding it. While Frankl wrote extensively about his spiritual beliefs in describing his survival of the Nazi death camps in World War II, he maintains that the practice of logotherapy is secular in nature. In other words, the goal is to help the client take personal responsibility for discovering meaning and purpose.

The goal of developing personal responsibility in existential counseling is often construed as necessitating the development of the client's personal world (*Eigenwelt*) in counseling. Existentialists believe this mode of being is often underdeveloped in comparison to other modes, such as being in the natural world (*Umwelt*). For example, May (1958) believed not in relieving symptoms but in helping clients fully understand their experience. To use the language of modes of being, a client in counseling may be overly focused on things that exist in the natural world such as symptoms of depression, including a loss of appetite and a lack of energy. Existential counselors believe that what is often missing is the meaning that a client attaches to this experience (*Eigenwelt*) and how it relates to the other modes of being.

Another important goal of existential counseling is to help clients transform their sense of meaning and their acceptance of personal freedom and responsibility into concrete actions in their lives. Existential counselors believe it is important for clients to distinguish between limitations that are placed on them by the outside world and limitations that they place on themselves (van Deurzen, 2002). Both May (1981) and Frankl (1988) wrote extensively about the need for clients to take concrete steps in their lives based on the sense of meaning developed in counseling. In other words, clients need to develop a sense of how they would like to lead their lives differently and then take actions to accomplish that goal. Specific methods that existential counselors use to accomplish this end will be described in the "Therapeutic Techniques" section of this chapter.

Process of Therapy

May (1958, 1983) summarized existential counseling as a series of client-therapist encounters in which the counselor attempts to help the client identify personal sources of meaning and then lead his life according to those values. May (1983) did not impose any particular structure on the process of counseling and, indeed, believed that what happened in the first few sessions of counseling could well resemble the content of the final sessions. Many existential counselors, however, do recognize at least some general ways in which the process of existential counseling unfolds.

First, in the initial phase of counseling, establishing an authentic relationship between the counselor and the client is paramount (Bugental, 1981). Craig (2000) described the nature of this relationship as "a human sanctuary within which the patient may experience the safety and freedom to know him/herself, to take up his/her own authentic possibilities for being-in-the-world" (p. 271). Recall that van Deurzen (2002) described the role of the counselor as a sage who can serve as a guide in the client's exploration of personal sources of meaning. In this way, the client is encouraged to explore the way in which he is currently leading his life, particularly with respect to the *Dasein*, or modes of being in the world. An example of how this might be explored was provided in the case of Tomas in the "Assessment" section of this chapter.

The existential approach focuses on universal concerns of human existence, those that are important for all human beings, and therefore it could generally be said that any client is a good candidate for existential counseling. However, in describing how they work with clients in time-limited existential counseling, Strasser and Strasser (1997) point out that "clients' expectations of any therapy are usually very high . . . these kinds of expectations need to addressed from the outset, the aim being to reduce any expectation on behalf of the client to a feasible and workable position" (p. 14). Such considerations apply not only to time-limited interventions but also to any type of existential encounter, since clients must recognize that the search for meaning lasts throughout the life span. Discussing the basic structure of the counseling process, including time limits for sessions, helps establish the boundaries, and importance, of the counseling relationship: "[T]he more regular and reliable our meeting times and the more transparent our arrangements, the greater is the sense of personal sanctuary for the patient" (Craig, 2000, p. 270).

Consider the example of Marie, a 30-year-old client who works as a technical writer and has been experiencing conflict with Nola, her partner of 1 year. Marie has become increasingly concerned about the frequent arguments she has with Nola, particularly when it comes to social activities. Nola works for a conservative high-technology company and is very concerned about concealing her sexual orientation from her coworkers. Marie, however, is very open about being a lesbian and longs to include her partner in parties with coworkers and other social functions. Nola is adamantly opposed to this for fear of being "outed" by running into a coworker in a public venue. Marie has become convinced that Nola needs to be more accepting of her sexual identity, even if it has repercussions in the workplace, and had hoped Nola would seek couples counseling with her. Nola refused, and Marie decided to seek out individual counseling instead. In the initial stage of counseling, the counselor attempts to balance the establishment of an authentic relationship with the structure necessary for a "human sanctuary."

See DVD

Chap. 5
Clip 1

Marie: Well, what I really want to do is fix my relationship with Nola. Can you help me work on that even if Nola won't come to counseling right now?

Counselor: Marie, we can certainly talk about how important the relationship is to you. However, it's also important for us to acknowledge that Nola is not here with us and that our work together will be different than couples counseling.

Marie: What do you mean? What would be different?

Counselor: Well, first off, in our work together, you and I will be working toward establishing an honest and authentic relationship between the two of us. This will give us a chance to explore the meaning of your relationships, including our own, and how they affect the way you live.

Marie: I think I see what you mean . . . I probably haven't spent much time considering my own personal values—I've spent most of my adult life in one romantic relationship or another.

In this example, we see that the counselor is attempting to establish an authentic relationship with Marie while at the same time educating her about the structure of their counseling session. He communicates to Marie that individual counseling is not couples counseling and that the focus will be on Marie rather than the relationship she has with Nola. In addition, the counselor is attempting to convey the importance of Marie's exploration of her own thoughts, feelings, and values about romantic relationships. At this early stage, the counselor has not yet explicitly addressed the complex factors associated with Marie's sexual identity or the possible societal discrimination she and her partner face. These factors will be very important, however, in understanding her present concerns and the problems she is having in her relationship with Nola.

During the middle phase of counseling, the primary focus is on a continuing examination of the client's present value system and the meaning that is attached to his experiences. There is a particular emphasis on helping the client explore his internal psychological world (*Eigenwelt*), which is the area where the client grasps what the world means to him (May & Yalom, 1984). While existential counselors can use a range of techniques throughout this phase of counseling, van Deurzen (2002) identified the Socratic method of questioning the client as a mainstay of this approach: "[T]he therapist will encourage close scrutiny of moods and emotions, indicating profitable ways of searching and giving some clues about what to look for, without ever forcing the issue or suggesting answers (p. 131)." van Deurzen (2002) suggested that the Socratic method of questioning can be used in such circumstances to remind clients how they can uncover the ideas and intentions that are obscured by their emotions and confusion.

Let us now return to Marie, who has seen her existential counselor for several sessions and has recently expressed anger about Nola's reluctance to come out about being a lesbian to her coworkers. She is having trouble understanding why a "grownup" like Nola would continue to live and put up with concealing her identity as a lesbian to her coworkers.

> **Marie:**   I just don't understand why Nola would want to live that way—pretending like she's straight at work, always having to think about what she says, what she does, and whether it would tip someone off that she is gay. I know it's not easy—I went through all that myself! But I'd hope that I'm important enough to her that she'll consider it and see what it's doing to our relationship.
>
> **Counselor:**   Well, let's take it step by step . . . it sounds like you have ideas about what's going with on Nola right now.
>
> **Marie:**   [*Pauses*] Yeah, I mean obviously I know how hard it is to come out to people, especially at work when you don't know how they'll react. And your livelihood is at stake.
>
> **Counselor:**   It sounds like a very difficult time for you . . . it took a lot of courage. It must have been very important to you; otherwise, you wouldn't have risked so much.
>
> **Marie:**   I just realized how much energy I spent lying to other people, lying to myself really. I just decided it wasn't worth it, no matter what happened to me.
>
> **Counselor:**   As if nothing could be worse than putting up a front, not being who you are?
>
> **Marie:**   Something like that, yeah. I had a lot of help—I had some close friends who were also gay, and it helped to talk to them. Plus I realized it mattered a great deal where I worked . . . I ended up switching jobs to a place I thought would be more gay friendly, you know.
>
> **Counselor:**   So coming out was really a career decision, as well as a personal decision. It really required changes on many levels, and that wasn't easy.
>
> **Marie:**   Yes, but to be honest, my career wasn't all that important to me—it wasn't so hard once I decided to do it. I think Nola would have a much harder time it if came down to it. She loves her job.

This vignette suggests how a Socratic method of dialogue can be used to explore existential themes with a client. Of course, there are rarely quick and tidy resolutions when it comes to the exploration of existential factors, but here we can see that the counselor is gently prodding Marie to consider what an important decision it was to come out to her coworkers and how this impacted her vocational life as well. While Nola is not the focus of the counseling intervention here, it is quite likely that Marie will need to consider her stage of identity development with regard to her sexual orientation and what she expects of a romantic partner.

During the latter stages of existential counseling, clients are encouraged to translate what they have learned about their values and purpose in living into concrete actions. Frankl's (1988) logotherapy strongly encourages the client to acknowledge the freedom and responsibility that come with purposeful living and to choose actions consistent with that understanding. A fuller discussion of logotherapy and some of the techniques used to accomplish these ends will be provided in the following "Therapeutic Techniques" section.

THERAPEUTIC TECHNIQUES

Existential counselors are not especially concerned with using formal techniques in counseling. As we have noted throughout this chapter, existential goals are achieved primarily through the counseling relationship and a quest for understanding and meaning shared by the counselor and the client. May, Angel, and Ellenberger (1958, cited in Frey & Heslet, 1975) noted the following technical approaches to counseling that existential counselors share. First, existential counselors are versatile and tend to use a variety of approaches based on what will help them best understand and work with a given client. Second, many existentialists, such as Frankl, May, and Yalom, were originally trained as psychoanalysts and use psychoanalytic ideas such as transference and repression to help understand client dynamics. Third, existential counselors avoid the use of techniques that create distance between them and their clients.

One of the few existential approaches that has emphasized the role of technique is Frankl's (1988) logotherapy, which incorporates several psychotherapeutic counseling techniques into the quest for spiritual meaning. Because of this emphasis, we have chosen to discuss Frankl's brand of existential counseling in this section, although logotherapy is a specific way to practice existential counseling rather than a technique.

Frankl believed that all helping professionals, including doctors, nurses, counselors, social workers, and educators, work with people according to their own personal values and worldviews, and that in counseling it is important that this be acknowledged, explored, and brought into the therapeutic encounter (Hillman, 2004).

In conducting logotherapy, Frankl (1963) assumed that even high-functioning individuals were occasionally beset with a sense of emptiness and futility in life, which he later referred to as the "unheard cry for meaning" (Frankl, 1978). Logotherapy assumes that while we have an innate need to overcome this emptiness, we are also internally driven to search for meaning in life, something Frankl (1988) described as the "will to meaning." The counselor therefore helps the client overcome the distress associated with feelings of emptiness by rediscovering his will to meaning through a variety of techniques and approaches, two of which are described below.

Paradoxical Intention This technique is most often used with clients suffering anxiety symptoms and is based on Frankl's belief that fears about life tend to escalate in a vicious cycle—in other words, the fear of something in our environment such as heights or dogs tends to be self-maintaining. We avoid that which we fear, and the anxiety caused by the extraordinary steps we take to avoid it, in turn, makes the object of our fear that much stronger. Frankl (1978) described this as the fear of fear increasing one's feelings of fear.

Paradoxical intention was a technique Frankl recommended to break this cycle. In paradoxical intention, the counselor suggests that the client engage in the very behaviors he fears most. For example, a client who is having trouble falling asleep would be instructed to stay awake as long as possible; a client who is afraid of fainting while speaking in public would be encouraged to actually try to faint while talking to a group of people. Although this technique is used in other theories and explained in different ways, Frankl (1978) and Yalom (1980) attributed an existential dimension to it: By engaging in the behaviors we fear, we change the meaning of that experience and step outside of our private fears and concerns.

In a brief example of this technique, let us imagine that a counselor is planning to use paradoxical intention with a client, Tom, who fears public speaking and is convinced that he will simply be overcome with anxiety and will black out if forced to do so. Paradoxical intention is being used to help Tom confront these fears because he has recently taken a new job in which he will be asked to occasionally make presentations to large of groups of people. Tom desperately wants to succeed at this job and has sought out a counselor to help him. Of course, an existential counselor does not use such a technique at the outset—he first needs to work with Tom long enough to understand his concerns and gain his trust in using such an approach. It is also important to connect the use of this technique to the meaning that Tom attaches to his work and personal life—the counselor wants Tom not to see the use of the technique as some sort of magic cure but rather to be able to understand how his fear of public speaking developed. But for the present purpose, we provide an example of how paradoxical intention might be introduced to Tom.

See DVD

Chap. 5
Clip 2

Counselor: Tom, we've been talking about the fear you have of public speaking and your desire to overcome it so you can do well at your new job. I wonder if you might be willing to participate in a little experiment.

Tom: What do you have in mind?

Counselor: Well, I wonder if you could find a safe way to speak to a group of people that you know, maybe a few friends, and actually try to make yourself faint while speaking in front of them. I'll explain it a bit more in a minute, but I wonder first off if you think that experience would be real enough for you. Do you get nervous in front of friends as well as people you don't know?

Tom: I sure do—I just hate it. Even when I have to do something like give a toast to people I know, I feel like I'm going to black out and I find a way out of it.

Counselor: OK, Tom, that sounds like a good place to start. You see, I believe that it's the fear of passing out that's really getting in the way for you, and the more you avoid situations like this, the harder it is to even think about them. So I'm proposing we test it out—you arrange for a few friends to get together and ask them if you can try that out with them. If you were to pass out, they'd be there to help you, so we know you would be safe. Would you be willing?

Tom: I guess so, if we talk a little more about exactly what I should do.

In this example, the counselor has already developed a good therapeutic relationship and has judged it would be an appropriate time to use the technique of paradoxical intention. The assumption is that even though Tom might be anxious about giving this talk, he will not actually pass out and might even surprise himself about how well he is able to do. If Tom can actually be convinced to *try* to pass out due to anxiety while giving this talk, it is assumed that his fear will decrease because he cannot simultaneously wish to pass out and fear passing out. To reduce his anxiety, the counselor might even evoke a little humor in getting Tom into the spirit of the activity by having him come up with something witty to say after his guests revive him from his panicked swoon.

According to Frankl, what is mobilized in paradoxical intention is the capacity to distance ourselves from our feelings and impulses in the pursuit of a larger purpose. This technique illustrates to clients that they do not have to be prisoners of their fears and anxieties. It is probably worth noting that using a technique such as this requires judgment and experience on the part of the counselor: It would not be appropriate to use this technique in a situation that could actually lead to a client's harm.

Dereflection This technique is used for clients suffering from hyper-reflection, defined as an overdose of self-preoccupation. For example, clients with some types of sexual disorders and somatoform disorders (the latter refers to physiological symptoms that are caused not by physical factors but by psychological factors) could be said to be suffering from excessive self-reflection. According to Frankl (1985), "Happiness is not only the result of fulfilling a meaning but also more generally the unintended side effect of self-transcendence. It cannot be *pursued* but rather must ensue" (italics in original, p. 270). In other words, one must give oneself over to a higher cause or purpose in order to experience self-fulfillment; one cannot pursue it directly. Using the technique of dereflection would therefore involve finding something that a client finds more attractive and engaging than hyper-reflection. The client is encouraged to focus on something or someone outside himself as a method of deemphasizing his self-preoccupation, thus reducing his symptoms.

In applying this method, Frankl (1978) was a precursor to behaviorists who recommended having clients engage in behaviors that are incompatible with their problematic behaviors. For example, a client who was extremely anxious would be asked to breathe deeply and consciously relax his muscles, which are not compatible with feeling stressed out. In describing how this technique could be used to treat sexual dysfunction, Frankl (1978) provided the example of a couple experiencing sexual incompatibility. According to Frankl, the wife complained that her husband was lousy at lovemaking, and he asked them to spend 1 hour in bed each evening nude, but without making love. When they returned to meet with Frankl a week later, they reported that while they tried to avoid having sex, they ended up making love three times. Upon hearing this, Frankl acted irate and asked them to follow his original instructions in the upcoming week. During the middle of that week, they called to tell him they were unable to comply. They were making love several times a day and did not return to counseling. A year later, Frankl learned the couple had no further difficulties with sex.

Interestingly, pioneer sex therapists William Howell Masters, a gynecologist, and Virginia Eshelman Johnson, a psychologist, developed a very similar method of treating male impotence using a behaviorist principle called sensate focus (Masters & Johnson, 1970). Just as Frankl described in the case above, in sensate focus it is assumed that the source of the impotence is anticipatory anxiety about sexual performance; this anxiety is incompatible with sexual arousal and therefore causes impotence. In the sensate focus technique, the sexual partners are asked to refrain from sexual intercourse and to focus only on touching each other in mutually pleasurable ways. By removing any expectations about sexual performance, anxieties about adequate performance are alleviated. Once the association of anxiety with sexual performance is eliminated, the couple is eventually able to have sexual intercourse.

Frankl acknowledged some of the behavioral components of dereflection but also saw the technique as tapping existential notions about finding meaning and purpose in life. The husband and wife described in his example are not merely altering their physiological responses. The use of this technique often includes focusing on the needs and feelings of someone else—which has the indirect effect of restoring one's own happiness.

MULTICULTURAL AND DIVERSITY EFFECTIVENESS

Many of the central tenets of existential counseling are directly applicable when working with persons from diverse backgrounds. Existential counselors are committed to helping clients examine their values, and therefore this approach could be adapted to working with clients whose cultural values are different from those of the majority culture. In fact, existential counselors encourage clients to live their lives not according to what is socially sanctioned at the time but according to what fits with their life ideals.

Eleftheriadou (1997) noted that existential counseling delves deeply into fundamental questions of human existence and is useful for exploring the experiences of persons relocated to different countries. In describing his work with a female client from an Arab culture living in England, Eleftheriadou noted:

> When there is a conflict between two cultures, often the therapist can rush the client to a resolution within one framework because it is so difficult to hold onto two. This was something I struggle with greatly, as I identified with her feelings of frustration as a woman who had restrictions in her Arab culture and yet had spent her adolescence in a different cultural framework. However, often this is exactly the goal of the counseling, that more than one culture can be retained alongside one another, sometimes in close connection and at other times in conflict. (p. 65)

This example of working with differing cultural frameworks suggests how existential principles can be used to work with clients who struggle with the differing values of their home and host cultures.

Ivey, D'Andrea, Ivey, and Simek-Morgan (2002) also noted that Frankl's logotherapy, which was developed out of his extreme experiences with cultural oppression, is particularly adaptable to working with diverse groups. A central tenet of logotherapy is the need to acquire meaning in the face of life's travails, and persons from cultural or ethnic groups who have encountered systematic discrimination could well benefit from such an approach. In developing logotherapy, Frankl relied heavily on his own religious and spiritual values, and this represents another dimension along which existential counseling can be used. Given its emphasis on understanding a client's religious beliefs and worldview, existentialism can be seen as offering the potential to understand a client's spiritual world (*Uberwelt*).

While persons of advanced age are not routinely considered in the multicultural and diversity counseling literature, they represent yet another type of human diversity where existential counseling can be applied. Existential themes such as the inevitability of death and isolation can be particularly salient for older persons with chronic health concerns, and Brody (1999) suggested that existential approaches can be used to help clients with severe medical problems who are facing an "existential vacuum" (p. 92). One example of an existential vacuum is the lack of purpose an individual can experience when physical limitations force him into long-term residential care.

While existential counseling offers considerable promise in working with individuals from diverse backgrounds, much of its theoretical foundation is drawn from Western European philosophies that place a premium on individuality. Each of the modes of living described previously in this chapter (physical, social, personal, and spiritual) is thought to interact with and impact the client's experience, but much of the existential literature focuses on development of the client's personal world. A therapist with limited experience in working with clients from diverse backgrounds might find it extremely difficult to incorporate aspects of each of the four modes of being into his attempt to understand the totality of a client's experience. A further limitation of the existential approach with persons from diverse backgrounds is the scarcity of literature suggesting how this approach can be used with specific ethnic and cultural groups.

PRIMARY APPLICATIONS

Medical Patients

Frankl (1963) noted that meaning is found in suffering and that it is our attitude toward life's travails that is important. We are often never more aware of the role of suffering in life than when faced with serious or life-threatening illnesses, which are usually unexpected and can have far-reaching implications for the way we lead our lives. Existential counseling has been applied to a wide range of medical concerns, including infertility (Goldenberg, 1997), advanced breast cancer (Spira, 1997), and illnesses associated with advanced age (Brody, 1999). Boss (1983) noted that "illness is always an impairment or limitation of a human being's freedom of movement, in the broadest sense of the word" (p. 251). Therefore, medical concerns can be seen as tied to fundamental concerns of existence, just as psychological concerns are.

The following example demonstrates an existential approach to working with Toni, an 85-year-old widow who is a resident of an assisted-living home. She is confined to a wheelchair and is in the early stages of Alzheimer's disease. She has some trouble with her memory and at times is unable to remember people she knows well. She was sent to the assisted-living home by her son and daughter because she increasingly had accidents in the apartment where she lived, such as leaving the stove or the iron on and setting fires. She feels quite lonely and isolated in her current living situation, and her son and daughter have arranged for her to see an existential counselor.

> **Toni:** I just hate it here sometimes. I don't know anybody and I miss my friends from my apartment building. Most of them can't make it here to see me, and I know my son and daughter can't visit me all the time—they are busy with their own families.
>
> **Counselor:** It sounds like you felt pretty close to the people in your building. That must have been a wonderful place to live.
>
> **Toni:** Yes, it was . . . I miss it so much . . . I feel even worse because now I'm forgetting the names of some of those people, even though I remember them most of the time. It just makes me feel even worse.
>
> **Counselor:** Would you like to talk to me about some of your memories now . . . I'll bet what's most important to you is how you felt about them, and not just their names.

In the above example, the counselor is attempting to help Toni find meaning in her current living situation by acknowledging the importance of the relationships she had before moving out of her apartment. The counselor might help Toni celebrate the importance of those relationships as a central source of meaning in her life and perhaps explore ways to keep some of those relationships going despite the fact that she has moved away. In addition, the counselor might use this discussion of Toni's current relationships to help her focus on the future and ways of establishing connections with those she is living with now.

Group Counseling

Yalom believed that attention to existential concerns is one of the most important therapeutic forces in group work. In his classic text *The Theory and Practice of Group Psychotherapy* (1995), he described how groups form a "social microcosm" in which the members re-create many of the same patterns of interacting with others that occur in their everyday lives. Once these themes and patterns emerge in the group, the group leader can draw them to the attention of the members and invite an examination of behavior patterns they may want to change. Because the counseling group will face many of the concerns and transitions common to other groups—for example, members leaving and entering the group, members making varying levels of commitment to the group—existential concerns can be addressed therapeutically.

Mullan (1992) wrote that existential group practice revolves around three factors: the maintenance of a highly experiential quality of interaction, the recognition of existential moments, and the support of patients by the therapist. The experiential quality of the interaction comes from the energy provided by exchanges among group members.

One example of an existential moment that is typically addressed in group work has to do with ending the group (Yalom, 1995). This is typically referred to as *termination* in counseling language; in a group, it can refer to the departure of an individual member or to the ending of the group as a whole. Termination in a group is expected to bring forth feelings that go along with endings in other parts of group members' lives, including feelings of loss, hope, and abandonment.

In everyday life, it is often easy for individuals to minimize or deny such losses. For example, many people acknowledge having a hard time saying "good-bye" and might elect to skip out on a farewell party for a friend who is leaving town. Existentialists, however, view such reactions as often reflecting existential anxiety about the finiteness of life and in extreme forms could lead to the avoidance of intimate relationships in order to protect against such feelings. In a group, the opportunity to work through such concerns is present and is typically accomplished by having members acknowledge endings as they occur, explore their reactions to these endings, and then work through feelings that prevent them from acknowledging endings in their everyday lives (Yalom, 1995).

Mullan's (1992) third factor, that of support of patients by the therapist and other group members, occurs frequently in existentially oriented groups for members who have recently suffered loss or illness in their lives. A controlled study of one such type of group by Lieberman and Yalom (1992) is presented in the "Research" section of this chapter. Spira (1997) described several beneficial characteristics of group psychotherapy for persons with advanced illnesses. First, such groups are an effective way to address the concerns of medical patients in a health system that is already overburdened with meeting the needs of its patients. Such groups can include up to 10–12 people working with a counselor, and since groups have been to shown to as effective as individual counseling (Yalom, 1995), such groups can be considered more efficient. Second, such groups can be highly experiential: "Because of the pressing issues of life and death, there is no need for abstract consideration of living in the face of dying. For these patients, existential issues are a reality they need little encouragement to address" (Spira, 1997, p. 166). Finally, existential groups can be used with a wide range of members experiencing advanced illness, and possibly their family members as well. Spira pointed out that in many cases persons who would be reluctant to seek out individual counseling because of the perceived stigma would be more open to group work with other members sharing the same types of concerns.

Couples Work

Existential couples therapy pays attention to the relationship between the couple and the therapist, as well as the freedom and responsibility, the opportunity for growth found in crisis, and the meaning and potential to be found in marital and family life (Lantz & Gregoire, 2000; Yalom,

1980). Lantz (2000) described how the therapist working with couples acts to "hold" the pain and conflict experienced in the relationship so that both members can evaluate the relationship in terms of what is working and what is not. Just as with other forms of existential counseling, the ultimate goal of such an intervention is to help both members of the relationship find meaning in the experiences they have had with each other.

BRIEF THERAPY/MANAGED CARE EFFECTIVENESS

Existential counselors have increasingly focused on brief therapy because of the demands of managed care models of health delivery (Ellerman, 1999). Strasser and Strasser (1997) pointed out that a main goal of existential counseling is to help clients understand the difference between limitations the outside world places on them and limitations they place on themselves. The limitation of time itself plays a central role in brief therapy, and the sense of finality it imposes creates a tension that can have positive and negative consequences for existential counseling. On the positive side of the ledger, the time pressure can increase the client's commitment to therapeutic work, since there is precious little time to waste. However, Strasser and Strasser also pointed out that the urgency of time-limited work can cause the counselor to become overly focused on meeting the client's expectations for success at the expenses of an authentic relationship. To counter this tendency, they recommend that therapists "bracket," or suspend, as much as possible their desire to help the client so they can focus on the development of the relationship.

Strasser and Strasser (1997) noted a number of characteristics of time-limited existential counseling. First, it usually lasts between 10 and 12 sessions, with 2 follow-up sessions that occur at 6-week intervals after termination. One issue Strasser and Strasser noted in time-limited work is the clients' usually high expectations for what can be accomplished in the course of counseling. While such expectations can be difficult to manage even in long-term work, in brief counseling the counselor needs to address such expectations at the outset so that reasonable goals can be established for the time available. Strasser and Strasser noted that in time-limited work it is important to avoid focusing on any one specific issue, since all counseling issues are inextricably linked. The overall aim is to help clients alleviate their initial concerns while absorbing the method and procedure of the process so they can be applied in other parts of their lives.

Strasser and Strasser (1997) noted that clarifying questions and challenging questions are used more often in time-limited therapy. The issue of the counseling coming to an end is also a central focus: "[K]nowing that there is an ending tends to evoke stronger emotion" (p. 15). In other words, emotions generated by the impending termination of counseling, such as fear, anger, and sadness, help clients evaluate their values and the strategies currently employed to act on those values.

In evaluating the overall applicability of existential counseling to managed care environments, it is obvious that patients in managed care settings grapple with existential concerns. Existential principles might therefore be very important to address in counseling. Given that Strasser and Strasser (1997) have suggested guidelines for using existential counseling in a briefer format, it seems very appropriate to consider using this approach in managed care environments.

However, it also seems important to note that a counselor using existential counseling in such a setting will encounter several obstacles. These include the lack of emphasis on diagnosis, as well as the paucity of research supporting its efficacy, which will be reviewed later in this chapter. Therefore, a counselor seeking to address existential themes in a managed care environment may need to combine this approach with other counseling models that provide for assessment and empirically validated treatment.

INTEGRATING THE THEORY WITH OTHER APPROACHES

Existential counseling has three characteristics that allow it to be integrated with other models of counseling. First, it emphasizes a genuine and caring relationship between the counselor and the client as the primary therapeutic ingredient of counseling, which is fundamental to many systems of counseling. Second, while Frankl utilized a number of specific techniques in his logotherapy approach, in general existential counseling does not emphasize one technique over another. It might therefore make sense to incorporate discussion of existential themes in counseling with other models that offer more in the way of structure and specified techniques for working on specific client concerns. Third, because existential counseling emphasizes what it means to be human, it addresses important values that are implicitly addressed in other counseling theories. van Deurzen (2002) has suggested that existential counseling is unique in its emphasis on the clients' spiritual beliefs (*Uberwelt*) and their relationship with themselves (*Eigenwelt*). Existential counseling can therefore be used to provide a philosophical and moral framework for addressing client values that are not made explicit in other counseling approaches.

Many of the major existential theorists, such as Frankl, May, and Yalom, were originally trained as psychoanalysts and wrote how some of Freud's ideas could be understood in existential terms. For example, Yalom (1980) wrote that Freud's belief that anxiety is caused by inner psychic conflict is replaced in existential counseling with an awareness that ultimate concerns in life are the source of anxiety. However, existentialists differ sharply with Freudians on the utility of defense mechanisms: Freud believed they were necessary to ward off id impulses, while existentialists regard defense mechanisms as barriers to authentic living.

While the emphasis in behavior therapy on environmental determinants of behavior would seem to contradict the existentialist belief in human freedom, in actuality Frankl's belief that "will to meaning" must be translated into action allows for integration of existential theory and behavioral practice. In fact, Frankl's techniques of paradoxical intention and dereflection are very similar to techniques used by behavioral counselors. Arbuckle (1975) pointed out, however, that problems exist in fully integrating existential counseling with approaches such as behaviorism even though they may share similar techniques. Existential counseling is a subjective rather than an objective approach and assumes that humans are free rather than shaped by the environment. Such differences in the fundamental tenets of the approaches could undermine the ability of the counselor to use both approaches in working with clients.

Finally, the emphasis on establishing the counseling relationship and understanding the client's subjective world allows existential counseling to be integrated with approaches such as person-centered and Gestalt counseling. Indeed, many experts refer to these three theories as representing a distinct, humanistic-existential school of counseling and psychotherapy.

RESEARCH

Existentialists take issue with systems of philosophy and psychology that seek to formulate explanations or laws that govern human activity. According to this view, our thoughts, our feelings, and the events of our daily lives are experienced directly and cannot be objectively understood through scientific means. Lantz (2004) noted that existential therapists have serious reservations about empirical research. He indicated several specific objections that existential counselors have to traditional empirical research, including (1) that it could limit human freedom and (2) that it could be considered superficial information.

With regard to the first point, Lantz (2004) wrote that existential counseling is based on the assumption that clients have freedom and must exercise that freedom in order to benefit. Therefore, any research suggesting the "best" way to practice existential counseling would necessarily limit a given client's freedom.

On the second point, that empirical research can be superficial, Lantz noted that many quantitative studies of counseling effectiveness tend to be based on data derived from client symptoms and standardized assessment instruments. This type of study tends to generalize information across large numbers of people and is criticized by existentialists as ignoring the richness and complexity of each individual client's experience. Prochaska and Norcross (2003) reviewed the existential and psychotherapy outcome literature and found no controlled studies evaluating the effectiveness of existential counseling in general or of logotherapy in particular. However, Frankl (1985) did point to a few studies that have evaluated the effectiveness of his technique of paradoxical intention, including studies by Ascher and Turner (1979) and Solyom, Garza-Perez, Ledwidge, & Solyom (1972).

Existential researchers tend to use other methods of inquiry, including participation reports, which, according to Lantz (Lantz, 2004; Lantz & Kondrat, 1997), include five basic modes of inquiry: case stories, case transcripts, single-subject designs, before-after field studies, and grounded theory studies. Case stories are in-depth descriptions of a client's experiences in counseling, such as those provided in Yalom's *Love's Executioner and other Tales of Psychotherapy* (1995). Case transcripts or tapes of counselor-client sessions can be reviewed in detail, often as a part of counselor training. Single-subject case designs, in which one person is studied in detail, rather than large groups of people, can be used in ways that respect the client individually, can be tailored to the client's specific needs, and do not entail withholding treatment from clients who are in a control group condition (Lantz, 2004). In before-after field studies, clients being treated are evaluated at several points in time (including the beginning of treatment and the termination), using both subjective and objective methods. This approach was used by Lantz and Gregoire (2000) in a description of existential psychotherapy with Vietnam veteran couples. Finally, grounded theory studies are those in which a researcher uses interviews or other qualitative information to develop theories about why clients changed, how they progressed, and why they were able to grow.

In sum, while there is a large body of research discussing how existential counseling is practiced, as well as descriptions of counselors work with clients, there are few empirical studies of its effectiveness. Existential theorists would note that this is because this type of research is contrary to its basic philosophy, not because there is no evidence as to the usefulness of this approach. Given the current climate of managed health care and its emphasis on empirical validation, existential counselors will continue to be challenged to find creative ways to demonstrate its effectiveness. While it has been noted that empirical existential studies are few in number

(Prochaska & Norcross, 2003), we provide one example of a group that was partially devoted to existential themes below.

SAMPLE RESEARCH: Brief group psychotherapy for the spousally bereaved: A controlled study

Goals of the Research

Lieberman and Yalom (1992) studied whether mid- and late-life bereaved spouses bene-fited from brief group psychotherapy focused on the existential themes that surface after the loss of a husband or wife.

Participants

Surviving spouses of individuals who died of cancer 4–10 months previously were recruited for the study. This timeframe was established because of evidence that the inter-vention might not be effective in the very early stages of bereavement (i.e., less than 4 months after the spouse's death). Individuals were eligible up to 10 months after the loss because, according to the authors, there is evidence that such individuals are still in the active stages of bereavement.

Methods

Fifty-six participants were included in the study: 20 served as controls for the study (i.e., they completed all of the measures used in the study but did not participate in the intervention), and 36 participated in one of four bereavement groups. Each of the bereavement groups was led by Yalom and an experienced senior psychiatric resident. The groups consisted of eight 80-minute sessions, involving considerable discussion of existential issues such as the brevity and preciousness of life, as well as helping each member move forward with life after the loss of his or her spouse.

Results

At the beginning of the study, the authors evaluated whether the control and experimental participants differed in terms of psychological symptoms and found them to be generally comparable. In addition, experimental participants in each of the four groups were not statistically different from each other in terms of the types of concerns and psychological symptoms they were experiencing.

Participants in the control and experimental conditions were given a lengthy question-naire to complete at the beginning of the study and 1 year later in order to evaluate whether there were any differences between the experimental and control subjects in the following domains: mental health (i.e., whether participants experienced anxiety, depression, and physical symptoms due to psychological problems), mourning (i.e., feelings of anger, guilt, and grief), positive psychological states (i.e., self-esteem, feelings of well-being and a sense of mastery of life), and social adjustment (i.e., how much role strain and perceived social stigma they experienced due to their new status as a "single" person).

At the 1-year follow-up, the authors found that group participants increased signifi-cantly more than controls on self-esteem and experienced significantly less difficulty in adjusting to their new status as a single person. However, these effects were not large, and the authors concluded that the group therapy used in this study did not demonstrate a powerful effect. Recall that persons were selected for the study randomly and not because they were necessarily having difficulties following the death of their spouses.

Implications of the Research

Because there were no large differences between the treatment and control groups, the authors concluded that these results suggested most persons experiencing such a loss did not necessarily need a preventive intervention such as the short-term group therapy used in this study. As evidence in support of this, the authors noted the finding that whether or not they participated in the treatment groups, the participants as a group gradually improved over time on the measures studied. However, the authors did point out the need for future research into whether individuals who felt the need for psychological assistance following bereavement could benefit from such a group. In other words, future research was necessary with individuals who demonstrated significant adjustment problems after the death of a spouse to determine whether a group intervention would be effective.

EVALUATION OF EXISTENTIAL COUNSELING

Existential counseling developed out of a philosophical understanding about what it means to be human and encourages clients to search for their own answers to the questions of what makes life meaningful. No other major system of counseling emphasizes such an approach, and this means that this counseling approach could have much to offer in working with clients with existential concerns, such those faced with severe or terminal medical conditions and the survivors of abuse or trauma. Such individuals are often very concerned with finding meaning in their experiences and their lives, and existential counseling is well suited to this type of work. Of course, persons who confront trauma, abuse, or medical concerns are not the only persons concerned with the meaning of life. In fact, all humans have such concerns and at various points in their lives might be highly motivated to discuss them with a counselor.

Another strength of existential counseling is its potential for integration with other models of counseling. As was noted earlier, many existential counselors were originally trained as psychoanalysts and found that many of Freud's principles could be incorporated into existential work. Further, many of Frankl's techniques for logotherapy are reflected in behavioral interventions and offer the counselor the opportunity to combine both approaches, analyzing both the concrete behaviors and the meanings the client attaches to those behaviors. The fact that most existential counselors are flexible in the techniques that they use means that approaches from other systems of counseling can be readily incorporated into their repertoire.

Another strength of existential counseling is the fact that it focuses on the spiritual and psychological emptiness that many scholars see as endemic to modern life (Cushman, 1990; McKnight, 1996; Richardson et al., 1999). Existential counseling explicitly focuses on such concerns, while allowing the client to ultimately make his own judgments about such matters.

Existential counseling is not without its limitations, of course. Lantz (2004) noted that existential therapists have serious reservations about empirical research, and while other methods of inquiry, including qualitative research and case studies, have been used, the lack of quantitative research can be problematic in a managed care era, in which empirically validated treatments are ascendant. Another potential limitation of this approach is the lack of a framework for utilizing specific interventions. While this criticism does not apply as strongly to Frankl's logotherapy, for the most part existential counselors rely far more on the counseling relationship than on any specific technique. Existential counseling offers the experienced clinician who is comfortable with the counseling process an opportunity to be extremely flexible, but it may be less suitable for a novice counselor who needs more structure.

Finally, it seems to us that another potential limitation of the approach is that in the end it offers few answers about what gives life meaning. Helping clients understand, and find meaning in, life's ambiguities is both an important and an extremely complex task. It may therefore be difficult for new professionals to feel adequately prepared to help clients confront such issues. Such questions, of course, can probably never fully be resolved, but it may also at times be problematic to embark on a therapeutic philosophical inquiry when one admits up front to not knowing the answers. A theistic existential counselor, working within the framework of a religious tradition, would be less vulnerable to this concern but in the end could offer answers only to those who already shared his religious framework.

Questions and Learning Activities

These questions and activities are designed to stimulate your thinking about this theory and to help you apply some of the ideas to your own life and experience. If possible, you should work with another person or with a small group. Getting others' points of view and sharing your own ideas and perspectives will be invaluable as a way to help you evaluate this theory and its applications.

Personal Application Questions

1. Existential counseling involves helping clients clarify their personal values and then act on them. What do you think the counselor's role should be in encouraging this type of exploration? Is it possible and desirable for the counselor to take a neutral position with regard to a client's values?
2. Some existential counselors believe that meaning in life is found theistically (i.e., through a belief in God), while others maintain that there is no God and that meaning must be created in spite of a meaningless universe. Do you believe that a theistic counselor could work with an atheistic client and vice versa?
3. Existential philosophy was spurred by the development of modern, industrial societies and the living conditions this created. What elements of modern society do you see as most conducive to leading a meaningful life? Which mitigate against finding meaning in life?
4. Many existentialists expressed themselves through art and literature. To what extent could artistic works be utilized in counseling? For example, could you envision asking a client to read an existential classic such *The Plague* by Camus?
5. What is the role of philosophy in counseling? Do you see concern with existential conditions as the appropriate role of a counselor?

6. Many existential counselors were concerned with political activism and the shaping of public policy in the societies in which they lived. What role, if any, should counselors play as political activists?
7. What are the core values and beliefs that you might bring to your work with clients?

Learning Activities

Examples of Techniques

1. Provide an example of the use of each of the following logotherapy techniques:
   Redeflection
   Paradoxical intention

Modes of Being

2. Existential counselors maintain that we live in four modes of being:
   a. *Umwelt*, the natural world, which includes all of our physical surroundings;
   b. *Mitwelt*, the public world;
   c. *Eigenwelt*, the "own-world," which refers to our experience of our own thoughts, perceptions, and feelings; and
   d. *Uberwelt*, the spiritual dimension.
   Take a piece of paper and draw two lines, one down the center and one across the middle, so that you create four quadrants. Label each according to the four worlds described above, and then draw pictures of ideas, objects, or people that inhabit all four worlds for you. Next take a moment to examine all four quadrants: Are some richer or more diverse than others? How do you feel about what you see in each quadrant? Discuss with a partner or in a small group.

Art and Existentialism

3. Make a list of 5 to 10 of your favorite movies or books. Next note any salient existential themes that occur in each, such as discovering the importance of love, learning to accept loss, or finding humor in life. Do you notice any existential themes or patterns among your favorites? Discuss with a partner or in a small group.

Dream Interpretation

4. Existential counselors sometimes interpret a client's dreams in terms of salient existential issues for that client. Do you have any recent dreams that you remember and can connect to existential topics that are important to you? Discuss with a partner or in a small group.

Reflections on Loss

5. Write a few paragraphs describing your reaction to a significant loss in your life (e.g., the death of a friend or relative, the loss of a relationship or a good friend). Do you see any existential themes in your reactions? Was your life changed by these losses? Discuss with a partner or in a small group.

Companion Website

Now go to the Companion Website at www.prenhall.com/archer to assess your understanding of chapter content with multiple-choice and essay questions, and broaden your knowledge with related Web resources and additional print resources.

CHAPTER 6

Gestalt Therapy

VOICES FROM THE FIELD: COUNSELOR AND CLIENT REACTIONS

Yes, it works for me

Client: At first, I didn't know what to make of my Gestalt counselor—she kept asking me about body movements, and later on I sat in a chair and pretended to have a conversation between two parts of myself. Kind of weird, but I learned a lot about myself, and I feel more together and balanced. I liked the fact that we always talked about the here and now.

Counselor: The Gestalt approach to counseling is pretty scary at first. I was afraid to do much with it until I had more training. You can really open someone up by such a strong focus on how they are feeling right at the moment. I really like the idea that clients can examine the different sides of themselves. Helping a client integrate different or opposite parts of herself has been helpful.

No, it doesn't work for me

Client: At first, I liked this approach. My counselor focused on my body language, and she really helped me get in touch with how I was feeling. But I also wanted to talk about the problems I'm having with my fiancé, and my counselor kept focusing on me and what I was doing—my facial expressions, my arm movements, everything. It was uncomfortable . . . I guess I wanted more of an understanding of my problems and how to solve them.

Counselor: I can see using some techniques from Gestalt therapy with another counseling theory, but I don't see using it exclusively. Helping clients get in touch with feelings and live in the moment is important, but it's not everything. I think clients also need to be able to examine their thought processes and learn specific life skills, like being assertive and making good decisions. Plus, I do not think I am the right personality type for this approach—I want to be supportive to my clients, and it is hard to be so intense and focused all the time.

Carl, an African-American male in his early fifties, is seeking counseling through the employee assistance program at the computer company where he works. Over the past year, Carl has been moved around to different departments in his company because of conflicts that seem to routinely emerge with his supervisors. Carl was threatened with termination from the company unless he agreed to counseling to learn to manage his temper better.

> **Carl:** I can't believe they're blaming all this on me! I got stuck with a few supervisors who don't know anything, and they say it's my fault . . .
>
> **Counselor:** I notice that while you said that, you started to clench your fist. Can you finish that gesture?

Carl: What do you mean—do this? [*Carl clenches his fist tightly*] I tell you, I would like to to punch my supervisor's lights out!

Counselor: Can you show me that? I'd like to see you develop that more.

Carl: [*Pounding the fist of his right hand into the palm of his left hand*] OK, I just feel it's unfair to constantly ask someone to retrain and learn how to work new machines because other people have been let go.

Counselor: If your supervisor was here right now, what would you say to her?

Gestalt counselors assume that we start life "whole"—that all of the various traits and characteristics that make us unique sum up to form one integrated self. As we grow older, we are challenged to take increasing levels of responsibility for our own lives and to learn how to negotiate meeting our own needs while still respecting those of others. Fritz Perls, the founder of Gestalt therapy, believed that awareness of what we are doing, feeling, and experiencing is the key to keeping a coherent sense of self. Focusing on the present moment allows us to take responsibility for the direction of our lives and to realize our potential. Bemoaning past failures or ruminating about future possibilities only distracts us from this present focus and can cause us to block off and lose touch with our current experiences. When this happens, our feelings, thoughts, and even memories become disjointed and fragmented, and we are no longer able to live creative and autonomous lives.

In the example above, the counselor focuses on Carl's gesture of clenching his fist as a way of helping him get in touch with his feelings, which in this case was obviously anger toward his supervisor. We might guess that Carl was not wild about the idea of seeking counseling, and a Gestalt counselor would not attempt to assign blame for his problems or immediately change his attitude about his supervisor or the company he works for. Instead, Carl would be encouraged to get in touch with his present experiences as fully as possible, and the counselor would likely use a variety of skills and techniques to promote his awareness of the thoughts, feelings, and experiences that have led to a fragmentation of his core identity. The guiding assumption here is that this heightened awareness will eventually help Carl live more purposefully and be able to negotiate meeting his own needs while still respecting those of his supervisor.

HISTORICAL BACKGROUND

Historical Context

Gestalt therapy became prominent in the late 1960s and early 1970s and is best known for both the powerful personality of its primary founder, Fritz Perls, and the innovative counseling methods and techniques he developed with cofounders Laura Posner Perls (his wife) and Paul Goodman (Harman, 1995; Wulf, 1998). The development of Gestalt therapy was strongly influenced by three sources: Freud's psychoanalysis, the study of human perception by Gestalt psychologists, and humanistic and existential philosophy (Latner, 1992). Fritz Perls was originally trained as a psychoanalyst and developed some of the groundwork for Gestalt therapy as he sought to address what he saw as gaps in Freud's thinking. While his early theorizing was couched (pardon the pun) in terms of psychoanalytic thought, over time Perls became dissatisfied with psychoanalysis and developed his own unique approach to counseling.

Perls took the name for his brand of therapy from Gestalt psychology. This was a branch of experimental psychology devoted to studying human sensation and perception that became prominent in the first half of the twentieth century through the work of Max Wertheimer, Kurt

Koffka, and Wolfgang Kohler. The German word *Gestalt* has no direct English translation, but it refers to a unified or meaningful whole. The Gestalt psychology movement was a reaction to the British empiricist tradition, founded by John Locke, which held that humans acquire knowledge and information passively as information is collected from the outside world through the sense organs. The Gestalt tradition differed by asserting that humans have intrinsic capacities for organizing sensations and experiences and that the mind is capable of imposing patterns or meanings that are more than just the sum of our individual perceptions. One concrete example of this phenomenon is our perception of the images sent by motion picture projectors: Images are flashed onto a screen so fast that we cannot see them individually. From the rapidly changing individual frames, the mind creates a seamless moving image.

When Perls made Gestalt psychology a central component of his approach to *psychological* counseling for personal difficulties, Gestalt psychologists criticized him for what they saw as the incomplete and haphazard way that he applied their principles. Perls acknowledged that academic Gestalt psychologists never accepted him, primarily because he did not favor the scientific methods they used (Perls, 1969a). Over time, Perls's Gestalt therapy departed from both Freud's psychoanalysis and the academic tradition of Gestalt psychology in order to reflect a combination of Perls's unique personality and beliefs and the existential and humanistic schools of thought. The latter influence was incorporated into Gestalt therapy with a focus on humans as meaning-making individuals who are ultimately responsible for their own lives and an emphasis on present experience rather than psychological history (Perls, 1947).

Development of the Theory

Frederich Salomon Perls, who later changed his name to Frederick and became best known as Fritz, was born into a lower middle class Jewish family in 1893 in Berlin. He was the youngest of three children and did well academically until middle school, when he failed the seventh grade twice. He persevered, however, and eventually joined the German army as a medic in 1916 during World War I. Following the war, Berlin was both an exciting and a turbulent place to live. Perls spent time as an actor and met Max Reinhard, whose emphasis on nonverbal communication had a strong influence on Perls (Wulf, 1998). During this same time, Jacob Moreno staged expressionistic experiments in theater that would later become the foundation for psychodrama, in which role-playing and movement are adapted to therapy (Wulf, 1998). Moreno's influence would later be evident in Perls's use of role-plays with his clients in Gestalt therapy.

Perls first learned how principles of Gestalt psychology could be used therapeutically when he became an assistant to physician and psychiatrist Kurt Goldstein at the Institute for Brain Injured Soldiers in Frankfurt, Germany, in 1920. Goldstein used principles of Gestalt psychology to help improve the perceptual functioning of the brain-injured patients at the hospital. Perls also credited Goldstein for introducing him to the term *self-actualization*. He admitted he did not fully understand what this meant until 25 years later, when the same expression was used by Abraham Maslow (Perls, 1969a). However, the idea struck Perls as a good thing, since it seemed to involve expressing oneself honestly and openly in a deliberate way. Fritz Perls met his future wife, Laura, during this time as well.

Later Perls trained at the Vienna and Berlin Institutes of Psychoanalysis. Karen Horney supervised his training and was his first analyst, and Wilhelm Reich followed Horney as his analyst (Sapp, 1997). Horney shared Perls's love of the theater, advocated a more active stance on the part of the therapist than was traditional for psychoanalysts, and viewed human problems holistically, thus encouraging Perls to work with the whole person (Wulf, 1998). Reich influenced Perls through his emphasis on the bodily experiences of his clients (Smith, 1976).

Early psychoanalysts thought that sensations and drives associated with various parts of the body played a key role in early human development but focused mainly on their symbolic role in working with patients' psychological defenses. In contrast, Reich moved out from behind the analyst's couch and sat beside his patients, where he could observe their nonverbal behaviors and gestures and they could see him as well. Reich believed that clients' psychological difficulties were manifested physically in such behaviors as rigid posture and tense face muscles, which he referred to as body armor. In other words, such behaviors were physical manifestations of psychological defensiveness. Reich believed that the therapist needed to work with *what* a client was *doing* physically rather than focusing on psychological explanations for *why* she was doing it. This notion would become an important element of Perls's Gestalt therapy.

Perls and his wife, Laura, left Germany for Johannesburg, South Africa, in 1934 to put themselves as far away as possible from Nazi rule (Perls, 1969a). It was here that they founded the South Africa Institute for Psychoanalysis. While they were the first to ever practice psychoanalysis in South Africa and lived very comfortably, Perls became increasingly dissatisfied with psychoanalytic thinking (Perls, 1969a). While attending the International Psychoanalytic Congress in Czechoslovakia in 1936, Perls presented a paper that was not well received and had a disappointing meeting with Freud (Smith, 1976). After living for over a decade in South Africa, Perls immigrated to the United States in 1946 with Laura and their children.

While Fritz Perls is the figure most strongly associated with the development of Gestalt counseling, both his wife, Laura, and Paul Goodman played important roles as well. Wulf (1998) points out that Laura deserves much of the credit for the existential themes evident in Gestalt therapy. She studied with existentialists Martin Buber and Edmund Husserl, both of whom emphasized that humans should be studied not from the "outside" using the scientific method of observation and experimentation but rather from a phenomenological perspective. Phenomenology refers to the study of how individuals organize, understand, and make sense of their experiences from *their* own point of view rather than from the perspective of an impartial outside observer (Wheeler & Backman, 1994).

Both Laura Perls and Paul Goodman, who was broadly educated and originally a follower of Freud, helped Fritz Perls with his first text on Gestalt therapy, *Gestalt Therapy: Excitement and Growth in Human Personality* (Perls, Hefferline, & Goodman, 1951); Laura, however, was not credited as an author. The book, which contained both exercises designed to develop awareness and a description of the principles of Gestalt therapy, was well received. The New York Institute for Gestalt Therapy was established in 1952 by the Perls and Goodman.

After establishing the institute, Perls traveled extensively and set up several Gestalt therapy training centers throughout the United States. By 1956, both Perls's physical health and his relationship with Laura had begun to deteriorate: Fritz was diagnosed with a heart condition and moved to Miami, Florida, without Laura. Although the two never divorced, they also never again lived together for any amount of time. While in Miami, Perls began a relationship with a patient of his named Marty Fromm, which he described as the most important of his life (Perls, 1969a). Today such a relationship between therapist and patient would be considered highly unethical, and it eventually ended when Marty fell in love with a younger man.

In 1960, Perls moved to the West Coast and in 1964, he became affiliated with the famous Esalen Institute, where he met highly prominent figures in the existential and humanist movements, including Rollo May and Abraham Maslow. It was here that Perls gave many of his famous demonstrations, transcripts of which were published in 1969 under the title *Gestalt Therapy Verbatim* (Perls, 1969b). Perls eventually moved to Vancouver Island, Canada, where he died of a heart attack after surgery in 1970.

The Gestalt therapy movement continued to grow after Perls's death, with students of Perls such as Gary Yontef and Miram and Irving Pollster playing leading roles. The visibility accorded Gestalt therapy by both Perls's personality and the uniqueness of Gestalt techniques represented something of a mixed blessing in the decades following his death. Many American cities have a Gestalt therapy institute, and there are now more than 100 institutes devoted to Gestalt counseling around the world. However, Mackewn (1997) points out that for many, Gestalt counseling remained synonymous with Fritz Perls. His large-group demonstrations of his techniques in the 1960s were compelling but ultimately represented just one's person unique approach to Gestalt counseling. Fritz Perls himself believed that awareness, creativity, and spontaneity were hallmarks of psychological health, and he did not wish to see his approach reduced to techniques or gimmicks (Perls, 1973). In the past few decades, Gestaltists have sought to build on the original creativity of the "Perlsian" approach to therapy and to supplement it with new developments in the practice of Gestalt therapy and the field of counseling and therapy in general (Mackewn, 1997).

ASSUMPTIONS AND CORE CONCEPTS

View of Human Nature

Perls has been criticized for developing a method of counseling without constructing a comprehensive theory of how healthy personalities develop (Sapp, 1997). However, he did have very strong ideas about what it meant to be fully human. Insight into his ideas can be gleaned from the Gestalt community he attempted to set up in the last year of his life in Cowichan, a small lumber town in British Columbia. Spitzer wrote about Perls's philosophy for this community in the introduction to *The Gestalt Approach and Eye Witness to Therapy*, a book Fritz Perls was working on before his death that was finally published in 1973. According to Spitzer, in Cowichan Perls had hoped to develop a community for training Gestalt therapists based on increased awareness, "with each person integrating disowned parts of his personality and taking responsibility for his own state of consciousness" (Spitzer, in Perls, 1973, p. x).

The principle of holism in Gestalt therapy refers to the notion that all of nature is a unified and coherent whole (Latner, 1973). While Gestalt psychologists studying human perception applied this principle to how the brain organized sensory information, Gestalt therapists extended the notion of holism to the larger context of people's lives. Humans are not seen as simply driven by internal drives or environmental rewards: Individual appetites, desires, and goals can all be important at various times, but ultimately our behaviors cannot be understood without reference to the overall purpose and meaning we assign to our lives (Wheeler & Backman, 1994). Perls believed that we have the potential to take responsibility for our lives, work cooperatively with others, and fulfill our potential, but our behaviors that move us toward or away from these goals cannot be understood in isolation.

For Perls, living in the present moment and viewing individuals holistically also meant giving them responsibility for the direction of their lives. Perls embraced the notion of individual responsibility and thought that a fundamental part of awareness was claiming the values and attitudes one wishes to live by and rejecting the values and attitudes forced on one by others. Perls emphasized personal responsibility, as is seen in the famous Gestalt prayer:

The Gestalt Prayer

I do my thing, and you do your thing.
I am not in this world to live up to your expectations.
And you are not in this world to live up to mine.
You are you, I am I,
And if by chance we find each other, it's beautiful.
If not, it can't be helped.

(Perls, 1969b, p. 4)

While individuality and personal responsibility were strong themes in Perls's writings, Mackewn (1997) pointed out that the early Gestalt literature also recognized that people are essentially social beings and that meeting one's own needs also involves consideration of others. It was self-evident to Perls that humans cannot live in isolation and are dependent on other people for such basic needs as food, water, shelter, and companionship. Psychological health for Gestaltists therefore rests on achieving a delicate balance between being responsible for oneself and remaining connected with others. Fritz Perls was probably best known for challenging others to take responsibility for their own needs rather than preaching the benefits of cooperative living. In fact, Mackewn (1997) maintained that the famous Gestalt prayer reprinted above was probably written by Perls in an attempt to goad people into personal responsibility rather than to seriously convey an "I'll do my thing, you do yours" attitude.

Core Concepts

Gestalt Formation As was noted earlier in this chapter, psychologists such as Max Wertheimer, Kurt Koffka, and Wolfgang Kohler believed that humans are hardwired to organize sensory information into gestalts. Recall that a *gestalt* is defined as a whole that is different from the sum of its parts and that has qualities of both completeness and meaning. Thus, the central idea that connects Gestalt therapy to its namesake, Gestalt psychology, is the notion that humans are innately predisposed to organize experiences into meaningful wholes. In order to demonstrate this idea, consider the dashed lines in Figure 6.1.

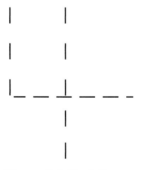

Figure 6.1 Gestalt example.

Is it possible for you to look at these dashed lines and *not* see the number 4? For most of us, the mind automatically imposes the gestalt "number four" onto our visual experience of this pattern of lines. With effort, you might be able to focus on individual dashes without your mind automatically completing the gestalt "number four," but this involves consciously overriding the mind's tendency to complete the gestalt.

A gestalt includes two elements: figure and ground. The *figure* is anything that stands out perceptually and serves as a focal point, while the *ground* refers to all the other elements of the sensory field that form the background for the figure. Note that the figure and ground are not fixed properties of the environment but rather are in the "eye of the beholder." Gestalt theory assumes that we have at least some control over what we focus on as the figure and what we allow to become part of the ground. Perls believed that this has as much to do with our internal beliefs, motives, and needs as it has to do with the perceptual information we receive. A famous example of how this happens in visual perception is shown in Figure 6.2.

In the figure, we can see either an older or a younger woman. Either can serve as the figure, and when it does, other elements of the image become part of the ground. If you see the picture as an older woman, what elements of the picture stand out to you? You may focus on the nose and long chin on the older woman's face and the fact that she appears to be looking slightly down. As you do this, your mind completes the gestalt that you are seeing a picture of an older woman. Next try changing the "figure": Notice that the nose of the older woman could also be seen as the jawline of a younger woman who is looking away. As you do so, a perceptual shift will occur. Elements of what was the figure in the picture now reorganize themselves and become

Figure 6.2 Figure/ground example. (From *American Journal of Psychology*. Copyright 1930 by the Board of Trustees of the University of Illinois. Used with permission of the University of Illinois Press.)

part of the ground—what was once the older woman's eye becomes the younger woman's ear, and so forth.

Changing one's perception in this way is an interesting visual trick; however, Gestalt therapists view the emergence of figures in the lives of their clients as something much more important. Figures that emerge can be meaningfully connected to the individual thoughts, feelings, and experiences of the individual. For example, whether you initially saw an older woman or a younger woman in Figure 6.2 could be seen not just as a visual trick of the eye but also in terms of your needs, wishes, feelings, and thoughts. Perhaps if some important event has occurred in your life involving an older woman, the figure that emerged out of the ground for you might have been the older woman. Conversely, if you had a recent experience that involved a younger woman, that figure might have emerged first from the background and become the figure.

A phrase that is often repeated in the Gestalt counseling literature is that the whole is more than the sum of its parts, and the notion that we are each motivated toward "wholeness" is fundamental to Gestalt therapy. Therefore, seeing an older woman or a younger woman represents a purposeful, unified, and coherent organization of experience.

Needs and Unfinished Business   The healthy person is both aware of sensations and able to form everyday experiences into gestalts that then fade into the background as new experiences emerge. This process can be derailed, however, if an individual is unable to meet basic needs, such as food, water, shelter, friendship, and sexual companionship. Forming and dissolving gestalts, a function crucial to the meaning-making we do in everyday life, involves being able to shift between different elements of our sensory field. At times, certain elements become the figure and others the ground, a process that is constantly shifting as we move throughout the day and our lives. Unmet needs, however, become figural and resist fading into the ground, tying up one's energy and focus.

As an example of this idea, consider the case of Juan, a person who has recently been downsized from a sales job in a telecommunications company. We might consider his everyday life as having been organized into a series of meaningful gestalts that were formed and dissolved as he moved through the week. Workdays may have been organized around specific tasks that needed to be accomplished each day: Near the beginning of the workweek, Juan completed paperwork, planned sales visits for the upcoming week, and participated in meetings with other sales personnel. In the middle of the week, he traveled to visit his clients, and toward the end of the week, he placed orders for clients and arranged travel plans for the upcoming week. Weekends may have been organized around housekeeping, visits with friends and family, and various hobbies.

One could easily imagine how the daily activities of Juan's life formed meaningful gestalts for him: Various challenges arose during the week, he dealt with them, and he moved on to the next task, each completing the gestalt of successful salesperson who also leads a fulfilling personal life. However, the traumatic event of being downsized from his job might throw this salesperson gestalt into disarray. His view of himself as a productive worker would be challenged, his contact with coworkers and clients would be abruptly terminated, and he would suddenly have to reorient his activities until he could find a new job. "Figure-ground" reversals might arise in his experiences. Where before he saw friends as people with whom he could spend leisure time, they may now become possible sources of job leads. The notion of workdays and weekends might also be rearranged as Juan finds himself networking, mailing resumes, and reading the want ads around the clock. Until his need to be a productive worker is met, and a new gestalt completed, it is likely to dominate Juan's experiences and serve as a focal point for his activities.

Polarization   Gestalt formation can be either facilitated or hindered by a process known as polarization. Through polarization, we categorize experiences into discrete evaluative categories such as good or bad and fun or boring. Organizing experiences in such a dichotomized manner can either help us in or hinder us from leading healthy and productive lives. For example, events can be labeled exciting or boring, our own feelings can be labeled good or bad, and other people can be labeled friends or enemies. The advantage of polarization is that it can make it easier to relate to the outside world. If the complex information we receive every moment of every day can be neatly encapsulated in categories, it is much easier to handle. However, the potential downside of polarities is that they can lead to a dull and routine existence. Also, once an individual has identified something with one end of a set of opposite characteristics, she is often highly motivated to maintain this view and can often miss or ignore contradictory information.

As an example, an adult might develop a polarized view of children as bothersome and unpleasant to be around, ignoring the fact that most children's qualities exist along a continuum with varying degrees of both positive and negative qualities. A highly polarized view of children as simply bothersome could well serve to simplify an adult's existence. Such a person would not have to consider whether to raise a family, she would not have to think about whether or not to attend events where young children might be present, and she could simply write off careers that involve interacting with young people. The following example demonstrates how a counselor might work with a client's polarized views. Elsa has been married for several years and has always vowed not to have children. Her husband initially agreed to this arrangement but now wants children, which has led to conflict in their marriage.

> **Counselor:** So the conflict seems to really be focused on your not wanting to have children.
>
> **Elsa:** Yes, I just don't like being around children, and I don't think I would be a good mother.
>
> **Counselor:** Can you think of an instance when you did enjoy being around kids?
>
> **Elsa:** Well, my sister has two really nice kids, and I enjoy visiting them, at least for short periods of time.
>
> **Counselor:** What do you enjoy about your sister's kids?
>
> **Elsa:** Oh, I just feel a lot of love for them and I like to play with them. It's fun to take them places like the zoo or just to the park. But they are pretty young . . . wait until they are teenagers.
>
> **Counselor:** Would it be fair to say that some part of you, then, does like kids?
>
> **Elsa:** I suppose so . . . a limited part.

In this example, the counselor is not trying to convince Elsa to have children; she is just getting her to focus on the polarity in her thinking about children. In this case, the counselor believes that Elsa's polarized view of children needs to be explored in more depth because it could be causing the conflict in her marriage. The counselor would, of course, not want to argue with Elsa about whether or not to have children. Instead, the goal is to explore Elsa's black-and-white thinking about children so that she and her husband can work on their relationship and make the best decision possible about whether or not to have children.

One of the more important polarities that Perls (1969b) wrote about is an internal struggle between what he labeled the *top dog* and the *underdog*. The top dog is something Perls developed from Freud's notion of a superego, which is an element of personality holding all of society's rigid prescriptions for acceptable standards of behavior. Perls believed that the top dog results from introjections from figures in authority, such as parents, teachers, and relatives, often when we are very young. The term *introjection* was also used by Freud and refers to a psychological process by which such standards are internalized, or taken as one's own, without much deliberation or evaluation. Thus, the top dog serves as an internal voice directing behavior, feelings, and attitudes that really come from these outside introjections.

Opposed to the top dog is the underdog, which Korb, Gorrell, and Van De Riet (1989) defined in this way: "[O]pposed to the top dog is the underdog, the manifestation of resistance to external demands. Essentially, the underdog agrees that the top dog's demands are appropriate; however, the underdog's internal sabotage assures that the demands will never be met" (p. 63). Korb et al. therefore describe the underdog as a "passive-aggressive" component of the personality, using whatever coping strategies are necessary to block the demands of the top dog without directly confronting it. The underdog is thus relating to the world as a fearful, threatening place that cannot be coped with through more assertive and forthright means.

Present Awareness The need for awareness of the present is a theme that runs through each of the concepts we have described so far. Perls emphasized that the past is over and the future may never arrive, so the healthy individual must be able to live in the present moment rather than wasting time and energy reliving the past or anticipating the future. The process of forming and completing gestalts in everyday life makes it necessary for a person to function in the here and now: "[A]ny experience or reactive pattern of behavior that is held over from the past, or anything that is being anticipated about the future, diminishes the amount of attention and energy persons can apply to the present" (Korb et al., 1989, p. 5).

Perls (1973) believed that clients encounter psychological difficulty because they lack awareness of both what is happening inside them and what is going on around them. This limits their ability to act creatively and spontaneously in the moment. A person who does not live in the moment is doomed to repeat old scripts about how he should behave, based on either past experiences or predictions about the future. The solution, Perls thought, was to get back in touch with what is happening right now: "[S]imply becoming aware that you are aware increases your potential area of operation. It gives a wider orientation and greater freedom of choice and action" (1973, p. 73).

Because of our unique feelings, goals, thoughts, and experiences, sensory information that comes into our awareness can be interpreted in many ways (Latner, 1992). Children engaged in a game of baseball may regard the setting of the sun as nothing more that an inconvenience that interrupts their play, while an older adult may build a porch on the back of her house just so she can watch the sun set on a clear day. The meaning that a child attaches to the setting sun, in this example, is simply losing a source of light, while for the adult it is a beautiful experience that marks the passage of time. Other types of sensory information, such as the intense pain caused by contact with a hot stove or the attention generated by a loud siren, may be met with a more universal reaction: Almost everyone will react with pain and withdraw when contacting a hot stove.

Contact Our present awareness is shaped by our contact with the outside world. *Contact* for Gestalt counselors refers to "the meeting of differences" (Wheeler, 1991, p. 18). Contact with something that is new, different, or outside of ourselves is a crucial first step in awareness. All organisms must interact with their environment to meet the basic needs of life, including food, water, shelter, comfort, and the companionship of others. In order to strike a healthy balance between the needs of the individual and those of other people, boundaries that regulate contact must be developed. These must be firm enough to establish one's uniqueness from other people but permeable enough that one is not isolated. According to Latner (1992), contacting the environment is how we grow: "[T]his creative activity is a given for us as we live. It *is* living. Out of our needs and appetites, our wishes and desires, our curiosity, we encounter the environment and work and rework it to suit our own interests. And . . . it encounters and molds us. The result is true universal ecology" (p. 28).

Avoidance of Contact (Resistance) While contact with the outside world is the growth medium for the development of the individual, it is also usually fleeting. Enright (1975) wrote that most Gestalt counselors assume that if a person can achieve a point at which she is fully aware of her experiences, she will no longer have a need for counseling and will be able to take responsibility for her own well-being. However, it is also assumed that most of us can tolerate contact with the outside world only for limited amounts of time, after which we must withdraw and process what has been experienced.

Because we are able to stand only a limited amount of time in contact with our experiences, Perls believed that we often develop defense mechanisms that serve to limit and distort our contact with the present. Some of the more prominent ones are briefly described below, and if you have read the chapter on psychoanalysis, you will note Freud's influence on several of the constructs.

INTROJECTION. This refers to behaviors that result from uncritically accepting the beliefs, opinions, and attitudes of others without measuring them against our own beliefs and experiences. As was noted in our previous discussion of the top dog and underdog, Freud hypothesized a similar process whereby the superego develops by introjecting the ideas of one's parents to counteract the demands of the id. For Perls, introjections are seen as problematic when they are accepted wholesale and are not evaluated against one's own experiences and beliefs. By accepting introjections, the individual ends up with internal voices nagging her, since the attitudes expressed have not been assimilated into her belief structures. She is not able to make decisions in the present based on her own opinions or values but rather has her energy tied up in passively accepting the attitudes of others.

PROJECTION. This is the reverse of introjection, in which characteristics or traits that the individual finds unacceptable about herself are projected onto another person. The use of projection as a defense mechanism may allow the individual to avoid the discomfort of recognizing these unacceptable parts of the self, but it also leaves her unable to take responsibility for change. For example, a person who is extremely stingy about giving money to other people might project this tendency onto other people and remain on the lookout for any sign that another person is trying to shortchange her. Such a person might overlook her own miserly tendencies, thus avoiding any responsibility for changing. In addition, this "blind spot" could lead to conflict in social situations: Who wants to go to dinner with someone who counts every last penny when the check arrives?

RETROFLECTION. This involves directing energy inward that should be directed outward, usually because the individual does not accept responsibility for her feelings. For example, a person in a state of retroflection may be afraid that she will lash out at another person, and rather than taking the risk, she might direct that energy inward by getting angry at herself.

DEFLECTION. This method of avoiding awareness or contact was first described by Polster and Polster (1973). A person avoids real verbal contact with another person through the excessive use of humor, questions, or intellectual abstractions, which keeps others at a distance (Sapp, 1997).

A person uses non-verbal deflection by avoiding eye contact or turning away from the other person. To the extent that deflection serves some practical purpose, such as averting conflict between nations when used in politics, it can be deemed useful. However, between individuals, deflection can cause both persons to feel disconnected, as well as interfering with their ability to honestly work through differences.

CONFLUENCE. With the previous four defense mechanisms, boundaries between the self and the outside world may be confused or distorted, but in the case of confluence, one's awareness of such boundaries is more seriously impaired. A person in a state of confluence does not experience herself as distinct from the environment but instead takes comfort in merging her identity with that of another, such as a family member, possession, or coworker. Meaningful contact cannot occur when this person is in a state of confluence because she has no sense of a distinct identity: she is simply the reflection of another person.

Layers of Neurosis Perls (1973) compared the unfolding of personality as the outside world is contacted to the peeling back of the various layers of an onion. Perls believed that most people are unable to sustain genuine contact with another for any length of time, so they use defense mechanisms such as those just reviewed to defend themselves from reality. Thus, when he met a client in a counseling situation, Perls did not expect an authentic, genuine contact to occur at the outset. Instead, he expected to encounter what he labeled the five layers of neurosis (1969b): first, the phony layer, followed in order by the phobic, impasse, implosive, and explosive layers.

According to Sapp (1997), when initially contacting the phony layer, Perls expected the client to play certain roles, such as a victim or helpless person, in order to avoid contact with him. In the phobic layer, the client presents a façade to the therapist because she is fearful that, if known, her true self would be rejected. In the third layer, the impasse, the client feels stuck and unwilling to assume personal responsibility. She may report feeling lifeless, and it is essential for the client to move past this stage to reestablish contact with her own senses and experiences. In the implosive layer, the client is finally able to stop playing roles and get in touch with her experiences. Implosion leads to the emergence of the self, which is followed by the explosive layer, in which the client is able to fully experience her own feelings and sensations.

THERAPEUTIC RELATIONSHIP

Counselor's Role

Gestalt therapists see their role as helping clients learn to use their sensorimotor equipment again in the service of heightened awareness—something Perls described as "losing your mind to come to your senses" (Stephenson, 1975). In this way, the therapist is encouraged to take an anti-intellectual stance, helping clients get in touch with what is obvious and right in front of their noses rather than coming up with complex explanations for past behaviors (Sapp, 1997). In order to do this, the gestalt therapist's main responsibility is to enter into an authentic relationship with a client in which both parties are fully present. Increased awareness is essential to bringing about change, and Gestalt therapists do this by balancing support and frustration with clients, which will help them live in the present, take responsibility for their current difficulties, and lead more creative and fulfilling lives. Korb et al. (1989) described the role of the gestalt therapist as that of an artist, "creating each moment of a therapeutic relationship with an appropriate ambience and set of tools related to the client's needs" (p. 109).

While the therapist takes an anti-intellectual stance in order to bring clients to awareness, this does not mean that the therapist's tasks in the therapeutic relationship are easy or trivial (Zinker, 1977). Being an effective Gestalt therapist requires a number of personal characteristics and professional abilities. Korb et al. (1989) noted three personal characteristics that are necessary to be an effective Gestalt therapist: being authentic, taking a phenomenological orientation, and believing that every person who enters counseling has the means to live a personally fulfilling life.

First, being authentic in the counseling relationship is a fundamental component of most humanistic and existential approaches to counseling, and in Gestalt counseling, it refers to having a high level of awareness of oneself and other people. This awareness allows the counselor to integrate her own personal reactions to clients with her professional training and experience in order to help clients gain increased awareness. Gestalt therapists believe that authenticity helps create trust between people, even when it leads to disagreement. Further, the counselor's awareness of herself and others allows her to notice discrepancies between the verbal and nonverbal behaviors of her clients.

Second, according to Korb et al. (1989), taking a phenomenological orientation entails a belief that "the therapist can work best with the client by entering into his or her phenomenological world, experiencing along with the client the client's perspective" (p. 110). This is similar to what Carl Rogers termed *empathy*, the ability to see the world as a client sees it and feel what the client feels. What is somewhat unique to Gestalt therapy, however, is the primary concern for what is going on in the current, immediate experience of the client. In other words, while a Rogerian counselor might be content to empathize with any events or experiences that the client brings up, including those from the past, the Gestalt counselor focuses on what the client is feeling at the present time so that unresolved conflicts can emerge and be resolved.

Finally, Korb et al. (1989) point out that "clients need to know that they are not crazy, that they are not beyond repair, and that what they experience is understandable" (p. 112). In other words, clients may come to counseling with negative self-images, a history of interpersonal difficulties, and perhaps a level of despair about whether they can truly effect change in their lives. It is up to the Gestalt counselor to help restore hope in her clients. In order to do this, of course, the counselor must genuinely believe that a client is capable of change, no matter what her current level of difficulty. This belief can then be communicated to the client in a variety of ways. It could be done, for example, in a very direct way by telling the client repeatedly that she is capable of change. Or it may be done in more subtle or indirect ways, as when the counselor is willing to continue working with the client over the course of weeks or months.

Each of these personal characteristics described by Korb et al. (1989) refers to who a Gestalt counselor *is*. It is also important to consider what the Gestalt therapist *does*—in other words, to consider the professional functions she is responsible for in the course of Gestalt counseling. Three key functions noted by Korb et al. (1989) will be described next: how a Gestalt counselor uses language, attends to the obvious, and notes patterns.

Dialogue is the primary form of contact between the counselor and the client in Gestalt therapy, and it is incumbent on the counselor to use language in a way that promotes awareness and genuineness in the relationship. Perls (1973) set out three questions designed to increase awareness on the client's part: What are you doing? What do you feel? What do you want? Note that Gestalt therapists rarely use questions that begin with Why? because these typically move the client out of present awareness into intellectual explanations for past behaviors. Gestalt therapists also use "I" statements whenever appropriate—for example, by saying "I feel uncertain" as a way to model openness and self-awareness.

With regard to attending to the obvious, Korb et al. (1989) noted that a therapist seldom errs by focusing on body language because it is far more difficult for clients to distort, rationalize, or explain away nonverbal communications than spoken words. Stephenson (1975) wrote that many persons trust their ability to rationalize, intellectualize, and explain things far more than they trust their capacity to live in the present moment. Once a person is made aware of some bit of incongruous or inexplicable nonverbal behavior, she is likely to jump on what Stephenson described as the "why merry-go-round," in which a person casts about for some explanation or reason for the behavior while repeating it over and over. Gestalt therapists therefore rely on directed awareness techniques that encourage a client to focus on what she is aware of, rather than why she is doing something, and to trust nonverbal behaviors at least as much as verbal behaviors.

As an example, during a session a client might be talking in a dispassionate tone of voice about the rude way a supervisor treated her at work and the counselor might note the client clenching her fist as she speaks. To attend to the obvious, the counselor might state, "You are talking very calmly about what happened at work, but notice what you are doing with your fist." The purpose of doing this would be to encourage the client to be aware of the totality of her experience (probably anger at the supervisor) and the message she is communicating to the outside world (I'm angry, but I won't admit it). Gestalt therapists assume that most of us are able to trick other people, and ourselves, quite easily through the words we use; in many cases, it is only by attending to nonverbal behaviors that one can comprehend the totality of a client's experience. It is not enough, however, for the counselor to merely notice such behaviors; this awareness must also be encouraged in the client by inviting her to note both verbal and nonverbal communication.

Finally, Korb et al. (1989) indicated that formal assessment and diagnosis are seldom used by Gestalt therapists but that careful attention to patterns exhibited by clients can be important. They caution that ultimately it is the client, not the therapist, who can attach meaning to such patterns. This will be explained further in the "Assessment" section of this chapter.

Counselor-Client Relationship

The relationship between the counselor and the client is the primary mechanism for change in Gestalt counseling. While Gestalt therapists emphasize freedom of expression and personal responsibility for both the counselor and the client, the two must form an alliance for counseling to be effective. In other words, the point of the relationship is not for the therapist and the client to be autonomous but rather for them to have authentic and meaningful contact that leads to greater understanding for both. In fact, when describing the importance of the therapeutic relationship, Gestalt theorists refer often to the work of Martin Buber, a philosopher, theologian, and Bible translator who believed that we can understand ourselves only in the context of our relationship with the outside world.

Buber (1958) believed that "I" has meaning only in the context of an I-It or I-Thou relationship. As was discussed in Chapter 5, by I-It relationships Buber meant the instrumental day-to-day interactions that keep the world running. These include buying goods and services, making appointments, and generally keeping things running smoothly. While such transactions are necessary, Buber contrasted them with an "I-Thou" relationship, in which the person is contacted in a truly spontaneous and authentic way. In Gestalt therapy therefore counselors seeks to establish an I-Thou relationship, which will lead to authentic contact.

While the notion of an I-Thou relationship between the counselor and the client accurately describes the philosophy of the Gestalt therapeutic relationship, it may also be considered a bit abstract, which is antithetical to actual Gestalt practice. Simkin and Yontef (1984) wrote that what is essential in the counselor-client relationship is that a dialogue be established that is distinguished by five characteristics. First is the notion of *inclusion*, which involves putting oneself as fully as possible into the experience of another person without judging or evaluating her. In many ways, this is similar to Carl Rogers's notion of unconditional positive regard and essentially means that the therapist establishes a safe and inviting atmosphere where the client will not feel judged or criticized. A second characteristic of dialogue between the counselor and the client is *presence*, in which the therapist demonstrates the importance of awareness and self-expression by communicating observations, preferences, personal experiences, and thoughts to the client when appropriate. These include observations about what is happening in the moment between the counselor and the client, as well as the therapist's personal reactions.

Simkin and Yontef also wrote that the counselor-client relationship should be characterized by *commitment to dialogue, refraining from exploitation*, and *living dialogue*. Commitment to dialogue means that contact between the counselor and the client should not be forced in any way but should be allowed to occur naturally and spontaneously. The counselor should not take on too much responsibility for the ebb and flow of dialogue by peppering the client with questions or filling gaps in the dialogue with everyday conversation. By refraining from exploitation, Simkin and Yontef mean that counselors must refrain from placing any demands or expectations on the client that could interfere with the integrity of the client's experience. For example, a beginning counselor might be overly concerned with her own competence and exploit the client by attempting to cover up any mistakes she might make. In order to serve the client's interests, the counselor should instead readily acknowledge areas where she feels uncertain or anxious. Finally, in suggesting that dialogue be lived, Simkin and Yontef emphasized the excitement and immediacy of *doing* rather than *talking about doing*. The dialogue between counselor and client should be conducted in the moment and not be confined to verbal exchanges. Zinker (1977) suggested that creativity is one of the hallmarks of an effective relationship in Gestalt work and can be expressed through movement, artwork, or song.

ASSESSMENT, GOALS, AND PROCESS OF THERAPY

Assessment

Formal assessment and diagnosis are not emphasized in Gestalt counseling. Reliance on such methods is not consistent with the Gestalt emphasis on present awareness and an authentic relationship between the counselor and the client.

Houston (2003) suggested that a number of tasks are typically conducted at the outset of counseling. These suggestions are particularly important if the counselor believes the intervention is likely to be short-term in nature. First, it is important for the counselor to gain an impression of the contact boundary created between client and counselor. At the outset of counseling, the counselor should assess both the client's capacity to move beyond the phony layer of personality and how pervasive the more superficial I-It relationships are in the client's life. Second, Houston recommended assessing whether enough trust can be established between the counselor and the client for a therapeutic bond to develop. Such impressions might be difficult to form with limited contact, particularly since most individuals are hesitant to trust complete strangers. However, the development of trust is essential for the kind of risks that need to be taken to move beyond the phony layer. Third, Houston suggested finding out as much as possible about the kind of difficulties that have brought the client to counseling. Important questions need to be addressed in each approach to counseling: What has happened to bring a client to counseling at this point in her life, especially when problems or situations have persisted for some time? Was there a specific event that triggered the decision to seek counseling? Gestalt therapists do not dwell on past events or historical explanations, but some understanding of these issues can be used to bring the client's concerns into present awareness.

Earlier in this chapter, we noted that Gestalt therapists are responsible for tracking patterns in clients' verbal and nonverbal behaviors so they can be brought into present awareness, which is a form of assessment. Gestalt therapists often use clients' reactions to experiences in their lives as a method for understanding them better, but they do so in a completely different way than therapists using other approaches. For example, a psychoanalyst using the Rorschach inkblot test as an assessment would ask the client to describe what she sees in each card. This information would then be used to gain insight into the inner workings of her unconscious mind because it is assumed that whatever reactions a client has to the ambiguous pictures presented in the inkblots say more about the client than about the picture. While a Gestalt counselor would probably agree that the way we react to perceptual information has as much to do with our own needs and motivations as it has to do with the sensory information we are receiving, she would use the information in a completely different way. Instead of analyzing a client's reaction and how it relates to the past, a Gestalt therapist would focus on what is happening in the present moment (the here and now).

Take, for example, the case of Edward, who exhibits characteristics of the top dog/underdog split. A Gestalt therapist observes that Edward, who is currently studying for exams in college, exhibits a pattern of holding himself to exceedingly high standards of performance (top dog) but then sabotages himself (underdog) when it comes time to study for an exam:

> **Edward:** Well, I tried to study last night, but I got so disgusted with myself for procrastinating that I ended up quitting and going out for a few beers.
> **Counselor:** And you are beating yourself up for it now.
> **Edward:** Yeah, I just put so much pressure on myself that I can't stand it . . . I just can't cope!
> **Counselor:** You seem frustrated . . . like this has happened before.
> **Edward:** It usually does when I have a big exam or something. Weeks before, I build up all these expectations for myself, and the closer it gets, the more I just want to run away.

In this short example, the counselor is attempting a type of assessment by making a connection between what Edward is currently experiencing and what has happened in the past. However, the counselor will not attempt to determine for Edward when in his life he might have introjected very high standards for test performance (top dog) and why he copes with internal standards through avoidance (underdog). Instead, the counselor will continue to make Edward aware of his experiences so that he can decide for himself what to make of his experiences. Korb et al. (1989) described this in the following way: "[W]hen the structural relationships of a problem are delineated, when the features are obvious in their functioning, and as they relate to the environment, the understanding emerges in a solid, well formed, and sharply focused pattern or gestalt" (p. 119). In other words, the counselor helps the client track such patterns and bring them into awareness, but it is up to the client to put the pieces together and decide what goals she has for counseling. The goals of Gestalt therapy will be described next.

Goals

Gestalt counseling does not need to revolve around specific problems; simply focusing on present awareness and the interaction between counselor and client is a legitimate goal. However, it is likely that most clients today will seek counseling for specific concerns, and Houston (2003) noted that establishing goals for Gestalt counseling includes exploring client expectations, formulating a hypothesis about what makes the client "tick," and coming to an agreement on what aspects of the client's life or difficulties need to stay in the foreground. By exploring client expectations, the counselor attempts to inform the client as much as possible about what is expected in Gestalt counseling, as well as encouraging the client to be as forthcoming about her impressions as possible (i.e., promoting awareness). Formulating a hypothesis about what makes the client "tick" might involve identifying what needs are unmet for the client and are causing distress.

Recall that once a gestalt is formed, the experience is completed, and it fades into the background as new experiences emerge in the foreground. If needs are met, "life becomes a series of emerging gestalten and the completion of these gestalten as the individual lives totally aware of the present and functions fully in the present" (Korb et al., 1989, p. 5). In other words, a healthy person is constantly involved in making sense of everyday experiences, and as she does so, that gestalt moves into the background so she can devote attention to making a gestalt of the next set of experiences. Unmet needs interfere with this process and tend to focus all of the individual's energy on the incomplete gestalt.

Finally, in coming to an agreement about what needs to stay in the foreground, the counselor attempts to understand what gestalts are currently incomplete or unresolved for the client and need the most attention in counseling. In effect, this refers to an initial working agreement between the counselor and the client that will guide at least the early stages of counseling.

Gestalt therapists attempt to help clients increase awareness of their experiences so they can activate their self-support system, which enables them to make responsible choices and facilitate contact with others. The goal of increasing awareness is something of a paradox in that clients must learn to be themselves in order to change. Perls (1973) described how awareness helps clients solve problems in this way: "[I]f [the client] can become truly aware at every instant of himself and his actions on whatever level—fantasy, verbal, or physical—he can see how it is producing his difficulties, he can see what his present difficulties are, and he can help himself to solve them in the present, in the here and now" (p. 62).

Process of Therapy

Marcus (1979) described the process of Gestalt therapy as consisting of three stages: contact, process, and experimentation. Contact refers to the nature of the relationship between the counselor and the client and is thought in many ways to resemble the types of relationships that a client has with important people in her world. Process refers to how the client does what she does, which is considerably more important to Gestalt counselors than what the client does. Marcus pointed out that the client's focus is usually on the content of what she is presenting, not the way she is presenting information but that most of the client's defenses are communicated through process. The final component of Gestalt therapy is the conduct of experiments. Marcus describes experiments as opportunities to behave, think, and feel differently within the safety of the therapeutic relationship. Gestalt counseling is perhaps best known for such experiments, in which the therapist might use a technique such as the "empty chair" to have the client role-play a conversation with some important figure in her life. Polster and Polster (1973) pointed out that experiments are not rehearsals for future events or postmortems of past experiences but are rather designed to experience what it feels like to move from awareness to behavior. In other words, a technique such as the empty chair is not a dress rehearsal; participation in the experiment may well lead the client to behave differently in the future, but such behavior may not at all resemble the experiment conducted in the therapy room.

Perls believed that by working together in this manner, the counselor and the client would eventually work through the five layers of neurosis described earlier in this chapter. When first encountering the phony or cliché layer, it is expected that the client will engage in social chatter and will tend to avoid the real concerns that have brought her to counseling. While the therapist should, of course, remain respectful, her primary aim at this point is to avoid such chatter herself. In the second layer, a façade is encountered, and it is expected that the client will resort to scripted manners of interacting with the counselor and will likely attempt to push the counselor into a complementary role—for example, helpless victim and rescuer. If the counselor takes up this role, it will prevent the client from gaining awareness. Therefore, the counselor should resist playing along and instead attempt to bring the client's attention to what is happening. At this point, experiments can be used to explore how the client relates to other people and seeks to meet her own needs.

Once the impasse is reached, the client is at a turning point in the counseling process: She has achieved awareness of previously used ineffective roles, but he is faced with the responsibility of what to do next. The client might be tempted to retreat to previously used roles to dispel the anxiety created at this level, and it is the counselor's responsibility to help the client tolerate what Perls termed the "safe emergency" of the therapeutic setting. In other words, the counseling process should create sufficient support for the client to tolerate the anxiety of living more authentically. If the counselor can do this, the client reaches the implosion stage, in which new possibilities for feeling and acting are explored. Finally, when the client reaches the explosion layer, energies and feelings are released that make it possible for the client to assume greater responsibility for her life. The therapist's task at this point is to remain engaged with the client as such realities are experienced. In these final two stages, the counselor finds the use of experiments less necessary, and the client assumes greater responsibility for the course of counseling.

THERAPEUTIC TECHNIQUES

Gestalt counseling is well known for the variety of creative and compelling "experiments" Perls and other Gestalt theorists pioneered to promote interpersonal awareness. While at the Esalen Institute near the end of his life, Perls demonstrated techniques such as the empty chair to large, enthusiastic audiences, so there is little surprise that his methods became quite popular and perhaps a bit detached from the overall philosophy of Gestalt counseling. Many counselors seeking to encourage awareness in their clients find these techniques to be quite effective and borrow them regardless of theoretical orientation. Considering Perls's emphasis on spontaneity and creativity above all else, it is ironic that a major contribution of this approach has been a set of "prescribed" techniques for increasing awareness.

We have found in our teaching that once students are exposed to an intervention such as the empty chair technique, they cannot wait to use it in role-plays with other students, even if they are just beginning to learn about Gestalt counseling. Zinker (1977) warned that counselors should anchor experiments in the spontaneous experience of an authentic relationship between the client and the counselor and that the counselor should avoid thrusting a favored technique or activity on a client simply because the counselor finds it appealing. Such interventions will lack any context or authenticity for the client and are therefore less likely to be helpful to the client.

Certainly, beginning counselors must try out techniques and theories if they are to learn how to use them, but with Gestalt therapy, we would urge extra caution because of the strong affect that can be evoked. In our view, the best way to learn to practice Gestalt therapy is to attend Gestalt training groups where the counselor can see the techniques used within the context of the overall Gestalt approach and can also experience them on a personal level. As with any other counseling technique, Gestalt experiments should not be used without proper training and supervision.

Giving Directives

Gestalt counselors are active and creative and in many cases will give the client specific directions designed to promote awareness during the counseling session. It is then up to the client to decide how such an experience applies to the rest of her life and the problems that have brought her to counseling. In order to demonstrate how a counselor might do this, we provide a short example of a Gestalt experiment in which a client is encouraged to act out a dilemma she is experiencing. Martha is a recently married Caucasian woman who has sought counseling because of her inability to trust her husband. The counselor in this situation gives her specific directions to bring such feelings into immediate awareness.

See DVD

Chap. 6
Clip 1

Martha: My husband and I got along so well before we were married, but once we finally did, it was like this big curtain just came down and I started getting suspicious all the time. And I really don't have a reason to be this way . . . at least I don't think so. I feel like I'm turning into my mother. She died several years ago, but I have all these memories of her hounding my dad . . . asking where he was at night, all that. It scares me. He eventually left us.

Counselor: Would you be willing to explore being like your mother now?

Martha: I sure would like to understand it . . . I'll tell you that. What do you mean, you want me to talk about my mother some more?

Counselor: Well, actually what I had in mind was if you could behave right now with me the way your mother does. . . like you are suspicious of me and don't really trust me.

Martha: I guess I could try that. You mean to pretend I am my mother?

Counselor: What if you just treat me with suspicion and mistrust the way your mother would, without worrying about getting into character. Just whatever comes to mind.

> **Martha:** OK . . . I don't think you really care about me at all. You are getting paid to listen to me, and you're probably thinking about your next client right now. Why should I spill my guts to someone like you?
>
> *[Martha pauses for a moment and a look of concern spreads across her face]*
>
> **Martha:** Uh oh, I hope I haven't offended you.
>
> **Counselor:** What are you experiencing right now?
>
> **Martha:** Well, I think some of that came from me, and some is coming from my mother. I guess I am a little concerned starting counseling with you, that you won't find my problems interesting enough or something. So that part seems kind of healthy, like you need to be cautious when you meet someone new. But what comes from my mother is not even letting someone earn my trust—like I push them away without giving them a chance.

This experiment might continue for some time and is an example of how a Gestalt counselor might use an experiment in the here and now to increase a client's awareness. After talking to the counselor as if she were her mother, Martha will be encouraged to evaluate how her reactions to the counselor in the present moment are similar or dissimilar to those of her mother. This experiment will hopefully allow Martha to consciously evaluate what aspects of her reactions to other people she might want to explore and modify. Note that the counselor did not ask Martha to participate in an elaborate or complicated activity—the experiment emerged spontaneously from the interactions between the two. And even though Martha's relationship with her mother deals in part with historical information, it is brought into the present through dialogue between the counselor and the client.

Staying with the Feeling

This is a rather straightforward technique in which clients are asked to sustain contact with an emotion that seems central to their current difficulties. This can be done verbally when the counselor asks a client to talk about a specific feeling more. The case of Martha above is an example of a counselor using directives; it also demonstrates how Martha was asked to stay with the feelings of suspicion and mistrust. Staying with the feeling can also involve nonverbal behaviors, as when a client is asked to develop a gesture that expresses emotions. For example, a client might clench her fist or tense her jaw muscles, and to develop the feeling attached to this gesture, the counselor might invite the client to notice the behavior and even exaggerate it to bring emotions into awareness.

Empty Chair

This is perhaps the most famous of all Gestalt experiments and is used when a client is having a conflict with an important figure in her life, such as a parent, partner, sibling, or child. To use the empty chair technique, the counselor asks the client to imagine that the person is sitting in an empty chair in front of her. The client is then asked to begin speaking to that person about concerns that have arisen during the counseling session. After this has begun, the counselor might ask the client to switch into the empty chair and speak back to the client as if she were that person. As the exercise continues, the client is asked to switch back and forth from one chair to another, alternating between speaking as herself and speaking as the other person. The counselor's role is to identify key points where the client should switch back and forth between the roles and to help the client stay "in character" as this happens.

The point of the experiment is to bring the client's feelings and experiences with this other person into the present awareness, although authors such as Zinker (1977) caution that such experiments should not used as dress rehearsals for future interactions with that person. The empty chair technique may well prepare the client to act differently in the future, but the point is to promote awareness, not to create a script for future activity.

Following the example of Martha we used earlier, the counselor might invite Martha to use the empty chair technique to "talk to her mother" about her feelings of suspicion and mistrust toward other people. Of course, a Gestalt counselor does not necessarily jump from one experiment to another, but for now, let us assume that some time has passed since the last experiment and that the counselor has had an opportunity to explain the purpose of the empty chair technique and to enlist Martha's cooperation in order to further explore her feelings.

See DVD

Chap. 6
Clip 2

Counselor: Martha, would you like to go ahead and talk to your mother about the mistrust and suspicion we talked about?

Martha: [*Looks at empty chair in front of her*] Mom, you never trusted anyone in your life, even me, and now look at me—I can't trust my own husband. I think that's why Dad left when I was very young . . . [*Martha looks down and tears up a bit*]

Counselor: I see that really touches a chord with you. Could you switch chairs now and respond as your mother?

Martha: [*Looking uncertain*] You mean just respond back to what I said, as if I were my mother?

Counselor: Yes, whatever comes to mind.

Martha: Well, my mother would probably say . . .

Counselor: Please try to talk as if you are her, and she is right here talking.

Martha: OK, Martha, you just don't understand . . . I didn't start things with your father. He's the one who didn't come home until late at night, never telling me where he was or what he was doing. What was I supposed to do, just keep going like the good little wife, never asking him anything?

This dialogue might continue for some time, with Martha continuing to alternate between being herself and being her mother in the conversation. As was shown in the example, the counselor can suggest points in the dialogue for the client to switch roles, as well as helping the client stay in each role in order to bring feelings into awareness.

Having Clients Talk to Parts of Themselves

The notion of wholeness or completeness is essential to healthy personalities in Gestalt work, and Perls believed that individuals could become stuck when certain feelings or experiences are disowned or disconnected from awareness. This experiment, a variation of the empty chair technique, helps clients recognize splits or conflicts within their personalities. Greenberg, Rice, and Elliott (1993) described markers for such splits as statements by the client that two parts of herself are in opposition. For example, a client who abuses alcohol might see intoxication as the only way she can be comfortable around other people and may therefore experience a split between the part of herself that wants to quit drinking and the part that wants to be the "life of the party." The empty chair technique could then be used to create a discussion between these conflicting experiences in order to bring them into awareness.

Playing the Projection

Like Freud, Perls viewed projection as a defense mechanism in which feelings and attitudes that are unacceptable to oneself are "projected" onto other people. An example we used earlier in this chapter was the selfish and miserly person who is on guard for such traits in others. In counseling, a Gestalt therapist might invite a client who is projecting such attitudes onto others (perhaps the therapist) to play the role of this other person—in this case, to be someone who is miserly— and explore these feelings as fully as possible. The point of this experiment is to work around the individual's defenses by having her immerse herself in a role assigned to another person rather than acknowledging her own tendencies right away. By playing the projection, the client will hopefully get in touch with her own feelings and be able to discuss them with the counselor.

MULTICULTURAL AND DIVERSITY EFFECTIVENESS

Gestalt theorists have not written extensively about the role of diversity in using this approach, but many of its principles are applicable within the contemporary emphasis on multicultural counseling. First, Perls stressed the importance of real and authentic relationships, and near the end of his life, he even attempted to extend these practices to community living in Cowichan, British Columbia (Ivey, D'Andrea, Ivey, & Simek-Morgan, 2002). This basic respect for the uniqueness of other persons and the importance of bridging "boundaries" between individuals suggests a fundamental regard for different cultural values and perspectives. Mackewn (1997) also suggested that the importance attached to the phenomenological experience of the client and her relationship to the outside world in Gestalt counseling offers considerable promise for working with persons from diverse backgrounds. Gestalt counselors are encouraged to understand each client as a real, authentic, and unique person and to use information about their relationship with the client to understand how that individual relates to the outside world.

Such a perspective can therefore assist in understanding the unique demands, barriers, and stresses that persons from minority cultural groups may face with respect to the majority culture. A Gestalt counselor who is truly open to experiencing her client will presumably also be open to exploring cultural oppression with a client and understanding how such factors have limited that person's ability to take responsibility for her own life. Houston (2003) warned, however, that without multicultural knowledge and skills, even a well-intentioned Gestalt counselor who is fully committed to awareness and experimentation can do a disservice to clients. She described, for example, the case of one Gestalt supervisee who was puzzled as to why a Thai client failed to come back to counseling after two sessions. It turned out that this therapist had been urging emotional expression in an early session with the client, unaware of the Thai concept of a "cool heart," a cultural prescription against displaying uncomfortable emotions.

Even if a client's culture does not discourage the expression of certain emotions, it is important to note that some clients may feel unprepared to reveal emotions early in counseling. For example, emotional guardedness might be entirely functional in the beginning for someone who has experienced trauma and abuse. As counseling progresses, she might be better able to experience strong emotions, but it would be unethical for a counselor to push her to do so before she has the necessary psychological resources.

A considerable body of literature exists on using Gestalt therapy with couples, an application that will be described in further detail in the "Primary Applications" section of this chapter, and this emphasis has increased the relevance of Gestalt counseling for working with gender dynamics and lesbian and gay clients. For example, Lapid (1980) described how Gestalt workshops could be used to explore the social context of sex-role socialization and stereotyping. Such workshops were concerned with understanding the individual in the context of her environment, and an emphasis is placed on increasing awareness of societal prescriptions for how men and women should behave. Curtis (1994) extended this type of work to lesbian couples, who must contend not only with the "typical" struggles faced by couples in a relationship but also with heterosexist cultural values. Such obstacles occur not only in the context of cultural values and beliefs but also in the legal privileges that are extended to heterosexual couples but denied to same-sex couples.

Sapp (1997) suggested that the Gestalt emphasis on wholeness and integrating various aspects of one's personality can be applied to the concerns of persons in minority cultures in the United States, as well as to those of people who emigrated from other countries. The notion of biculturalism, in which a person might have varying levels of acculturation to both her native culture and the majority culture in the United States, might be approached productively using Gestalt therapy. For example, this approach could be used to help such an individual integrate the values and customs of the two cultures, and to reconcile any conflicts produced when attempting to do so.

As has been noted in this chapter, Gestalt counselors favor an active, creative approach (Zinker, 1977). This may or may not represent a good fit with a given client, depending on both gender socialization and cultural values. With respect to gender roles, males in the U.S. culture are typically socialized to inhibit emotional expression, while females may be socialized to be less inhibited about expressing emotions. Examining the role of such societal expectations in a couples' relationship could be done using a Gestalt approach (Lapid, 1980). For example, both partners could be encouraged to examine what it would be like to behave more authentically and spontaneously with their partner. However, whether working with individuals or couples, the counselor would need to be sensitive to the fact that many clients may be uncomfortable with open and spontaneous emotional expression. The same can also be said for persons from diverse cultural backgrounds—an emphasis on spontaneous expression of emotions, experiments, movement activities, and a highly active therapist could represent either a good or poor fit, depending on the client's cultural frame of reference.

While Gestalt therapy has several potential strengths with respect to multicultural and diversity applications, there are several limitations worth noting. First, while many of the ideas and philosophies associated with Gestalt therapy can potentially be applied to clients from diverse backgrounds, a solid theoretical and empirical foundation for doing so has not been established. Gestalt counselors seeking to work with clients from diverse backgrounds may find little specific direction as to how such ideas can be used in practice. The emphasis on individuality and personal responsibility-taking probably is a good cultural fit for clients from many Western industrial nations, but such an approach may be inappropriate for use with persons from more collectivist backgrounds. Additionally, whether or not clients' values are consistent with notions of personal autonomy, persons who have faced systematic discrimination and barriers due to culture, ethnicity, sexual identity, disability, gender, age, or other factors may resent the suggestion that their difficulties stem from a lack of initiative on their part.

Saner (1989) has noted that the America Gestalt movement, in particular, has emphasized individuality more so than European Gestalt therapists. Fritz Perls was well known for the Gestalt prayer reprinted earlier in this chapter, which emphasizes individuality and personal responsibility, but there is some controversy as to whether he actually intended this as a serious statement of philosophy or whether it was an attempt on his part to be provocative (Mackewn,

1997). The emphasis on personal responsibility in Gestalt counseling is therefore not given, and has much to do with the approach taken by the therapist.

A final point worth noting is raised by Sapp (1997), who contended that the deemphasis on intellectual explanations of a client's concerns and behaviors could represent another limitation of Gestalt counseling. The multicultural literature emphasizes the importance of knowledge, abilities, and skills on the part of both counselor and client in coping with a diverse world (Ivey et al., 2002). Therefore, a deemphasis on explanation could result in important information about culture not being discussed.

PRIMARY APPLICATIONS

Group Work

As Gestalt therapy emerged in the 1960s and 1970s, its practitioners were as well known for group work as for individual work (Frew, 1988). In *Gestalt Therapy Verbatim*, Perls (1969b) declared his belief that individual counseling was an outdated modality and that clients stood to learn more from group interactions. While at the Esalen Institute, Perls did much to popularize Gestalt therapy by conducting demonstrations of his techniques in front of large groups of people. A common early method for conducting group interventions was the *hot seat*, a variation of the empty chair technique. Using this technique, a group member is invited by the leader to conduct a dialogue with an important person in her life, just as is done in individual counseling. While the leader and the member work through this exercise, the other members are invited to observe and later offer their comments about the experience. Perls believed that the observing members, who would later have their own opportunities to sit in the hot seat, stood much to gain: "[Y]ou learn so much by understanding what's going on in the other person, and realize that so much of his conflicts are your own, and by identification, you learn" (p. 73).

The early focus of Gestalt group work on the hot seat and one-to-one and the interaction between the group leader and individual members of the group came to be criticized for overlooking the dynamic processes that go on between members (Harman, 1984a). Harman wrote that Gestalt group leaders have increasingly paid attention to the process by which group members interact with each other and the leader and that groups tend to develop according to Perls's (1969b) neurotic layers: (1) phony, (2) phobic, (3) impasse, (4) implosive, and (5) explosive. The phony layer is that polite, surface-level manner of interacting that most of us use in day-to-day life, as when we ask a passerby, "How are you?" According to Harman, "[B]ehavior at this stage is robot-like and conveys little meaning" (p. 479). As group members have some time to interact, they enter stage two, in which they engage in familiar roles they have played throughout life, such as that of bully, parent, victim, and so forth.

Harman (1984a) wrote that neither of these first two stages provides much satisfaction for members, and as such stereotyped roles are left behind, they enter the third stage, that of impasse. At this point, the members may feel stuck, just as those in individual counseling do at this stage, because they have not yet developed the awareness or confidence to behave creatively or spontaneously. They might feel a lack of energy and be tempted to quit the group. At this point, the group leader must work hard to help the group move past this crucial stage. Harman suggested that the leader acknowledge members' difficulties so that such feelings can be brought into awareness and the group can move into the implosive layer, where members feel a renewed sense of energy. However, in the implosive layer, members are not yet ready to share this energy with other members. It is only in the final stage, the explosive stage, that members will be able to express this energy and engage in more authentic contacts with other members.

We note that this overview of group stages provides only a very general sketch of how a group might develop according to Perls's (1969b) layers of neurosis. In the past several decades, Gestalt groups have been extended to a variety of different applications, many of which were outlined in Feder and Ronall's *Beyond the Hot Seat* (1980). Contributors to this book described how Gestalt group techniques could be used with college students, in counselor training, and in organizational development, for example.

Couples Work

The empty chair technique, a staple of both individual and group work in Gestalt counseling, involves having a client talk to an important figure in her life as if that person was actually sitting there in the room. It follows that a natural application of Gestalt therapy is to actually bring that person into the room so that couples can work on their relationship. Wheeler and Backman (1994) pointed out that the couple gestalt is fundamental to human relationship patterns and that as far as we know every human society has been built around the notion of long-term pair bonding of one sort or another. Earlier in this chapter, we described psychological health in the individual as marked by holism and the taking of responsibility for one's needs. Wheeler and Backman described health in the couple relationship as marked by support for the ability to achieve common goals, such as financial stability and child rearing, and autonomy to pursue individual goals, such as career advancement.

Harman (1989) wrote that in Gestalt couples work the "relationship is the patient" (p. 73) and that two important objectives to be addressed in couples work are awareness and contact. The first goal is to help the members of the couple become aware of what they are thinking, planning, and interpreting as contrasted with what they are feeling and sensing. Harman suggested that it is essential for both persons in the relationship to avoid confusing these spheres of awareness. Otherwise, their manner of relating can unfold as if following a script, with both members assuming they know what their partner will do or say next. Promoting current awareness of feelings and perceptions of the outside world, and the difference between the two, allows for the possibility that the couple will relate differently in the future.

Harman (1989) also wrote that awareness of contact boundaries between the members of the couple, and between each client and the therapist, is an essential component of Gestalt couples work. According to Harman, "[H]ealthy relating in couples is characterized by good, clear contact. Another ingredient for a healthy relationship is respect for individual autonomy" (p. 74). In other words, having an appropriate sense of the boundaries between self and others allows partners in a relationship to assume responsibility for their own needs and negotiate with each the other to achieve mutually satisfactory goals.

Harman (1989) noted that Gestalt counselors have several roles to play in couples work that are different from those they play in individual counseling. First, the counselor may play a less active role and allow the clients to interact with each other as much as possible. This may be particularly true in the early stages of counseling as the therapist is attempting to ascertain the types of boundaries that each member of the relationship has. The counselor may still use direct suggestions to promote interactions between the clients, such as by asking them to speak directly to each other rather than through the counselor. The therapist will also use the clients' own

reactions to what is happening in the room as the couple interacts as a way to promote awareness. For example, if there seems to be little energy or enthusiasm in the room, the therapist
might comment on this in order to bring the situation to the couple's attention.

Child and Adolescent Counseling

The emphasis on creativity and personal responsibility found in Gestalt counseling has led to a
number of applications with children and adolescents. Oaklander (2002) pointed out that nothing happens in Gestalt counseling without the establishment of a therapeutic relationship, and
with children, it is important to make it as egalitarian as possible. The counselor should not
jump into a teacher or parent role with the child or place expectations on the child.

A number of Gestalt modalities can be used effectively with children and adolescents. For
example, Tervo (2002) pointed out that bodily awareness is an important aspect of self-organization
and that disconnected feelings and experiences can be brought into awareness through greater
attention to physical processes. "Children/adolescents are often numb or deadened in part of
their body. Gradual increases in sensation help the client develop support for self and contact
with others" (p. 129). This can be done by teaching breathing exercises and concentrating on
physical sensations in different parts of the body. Play therapy, in which a child or adolescent is
encouraged to express herself through drawing, playing with toys, or playing in a sandbox, can
also be used (Oaklander, 2002).

Ferguson and O'Neill (2001) suggested that children in adolescence face a number of
unique tasks that can be addressed using Gestalt techniques. These tasks involve increasing
awareness and reorganizing relationships with peers and adults as adolescents mature and
face increasing responsibility. For example, they may need to reorganize relationships with peers
that are now less centered around play activities and with adults who may grant them more
autonomy.

BRIEF THERAPY/MANAGED CARE EFFECTIVENESS

Gestalt therapists face the same pressures to provide services in a brief and economical format that
other therapists do. Dierks (1996) suggested a short-term approach to Gestalt counseling
that emphasizes both cognition and affect, and Houston (2003) described a short-term approach
that emphasizes an initial assessment of the client and an evaluation of whether or not short-term
interventions are suitable for her.

Harman (1995) suggested that Gestalt therapy can be conducted in such a way that each
session is a "whole" without necessarily making major changes in the way Gestalt counseling is
practiced. The difference in short-term interventions is that the counselor and the client must
prioritize the client's concerns in order to see what needs to be worked on first. In Gestalt terms,
is there a concern in the foreground of the client's experience that is specific and can be
addressed in a short period of time? The next step is for the client and the counselor to work
together to bring everything associated with that concern into the client's present awareness, perhaps with the use of experiments. Harman pointed out that the here-and-now emphasis of
Gestalt counseling lends itself well to short-term approaches, and the main adaptation that must
be made is to identify and work with client concerns as quickly as possible.

INTEGRATING THE THEORY WITH OTHER APPROACHES

The techniques and experiments that Fritz Perls and other Gestalt therapists pioneered, such as the empty chair technique, have been widely applied to other counseling approaches. While potentially powerful, the theoretical background for Perls's techniques often receives less attention when an experiment is integrated with another counseling approach. However, many of the central theoretical principles of Gestalt therapy are, in fact, consistent with those of many other counseling approaches.

Both Gestalt therapy and client-centered counseling emphasize the centrality of the therapeutic relationship and recognize that this bond is necessary for change to occur. Just as Carl Rogers considered accurate empathy to be essential in establishing this relationship, Gestalt therapists are encouraged to enter into an authentic relationship with a client in which both parties are fully present. While Gestalt therapists view historical explanations and intellectualizing as anathema to their approach, a number of authors have suggested methods for integrating the emphasis on experiencing emotions with cognitively oriented approaches. For example, Dierks (1996) suggested how a cognitive model could be used with Gestalt techniques for short-term counseling, and Greenberg et al. (1993) have written extensively on an experiential approach to counseling that combines Gestalt techniques for increasing awareness of emotional functioning and cognitive models for understanding such processes.

While the emphasis on awareness of the present allows Gestalt therapy to be combined with other approaches to counseling that emphasize the importance of the counseling relationship and getting in touch with one's emotions, it is more difficult to apply with counseling theories that take a more historical approach to understanding clients' concerns. For example, while Perls was originally trained as a psychoanalyst and adapted many of his ideas about personality functioning from Freud, the process of conducting therapy that Perls pioneered was quite different from psychoanalysis. Classical psychoanalysis involves a more detached therapist who seeks to analyze a client's current difficulties by investigating her psychological history. This is the reverse of what happens in Gestalt therapy, in which the client gets in touch with emotions *first*, and explanations happen later, if at all. Contemporary psychodynamic theorists, however, emphasize the role of the counselor-client relationship more than Freud did. For example, in the more interpersonally based dynamic therapies, much of the curative part of the treatment is said to come from what the client learns from the therapeutic interaction with the counselor.

While authors such as Greenberg et al. have suggested methods for integrating Gestalt with cognitive approaches, to the extent that such approaches emphasize explaining and understanding one's behaviors, the ability to integrate Gestalt counseling would be diminished. Cognitively oriented therapists can use Gestalt-like techniques to elicit emotion as a way of helping clients understand the connection between their thoughts and feelings. This integration is demonstrated in the following example, in which a client named Janet is distressed because she has to call her former husband to ask him to take their children while she goes on a business trip.

Janet: I just get so damn nervous whenever I have to ask that SOB for anything; he is so condescending.

Counselor: Can you identify some of the thoughts that you are having when this happens?

Janet: I don't know—it's just so typical of him.

Counselor: Janet, would you be willing to try an experiment so that we can better understand what goes on with Eric?

Janet: I suppose, if it will help.

Counselor: OK, I want you to imagine that Eric is sitting in this chair and you are asking him for a favor. I'd like you to pay attention to how you are feeling and what thoughts are going through your head right at this moment in time.

The counselor in this example is primarily interested in the connection between Janet's thoughts and feelings but suggests the empty chair technique as a way to access her feelings. This would then be followed by an examination of the thoughts that lead to her feelings. This example shows how Gestalt experiments can be used with other approaches, such as cognitive therapy, particularly to bring out client feelings that can then be addressed in counseling. We do, however, note that counselors must think carefully about how to integrate these gestalt techniques in a meaningful way with other counseling theories. Gestalt experiments can seem quite compelling as a means to help clients get in touch with feelings, but counselors must consider the appropriate time to do this and have therapeutic goals for working with the feelings that do surface.

RESEARCH

Systematic empirical research investigating the claims made by Gestalt theorists is lacking, particularly when compared to approaches such as behavior therapy, cognitive-behavioral techniques, and person-centered counseling, which have more research support. Harman (1984b) classified the existing Gestalt research into five categories: (1) studies of the effectiveness of Gestalt marathon groups, (2) analyses of Fritz Perls's demonstrations of his technique in the Gloria film (listed under videos in the Web site that accompanies this text), (3) comparisons of Gestalt therapy to other theoretical orientations, (4) analyses of specific Gestalt techniques, and (5) doctoral dissertations. While Harman noted that several studies conducted in the 1970s indicated support for the use of Gestalt weekend marathon groups in improving members' self-actualization tendencies and self-concept, Lieberman, Yalom, and Miles (1973) found at least some Gestalt marathon groups to be less effective than marathon groups conducted using other theoretical approaches. Marathon groups, and their effectiveness, are discussed in more detail in Chapter 4.

Harman's review of dissertations and studies of the Gloria film sheds little light on the effectiveness of Gestalt therapy. Most of the dissertations he found were theoretical rather than empirical in nature, and analyses of the Gloria film reflect Perls's work with only one client under rather artificial circumstances.

Smith, Glass, and Miller's (1980) meta-analysis of the counseling outcome literature does include a small sample of Gestalt studies. Overall, the effectiveness of Gestalt therapy was roughly equal to that of most other counseling approaches, but there were far fewer studies available on Gestalt counseling than on most other counseling theories. Sapp (1997) cited a similar finding by Bretz-Joachim, Heekerens, and Schmitz (1994), who conducted a meta-analysis of 38 studies carried out between 1970 and 1986: Overall, Gestalt therapy was found to be as effective as other counseling approaches.

Research is available that supports the empty chair technique. Leslie Greenberg and his colleagues have been leaders in this area and have shown the effectiveness of the empty chair technique for encouraging the expression of unresolved feelings (Paivio & Greenberg, 1995) and reducing the client's level of indecision about career issues (Clarke & Greenberg, 1986). The latter study is described in more detail next.

SAMPLE RESEARCH: Differential effects of the Gestalt two-chair intervention and problem solving in resolving decisional conflict

Goals of the Research

Clarke and Greenberg (1986) compared the use of the Gestalt two-chair intervention and cognitive-behavioral problem solving to determine which was more effective in helping clients resolve career decision conflicts.

Participants

Forty-eight people who wanted help in resolving a career-related conflict were recruited. They ranged in age from 16 to 73.

Methods

The participants were divided randomly into three conditions: (1) a group that used the Gestalt empty chair technique to help resolve conflict, (2) a group that used cognitive-behavioral methods (defining the problem, generating alternatives, making a decision, and then evaluating the results of the choice) to help resolve conflict, and (3) a wait-list control group that received no treatment. Those in the groups that received treatment were seen by doctoral-level psychologists and graduate students in training. In order to compare the results for each of the three conditions, the participants' degree of career undecidedness before and after treatment was measured. In order to represent the goals of the two types of treatments, two measures of outcome were used, one that assessed feelings of undecidedness and one that emphasized cognitive factors such as movement through decision-making stages. The clients met two times with their counselors.

Results

The results indicated that both of the treatment groups showed statistically significant decreases in undecidedness compared to the no-treatment group but that the group using the empty chair technique improved more than the group receiving the cognitive intervention. The authors found neither treatment affected the cognitive outcome of movement through decision-making stages.

Implications of the Research

The authors concluded that the two-chair intervention reduced indecision more effectively than the cognitively oriented problem-solving intervention.

EVALUATION OF GESTALT THERAPY

Gestalt therapy is often classified as an existential/humanist approach, and while it has generated little empirical research, Perls's approach has been continually refined and updated, a sign of interest in and continued commitment to this approach. In our view, the applicability of Gestalt counseling has been increased as it has continued to change and adapt since its initial "Perlsian" stage, in which Fritz's personality dominated the approach. As other pioneers such as Zinker and the Polsters have refined the approach, it has become more accessible to counselors attracted by its ideas and interventions but wary of Perls's confrontational style.

The numerous experiments devised by Perls and his followers continue to be popular and are frequently integrated into other counseling approaches. Perls's emphasis on experience, expression, and awareness of emotions represents a unique contribution of this approach—one that has allowed it to survive despite the paucity of empirical research attesting to its effectiveness. Emotional functioning is an essential aspect of healthy personalities, and it is difficult to think of another counseling theory that has as much to offer as Gestalt counseling for accessing clients' feelings.

The emphasis on clients getting in touch with their emotions also represents one of the potential drawbacks of this approach. The encounter group movement that started in the 1970s was spurred by humanistic/existential theorists such as Rogers and Perls and involved large groups of people retreating to the wilderness or other places of solitude to "get in touch with their feelings." Such groups were often led by individuals with little training in counseling, and the movement unfortunately produced some negative effects for clients, which are described in Chapter 4. It is, of course, not fair to lay the sins of the encounter group movement entirely at the feet of Gestalt counselors. A number of books have been written by Gestalt theorists suggesting ethical and appropriate methods for accessing client feelings. Nevertheless, a new counselor can easily become attracted to Gestalt experiments without properly understanding the theory, which is a potential danger to clients.

Finally, it is difficult to look past the lack of empirical research on Gestalt therapy. This dearth of research is due to a number of factors, including Perls's own discomfort with empirical research and the fact that the philosophy of present awareness and spontaneity does not lend itself to empirical investigations. However, in today's managed health care environment, such a lack can serve to limit the applicability of the theory to settings where empirical validation is strongly encouraged.

Questions and Learning Activities

These questions and activities are designed to stimulate your thinking about this theory and to help you apply some of the ideas to your own life and experience. If possible, you should work with another person or with a small group. Getting others' points of view and sharing your own ideas and perspectives will be invaluable as a way to help you evaluate this theory and its applications.

Discussion Questions

1. The emphasis of Gestalt therapy on self-expression and present awareness seems uniquely suited to cultural attitudes prevalent in the United States and elsewhere in the 1960s and 1970s. How applicable are such notions in today's culture? Would you argue that gestalt therapy's central theoretical foundations need to revised or modified in any way?

2. Fritz Perls conducted Gestalt therapy in a controversial way by using personal confrontation and self-disclosure. What is your reaction to such methods?

3. Techniques such as the empty chair could make clients feel uncomfortable and psychologically vulnerable. In your mind, what are the pros and cons of using such exercises?

4. Beginning counselors often find Gestalt experiments such as the empty chair quite compelling. How do you account for the popularity of such approaches? Might clients

find such interventions awkward and strange? How can novice counselors ensure that they don't misapply such techniques?

5. A primary goal of Gestalt counseling is to facilitate present awareness. Which techniques seem most appropriate to you for facilitating this awareness?

6. Does Perls's theory of layers of neurosis fit with your own experience? Have you noticed a similar pattern in your interactions with other people?

7. Perls believed that our intellect can sometimes override our common sense and interfere with what is in front of our face. How relevant are such ideas to our current information society, in which we are bombarded with information all the time? Could this get in the way of being spontaneous and creative in everyday life?

8. Another important notion in Gestalt counseling is that of unity of personality—i.e., that the healthy person has integrated experiences and feelings. Does this strike you as a realistic and desirable goal?

9. How do you reconcile Perls's emphasis on personal responsibility with the suggestions of multicultural researchers that certain segments of our society have faced barriers to full participation in our society?

Learning Activities

The Empty Chair

In a group of three or four people, take turns practicing the empty chair technique. Allow sufficient time for each member of the group to be both the counselor and the client. When being the client, the group member should pick a person in her life with whom she has unfinished business. For the purpose of this exercise, it is important that this be a relatively minor conflict that the individual does not mind sharing with the group: for example, an old roommate who did not clean up after herself or a neighbor who left her barking dog out all night. While the member pretending to be the client talks to that person as if she was sitting there, another member of the group takes the role of the therapist and directs the action. The person playing the therapist should encourage the person playing the client to switch back and forth between roles when it seems appropriate. The other members of the group serve as observers and share their reflections once the empty chair dialogue has taken place. Discuss how this technique might be safely integrated into actual counseling practice.

Remember that Gestalt techniques can bring up powerful emotions. Don't participate in this exercise if you have any hesitations, and don't use a person in your empty chair conversation with whom you have serious unfinished business or a current conflict.

Gestalt Defenses

With a partner or in a small group, try to identify examples of the following defense mechanisms (if possible from your own observations or experiences). Your first task is to make sure that you understand what they mean, as you will probably need to review their definitions and examples.

Introjection

Projection

Retroflection

Deflection

Confluence

Gestalts

A central notion of Gestalt psychology is the tendency of the human mind to complete gestalts of our sensory experiences. Early in this chapter, we suggested that one example of Gestalt completion is the mind making a moving image out of the individual frames of films. Can you think of other patterns of sensory experiences that are automatically completed?

Unfinished Business

Gestalt theorists suggest that incomplete gestalts become a source of unfinished business for us, tying up our energy and interfering with our ability to move on and complete other gestalts. Can you think of experiences in your own life that represent incomplete gestalts and have become a source of unfinished business for you? Discuss this with a partner or in a small group. Again, be careful not to discuss unfinished business that is too difficult for you to talk about in this setting.

Nonverbal Communication

Gestalt therapists believe that it is much easier for us to obscure the messages we send verbally than nonverbally. In other words, a person's true feelings are more likely to be revealed in body language than in spoken language. Make a list of common nonverbal gestures and what they typically mean. For example, what can you conclude about a person not making eye contact in conversation? What about movements such as crossing one's arms? With a small group, videotape a conversation. Replay the tape and discuss the nonverbal behavior and what it might mean.

Waking Up

Spend a few moments reflecting on what conditions facilitate your own awareness of your feelings and experiences. In other words, when are you most aware of your own surroundings? For example, do you need to be around other people to do this, or do you need peace and quiet?

Awareness Journal

For at least part of one day, attempt to keep a log or diary of how much time you spend actually being aware of your environment and how much time you spend on "autopilot"—that is, going through everyday activities without being aware of what you are doing. How much of your day is spent on autopilot, and how much is spent being creative and spontaneous? How does time spent in each state contribute to your own happiness and welfare?

Companion Website

Now go to the Companion Websites at www.prenhall.com/archer to assess your understanding of chapter content with multiple-choice and essay questions, and broaden your knowledge with related Web resources and additional print resources.

CHAPTER 7

Reality Therapy

VOICES FROM THE FIELD: COUNSELOR AND CLIENT REACTIONS

Yes, it works for me

Client: At first, I was surprised at what my counselor did. He didn't really want to talk about my feelings all that much, although he was easy to talk to. He helped me understand that I have a lot of choices about how I react to things. I learned that it's up to me to take charge of my life and accept responsibility for my feelings and behavior.

Counselor: Reality therapy is very action oriented and gives control to the client, not the counselor or somebody else in the client's life. When I first learned about it, I didn't like it much. It seemed as if everything was being blamed on the client. But then I realized how much freer people are when they realize the wide range of choices that they have about how they live their lives.

No, it doesn't work for me

Client: It seems like my counselor is blaming everything on me. He keeps saying that I can choose to feel differently . . . but he doesn't realize how tough things are for me. After all, I didn't choose to grow up in such a weird family, and I certainly didn't choose to get fired from my job! I want somebody who can understand the problems I face.

Counselor: Glasser's choice theory certainly is a useful way to tackle some problems. After all, I think the counseling profession has relied too much on unconscious or biological explanations for behaviors. But overall I think the theory simplifies the environmental context of clients' lives too much—external factors play an important role in shaping behavior, and it doesn't always seem appropriate to think that people can just choose to cope with whatever comes their way. What about clients who are subjected to racism or who are abused sexually?

Edward is a 14-year-old high school freshman who was referred to his school counselor after being suspended from school for multiple incidents of fighting with other students. His teacher has tried unsuccessfully to establish behavior contracts with him to cut down on his fighting with other students and in desperation referred him to the school counselor.

> **Counselor:** Edward, I'm glad to have the chance to talk with you. I don't get the chance to sit down with students one on one as much as I'd like.
>
> **Edward:** You don't care. I'm just here because I have to be, and so are you. It's just your job, and you're on their side.
>
> **Counselor:** You're right that this is part of my job, but I do mean it when I say that I'm glad to have the chance to talk to you.

Edward: Well, what is it you want me to talk about? Am I going to get in trouble because of what I say to you?

Counselor: Edward, I'd like you to talk about whatever is important to you. And no, you're not going to get in trouble for what you tell me. You've been punished quite a bit so far this year, and it just doesn't seem like things have improved at all. So let's take a different approach: You tell me what's going on.

Reality therapy is based on choice theory, developed by William Glasser to explain how all humans have fundamental needs and wants, as well as the capacity to choose behaviors to satisfy them. Accordingly, the outside world is viewed not as controlling our actions but rather as providing information that we can choose to act on. Control theory also suggests that we store concrete images of need-satisfying conditions in a mental "photo album" called the quality world. When this is discrepant from the information we get from the real world, a unified system of actions, thoughts, feelings, and physiology must be brought into play to better meet our needs.

Reality therapists reject systems of psychology that emphasize external control of human behavior. A counselor using reality therapy first establishes a warm and trusting relationship with his client so he can help his client evaluate choices made to meet the basic needs that all humans have for survival, belonging, power, freedom, and enjoyment. Together the counselor and the client decide whether different choices need to be made to meet the client's goals. In this example, we can assume that Edward is used to rebelling against external controls, and in using reality therapy, his counselor will make sure at the outset to avoid being a part of the same external control system. Instead, he will attempt to have Edward describe some of his own needs and wants, particularly at school, and then will attempt to help Edward choose different behaviors so he will be successful in meeting those needs.

HISTORICAL BACKGROUND

Historical Context

William Glasser, the founder of reality therapy, began training as a psychiatrist in the early 1950s. He became a consultant for a California institution for delinquent girls in 1956, and in 1957, he completed his psychiatric training at the Veterans Administration Hospital in Los Angeles. During this time, Glasser found that his psychoanalytic training was ill-suited to the needs of his patients. In his view, a therapist working in such settings needed to be personally involved in a therapeutic relationship that focused on helping clients make concrete changes in behavior. This contrasts rather sharply with Freud's emphasis on the analyst as a distant authority figure who analyzes unconscious conflict.

Glasser (1965) developed reality therapy to help clients successfully meet internally derived needs in the outside world—in other words, to cope successfully with reality. Robert Wubbolding, who was important in helping refine Glasser's ideas into a systematic approach to teaching and practicing reality therapy, defined it as a method for helping clients regain control of their lives (Wubbolding, 1988). Both Glasser and Wubbolding stressed the importance of human freedom and rejected deterministic models of human behavior.

Glasser's underlying assumption that we all have the innate power to choose our behaviors fit well in an era when Freudian psychology and its deterministic view of human behavior were under great challenge. Institutions such as elementary and secondary schools, community counseling centers, psychiatric hospitals, and prisons played increasingly prominent societal roles in post–World War II America and were concerned with helping as many people as possible to become productive members of society. As is true for many of the counseling models developed in this time period, part of the attractiveness of Glasser's ideas was the focus on human choice and on concrete results.

In one particularly revealing example of Glasser's early thinking, Howatt (2001) described how Glasser conducted a simple informal experiment during his residency in a Veterans Administration hospital. He moved all of the pinball games that patients used for recreation into one corner of the ward and clearly demarcated this area as a place where no "crazy" behavior was allowed. Patients were free to act as "crazy" as they chose outside of this area, but in order to play the pinball games, they had to choose to suppress these behaviors. Glasser found that the patients' desire to play these games was more important than their need to act "crazy." Insights of this nature propelled him to create a new psychology based on human freedom, choice, and responsibility.

Reality therapy grew in popularity in the 1960s and 1970s but was mainly viewed as a set of counseling methods rather than a comprehensive theory (Wubbolding, 2000). Reflecting the strengthening of its theoretical foundations and its application to a wide range of settings, Glasser's label for his approach had evolved from reality therapy to control theory to choice theory. This progression will be further detailed in the next section, and throughout the chapter, we use the terms *reality therapy* and *choice theory* to describe this approach.

In his book *Counseling with Choice Theory: The New Reality Therapy* (2000a), Glasser noted that his emphasis on personal responsibility in addressing human problems is just as necessary today as it was during the ascendancy of psychoanalysis several decades ago. Glasser thought it unfortunate that Freud's deterministic view of human behavior, shaped by unconscious psychic conflict, had been replaced with models of biological causation that are just as deterministic. In other words, he viewed many mental health professionals as still trapped in a view of human behavior as outside the control of the individual.

Reality therapists today continue to place an emphasis on educating and training professionals and the public in the principles of taking personal responsibility and making effective choices. The William Glasser Institute, founded in 1967, provides intensive training in reality therapy and has certified thousands of professionals in this approach. A number of reality therapy training institutes exist in the United States and abroad, offering training and certification for interested professionals.

❋Development of the Theory

William Glasser was born in 1925 to immigrant parents and grew up during the Great Depression. He received a bachelor's degree in engineering and spent an unfulfilling year working as a chemical engineer. Believing that he could not gain admittance to medical school because of low grades in college, Glasser switched professional tracks to pursue graduate work in clinical psychology. After he completed his master's, a professor convinced him to follow his dream of attending medical school, and he was accepted at Case Western Reserve University. After graduating with a medical degree in 1953, Glasser received psychiatric training at the Veterans Administration Center in Los Angeles. During this time, he also became a consulting psychiatrist at the Ventura School for Girls, which was a California state facility for delinquent adolescents.

As he worked in these settings, Glasser found a gap between the psychoanalytic focus of his psychiatric training and what actually seemed to work with his patients. In his first book, *Mental Health or Mental Illness?* (1961), he challenged the prevailing notion that mental illness was caused by unconscious, unresolved psychological conflicts. In fact, Glasser rejected the very notion of mental illness and instead viewed "disordered" behaviors as simply the individual's best attempt to fulfill unmet needs. In other words, it is not useful to label behaviors as abnormal. Doing so means that such behaviors are considered the purposeless consequences of mental disease. The behaviors may be ineffective in accomplishing one's goals, but the individual still has control over them and can choose to behave differently in the future.

The publication of *Reality Therapy* (1965) was an important landmark for Glasser, as it signaled his movement from just offering opinions about what did and did not work in psychiatry to developing a new theory (Lennon, 2000). It contained several significant departures from current psychiatric practice, including the centrality of client responsibility, a preference for dealing with the present rather than the past, an emphasis on new behavior rather than the development of insight, and an active role for the therapist in counseling. While not initially greeted with enthusiasm by the medical profession, reality therapy gained acceptance in other fields such as education, corrections, and counseling (Collins, 1997). The last chapter of *Reality Therapy* dealt with its application to educational settings, and in *Schools Without Failure* (1968), Glasser advanced his view that too many students were failing in schools because of the educational system's reliance on external control over student behavior.

Despite its impact, reality therapy was still criticized at this time as being a set of useful techniques rather than a counseling theory (Wubbolding, 2000). Glasser published *The Identity Society* (1972) to provide a sociocultural foundation for his approach. In it, he identified three developments that he believed had fundamentally changed life in Western industrialized nations. First, such societies had developed and strengthened institutions and laws that guaranteed basic human rights. Second, most had achieved a level of economic prosperity where they did not need to worry about basic survival. Third, modern technology allowed instantaneous communication worldwide. In Glasser's view, therefore, so-called identity needs for belongingness, achievement, freedom, and enjoyment had supplanted the need for survival as an organizing force in human activity. Accordingly, all persons are viewed as capable of taking responsibility for meeting their own needs and wants, particularly connections with other people.

The Identity Society provided a context for the importance of reality therapy, but it was not until almost 20 years after its introduction that Glasser articulated a cohesive theoretical foundation for this approach with the publication of *Control Theory* in 1984. Control theory began as a model of brain functioning developed by Powers (1973), and Glasser incorporated control theory into his approach by describing the brain as an input control system that regulates behavior like a thermostat (Wubbolding, 2000). Glasser disagreed with the classic behaviorists' notion that all behavior is shaped by the environment and instead believed that our motivations are internal. An essential component of control theory is the idea that all behavior is the result of people trying to meet needs, and it is the brain that regulates behaviors to help us reach these ends. Control theory will be further described in the "View of Human Nature" section of this chapter.

Glasser maintained a private practice from 1956 to 1986, at which time he stopped his clinical work to focus on educating, training, and writing about reality therapy. A further refinement of the theory came with Glasser's announcement in 1996, while speaking in Australia, that he would no longer use the term *control theory* in his approach; instead, he would use *choice theory*

He had become concerned that the term *control* connoted an emphasis on coercive influence, rather than responsibility for one's own actions (Lennon, 2000), and thus did not represent his philosophy. In 1998, he published *Choice Theory: A New Psychology of Personal Freedom*, in which he emphasized the damage caused by external control systems that he thought dominated much of society. In addition, he focused on the fundamental human needs for satisfying relationships and a balanced and flexible approach to life (Skeen, 1998).

Glasser's name has been more or less synonymous with reality therapy, but many others have contributed to its development (Wubbolding & Brickell, 2000). Robert Wubbolding, a psychologist who is currently the director of the Center for Reality Therapy in Cincinnati, Ohio, and a professor emeritus at Xavier University, is foremost among these. Wubbolding's background in academics complemented Glasser's focus on practice and training, and he made many important contributions to refining reality therapy as a systematic approach to counseling. Perhaps most important, Wubbolding (1989) developed the WDEP system, a pedagogical tool for learning and practicing reality therapy, which will be described in more detail in the "Process of Therapy" section of this chapter.

ASSUMPTIONS AND CORE CONCEPTS

View of Human Nature

The view of human nature that is foundational for the practice of reality therapy is control theory, later relabeled choice theory; it is now used interchangeably with reality therapy in referring to Glasser's counseling model. Reality therapy is based on the assumption that all needs are internal and that human beings act on the world purposefully to satisfy their needs and wants. As was noted in the introduction to this chapter, Glasser eventually dropped the term *control theory* in favor of *choice theory* because the former term created the false impression that the theory was based on controlling other people's behavior rather than one's own. Wubbolding (2000) has provided the following overview of choice theory:

1. Human beings are born with the five needs described in the "Core Concepts" section of this chapter, which serve as the motivation for all behavior.
2. Reality therapy rests on the assumption that all human behavior is internally driven and results from the difference between what we want and what we perceive ourselves as getting. The source of our behavior therefore is not our unconscious or previous learning experiences but rather our present perception of our success in meeting our needs, goals, and wants.
3. While we usually define behavior by its most obvious or apparent characteristic, all human behaviors are total and composed of four elements: doing (acting), thinking, feeling, and physiology. For example, the feeling component is most obvious for people who are labeled "anxious," but this behavior includes not just feelings of worry or dread but also actions (asking for reassurance from others, avoiding feared situations), thoughts (thinking negative thoughts about what might happen in the future), and physiology (experiencing a rapid heartbeat as elevated blood pressure).
4. Humans are responsible for their behavior and are capable of change. Wubbolding (2000) wrote that we have the most control over acting, and, secondarily, thinking,

and these are the two elements of behavior that usually serve as the starting points for counseling. Clients are initially encouraged to talk about the actions they are choosing at the present and how successful they are in meeting needs.

5. Exploring perceptions of the outside world and their helpfulness in meeting needs is an important component of counseling. At a low level of functioning, individuals are able only to recognize and label components of the outside world, while at a higher level, they are able to put a positive or negative value on their perceptions of the world.

Glasser (1989) believed that almost all clients come to counseling because they are not able to cope successfully with what is happening in their lives. However, a fundamental tenet of choice theory is that persons who are not coping effectively are capable of choosing better behaviors to manage life effectively. Reality therapy does not deny that suffering exists or that events over which we have no control can conspire to make life difficult. However, according to Glasser, in the end the only behavior we can control is our own, and that is where this approach to counseling begins.

Core Concepts

Basic Needs Glasser's view of human nature includes basic types of needs that Wubbolding (2000) described as similar to Abraham Maslow's hierarchy. However, according to Maslow, basic needs such as hunger, thirst, and reproduction form the foundation for higher-level needs such as social belonging and personal growth. While agreeing on the types of needs that are important, Glasser and Wubbolding did not view these needs hierarchically but rather saw them as interconnected and mutually dependent. Wubbolding (2000) used the analogy of legs on a chair to describe how needs function in choice theory: All must be present and in balance. The five basic needs Glasser identified are described below.

SURVIVAL. Glasser (1998) wrote that "[A]ll living creatures are genetically programmed to struggle to survive" (p. 31). For Glasser, the Spanish word *ganas* summed this need up better than any other; it refers to the desire to work hard, do what it takes to survive, and move beyond just survival to longer-term security. As Glasser noted in his book *The Identity Society* (1972), in many nations, especially those in the West, obtaining the base necessities of life is no longer a primary concern, since they are assured to most people. Glasser, of course, does acknowledge that in parts of the world millions of people face critical shortages in food and medicine, which are pressing survival concerns. Glasser (1998) also wrote that the other aspect of survival, the survival of the species, is based on sexual pleasure. Glasser pointed to this aspect of survival as an example of how the five basic needs are interconnected and mutually dependent. Sexual activity is associated with the needs for belonging and fun, as well as the need for reproduction (survival).

BELONGING. Most animals have the need to form groups and cooperate for mutual benefit. Humans belong to many such groups, including families, work groups, social clubs, schools, neighborhoods, and religious organizations. In *Counseling with Choice Theory* (2000a), Glasser made it clear that the source of most clients' concerns is the lack of satisfying relationships. He used the term *disconnected* to refer to such individuals and believed that in the majority of cases they attempted to meet their needs for connection by resorting to external controls over such persons. Such efforts, he believed, are ultimately doomed to failure, as attempts to control another person only lead to further disconnection. For example, a teacher who has a misbehaving student in class might attempt to control her behavior by threatening a poor grade, or a parent might attempt to control a disobedient child by cutting off his allowance. Such attempts at external control can rupture the relationship with the child and interfere with the need for belonging that both children and adults have.

POWER. This refers to the need for achievement, competence, and accomplishment. Glasser (1998) noted that the need for power for its own sake is unique to human beings. Other animals attempt to gain dominance over each other to assure their survival and ability to reproduce, but humans alone seek power even when it is no longer needed for survival. Wubbolding (2000) stressed that power does not simply refer to gaining control over others but also includes the human need for competence and accomplishment. Thus, the need for "power" does not need to be met at another person's expense: It can be developed cooperatively with others and, indeed, can lead to the fulfillment of other needs such as belonging. Power is therefore viewed as an internal quality that allows one to feel more control over his life through accomplishment and the refinement of skills necessary to succeed in life. For example, academic achievement could be seen as meeting this need because it contributes to both the individual's personal development and his ability to access quality employment.

FREEDOM OR INDEPENDENCE. Glasser (1998) wrote that the need for freedom and independence is nature's attempt to balance others' desires to control our lives and our own need to be free of these influences. He believed that this balance is best expressed by the Golden Rule of "Do unto others as you would have them do unto you." To function effectively, we must have the opportunity to choose among various possibilities and to act on these possibilities without unreasonable constraints. Glasser saw our freedom as the foundation for our creativity and our ability to cope effectively with our environment.

FUN OR ENJOYMENT. Glasser (1998) noted that even as infants we have an innate need to play. Through play, we are able to explore our world and establish connections with other people. As adults, the need for fun or enjoyment is a prime motivator, and we can quickly become bored without it. For example, many adults become dissatisfied with jobs that do not allow them to at least occasionally experience enjoyment in the workplace.

Quality World An important element of choice theory is the notion that the brain stores need-satisfying images that serve as a guide to behavior. Glasser (1998, 2000a) labeled this kind of mental file drawer the *quality world*. We begin filling it early in life, and there must be at least one satisfying picture for every need (Collins, 1997). These pictures can be updated as a function of our experience with need satisfaction, and in this way, the quality world functions as a type of picture album against which to compare our current experiences. We are motivated to change our behavior when a discrepancy exists between our perceptions of the real world (people, things, and situations) and our quality world.

Total Behavior As was noted in the "View of Human Nature" section of this chapter, Glasser believed that all human activities are total behaviors comprised of the following elements: acting, thinking, feeling, and physiology (Glasser, 2000a). Total behaviors are purposeful, internally generated, and designed to maneuver the external world so that our needs are met (Wubbolding, 2000). While all of our behaviors consist of these four elements, some may be more obvious than others at times, and Glasser maintained that it is our actions that are most directly under our control. As an example, consider a college student who wants to pass a challenging exam. In order to successfully prepare for the exam, the student will need to take actions, the behavior over which the student has the most direct control; in this case, these actions will be studying behaviors, such as reviewing the textbook and class notes. However, each element of that student's total behavior will come into play in preparing for the exam: The student will likely experience feelings such as anxiety or confidence, which can be used to accomplish this goal. Thinking will, of course, come into play as the student rehearses the material, commits it to memory, and organizes it cognitively in order to be able to answer questions about it. Physiology also comes into play in preparing for an exam: At times, the student may feel alert or weary or have trouble sleeping.

Wubbolding used the metaphor of a car's four tires to describe the notion of total behavior: All four tires are necessary for the car to operate, just as all four components of the total behavior system are necessary for a human being to operate effectively. The idea that acting and thinking are under more complete control than feeling and physiology is also a part of this example: In a car, the front two tires (acting and thinking) direct the forward motion of the car, while the rear tires follow along (feelings and physiology). This illustrates the idea that in the total behavior system, it is actions and thoughts that can be changed most quickly.

The notion of effective control is important when understanding how total behaviors help us meet our needs. Each of the behaviors described above must be integrated and balanced for the student to perform at an optimal level in meeting the need to successfully prepare for and do well on the exam. If the student neglects physiology, for example, by not getting enough sleep, it could become very difficult to concentrate on the course material (thinking). Anxious feelings about the exam could also interfere with the student's ability to prepare for an exam (thinking) and to get enough rest (physiology). Wubbolding (2000) noted that relationships with other people are essential in effective total behaviors. In the above example, a student who prepares with other students, consults with the professor or a teaching assistant, and maintains a healthy social support system is far more capable of performing well on an exam than one who is isolated from other people.

External Control Psychology This refers not to a principle of reality therapy, but rather to what Glasser viewed as the harmful approach traditionally used by society to control behavior. As he wrote in his book *Choice Theory* (1998), "The seeds of almost all of our unhappiness are planted early in our lives when we begin to encounter people who have discovered not only what is right for them—but also, unfortunately, what is right for us" (p. 4). External control psychology is based on punishing those deemed to be doing something wrong and then, once they have stopped, rewarding them so they continue to do what is "correct." In other words, the system of control, whether it is based on punishments or rewards, is external to the individual. Glasser maintained that principles of external control psychology have been used throughout human history because they serve the interests of those in power, whether they are government authorities, religious leaders, people in business, teachers, or parents. This system is used because, quite simply, it works, at least to a certain extent, and the persons over whom the control is exerted come to accept it because it provides security and because it seems there are no other options (Glasser, 1998).

What is wrong in using methods of external control psychology that have been with us for thousands of years? In Glasser's view, it is the source of most of human misery. Glasser viewed his approach as a prorelationship theory and believed the basis of happiness is fulfilling relationships. External control psychology is "a terrible plague" that destroys happiness, marriages, families, educational systems, and work settings because neither the people in control nor those over whom they exert control can have mutually beneficial relationships in which each party is able to fulfill his needs as he sees them. Instead, all systems of control are based on external rewards and punishments that undermine relationships.

Psychopathology and Glasser's Choice Theory Perhaps the most controversial aspect of reality therapy is Glasser's belief that mental disorders, and to a certain extent physical disorders, are actually under our control (Glasser, 1998). Glasser (2000) wrote that clients are responsible for their behavior and should not be labeled mentally ill. Instead, Glasser believed that what is labeled mental illness is actually the many ways that people behave when they are unable to meet their needs to the extent that they want. He contended that when clients make better or more need-satisfying choices, the symptoms labeled mental illness tend to disappear.

Glasser did not deny that biochemical forces have a role in human behavior, particularly in instances such as Alzheimer's disease, where there is a clear connection between mind and body. But he maintained that the traditional models of counseling and medicine strip the individual of personal responsibility and overemphasize the role of external factors in the change process. Glasser (2000a) was particularly concerned that psychiatrists now are overreliant on psychopharmacology (i.e., prescribing drugs) in working with patients.

Glasser (1998) wrote that in choice theory, all complaints are changed from adjectives and nouns to verbs to emphasize (1) that clients are actively choosing what they are complaining about and (2) that they can learn to make better choices to get rid of the complaints. We choose our own behavior and are responsible for our emotional, behavioral, and physical problems. For example, we don't *have* a headache; we are headaching. We aren't depressed; we are depressing.

Glasser therefore denied the very existence of disorders that have been established over the past several decades by the counseling profession. Sommers-Flanagan and Sommers-Flanagan (2004) pointed out that this is one of the most controversial parts of reality therapy but also indicated that according to Wubbolding it is not necessary to share this belief of Glasser's in order to practice reality therapy. It has been emphasized that in practice Glasser used the notion of a client's control over his symptoms not to confront or blame him, but rather to convey an interest in helping him manage his life better.

Stages of Mental Health Both Glasser and Wubbolding have described mental health in terms of regressive and positive stages of development. Wubbolding (2003) noted that regressive mental health is viewed not in terms of pathology but rather as ineffective attempts to meet one's needs. In contrast, the positive stages are effective ways to fulfill human needs that serve to balance the regressive stages and can be presented as goals for counseling. Both types of stages are not seen as absolutely discrete, and humans can display both types of behavior at different points in time. Wubbolding (2003) noted that even highly functional people occasionally choose ineffective behaviors and that the most disturbed people sometimes choose effective behaviors.

REGRESSIVE STAGES. The first stage of this process is the brief transition that occurs when the individual gives up after having attempted unsuccessfully to fulfill his needs. After meeting with frustration, the individual eventually gives up and ceases to try any further, which gives rise to the negative symptoms that characterize the second stage. These negative symptoms can be manifest in all of the behaviors that the individual chooses. For example, he may *act* destructively by harming himself or others. Negative symptoms can also be apparent in his *thoughts*, as when he is chronically pessimistic, and in his negative *feelings*, when he is as depressed and anxious. On a physiological level, he can choose *physical* symptoms such as headaches or pain. The final regressive stage includes negative addictions, such as alcohol, drugs, gambling, or overwork, in an ineffective attempt to meet needs.

POSITIVE STAGES. Wubbolding (2003) wrote that the initial positive stage of change is brief and is characterized by the attitude "I am committed to change." This is followed with positive symptoms that are the opposite of those described in the regressive stages in that they fulfill needs and lead to less frustration. The individual may engage in effective *actions* that help him get what he wants while contributing to society. For example, by being effective in the work-place, a person is able to contribute to society by producing goods as well as to earn money needed by those who depend on him. Realistic *thinking* is characterized by acceptance of what can and cannot be changed in life and acknowledgment of one's responsibility for his own behavior. Positive *feelings* include tolerance, acceptance, and hope, and positive *physiology* is characterized by an effective lifestyle that attends to one's physical needs.

Glasser (1976) stated that positive change can result in something he labeled *positive addictions,* which enhance one's well-being and are intensely need satisfying. Examples of positive addictions are running and meditation, practices that are the opposite of negative addictions in that they contribute to one's overall health and well-being. According to Glasser, such activities are regularly, but noncompulsively, chosen for a limited amount of time each day (for example, 45 minutes to an hour in the case of exercise) and are practiced in a noncompetitive way.

THERAPEUTIC RELATIONSHIP

Counselor's Role

According to Glasser (2000a), the reality therapist's role is that of an expert who teaches clients about the fundamentals of choice theory. The counselor plays an active role in the counseling relationship by asking clients questions about their current behaviors and helping them evaluate whether or not these are useful in meeting their needs and wants. Glasser thought it was important to communicate to a client during their initial meeting that the client has control over behaviors that currently seem unmanageable to him. This, of course, necessitates trust in the counselor as an expert, and trust is encouraged by the counselor's openness and honesty. Glasser suggested that the counselor also point out that this trust is a two-way process: The counselor places trust in the client as well—for example, by entrusting the client with the responsibility to show up for appointments and pay for services in a timely manner.

Wubbolding and Brickell (1998) noted a number of professional characteristics that are important for an effective reality therapist. First is the ability to reframe problems as opportunities. They noted that for reality therapists, "a lazy person has great potential, a resistant person has deep convictions, and a manipulative person is creative" (p. 48). In other words, a central component of reality therapy is the ability to "turn the tables" on clients and use what they perceive as problems or weaknesses as potential strengths that have yet to be tapped. Wubbolding (2003) also stressed the importance of doing the unexpected in counseling. For example, while a client may expect to talk about problems or weaknesses, the counselor may instead focus on the client's strengths and situations where he has chosen effective behaviors that help him meet needs successfully.

The ability to communicate hope was also noted by Wubbolding and Brickell (1998) as an essential characteristic of effective reality therapists. This does not mean that the counselor should function as a cheerleader or a Pollyanna but rather that reality therapists are committed to looking at what the client can do, exploring possibilities, and never giving up no matter how much frustration or pessimism a client expresses.

Counselor-Client Relationship

Wubbolding (2000) noted that at the outset of counseling, reality therapists rely on many of the same fundamental counseling skills pioneered by Carl Rogers to facilitate rapport and create a safe climate in which clients can convey their concerns. Examples of such skills include active listening, reflection of feelings, and the use of clarification questions. In the counseling relationship, clients are encouraged to assume as much responsibility as possible for meeting their own needs and choosing effective behaviors.

Another important component of the relationship between counselor and client in reality therapy is the focus on defining problems in solvable terms. Wubbolding and Brickell (1998) noted that very general or vague goals are ineffective: If the specific actions necessary to meet the client's needs and wants cannot be identified, the therapy is unlikely to succeed. Let us briefly consider how a reality therapist might work with a client, Jerry, who is unhappy with his job.

> **Jerry:** Well, I've been working at this software company for over a year, and I'm ready to quit. I feel like nobody really knows or cares about me; people just don't seem that friendly. It's pretty hard to get up and go to work every morning when it seems like nobody there even knows my name.
>
> **Counselor:** I think most people would feel the same way in a workplace where they feel anonymous. Have you figured out what gets in the way of your feeling better about your job?
>
> **Jerry:** Well, I work alone most of the time at my computer—that's just my job and it's not going to change. But I'd like to have people I can go to lunch with a few times a week, you know, maybe get together every now and then for a beer after work.
>
> **Counselor:** In other words, finding some people you can socialize with every now and then?
>
> **Jerry:** Yes, that would help a lot—it just makes me nervous even thinking about asking someone if they want to go lunch. I've always been that way.

In this example, the counselor attempted to get Jerry to be as specific as possible about his unmet needs for fun and belonging. The counselor did not assume he knew what Jerry meant when he expressed his displeasure about his current situation. He worked at getting more information about why Jerry's needs were not getting met and at the same time let him know that other people might feel the same way. One of his goals will be to help Jerry further clarify his needs for belonging and fun at work and then examine the choices he has to get those needs met. For example, he might talk to Jerry about how he has gotten similar needs met in the past, but he would not spend time analyzing the past or trying to figure out why Jerry has such a hard time socializing. He would continue to form a friendly relationship and provide hope and encouragement.

ASSESSMENT, GOALS, AND PROCESS OF THERAPY

Assessment

Reality therapists do not typically employ traditional methods of assessment, and they reject such methods as the analysis of dreams and the application of diagnostic labels. According to Glasser (2000), "[T]ime spent on dreams is time wasted" and "[C]lients should not be labeled with a diagnosis except when necessary for insurance purposes" (p. 24). Since formal assessments are typically used to diagnose and label individuals, something Glasser rejected, these methods do not play a prominent role in the practice of reality therapy.

Reality therapists do, however, conduct an informal type of assessment at the outset of counseling by evaluating a client's descriptions of his current problems and gauging how much internal locus of control he perceives in his everyday life (Wubbolding, 2000). This allows the reality therapist to assess how much responsibility and perceived control the client experiences at the present time, which helps establish goals for the therapy and types of changes the client desires to make in his life.

In the following excerpt, a reality therapist is meeting with Jane for the first time. She recently married Mario, who comes from a very traditional Mexican-American family. While Mario holds very egalitarian notions about male and female gender roles, his family subscribes to the more traditional notion that men should act as breadwinners for the family and that women should concentrate their efforts on child rearing. Jane has experienced considerable pressure from her in-laws to give up her successful career in banking to have children and is becoming increasingly angry and despondent that Mario does not stick up for her more with his family. This has caused considerable tension in their fledgling marriage, but she has been unable to convince Mario to come with her to counseling. She has therefore decided to see a reality therapist on her own. The following example briefly portrays how a reality therapist might use the initial session to evaluate how much responsibility Jane is currently able to assume for her behaviors.

> **Jane:** It's just so different now that we're married. I didn't see Mario's parents all that often when we were dating, and they were always nice and friendly, but once we got married, boy, the hammer came down. Now they keep asking, When are you going to have kids? When are you going to give up your job? That kind of stuff.
>
> **Counselor:** That sounds like a very difficult situation—your career seems very important to you. I'm wondering what kinds of discussions Mario and you might have had about having children and who would do what in taking care of them?
>
> **Jane:** Well, we both knew that we wanted to have children—we talked about that. But I just assumed we would work out a way for both us to keep our careers when we had kids. I certainly didn't know I'd get all this pressure from his parents or that he would more or less agree with them by not saying anything when they bring it up! I just shut down when that happens, and I just want to get out of there as quickly as possible. I just get so mad at Mario, too, when that happens. After a visit with his parents, we usually fight all the way home.
>
> **Counselor:** Could you choose to handle the situation differently—perhaps by saying something to his parents about your own feelings on the matter?
>
> **Jane:** What do you mean—telling them to mind their own business?
>
> **Counselor:** Well, I'm guessing that would make them angry and not help things very much. I'm thinking more of figuring out some way that you and Mario can work together in finding a way to acknowledge how important family is to them but also to let them know that it's something you and Mario are still working out.
>
> **Jane:** Well, I think that's Mario's responsibility—he needs to defend me to his own family. It's not really my place.
>
> **Counselor:** Well, it sounds like right now that's not working—Mario's not doing that. So is there a more effective way for the two of you to handle this situation?

In this exchange, we see that Jane had the opportunity to describe some of her current concerns, and her counselor had the chance to check out whether she is willing to take responsibility for the behaviors she is choosing in her interactions with her in-laws. At this point, we can see that Jane sees herself as something of a victim and that she is waiting for Mario to take control and more or less defend her from his parents. At this early point in counseling, we can guess that Jane may not be ready to assume responsibility for the behaviors she has chosen, but she has provided important information to the counselor about where their work needs to begin. The final statement by the counselor represents a classic reality therapy method. Jane seems to be somewhat resistant to taking any more responsibility, so the counselor suggests that this isn't working (isn't helping her meet her needs) and that further work is needed to figure out an effective way to meet her needs.

One type of assessment that can be used in reality therapy is an objective checklist that evaluates the client's current needs. Such a checklist is particularly useful as a convenient and fast way to assess a client's needs outside of the actual counseling sessions. For example, Dialessi (1999) developed the Student Self-Rating Scale to help school professionals understand their students from a choice theory perspective. The survey includes items on students' interest in reading, how they study, and their attitudes about the school. In addition, the instrument prompts students to label a successful experience in school and to describe the factors that led to their success. Another example is the Need-Strength Profile created by Glasser and Glasser (2000) and used to assess the relative strengths of the five basic needs for each partner in a relationship. This measure is based on the assumption that discrepancies in the strength of each need for partners in a relationship can lead to difficulties. It should be noted that while such measures are used in empirical research, they were mainly developed for clinical applications in counseling rather than as research tools (Huffstetler, Mims, & Thompson, 2004).

Goals

Glasser viewed the counselor's role as helping people define their wants, evaluate their behaviors, and make concrete plans for fulfilling their needs (Glasser, 1998, 2000a). The positive stages of mental health described earlier in this chapter are effective ways to fulfill human needs that serve to balance the regressive stages and can be presented as goals for counseling. Over time, Glasser (2000b) increasingly came to view the core concern of all clients as social in nature: "[A]lmost all the pain or abnormality associated with the choices that are commonly called mental illness are a genetic warning: We are not involved in a relationship that satisfies what our genes demand" (p. 1). Therefore, the central goal of reality therapy is to teach clients the principles of choice theory (we choose all of our behaviors) so they can effectively meet their need for satisfying relationships.

Recall that Glasser (1998) believed that all human activities are comprised of acting, thinking, feeling, and physiology and that each of these behaviors is purposeful, internally generated, and designed to maneuver the external world so that our needs are met. He believed that it is our actions that are most directly under our control, followed by our thoughts, our feelings, and finally our physiology. Therefore, reality therapists typically start by evaluating the effectiveness of a client's behaviors, which are most amenable to change and, secondarily, his thoughts.

For example, a client who describes constant fear that he is sick and who is constantly seeking out doctors' reassurances that nothing is wrong might be told by a reality therapist that counseling cannot start by addressing his anxieties about illness. Instead, counseling might start with what the client is actually doing: perhaps constantly reading about illnesses on the Internet, asking friends whether they notice anything different or "wrong" with him, making doctor appointments, etc. The counselor would teach the client that he does have control over these behaviors, and the thoughts behind them, but that he must first evaluate whether these behaviors are effective in getting him what he wants: satisfying relationships. Once the client decides to choose different behaviors, and different thoughts, changes in his feelings of anxiety are possible.

Process of Therapy

Glasser (1998, 2000a) asserted that our behaviors are the result of choices we make, and if these behaviors are not effective, most of us have options for choosing different behaviors in the future. As a result, the objective of his approach to counseling is not to provide clients with insight into the historical reasons for their current choices but rather to change their current behaviors so they have a better chance of meeting their needs. These fundamental needs include the physiological need for survival, as well as the psychological needs for belonging, achievement, freedom, and enjoyment.

In his books, Glasser used mainly case examples to demonstrate principles of reality therapy; it is Wubbolding (1988, 2000) who provided a systematic process for the practice of reality therapy, which he labeled the WDEP system: W (wants), D (doing), E (evaluation), and P (plans). Wubbolding (2003) emphasized that the WDEP system provides a cyclical system for the practice of reality therapy. It should not be interpreted as a strictly linear process that must be followed mechanistically. In fact, Wubbolding noted that younger persons might at first have difficulty describing their wants, and thus it might be more useful to begin counseling with an exploration of what they are currently doing. We now describe this system in further detail, using the case of Jane, introduced earlier in the "Assessment" section of this chapter.

W (Wants): Exploring the Client's Wants, Needs, and Level of Commitment Counseling may begin with a discussion of the client's wants, needs, and perceptions (Wubbolding, 2000). Wubbolding described some basic types of explorations that are useful, including (1) wants the client has that are, in fact, currently being met; (2) wants the client has that are *not* being met and (3) things the client is currently getting but does not really want. In reality therapy, it is assumed that all wants are connected to the five basic needs of belonging, power, freedom, fun, and survival, and it is therefore important to connect each of these needs to the client's wants. For example, a teenager wanting his parents to "get off his back" may be expressing a need for freedom, while a middle-aged manager who feels dissatisfied with his job may be expressing a need for fun or possibly power.

As part of the exploration of the client's wants, the counselor may choose to share some of his own wants and needs with respect to what is happening in the relationship with the client and possibly in the counselor's personal life as well (Wubbolding, 2003). The counselor may even make suggestions about specific ways in which the client can choose behaviors to meet his own needs and wants. However, at all times the counselor should be careful never to assume responsibility for the client's behaviors; instead, the counselor should function as a coach or mentor in helping the client choose the best behaviors to meet his needs.

Wubbolding (1988) also noted the importance of enlisting the client's cooperation early in the process and determining the level of motivation that he has for change. He identified five such levels, described by the following statements: (1) "I don't want to be here," which connotes a client who is resistant to counseling; (2) "I want the outcome but not the effort," the statement of a client who may want to change but is not committed to the behaviors necessary to effect change; (3) "I'll try; I might," indicating a client who has a higher motivation than clients in the first two stages but who is still "on the fence"; (4) "I will do my best," the statement of a client who will attempt changes in behavior but who will still allow for the possibility of failure; and (5) "I will do whatever it takes," which indicates a no-excuses commitment to change. Wubbolding (1988) noted that these stages are developmental, meaning that they can change over time, and that clients should not be pushed beyond their current level of commitment.

In order to examine what this stage of reality therapy might look like in actual practice, we will now return to the case of Jane, who is unhappy that her husband, Mario, has not intervened with respect to the pressure his parents are putting on Jane to give up her career and have a family. In this early stage of counseling, the counselor is attempting to identify exactly which of Jane's needs and wants are not being met.

See DVD

Chap. 7
Clip 1

Jane: I just wish Mario would say something when we are visiting his parents and they start in on me about giving up my career. I try to be polite, and I wait and wait for him to say something, but he just changes the subject.

Counselor: Is there something you would like to say to his parents?

Jane: Obviously, yes, I'd like to tell them to butt out! But I can't do that—it would upset them and probably Mario, too.

Counselor: What type of relationship would you like to have with Mario's parents? If they weren't focusing so much on the two of you having a family, what would you like them to discuss with you?

Jane: Good question. I guess my own parents are not really involved that much in our lives, and they live far away, so I'd like to have family around that we can visit on holidays, ask for advice, that kind of thing. But not advice on having a family! Just the kinds of things that people who are newly married need to deal with: buying stuff for our house, that kind of thing.

Counselor: So you'd like some support for your new relationship as a married couple, and not necessarily as prospective new parents.

In this exchange, we can see that one of Jane's needs not currently being met is her need for a relationship with her in-laws that will support her new marriage and not necessarily rush her to the next stage of having children. Part of this unmet need may come from her distant relationship with her parents, and perhaps her feelings that they do not support her marriage to Mario. A counselor working with Jane would, of course, need to be aware of cultural factors that might also be at play in this situation. We know that Mario comes from a traditional Mexican-American family, and he therefore may not feel it is appropriate to disagree publicly with his parents about family matters. It might be important for a counselor working with Jane to explore how much she has discussed family expectations with her husband and how he is accustomed to interacting with his parents.

It is difficult at this early stage to gauge Jane's level of commitment, but she seems at least motivated to change her current situation. Whether or not she will be open to changing her own behaviors to meet this need will become more evident in the following stage, in which the counselor explores what Jane is doing.

D (Doing): Exploring What the Client Is Doing This stage of counseling is marked by the generic question "What are you doing?" which was the title of one of Glasser's (1980) books. Wubbolding (2000) noted that each word in this question is important in the overall context of reality therapy: "What" implies a precise evaluation of exactly what the client is doing, "are" focuses on present behaviors, "you" makes it clear that it is the client who is responsible, and "doing" refers to the total set of behaviors chosen by the client. As part of this discussion, the counselor may ask the client to focus on the consequences of his behaviors by asking him to speculate about what will happen if he continues on his present course in the upcoming days, weeks, and months.

Let us now return to the case of Jane and examine an exchange in which the counselor asks her to examine exactly what she does during a visit to her in-laws.

See DVD

Chap. 7
Clip 2

Counselor: Jane, we've talked about the feelings of anger you have when your in-laws question you about having a family—anger at both them and your husband. I wonder if we might talk more about exactly what you do during a visit in which they bring this up.

Jane: Well, what I do is get angry!

Counselor: There's no question about that, but besides the feelings you have, I wonder if we could talk about what you do or say.

Jane: Usually, I try to brush it off and change the subject. I can feel my anger rising, so I often make up an excuse to leave the room. Then on the way home, I let Mario have it for not saying anything!

Counselor: What kinds of things have happened, or would happen, if you told them how you feel?

Jane: Well, I tried that early on, but they were just patronizing. I said that my career was important, but then they said, "Don't worry, dear, you'll feel differently later on." Then I made it clear to Mario that I didn't like that and asked him to say something; then we'd just fight about it. He said that he was raised to obey his parents.

Counselor: And since then, you're tried to more or less avoid his parents when this comes up. I guess you're pretty much hoping it won't get brought up again?

Jane: Yes, I guess so. I try to make sure we stay off the subject as much as possible. Sometimes I talk and talk just so there won't be gaps in the conversation where they can jump in and ask us about having a family.

We can see from this exchange that Jane's behaviors in interacting with her in-laws are more or less oriented around avoiding the subject of Mario and her having children. She is using avoidance behaviors, such as leaving the room, changing the subject, and talking incessantly, just to avoid having them bring up this subject. If Mario's parents are behaving in part according to cultural expectations about their role in the family, it is obvious that simple avoidance of the subject will not be successful in effecting change. We might assume that since Jane really wants to have a close relationship with her in-laws, these behaviors are not meeting her needs and instead are probably distancing her from them, and from her husband as well.

E (Evaluation): Working with the Client to Conduct Evaluations Wubbolding (2000, 2003) noted that the evaluation component of reality therapy is foundational and to a certain extent makes it a cognitively oriented approach to counseling (similar to the cognitive therapies of Beck and Ellis covered elsewhere in this book). Clients are asked to evaluate their current behaviors to determine whether their current needs are being met and to take responsibility for choosing new behaviors as necessary. Because self-evaluation is critical to the process, a certain amount of cognitive restructuring may need to take place. As is described in Chapter 9, covering cognitive therapies, cognitive restructuring involves assisting clients in finding alternate, and hopefully more adaptive, perspectives on their thoughts, feelings, and behaviors. For example, a client may need to restructure his belief that working hard for extremely long hours will bring him satisfaction. It may indeed earn him more money, but such devotion to work may also decrease the amount of time he can invest in family relationships.

According to Wubbolding (2000), in order for change to occur, clients must come to the conclusion that some component of their total behavior system is not getting them what they want. Wubbolding noted that such as evaluation consists of the following elements:

1. **Evaluation of behavioral direction**. This portion of the evaluation considers the overall direction of a client's life. Is the totality of the client's behaviors positive or negative? If carried into the future, will these behaviors ultimately result in getting the client's needs met?

2. **Evaluation of specific actions**. In addition to global evaluations of behavior, it is important to evaluate specific instances of behavior. For example, if a client recalls a specific instance in which he drank too much at a party, a dialogue might ensue in which the client is asked to evaluate the pros and cons of such behaviors. Wubbolding noted that generalities will not suffice to help the client choose different behaviors: In order to plan changes, it is essential that specific instances of problem behaviors be identified and described.

3. **Evaluation of wants**. Clients are asked about the appropriateness and feasibility of their wants. For example, a student might be asked if it is realistic to want all teachers to leave him alone, or a single person seeking companionship might be asked if it is realistic to want to never experience rejection.

4. **Evaluation of perceptions and viewpoints.** Glasser (1980) believed that perceptions are not easily changed and that this must be accomplished indirectly by changing behaviors rather than simply by deciding to change a perception. Wubbolding (2003) noted that "human beings seek the perception of being adequate, popular, skilled, in control, helpful to others, and comfortable" (p. 274). Thus, while it might not be useful to try to change a perception until later in counseling, at the outset it can be important to have a client evaluate the extent to which his perceptions are useful in meeting his needs. For example, the client might be asked whether it is useful to see all her coworkers as hostile competitors or all prospective dating partners as lying cheats.

5. **Evaluation of new behaviors.** Evaluation can occur with potential new behaviors that clients might choose, especially by asking hypothetical questions such as "What impact would it have to see your coworkers as allies rather than competitors?" or "To what extent might your social life be more satisfying if you didn't automatically assume dating partners were liars?"

6. **Evaluation of plans.** Before moving to the next and final stage of the WDEP cycle, planning, clients are asked in this stage to evaluate possible new directions for the behaviors they might choose. For example, a client might be encouraged to take very

small, discrete "baby steps" in moving toward his goal rather than attempting to institute sweeping changes in his life. A client seeking better physical fitness might be encouraged to begin by taking a short walk in the evening and then building toward running short distance, rather than jumping right into preparing for a marathon.

We will now return once again to the case of Jane to provide a brief example of the evaluation stage.

> **Counselor:** Jane, we've talked a little bit about what you're doing right now when you visit your in-laws, and some of the feelings you've had, and I wonder if I could ask about the type of relationship you'd like to have with them, and with your husband. I guess one thing that occurs to me is that it might not be realistic to expect that they are never going to ask you about your plans for having a family. Does that ring true to you?
>
> **Jane:** Yeah, sure, it's fine for it to get mentioned every now and then. But what steams me is that I know that behind that question is what they really want: for me to give up my career. And I think that's what really sets me off.
>
> **Counselor:** So the two things have become connected: They ask about your plans with Mario for a family, and what you also hear is "Give up your career."
>
> **Jane:** Yes, I think so.
>
> **Counselor:** And how realistic is it for you to expect that Mario is going to jump into that conversation when it starts?
>
> **Jane:** Well, given his past history, it's not very likely.

This process demonstrates an evaluation of Jane's wants, in which she is asked to contemplate how realistic it is to expect certain changes in behaviors from others. Again, as the session progresses, we might expect that a culturally sensitive counselor would help Jane explore the role of cultural factors in her interactions with both Mario and his parents. As this process continues, a reality therapist would likely look for opportunities to suggest to Jane that ultimately she cannot dictate the behaviors of others, particularly when cultural values are at play, but that she can control her own and that an important goal of counseling will be to help her identify behaviors that might be more useful in getting her needs met.

P (Planning): Developing Specific, Attainable Positive Plans Both Glasser and Wubbolding noted the importance of having clients make specific plans for change but also cautioned that planning is often mistaken as the focus of reality therapy. Instead, they believed that planning is useful only when the client has first progressed through the W, D, and E phases of the counseling process. In other words, making concrete plans is effective only if the client is on board with the plan and if it has a reasonable chance of succeeding. Wubbolding (2003) noted eight qualities of successful plans, which he summarized with the acronym $SAMI^2C^3$:

1. **Simple.** The plan should not be complicated.
2. **Attainable.** The plan should be realistic.
3. **Measurable.** Concrete indicators of the success of the plan should be used.
4. **Immediate.** The plan should be carried out as quickly as possible.
5. **Involved.** If possible, both the counselor and the client should be involved in the plan.

6. **Controlled.** The client should carry out the plan, and it should not depend on the actions of another person.
7. **Committed.** The counselor should make sure the client is motivated to carry out the plan.
8. **Consistent.** Plans have a better chance of succeeding if they involve something a client can do every day and practice over and over.

Returning to our case study of Jane, it is not possible to predict exactly what plan the counselor and Jane might develop from the limited exchanges we've presented, but we can anticipate some elements of what the plan might look like. First, the counselor will not want Jane to develop a plan that depends on a certain response from her husband or her in-laws. The plan should only involve Jane's choosing new behaviors; she should not count on specific reactions from other people. Ideally, the plan should involve something that Jane can do right away rather than waiting until the next time she visits her in-laws. Also, it would be important to have Jane choose behaviors that are simple and that she can practice every day. Jane might decide that she is not assertive enough with other people besides her in-laws and might practice a few elements of assertive communication every day: For example, she could learn polite but direct ways to be clear about her needs and desires with other people.

A central tenet of reality therapy is to "never give up." No matter what successes and failures clients experience in implementing their plans, the reality therapist will encourage them to continue experimenting with behaviors that will better meet their needs. As noted before, the WDEP process is seen not as linear but rather as continuous, and the counselor and the client might recycle through the process as necessary. Persistence is viewed as essential to ultimate success.

THERAPEUTIC TECHNIQUES

William Glasser described the practice of reality therapy as a series of conversations aimed at helping clients identify needs and wants and then helping them choose behaviors that will be effective in meeting those needs. Reality therapists are encouraged to be flexible in this approach, and the use of one specific technique over another is not emphasized. Therefore, there are no specific techniques that are unique to the practice of reality therapy. In this section, we will present a sampling of interventions that can be used in reality therapy, but none is synonymous with it.

Using Questions

Wubbolding (2000) identified the use of questions as a cornerstone in the practice of reality therapy in order to help clients examine their life directions. As was noted in the "Process of Therapy" section of this chapter, the WDEP system of reality therapy begins with a discussion of the client's wants, needs, and perceptions, and questions revolve around the following categories: (1) What do you want that you are getting? (2) What do you want that you are not getting? (3) What are you getting that you don't want? Other types of questions include these: "How much do you want to get it?" "What are you willing to settle for?" "What would you have to give up to get what it is that you want?" (Wubbolding, 2003). The use of questions is emphasized more in reality therapy than in many other systems of counseling. However, the counselor must still be careful about overusing questions, which could lead to his taking too much control over the session and establishing himself as an "examiner" rather than a helper. A counselor who peppers his client with question after question may also undermine rapport, create defensiveness in the client, and reduce their exchanges to a monotonic question-and-answer session (Wubbolding, 2000).

Wubbolding (1988) identified the following purposes for using questions in the practice of reality therapy:

1. **To enter the client's quality world.** By asking questions about various facets of the client's experience—wants, needs, perceptions, and plans, for example—the counselor can come to be seen by the client as part of his quality world. In other words, the counselor becomes a part of the system of the client's total behaviors and an ally.

2. **To gather information.** This is a central goal of the early part of reality therapy, and questions are used to gather as much information as possible.

3. **To provide information.** Asking questions is a two-way street for providing information. By asking questions, a counselor not only gains important information about a client but also can subtly impart it as well. A question such as "What other strategies could you use to get along with other students?" conveys the assumption that options for behaviors exist that have not yet been attempted.

4. **To help clients gain more effective control.** Through the self-evaluation process that follows the counselor's use of questions and the planning of alternative behaviors, clients can gain more effective control of their lives.

As an example of how questions are used in reality therapy, let us return to the case of Edward, who was briefly introduced at the outset of this chapter. Edward was referred to his school counselor for numerous incidents of fighting with other students.

Counselor: Edward, we've talked about the fight that you had with Tad and how angry you got that your teacher blamed the fight all on you. What would you like to have happened in that situation?

Edward: I wish she'd stop blaming it all on me.

Counselor: Do you believe that if you get into fights with other students, you won't get at least part of the blame?

Edward: [Pauses] No, I usually get all of the blame! And it makes me mad.

Counselor: So the more you get into fights, the more it seems they blame you?

Edward: Yeah, if there's a fight, I'm going to get blamed for it.

Counselor: What do you think it would take to stop all that blame coming your way?

Edward: I know what you're going to say . . . stop fighting. Easy for you to say.

In this exchange, we can see that the counselor used several questions to attempt to help Edward explore what was happening when he got into fights with other students, the types of reactions this prompted in the teachers, and whether Edward might prefer another outcome in the future. Obviously, this would entail avoiding fights with other students, and Edward's last response to his counselor may have been a bit sarcastic. A reality therapist would not assume at the outset that Edward would actually trust that he could choose other behaviors than fighting at school or that this would lead to positive outcomes for him. However, it is at least an encouraging sign that Edward was the one to announce that he would eventually have to stop fighting, even if his enthusiasm in questionable at this point.

Doing the Unexpected

Wubbolding (2003) noted that unpredictability is a quality that can enhance the psychotherapeutic environment by expanding a client's ways of thinking about himself and the world. Doing the unexpected can be as simple as focusing on a client's strengths or successes, rather than the problems he is currently focused on, to underscore points in his life when he was in effective control of his behaviors. A client demonstrating negative symptoms invariably displays positive symptoms, and discussion of this can energize counseling sessions and restore the client's optimism about the future.

Other examples of "doing the unexpected" can include reframing the client's perceptions and using paradoxical techniques. In an example of reframing a client's experience, bullying behaviors could be relabeled as examples of leadership and striving for achievement that need to be redirected. Paradoxical techniques involve directing a client to perform a symptom in an effort to either establish his control over the behavior or eliminate the symptom. For example, a client who has trouble getting to sleep at night because of persistent worries about his work might be directed to stay up as late as possible that night worrying. If the client does so, it establishes his control over the behavior, and if the client does not, the symptom is eliminated.

Using Bibliotherapy

Glasser (2000a) believed that an important component of reality therapy is teaching clients the principles of control theory, in part by having them read his books and those of other reality therapists. Clients are encouraged to read *Choice Theory* (Glasser, 1998), and of course, counselors using reality therapy must be thoroughly familiar with the book. Couples working on their relationship are encouraged to read his book *Getting Together and Staying Together*, cowritten with his wife, Carleen Glasser (Glasser & Glasser, 2000), and it is suggested that parents and teachers read *Unhappy Teenagers: A Way for Parents and Teachers to Reach Them* (Glasser, 2002).

Allowing or Imposing Consequences

Wubbolding (2003) noted that counselors and therapists have fewer opportunities to use this element of the environment than do persons who actually work in school, business, or correctional settings. And of course, ethical concerns come into play if a counselor contemplates allowing clients to experience the environmental repercussions of the behaviors they choose: A counselor's first concern is always the welfare of their client. However, in some circumstances, it can be appropriate and beneficial to allow clients to experiment with various behaviors and to learn from their experiences which are most effective. For example, a student who is struggling academically might be allowed to choose a method for preparing for a test that the counselor deems ineffective but that will restore the student's sense of control over his behaviors. If the student performs poorly on the test, it will be framed as useful information from the environment that can be considered when choosing future study behaviors.

Incorporating Physical Activity and Meditation

Glasser (1976) described running and meditation as the most common positive addictions, which induce a positive trancelike state that joins mind and body and allows for increased energy and creativity. While creating these beneficial results can take time and dedication to such activities, Glasser believed it was an important part of a client's total behavior system: acting, thinking, feeling, and physiology. Counselors may therefore want to educate their clients about such practices and incorporate them into treatment strategies.

Using Humor

Wubbolding (2003) wrote: "[T]o function fully as a human being, as a person who is in effective control who is characterized by positive symptoms, it is advantageous to have a sense of humor" (p. 268). Therefore, counselors can help their clients by laughing with them and bringing humor into the counseling session when appropriate.

Listening for Metaphors

Metaphors include analogies, symbols, and figures of speech that quantify experiences and make them manageable (Wubbolding, 1991). Metaphors can be used to put problems in perspective and help clients increase their sense of control. For example, a client who feels like he has a "monkey on his back" could be asked to describe what the monkey feels like, what it would take to get rid of the monkey, and how life would be different if he was not carrying the monkey on his back.

MULTICULTURAL AND DIVERSITY EFFECTIVENESS

Glasser believed that the five basic needs are universal and that choice theory and reality therapy can be used with individuals from any culture. Further, his rejection of external control psychology — the imposition of external constraints on individual actions by societal institutions and those in power—would seem consistent with the interests of those who have been subject to discrimination and exclusion from the mainstream culture. Further, Glasser's notion that each individual is capable of choosing effective behaviors to meet his needs is congruent with a focus on diversity and multicultural counseling because it suggests that persons of diverse backgrounds can overcome societal obstacles and enhance their welfare. However, in our view there are two obstacles to using reality therapy with persons of diverse backgrounds.

First, while there is an increasing literature on the use of choice theory and reality therapy with clients from diverse backgrounds, most of it involves suggestions for practice and case studies, not empirical research. Therefore, while we know that the principles of reality therapy *can* be used with diverse clients, we have less evidence as to whether it is truly effective in these contexts. For example, while Glasser (1998, 2000a) has provided numerous case studies in his books demonstrating effective clinical practice and has recently come to focus on satisfying relationships as the cornerstone of mental health, when it comes to romantic relationships, he has focused mainly on the needs of heterosexual couples (Glasser & Glasser, 2000). Therefore, it is unclear whether the extensive body of clinical successes he described in such volumes would translate to same-sex romantic relationships.

A second concern arises when applying the assumption of personal responsibility for choosing effective behaviors to those who have faced systematic discrimination. In one respect, such a philosophy represents an optimistic belief that no matter how many obstacles one encounters, it is possible to overcome them and lead a rewarding and need-satisfying life. And it should be noted that Glasser has consistently called for abolishing mechanisms of external control, which he views as counterproductive and harmful, throughout society. However, Brickman (1982) noted some of the drawbacks with counseling theories that assume clients are not responsible for their problems but are responsible for their "cure." This "compensatory" model has been applied in other areas of society, such as the modern civil rights movements, whose leaders have told members of ethnic minority groups they are not responsible for their circumstances but they are responsible for doing something about them.

The advantage of a compensatory model, which describes the practice of reality therapy with persons from diverse groups in our view, is that it allows people to direct their energy outward and not spend time in self-blame for their circumstances. It also has the potential to garner respect from the larger society, as members of such a group are seen not as "complainers" but rather as "doers" (Brickman, 1982).

The potential deficiency of such a model is that members of groups who are constantly compensating for external barriers can become discouraged and even hostile toward and suspicious of the culture at large. In fact, in the field of multicultural counseling, the term *healthy cultural paranoia* has been used to describe the naturally suspicious attitudes of those who have been oppressed toward their oppressors. With respect to the practice of reality therapy, therefore, a counselor might have a great deal to offer a client experiencing oppression by expressing a belief in the client's ability to overcome such barriers, but he should also guard against overlooking the potential discouragement, cynicism, and hostility that such an individual could experience from constantly having to overcome such obstacles.

Despite such potential limitations for clients from diverse backgrounds, those who practice reality therapy have devoted considerable effort to exploring its multicultural applications. For example, Wubbolding et al. (1998) endorsed the Essential Attributes of Culturally Skilled Counselors issued by the Association for Multicultural Counseling and Development. They further stressed the importance of adapting counselor interventions to the specific needs of each individual client. In other words, Wubbolding et al. believed that reality therapy should not be viewed as monolithic and should be adapted to meet the needs of people from diverse backgrounds. Counselors must be able to appreciate each client's worldview and to examine their own attitudes, knowledge, and skills in order to understand how different cultures impact the quality world of diverse individuals.

Sanchez (1998) noted that with respect to the integration of quality world and culture, "[C]ulture in the broadest sense provides the organizing values behind the pictures in our perceptual system of what our quality world should be" (pp. 13–14). In other words, each individual is embedded in a culture that to a large extent shapes perceptions of how basic needs are best met. A reality therapist must therefore understand each client's cultural context in order to help him choose effective behavior that will suffice to meet those needs.

Several authors have made suggestions for the practice of reality therapy with members of specific ethnic groups. For example, Moore (2001) described how reality therapy could be used to treat the substance abuse problems of African-American male adolescents. She noted that it is important to communicate that such persons are not responsible for negative societal forces; they are responsible for their reactions to them and the consequences of their actions. In using reality therapy, Moore recommended focusing attention on the possibility for future positive behavior, rather than past negative behavior, and allowing the adolescent to decide for himself which behaviors are most appropriate.

Cheong (2001) discussed how choice theory and reality therapy could be utilized in the Korean culture. For example, while individualism has been expanded in modern Korean culture, family relationships still maintain a central role, and therefore the central principle of choice theory that belongingness is essential applies very well. In contrast, the heavy reliance on direct questioning may not be a good fit with Korean culture and, in fact, could be offensive; Koreans' communication methods tend to be indirect, and nonverbal expression is often more important than what is said verbally. Cheong suggested that certain questions used by reality therapists can be reworded to be less direct. For example, "What are you looking for?" may be more appropriate than "What do you want?"

Sanchez and Thomas (1998) described how the Americans with Disabilities Act (ADA) can be interpreted as facilitating the attainment of basic needs for persons with disabilities. They pointed out that persons with disabilities often face unique challenges in meeting the five basic needs: survival, belonging, power, freedom, and fun. Various provision of the ADA, such as those protecting such individuals from discrimination and requiring ramps or elevators for those with mobility impairments in public buildings, can be viewed as helping such persons meet basic needs. Sanchez and Thomas noted how the disability rights movement was modeled after the civil rights movements of the 1960s and called on reality therapists to act as public advocates for persons with disabilities. In others words, to meet the needs of such clients, reality therapists would have to expand the scope of their role to include being an activist for public policy.

Applications of reality therapy to clients' religious and spiritual needs have also been suggested. Dettrick (2004) noted that reality therapy is not a Christian process but that its underlying assumptions are consistent with biblical principles. For example, he maintains that choice is a recurring theme in the Bible, as are suggestions that humans need to take responsibility for their behaviors and are capable of change. Consistent with the principles of choice theory, it is emphasized that the range of choices available depends on one's life experience and his creative ability to reorganize behaviors. Linnenberg (1997) also suggested that reality therapy and choice theory can be used to help clients connect with their spiritual needs for a higher power. In doing so, he suggested that reality therapists need to help clients examine their spiritual journey by asking them what they want from their relationship with God. While these authors wrote mainly about Judeo-Christian spiritual factors, we note that these basic ideas would be applicable for clients from other religious traditions as well.

PRIMARY APPLICATIONS

School Settings

William Glasser wrote several books describing how choice theory could be applied to educational settings, including *Schools Without Failure* (1968) and *Control Theory in the Classroom* (1986). Glasser believed that many, even most, students perform far below their ability because educational systems are by and large ruled by external psychology principles. According to Glasser (1998), this means that school professionals "adhere rigidly to the idea that what is taught in school is right and that those who won't learn it should be punished" (p. 237). Glasser labeled such ineffective practices *schooling*, which he thought emphasized mundane practices such as memorizing facts and drilling students in mathematical calculations rather the ability to think critically and apply knowledge to real-life situations. In Glasser's view, therefore, *schooling* entails two undesirable features: first, students are forced to acquire and memorize facts that have no value for anyone, and second, when students are forced to learn facts that may have some relevance in the real world, these facts are usually nowhere nearly important enough to justify flunking students out of school if they do not learn them.

Glasser believed that education is best defined as learning how to use knowledge, not necessarily acquiring it. He further thought that the ineffective practice of *schooling* interferes with a student's ability to use knowledge. In *Choice Theory* (1998), Glasser used the example of students in elementary school being forced to perform calculations over and over in school, beginning in the early grades. For example, students learn how to do addition and subtraction, and then memorize multiplication tables, and then learn long division. Glasser believed that in the real world, however, math boils down to just one thing: solving story problems, which means being able to analyze situations where numbers are involved to the point where simple calculations can be used to arrive at an answer. At this point, calculators are more efficient and accurate than humans ever will be, and Glasser believed it pointless to spend endless hours practicing calculations and little time solving story problems. Students, he believed, are far more likely to be motivated to apply themselves to solve real-world problems, where their higher intellect is needed, than to churn out one calculation after another.

Glasser (1968, 1986) did not just believe that *schooling* was a waste of time; he also believed that it was responsible for forcing promising young people out of the educational system and blocking off any possibility of their becoming productive citizens. *Schooling* forces students to memorize rote facts and punishes them if they do not perform. This, he believed, leads many students to be discouraged, and they ultimately give up on school early in life.

In order to understand the role of the school counselor in what Glasser referred to as "quality schools," we must return to the notion of need satisfaction and the notion that we each have pictures in our heads of quality worlds in which our needs are met. Unless students view schools as meeting their needs (i.e., unless schools are pictures they have in their quality worlds), they are unlikely to behave in school for any length of time. Such students are likely to be consistently disruptive, and according to Glasser (1986), the only effective ways to counsel such students are those that can lead to more effective need satisfaction.

A school counselor using reality therapy would ideally be working in what Glasser labeled a quality school. Quality schools are those in which external controls are replaced with the principles of choice theory. Of course, creating a quality school is quite complex and beyond the scope of this chapter. But in order to demonstrate something of what it means, Glasser (1998, p. 282) listed the following six principles as criteria for a quality school:

1. All disciplinary problems, not incidents, will be eliminated in 2 years. A significant drop should occur in the first year.
2. At the time the school becomes a quality school, achievement scores on state assessment tests should be improved over what was achieved in the past.
3. Glasser believed that in quality schools, only competent work should be accepted as satisfactory, something he referred to as "Total Learning Competency" or TLC. In other words, schools should not reward substandard school performance with passing grades, such as a C or D: a B is the minimum grade needed for passing. Students in quality schools will have to demonstrate competence to their teachers to get credit. All *schooling* will be eliminated and replaced by useful education.

4. All students will do some quality work each year—that is, work that is significantly beyond competence. This criterion gives hardworking students a chance to show they can excel.
5. All staff and students will be taught to use choice theory in their lives and in their work in school. Parents will be encouraged to participate in study groups to become familiar with choice theory.
6. It will be obvious by the end of the year that this is a joyful school.

Even if they do not work in quality schools, school counselors can still choose to use choice theory with challenging students (Richardson & Wubbolding, 2001). Such interventions will revolve around helping teachers and students understand that student misbehavior should be interpreted as ineffective attempts on the part of students to meet their needs or as effective behaviors that are being punished by an external control system. When working with students, the counselor does not seek to reinforce these external controls but rather helps them find more effective need satisfiers.

In order to demonstrate how this might be accomplished, we will use the example of Maria. She is a third-grade student referred by her teacher, Mr. Green, to her school counselor for talking in class and generally being disruptive throughout the day. While the teacher may simply want such behaviors to stop, a counselor using reality therapy would be seeking to first establish a relationship that is not based on external controls. In other words, the counselor would not attempt to threaten Maria or force her to alter her behaviors. Instead, he would attempt to find out what current needs are being met, and not met, when Maria acts disruptively and then attempt to help her choose more effective behaviors.

> **Maria:** I know Mr. Green is mad at me, but it's not my fault.
> **Counselor:** Mr. Green sent you to me, and I don't know what he's feeling, but I do know that I'm not mad at you, and I'd like to talk about what's going on.
> **Maria:** All the boys pick on me at recess.
> **Counselor:** I don't think I'd like recess very much if I felt like people were picking on me.
> **Maria:** No, I hate it. So that's why I try to get those boys in trouble after recess in class. I pass them notes, I throw things at them, and they get in trouble.
> **Counselor:** Sounds like you get in trouble, too.
> **Maria:** [Looks down] I guess, but I'm not going to let them get away with it.
> **Counselor:** I understand that, but I wonder if there is a way to make them stop that doesn't get you in trouble?

In this exchange, we can see that Maria is upset that she is getting bullied during recess, and her attempt to get back at her persecutors is causing the trouble with her teacher. Reality therapists believe that children are responsible for their choices and that each choice is the child's best attempt to meet his needs (Beck, 1997). Maria's counselor would avoid blaming her for her behavior, and he would work at helping her choose more effective behaviors that would end the recess taunting but not get her in trouble with her teacher. As we can see at the end of this example, the counselor is attempting to point out to Maria that her current behaviors are not effective and that it will be in her own interest to choose more effective ones.

Couples Counseling

Glasser believed that successful intimate relationships are essential to need satisfaction. In *Reality Therapy in Action*, Glasser (2000b) wrote: "[T]o satisfy every need, we have good relationships with other people. This means that satisfying the need for love and belonging is the key to satisfying the other four needs" (pp. 22–23). In his 1988 book *Using Reality Therapy*, Wubbolding noted that the application of reality therapy to couples and family counseling was in its early stages and that there existed no comprehensive models for its application. Since that time, Glasser wrote *Staying Together: The Control Theory Guide to a Lasting Marriage* (1995) and *Getting Together and Staying Together: Solving the Mystery of Marriage* (Glasser & Glasser, 2000) to describe how principles of choice theory could be used with married heterosexual couples. These books were written to show the general public how to apply principles of choice theory to their lives and in their marriages rather than to guide counselors in using reality therapy to work with couples. As was noted in the "Multicultural and Diversity Effectiveness" section of this chapter, Glasser did not write about romantic relationships between same-sex couples, which may limit the applicability of his approach to working with such clients.

Glasser (2000b) labeled his approach to marital counseling *structured reality therapy* and emphasized that the focus needed to be on what was good for the marriage rather than for each individual in the relationship. At the same time, Glasser believed it essential to make it clear that attempts to use external control psychology on the other partner would harm the relationship: Choice theory teaches that we can control only our own behavior. Instead, each member of the relationship was encouraged to focus on how to change his or her behaviors to make the relationship work better, assuming he or she was committed to saving it.

Reality couples therapy attempts to steer couples away from venting their feelings about their spouses and toward the realization that they can control only what they are doing in the relationship. Glasser (2000) emphasized that the role of the counselor was not to take sides in any disputes between the partners, but rather to be on the side of saving the marriage and to help each partner decide on behaviors that can contribute to improving it. In order to do this, each partner must understand the extent to which his or her own needs are being met in the relationship.

In *Getting Together and Staying Together: Solving the Mystery of Marriage* (2000), Glasser and his wife, Carleen, suggested that individuals vary in the importance they attach to each of the five needs that are a part of choice theory (survival, belonging, power, freedom, and fun) and that this can be an important determinant of the success of a marriage. Glasser and Glasser suggested that the strengths of these needs follow the famous "bell curve": Most of us have average-level need strengths, while a few people have either very high level or very low level strengths for some needs. Glasser and Glasser developed what they called the Need-Strength Profile to describe these needs. Individuals are asked to rate themselves between 1 and 5 for the strength of each need, with 1 representing a very low level of need strength and 5 representing a very high level. As noted, most individuals fall toward the middle of this scale.

While it is beyond the scope of this chapter to provide much detail about how the Need-Strength Profile can be used to evaluate the compatibility of two people, it is instructive to consider the types of problems that can develop in a relationship if the levels of a given need are incongruent. Glasser and Glasser noted that a marital relationship's prospects for survival are enhanced if both members have a high need for love, which they found to be central to human happiness. When one or both of the members of the relationship have a moderate or low-level need for love, they may be unwilling to invest the energy and commitment necessary for a long-lasting marriage.

The need for survival typically manifests itself as the degree of risk each member of the relationship is willing to take with important matters such as finances. Glasser and Glasser noted that those who have high survival needs and thus are careful with their money are sometimes attracted to "big spenders," who have lower needs for survival, because such individuals seem liberating and fun, but a mismatch on this dimension can often become a source of conflict in a long-term relationship. Glasser and Glasser also stated that high needs for power and control are among the greatest obstacles to successful romantic relationships and that people with lower needs for freedom are sometimes better prospects for successful romantic relationships. Finally, they noted that with respect to the fifth basic need, fun, a mismatch can be difficult for the person who has the higher need. He might constantly find himself trying to coax his partner to participate in whatever it is that he considers fun. Glasser and Glasser also described what they called the "specific search for fun"—in other words, a hobby or recreational activity that one enjoys. They pointed out that partners in a relationship who share such interests often have an easier time meeting this type of need.

As has been noted throughout this chapter, an essential tenet of choice theory is that needs are internally derived and difficult to change. Glasser therefore believed that in marital relationships it was important that the couple start out with similar levels of each of the five basic needs. However, Glasser and Glasser (2000) did not believe that it was impossible for couples to overcome differences in the strengths of their needs; they noted that it was to be expected that couples would not have the exact same need strengths.

In the following example, a reality therapist is working with a heterosexual married couple, Joan and Bob. During the first session, the counselor is introducing a basic tenet of reality therapy: that both members of the relationship need to understand that they can control only their own behavior and that the counselor will not take sides during the therapy. The counselor is on the side of the marriage. At the outset of this exchange, the counselor is attempting to help the couple understand this and to discern whether or not they are committed to saving the marriage.

> **Bob:** I really wish you'd tell Joan to get off my back—she's always after me about my long hours at work.
>
> **Counselor:** Let's remember my suggestion that we focus on what each of you can do to improve the marriage, not focus on what you think the other person should do differently.
>
> **Joan:** I'd love to improve the marriage, but I don't see how we can get anywhere with Bob and his temper—he gets angry so easily.
>
> **Counselor:** Joan, Bob, I think we need to revisit what we talked about at the beginning of this meeting: Do you both want to work to improve this marriage, or have you made up your mind to divorce? Because unless both of you are willing to work on the marriage, not each other, I can't really help you improve it.
>
> **Bob:** Yeah, I remember what you said. I'd really like to work it out if we can.
>
> **Joan:** I would, too, I guess. But I can't say I'm too optimistic at this point.
>
> **Counselor:** OK, let's start with that. Bob, is there anything you could do to improve the marriage?

Bob: Well, I know what Joan wants me to do: work less!

Counselor: I think it will be hard for you to feel more positively about the marriage by doing what you think Joan wants. Am I right?

Bob: Darn right!

Counselor: OK, then what could you do to improve the marriage?

Bob: Well, I'd like to have a little more fun in my life. I wouldn't mind arranging things at work to leave early if Joan and I could do something fun.

Counselor: Joan, how about you? What could you do to improve the marriage?

Joan: I wouldn't mind a little more happiness in my life either.

This vignette demonstrated that a counselor using reality therapy with a couple first establishes whether or not both members of the relationship want to commit to working on the marriage: Choice theory dictates that if the idea of being married to the other person is not part of one's quality world, no amount of counseling is likely to work. Once this commitment is established, at least tentatively, the counselor then focuses on teaching the members of the couple that they cannot control each other's behavior and must instead focus on what they can do to improve the marriage. Couples in reality therapy are encouraged not to vent their feelings about one another but rather to focus on specific actions that they can take. Toward the end of the vignette, the counselor introduces the idea of need satisfaction, particularly with respect to Bob wanting a little more fun in his life. Joan seems to agree on this point, and later in counseling, the Need-Strength Profile might be administered in an attempt to help Bob and Joan examine their compatibility on the other basic needs identified in choice theory.

Group Counseling

Glasser's efforts to make the principles of choice theory readily accessible to the public mean that he has focused on many alternative methods of communicating it besides individual counseling. In addition to formats such as workshops and public lectures, reality therapy is commonly practiced in groups. Many of the settings in which reality therapy is typically used, including school, workplace, and correctional settings, often have far more clients in need of counseling services than can be accommodated by a counselor working with clients individually. For this reason, and because groups provide a setting in which principles of choice theory can be reinforced by group members facing similar circumstances and concerns, group interventions are commonly used by reality therapists.

Many of the same general principles for practicing reality therapy with individuals are used in groups, particularly Wubbolding's (2000) WDEP system: W (wants), D (doing), E (evaluation), and P (plans). However, in group settings, after members are introduced to the principles of choice theory, they are asked to assist each other, and the group leader, in each stage of the process. For example, each member of the group might be given a set amount of time to talk about his quality world (wants) and the extent to which his needs are being met by his current behaviors (doing). This type of sharing from group members can be useful in creating a climate of trust and cooperation among the members. During this time, the group leader would be teaching members about the importance of the five basic needs; he would emphasize that it is current behaviors that should be focused on and that establishing close relationships is essential to successfully meeting one's needs. Groups, of course, are a very appropriate format for working on interpersonal relationships.

The evaluation and planning stages of Wubbolding's model can also be accomplished by groups because the leader has the perspective of all members to draw on in helping members evaluate the effectiveness of their current behaviors and decide on what new behaviors might be used to better meet their needs. Particularly once the group members have learned about the tenets of choice theory, they can be an invaluable resource for helping each other choose new behaviors. Since relationships are central to happiness in Glasser's approach, new behaviors could even be tested out in the group so that members are better able to decide whether to try them in other parts of their lives.

Work Settings

Glasser (1998) noted that work is central to adult life; it is where most people spend much of their waking time. Many counselors today work in such settings, usually in employee assistance programs (EAPs), and it is worthwhile to consider how reality therapy and choice theory apply to workplaces. It is no coincidence that Glasser focused on the application of choice theory in schools, work settings, and relationships, for he saw these as integral to the lives of most individuals. Just as in the schools, Glasser believed that far too many workplaces are dominated by external control psychology, in which managers become *bosses* who lead by instilling fear and pitting one worker against another. In such a climate, workers focus mainly on saving their jobs and use a "dog eat dog" mentality when relating to their coworkers. In Glasser's view, not only are such workplaces extremely unpleasant, but also they result in inferior work products and high costs of doing business.

Glasser (1998) described four key elements of "boss management":

1. Bosses set standards for the work to be done without consulting the workers. Any challenges to the bosses' authority are met with severe reprisals, including the loss of a worker's job.
2. A boss usually tells workers what needs to done, rather than demonstrating it, and rarely asks for input from workers as to how the work could be done better.
3. The boss, or someone the boss designates, evaluates the workers' performance, again without any input from the workers. Employees working in such a system focus only on what will get them passing marks in such an evaluation and not on what will truly improve the quality of their work.
4. When workers inevitably attempt to resist such external controls, the boss retaliates with additional threats and punishments designed to bring workers back into line. This vicious cycle creates a climate in which adversity is seen as the norm.

Glasser (1998) noted that "lead management is to boss management as choice theory is to external control psychology" (p. 289). Lead managers use choice theory in working with their supervisees and put the workers, their product, and the stockholders in their quality world. The following four elements of lead management contrast with those Glasser used to describe boss management:

1. Lead managers engage workers in an ongoing discussion of the quality and cost of the work they are doing and incorporate workers' suggestions as to how to improve quality and lower costs.

2. The lead manager, or someone designated by her or him, models the work to be done rather simply telling the workers what to do. Workers' input as to how to do the work better is considered.
3. Workers are responsible for monitoring the quality of their work, and it is understood that quality work is valued over cutting costs. Glasser believed that this expectation could be met only when there is a climate of trust between workers and supervisors, but if such trust was established, work quality would rise and costs would be lowered.
4. The lead manager continually emphasizes that the essence of quality is continued improvement.

The notion that human relationships are central to need satisfaction is just as important in workplaces as in other settings, and therefore counselors can use choice theory with both workers and supervisors to improve workplace settings. Just as in school settings, if an external control mentality dominates a business, a counselor will face an uphill struggle in helping workers improve the quality of their lives. Therefore, Glasser went to great lengths in his books and in his workshops and public appearances to argue for the importance of using choice theory in all facets of the workplace.

BRIEF THERAPY/MANAGED CARE EFFECTIVENESS

In their descriptions of reality therapy, Glasser (2000) and Wubbolding (2000) noted that reality therapy is essentially a short-term approach and can therefore be quite effective in settings where this is important. Managed care environments are one such example, but as noted in the previous sections, school, correctional institutions, and businesses have also embraced reality therapy because of the practicality and brevity of the approach. Watson and Buja (1997) suggested that reality therapy can be used in health care settings for physiological complaints. Recall that in choice theory, it is assumed that all components of clients' behavior—acting, thinking, feeling, and biology—are part of a total system, but that acting and thinking are more directly under our control than feeling and biology.

Kelsch (2002) wrote that choice theory could be effective in gaining control over multiple sclerosis (MS), for example. MS is a disease that attacks the central nervous system and is thought to have physiological, neurological, and psychological components. The physiological and feelings components associated with the disease cannot be dealt with directly, so patients must choose ways of acting and thinking that will help them meet their needs and ultimately improve their physiological health. For example, many people suffering from MS are forced to give up their jobs, which causes them to become more isolated from others and despondent. Kelsch wrote that the principle of choice theory suggests that instead a counselor could work with such a client to help him access supportive resources available under the Americans with Disabilities Act, which could be used to help him retain his job and thereby enhance his overall well-being.

One aspect of reality therapy that may limit its application to managed care environments is the rejection of the disease model and psychiatric diagnoses. Obviously, such ideas are an important part of the medical system, and diagnoses are used in determining whether psychological services are reimbursable under third-party payment systems. Glasser (2000) suggested that labels can be used as necessary for such purposes but that counselors should work to make sure that clients do not identify themselves with such labels.

INTEGRATING THE THEORY WITH OTHER APPROACHES

Reality therapy is often identified with the "third force" of existential/humanistic counseling theories, which includes the existential, person-centered, and gestalt models of counseling. Reality therapy can be viewed as consonant with these approaches, since it emphasizes human freedom, the establishment of an alliance between the counselor and the client, and the importance of understanding a client's phenomenological world. Reality therapy is distinct from these other approaches in its emphasis on personal responsibility and its practical approach to helping clients make the best choices possible to meet their needs and wants.

Both Glasser and Wubbolding noted that many of the core counseling skills identified by Carl Rogers, such as empathy, reflection, paraphrasing, and warmth, are necessary to form a solid therapeutic alliance in reality therapy. Both person-centered therapy and reality therapy suggest that humans have a fundamental need for connections with others and must also trust their internal experiences: Rogers emphasized the organismic valuing process, while reality therapy focuses on the five basic needs. However, the two approaches depart on the point of what is necessary for optimal psychological health: Rogers believed that unconditional acceptance from others "unlocks" the human potential for growth, thus obviating the need for further intervention. In contrast, reality therapists maintain that after identifying basic needs and wants, effective behaviors must still be chosen to satisfy such needs in the outside world.

Both existential counseling and reality therapy place a heavy emphasis on the client's personal freedom and responsibility for making choices about his life. Existential counselors believe that humans have a fundamental need to find meaning in life and have the freedom to orient their lives around this need. While Glasser did not identify meaning as one of the five basic needs of control theory, the needs for belonging, power, and freedom are consistent with existential practice.

Glasser (2000) noted that reality therapy is often classified as a cognitive therapy, and his approach is congruent with many of the tenets of Ellis's and Beck's cognitive theories. Control theory maintains that thinking is one of the activities that humans can control most readily, and cognitive theories have well-defined systems for changing cognitions.

In contrast, however, strictly behavioral systems of counseling represent a poorer fit with reality therapy, since these systems have opposite notions of where control lies in human behavior: Glasser thought humans are free to choose any behavior they wish, while behaviorists take the view that it is the environment that controls behavior. One point of similarity between these theories, however, is that client behaviors must be identified, quantified, and measured in order to lend themselves to counseling interventions.

It is difficult to imagine how reality therapy could be successfully integrated with counseling theories that emphasize unconscious processes, such as psychoanalysis, and the client's psychological history, such as Adlerian counseling. In fact, Glasser initially developed reality therapy in reaction to the fundamental principles of psychoanalysis, which he found to be ineffective in the settings where he worked.

Reality therapy may be appropriate to integrate with solution-focused counseling because of its emphasis on the client's innate ability to make choices and control how he meets his needs. In solution-focused counseling, one of the main techniques is finding exceptions—in other words, times where the client was successful in coping with a difficult situation. The idea is to focus on the positive exceptions and get the client to do more of whatever allowed for the exception. In a sense, this is similar to the reality therapy concept of never giving up. The solution-focused therapist never gives up looking for exceptions and strengths in the person, and the reality therapist never gives up trying to help the client find a way to satisfy his needs. Both are inherently optimistic about people's capabilities to choose and to get what they want.

RESEARCH

Reality therapy practitioners and scholars have historically focused on developing the theoretical and practical applications of choice theory rather than conducting empirical evaluations of the effectiveness of this approach. With that noted, however, empirical evidence for the effectiveness of reality therapy has started to emerge and is reasonably supportive of the approach. For example, Murphy (1997) reviewed the literature on the use of reality therapy in the schools from 1980 to 1995 and found six studies on its efficacy. However, while each of these studies found to one degree or another that reality therapy was effective, many lacked sufficient experimental rigor in such areas as participant recruitment, sample size, and adequacy of the measures used. Some of the positive effects noted in these studies after reality therapy was used with students were increased positive attitudes toward school, decreased disruptive behaviors, and increased self-esteem.

Radtke, Sapp, and Farrell (1997) also completed a meta-analysis of 21 reality therapy studies conducted in a variety of settings, including schools, correctional institutions, and treatment facilities. Meta-analysis allows for a numerical comparison of treatment gains across different studies using a common metric, called an *effect size*. None of the studies reviewed by Radtke et al. overlapped with those reviewed by Murphy (1997), although it was unclear from the article what criteria Radtke et al. used to include or exclude studies in their meta-analysis. They found across the studies reviewed a medium effect size, although this effect was not statistically significant. In other words, treatment differences were found across the studies, but this effect was not reliable enough to be statistically significant. This may have been due to the small number of studies used in the analysis. Similar to Murphy's meta-analysis, many of the studies were school-based, and the methodological rigor of the studies varied considerably.

In his book *Reality Therapy for the 21st Century*, Wubbolding (2000) reviewed numerous studies conducted on reality therapy, many of which were applied to persons from diverse ethnic backgrounds. While Wubbolding found general support for the effectiveness of reality therapy, many of the studies reviewed were case studies or applications of reality therapy principles in a single setting. Many of the studies also did not possess the highest levels of empirical rigor, and the *International Journal of Reality Therapy* was the scholarly outlet for many. While the latter point is not necessarily problematic, the publication of such studies in outlets not specifically identified with reality therapy would provide more evidence for the objectivity of these findings. Wubbolding called for more research into the effectiveness of reality therapy, which he noted has increased in recent years. Perhaps one of the more important items on the research agenda for future years should be comprehensive studies of the effectiveness of reality therapy using tight experimental controls (Sansone, 1998).

SAMPLE RESEARCH: The effect of a reality therapy program on the responsibility for elementary schoolchildren in Korea

Goals of the Research

Kim (2002) evaluated a Responsible Behavior Choice Program (RBCP) for elementary schoolchildren in South Korea. In this program, students are taught to take responsibility for their behaviors as a basis for taking effective control over their lives.

Participants

The RBCP was taught in a small-group format to 12 students who were randomly assigned to participate in the group, while 13 other children were randomly assigned to serve as a control group.

Methods

Students in the experimental group met for eight sessions and, using a variety of group activities, covered such topics as identifying needs and wants, clarifying their quality world, finding happiness, and taking responsibility for their actions. The experimenters gave students in both the experimental and the control groups a measure of internal locus of control, assessing whether they made internal attributions for the things that happened to them, and a measure of social responsibility as both pre-tests and post-tests.

Results

The researchers found that students in the experimental group increased their scores on both measures more than students in the control group, thus providing some evidence for the utility of this intervention.

Implications of the Research

Given its lack of empirical rigor, this study provided only preliminary evidence at best for the effectiveness of the RBCP. For example, while the students were randomly assigned to the experimental and control groups, it was not clear whether the improved scores had to do with reality therapy principles or the extra attention members in the experimental group received compared to those in the control group. In addition, the study used a small sample size and was conducted in only one school; it is therefore difficult to know how these results would generalize to other students in other settings.

EVALUATION OF REALITY THERAPY

Reality therapy is a practical, optimistic, and theoretically grounded approach to working with clients in a variety of settings. The notion that humans are capable of choosing effective behaviors to meet their needs is in our view a productive and proactive approach to counseling, particularly for counselors working with higher-functioning clients in educational settings such as schools and colleges. We tend to agree with William Glasser's notion that at times the mental health field has overemphasized external control of individual behavior, whether it be Freud's ideas of unconscious psychological conflict or more recent biochemical models of brain functioning. Placing the responsibility for choosing new behaviors with the client may allow some individuals to overcome persistent patterns of ineffective behaviors and feelings of hopelessness about the future.

However, we do believe that there can be utility in recognizing external factors that impact human behavior, and this may at times be downplayed in the practice of reality therapy. For example, studies investigating a gene for alcoholism and chemical imbalances in the brain that lead to schizophrenia were welcomed by persons afflicted with these disorders because they had previously been "blamed" for their circumstances. Earlier in the last century, chemical dependence was seen as a moral failure, and such persons were generally regarded as weak and lacking in virtue. Parents, particularly mothers, were also "blamed" for being ineffective or failing to provide proper warmth when their children displayed schizophrenia. Evidence for biological causation lifted at least some of the stigma attached to these disorders and in many cases allowed their victims to seek proper treatment. Therefore, any approach to counseling that places responsibility for change squarely on the shoulders of clients runs the risk of at least implicitly blaming the victim.

Glasser did go to great lengths in his writing, teaching, and public speaking to acknowledge that it is the systems of external control, not the individuals living within them, that are largely responsible for much of human misery. And a significant portion of Glasser's life has been devoted to changing such systems in order to give individuals the freedom and responsibility to be productive members of society. However, in our view, counselors seeking to apply reality therapy principles in settings that still operate according to external control psychology principles face a complex task in helping clients choose effective behaviors while still acknowledging the limitations and oppression that can exist in such systems.

Reality therapy has been used throughout the world, and numerous articles have been written about how to adapt it to the cultural values of different societies. Nevertheless, limitations still exist in using reality therapy with members of historically oppressed groups. Given that reality therapy does not fully address social influences on individual behavior, placing responsibility for finding effective behaviors that will meet clients' needs seems particularly problematic for those contending with systematic discrimination. Such persons may have drastically reduced options for choosing alternative behaviors compared to persons who do not face such barriers. For example, in the United States, African Americans and Latinos have sometimes been unfavorably compared to Asian Americans (sometimes called a "model minority") in terms of their educational progress and economic prosperity. It is certainly desirable that all members of society increase their level of education. However, it also important to recognize that all members of society do not have equal access to such resources and that some groups have faced unique obstacles and barriers to success in this and other cultures that can restrict the range of desirable choices open to them.

A similar potential limitation of reality therapy pertains to victims of abuse and trauma, including rape survivors, political refugees, and survivors of natural disasters. Reality therapy's emphasis on actions, rather than feelings, would seem ill-suited to such clients, who may have a need to talk about their feelings at length with a counselor rather than changing any of their actions.

Perhaps most controversial among Glasser's views is his idea that manifestations of psychological disorders are, in fact, behaviors that we choose. In the case of depression, for example, Glasser thought that clients made a "choice to depress"; they did not have depression. We believe that in this provocative view Glasser may have been attempting to act as a gadfly for mental health professionals overly comfortable with traditional diagnostic labeling systems. It seems to us entirely appropriate to question the validity of such systems, but given scientific evidence for biological factors for many disorders in the *DSM*, it seems premature to discount the lack of control clients may have over such conditions. Wubbolding (2003) seems to take a somewhat more nuanced position in his writing by pointing out that the diagnostic labels in the *DSM* should not necessarily be rejected but also should not be accepted as fixed properties of the client.

The concrete principles and ideas of reality therapy can be viewed as both potential strengths and potential weaknesses of this approach. In our view, the emphasis that reality therapy practitioners have placed on making their approach understandable to the layperson and on effectively training individuals in the principles of choice theory is a benefit to both counselors and their clients. Because reality therapists have placed such a strong emphasis on teaching choice theory to clients, organizations, and the public, they have had a strong impact on educational, business, and correctional settings eager to incorporate their ideas.

Glasser (2000a) noted that while the overarching ideas of reality therapy are easy to understand, putting them into practice can actually be complex. In our view, reality therapy is still vulnerable to the charge that it oversimplifies much of human behavior. For example, the notion of total behaviors—that all of our actions, thoughts, feelings, and physiology can be viewed as an integrated system of behavior—does not have extensive empirical support. While control theory attempts to describe how the human mind organizes all of our activities for purposeful action, brain researchers have not been able to identify any central "control system" in the brain that integrates all these functions. Indeed, it seems that the more we understand the brain, the more localized its activities appear to be. Visual stimuli are processed in one part of the brain, while smell and other sensations are processed in other areas. While we experience our consciousness as singular and uniquely "us," we have yet to discover how the brain does this.

Such concerns underscore an additional limitation of reality therapy: the lack of an empirical research base. While empirical research evaluating various propositions of reality therapy and control theory is starting to accumulate, few rigorous studies of the overall approach have been conducted. This remains a concern in the counseling field, where empirical validation of counseling approaches continues to be important.

Questions and Learning Activities

These Questions and activities are designed to stimulate your thinking about this theory and to help you apply some of the ideas to your own life and experience. If possible, you should work with a small group. Getting others' points of view and sharing your own ideas and perspectives will be invaluable as a way to help you evaluate this theory and its applications.

Personal Application Questions

1. Do you believe that individuals are responsible for their own problems and can choose effective behaviors to better meet their needs? How does this notion apply to individuals who face systematic discrimination, such as women, ethnic minorities, or lesbian, gay, bisexual, or transgendered persons?

2. Glasser viewed a lack of satisfying relationships as the core reason for psychological distress. In your view, is such a belief warranted, or can you think of exceptions?

3. In perhaps the most controversial part of his theory, Glasser refused to accept the notion of mental disorders and labeled such conditions with verbs, rather than nouns, to highlight the fact that we choose these behaviors. For example, we are not depressed; we are depressing. What is your reaction to this idea?

4. Glasser believed that institutions such as schools and businesses rely far too much on external control systems and could be better built around giving individuals the freedom to meet their needs. In your view, would such organizations function better using choice theory as opposed to external control psychology?

5. Glasser and Wubbolding wrote about regressive and positive stages in mental health, in which either negative or positive symptoms are generated by the choices we make. Do you believe that we can characterize persons as exhibiting mainly regressive or positive stages of mental health, and are these choices actually under their control?

Learning Activities

Developing Your Quality World

Quality world refers to mental "photo albums" that we all have of need satisfiers. Take a few moments to think of each need identified by William Glasser—belonging, power, freedom, fun, and survival—and see what pictures or visual images come to mind. Make notes of your need satisfiers for your quality world, and discuss them with a partner or in a small group.

"What Are You Doing?"

This is perhaps the fundamental question asked in reality therapy. Consider your plans for today: What are you doing today? How will your activities meet your needs and wants? What wants and needs will go unmet? In a group of three to four people, share your answers to these questions, and provide each other feedback about behaviors you could choose today to get closer to your quality world.

Total Behavior

In the total behavior system, actions and thoughts are believed to be under more direct control than feelings and physiology. Identify a feeling or physiological condition you would like to change. How could altering your actions or thoughts accomplish this?

Positive Addictions

Glasser noted that positive addictions, such as physical exercise and mediation, are self-reinforcing and help us to live creative and energetic lives. Are there examples of positive addictions in your life? List one such example and identify how it meets some or all of the five basic needs identified by Glasser.

Companion Website

Now go to the Companion Website at www.prenhall.com/archer to assess your understanding of chapter content with multiple-choice and essay questions, and broaden your knowledge with related Web resources and additional print resources.

CHAPTER 8

Behavior Therapy

VOICES FROM THE FIELD: COUNSELOR AND CLIENT REACTIONS

Yes, it works for me.

Client: I really liked working with Dr. BT. I was afraid that we would spend a lot of time hashing over my past and blaming my Mom for everything, but we didn't. Instead, we got right to a discussion of what was causing me to feel so bad, and we were able to set up some concrete ways I could work toward making my situation better. At first, I didn't like the idea of doing homework, but as Dr. BT explained to me, the changes would have to occur in my real life, not in the therapy sessions. I learned a lot just during the first week when I started keeping track of all of the details and situations when I feel anxious.

Counselor Trainee: Finally, I have found a therapy that seems to work for me. I know that you have to establish a rapport, but if you don't really get down to the specific problem behaviors, how can you help someone? I really like helping someone figure out what she wants to change and how to do it. I loved experimental and behavior analysis psychology, and this seems like a logical extension. I feel like I am really offering my clients something, and I love all of the behavioral techniques that are researched and available to use.

No, it doesn't work for me.

Client: Dr. BT was a nice woman, but I didn't really feel like she understood what I was going through. She asked a lot of questions and seemed to think that I could work out my problems just by changing some things I do and learning how to relax. I don't think she really understood what was going on inside of me. Counseling wasn't at all what I expected. I thought I would have a chance to figure out how my past has gotten me into this situation and to talk about changing my philosophy of life so that I can be a happier person. And I really didn't like all of that homework. I just couldn't remember to write all of those things down, and I didn't really see the value of it.

Counselor Trainee: I really don't feel comfortable with behavior therapy. It seems so superficial. If you help a person change one behavior, won't the problem just crop up somewhere else? If you can't help a person really find some meaning and direction in his life, what good is counseling? I went through the whole relaxation, desensitization thing with one of my clients, trying to help her get over an anxiety reaction to going out on dates. After several sessions of trying this, she finally told me that she just didn't feel that she was a worthwhile person and that she was anxious because she didn't want any of her dates to find out that there wasn't really anything behind her façade.

Arnie is a 70-year-old man who recently retired from a position as an insurance adjuster. He has come to counseling because he has been diagnosed with diabetes and he wants to stop eating and drinking so much.

Counselor: Arnie, tell me about the last time you had too much to eat or drink.

Arnie: Well, it happens just about every day. In the afternoon, I usually have a few beers, and then I start snacking on anything in sight until my wife comes home and fixes dinner.

Counselor: Do you think snacking is connected to having a few beers?

Arnie: I suppose so. When I'm hanging around the house, I just seem to get the urge to go to the fridge and have a beer.

Counselor: So feeling bored seems to trigger your wanting a drink.

Arnie: I don't know exactly. I guess you could say that.

Counselor: And what does it feel like when you have a few beers and snacks?

Arnie: Well, it feels good, but then I start to feel guilty.

As the term implies, *behavior therapy* focuses on behavior. It is characterized by a reliance on learning theory principles applied to human behavior in a scientific manner. The underlying assumption is that human behavior is governed by a set of laws or principles, and the therapist's primary role is to help clients apply these laws to change problematic behavior(s) or to add new behavior(s) to their repertoire. In its early, more radical form, little attention was paid to cognitive processes. Later, behavior therapy was integrated with cognitive therapy and became more complex. In the example above, Arnie's counselor is exploring the situations that trigger his drinking and eating behavior and also trying to determine what rewards Arnie gets out of drinking and eating. Since the counselor is using a behavioral approach, we can guess that the focus will remain on Arnie's problem behaviors and will probably also address his boredom by trying to build new behaviors that might substitute for eating and drinking.

HISTORICAL BACKGROUND

Historical Context

When behavior therapy began to emerge in the 1950s as a viable therapeutic modality, psychoanalysis was still the dominant force in counseling and psychotherapy. However, as the need for different kinds of counseling emerged, various kinds of alternative approaches developed. Many regarded classical analysis as a long, unfocused approach, accessible only to those wealthy enough to afford years of extensive therapy. Most theorists in this era, including behavior therapists, were trained as analysts and developed their own approaches because of varying degrees of dissatisfaction with the analytic approach.

Behavior therapy became more popular and more widely used in the 1960s and 1970s, partly as a result of a need for more specific approaches to deal with all kinds of societal problems and needs. Schools, juvenile justice systems, alcohol and substance abuse programs, businesses, and a multitude of other societal institutions were fertile ground for the application of behavior therapy principles. Growing confidence in science and in the empirical approach embodied in the booming industrial society of post–World War II America led to a kind of optimism that a scientific model of behavior could be applied to human beings.

Development of the Theory

Although behavior therapy had its roots in the early learning research of Ivan Pavlov, John Watson, and E. L. Thorndike in the late nineteenth and early twentieth centuries, it wasn't until the mid–twentieth century that the application of learning principles to therapy began to take hold. The early behavior therapists took the view that changing behavior was dependent on modifying conditions in the person's environment, a radical departure from the then-popular psychoanalytic theory, which emphasized a rather complex formulation of the mind and its inner workings.

Early behavioral research and theory emphasized conditioning, counterconditioning and reinforcement as the most important aspects of learning. These are usually called classical and operant conditioning, respectively. Early counseling applications of these learning theories involved methods to decrease anxiety through counterconditioning and a variety of methods to help clients manage behavior by changing antecedent conditions and reinforcements (these terms will be discussed in detail later in the chapter). There was a strong emphasis on identifying and defining specific conditions and behaviors, with no emphasis on discussing inner cognitive processes that might be affecting behavior.

One of the strongest criticisms of early behavior therapy was aimed at the notion that there was no room for considering internal processes. Albert Bandura's research on social learning theory added a more complex dimension to learning theory and was a welcome addition to behavior therapy because there was more of an emphasis on internal processes associated with learning. Research by Bandura, including the influence of role-modeling (the idea that people learned things just by watching others), brought a greater emphasis on the importance of cognitive processes in learning. In order for us to learn from role models, for example, we must selectively attend to events in our environment. The last decades of the twentieth century saw a kind of convergence of the behavioral and cognitive approaches into a more integrative cognitive-behavioral approach.

Three stages of development can be identified for behavior therapy. Each stage corresponds with historical developments in learning theory and with specific techniques that will be discussed in more detail later. Stage one might be called the *conditioning approaches* stage and is most closely associated with Joseph Wolpe (1958, 1990). Stage two, which could be labeled *self-management approaches*, represents an integration of operant conditioning and social learning theories with classical conditioning approaches. This stage is associated with several theorists including B. F. Skinner (1971) and Albert Bandura (1969, 1986, 1997). The third stage might be called the *integration* stage because cognitive and behavioral approaches essentially merged into what is now called cognitive-behavioral therapy. We will discuss a number of these integrative cognitive-behavioral approaches in Chapter 9, which covers cognitive approaches. Each of these stages will be discussed in this chapter.

ASSUMPTIONS AND CORE CONCEPTS

View of Human Nature

Human Behavior Is Governed by Basic Learning Principles   The most basic assumption underlying behavior therapy is that the scientific study of learning theory can explain human behavior. Human behavior, although complex, can be understood and studied, and the principles that govern all animal behavior also govern human behavior. The way that humans learn is viewed somewhat differently in the various theories of learning, but the basic assumption that behavior is based on observable principles applies. Even with the addition of cognitive approaches to behavioral approaches, and the attendant realization that behavior is mediated by thinking, the underlying assumption that this occurs according to some set of principles remains. The growing attempt to understand the brain and its specific functions might be seen as an attempt to discover the biochemical principles on which behavior is based.

Humans Are Neither Good nor Evil; They React to Their Environment Humans are neither inherently good nor inherently bad. They have evolved, as have other species, with the motivation to survive. They adapt to a particular environment in order to survive and to maximize their levels of comfort and satisfaction. This adaptation involves many social behaviors, and humans must have the ability to operate successfully within a social context.

All People Are Capable of Modifying Behaviors Under the Right Circumstances Human behavior can be changed, and humans are capable of developing new behaviors throughout their life span. Although physical or intellectual limitations do exist, there is still great potential for change and modification.

Core Concepts

The basic principles of behavior therapy can best be described by examining the work of three men—Joseph Wolpe, B. F. Skinner, and Albert Bandura—and their contributions to the application of learning theory to behavior therapy. Each of them has had a profound influence on psychology and on the evolution of behavior therapy.

Joseph Wolpe and Classical Conditioning Joseph Wolpe (1915–1997) might be called the father of behavior therapy. His approach was based on classical conditioning, a model developed by Ivan Pavlov and other learning theory researchers. Wolpe's book *Psychotherapy by Reciprocal Inhibition* (1958) was clearly a major force in the beginning of behavior therapy. Also, his book *The Practice of Behavior Therapy* (1990) was published in four editions and is a classic in the behavior therapy literature. Wolpe was born in South Africa and attended college there. He became a psychiatrist and was drawn to Freud's theory initially. As a medical officer during World War II, he worked in a military hospital, treating what are now called post-traumatic stress disorder victims. He and his colleagues attempted to use drug treatments but were generally unsuccessful.

After the war, having become more interested in learning theory than psychoanalysis, he began experimenting with animals. From his experiments with cats, he developed the basis for the counterconditioning methods used in behavior therapy. Wolpe collaborated with colleagues at the University of Witwatersrand, notably Arnold Lazarus, in applying these counterconditioning principles to humans, and with the publication of his 1958 book, his work spread rapidly. He then moved his research program to the United States and remained there until his death in 1997. He received many awards and accolades, including the American Psychological Association's 1979 award for distinguished scientific contributions.

Pavlov's classic study of dogs and the way in which they learned to salivate set the stage for the basic classical conditioning paradigm used by Wolpe. Pavlov observed that dogs automatically salivated at the sight of food, a response that is "hardwired" into many animals to facilitate digestion. The food is the *unconditioned stimulus* (UCS) and the behavior of salivation an *unconditioned response* (UCR). The terms *UCS* and *UCR* can be applied to any event that automatically triggers a behavior.

.   Pavlov observed that when he presented (paired) some other stimulus like a sound with the UCS, over time this new stimulus produced the same response (salivation) as the UCS. The new stimulus is called a *conditioned stimulus* (CS). When a behavior, such as salivation, is elicited through this type of learning, it is labeled a *conditioned response* (CR). So when a dog salivates after smelling a juicy steak, we can refer to the steak as the UCS and its salivation as a UCR. However, if we continually ring a bell every time we place the steak in front of the dog and the dog eventually learns to salivate after hearing a bell, even if the steak is not presented, we would refer to the bell as the CS and the salivation as a CR.

John Watson is considered a pioneer of behavior therapy, and in the early 1900s, as a faculty member at Harvard, he experimented with applying this kind of learning to humans. In his famous "Little Albert" studies, he conditioned a young child to experience fear at the sight of a white lab rat by surprising the child with a loud sound every time the child came near the rat. While such an experiment would be considered unethical today and many have questioned the scientific rigor he used in these studies, he was nevertheless quite effective in popularizing ways in which such methods could be used with humans.

Wolpe used cats to demonstrate how learned associations such as Little Albert's fear of rats could be "unlearned," something he labeled *counterconditioning*. This involved mildly shocking cats in particular surroundings and during specific sounds, thereby conditioning the cats to associate these surroundings and sounds with fear—much like Pavlov's dogs and Little Albert were conditioned. Wolpe, however, was able to get the cats to unlearn the fear they associated with these sounds and surroundings when he later replaced the shocks with food in the presence of the same sounds and surroundings. This counterconditioning paradigm was the beginning of early behavior therapy.

For Wolpe's cats, food was used to countercondition the fear that had been paired with shock, and for humans, in systematic desensitization, relaxation is used to countercondition anxiety that has been paired with different stimuli. Relaxation is paired with whatever stimulus creates anxiety for the client (fear of tests, airplanes, elevators, parties, etc.). If she is counterconditioned to feel relaxed, then the anxiety is inhibited. This counterconditioning occurs because we can't experience the physiological aspects of anxiety (increased heart rate, faster breathing, higher blood pressure, etc.) and, at the same time, feel relaxed. Systematic desensitization and several other specific behavior therapy techniques using counterconditioning will be described later in the "Therapeutic Techniques" section.

B. F. Skinner and Operant (Instrumental) Conditioning B. F. Skinner (1904–1990) is best known for *operant* or *instrumental conditioning*. Skinner was born in a small Pennsylvania town, and he loved the outdoors and school. He was somewhat of a misfit at Hamilton College. He didn't fit into the fraternity/football culture, he wrote critical articles about the school in the school newspaper, and he identified himself an atheist (Hamilton College was church-related at the time). He wanted a literary career writing fiction and poetry, but after little success in this endeavor, he returned to school at Harvard. He was strongly influenced by Bertrand Russell, Watson, and Pavlov and began to do research in psychology. After teaching at the University of Minnesota and Indiana University, he returned to Harvard in 1948 and remained there for the rest of his career. His most famous experiments involved the Skinner box, where he held animals in a controlled environment and gave them food pellets to reward and shape their behavior.

Skinner was a tireless crusader for his form of behaviorism, and his controversial book *Walden II* (1948, 1976), described an ideal society set up on behavioral principles. He responded to the criticism with another book, *Beyond Freedom and Dignity* (1971), in which he continued to argue the importance of rewards as the driving force of society.

Operant conditioning includes a number of important concepts:

Positive reinforcement. This is a stimulus after a behavior that increases the probability of that behavior in the future. For example, a child receives a cookie whenever she sits and reads a book. She is therefore more likely to carry out this set of behaviors in the future. Reinforcements can be basic things like food, drink, sex, or a hug, or they can be verbal phrases like "good job" or "excellent work."

Negative reinforcement. Negative reinforcement involves the removal of an unpleasant consequence in order to reinforce/produce a behavior. For example, a student is constantly harassed by his friends because he does not play football with them. When he finally plays football with them, the harassment (negative reinforcement) stops, thereby reinforcing the behavior of playing football.

Punishment. This occurs when a negative stimulus follows a behavior and decreases the likelihood that the behavior will occur in the future. For example, a husband leaves his clothes on the floor, and his wife gets angry and verbally chastises him. The probability that he will leave his clothes on the floor is decreased because of the aversive stimulus (punishment).

Reinforcement schedules. These schedules determine the rate or ratio of reinforcement. The schedule of reinforcement that is most effective for maintaining a behavior is a variable (intermittent) schedule, where the reinforcement comes randomly. Gambling on a slot machine is a perfect example. A person who plays the slots wins periodically (a random intermittent schedule), and it is difficult to extinguish this behavior (at least until the person runs out of money).

Extinction. This refers to the gradual elimination of behaviors that are no longer reinforced. For example, if a child is initially reinforced for cleaning up her room with an allowance payment, this behavior may eventually extinguish if the child stops receiving the allowance. Extinguishing behaviors like smoking, where a physical or psychological addiction is present, can be very difficult.

Shaping. This refers to reinforcing some ultimate desired behavior by starting with a behavior that is similar to the one that one wants to reinforce. This is the most effective way to develop new behaviors. For example, a teenager's parents are trying to get him to do his homework instead of watching TV. They start shaping by rewarding him whenever he is in his room without the TV on. Then they reward him when he is reading something. And finally, they reward him when he takes out a schoolbook. This approach is probably easier with young children or animals.

Token economies. Token economies involve tokens (sometimes called secondary reinforcers) that are given as rewards and can then be used to buy or trade for items that an individual desires. Money can be considered a token. If you perform certain work tasks, you receive money that you can then trade for items that you desire. Other kinds of token economies are often used in institutional settings and in schools.

Stimulus control. Stimulus control involves narrowing the stimulus that might trigger a certain behavior so that this behavior is triggered only in certain circumstances. For example, in weight control programs, clients are often warned not to fill their kitchens or refrigerators with fattening snacks like cookies or ice cream. Keeping only healthy snacks will narrow the stimulus to eat to those items alone.

Albert Bandura and Social Learning Albert Bandura (1925–) was born in northern Alberta, Canada, and received his doctorate in psychology from the University of Iowa in 1952. He was stimulated by the intellectual ferment in psychology that he found at Iowa, and he moved to Stanford University as an assistant professor in 1953, where he is now a distinguished professor emeritus. His early work focused on the important role of modeling in learning, which refers to how one organism can learn behaviors by simply *watching* the behaviors of another rather than experiencing rewards and punishment themselves. He found that modeling could influence motivation and values and could help teach skills. This idea and his later research demonstrated that learning was more complex than was accounted for in the classical and operant conditioning models, and this had a strong influence on the entire field of psychology.

Bandura's books *Social Learning Theory* (1977) and *Social Foundations of Thought and Action: A Social Cognitive Theory* (1986) included theory and research indicating that internal processes like values, preferences, beliefs, self-awareness, and anticipations could affect learning and behavior. He suggested that perceptions and cognitions interacted with the environment to produce learning and self-directed behavior. In other words, people both created their environment and were products of that environment. His work helped pave the way for the acceptance of cognitive theories and their incorporation into what has become cognitive-behavioral therapy. His 1997 book, *Self-Efficacy*, further refined his ideas and expanded his work on self-efficacy (a person's confidence that she can produce a particular behavior). Dr. Bandura has won many awards, including the American Psychological Association's Distinguished Scientist award, and the American Psychological Society's William James Award, and he is considered one of the most prolific and influential psychologists of the twentieth century.

We will now examine some of the fundamentals of social learning.

OBSERVATIONAL LEARNING/MODELING. According to Bandura (1977, 1997), observational learning has four components. The learner must pay attention to and perceive the model, the behavior of the model must be remembered, the learner must have the physical skills to perform the modeled task, and the learner must be motivated to perform the behavior. Motivation can come from internal reinforcement, when the learner achieves a personal goal or expectation; from vicarious reinforcement, when the learner sees the model being reinforced for the behavior; or from the imagined promise of positive reinforcement.

Let's take the clinical example of Rodney, a young man who is very anxious about talking to women and who has come to counseling to get over this fear and to be able to start conversations. To use observational learning, the therapist must get Rodney to pay attention to and remember a particular positive modeling situation. For this example, he might have to observe a friend who talks easily to women, and remember what he saw. He must also have the social and verbal skills to interact, and he must be motivated. As you can see, the use of modeling in a therapeutic context will probably involve more than just modeling itself. In this case, it could involve skill building, perhaps anxiety management, and motivation building.

ROLE-PLAYING. Role-playing involves the client and the therapist taking on roles and interacting as if they were in a particular situation that is difficult for the client. The client might take the role of herself, or the therapist might play the client and the client might play another person in the client's life. In reality, role-playing involves learning based on all three major learning theories. It involves classical conditioning because often, when the client role-plays a difficult situation, her anxiety about the situation lessens as she pairs the comfort and safety of the role-play situation with the real situation. It can also involve operant learning in that the therapist is very likely to reinforce the client after she successfully plays a particular role. The client also learns by observing the interpersonal behavior of the therapist while playing her role.

SELF-EFFICACY. Self-efficacy can be defined as the person's perception of how well she can perform a particular behavior in a particular situation. She may have the skill to perform a particular task, but the chances of her doing it are greater if she has confidence in her ability. According to Bandura (1997), people develop self-efficacy in four ways: from previous success with the behavior, opportunities to observe models and experience doing a behavior vicariously, verbal persuasion from others, and lowered emotional arousal (anxiety), which allows the person to perform the behavior without being too anxious.

Imagine the case of a woman who comes to counseling because she is very anxious about getting AIDS. She is afraid to have sexual relationships because she knows that she might contract HIV. After the therapist and the client discuss the subject in some detail and the therapist ensures that the client understands the facts about AIDS and HIV transmission and the risks of various kinds of protection, the client decides that she would feel comfortable if her partners used a condom along with a virus-killing spermicide. She then reports that she has already tried to do this but that she just can't bring herself to discuss protection with potential partners ahead of time. She says that she knows what to say and is convinced that it needs to be done, but she just can't seem to get it out. If we examine this from a self-efficacy perspective, it appears that she does not have confidence in her ability to perform this set of behaviors.

In order to increase the client's sense of self-efficacy, the therapist must examine the four ways to develop self-efficacy. The first, and incidentally the most powerful, is previous performance success. In this case, she has not performed the behavior yet. The therapist may be able to help her recall instances where she was able to be assertive with men in sexual situations (perhaps saying no to sex or refusing particular sexual requests). The therapist may also verbally persuade her that she can perform the task, and the therapist may be able to help her develop ways to lessen her emotional arousal (in this case, it may be anxiety and sexual arousal combined) so that she can be more in control of what she wants to say. The therapist might also provide her with a training videotape in which a woman models a discussion of protection, or lacking this resource, the therapist might role-play a woman discussing protection well before a sexual encounter begins. Some discussion of the factors that seem to block her performing the behaviors (embarrassment, worry about being perceived as too forward, etc.) might also help decrease anxiety and persuade her to try the behavior. She might even be asked to role-play taking the initiative in a discussion of sexual protection with a male friend her own age with whom she is not romantically involved.

THERAPEUTIC RELATIONSHIP

Counselor's Role

One very common misconception about behavior therapy is that the therapist is a distant, cold figure, imposing various behavioral techniques on the client. Some even imagine that the therapist surreptitiously controls the client. In reality, behavior therapy requires a productive counseling relationship, and behavioral counselors are usually warm and understanding people.

The counselor's role is to provide expertise in behavioral assessment and the application of learning theory to behavior change. The counselor serves as an educator and guide but does not impose her goals on the client. The criticism that behaviorists control behavior is true in some situations, largely in institutions where token economies are set up to produce socially acceptable behavior. This most often occurs in criminal justice or inpatient facilities.

Counselor-Client Relationship

Although the behavior therapist is likely to be a warm and caring person, the nature of the relationship between client and counselor is one of expert and client. The counselor is the expert on using behavioral techniques, assessing the behaviors that need to be changed, and prescribing what methods are to be used. This is not to say that the counselor establishes the goals. The counselor and the client discuss the goals for counseling and mutually agree, but then the behavior therapist takes the initiative in developing assessment and intervention techniques. The techniques are not secret, however. In fact, a hallmark of behavior therapy has been the transparency of the methods. This is largely because the methods are straightforward, and the client must understand the methods in order to become an active participant.

Another aspect of the client-counselor relationship is significant. From a learning theory perspective, the relationship with the therapist can be a powerful reinforcer. If an effective relationship is formed, just gaining the approval of the therapist may be a great help in changing negative behavior and producing positive change. Behaviorists have suggested that verbal and nonverbal reinforcement is perhaps the most powerful influence of the therapeutic relationship.

ASSESSMENT, GOALS, AND PROCESS OF THERAPY

Assessment

One of the most important parts of behavior therapy is a careful assessment of behavior. A treatment plan and program cannot be developed unless this assessment has been made. The traditional psychopathological diagnostic categories of the *Diagnostic and Statistical Manual of Mental Disorder* (*DSM*—currently *DSM–IV*; there are periodic updates) are not typically part of this assessment, although in most settings and agencies, behavior therapists are required to complete a *DSM* diagnosis to comply with agency rules or to get insurance reimbursements. Formal assessment instruments, such as personality or psychopathology tests, are also typically not used, although behavior inventories in which the client or the client's parents or partner complete behavior frequency categories might be used. The Beck Depression Inventory (BDI–II) (Beck, Steer, & Brown, 1996) is an example of one such behavioral inventory. Checklists for parents, teachers, and peers are also used. For example, this is currently the most common way of assessing attention deficit hyperactivity disorder (ADHD). In addition, assessment techniques include observation of the client's in-session behavior and charting (in which the client records self-observations outside of the counseling sessions). Following are further explanations and examples of some of these assessment techniques.

Behavioral Interview In the basic interview, the therapist attempts to learn more about the problem and to help the client be as concrete as possible. This allows the therapist to gain an understanding of what behaviors or lack of behaviors are a problem and in what situations difficulties occur. The degree of severity, as well as the conditions that seem to trigger the problem behaviors or feelings related to the behavioral deficits, is explored. The thoughts and feelings related to the problem situation are examined, as are the relationships with peers and family members who seem to be involved. Although behavior therapists do not subscribe to the notion of an unconscious, this interview is designed to bring out all factors that might be relevant to the problem, and some of these factors may not be obvious to, or even understood by, the client. Here is a brief example of part of a behavioral interview with Manny, a 25-year-old Hispanic male.

See DVD

Chap. 8
Clip 1

Counselor: Manny, what brings you in for counseling?

Manny: My family has been worried about me. I seem to be really down a lot.

Counselor: What kind of worries do they have, Manny?

Manny: Well, you know Hispanic families are really close, and my mom can tell that things are not right.

Counselor: What does your mom see that makes her think things aren't right?

Manny: She sees that I am not happy and that I don't go out on weekends.

Counselor: It sounds like you might be feeling depressed. Can you tell me how often you feel really down and when it occurs?

Manny: I feel this way quite a bit, almost all the time on weekends.

Counselor: How does feeling depressed like this affect you? Does it keep you from doing things that you want to do?

Manny: Yes. I am not doing so well at work, and I tend to sleep a lot on weekends.

Counselor: How does it affect your work?

Manny: I can't seem to get very much done. My boss has been down on me lately.

Counselor: What kinds of things can't you get done?

This is just the beginning of a long interaction to help the therapist and the client define the problem more concretely. Note that the therapist does not avoid talking about the client's feelings and even defining the feeling of depression, but the emphasis is on learning more about the details of the behavior and the circumstances. Contemporary cognitive-behavioral therapists would also explore what the client is thinking. Applications of other assessment techniques that follow will illustrate more about how this case might be assessed.

Inventories and Ratings Behavioral inventories might also be used to learn more about behaviors related to the client's problems. In the example above, the Beck Depression Inventory (BDI–II) is a logical choice. It will provide the therapist with a quick assessment of the severity of the depression. A lethality assessment of suicide danger is always recommended when a client reports feeling depressed, and the BDI–II can provide valuable information.

Behavior ratings by family members, spouses, or peers can also be useful. People in the environment may be able to provide valuable insight into the behavior of the client. A behavior therapist may ask significant others in the client's environment to attend counseling sessions as part of the basic assessment. Note that since Manny is from a Hispanic family, gathering accurate information about the culture and environment will help the therapist become attuned to cultural factors. This, of course, would be with the client's consent. Here is an example of how that might work in our sample case.

Counselor: Manny, you mentioned that you are having a rough time on weekends. Since you live at home with your family, I wonder if you would mind if I talked with them to get a better idea of how they see what is going on with you. I don't want to force this on you, and if you are uncomfortable with doing this, we don't have to do it. You may, however, be able to learn some things about yourself by getting some more systematic observations from others.

Manny: Well . . . I don't know. My mom is really the one who is worried and who knows what is going on. My dad really doesn't believe in counseling. He thinks the family should solve its own problems, but my mom is different. I think she would be willing to come in and talk with you. Should she come in at the same time I do?

Counselor: Yes, that would be easier. But let's make sure that her coming in doesn't cause you any family problems. I think you need to make sure her coming in isn't a problem for your dad.

Manny: No, it won't be. He's already said that even though he doesn't think it will help, he is OK with counseling as long as he doesn't have to come.

Bringing in family members isn't always necessary or even a good idea, but they do have the potential for providing important information. In this assessment phase, the family member or significant other is there just to help with the assessment. Later on in counseling, it might be desirable for that person to participate in whatever interventions are decided on. Note that the therapist here is sensitive to family and cultural dynamics and possible resistance to counseling by asking about the father's reactions. It is also important to note here that in behavior therapy the therapist is open with the client about what is going on and why. As part of the approach, the therapist explains the rationale for whatever is going on in counseling and gives the client the opportunity to decide if he wants to proceed.

Personal Behavior Recording/Charting In order to get a clearer picture of the problem behaviors or lack of behaviors, frequency of problem situations, antecedent conditions, and consequences, clients are sometimes asked to keep a record or chart of the circumstances surrounding the reported problem. The format of the chart might depend on the type of assessment needed. It might consist of the client recording only the time and frequency of a certain behavior or feeling, or it might involve a more extensive recording of feelings, thoughts, and specific stimuli or reactions from others. Some clients gain insight and change behaviors just by keeping a record of certain activities for a week. For example, clients with time management problems often don't realize how they are spending their time, and when they see how much time they waste, they are sometimes surprised and motivated to make changes. In the case of Manny, the following kind of initial self-observation might be used.

Counselor: Manny, I wonder if you would be willing to keep a kind of diary for a week so that we can get more information on what is going on for you?

Manny: Do you mean I would have to write about my feelings at the end of the day?

Counselor: Well, that isn't a bad idea, but what I have in mind is much more specific. I would like you to jot down on this chart each time during the next week when you feel depressed. Indicate the time, location, who you are with, intensity of the experience, and what you do. Also, if you can, write down what you think might have triggered your depression. I have a kind of chart I will give you that will help you remember what to write down.

Manny: What do you mean by triggered?

Counselor: Well, for example, if you are watching TV and something you see seems to set off a kind of depressive cycle, write down what you saw. Or if someone says something to you that seems to trigger these feelings, mark that down. Don't worry if you can't identify the causes; just record as much as you can about the situation.

Manny: This seems like a lot to do. I'm not sure I can do it.

Counselor: Do the best you can. Just try it out. It will really be helpful to us if we can identify some patterns. This will be the first step toward setting some goals and working out a plan that will make you feel a lot better.

A good assessment is the foundation of successful behavior therapy. If the therapist cannot define a problem as a set of detailed and concrete behaviors or behavioral deficits and also sort out the related stimulus and response patterns, behavior therapy cannot proceed. It is sometimes easy for the beginning student to underestimate this aspect of behavior therapy because of the specific nature of the behavior therapy treatment options. Practice and skill in behavioral assessment are essential.

Goals

As we have discussed, in the more modern forms of behavior therapy, the earlier, almost exclusive focus on behavior has given way to a much greater inclusion of the domains of thinking, feeling, and behaving. It is still fair to say, however, that behavior is at the heart of behavior therapy. Since behavior is the most significant focus, the counselor and the client will agree on behavioral goals for therapy.

Let's examine the case of Manny discussed earlier. From the brief assessment examples, you can guess that the therapist is trying to identify some specific cues that lead to the depression. Later on, in the treatment planning part of this case, the therapist will attempt to help Manny identify behavioral goals that will help him feel less depressed and that will help him avoid situations where he feels depressed.

From the information we have so far, we can only guess at many possibilities. Manny may feel depressed when he is alone and feeling lonely. This could be a result of not being able to form relationships or perhaps of being too dependent on his parents (this could be a complicated acculturation issue, with Manny caught between his parents' cultural values and the dominant culture values he has accepted). Or it might be a result of inactivity and few interests. Or maybe his poor performance at work is triggering most of the depression, and the problem is related to difficulty in talking to those in authority or even in managing those who work for him. The importance of a thorough assessment becomes obvious as we consider all of the possibilities.

Process of Therapy

In classic behavior therapy, the process is fairly straightforward. An assessment is completed and the target behaviors are identified. The client and the therapist form some type of contract regarding these behaviors, and the therapist discusses treatment options. A treatment method is determined and a specific technique is applied. Insight into the causes of these behaviors is not something that the therapist typically spends a great deal of time on; the emphasis is on the present and on changing behaviors. For example, in behavior therapy, it would not be important for Manny to spend a lot of time exploring his childhood experiences so that he could understand why he is overly dependent on his parents. It would not be unusual, however, for a behavior therapist to ask some questions about his past, particularly in regard to how and when problem behaviors first started.

Spiegler and Guevremont (1998) and Kazdin (1994) have identified the following core characteristics of the practice of modern behavior therapy:

- The client is an active participant in therapy, and the treatment is action oriented.
- The counselor and the client develop goals together.
- The focus is on current behavior.
- The client is expected to work outside the session (homework).
- The therapist is an expert in behavioral principles/techniques.
- The client is fully informed about the purpose of and rationale for all treatment methods to be used.
- The therapy is often relatively brief.
- The treatment is based on the application of scientific learning theory principles.
- The treatment usually focuses on observable behaviors and situations.

THERAPEUTIC TECHNIQUES

Systematic Desensitization and Relaxation Methods

The first step in the desensitization process is to teach the client progressive deep muscle relaxation. Using this technique, which was developed by Jacobson (1938), the therapist asks the client to tighten and then relax various muscle groups and to focus on the sensation of relaxation as he relaxes the muscles. This heightened sense of relaxation as the muscles relax helps the client develop a kind of conditioned progressive relaxation response.

This relaxation response is then used to help decrease a person's anxiety by what is called *reciprocal inhibition*. In other words, one can't feel anxious and relaxed at the same time. One of the key elements of this technique involves what has become known as the mind-body connection. In this case, an individual's emotion, anxiety, is directly tied to body sensations (tense muscles, fast heart rate, sweating, etc.). When she feels anxious, she has the body sensations that go with it. The relaxation response works the same way; therefore, if the client begins to relax physically, she will also feel less anxious emotionally.

Originally, progressive deep muscle relaxation was primarily used with systematic desensitization, first developed by Wolpe (1958, 1990) from the classical conditioning paradigm described earlier. However, in the last several decades, it has become a primary component in many different stress management programs and is often used by itself in counseling just as a way to help clients who have a high level of stress and anxiety learn to relax. When it is used in this way, the client is taught the technique or some variation of it and asked to use it for 10–15 minutes twice a day. Meditation has also become a popular technique used as a counseling adjunct to produce a relaxation response. Benson (1975) did a series of studies in the 1970s demonstrating that what he called a *relaxation response* could be obtained in a variety of ways and could have positive emotional and physical effects.

When using a general relaxation technique, such as deep muscle relaxation, a major emphasis for the therapist must be on helping the client develop a plan to actually practice this particular homework. Archer (1991), in a stress management workbook, offered four suggestions for this plan: Create a satisfactory environment, practice at the same time every day, use social reinforcement, and expect different experiences. Literally hundreds of books and videotapes have been developed in the last 30 years to help clients and people in general learn stress management, and all of these have suggestions for ways to develop a successful relaxation technique.

Many relaxation scripts have been developed for therapists to use to teach deep muscle relaxation. All of these are based on the original scripts developed by Jacobson (1938) and Wolpe (1958). Counselors typically devise a script that works best for them and also tailor the script to particular clients. The role of suggestion appears to play an important part in the process, with the therapist often telling the client that she is feeling progressively more relaxed. It is not unusual for the client to feel some hesitancy when a counselor suggests this procedure. The client may experience considerable vulnerability with a focus on body muscles and the need to close her eyes and let down her defenses to relax. The client may also confuse deep muscle relaxation with hypnosis because hypnotic induction often follows a similar relaxation pattern.

Typical Relaxation Script

General Directions

Sit back quietly, relax, and breathe deeply. Begin to imagine that all the tension is slowly going out of your body. As you go through the progressive deep muscle relaxation, you will feel more relaxed each time you tighten and relax a specific muscle group. In order to develop a conditioned response, say the word "relax" to yourself every time you relax a muscle group. Keep your eyes closed and try to screen out any external noises or distractions. Begin with the muscles in your arms and shoulders.

Arms and Shoulders

1. Put your arms out in front of you and clench both fists (keep the muscles tensed for five to fifteen seconds). Note tension in your forearm and hand. Relax. Notice the difference between tension and relaxation. Repeat.
2. Now, put your arms out in front of you with palms up and bring your fingers up until you touch your shoulders. Notice the tension in your biceps and upper arms. Now relax. Notice the difference between tension and relaxation. Repeat.
3. Straighten and stretch out your arms with your fingers spread out and forward as far as possible. Note the tension in your upper arms and fingers. Relax. Notice the difference between tension and relaxation. Repeat. Remember to breathe deeply and notice how your body is getting more and more relaxed.

Face, Neck, and Shoulders

1. Wrinkle your forehead. Note the tension around your eyes, temples, and forehead. Relax. Notice the difference between tension and relaxation. Repeat.
2. Close your eyes tightly. Note tension around your eyes and temples. Relax. Notice the difference between tension and relaxation. Repeat.

(continued)

3. Press your tongue up on the roof of your mouth. Note tension in your mouth and jaw area. Relax. Notice the difference between tension and relaxation. Repeat.
4. Press your lips together tightly. Notice tension in the mouth and lower jaw. Relax. Notice the difference between tension and relaxation. Repeat.
5. Press your head back until you feel tension in your neck and shoulders. Relax. Notice the difference between tension and relaxation. Repeat.
6. Push your head forward, moving your chin down toward your chest until you feel tension in your throat and neck. Relax. Notice the difference between tension and relaxation. Repeat.
7. Shrug up your shoulders. Raise them until you feel tension in the shoulders and neck. Relax. Notice the difference between tension and relaxation. Repeat. (Remember to breathe deeply and notice that you are becoming progressively more relaxed.)

Chest, Stomach, and Lower Back

1. Arch your back, move away from your chair, and push your elbows back. Note tension all along your spine. Relax. Notice the difference between tension and relaxation. Repeat.
2. Take a deep breath and hold it. Notice the tension in your chest and stomach. Relax and exhale slowly. Notice the difference between tension and relaxation. Repeat.
3. Suck in your stomach and try to make it reach your spine. Notice the tension in your stomach and lower back. Relax. Notice the difference between tension and relaxation. Repeat.
4. Push your stomach out. Note the tension in your stomach and along your sides. Relax. Notice the difference between relaxation and tension. Repeat. (Remember to breathe deeply and notice how you are becoming very, very, relaxed.)

Hips, Thighs, Legs, and Feet

1. Tense your buttocks by lifting up. Note the tension in your buttocks, back, and upper legs. Relax. Notice the difference between tension and relaxation. Repeat.
2. Straighten your legs out so that your knees are stiff, your legs are up off the chair, and your toes point away from you. Note the tension in your legs, calves, upper feet, and knees. Relax. Notice the difference between tension and relaxation. Repeat.
3. Straighten your legs out so that your knees are stiff, your legs are up off the chair, and your toes are pointing toward you. Note tension in your legs, calves, ankles, and knees. Relax. Notice the difference between tension and relaxation. Repeat. (Keep breathing easily and deeply. You are becoming more and more relaxed.)

After you complete the muscle relaxation, take some time to enjoy the relaxed state. You may want to use a visualization to further deepen your relaxation. (Copyright 1991 from *Managing Anxiety and Stress* by J. Archer, pp. 48–50. Reproduced by permission of Routledge/Taylor Francis Group, LLC.)

After the client has learned the conditioned relaxation response, desensitization can proceed. First, the counselor helps the client create an anxiety hierarchy, which is a listing of scenes related to a particular situation that creates anxiety. The aim is to identify six to eight scenes that provide a range of anxiety levels, measured on a scale of 0 to 100 subjective units of stress or SUDs. Here is a dialogue in which a client, Janet, and her counselor are creating an anxiety hierarchy.

Counselor: Janet, now that we have established that you want to work on your fear of talking to your boss, I would like you to imagine some scenes related to that fear and rate the degree of anxiety and fear that you feel in each situation.

Janet: What do you mean by scenes?

Counselor: These are just situations when you can remember feeling very anxious about talking with your boss. For example, could one scene be when he calls you on the phone to come into his office?

Janet: Oh, yes! He doesn't do that very much, but when he does my stomach gets tied in a knot.

Counselor: OK, good. Let's use that one. On a scale of 0 to 100, with 100 being the absolute highest stress you feel around this issue, how would you rate this?

Janet: Oh, it's pretty high. I don't know, maybe about 90.

Counselor: Great! Now can you think of one that is in the lower ranges?

After the anxiety hierarchy is established, the counselor has the client produce the relaxation response (by this time, the client would have practiced at home and should be able to become very relaxed fairly easily). While the client is in a very relaxed state, the therapist asks the client to imagine the lowest-rated anxiety situation and to signal by raising a finger when she has the situation in mind and when she begins to feel any anxiety. When she signals that she feels some anxiety, the therapist reminds the client to relax and to go back into a deep state of relaxation. The idea is to pair the anxiety-producing stimuli with the relaxation response so that the anxiety is inhibited. It may take several tries with each item of the hierarchy before the client experiences no anxiety when imagining a particular sequence.

In Vivo Desensitization

In vivo desensitization occurs when the desensitization is done in the real-life situation. It may involve the therapist accompanying the client as she gradually approaches the feared situation. The therapist's role is to help the client produce the relaxation response in order to inhibit anxiety. A classic example of this is dealing with a fear of dogs. A therapist might first accompany a client to a place where a dog is penned in a yard. The first step might be just to come within 25 feet of the pen. Progressively, the therapist and the client would approach the dog, using the relaxation methods to inhibit fear, until finally the client can approach the dog and pet it. Of course, the therapist would want to use a friendly dog!

Since it is not usually practical for a therapist to accompany clients in vivo, the client can be instructed to work on the in vivo desensitization by himself or with a friend or relative who is willing to assist. In the dog example, this would probably require some rehearsal with the therapist. Then the client would use the learned relaxation progressively as she approached the dog pen. A friend or family member may also accompany a person in this kind of situation.

The use of relaxation by the client in the actual situation has been called *cue-controlled relaxation*. The client is taught the relaxation response and can then produce the relaxation on cue in any situation. The cue is often taking a deep breath. The relaxation training is similar, except there is an emphasis on being able to produce the response on cue in different situations. The following counseling segment with Janet, who was afraid to talk with her boss, shows how cue-controlled relaxation might be used for an in vivo desensitization.

Counselor: Now that you have learned to deeply relax and have practiced in different settings, including at work, do you think you are ready to try to use it in some conversations with your boss?

Janet: Well, I don't know. Do you think it will work?

Counselor: Well, you have really been diligent in practicing. I think it is going to work for you.

Janet: OK, I'll try it.

Counselor: Let's think of a situation with your boss that would be a good one to start with. . . something that would not be too difficult.

Janet: Well, I usually get nervous when I just pass him in the office and say "Hi." I guess I could try it just when I see him.

Counselor: That sounds like a good place to start. Later on we can get to the tougher stuff like your going into his office.

Note in this segment that the therapist creates a positive expectation and that the difficulty of the situations is graduated just as the imagined situations are in the anxiety hierarchy.

Virtual Reality Exposure Therapy

This approach is similar to in vivo desensitization, except the person encounters the phobic situation via a computer-generated scene. Again using the example of desensitization to dogs, the person would experience a virtual reality that gradually increases his exposure to dogs. The advantage to this approach is efficiency. The person can be desensitized in a computer lab right at the counselor's office. Biofeedback can also be used as part of the process to help the client learn to monitor and control her anxiety while experiencing the stimulus.

Assertiveness Training

Wolpe spawned an entire industry when he developed assertiveness training. It is safe to say that assertion training has become one of the most popular self-help techniques in the last 30 years. In 1978, Alberti and Emmons (1990) were the first to popularize the idea in a self-help book. Many others followed, and the idea of teaching women to become more assertive and speak up for themselves was a mainstay of the women's liberation movement during the later decades of the twentieth century.

Wolpe's original idea of assertiveness training was directly related to counterconditioning. People feel anxiety when they want to say something and don't or when they overreact and get angry and are out of control. However, an assertive response tends to counter the anxiety in a way that is somewhat similar to what happens in desensitization. For example, if a person is afraid to say no to her best friend and always goes along with what the friend wants to do, she feels anxious each time she wants to say no but doesn't. When she does respond in an assertive manner, the act of responding inhibits anxiety.

Assertiveness training basically teaches clients to verbally express their opinions and feelings to others. Although assertiveness training was developed as a counterconditioning technique, it seems clear that over time other types of learning have been included. These include role-playing, social reinforcement, and modeling and are sometimes conducted in group settings.

Archer (1991) summarized typical assertiveness training steps: (1) Learn the differences among assertive, nonassertive (passive), and aggressive responses; (2) assess your assertive, nonassertive (passive), and aggressive responses; (3) develop new assertive responses for specific situations; (4) think through and discuss the risks of your being assertive; (5) rehearse your assertive behavior; (6) try out assertive responses in a real situation; and (7) maintain assertive behavior by constant reevaluation and reinforcement (pp. 177–179). Also, before any assertiveness training steps can be successful, the client must come to believe that he deserves to have his feelings and opinions expressed. A client who has a long history of passivity and an image of herself as unworthy and undeserving of being heard may have difficulty with the method and may need more extensive preparation before she is ready for the training itself. The following is an example of an assertiveness training session.

See DVD

Chap. 8
Clip 2

Leslie: I think I understand what I need to do to be assertive, but I don't know if I can really do it with Melinda. She is such a strong person, and when I want to disagree with her, I just feel so anxious and think she won't listen to me anyway.

Counselor: Remember how we talked about everyone having the right to express their feelings and opinions in a respectful way? Don't you think that you have that right?

Leslie: Yeah, I do think I am entitled to disagree with her. It's just. . . .

Counselor: Let's take a minute to practice what you might say to her that would be assertive and that would help you feel a lot less anxious.

Leslie: OK.

Counselor: Can you think of a situation that might come up soon?

Leslie: Yes, tonight she is going to have her boyfriend over again to spend the night, and. . . I just don't like them taking over the apartment all the time.

Counselor: OK, when would be a good time to talk with her about the situation, and what feelings do you want to express? Remember, this is just going to be a practice. You can decide when you are ready to actually be assertive with your roommate.

In the example, the therapist reminds the client that she is entitled to express herself and checks to see if she really agrees. The therapist then prepares to do a role-play by carefully setting up a situation that might occur. The therapist is also careful to let the client know that she doesn't have to confront her roommate until she is ready. The therapist will also, at some point, need to discuss the possible consequences that being assertive might have and the risks involved.

Self-Management

The operant conditioning principles, which are most closely associated with B. F. Skinner, have been very important in the development of the self-management aspects of behavior therapy. James and Guilliland (2003) here provided a detailed summary from a review of the self-management literature. The five basic steps are (1) conceptualizing and defining the problem and selecting appropriate outcome goals in behavioral terms, (2) managing and monitoring target behavior, (3) changing precipitating conditions and setting events and generating appropriate action steps, (4) generating appropriate reinforcement contingencies and establishing consequences that are meaningful to the client and effective in maintaining the targeted behavior; and (5) maintaining and consolidating gains. The level of complexity of the self-management plan will depend on the client, the complexity of the problem, and the time available. For example, let's take the case of

Morgan, a 35-year-old man who comes to counseling complaining that he is just not at all happy with the way people treat him at work. He further complains that this makes him anxious and angry.

Step 1: Setting a goal. After defining the problem (poor relationships with fellow workers), the therapist and Morgan might pick a starting outcome goal that would require Morgan to spend more time talking informally to fellow workers (this assumes that an assessment has determined that at least part of the problem is that Morgan is reclusive and is not friendly with his fellow workers). The initial behavioral goal could call for Morgan to spend 5 minutes in the coffee room daily.

Step 2: Monitoring behavior. This could be accomplished with a chart, personal digital assistant, or daily journal.

Step 3: Altering environments and generating action steps. To accomplish the goal of having Morgan spend 5 minutes each day in the coffee room (the first in a series of goals), the counselor might develop several action steps: Morgan will set his watch for 10:00 A.M., and when the alarm goes off, he will go into the coffee room. If his anxiety prevents this, then some anxiety reduction work might need to be done.

Step 4: Generating reinforcements. This might be tricky, since one of the major reinforcements on which the therapist might depend would be a positive reaction by fellow workers; however, even if Morgan does not interact with others in the coffee room, his initial behavior of spending 5 minutes in the coffee room can be reinforced by the therapist and perhaps by the charting that he is doing. Or some other reinforcer might be developed—say, a soda or snack. This example illustrates how difficult it can be to subdivide behaviors into small parts. The first small goal here is for Morgan to spend 5 minutes in the coffee room, but he can't really do that without encountering his fellow workers, which requires him to converse with them. If he is afraid to talk to them, then some additional strategy, like cue-controlled relaxation or role-play rehearsal may be necessary.

Step 5: Maintaining and consolidating gains. The idea here is that by appearing and being friendly, Morgan will be more accepted by his fellow workers, and by being friendly to and accepting of him, Morgan's fellow workers will further reinforce his behavior.

The many possible pitfalls of this application, which are not atypical, should be apparent to the reader. What if Morgan can't learn to converse with his fellow workers? What if the problem has more to do with his being angry because of a recent divorce? What if he is being treated very poorly by some fellow workers and has a right to feel angry and resentful? According to self-management theory, none of these pitfalls is likely to occur if an accurate assessment of the problem and the situation is done and if the behavioral contingencies and reinforcements can be correctly modified.

Multimodal Therapy

We have included a brief discussion of multimodal therapy, which was developed by Arnold Lazarus (1971, 1989, 1997), as a behavioral approach because Lazarus work came out of a behavioral paradigm developed it in the 1970's. However, it might also be seen as a precursor to the integrated approaches that became so popular in the late 1900's. Multimodal therapy includes techniques from a number of different therapy systems, and Lazarus argued that this kind of "technical ecclectisicm" does not borrow from these other approaches unsystematically, but rather takes into account a holistic view of the client's life with an understanding of how the different areas of functioning fit together and affect the whole person.

The keys to using the system effectively are a careful initial assessment and a thoughtful decision on the part of the therapist as to what approaches to use in the treatment plan. The reliance on the therapist to take primary responsibility for assessing and deciding what approach is best, and also to be flexible and skilled in many different therapeutic modalities, is noteworthy.

One of the most appealing aspects of multimodal therapy for the counselor is the structured way in which all of the important life areas are examined. Lazarus (1971, 1989, 1997) used what he calls the BASIC ID as a shorthand for the life areas in which a client should be assessed:

B — Behavior

A — Affect (emotion)

S — Sensations (physiological reactions)

I — Images (cognitions in the form of pictures, scenes)

C — Cognitions (thoughts)

I — Interpersonal relationships

D — Drugs (state of physical functioning, exercise, nutrition, etc.)

When a client comes in initially, the first step is to assess her functioning in each of these areas. A multimodal counselor will typically use an extensive precounseling questionnaire to gather information about the client in each of these areas. It is interesting, and perhaps surprising, that Lazarus has not added an assessment area for race and culture. The understanding that a person's race and cultural background, and perhaps her experiences of discrimination if she is not a member of the majority culture, can have strong influences has become more widespread in recent years.

After the assessment is made, the counselor, with consultation from the client, decides on one of the BASIC ID areas as a starting point, keeping in mind the close connections and interrelationships among the different areas. For example, if a client reports feeling depressed (A—Affective) and she begins to cut down on alcohol use and to exercise and eat more nutritiously (D—Drugs), then some of the depression may lift. The relative importance of the client's life areas may influence where the therapist begins and how the course of therapy is planned.

Let's examine a case and see how a multimodal counselor might proceed. Erika is a 35-year-old, divorced mother of two children. She comes to therapy reporting that she is very stressed and is having a very difficult time dealing with her teenaged son. In brief, simplified form, here are the results of her preliminary BASIC ID survey:

B — Behavior: She is yelling a lot at her son, missing work too often, neglecting her friends, and having difficulty sleeping.

A — Affect: She feels anxiety, depression, and anger.

S — Sensations: She has tired and sore muscles and a feeling of tenseness in her neck and stomach.

I — Images: No images were reported, but she does have some disturbing dreams.

C — Cognitions: She is very critical of herself, telling herself that she is a bad mother and that she is incompetent.

I — Interpersonal relationships: She has friends but seems to be distant from many of them.

D — Drugs: She doesn't report drug or alcohol abuse, but she does report that she is very tired and feels that she is not very healthy.

The question is where to begin and how to determine what approaches to use with Erika. Although the therapist is called on to use her expertise to determine an effective treatment plan, the client's goals and degree of distress must also be taken into account. In this case, let's say that Erika is most focused on her sense of anxiety and her tiredness. This could be a clue to begin some kind of stress and anxiety management program that would help Erika manage the negative body sensations, as well as her feelings of stress. This might, in turn, help her better manage her behavior toward her son and also reconnect with some of her friends. And, of course, work on a healthier lifestyle would fit nicely into the picture. It is quite possible that there might be complications in this case. For example, Erika might have muscle or stomach problems that would require medical attention and consultation. She might respond well to a brief round of antianxiety medication or muscle relaxants to give her some immediate relief. This might also empower her to get to a point where she could profit from therapy. Another option here would be family therapy to work on her relationship with her son.

It becomes obvious by examining this case that the multimodal approach offers a wide variety of possible counseling interventions but also challenges the therapist to be "technically eclectic" and develop a treatment plan tailored to a specific client. Lazarus (1989, 1997) has offered a much more complex and comprehensive discussion of ways to use multimodal therapy in his books describing the multimodal model.

MULTICULTURAL AND DIVERSITY EFFECTIVENESS

Although culture (ethnicity, race, nationality) was not originally considered in behavior therapy, the environment, including the social environment, has always played an important role. Behavior therapists in a multicultural society must understand the environment and the social reinforcers, as well as specific cultural norms. Ivey, D'Andrea, Breadford, Ivey, & Simek-Morgan (2002) note that the behavioral approach, with its emphasis on changing specific behaviors, is often viewed positively by minority groups. Clients from low socioeconomic groups, who are often minorities, don't usually have the luxury of long-term counseling for insight or self-understanding. On the other hand, Helms and Cook (1999) pointed out that the clear separation of human functioning into discrete elements—cognition, behavior, and emotion—may create confusion for clients whose cultures consider these aspects to be inseparable.

The issue of control must be addressed in this context. The token economies used in drug rehabilitation and prison settings are clearly designed to control inmates and produce certain behaviors. Since these settings often have a disproportionate percentage of minorities, particularly African-American males, one must closely examine the ethics of using behavioral methods for control. In school systems, where behavioral methods are often used in special education, there has been considerable controversy about the high percentage of minorities. Critics contend that minority children are disproportionately put into special education in order to segregate these students and control their behavior. These are difficult issues to confront, but they really relate more to how behavioral methods are used than to some inherent defect in the methods. We note that for behavior modification programs in institutional settings to be effective, those designing them must understand cultural norms and differences. The meaning of reinforcers and even of language is often dependent on culture.

We suggest three important considerations when using behavioral interventions in a multicultural context:

1. **Identification of goals.** Behavior therapists working with clients from diverse backgrounds need to be especially careful about making sure that goals for treatment are consistent with a client's cultural background, worldview, and issues of acculturation. A school counselor working with a student from an immigrant background, for example, who is struggling in school may be faced with conflicting goals: what the child wants (for example, "I want to be able to spend time with my friends") versus what the immigrant parents want ("Our child should be at the top of the class no matter what it takes").

2. **Role of the environment.** Since behaviorists stress the application of principles of environmental learning, it is important to take into account the unique environmental factors that persons from ethnic minority groups can face. For example, some have used the term *healthy cultural paranoia* to describe the adaptive heightened sense of suspicion that minority group members may have toward the intentions of members of the majority culture. Behaviors considered to be inappropriate responses to the environment by European Americans might not be viewed the same way by members of other ethnic minority groups.

3. **Skill development.** The teaching and educational functions of behavior therapy must also be viewed through a cultural lens. For example, an Asian-American adolescent female may state her desire to communicate more clearly with her mother. A counselor could take this to mean clear, assertive communication. But it is entirely possible that the client's mother has a different attitude about the nature of mother-daughter communication than the therapist (and perhaps even the daughter).

PRIMARY APPLICATIONS

Because of its concrete, practical, and short-term nature, behavior therapy has been used with a wide range of counseling populations and settings. These include work with couples, families, children and adolescents, and groups and in substance abuse, career counseling, behavioral medicine, and many other settings.

Children and Adolescents

Behavior therapy is widely used with young people. Because young children and many adolescents may not possess many of the intellectual capacities necessary for the "insight" work required by many other counseling approaches, behavior therapy is often the treatment of choice. Furthermore, many children and adolescents are not self-referred to counseling. Usually, a parent, teacher, or some other person in a position of authority wants the child or adolescent to change specific patterns of behavior. While the behavior therapist must ensure that her interventions are consistent with the best interests of the child in treatment, targeting problematic behaviors for intervention that are causing conflict with adults can often have a dramatic positive impact on both the child and the parents.

The use of behavior therapy with children and adolescents is well established for anxiety, social phobia, anorexia nervosa, post-traumatic stress disorder, conduct disorder, ADHD, mental retardation, elimination disorders (enuresis and encopresis), and alcohol and drug abuse (Hersen, 2002). A number of common steps are used for behavioral interventions addressing these disorders. First, a behavioral assessment is conducted to comprehensively evaluate past and current symptoms and behaviors, as well as environmental factors that seem to be triggering or maintaining the behavior. As was noted previously in the chapter, this initial assessment might also include administering a self-report checklist to identify various problems the child or adolescent may be experiencing. Specialized inventories (for example, the Children's Yale-Brown Obsessive-Compulsive Scale and the Children's Depression Inventory) have been developed for use with children complaining of specific mental disorders.

In many cases, family members participate at least part-time in the counseling work. When behavioral interventions involve education and skills training, the participation of family members is vital in order to teach and reinforce new behaviors. In other respects, the course of treatment in behavior therapy with children is similar to that conducted with adults. Behavior therapy has been particularly well received in educational settings, and behavioral methods are often used by counselors in K–12 settings. In fact, it could be argued that as long as schools have existed, rewards and punishments have been used to modify behavior. A number of behavioral principles are routinely used by a variety of school personnel—teachers, administrators, coaches. Following are a number of techniques typically used by school counselors and psychologists.

Social Skills Training Cartledge and Milburn (1986) pointed out that development of social skills is a hidden component of the school curriculum. School counselors can use behavioral interventions, with individuals or groups, to help schoolchildren develop social skills. A socially skilled person is someone who has found the right balance between adapting to the expectations of others (doing what others expect) and influencing the environment so that the person's wishes are taken into account (getting the environment to do what the person wants) (Swager, 1995). The counselor might first provide a model for appropriate communication (for example, a demonstration of how to say something positive about oneself or another person) and then give children an opportunity to practice these skills with each other. School counselors often focus on communication problems that typically arise in school settings, resulting in interpersonal conflict, fighting, teasing, and poor classroom participation.

Motivation Van Bilsen (1991) described a behavioral intervention to increase student motivation predicated on behavioral principles and the notion that students must be motivated to change through an awareness of the problem, sufficient concern about the importance of the problem, and the belief that they can take steps to improve the situation. Van Bilsen described four steps in this process: (1) creating a willingness to change, (2) analyzing the problem in behavioral terms, (3) negotiating learning objectives and methods, and (4) developing the treatment. Treatment usually begins with a reasonable plan that has a good chance of succeeding. For example, if the goal is to increase time spent on homework, an initial goal might be to increase the time spent on homework by 10 or 20%, with powerful reinforcers included for goal attainment.

School Phobia Mattis and Ollendick (2002) pointed out that the term *school phobia* was first used to describe extended absences from school presumably motivated by an overdependence on one or both of the parents. More recently, however, researchers and clinicians have come to understand that school phobia can be a symptom of a variety of underlying disorders. Through assessment of the specific behaviors associated with the phobia, including when the symptoms started, how long they have persisted, and any possible "benefits" the child may experience by avoiding school, is essential in determining appropriate behavioral interventions. Mattis and Ollendick also pointed out that a thorough medical evaluation is necessary if any physical symptoms, such as stomach pains, are causing the child to miss school.

Behavioral treatment of school phobia might begin with a psychoeducational component in which the child learns about the nature of anxiety and its attendant physical, behavioral, and cognitive components (Mattis & Ollendick, 2002). The therapist can then use behavioral methods to provide the child with the necessary tools to return to school. The child can be taught relaxation techniques, such as muscle relaxation, as well as methods for monitoring her own thoughts about school (e.g., fears that others will make fun of her). The therapist and the parent can serve as role models for entering the school environment without fear. Eventually, the counselor and the child establish a contract under which the child spends progressively longer days in school and is rewarded for success after each week in school.

Career Counseling

John Krumboltz, a psychologist at Stanford University, applied principles of human learning theory to career development interventions (Krumboltz, 1994; Mitchell & Krumboltz, 1996). According to Krumboltz, people choose occupations based on genetic characteristics (i.e., characteristics or abilities that are innate), environmental conditions (i.e., factors affecting job choices such the state of the economy and the vocational opportunities for women and members of minority groups), learning experiences (instrumental, associative, and observational), and task-approach skills. Task-approach skills are acquired throughout life as a result of learning experiences, and those related to career development can include setting goals, searching for occupational information, and making decisions.

Krumboltz is one of the few theorists to emphasize the role of learning in career development. A career counselor using this approach will seek to gather as much information as possible about the learning experiences that influence a client's career concerns. For example, a client might have developed the belief early in life that she has limited math skills (perhaps acquired from a less than supportive math teacher), and her current lack of education in this area might be limiting her vocational prospects. As a first step, a counselor using this approach will investigate, through an analysis of the client's learning experiences, exactly how this belief was acquired. Does the client's academic record support this belief, or is it possible that she has erroneously acquired this belief? Has the client developed the proper task-approach skills to remedy the situation (i.e., does she have the proper study habits to "skill up" in math)?

After identifying the learning experiences that have led to the client's current difficulties, the career counselor might then use a number of behavioral interventions to help the client achieve her career goals. For example, the counselor might reinforce desired behaviors in order to encourage the client to explore occupational alternatives. She also might assign homework, such as completing specific occupational research at a university career resource center. Following successful completion of the assignment, the counselor would provide verbal praise for the client. Other behavioral techniques for career counseling using this approach include the use of role models and simulation activities. The former are widely used in school settings when parents and members of the community are encouraged to visit classrooms and describe their daily work routine. Simulation activities provide clients an opportunity to practice necessary job search skills such as through mock interviews.

Group Work

Since behaviorists assume that other people are sources of reinforcement and punishment in the environment, groups are a natural setting in which to change behavior. Behavioral groups can be used to address a variety of topics, ranging from learning life skills (such as dealing with anger) or interpersonal skills (such as assertiveness) to treating specific disorders (such as phobias or depression). Obviously, the key to using behavior therapy in groups is involving the other members of the group in the treatment. Each member of the group should have the opportunity to practice behavioral principles with the other members of the group, discuss ways to apply those to their own lives, and have the opportunity to learn from other members' experiences and ideas. A behavioral leader will likely take an educationally oriented approach with a group—a significant amount of time is usually spent teaching group members about principles of behavior therapy and using exercises and activities designed to help members apply these ideas to their own lives.

Rose (1989) developed a multimethod group approach that uses a small-group format to teach coping strategies (e.g., relaxation, behavioral rehearsal, assertiveness) previously reviewed in this chapter. In the initial stage, the group leader typically attempts to build group cohesiveness and trust, familiarize the members with the structure of the group, and identify goals for each of the group members. Once these have been established, the group moves into the working stage. At this point, the group leader makes decisions about which behavioral interventions might best serve the goals and needs of the group. For example, the group leader can use reinforcement strategies by asking members to report their progress during the previous week. Or the group leader can model a particular skill, such as assertive communication, and then have members practice such skills on their own. In the final stage of this type of group, increasing attention is paid to transferring learning that has taken place in the group to the members' everyday lives. Members may be increasingly encouraged to take responsibility for their own treatment as the group progresses. Members are prepared for coping without the presence of the group and for managing the possibility of a relapse in their symptoms.

Alberti and Emmons (1990) described the use of groups in assertiveness training, previously discussed as a major behavior therapy technique. A key part of group training in this area is having members practice assertive communication (for example, clearly communicating their wishes using "I" statements), while still respecting the rights of others. Group members might be encouraged to role-play problematic situations in their own lives and receive feedback about their assertive behaviors from other group members. Contrast the power of the feedback, practice, and reinforcement of this technique in group and individual therapy settings. Clearly, the group provides considerable advantages because of the modeling and reinforcement possible from peers.

Other Applications

The use of behavioral methods has gained widespread acceptance in medical settings. Called *behavioral medicine*, behavioral approaches are often used as a component of medical treatment. Many of the health complaints brought to physicians have psychological components that have caused or exacerbated these conditions, and changes in lifestyle are often necessary. For example, patients with cardiac illness usually need to make substantial lifestyle changes, including changes in diet, exercise, and stress management. Behavioral interventions are often utilized in such settings because they are relatively easy to teach to patients (but gaining patient compliance is much more difficult) are widely accepted by medical personnel interested in concrete changes in the lives of their patients, and readily complement medical treatments.

Behavior methods and techniques lend themselves well to *prevention programs* (programs to prevent mental health and emotional problems) because they are based in large part on education. Many principles of behavior therapy are rather straightforward and easy to self-administer, either individually or in groups. For example, a company might offer stress management training to its employees in an attempt to increase morale and decrease absenteeism. This stress management training could include a number of behavioral approaches, such as relaxation, time management, and assertiveness training. The employer, in this case, is attempting to prevent problems that have a negative effect on the bottom line.

A behavioral approach to *substance abuse* counseling involves clearly defining the target behaviors to be modified (in this case, substance use and related behaviors) and then specifying environmental precipitants. The notion of stimulus control can be important here: that is, helping the substance abuser identify circumstances in which her substance abuse is likely to occur (e.g., a social occasion where alcohol is served) and then helping her either avoid such circumstances or find ways to modify her behavior if the situation cannot be avoided. Attention to finding alternate sources of reinforcement is also a key component of this approach. Using and abusing substances initially result in positive feelings, so a behavioral counselor will seek to identify other sources of reinforcement (such as exercise or involvement in a hobby) that might be used as substitutes for the problematic behavior. Participation in groups like Alcoholics Anonymous, which is a well-accepted part of many substance abuse treatment programs, provides an opportunity for regular group reinforcement for behavior change.

Many *criminal justice* settings use elements of behavior therapy. Because the people who run prisons have a great deal of control over the environment of prisoners, and their sources of reward and punishment, many have found the application of behavior therapy to work quite effectively. And since the very idea of a correctional institution is to rehabilitate persons whose behavior has been deemed unacceptable by society, it is often possible to identify the behaviors that a prisoner needs to correct.

Perhaps the most famous application of behavior therapy to criminal justice settings is the use of a token economy, which was discussed earlier. Token economies are established in small communities to promote desired behaviors and discourage unwanted ones. Setting up a token economy requires careful identification of the behaviors the institution wants to reward and those it wants to discourage. Then, based on the assigned importance of each type of behavior, a rate of exchange is established in which prisoners earn specified amounts of points for desired behaviors and lose specified amounts of points for undesirable behaviors. The advantage of such a system is that it clearly specifies desired behaviors and provides a strong incentive for participants to follow the rules. One disadvantage of such a system is that it can take considerable effort to establish and maintain a token economy. As was noted above, rates of exchange must be established, points earned and lost must be carefully tracked, and each of the participants must be closely monitored.

Clinicians who use behavior therapy with *couples and families* focus mainly on how each member of the family or couple can learn to reward the other(s) more and punish the other(s) less (Young & Long, 1998). This may necessitate learning new skills, such as assertiveness or active listening. Young and Long outlined some of the premises for application of the behaviorist approach to couples: Relationship history is important only insofar as the behaviors learned contribute to the couple's problems; the focus of treatment is usually educational and related to learning more effective relationship skills; sexual relationship problems, if not medically caused, are usually treatable with behavioral methods; and changing reward and punishment patterns in relationships can lead to effective counseling outcomes.

BRIEF THERAPY/MANAGED CARE EFFECTIVENESS

Because of the focus on changing client symptoms, behavioral approaches to counseling work very well in a managed care environment. The various managed care mental health providers, the Veterans Administration, health maintenance organizations, preferred provider organizations, and employee assistance programs prefer the symptom-removal focus that behavioral approaches offer. These organizations want to know in concrete, measurable terms whether or not the treatment they are paying for is working. They are generally interested not in the root causes of their clients' problems but rather in how those clients can regain effective functioning.

As we noted earlier, those in the empirically supported treatment school of thought tend to favor behavioral and cognitive approaches because they can develop concrete treatment protocols for different problems. This fits rather well with a medical model, where a problem is diagnosed and specific treatments are generally accepted as effective. We note that this idea of a clear-cut cure is often more of a myth than a reality, even in medicine. The ideal counseling scenario for managed care is a clearly diagnosable problem with a standardized treatment protocol that is time limited and successful. Although we are rather skeptical that this ideal will ever be completely realized, in either medicine or counseling, behavioral approaches certainly have more potential to move in that direction than do most other counseling approaches.

INTEGRATING THE THEORY WITH OTHER APPROACHES

Behavioral approaches fit well with a number of other theories. For example, the counselor may use techniques drawn from a client-centered perspective, such as active listening and empathy, to help clients feel understood and clarify their feelings about their current concerns. Combining such approaches with behavioral assessment can help the counselor gain a fuller understanding of her client's strengths, as well as things the client might seek to change in counseling.

While approaches to counseling and psychotherapy such as the Adlerian and object relations theories stress the importance of clients' early childhood experiences, Goldfried and Davison (1994) acknowledged that behavior therapists typically focus on the current determinants of behaviors. However, they asserted that it would be a mistake to assume that behavior therapists consider early experiences to be unimportant. Rather, behavior therapists assume that while early experiences are extremely important in determining how a person is currently behaving, such forces are unlikely to still be operating in a client's life. Adlerian and other dynamic cognitive and insight-oriented approaches might be used as a way to help the counselor gain a more in-depth understanding of how particular behaviors were learned.

Several authors, including Carkhuff (1993) and Hill and O'Brien (1999), here recommended using behavioral approaches in counseling if specific skill deficits have been identified that might be amenable to behavioral interventions. For example, a client who enters counseling with a history of isolation and loneliness might initially be treated using a client-centered perspective. The counselor might demonstrate empathy and concern in sensitively responding to the client's feelings of loneliness, thereby helping the client feel less isolated. Over time, the counselor might even use an insight-oriented approach to help the client explore what happened in her early life that may have caused her to feel lonely as an adult. However, at some point in therapy, the client, with the help of the counselor, might state, "I want to start acting differently. I understand my history with this problem, how it started, and where it has led me, but I want to do things differently now." At this point, the counselor can use a behavioral technique, such as social skills training, to help the client reach her goals.

Behavioral methods are also used a great deal in reality therapy and solution-focused therapy. The foundation of reality therapy is existential, in that a client's choice is emphasized, but the counselor uses behavioral methods to help the client develop a plan to reach his goals. Although solution-focused counseling is considered postmodern because it emphasizes the importance of language and the constructs of communication between the client and the counselor, helping the client find ways to achieve solutions is often concrete and behavioral. In a general sense, whenever a therapist, no matter what her theoretical orientation, begins to focus on concrete behavior change, she is probably using learning theory in some way.

RESEARCH

The behaviorist tradition first took root in college and university research laboratories. Pioneers such as Ivan Pavlov and B. F. Skinner spent years conducting rigorous experimental evaluations of animal behavior and formulating learning theory principles before these were applied to human behavior. It would not be unreasonable to contend that behavior therapy has the strongest scientific foundation of all the counseling theories.

A number of classic studies have been conducted comparing behavioral approaches with other theories. This in large part explains why it is the most thoroughly researched of the counseling theories reviewed in this book (indeed, it is the most researched of *any* counseling theory). Literally hundreds of studies have been conducted over the past several decades using behavioral interventions with different types of disorders, with different types of clients, in varying formats (e.g., individual counseling, group counseling), and in different settings.

Does behavioral counseling work better than other approaches? Luborsky, Singer, and Luborsky (1975) conducted an extensive review of research on the various psychotherapeutic approaches using "box scores." They accomplished this by tallying the results of existing studies in order to determine whether a preponderance of the research comparing various counseling interventions supported the efficacy of one approach over another. They found that behavior therapy appeared to be particularly well suited to the treatment of phobias, but in general, they were unable to conclude that any one counseling intervention was better than another, including behavior therapy. They cited a famous phrase of the Dodo bird from the book *Alice in Wonderland*: "everyone has won and all must have prizes."

A few years after the Luborsky et al. study, Smith and Glass (1977) and Smith, Glass, and Miller (1980) pioneered a quantitative method of comparing the statistical results of many different studies, called a *meta-analysis*. Smith and Glass (1977) found that the typical therapy client is better off than 75% of untreated individuals, but there was no difference in the effectiveness of behavior therapy as compared to other forms of counseling interventions. Using the meta-analysis technique, Smith et al. (1980) were able to quantitatively rank the average "effect" of existing counseling theories based on 475 existing studies. While a specific type of behavioral treatment, systematic desensitization, was ranked 4th among the various theories evaluated, in general the overall effectiveness of the counseling theories reviewed was so similar that they concluded there was little evidence to suggest that one theory of counseling was superior to any other. In a move recent meta-analytic study (Grawe, Donati, & Bernauer, 1998) researchers have found that cognitive and behavioral methods were more effective than client-centered and psychodynamic approaches. Clearly, there is considerable disagreement among researchers about the effectiveness of any one treatment compared to another.

Much of the research on behavioral treatments has focused on specific disorders such as depression, generalized anxiety, phobias, and obsessive-compulsive disorder. Although the question of relative efficacy as related to other theoretical approaches has not been answered, there is evidence that behavioral and cognitive-behavioral approaches work for a number of specific disorders (see the sample study below). Because cognitive-behavioral theory itself is based on scientific principles and because it involves observable behavior changes that can be measured, the research support for cognitive-behavioral approaches tends to be more scientific and empirical. Some of the more recent integrated approaches that include a number of specific therapy steps and techniques have been researched. Although these approaches are complex and often include cognitive, behavioral, and sometimes other kinds of techniques, the fact that the treatment is set out in great detail allows researchers to more accurately assess the effects of the treatment itself.

SAMPLE RESEARCH: Treating Obsessive-Compulsive Disorder with Exposure/Ritual Prevention

Goals of the Research

Franklin et al. (2000) studied an exposure/ritual prevention (EX/RP) treatment for obsessive-compulsive disorder (OCD), a type of anxiety disorder in which the individual is afflicted with recurrent obsessions (for example, that something terrible will happen to a loved one) that cause intense anxiety. People usually develop compulsive repetitive behavior or rituals as an attempt to manage the anxiety.

The researchers wanted to evaluate whether EX/RP worked as well in a less-controlled outpatient setting as it did in laboratory settings using highly selected groups of OCD patients. In order to achieve higher levels of internal validity, those conducting laboratory studies of the use of EX/RP with OCD patients often select patients who received only that diagnosis, while in the real world persons with OCD often suffer from depression or other anxiety disorders as well. In addition, laboratory studies often rely on manualized treatments, in which therapists follow very specific rules and procedures for implementing treatment.

Participants

Franklin et al. studied 110 adult outpatients treated at the Center for the Treatment and Study of Anxiety at the University of Pennsylvania Medical School.

Methods

The treatment in the Franklin et al. study, exposure and ritual prevention, is really an application of Wolpe's systematic desensitization technique, in which persons gradually expose themselves to an anxiety-provoking situation until the feelings have abated. With OCD, ritual prevention is necessary as well as exposure in order for the association of anxiety to be extinguished.

During EX/RP, the OCD patient is exposed to whatever stimuli cause her anxiety. This can involve coming into contact with something perceived as "dirty" (for example, a kitchen floor or a bodily fluid such as urine). She is then "prevented" (not by force but through mutual agreement with the therapist) from performing whatever rituals she normally carries out when this contact occurs (for example, washing her hands). In so doing, she is desensitized to the anxiety provoked by her thoughts, and eventually the compulsions used to ward off those feelings abate.

The researchers used treatments that were less controlled than did the laboratory studies. All of the outpatients in this study received EX/RP for OCD, which typically involved 3 treatment planning sessions, followed by 15 sessions of treatment for about 2 hours at a time The clinicians in the Franklin et al. study were trained by reading a training manual and sitting in on and assisting in the treatment provided by another therapist. Patients were not assigned randomly to therapists but rather were assigned according to clinical factors such as the severity of the case, the preferences of the client (such as for a male or female therapist), and practical matters such as therapist availability.

Results

The researchers compared their findings to those of four more highly controlled laboratory-based studies using similar outcomes measures (the Y–BOCS to measure OCD symptoms and the BDI to measure depressive symptoms) and found very similar patterns of symptom reduction. In other words, the participants in the study that involved more real-world conditions showed comparable levels of improvement.

Implications of the Research

This study added to the evidence for the external validity of this procedure (in this case, the validity of generalizing the results to real-world clinical situations), which had not been well established by laboratory studies that were different from real-life clinical situations. By using the same measures as previous laboratory studies and comparing their results with the previous results, the researchers were able to creatively look at applying this treatment in the field.

EVALUATION OF BEHAVIOR THERAPY

By now, it should be very clear that behavior therapy is an approach that focuses primarily on behavior but that it does not necessarily have a mechanistic or simplistic focus only on behavior. The role of insight and past history is not emphasized, except that behavior therapists work on helping clients understand factors that are maintaining behaviors that need to be changed or preventing new and more functional behaviors. Although thoughts and feelings are not neglected in modern approaches to behavior therapy, neither are they viewed as the preferred starting point for therapeutic interventions.

One of the contributions of behavior therapy to the field of counseling is the development of a range of specific techniques. Information about techniques such as assertive communication, systematic desensitization, and token economies can be communicated to both clinicians and their clients in understandable language and used in a wide range of settings. In fact, one does not even need to know very much about principles of learning to apply these techniques to problems in everyday living. The myriad of useful applications (criminal justice, substance abuse, behavioral medicine, etc.) was outlined previously.

While the gulf between practice and research can be wide for some counseling approaches, from the beginning, behavior therapists have been committed to demonstrating empirically the usefulness of this approach. As we have noted, this has been easier with behavior therapy because of the focus on concrete, measurable goals. Nonetheless, this commitment has produced an extensive research literature on behavior therapy.

One of the major criticisms levied against behavior therapy is that it is too focused on external influences and neglects innate characteristics of the client. However, modern behavior therapists would argue that while traditional approaches to behavior therapy emphasized the role of the environment almost exclusively in explaining human behavior, contemporary behavior therapy focuses on the interrelationship of the person and the environment; that is, while we learn and modify our behavior based on feedback from the environment, the role of human cognition in filtering, organizing, and attaching meaning to these experiences is now recognized. Additionally, human relationship factors are seen by modern behavior therapists as essential on at least two levels: First, the behavior therapist and her client must have a collaborative, trusting relationship in order for the therapy to have a good chance of working. The client must trust the therapist enough to complete homework assignments, apply what is learned to her life, and report her successes and setbacks honestly to the therapist. Second, behavior therapists recognize the importance of clients' healthy relationships with others in their lives as a key component of behavioral interventions. Interventions such as communication skills and assertiveness training are designed to improve the bonds that clients have with other people as a way of restoring healthy functioning.

As we have noted several times, behavior therapists have traditionally focused a great deal on the environment and how it impacts their clients; however, they have not typically noted in particular the influence of culture, race, gender, or other social environmental factors. Because of greater awareness of these issues in recent years, an analysis of the influence they have is compatible with a behavior therapy framework. For example, workplace discrimination could certainly affect a client's behavior at work. Favoritism-based discrimination or lack of positive reinforcement would certainly be an important factor in treating a worker for depression related to decreasing job performance.

Some critics contend that although behavior therapy may be effective in at least temporarily altering external behaviors, it neglects "deeper" aspects of the human experience, such as our cognitive, emotional, and even spiritual lives. Theorists who stress the importance of the varying levels of consciousness—for example, Freudian psychoanalysts—argue that changing external behaviors is not helpful until the underlying causes of the dysfunction are identified in the client's unconscious mind and brought into conscious awareness. Client-centered therapists, using Carl Rogers's approach to counseling, argue that it is far more important for the client to experience a trusting, warm, and empathic relationship that will unlock her human potential than it is to teach her new behaviors.

In part, this debate centers on whether behavior therapy is overly focused on client symptoms rather than underlying causes of these symptoms. Goldfried and Davison (1994) defended behavioral approaches by pointing to the many complexities that exist in trying to understand the environmental factors that are impacting a client's behavior. In other words, just because behaviorists see the environment, rather than intrapsychic factors, as a main determinant of client behavior does not make the approach inherently superficial or trivial. Environmental contingencies that influence complex behaviors can be just as challenging to understand as the workings of the unconscious.

Some criticisms of behavior therapy stem from attempts to "reward," "punish," or otherwise override a client's potential for self-determination. Indeed, some applications of behavior therapy have been used in prisons and hospital where "clients" are not entirely free to make choices about important aspects of their lives. For example, autistic patients who repeatedly injured themselves were exposed to mild shocks as a way of decreasing this self-injurious behavior. Behaviorists contend that BT allows a client to have more control over their behavior and therefore live a more rewarding and satisfying life. Even in the example of the autistic child being punished, the ultimate goal is to improve the client's quality of life.

Questions and Learning Activities

These questions and activities are designed to stimulate your thinking about this theory and to help you apply some of the ideas to your own life and experience. If possible, you should work with another person or with a small group. Getting others' points of view and sharing your own ideas and perspectives will be invaluable as a way to help you evaluate this theory and its applications.

Personal Application Questions

Consider and discuss with another student or in a small group the following questions:

1. Do you think that behavior change should be the main focus of counseling?
2. Can positively changing behavior change a client's negative feelings and attitudes?
3. Can you see yourself as a kind of teacher/expert, helping your clients apply the various behavior therapy approaches and techniques to their problems?
4. Will you be able to help clients define problems in terms of behavior, using various assessment techniques?
5. Do you think that for some problems all clients need to do is express and explore their feelings? If so, how could you define this in terms of behavior?
6. How does behavior therapy seem to fit in the setting or with the population with which you want to work (school, private practice, agency, teenagers, etc.)?
7. Are you comfortable with the control that you might have over your clients because you will be a big influence in helping them use learning theory to create or change behavior?

Learning Activities

Cue-Controlled Deep Muscle Relaxation

Use the deep muscle relaxation protocol presented earlier to practice deep muscle relaxation by yourself. Then practice with a classmate to get a feel for what it will be like to use the protocol with a client. Practice the technique on yourself at home for a week or two, and using a cue, see if you can develop a conditioned cue-controlled relaxation response. Try it out in an environment or situation that normally makes you anxious.

Personal Anxiety Hierarchy

Identify a situation in which you feel anxious (e.g., taking a test, asking someone for a date, crossing a bridge, discussing condom use with a new partner) and make up an anxiety hierarchy as if you were going to use systematic desensitization on yourself. Remember to have at least six to eight items in the hierarchy and a spread of anxiety ratings between 0 and 100 SUDs.

Assertive Responses

List several situations in which you have a problem being assertive. If you can't think of personal situations, think of situations you have observed with friends. Here are some examples: being afraid to speak up in class, being afraid to ask someone for a date, not speaking up when someone is rude, and not speaking up when someone is putting down a friend. After you have listed your own situations, see if you can come up with angry, assertive, and passive responses for each.

Example

Speaking up when someone is rude to you:
1. *Angry*—You SOB, don't talk to me that way.
2. *Assertive*—I don't appreciate your talking to me that way. It makes me feel angry and upset, and I won't put up with being treated disrespectfully.
3. *Passive*—I'm sorry if you feel that way.

Remember that a passive response is one in which you do not stand up for yourself or express your feeling, opinion, or point of view. An angry response is one in which you lash out in anger and are somewhat out of control, often because you have been passive for a period of time and have not expressed yourself in an assertive way. And an assertive response is one in which you express your feeling, opinion, or point of view and continue to respect the other person.

Problem Definition

Practice defining problems in behavioral terms by listing some of the questions or methods you might use to get to behavior in the following scenarios. Remember that as a behavior therapist you are also trying to build rapport, so there is still a need to express empathy and understanding.

Scenario 1—I am feeling really depressed. All I do is sleepwalk through life. Nothing seems to have any meaning. I haven't felt connected to others for a long time. I wish life had more meaning for me.

Scenario 2—I just don't get it. Why are all these people so materialistic? It seems like everyone spends most of his time chasing the mighty buck. It is just work, work, work so that you can buy a new car, buy a big TV, or eat at a fancy restaurant. Why can't people care more about each other and spend more time doing something socially useful? Sometimes I just feel like moving to a desert island.

Scenario 3—My partner just doesn't understand me. He is always assuming that I want to do what he wants to do. I know that he knows better, but he just keeps doing it. When I point out how overbearing he is sometimes, he apologizes and says he will do better, but he just goes back to the same old thing. I'm thinking about leaving him.

Multimodal Assessment

Assess a role-played problem situation with a partner using BASIC ID. Have a sheet of paper with each category in front of you—you are allowed to ask questions and take notes, but see if you can accomplish this as part of an interview rather than just asking the questions.

Companion Website

Now go to the Companion Website at www.prenhall.com/archer to assess your understanding of chapter content with multiple-choice and essay questions, and broaden your knowledge with related Web resources and additional print resources.

CHAPTER 9

Cognitive Approaches

VOICES FROM THE FIELD: COUNSELOR AND CLIENT REACTIONS

Yes, it works for me

Client (Cognitive): Working with Dr. C was quite an experience. He had a way of asking me questions that really helped me see what was going on in my head. Using that chart to see what my thoughts are when I am feeling stressed really helped me see that I am sometimes my own worst enemy. But it is pretty hard to stop telling myself that I am going to fail. I have been doing that for a long time.

Client (REBT): I was kind of surprised when I got into Dr. R's office. He started right in asking me questions about my situation, and before the session ended, he was teaching me how to recognize my irrational thoughts. I expected that he would be more of a listener and just let me get it all out. I was impressed, though, that we could start right in on my problem. I guess that is what counseling is all about. I'm not sure I agree that it really is my thinking that causes me to be so frightened of people, but I am willing to try using the ABC method to work on some ways to dispute what Dr. R called my irrational thoughts and beliefs.

Counselor (Cognitive): Learning to do cognitive therapy was difficult. It was hard to help the client discover her automatic thoughts for herself. I wanted to just tell her what they were and move right on to changing them. But I really liked the idea that a client can analyze the thoughts that are causing her a problem and work on changing them. I also really liked the fact that there are a number of specific techniques to use with clients. I think it is helpful for a client just to learn how his thoughts affect feeling and behavior, although the connections can get pretty complicated.

No, it doesn't work for me

Client (Cognitive): Dr. C was nice, but I just can't buy into this idea that I am causing my depression by the way I think. It sounds so easy: Just change your thoughts and the depressive system that you have going will change. It's true that I have always had a pretty negative view of life, but coming from my family, it is pretty understandable. When you are treated like crap the way I was, you are bound to think life sucks big time. I have tried to change this negative view of life a lot, but I just can't.

Client (REBT): Wow! That counselor didn't even give me enough time to tell him much about anything, let alone the abuse I suffered as a child. He started telling me how I am causing all of my problems by the way I think. Does he think the beatings I took from my dad were my fault? He wasn't anything like my previous counselor. I really need someone to help me understand how my past keeps coming back to haunt me. I just don't think I can do that with this counselor.

Counselor (Cognitive): I guess I am just not cut out to be a cognitive therapist. I don't like trying to argue clients out of their problems. I agree that people often have negative thoughts, but I am just not good at getting them to change their thoughts by seeing all of these different kinds of logical fallacies. I do think that people can have negative attitudes, but I think it is going to take something powerful to change these attitudes—maybe something like psychoanalysis or Gestalt therapy or participation in a therapy group where they can learn some new attitudes from many different people.

Yes, it works for me	No, it doesn't work for me
Counselor (REBT): I really like this REBT counseling approach: it gets right to what is causing problems for people. I think the ABC method really helps clients identify their problems and gives both the counselor and the client a chance to confront the problem and the irrational thinking that goes with it. It fits my personality pretty well. I like to analyze things, I have always been good at figuring out alternatives, and I like to take an active role in counseling. After all, counseling is really about teaching clients how to live better lives.	**Counselor (REBT):** I just can't do this REBT. I want to take time to understand a client's feelings. I also think that the past is important and that clients usually need to talk about what has happened to them as children so that they can understand some of their problems in the present. And I don't really think telling someone that he is thinking irrationally is helpful. I just don't like the idea of taking so much responsibility as a counselor and deciding what client beliefs are irrational. Maybe what is irrational to me is rational to them.

Dana is an interpreter for the United Nations. She is originally from Sweden but has been working in New York for several years. She is very tall and attractive and is uncomfortable around American men. She had a couple of very bad experiences when she first arrived and has avoided them since then. She has been unhappy about this and sought out a counselor.

> **Dana:** I don't know. . . I just don't trust any men these days.
> **Counselor:** Does that make life difficult for you?
> **Dana:** Sure, I am pretty lonely. Men just seem to be after sex. I'm thinking of going back to Sweden; they have a healthier attitude about men and women.
> **Counselor:** You must have encountered a very large number of American men who didn't treat you well.
> **Dana:** Well, not really, but I just got scared after a few bad situations.
> **Counselor:** When you say bad situations, what do you mean?
> **Dana:** Because I have a slight accent, because of the way I look, men just act like jerks around me, showing off, trying to impress me.
> **Counselor:** So they make assumptions about you and treat you differently because of the way you look?
> **Dana:** Well, I do think that American men have a thing about tall, Swedish women.
> **Counselor:** Do you think that all American men are like that?

The major variations of cognitive therapy developed by Beck and Ellis both stress the importance of understanding the relationships among thoughts, feelings, and behavior. The emphasis is on thoughts and how they relate to client problems and unhappiness. In this example, you can see that the counselor is trying to ask questions that will help Dana begin to look at her own attitude about American men. She seems to have an automatic thought that all American men only want sex and will treat her badly. As this Socratic dialogue progresses, she may also uncover some other problematic thoughts, perhaps related to her uncertainty about how to judge men or about how to stay in control. This particular style of interaction is somewhat different than what you will see later related to Ellis's rational emotive behavior therapy (REBT).

HISTORICAL BACKGROUND

Historical Context

The concepts underlying cognitive counseling have existed since humans began walking on two legs. We have also used our thinking capacity as both a way to deceive ourselves and a tool to encourage ourselves. In fact, the ability to carry on a kind of internal dialogue and to think about thinking is a major characteristic that makes human beings unique. However, it is only within the last several decades that a science of human cognition has developed and has been applied to counseling and therapy.

A number of important theories of counseling began to take hold in the 1950s. Both cognitive and behavioral theories, as well as humanistic-existential theories, were developed during the mid–twentieth century. The primary reasons seem to be reactions to psychoanalysis coupled with clinical experience and emerging research. New and creative applications of science and philosophy began several decades of growth in ways to provide counseling and psychotherapy. One also might speculate that the increasing complexities of industrial society created a greater need for counseling and psychotherapy, as well as more leisure time and wealth to spend on the pursuit of happiness.

Both Ellis and Beck began to develop their theories in this mid-twentieth-century time period, partially because of dissatisfaction with psychoanalysis. Aaron Beck developed cognitive therapy because of the negative results of research he was doing on psychoanalytic approaches to depression, and Albert Ellis developed rational emotive therapy (now rational emotive behavior therapy or REBT) when, as he began to practice, he came to believe that taking a more active role by giving advice and direct interpretations worked better than psychoanalysis. In this chapter, we will initially discuss each theory and the related techniques separately. Later we will cover the theories together in the sections on applications, integration, research, and evaluation.

The integration of cognitive and behavioral approaches into what is now called cognitive-behavioral therapy (CBT) is an excellent example of how counseling approaches and theories evolve and are integrated into new methods and practices. The classic behavioral approaches, paying little attention to cognitive process, were eventually profoundly affected by cognitive psychology, and similarly, the original cognitive approaches, focusing mainly on cognitions, took on more and more behavioral elements. To us, this is a striking example of how science and practice develop and move forward.

DEVELOPMENT OF REBT

Albert Ellis was raised in New York City and had a serious kidney disorder as a child. This illness and a difficult family situation led him to an interest in reading and in understanding people. As a young man, he worked in business and also wrote books, plays, and poetry. When he couldn't get any of these published, he began working on a book about the family and sex, a topic in which he had become interested. He became somewhat of an expert on the topic. Friends often asked him for advice, and he learned that he liked counseling and giving advice. He received a master's and doctorate in clinical psychology from Columbia University and, upon receiving his doctorate in 1947, began training as a psychoanalyst.

Ellis held teaching and clinical positions in the late 1940s and began to feel that psycho-analysis did not work as well as a more direct approach. He formulated what he then called rational therapy from some of his own experiences while he underwent psychoanalysis. This formulation was strongly influenced by his study of a number of philosophers. The quote "What disturbs people's minds is not events but their judgments on events" by Epictetus (100 A.D.), is often used as an introduction to his theory. He uses it as the heading for the Web site of his institute.

By the early 1960s, Ellis's approach had become well known, and he had begun a long and distinguished career as founder and very strong advocate of a cognitive approach to counseling and therapy. In 1961, he changed the name of his approach to rational emotive therapy (RET) in order to emphasize the fact that this approach also considered the role of feelings in counseling and psychotherapy. He changed the name again in 1993 to rational emotive behavior therapy (REBT), reflecting the growing integration of cognitive and behavioral approaches (Seligman, 2001). He has published 54 books and over 600 articles and is clearly one of the most well known psychotherapists of our time. In Ellis's biography on his institute Web page, Gary Greg (2003) provides a useful insight into Ellis's personality:

> "There is virtually nothing in which I delight more," says Albert Ellis, "than throwing myself into a good and difficult problem." Rational emotive behavior therapy is a direct and efficient problem-solving method, well suited to Ellis' personality. His self-assurance—some would even say arrogance—enables him to confront his clients about their beliefs and tell them what is rational and what isn't. The success of his clinical practice, his training institute, and his books testify that his methods work for many and that he is one of America's most influential therapists. (p. 1)

ASSUMPTIONS AND CORE CONCEPTS: REBT

View of Human Nature

Ellis contends that humans are born both rational and irrational. He views people as being both highly capable of growing through a creative, reflective, and rational approach to life and quite capable of being very self-destructive, making the same mistakes over and over again. Although students who view tapes of his counseling sessions often find him abrasive and overbearing, Ellis believes that human beings are worthwhile and worthy of self-respect. Like Rogers, he thinks that people should have unconditional positive regard for themselves (Ellis, 2000; Ellis & Dryden, 1997). He has written that people can be "self-preserving," "creative," "sensuous," and "interested in other people" and can "actualize their potentials for life and growth" (Ellis, 2000, p. 169). Critics have suggested that REBT therapists attempt to impose their value system on clients and that this implies that the theory somehow devalues individuals; however, Ellis has argued in nearly all his work that his theory is humanistic and places a high value on every individual.

In some of his later writing (Ellis, 2001b), Ellis identified himself as having moved from a logical positivist point of view (the modern, scientific approach with the underlying assumption that truth exists and is discoverable) to a constructivist postmodern point of view (a more recent philosophy with the underlying assumption that there is no absolute truth and that meaning is always constructed, at least partly, by the individual observer). In discussing this change, he acknowledged his belief that our views are largely constructions and that "we do not have any absolute certainty about what reality is or what it will be—despite our often being strongly convinced that we do" (Ellis, 2001b, p. 38). He also indicated that "although human personality has some important innate and fairly fixed elements, it also largely arises from relational and social influences and is much less individualistic than is commonly thought" (p. 38). He further acknowledged his belief in multiculturalism and the fact that different cultures or cultural beliefs have equal validity.

In addition to seeing human beings as capable of rationality and growth, Ellis suggests that we have a biological tendency (that interacts with the environment) toward irrationality. He listed 10 of these irrationalities in a 1997 book (Ellis & Dryden, 1997):

1. Virtually all humans, including bright and competent people, show evidence of major human irrationalities and self-defeatism.
2. Virtually all the disturbance-creating irrationalities (absolutistic shoulds and musts) that are found in our society are also found in just about all social and cultural groups that have been studied historically and anthropologically.
3. Many of the self-destructive behaviors that we engage in, such as procrastination and lack of self-discipline, go counter to the teachings of parents, peers, and the mass media.
4. Humans—even bright and intelligent people—often adopt new irrationalities after giving up previous ones.
5. People who vigorously oppose various irrational behaviors often fall prey to these very irrationalities. Atheists and agnostics exhibit zealous and absolutistic philosophies, and highly religious individuals act immorally.
6. Insight into irrational thoughts, feelings, and behaviors helps only partially to change them. For example, people can acknowledge that drinking alcohol in large quantities is harmful, yet this knowledge does not necessarily help them abstain from heavy drinking.
7. Humans often fall back into self-defeating habits and behavioral patterns even though they have worked hard to overcome them.
8. People often find it easier to learn self-defeating than self-enhancing behaviors. Thus, they very easily overeat but have great trouble following a sensible diet.
9. Psychotherapists, who presumably should be good role models of rationality, often act irrationally in their personal and professional lives.
10. People frequently delude themselves into believing that certain bad experiences (e.g., divorce, stress, and other misfortunes) can never happen to them. (A. Ellis and W. Dryden, *The Practice of Rational Emotive Behavior Therapy*, 2e, © 1997, pp. 6–7. Used by permission of Springer Publishing Company, Inc., New York 10036.)

In his 1997 collaboration with Dryden, he talked about two major categories of psychological disturbance, ego disturbances and discomfort disturbances. The ego disturbances essentially involve demands on the self that are not met and lead to self-damnation. Believing that one should be perfect in all endeavors and that one should be liked by everyone she meets are examples of beliefs that are ego disturbances. Discomfort disturbances basically involve beliefs that lead to an inability to deal with frustration when things in life don't go as one wants or expects. Things become terrible and awful when one is treated unfairly or blocked in some avenue of life.

Core Concepts

Two general principles are most prominent in REBT. First is the notion that a person's current thoughts play a major role in determining how he feels and behaves and therefore play a major role in emotional and psychological disturbances. It is the thoughts occurring in the present moment, not the past history of how these thoughts developed, that become the focus of therapy. Second is the idea that therapy needs to be active and that the therapist must actively help a person confront irrational and dysfunctional beliefs. You will see how these principles apply as we describe the basic ABC theory and later when we discuss therapy methods and techniques.

The ABC method has been at the heart of REBT for many years. According to Ellis and Dryden (1997), the original formulation was fairly simple. A was the activating event, B was the belief about the event, and C was the person's emotional and behavioral responses. As the theory developed, a more complex way of viewing the ABC assessment method also developed:

A = The event or activator. It is often related to the goals a person wants to achieve. It may be an actual event, or it may be an internal thought or feeling related to the past, present, or future.

B = The beliefs (thoughts or cognitions) a person has about the activating event. In other words, B involves the normal evaluations or processing that we do whenever we encounter some kind of event or have some kind of internal stimulus.

C = The consequences of the interaction of A and B. These consequences, in terms of counseling, would involve the emotional upset or negative behavior that results from the AB interaction.

In explaining the more complex relationships of A, B, and C, Ellis and Dryden wrote: "People largely bring their beliefs to A; and they prejudicially view or experience A's in the light of these biased Beliefs (expectations, evaluations) and also in the light of their emotional Consequences (C's). Therefore humans virtually never experience A without B and C, but they also rarely experience B and C without A" (1997, p. 9). Because of Ellis's assumptions about the propensity toward irrationality and the resulting ego and discomfort disturbances, we have this basic idea that human evaluation of events is often distorted and that this distortion causes many of our problems and difficulties.

Let's take two kinds of examples, one involving a fairly concrete activating event and one involving an internal event. In the more concrete event, Sharon, a woman of 32, is visiting her mother for a few days. Her mother shows her a picture of her younger sister's latest baby (her sister has been married for several years and has three children). Her mother remarks, as she is showing off her latest grandchild, that these grandchildren are the only things that really make her life worthwhile. So the event, A, is Sharon being shown the picture by her mother. As her mother is showing her the picture, Sharon begins to feel anxious, angry, and hurt and abruptly excuses herself and goes out. Sharon's emotional reactions and her hasty departure are C, the consequence of A, the activating event. Now, according to REBT, her interpretation of A and her irrational beliefs related to that are what caused the emotional upset of C. Sharon is a single career woman who has not married. She has never been as popular with men as her younger sister, and although she is successful and generally happy, this event has triggered a long-standing belief that she is not a good enough daughter or woman because she isn't married with a family. Thus, we learn that her interpretation of this rather innocent event—being shown a picture of her niece—has created some negative consequences for Sharon, and probably her mother. Note here that her mother's feelings and reactions, although they may have contributed to Sharon's irrational beliefs, are not the cause of her disturbance. It is her negative beliefs and expectations about herself that caused the problem.

> A = Sharon's mother showing her the picture of her sister's baby and remarking that her grandchildren are the only things that really make her life worthwhile.
> B = Sharon's irrational beliefs that she is not a perfect daughter (woman) because she doesn't have a family/children that she is not a worthwhile person because of this, and that her mother must approve of the lifestyle choices she (Sharon) makes.
> C = Sharon's feeling anxious, angry, and hurt and abruptly leaving.

In the second example, using an internal activating event, let's say that Charles, a 55-year-old accountant who has been a devout Catholic his whole life, is out jogging and mentally reviewing his unhappy divorce (something he does regularly). He once again sees in his mind's eye the scene in which he found his wife in bed with another man when he came home unexpectedly. He immediately feels angry, sad, and inadequate and resolves never to be hurt that way again. He also feels a great deal of guilt because he divorced his wife, an act that goes against his religious training.

The activating event (A) is Charles's memory and review of his divorce, and the consequences (C) are his feelings of anger, sadness, and inadequacy, which reinforce his decision not to attempt any more relationships with women. Again, we must examine his interpretation of the memories of his divorce and the bedroom scene. What is he saying to himself about what happened? Since he feels inadequate and is swearing off relationships, one of his irrational beliefs (B) must be that his wife's infidelity was his fault—because he was an inadequate husband, lover, and provider. He probably believes that he should have been able to prevent his wife's behavior. Perhaps other thoughts about how awful it was to have others know what happened, how poorly he handled the divorce settlement, and how disobedient he was to go against his religion are also involved. You can see that probing beliefs (B) is complicated and that a number of feelings, thoughts, and behaviors are involved.

> A = Charles thinking about his divorce, the bedroom scene, and the consequences.
> B = Charles thinking that he was an inadequate husband, that the divorce was his fault, and that this has ruined his life forever.
> C = Charles feeling sad, hopeless, guilty, angry, worthless, and despairing; giving up on relationships.

You will see later how REBT might be conducted in both these examples. After the ABC's are established, the treatment involves D (disputing the irrational belief) and E (developing an effective and rational philosophy of life). The methods and techniques for disputing irrational beliefs will be covered in greater detail under "Therapeutic Techniques."

THERAPEUTIC RELATIONSHIP: REBT

Counselor's Role

There is not a great emphasis on the therapeutic relationship in REBT. In fact, Carl Rogers and Albert Ellis were involved in several debates at national conventions over the years, with Ellis taking the position that the best way to form a relationship is by helping the client examine and change her irrational beliefs. In REBT, the counselor is clearly an active teacher. His job is to teach the client the REBT method of analyzing irrational thoughts and then to work actively to persuade the client to give up those beliefs. From our observations, we would say that the counselor must be able to think on his feet and to quickly and easily point out irrational thoughts.

Counselor-Client Relationship

Many students who have observed Albert Ellis counseling clients on film or videotape conclude that REBT requires a hard-hitting, argumentative approach. They contrast what they see with the gentler, more empathic approaches to counseling. It is true that Albert Ellis seems a bit abrasive at times (some would say that this is putting it mildly), but if you look closely at his practice demonstrations, you can see an unconditional acceptance of the client. Ellis, as we have seen, believes and argues that the most effective way to form a helping relationship is to actively work on the client's problems; empathy is not enough.

Since Ellis is such a dominant figure in REBT, it is particularly important with this theory to remember that the practice of the different theories can vary considerably, depending on the therapist's style. Imagine, for example, a soft-spoken, warm, motherly woman as an REBT therapist. She would still need to be active and help the client confront irrational beliefs, but she might do so in a very different way than an REBT therapist with a more direct, confrontational style. The bottom line, however, is that the therapist must take an active role and help educate the client regarding irrational beliefs and how they impact feelings and behavior. The counselor serves, in many ways, as a teacher or instructor.

ASSESSMENT, GOALS, AND PROCESS OF THERAPY: REBT

Assessment

The basic goals of REBT assessment, according to Ellis and Dryden (1997), are to determine the level of disturbance and whether the client can benefit from therapy. Factors such as the possible length and difficulty of therapy and the types of REBT techniques to use are also examined. The most effective stance of the therapist (active, supportive, etc.) is also assessed, as are skill deficiencies such as social and communication skills, which may need to be provided as part of or outside of therapy. Since REBT includes cognitive, emotive, and behavioral aspects, Ellis and Dryden (1997) suggested several factors that should almost always be part of an REBT assessment. These include the client's description of his self-defeating feelings and behavior, the client's identification of activating events and of his irrational beliefs and second-level irrational beliefs (related irrational beliefs), and the client's expression of anxiety and depression about being anxious and depressed.

There is typically no *formal* assessment phase to REBT. As you can see from the above description of assessment, the therapist typically moves quickly into an analysis of the ABC's and an active educational process about the role of irrational beliefs and thinking. As Ellis and Dryden (1997) put it, "Although assessment interviews and some standard diagnostic tests may at times be useful in exploring clients' disturbances, perhaps the best form of assessment consists of several REBT sessions with the client" (p. 32). If a client has difficulty verbally reporting irrational beliefs and consequences, Dryden (1984) has suggested other methods, such as the Gestalt two-chair dialogue, psychodrama, imagery, and an emotional diary. All these techniques help a person relive an experience and remember what she was saying to herself.

Ellis did develop a personality data form that can be used to get an overall picture of several dimensions of a client's functioning. The scales include acceptance, frustration, injustice, achievement, worth, control, certainty, and catastrophizing. Each scale has several items for which the client rates the frequency of his feelings. For example, on the worth scale, an item states "I feel that I am a pretty worthless person" (Ellis & Dryden, 1997, p. 39). In REBT, however, by far the most commonly used assessment instrument is a simple ABC chart. You will see an example of this chart in the "Therapeutic Techniques" section.

The following dialogue will give you an idea of what the beginning of a counselor-client interaction regarding assessment might be like. According to Ellis and Dryden (1997), the therapist should look for four kinds of irrational beliefs: dogmatic demands, awfulising, low frustration tolerance, and self/other downing. Patrick is a 70-year-old male of Irish descent. He has been extremely depressed since his wife died and has come to a counselor only because his children insisted.

> **Counselor:** So you have been telling me that you don't even feel like getting out of bed in the morning and that you just want to be left alone. It certainly sounds like you are still very depressed, is that right?
>
> **Patrick:** Of course, I'm depressed. I don't need a counselor to tell me that. I don't want your sympathy!
>
> **Counselor:** I'm not here to give you sympathy. I want to get you out of bed!
>
> **Patrick:** So how are you going to do that?
>
> **Counselor:** Well, would you agree to try out a way of looking at this problem that might help? What the hell, since your kids dragged you in here, we have some time together anyway.
>
> **Patrick:** OK, what do you want to know?
>
> **Counselor:** Well, I want us to examine for a while some of what is causing you to stay depressed and not be able to do anything.
>
> **Patrick:** That's easy—my wife died.
>
> **Counselor:** True, but what has that event meant to you? If it's OK with you, we can use a system with A, B, and C standing for different parts of what is going on.

Of course, this is a brief segment, but you can see that the counselor is working toward explaining the ABC system so that he can then begin to assess the irrational beliefs. It seems possible that Patrick might have irrational beliefs in all four categories. He might have beliefs related to *dogmatic demands* (I must have a wife to be happy); to *awfulising* (My wife's death was a terrible blow from which I will never recover); to *low frustration tolerance* (I just can't stand to be alone); and to *self/other downing* (I was never a good enough husband and now I am paying the price). Any of these are possible, and it is the job of the therapist to help the client get explicit about what irrational beliefs are at play. Explaining the ABC system and how thoughts and interpretations affect feeling and behaving is always a part of REBT.

In his earlier writing, Ellis provided a list of frequent irrational beliefs.

1. I MUST do well or very well!
2. I am a BAD OR WORTHLESS person when I act weakly or stupidly.
3. I MUST be approved or accepted by people I find important!
4. I am a BAD, UNLOVABLE PERSON if I get rejected.
5. People MUST treat me fairly and give me what I NEED.
6. People who act immorally are undeserving, ROTTEN PEOPLE!
7. People MUST have few major hassles or troubles.
8. My life MUST live up to my expectations or it is TERRIBLE!
9. I CAN'T STAND really bad things or very difficult people.
10. It's AWFUL or HORRIBLE when major things don't go my way!
11. I CAN'T STAND IT when life is really unfair!
12. I NEED to beloved by someone who matters to me a lot!
13. I NEED a good deal of immediate gratification and HAVE TO feel miserable when I don't get it. (J. Sichel and A. Ellis, *RET Self-Help Form*, © 1984. Used by permission of Institute for Rational-Emotive Therapy, New York.)

Goals

The goals of therapy are negotiated between the client and the therapist, with considerable help from the therapist. Because REBT does not place much, if any, emphasis on the past, it is not likely that "underlying" problems from the past will surface. The therapist is likely to ask the client what is wrong and then fairly quickly dig into those problems via changing irrational beliefs. In practice, however, it is often not that simple, and the therapist frequently has to help the client clarify and identify the problem. The active REBT therapist typically does not hesitate to provide this help. The major goal of REBT is to help clients learn to identify and modify irrational beliefs, but in a more general sense, the goals of REBT are to help clients learn to have a rational philosophy of life and live a rational lifestyle. This usually means that clients learn to use the ABC system to analyze their problems and to examine the underlying beliefs.

Process of Therapy

In REBT, thinking is emphasized throughout counseling. During the initial exploration stage, the counselor and the client explore the connections among the ABC's and, in particular, how the client's irrational beliefs play a prominent role in maintaining the problem. Thinking is clearly emphasized in this stage, although feelings and behavior are also explored. While insight in the traditional sense (insight into past causes of behavior or feelings) is not relevant, insight into the connection between thoughts and feelings is crucial. In fact, this is one of the major goals of REBT because the client must understand and believe in this connection for the therapy to work. In the action stage, the therapist finds ways to help the client give up irrational beliefs and substitute rational ones. You will see how this works in the "Therapeutic Techniques" section.

THERAPEUTIC TECHNIQUES: REBT

After the ABC's are identified, the therapy begins. The main curative effort in REBT is to get the client to dispute and change the irrational beliefs. According to the theory, when this occurs, the negative consequences (C) will stop or be diminished. There are three ways for the therapist to help the client change irrational beliefs: cognitive, emotive, and behavioral techniques. Each requires considerable skill on the part of the therapist. He is the primary force in the disputing process. In an active, directive kind of therapy like REBT the therapist must be skilled. Let's take the case of Sharon, discussed earlier. Recall the ABC's in this case:

A = Sharon's mother showing her the picture of her sister's baby and remarking that her grandchildren are the only things that really make her life worthwhile.

B = Sharon's irrational beliefs that she is not a perfect daughter (woman) because she doesn't have a family/children and is not good-looking, that she is not a worthwhile person because of this, and that her mother must approve of the lifestyle choices she (Sharon) makes.

C = Sharon's feeling anxious, angry, and hurt and abruptly leaving.

Here is a segment of the REBT therapy that might go on after these ABC's have been identified.

See DVD

Chap. 9
Clip 1

Counselor: So seeing this picture brought up a lot of negative feelings about yourself. Do you see how your irrational beliefs played into what happened?

Sharon: Yes, but I just can't help thinking that I am not a good enough daughter and that I will never make my mother happy.

Counselor: Well, let's take one of those at a time. Why is it your responsibility to make your mom happy?

Sharon: Well, it isn't really, but she is my mom and I know she would like me to get married and give her some grandchildren.

Counselor: Has she told you that, said something like "Sharon, I am just not going to be happy until you give me grandchildren".

Sharon: No, she hasn't, but I know she thinks it.

Counselor: So what if she does think it and would be happy to have you give her grandchildren? Does that mean you *have* to make her happy? Should you dedicate your life to that?

Sharon: Well, no, not really.

Counselor: So you agree that it is irrational for you to take responsibility for your mother's happiness?

Sharon: Well, when you put it that way, yes, it doesn't make too much sense.

Counselor: So is there a way to change that irrational belief that "I have to make my mother happy" to a rational one?

Sharon: Well, I suppose, it is more rational to say that I would like to make my mother happy.

Counselor: And I would add another sentence: "And I can't really control how my mother feels."

This kind of disputing of beliefs is the technique most commonly used in REBT. Ellis is a master of this technique, and in our judgment, REBT therapists typically think fast and are good at this kind of disputation. In this example, the counselor disputes Sharon's irrational beliefs with questions like "Why is it your responsibility to make your mom happy?" and "So what if she does think it and would be happy to have you give her grandchildren? Does that mean you *have* to make her happy? Should you dedicate your life to that?" As you can see, these disputations will all lead to more rational thoughts like "My mother may be disappointed that I am not married with children, but that's her business" and "I will be a good daughter and do what I can for my mother, but I am not responsible for her happiness!"

> **D** = The irrational belief that Sharon must always please her mother and be the perfect daughter is successfully disputed and changed to a more rational one.

> **E** = Sharon is not anxious or guilty, although perhaps disappointed, about not pleasing her mother and being the "ideal" daughter.

There are a variety of self-help forms using the basic ABC method with instructions on the method and how to challenge irrational beliefs. Ellis' form is for sale at his institute and a number of others can be found on the internet.

Although REBT, and Ellis, has most often been seen as using direct disputation of irrational beliefs, Ellis and Dryden (1997) contended that this criticism of REBT that it ignores the emotional side of life is unfair. They listed several emotion-oriented techniques that are used, including unconditional acceptance, humor, stories, and parables. Ellis has composed a number of humorous songs to help illustrate irrational beliefs. Ellis and Dryden (1997) provide one of them (sung to the tune of "God Save the King"):

God save my precious spleen
Send me a life serene
God save my spleen
Protect me from things odious
Give me a life melodious
And if things get too onerous
I'll whine, bawl, and scream. (p. 62)

Other emotive techniques include role-reversal, shame-attacking, and risk-taking exercises. An example of a shame-attacking and risk-taking exercise will provide you with a sense of the creative and active methods used in REBT. Tim is a 32-year-old man who has always been very self-conscious about his body type. He is quite thin and has several irrational beliefs about how he must be more muscular and masculine looking to be accepted by others.

> **Tim:** I know it is wrong, but I still feel really self-conscious about how I look. I'm as skinny as a rail.
> **Counselor:** Is that why you have on loose clothes again?
> **Tim:** Yeah.
> **Counselor:** Well, you remember how we identified the irrational statements that you make to yourself about your body—like "I'm not a real man unless I have good body" and "I can never have a happy life with this body."
> **Tim:** Yes, I know those things are irrational, but I just keep thinking them.
> **Counselor:** OK, would you be willing to try something to help yourself get rid of those irrational thoughts?

> **Tim:** OK.
>
> **Counselor:** I want you to get some tight-fitting clothes and go out in public in them.
> Then I want you to say hello to several people and exchange pleasantries with them.
>
> **Tim:** Oh. . . I don't know if I can do that!

The idea is to get Tim to get over his irrational thinking about his body shape by parading around in tight clothes and "shaming" himself; eventually, he can say something like "So they've seen my skinny body and it wasn't that big a deal!"

Ellis was one of the first theorists to advocate the use of homework as a part of counseling. Many of these homework assignments involve behavioral methods and tasks. Ellis and Dryden (1997) cited the following as behavioral methods that can be used with REBT: in vivo desensitization, flooding, staying in uncomfortable situations in order to build tolerance of fear and frustration (another type of desensitization), antiprocrastination exercises (clients start tasks early rather than later), rewards and punishments, and skills training. Behavioral methods were discussed in Chapter 8.

DEVELOPMENT OF COGNITIVE THERAPY

Aaron Beck was born in Providence, Rhode Island, in 1921. He grew up in a middle-class family and was active in sports and the Boy Scouts until the age of 8, when he was hospitalized for a life-threatening infection. After being hospitalized for a month, he changed from a very active boy to one who liked reading and quieter pursuits. He also developed a strong fear of hospitals, blood, and the smell of ether. He dealt with these fears rationally: "I learned not to be concerned about the faint feeling, but just to keep active" (Spear, 2003, p. 1). This experience probably had something to do with his development of a cognitive theory of counseling.

Beck received an M.D. from Yale University in 1946 and completed a residency in neurology. He worked at the Valley Forge Hospital during the Korean War in the early 1950s, attended the Philadelphia Institute of Psychoanalysis, graduated in 1958, and began working on the faculty at the University of Pennsylvania. Early research on the efficacy of psychoanalysis for depression led him to develop cognitive therapy. He created the Beck Institute for Cognitive Therapy and Research, now directed by his daughter Dr. Judith Beck. Beck has received many professional honors and has published over 375 articles and 14 books (Biography, 2003). He is also the author of BDI–II, certainly the most widely used inventory of depression.

In a *New York Times* article, Goode (2000) described Beck and provided some comments from some of his students:

> And in its way, cognitive therapy—practical, cerebral and to the point—is also a fair reflection of the man who conceived it. He is 78 now, an emeritus professor of psychiatry at the University of Pennsylvania, four times a father, eight times a grandfather. Yet even as a younger man, his former students say, Dr. Beck, with his white hair and the bow tie he carefully affixed each morning, projected a grandfatherly air, offering a nurturing presence, a passion for collecting data, a conviction that evidence always trumps opinion. (© 2000 by The New York Times Co. Reprinted with permission.)

As with most theories, Beck's cognitive approach has evolved over time with research and practice experience. Beck identified the earlier stages as involving a "linear" relationship between a person's cognitions (thoughts, interpretations) and her subsequent feelings, motivation, and behavior (Beck & Weishaar, 2005). His more recent formulations (Beck & Weishar, 2005) suggested that the four systems that are involved in survival—the cognitive, behavioral, affective, and motivational systems—work together in modes. "Modes are networks of cognitive, affective, motivational, and behavioral schemas that compose personality and interpret ongoing situations" (Beck, 2005, p. 239).

ASSUMPTIONS AND CORE CONCEPTS: COGNITIVE THERAPY

View of Human Nature

Clark and Steer (1996) suggested four basic assumptions of Beck's cognitive therapy regarding how humans function in the world: (1) Individuals actively construct their reality, (2) cognition mediates affect and behavior, (3) cognition is knowable and accessible, and (4) cognitive change is central to the human change process (pp. 76–77).

Although these are focused in a somewhat different way, they are similar to Ellis's beliefs that individuals cognitively process events and that their reactions are a result of how they interpret information. Beck and other cognitive therapists stress that this is an information-processing mode. REBT and cognitive therapy also share the idea that a person can become aware of these thoughts that are affecting his behavior and that he can change them. This contrasts somewhat with the Freudian idea of an "unconscious" that contains thoughts, feelings, and memories that are not within our awareness. One might argue, however, that a client's irrational thoughts and feelings are not really within his awareness until he becomes aware of the importance of cognitions and begins to analyze his previously "automatic" negative thoughts.

Although not specifically emphasized, Beck's use of the Socratic method implies that he has considerable confidence in his clients' abilities to uncover their own irrationalities and change them. Although emphasizing cognitions, Beck has a deep respect for human emotion, and observations of his work and reports from his students lead one to believe that he sees humans as complex and multifaceted creatures.

Core Concepts

Automatic Thoughts and Schemas Beck's early theory was primarily based on work with depression and anxiety. The "linear path" that he originally developed included a model with these steps:

Schemas > Automatic Thoughts > Negative Interpretations > Emotional/Behavioral Problems

Schemas are core beliefs, developed throughout life, similar to Adler's notion of lifestyle beliefs that affect one's interpretation of events. These interpretations often become automatic and are called automatic thoughts. Here is an example involving Stephan, a client whose life schemas have produced recurring automatic thoughts that have then led to chronic depression.

Stephan: Well, here I am again. As usual, people at work acted as if I wasn't even there and I feel really depressed.

Counselor: What happened?

Stephan: A group of people was going out to lunch and didn't even ask me to go.

Counselor: Well, did you ask if you could go?

Stephan: No, they don't want me around.

Counselor: Well, how do you know that if you didn't ask?

Stephan: Let's face it, Doc. I'm not a very interesting or fun person. I've always been the oddball in any group.

Counselor: What thought was going through your mind when you saw those people going out to lunch?

Stephan: Nobody wants to be around me.

Counselor: Do you remember our discussion before about these kinds of thoughts? You weren't very sociable growing up, but does that mean you will always be rejected by everyone?

Stephan: Well, I've felt that way for so long, it's hard not to have those thoughts.

What you see here is what Beck (2000) called the *cognitive triad*, a term that, in general, describes the schemas of chronically depressed clients. The depressed person has a negative view of himself, the world, and the future. In the above example, Stephan has come to believe that he is just not a person who other people like. He feels that he has nothing to offer others and that he never will fit in. Because of this schema, he has "automatic" thoughts about himself and how others will treat him. In the above example, the automatic thoughts might be "Nobody wants to be around me," "I don't have anything interesting to say," and "I'm worthless." You can see how these distorted automatic thoughts make sense, given this client's view of the world (schema). You can also see how this schema and these thoughts might lead to feelings of depression and hopelessness and to interpersonal avoidance behaviors. Cognitive therapy seeks to change these schemas and thoughts.

Thinking Distortions Cognitive therapy, like REBT, involves teaching clients to consciously control their thoughts and thereby their interpretations of events. Where Ellis focuses a great deal of attention on the different kinds of irrational beliefs, Beck's theory focuses on thinking distortions. He has listed and discussed these distortions in many of his books and chapters (Beck, 1967; Beck, Rush, Shaw, & Emory, 1979; Beck & Weishar, 2005). A brief definition and an example follow for each.

ARBITRARY INFERENCE Here a person comes to a conclusion inappropriately when there is really no evidence, or even contrary evidence, for the conclusion. For example, a student gets a C on a particularly hard test and concludes that he just isn't smart enough for college. He has failed to consider other evidence—that he has a solid B average and that this was a very difficult exam.

SELECTIVE ABSTRACTION This involves paying attention to a selective piece of information without looking at the other information or considering the situation as a whole. For example, a teenage boy walks past a girl at school and she doesn't say hello. He concludes that she is not really interested in him when, in fact, she was very involved in thinking about her next class and really has a crush on him.

OVERGENERALIZATION In this logical fallacy, a person draws a conclusion from very limited data. For example, a woman who is lonely calls two people she knows and asks them out for coffee, and both tell her they are busy. From this, she erroneously concludes that people don't want to be friends with her.

MAGNIFICATION AND MINIMIZATION   These consist of placing far too much importance on a particular event or situation and not placing enough importance on an event or situation, respectively. An example of magnification is a young man who looks in the mirror, sees a zit on his nose, and immediately decides he looks so awful that he can't go to school. An example of minimization is an older woman who doesn't see her adult son as dependent, even though he calls her several times a day to ask for her opinion on even the most trivial decisions he has to make and constantly asks for money.

PERSONALIZATION   We have all heard the expression "Don't take it so personally." This means that you shouldn't imagine that whatever happens (usually something bad) is necessarily related to you or something you have or haven't done. A retired man whose wife comes home from shopping and seems angry and on edge immediately thinks that she is mad at him when in reality she ran into a friend who made her very angry and she just doesn't want to talk about it.

DICHOTOMOUS THINKING   Another term for this is black-and-white thinking. It means that a person interprets something as either one extreme or the other. For example, a counselee finishes her first session with a counselor and concludes that since she didn't solve her problem, the counseling is going to be worthless.

Dysfunctional Modes   In their later writings, Beck & Weishar (2005) suggested that the view of schemas and thoughts as directly triggering feelings, motivation, and behavior is more complicated. He wrote that schemas form modes, which are "networks of cognitive, affective, motivational, and behavioral schemas that compose personality and interpret ongoing situations" (Beck, 2005, p. 239). In terms of treatment, he talked about "discharging and modifying the modes."

> There are three major approaches to "treating" the dysfunctional modes: first, deactivating them, second, modifying their structure and content, and third, priming or "constructing" more adaptive modes to neutralize them. In actual practice, the first and third procedures are carried out simultaneously (for example, demonstrating that a particular belief is wrong or dysfunctional and that another belief is more accurate and adaptive). (Beck, 1996, p. 15)

Beck suggested that different pathologies can be viewed in terms of the "primal" modes. For example, for a specific phobia, the primal mode would include the following: cognitive—the belief that the phobic stimulus is dangerous; affective—anxiety; behavioral—escape or avoidance; and physiological—autonomic nervous system activation (Beck, 1996). In discussing the role of medication in modifying these modes, Beck said, "From a neurochemical perspective, the modes can be viewed as consisting of patterns of neural networks, as yet undefined" (Beck, 1996, p. 18). If this is true, then pharmacological agents have the potential to deactivate negative modes. According to Beck, the pathway to the brain is different "for drugs and life experience (including psychotherapy): Drugs affect the mode through direct entry into the brain via the bloodstream and modify neural activity. External events are funneled through sensory channels, such as vision and hearing, and after preliminary processing are transformed into the neural activity that culminates in the modal activation or deactivation" (1996, p. 18). In other words, Beck is saying that treatment (defined in this later evolution of his theory as deactivation of the modes) with drugs may give an effect similar to psychotherapy.

Young's Expansion of Schemas Beck's theory has evolved from a specific treatment for depression to a more general cognitive approach to general problems and pathology. One interesting development has been the work of Jeffrey Young in expanding cognitive theory into what he calls *schema therapy*. Young (2003) proposed an expansion of the concept of schemas into four main constructs: early maladaptive schemas, schema domains, coping styles, and schema modes. The general goals are to help clients stop using maladaptive coping styles and to repair their early maladaptive schemas. Early maladaptive schemas are patterns of negative ways of thinking that tend to be repeated. Young and his colleagues have identified 18 different maladaptive schemas. The early maladaptive schemas are grouped into five schema domains according to what basic needs are not satisfied in childhood. Coping styles are the ways in which children learn to adapt to the negative childhood experiences and their subsequent maladaptive ways of thinking. A schema mode is a person's particular emotional state and the related coping behaviors he is using at a particular moment. These modes shift, and part of the therapy is to help the client move back out of negative modes as quickly as possible. This is a fascinating and complex theory that has been developed with a focus on working with personality disorders. See the book Web page for information on references that describe the theory in more detail.

THERAPEUTIC RELATIONSHIP: COGNITIVE THERAPY

Counselor's Role

Beck & Weishar (2005) stressed the therapist's need for flexibility and effective interpersonal skills. He noted that different kinds of problems call for different kinds of relationships: "For example, the inertia of depression responds best to behavioral interventions, while the suicidal ideation and pessimism of depression respond best to cognitive techniques" (p. 252). As you learned in the section describing Dr. Beck, he is a warm, grandfatherly man, and consequently, some of this kind of relationship flavor has been associated with cognitive therapy. The nature of the relationship between client and counselor in REBT is often contrasted with that of the relationship in cognitive therapy. In our view, there are, indeed, some structural differences. REBT, as we have mentioned, can involve rather direct challenges of a client's irrational beliefs, while cognitive therapy, which relies on the Socratic method, is more of a leading than a confronting approach. We don't believe, however, that the contrast should be overemphasized. The therapist's personality will also play an important role in how he practices either REBT or cognitive therapy.

Counselor-Client Relationship

Beck & Weishar (2005) have described Beck's approach to working with clients as "collaborative empiricism." He sees the client and the counselor working together, with the client as a "practical scientist" who has gotten into trouble because of faulty interpretation of information. He also discusses "guided discovery" as a way of helping the client connect his current distorted beliefs to the past. The relationship is one of trust and respect, but the client is not an equal of the counselor, who facilitates the movement of the therapy. *Socratic dialogue*, the model for client-counselor interaction, is a form of questioning designed to facilitate new learning. According to Beck & Weishar (2005), there are four purposes for Socratic questions: to clarify or define problems; assist in the identification of thoughts, images, and assumptions; examine the meanings of events for the client, and assess the consequences of maintaining maladaptive thoughts and behaviors. (p. 252)

Here is a brief example of a Socratic dialogue.

> **Counselor:** So what happens when you keep telling yourself how scared and incapable you are of confronting your father?
> **Client:** Well, that's obvious, I don't confront my father.
> **Counselor:** And that makes you feel. . . ?
> **Client:** Angry, childish, and pissed off at myself.
> **Counselor:** So what would happen if you were able to stop believing this about yourself, at least for a while?
> **Client:** I guess I might confront my father. That is still pretty scary.
> **Counselor:** Yes, but then how does this interfere with your relationship with him?

Clearly, the therapist makes some decisions about what needs to be asked, but he does not push the client into the conclusions that he has drawn. There is somewhat of a paradox here in that the therapist is a kind of "expert" but at the same time works with the client to discover misinterpretations and dysfunctional thoughts. The relationship is warm and empathic but is certainly not client-centered in the Rogerian sense.

ASSESSMENT, GOALS, AND PROCESS OF THERAPY: COGNITIVE THERAPY

Assessment

Assessment in cognitive therapy, as in REBT, is most often a part of the initial interview. Instruments like the Beck Depression Inventory, which measures depression, may also be used. This instrument is also sometimes used to gauge session-by-session progress for depression. As in REBT, assessment mostly involves identifying the connections among automatic thoughts, schemas (modes), and the problem feelings or behaviors. Thus, a chart or form with the column headings Situation, Automatic Thought, Emotion, and Behavior is often used for assessment.

The therapist would likely use this type of chart as he talks with the client, pointing out connections among the four areas. Typically, the client would then be asked to use this same method as homework, recording situations and automatic thoughts related to problem emotions or behaviors. As in REBT, a kind of client education is going on as the therapist attempts to assess the thoughts, emotions, and behaviors related to the situation. The therapist begins early to try to get the client to see the connections among thoughts, feelings, and behaviors.

In discussing the automatic thoughts, the therapist may also move in the direction of discussing the schemas underlying the automatic thoughts, but this would probably come a bit later when the therapist has a better idea of what kinds of schemas might be involved. The length of therapy will determine how extensively the therapist will be able to address these underlying schemas. Dealing with them may be quite complex. Let's take an example from an interview where the therapist is assessing the thoughts and schemas and at the same time working to educate the client. In this example, the client is Tom, a 38-year-old Caucasian male who has been experiencing stress and anxiety.

Tom: The stress is really getting me down. I can't sleep. I've lost weight.

Counselor: It does sound really difficult. Let's take that one situation you described earlier, where your father called and was so worried about your brother. You felt really anxious after that call, right?

Tom: Yes, I didn't know what to do . . . my brother left rehab again and my dad was crying. I felt like I was going to throw up.

Counselor: Can you remember what thoughts were going through your head when this happened?

Tom: I was thinking. . . damn, not again, and I don't know what to do, how to help my dad. I wish Jan and Ansel could help.

Counselor: Who are Jan and Ansel?

Tom: My sister and brother. Neither of them is very good at being supportive.

Counselor: So was another thought "I've got to help my Dad, because nobody else can"?

Tom: Well, something like that. I'm the one he always turns to.

Counselor: So is that phrase "I've got to help" one that comes to you kind of automatically?

Tom: I suppose that's true, more so for people I really care about.

Counselor: And if you can't help, you feel really rotten—sometimes even to the point of getting ill or not sleeping.

Tom: Exactly!

Counselor: So what's the connection between that thought that "I've got to help" and feeling rotten?

Tom: I see what you are getting at. When I have those thoughts that I have to help, sometimes I know I get too involved, but jeez. . . this is my dad.

So we see here that the therapist is beginning to help Tom identify what automatic thoughts trigger his anxiety. They seem to be related to Tom's feeling that he must always be able to help his Dad or take away his pain.

Situation	Automatic Thought	Emotion	Behavior
Father calls, in distress	I am responsible, I must be able to help	Stress, anxiety, guilt, pressure	Drop everything, take responsibility

The therapist will probably hypothesize that Tom has problems with these automatic thoughts in other situations whenever someone asks him for help or tells him about a problem. The therapist might further imagine that perhaps people who know Tom also know that he will always take responsibility for helping them. They may even "use" him because he has this "automatic" responsibility-taking characteristic. In the assessment phase, which we are demonstrating here, the therapist will work to better understand the automatic thoughts and the schemas underlying them and also begin to teach Tom about the connections among thoughts, feelings, and behaviors. In the case of cognitive therapy, the therapist will focus on how thoughts trigger feelings and behaviors.

Here the underlying schema seems to jump out at us: Tom has taken on or been given the role of "fixer" in his family—he is the go-to guy, the responsible one. There may be a connection between Tom's gender socialization and this schema that he has taken on. For example, he may be the only strong male in the family, and by virtue of this male role, he may be expected to take charge and help other family members. Or perhaps Tom's dad is an alcoholic, and Tom's role has evolved from his experience in the family. Learning this background may be useful, but the focus in cognitive therapy will ultimately be on changing Tom's current distorted thinking and the underlying schema that are causing him problems—that is, changing Tom's automatic thoughts that flow from the schema that he must always be the responsible one and take care of everyone.

Although assessment instruments, other than informal charts or surveys, are not necessarily used in cognitive therapy, a number are available, particularly to assess anxiety and depression. Blankstein and Zindel (2001) provided a comprehensive discussion of these, including instruments like the Penn State Worry Questionnaire, the Meta-Cognitions Questionnaire, the Panic Appraisal Inventory, and the Automatic Thoughts Questionnaire. These inventories have varying degrees of reliability and usefulness in clinical settings. In our view, given the current press for brief therapy, a clinical interview, and perhaps a brief assessment such as the Beck Depression Inventory (BDI–II), makes the most sense, because therapy can begin almost immediately. The BDI–II is by far the most well known of the assessment instruments that might be used in cognitive therapy. The initial form was developed by Beck during his early work with depression. It is brief and gives a quick picture of the mood of a client. It is based on Beck's theory in that it asks the client to rate basic beliefs. For example, there are questions on a person's degree of pessimism, her sense of failure, and so on.

Beck also identified "profiles" related to different disorders, similar to the cognitive triad for depression that we discussed earlier. These are essentially generalizations about what Beck & Weishar (2005) call "systematic bias in processing information" (p. 247). For example, the profile for panic disorder is "Catastrophic interpretation of bodily/mental experiences" and for obsession, "Repeated warning or doubts about safety" (p. 251). These profiles can serve as guides for therapists when exploring the basic modes that might be involved in the distorted interpretation of situations and events that create the pathology.

Persons and Davidson (2001) suggested a five-component case formulation plan to guide the process of therapy. This includes a problem list, diagnosis, working hypothesis, strengths and assets, and treatment plan. In the working hypothesis, "the therapist tells a story that describes the relationships among the components of the Working Hypothesis (Schemata, Precipitants/Activating Situations, and Origins), tying them to the problems on the Problem List" (p. 96). The treatment plan becomes a map for the treatment process. Persons and Davidson suggested that the case formulation can be helpful to a therapist by clarifying treatment goals, keeping a therapeutic focus, and helping the client play an active and collaborative role. The idea of a more formal treatment formulation and plan may be particularly appealing to new therapists who are attempting to use cognitive therapy and who need structure in the process of therapy.

Goals

The primary goal of cognitive therapy is to modify thinking that leads to problem behaviors and feelings. In modifying this thinking, the therapist and the client will likely need to examine and change or modify the life schemas that underlie the automatic thoughts. The degree to which this can be a viable goal depends on the length of time available and the nature of the schema that needs changing. Two examples, using the same client, will illustrate the different ways that life schemas can influence the nature and length of therapy.

See DVD

Chap. 9
Clip 2

Example 1: Christian is a 21-year-old community college student. He has always been just too shy to be able to get involved with the gay community. He is certain about the fact that he is gay and feels OK about this. He admits, however, that he still feels some guilt about being sexually attracted to men. He wants to meet people and to have a romantic relationship, but whenever he tries to get up the courage to go to a meeting or speak to someone, he freezes up. In cognitive therapy, he soon learned that he has some automatic thoughts that come up every time he starts to do something socially: "Everyone is better looking than me, I don't have anything to say, and I always make a fool of myself. Maybe being gay is weird."

Christian and his counselor were able to discuss the fallacies and logical inconsistencies of these statements, and they found ways to challenge them. For example, the therapist had Christian role-play an encounter with someone he was meeting for the first time and coached him through a conversation. This helped convince Christian that the automatic thought that he had nothing to say was not totally true, and he agreed to try to have a conversation with someone who might be a potential date during the next week. Christian and his counselor also discussed his guilt about being gay. Christian emphasized that he really did feel OK about his sexual orientation and that he felt this was just leftover homophobia that he had from growing up in an essentially homophobic culture. They also talked a bit about Christian's coming-out process and how well that had gone with his parents and most of his friends.

After some practice and work on learning how to challenge his negative automatic thoughts as they came up, Christian was able to function better socially, and he soon developed a social network and began to date. There was no real need to delve further into his life schemas to see which ones were related to his automatic thoughts. He was able to modify his thoughts and move on in a relatively short course of counseling.

Example 2: Christian is a 21-year-old community college student. He has always been just too shy to be able to get involved with the gay community. He is certain about the fact that he is gay and feels OK about this. He admits, however, that he still feels some guilt about being sexually attracted to men. He wants to meet people and to have a romantic relationship, but whenever he tries to get up the courage to go to a meeting or speak to someone, he freezes up. In cognitive therapy, he soon learned that he has some automatic thoughts that come up every time he starts to do something socially: "Everyone is better looking than me, I don't have anything to say, and I always make a fool of myself. Maybe being gay is weird."

As the cognitive therapist began to work with Christian to identify his automatic thoughts, he learned that Christian had a history of depression, that he had been tossed back and forth between his mother and father during his childhood, and that in his perception neither of his parents had loved him. Both parents were from very fundamental-ist homes and had outright rejected Christian after he came out as a gay. He reported that his mother had been telling him how fat and worthless he was since he was a little boy.

In this case, the therapist realized that a relatively brief intervention focused mostly on automatic thoughts would probably not work. He decided that more time needed to be spent sorting out the negative life schemas that Christian had developed and finding ways to help him challenge the schemas and learn new, more positive schemas about himself. This might take a while.

In these examples, then, it becomes obvious that the goals of counseling might be quite dif-ferent depending on the client and his situation. We will discuss some of the briefer methods for working with schemas, but in these examples, we wanted to point out the importance of consid-ering the client and his situation before establishing goals. It was quite appropriate in the first example for the counselor to work quickly to challenge Christian's automatic thoughts, but in the second example, which looked very similar on the surface, it is clear that more consideration needed to be given to setting goals and interventions.

Process of Therapy

Beck & Weishar (2005) identified three stages of counseling: initial sessions, middle and later sessions, and the end of treatment. In the initial sessions, the therapist works on building a rela-tionship, on educating the client about the relationship between thinking and feelings, on defin-ing and assessing the problems, on achieving symptom relief (through problem solving, goal setting, hope), on giving homework to help the client recognize connections, and on providing ongoing feedback about the process. The therapist is active in this stage.

In the middle stage, the emphasis is on getting the client to think and challenge automatic thoughts. Underlying assumptions (schemas) can also be examined. "In later sessions, the patient assumes more responsibility for identifying problems and solutions and for creating homework assignments. The therapist takes on the role of advisor rather than teacher as the patient becomes more able to use cognitive techniques to solve problems" (Beck & Weishar, 2005, p. 254).

Treatment ends when the client is able to use cognitive therapy to solve his own problems without the aid of a therapist. According to Beck (2000), it is important to help the patient understand that he will have setbacks and that these are normal and expected. This is called *relapse prevention* and is important because it helps keep the client moving in a positive direction rather than giving up when he does have a setback. Beck also recommended "booster" sessions to help keep the client on track.

THERAPEUTIC TECHNIQUES: COGNITIVE THERAPY

Once the assessment, with the client, determines how dysfunctional thinking and related modes (networks of cognitive, affective, motivational, and behavioral schemas) are involved in the client's problems, the therapist must help the client change these patterns of interpretation. In the earlier version of cognitive therapy, as we have noted, a kind of linear chart was used to help conceptualize the connections among the situation, schemas, automatic thoughts, and negative emotions/behaviors, with additional columns used to represent analysis of distorted thinking and new ways of feeling and thinking that could come out of changing the distorted automatic thoughts. The newer conceptualization of modes involves a more complex and less linear way of looking at schemas and automatic thoughts, but the methods for challenging and changing them are similar to earlier methods and techniques.

A number of different cognitive and behavioral techniques have been developed by Beck and other cognitive therapists (Beck & Weishar, 2005; Beck, 1995; Padesky & Greenberger, 1995). Following are descriptions of several cognitive techniques with brief counseling dialogues that show how each technique might work.

Identifying Automatic Thoughts

As with REBT, just becoming aware of the connections among thoughts, feelings, and behaviors and, in this case, the influence that thoughts have on negative feelings and behaviors can be quite helpful. In the language of cognitive therapy, this begins with the identification of automatic thoughts. As you have learned, however, just identifying automatic thoughts doesn't really get at the underlying schemas that may be triggering these thoughts. Nonetheless, just identifying the thoughts can be useful.

> **Counselor:** OK, so you once again got really nervous when your boss asked you a question in the sales meeting. Remember our talk about how your thoughts influence how you feel. What were the thoughts that you had when you were feeling so nervous?
>
> **Client:** I was thinking that I would make a fool of myself. . . you know, not be able to give a good answer.
>
> **Counselor:** So if I were to put that into a short, succinct automatic thought statement, would it be something like "I'm going to screw up."
>
> **Client:** Something like that; maybe more like "I'm really nervous."

Using Logical Analysis

In addition to simply recognizing them, we can test automatic thoughts with evidence to identify logical distortions.

> **Counselor:** You said that you always do yourself in and that you are incapable of taking care of yourself, right?
>
> **Client:** Right, I'm always doing things that aren't good for me; I have some kind of need to be self-destructive.
>
> **Counselor:** Well, let's look at that thought that you have all the time a bit more closely. How do you explain the fact that you have come in for counseling? Aren't you trying to take care of yourself here?

In this example, the therapist is gently encouraging the client to examine whether evidence actually exists for the belief that he cannot take of himself, particularly by providing the contradictory evidence that he is taking care of himself by coming to counseling.

Avoiding Reattribution

Clients sometimes take on blame or responsibility for any event that goes wrong, thereby creating negative emotions and behavior. This technique helps clients explore alternate ways of looking at who is responsible for events.

> **Client:** It happened again. I screwed up another situation at work. My boss was pissed off all afternoon.
>
> **Counselor:** Well, let's take a look at that situation. Did your boss directly tell you that she was pissed off at you?
>
> **Client:** Not exactly, but I had just turned in a big project, and I don't think she liked it.
>
> **Counselor:** Has your boss ever been pissed off before because of something that is not at all related to work?
>
> **Client:** Well, she does have her moods. I think her kids get to her sometimes.
>
> **Counselor:** So maybe she just had a bad morning with the kids.

Decatastrophizing

Some clients tend to see everything that happens as a catastrophe. They always imagine the worst possible outcome. To challenge this kind of distorted thinking, the "what if" technique is often used. The client is asked to image what might really happen as a result of what seems catastrophic.

> **Client:** I haven't slept for three nights. I've been worrying about my Dad. He fell down the other day, and I'm scared to death that he is going to break a leg or hip or something. He's getting pretty old.
>
> **Counselor:** That would be difficult. Has he fallen a lot? Or broken anything?
>
> **Client:** Well, not really, but I just have this feeling.
>
> **Counselor:** Well, what if he does fall again, or even break his leg? What would happen?
>
> **Client:** Well, it would be terrible. My Mom would be really upset and Dad hates hospitals.
>
> **Counselor:** Well, it would be a very difficult situation for the family. Do you think you all could handle it?
>
> **Client:** Well, I guess we could. It would be hard. My sister would probably help, and the people at church are pretty supportive.

Challenging Maladaptive Assumptions

Clients often make assumptions about themselves of which they are not completely aware. For example, a client might have assumed for years that she is just not the type to have an intimate relationship. Underlying this may be a somewhat unexamined assumption that she is not sexually appealing.

> **Client:** I did have a conversation with a guy. He seemed nice, but he would never be interested in me.
>
> **Counselor:** Why?
>
> **Client:** Well, guys are just not that interested in me.
>
> **Counselor:** Why is that?

Client: Well, I've never really had a boyfriend. Everybody just wants to be "friends."
Counselor: Why is that?
Client: Well, I guess that I'm just not a very sexy person.
Counselor: So you have basically always believed that you aren't attractive.
Client: Well. . . I guess I have.

Thought stopping, positive imagery, and positive self-talk are also often used in cognitive therapy. Positive imagery—asking the client to imagine a positive outcome—can help challenge negative automatic thoughts. Thought stopping—doing something like shouting "Stop" to oneself—is used as a way to break the negative thought cycle. Positive self-talk—saying positive, affirming things to oneself—is also a way to interfere with the negative thought cycle.

Modifying Cognitions with Behavioral Techniques

Beck & Weishar (2005) suggested a number of behavioral techniques that are primarily aimed at modifying cognitions, as opposed to behavioral techniques that are used to modify behavior without any thought to the cognitive mediation. Here are some of these.

Homework In both REBT and cognitive therapy, homework is an important technique. It can include having the client actually try out his new awareness of the concept of automatic thoughts by having him attempt to modify them in some everyday situations between sessions. This is really a hallmark of most cognitive and behavior therapies.

Hypothesis Testing In this activity, the client is asked to evaluate a negative hypothesis about herself by testing it out in real life and by discussing it with the therapist. For example, a client who believes that she is not a very good mother and spouse might be asked to list all of the things she does for her children and husband over several days. The therapist could then help her examine the list and encourage her to take note of the many different contributions she makes. A variation of this is called *activity scheduling* and might involve having a client who says that she is depressed all the time keep a record of her level of depression/pleasure for each activity in a day. The therapist could then help her see that there are times when she does feel better and perhaps help her plan ways to increase those times.

Role Playing This involves having the client practice interpersonal behaviors in order to improve his skills and confidence. When used in cognitive therapy, this technique challenges a person's beliefs that he can't engage in some interpersonal activity. Following is a counseling segment with Marvin demonstrating this.

Marvin: I am just not able to carry on a simple conversation with a woman.
Counselor: What happens when you try?
Marvin: I just get tongue-tied and don't know what to say.
Counselor: Would you be willing to try an experiment to see if you can learn to carry on a conversation?
Marvin: Well, it depends. What is it?
Counselor: Well, I want you to pretend that I am a woman you're sitting next to at the snack counter at your health club.

> **Marvin:** Yeah, I've seen this done—it's called role playing, right?
> **Counselor:** Yes. So can you try it?
> **Marvin:** I don't know. . . OK.
> **Counselor:** Now if you get stuck, just raise your hand and we can talk about what you are experiencing and what you might say.

You can see that the therapist serves as a kind of coach, helping the client develop his skills and also decrease anxiety. But, again, the main goal is not to develop the client's skills, at least from a cognitive therapy perspective. Rather, the main goal is to change the client's distorted thinking related to his interpersonal abilities.

All of these techniques are used in cognitive therapy to help the client change negative automatic thoughts and the underlying negative schemas that he has developed about himself. Beck & Weishar (2005) have emphasized in his later writings that these negative schemas are part of a system of modes that includes cognitive, affective, motivational, and behavioral aspects. Thus, all of these parts of the system are affected when automatic beliefs and schemas are modified. Beck & Weishar (2005) have described the overall therapeutic process in the following way:

> The therapy attempts to improve reality testing through continuous evaluation of personal conclusions. The immediate goal is to shift the information-processing apparatus to a more "neutral" condition so that events will be evaluated in a more balanced way. There are three major approaches to treating dysfunctional modes: (1) deactivating them to neutralize them, (2) modifying their content and structure, and (3) constructing more adaptive modes to neutralize them. (p. 240)

INTEGRATED COGNITIVE-BEHAVIORAL TECHNIQUES

As we mentioned in the previous chapter on behavior therapy, cognitive and behavioral approaches have been integrated into what is now called *cognitive-behavioral therapy* (CBT). You can see this integration in both Ellis's and Beck's theories, as behavioral techniques are important aspects of their approaches. A number of other integrated CBT techniques have been developed, although we will cover only a few of these: Meichenbaum's (1974, 1985, 1993, 1997) stress inoculation and his more recent constructivist cognitive behavioral treatment; eye movement desensitization reprocessing (Shapiro, 2001); problem-solving therapy, described by D'Zurilla and Nezu (1999); and treatment protocols.

Stress Inoculation

As the name implies, this method attempts to inoculate a person by going through a kind of stress rehearsal (much like the body rehearses its reaction to viruses or bacteria by forming antibodies after a vaccination). Meichenbaum (1985) used a three-stage treatment model with a conceptual phase, a skills acquisition phase, and an application phase.

Conceptual Phase In this first phase, the counselor establishes a collaborative relationship, discusses the stress problems, and uses various methods (interview, questionnaire, self-monitoring) to gather information about the problem and situation. The therapist then, with the client, establishes goals and forms a treatment plan. The counselor educates the client about stress and coping and the role of thinking and emotion in maintaining stress. Finally, the counselor helps the client reconceptualize her stress by helping her understand more about how the stress process works for her and how she might think about it in some different ways. This typically helps the client feel a bit more in control of the process and allows the therapist to begin to lay the groundwork for positive change. The following dialogue between a counselor and Anita, who has come to counseling because of stress related to making presentations to large groups, illustrates part of this conceptualization process.

> **Counselor:** Anita, we've been talking quite a bit about the perceptual nature of stress—that you seem to give yourself a vote of "no confidence" when you step in front of a group of people, mainly by focusing on what could go wrong rather than having confidence in your own skills and thorough preparation. Now that we have discussed your stress situation a couple of times and used the information that you gathered last week about your thoughts and feelings, do you see the whole situation any differently?
>
> **Anita:** Well, I realize that I seem to tell myself that the audience has it out for me when I know they probably don't. It only gets in the way, thinking like that.
>
> **Counselor:** What do you mean?
>
> **Anita:** Well, I never really realized how the stress kind of builds up and how what I do and say seems to add to it.
>
> **Counselor:** Yes, it is a pretty complicated process, involving a lot of different internal and external factors.

This can be a much more complicated stage than our counseling vignette implies. The therapist uses a Socratic method to help the client discover new ways of looking at the problem and to develop some sense of hope and control.

Skills Acquisition Phase In this phase, the counselor teaches the client coping skills that can be used in stressful situations. The therapist is careful to help the client understand that the goal is to lessen the anxiety and cope with the situation, not to eliminate stress altogether. In fact, the earlier conceptual phase should have included a discussion of how stress can be helpful unless it becomes too intense. One major aspect of this phase consists of combining cue-controlled relaxation training (which was described previously) with the development of positive coping self-statements. The idea is to teach the client to cue the relaxation response and at the same time use the positive self-statements that are developed here. In developing the coping self-statements, the stress sequence is divided into four stages: preparing for a stressor, confronting and handling a stressor, coping with feelings of being overwhelmed, and evaluating efforts and providing self-rewards. Following are examples of some possible coping self-statements for each phase for Anita, who fears making presentations to large groups:

Preparing for a stressor

I know I will be nervous, but I can handle it.

I am very prepared for the presentation.

Is there anything else I need to do to prepare?

Confronting and handling a stressor

Just relax. Take a deep breath and relax.

I'm in control, even though I feel some stress.

Some stress is OK. I can use it to do well.

Coping with feelings of being overwhelmed

It is bad right now, but it will get better.

Just take a deep breath, relax.

Slow down, take things a step at a time.

Evaluating efforts and providing self-rewards

I did it—I coped with the stress.

I will improve my coping skills next time.

I was able to relax when I took a deep breath.

Other coping skills, such as problem solving (to be discussed in some detail later), might also be included in this phase. For the inoculation to work, the skills must be learned. The client must take the time to learn cue-controlled relaxation and to develop and memorize the self-statements.

Application Phase   The primary goal of the final phase is to help clients practice the skills that they have learned and to encourage them to apply them. Meichenbaum (1985) suggested several activities for this phase: imagery rehearsal; behavioral rehearsal, role-playing, and modeling; graduated in vivo exposure; relapse prevention; and followthrough (follow-up booster sessions). This listing of application activities demonstrates how well this model integrates many different behavior therapy methods. Methods from all three of the major branches of learning theory (classical conditioning, operant conditioning, and social learning theory) are present.

Constructivist Cognitive-Behavioral Treatment

This approach represents a more current evolution of Meichenbaum's thinking. His more recent writings (Meichenbaum, 1993, 1994, 1996) have taken what he calls a postmodern, constructivist approach: "Common to each of these proponents is the tenet that the human mind is a product of personal meanings that individuals create. It is not as if there is one reality and clients distort that reality, thus contributing to their problems; rather, there are multiple realities, and the task for the therapist is to help clients become aware of how they create these realities and of the consequences of such constructions" (Meichenbaum, 1993, p. 203).

Meichenbaum summarized this newer constructivist cognitive-behavioral, which has components that appear to be very similar to those of his earlier formulation of stress inoculation, in a manual that accompanies a video published in 1996 (Meichenbaum, 1996). Following are the seven major steps that he mentions:

1. Develop a therapeutic alliance and help clients tell their stories.
2. Educate clients about the clinical problem.
3. Help clients reconceptualize their "problems" in a more hopeful fashion.
4. Ensure that clients have coping skills.
5. Encourage clients to perform "personal experiments."
6. Ensure that clients take credit for changes they have brought about.
7. Conduct relapse prevention. (pp. 15–18)

In essence, this newer, constructivist cognitive-behavioral approach seems to be less structured and more client-centered, using many of the basic cognitive-behavioral techniques included in stress inoculation.

EMDR (Eye Movement Desensitization Reprocessing)

Francine Sharpiro (2001) originally developed this theory by accident. While walking, she noticed that when she had disturbing thoughts, her eyes began to move up and down in a diagonal direction. She further noted that when she brought those thoughts to mind again, the "negative charge" of the thoughts was reduced. In 1987, when she originally began her research on the method, the emphasis was on the eye movements, and the method was originally called eye movement desensitization (EMD).

Shapiro later changed the name to EMDR, adding the word *reprocessing* to indicate that more than just desensitization was occurring. Shapiro now believes that the method is much more complex and less dependent on eye movements and indicates that she would call the approach *reprocessing therapy* if she was to name it today. "On the basis of the observation of thousands of EMDR treatment sessions, the earlier desensitization paradigm was replaced by this model (adaptive information processing)" (p. 16). The complexities of this model are too involved for a discussion here, but Shaprio provided a simplified explanation:

> Briefly stated, the model regards most pathologies as derived from earlier life experiences that set in motion a continued pattern of affect, behavior, cognitions, and consequent identity structures. The pathological structure is inherent within the static, insufficiently processed information stored at the time of the disturbing event. In a wide variety of cases, ranging from simple PTSD and phobias to more complex conditions such as panic disorders, some forms of depression, dissociation, and personality disorders, pathology is viewed as configured by the impact of earlier experiences that are held in the nervous system in state-specific form. (p. 16)

Shapiro goes on to say that a person's current life situations and events continue to elicit the negative affect and beliefs related to the past memories and that a person's behavior is influenced by these feelings and beliefs. For example, Martin, an adult male, has poor relationships, has a poor self-concept, and is depressed. These problems could be a result of his being physically abused by his father. The negative feelings (guilt/depression) and thoughts (I deserve this, I am a bad boy), because they were not adequately processed in the brain, cause the same thoughts and feelings to continue into adult life. EMDR promises a brief, albeit complex, method for reprocessing these memories.

Although EMDR was used primarily for post-traumatic stress disorder early on, Shapiro (2001) provided specific protocols for a number of other problems, including current anxiety and behavior, recent traumatic events, phobias, excessive grief, and illness and somatic disorders. EMDR is a multifaceted, integrated method that requires advanced therapeutic skills and training. An EMDR Institute is available to provide this training.

Problem-Solving Therapy

Problem-solving therapy is another example of an "integrative" approach. It is broad enough to include a great variety of behavioral techniques, which are all integrated into a problem-solving model. D'Zurilla and Nezu (2001) suggested helpful definitions of problem solving, problem, and solution: Problem solving "may be defined as the self-directed cognitive-behavioral process by which a person attempts to identify or discover effective or adaptive solutions for specific problems encountered in everyday living" (p. 212). "A 'problem' (or 'problematic situation') is defined as any life situation or task (present or anticipated) that demands a response for adaptive functioning, but for which no effective response is immediately apparent or available to the person, due to the presence of some obstacle or obstacles" (p. 212). "A 'solution' is a situation specific coping response or response pattern (cognitive and/or behavioral), which is the product or outcome of the problem-solving process when it is applied to a specific problematic situation" (p. 213). They went on to point out that problem solving and solution implementation must be viewed as conceptually different. Problem solving involves finding a solution, and solution implementation is carrying out that solution. In counseling, these relate to very different stages in the counseling process.

Let's say a client, Tony, comes in for career counseling and reports feeling confused, angry, and depressed. He is from a very close Italian family where everyone has gone into the family business for three generations. He reports a great deal of conflict with his family. After talking with the counselor for a while, Tony and his counselor decide on a statement of the problem. Tony does not want to major in accounting, but his grandfather and his father have decided that he should major in math because the family business needs a comptroller. He hates math, although he is good at it. He really wants to be an artist. So the problem is identified and is complex because of his strong feelings of affection for and allegiance to his family. He doesn't want to displease his family, but he wants to be fulfilled by doing something that interests him. Defining this problem, although it took building alliances and overcoming Tony's hesitation to face his problem, was the easy part.

D'Zurilla and Nezu suggested that this method may be especially helpful if the client has deficits in problem orientation or problem-solving skills. Tony seems to fit this definition, since he feels immobilized and does not have a problem orientation. He is not approaching this as a problem that might have solutions. He also appears not to have the skills necessary to find and carry out a solution. The observant reader can see a possible paradox here. Although Tony fits the definition of someone who can use problem-solving therapy, his problem seems almost insoluble. What if there are no solutions? Is this a major weakness of this approach?

We can explore this more by applying the basic problem-solving method to this case. There are four basic steps: (1) problem definition and formulation, (2) generation of alternatives, (3) decision making, and (4) solution implementation.

Problem Definition The problem can be defined here as a conflict between Tony and his family regarding his choice of a career.

Generation of Alternatives On the surface, the alternatives seem limited. Either Tony majors in accounting and satisfies his family, or he majors in art or something related and satisfies himself. A major part of the counselor's job in this instance is to help Tony generate other, creative alternatives. He might, for example, be able to do a double major. Or perhaps he could major in accounting and minor in art. Or maybe he could talk with someone else in the family and get her to intercede with his grandfather and father. Maybe he would want to put off making a choice until he is clearer about what to do. The goal here is to generate many different, and perhaps initially unrealistic-sounding, alternatives. This requires the counselor to be able to help the client reconceptualize the problem in different ways.

Decision Making After the alternatives are listed, Tony and his counselor will go over each alternative and discuss the pros and cons and the consequences. This will include an assessment of Tony's skills and his ability to carry out the different alternatives. In this particular case, the family situation and the cultural influences of a large, close-knit Italian family will need to be addressed. What would it mean to Tony's relationship to his family if he attempted a compromise? How would he feel if his efforts were rebuffed? How much alienation would he be willing to accept in order to follow his own path?

Solution Implementation Tony might require several different kinds of behavioral interventions before he is ready for implementation. For example, he might need some desensitization if he is terribly fearful about discussing the issue with his family. Or he might need role-playing and reinforcement to help him learn ways to go about starting a discussion. Assertiveness training might also be a part of this. Tony might even want to discuss his situation with some cousins or others who understand the cultural and family dimensions of his situation. He might find some models in this process.

An integrative approach like problem-solving therapy often includes elements of theories other than those based on learning theory. In this case, for example, it might be useful to explore some of Tony's past history with his family. Perhaps more insight into the acculturation process and what he has come to believe as he has grown up would help. These are not behavioral approaches, but they might still be integrated into a problem-solving approach.

Treatment Protocols

Treatment protocols have developed in the last decade as a result of several factors. First has been the effort by a number of psychologists to move toward empirically based treatments. These are structured treatment programs (also called manualized treatment programs) that are based on the most current outcome research. For a specific treatment to be effectively researched, it must be replicable and specific. As we have seen, this kind of very concrete and sequential description of counseling treatment is very difficult with many of the theories covered so far. The cognitive-behavioral approaches most easily lend themselves to this method of describing and specifying treatment—and therein lies much of the controversy over this notion of empirically based treatments. Those who consider therapy a kind of "art" that is essentially created for each client and each situation feel that this idea is untenable. It seems to also fly in the face of the postmodern notion that reality is co-created by the counselor and the client.

On the other hand, the idea of a treatment program with a specific number of sessions that has been proven to work for a particular problem has great appeal to managed care and insurance companies, which are always striving for efficiency. Also, agencies hard-pressed to provide the services demanded with limited staff find the idea of brief and proven treatments attractive. One aspect of treatment protocols that appeals to counselors is the availability of structured materials and in some cases the availability of a client manual. For example, one company offers counselor and client treatment protocols for agoraphobia, anger, depression, generalized anxiety, obsessive and compulsive disorder, post-traumatic stress disorder, and specific phobias.

White's protocol *Overcoming Generalized Anxiety Disorder* (1999) is one example. The introduction to the therapist includes information on symptoms, etiology, prevalence, concurrent pharmacological treatment, research, assessment, and the rating scales used. The approach is cognitive-behavioral and includes 10 sessions: (1) Getting started; (2) Scheduling worry, time; (3) Relaxation; (4) Risk assessment; (5) Problem solving; (6) Worry exposure; (7) Reducing safety behaviors; (8) Thought-stopping; (9) Revising core beliefs; and (10) Relapse prevention.

The client manual includes the same 10 sessions but has a more "self-help" tone and adds cartoons and homework assignments. For example, session 6 includes a preview of the session, skill-building exercises to help the client learn worry exposure (desensitization to various worries), a review of cue-controlled relaxation, a blank form for a thought record and a daily worry record, and quotes from famous people about worrying (Oprah Winfrey about being fat and Jack Nicholson about premature ejaculation).

For the cognitive-behavioral therapist who wants to use an integrated set of techniques, these protocols, with accompanying client manuals, could be very useful. White (1999) said that "the protocol here serves as a table of contents for you and your client to bring together the best researched methods in support of ongoing therapy so your client can overcome her anxiety" (p. 1). He also stated that the average number of sessions is between 10 and 12, even though the protocol contains 10 sessions. This seems to imply a certain flexibility in terms of the duration of treatment, although the program appears to be highly structured.

MULTICULTURAL AND DIVERSITY EFFECTIVENESS: REBT AND COGNITIVE THERAPY

Cognitive therapy and REBT have been criticized for their failure to take into account the context within which a person's irrational or dysfunctional thinking occurs. Culture and gender are not specifically mentioned, and Ivey, et al. (2002) suggest that an additional column for gender and culture be added to the traditional chart that records the situation, thoughts/schemas, emotions, and behavior. They also recommend that counselors ask their clients to examine their emotions and automatic thoughts in light of gender, culture, religion, and other contextual frameworks.

The tendency in both of the cognitive therapies is to focus on the individual and her interpretation of events as the key to relieving the client's distress. According to Ivey, et al. (2002), "There is a pronounced tendency in cognitive-behavioral psychology to ignore gender and multicultural matters. However, multicultural theorists often stress that external reality must be dealt with if clients are to achieve mature cognitions and emotions" (p. 215). For example, in our dialogue between the counselor and the client who was depressed and reported that people never invited him to lunch, it could be that the client is African American and that he is not invited to lunch because of racism. This would certainly be a contextual variable, not a result of his thoughts "interpreting" the situation.

Ellis has been active in discussing the criticism of REBT by multicultural theorists. He has participated in several symposia at national conventions, and in a chapter titled "Issues in Counseling in the Postmodern Era" (Ellis, 2001b), he responded to a criticism of cognitive therapy by Rigazio-DiGilio, Ivey, and Locke (1997):

[Criticism] Theories of counseling that primarily address the thought and action process of individuals (e.g., REBT, psychoanalysis, CBT, Gestalt Therapy, Reality Therapy) offer unique perspectives on mental health and how to achieve it, but omit action with and reflection on the wider social systems that may have contributed to or labeled the distress. (p. 324)

[Response] Let's face it: These critics of various therapies are partly accurate and make an important point. [However,] I took a firm stand against the social-sexual system that endorsed Puritanism, encouraged machismoism in men, downgraded women in many respects, and otherwise helped to cause many cultural and personal emotional evils. (pp. 51–52)

PRIMARY APPLICATIONS: REBT AND COGNITIVE THERAPY

Cognitive therapies have been incorporated into a great variety of treatment and educational programs. The applications discussed here include couples/family counseling, group work, and work with children in school and criminal justice settings.

Couples/Family Counseling

Cognitive therapy has been widely used in couples and family therapy (Dattilio, 1998; Epstein, 2002; Faust, 2000; Graham, 1998; Morano, 2002. Russ, 1999). In general, the ideas used in individual work are adapted to work with a partner or family members. Ellis calls this REBCT (Rational Emotive Behavior Couples Therapy). (Ellis & Dryden, 1997).

In discussing the nature of couple problems, Ellis differentiated between a couple's dissatisfaction and a couple's disturbance. A couple's dissatisfaction comes when either or both of the partners are not getting what they want, and a couple's disturbance comes when either or both become emotionally disturbed about the dissatisfactions (Ellis & Dryden, 1997). Ellis and Dryden suggested that dissatisfied couples can solve their own problems if they have the necessary communication, problem-solving, and negotiation skills. Thus, counseling with these couples could involve teaching them these skills. For disturbed couples, their irrational thinking and beliefs, particularly about the relationship and their partner, must be examined and made rational. Ellis and Dryden discussed several kinds of irrational thinking that need to be changed to rational thinking (pp.115–116). Two of these are "desiring vs. musturbation" and "tolerating vs. I can't stand it."

Following is a dialogue illustrating a point in couples counseling where some of these issues are being discussed.

> **Counselor:** Oscar, you have said many times that Melissa *MUST* pay more attention to her appearance. Why must she?
>
> **Oscar:** Well, you have to give some kind of a damn about how you look.
>
> **Melissa:** Jeez, Oscar, do you know how hard it is to fix yourself up when you are trying to manage two kids? And, anyway, I usually look fine.
>
> **Oscar:** Well, if you would fix yourself up, I would feel better.
>
> **Melissa:** You know damn well that I'm not as compulsive as you are about how I look, and I really don't care a hell of a lot what people think. When I don't feel like dressing up, I don't.
>
> **Counselor:** OK, stop! Let's take a time-out and look at what is going on here. Oscar, does the fact that Melissa doesn't pay as much attention to her appearance as you would like mean that life can't go on?
>
> **Oscar:** Well, of course not, but it really bothers me.
>
> **Counselor:** So would it be fair to say that you *want* her to dress up more but that it isn't an absolute necessity? That it would make you feel better if she paid more attention to her appearance?
>
> **Oscar:** Well, I guess that's true.

This session can then go on with the therapist working further to get Oscar to realize that he is "musturbating" when he believes that his wife *must* improve her appearance. If he realizes that he *desires* her to look better, he might get less agitated and angry and perhaps have a better chance of getting her to pay attention to his concerns.

Couples therapy generally has two stages, overcoming the couple's disturbance and enhancing the couple's satisfaction. The techniques used appear to be similar to the general disputing methods, and REBCT is flexible in terms of how it is structured—that is, whether and when the clients are seen individually and together.

In family therapy, the ABC method is again applied, with the activating event (A) typically being a family situation that causes conflict and negative behavior and emotion (C). The family therapist must help the partners and children learn to dispute the irrational beliefs and thinking (B) that lead to the consequences. Ellis and Dryden (1997) listed several ways in which acceptance is important in family therapy. In essence, these could be called general goals of family therapy: (1) acceptance of human fallibility, (2) acceptance of human demandingness, (3) acceptance of uncaringness and unlovingness; (4) acceptance of proneness to human disturbance; (5) unconditional self-acceptance and other acceptance, and (6) acceptance of unchangeable frustrations.

Dysfunctional automatic thoughts can lead to problems in couples and families. A typical example would be when one member of a family interprets the behavior of another erroneously as a result of automatic thoughts. Take the example of a teenaged boy who was in an automobile accident and did considerable damage to the family car. When his mother asks him where he is going and who he will be with, his automatic thought might be "I made one mistake and she will never trust me again," when, in fact, his mother might just be doing what to her is good parenting by finding out about her son's activities. He gets angry and says in a huff, "Out! Will you get off my case?" She then gets angry, and her automatic thought is then elicited: "I just can't trust him; he is just too secretive." You can see how difficult communication can become in families (no doubt you have experienced it yourself). The cognitive therapist's role here is to bring out the faulty interpretations, by both the parent and the son, and attempt to facilitate more rational thoughts.

No discussion of cognitive therapy with couples can neglect Ellis's role in pioneering sex therapy. In fact, as we discussed in our short biography, Ellis's work as a sex therapist led him to develop REBT. One of his most significant contributions has been the use of REBT to educate and challenge the guilt that often causes sexual dysfunction. Ellis was one of the first psychologists to recognize that the problem that gay and lesbian clients had was a result of irrational beliefs about sexuality promulgated by society and many religions. In his groundbreaking book, *Sex Without Guilt* (1965), Ellis pioneered the way for the more open discussion of sexual problems and ultimately specializations in sex therapy.

Children/Adolescents

Cognitive therapy has been used with children and adolescents in a number of settings, including schools, juvenile detention facilities, substance abuse programs, and psychiatric hospitals. Generally, this work requires creativity and imagination on the part of the therapist to help young people understand the principles and stay involved in the counseling process.

Analogies and metaphors are often used. Platts and Williamson (2000), in a case study, discussed using an analogy with a teenage girl who was very critical of herself and was generally unhappy. The therapist asked the client to think of her favorite car and then asked her if she would junk the car if one of the tires had a puncture. When she said no, the therapist asked her why she would want to "junk" herself when one thing went wrong. This led to fruitful discussion of her underlying negative beliefs and cognitive distortions. Rowen (1997) reported using a metaphor to help young people understand the concept of automatic thoughts:

> I ask the child to draw a river in the direction in which it flows. Then I ask: "If we want to change the direction of the water, what can we do?" I illustrate the answer on the drawing: "We need to dig a new canal or ditch, and to build a dam over the old one. Up until now the river would automatically flow that way. Now it can flow in a new direction—this way. This is what happens with the brain's old, automatic commands and how we can change them into a new, mediated one." (p. 80)

Simpler versions of the automatic thought record or the ABC chart are typically used and discussed; however, the key is to present the material in a way that a youngster can understand.

Zarb (1992) suggested a four-phase cognitive restructuring approach that adapts techniques often used in cognitive therapy and in REBT for use with adolescents. She cautioned that explanations should not be overly abstract and that adolescents may vary greatly in their abilities to introspect and reflect on their day-to-day thoughts and feelings. She suggested more behavioral methods for those who are not ready or willing to introspect. Her four phases are (1) techniques for eliciting cognitive data, (2) techniques for analyzing cognitions, (3) cognitive-change techniques, and (4) experiments to test interpretations and beliefs. In each phase, she suggested techniques that may be especially helpful for use with teenagers.

One of the techniques Zarb suggested to elicit cognitive data is to use a list of negative feeling words (e.g., helpless, hopeless, angry, anxious) as a starting point to elicit discussion of negative moods and then the negative thoughts that go with those moods. This exercise illustrates the fact that with children and adolescents the therapist must often find ways to "get into" conversations and discussion about important material. To help clients distinguish between observations and interpretations, she asks them to examine some of their activating events from the perspective of a reporter who is going to write a story. One of her suggestions to help produce cognitive change involved an analysis of "upsetting social interactions in daily life" (p. 81). These might be things like "A friend passed me in the hall and didn't say Hi" and "I thought Gino really liked me, but I heard he was hanging out with Charlene all day Saturday." Clients are again taught to distinguish between observations and interpretations.

Many of these techniques for adolescents (and for adults, too) work particularly well in group settings where participants have common problems and can help each other learn to give up negative and dysfunctional thoughts.

Group Work

Cognitive therapy groups often use a combination of psychoeducational and process-oriented techniques. In the first sessions, the group is taught the cognitive system. Group members learn the REBT approach, or they learn to use Beck's cognitive therapy. This could involve several sessions, with practice in identifying and analyzing irrational and dysfunctional thoughts and the connections to feelings and behavior. As the group progresses, it may become more process-oriented, with the therapist taking a more facilitative role and using material the group members bring in or interactions in the group itself. Following is an example of an interaction between a leader of a cognitive group for people who are depressed and two group members:

Leader: Does anyone have something they want to discuss today?

Elijah: Yes, I had that same old feeling of being down in the dumps again this week.

Leader: Can you say more about it?

Elijah: Well, I stayed at home again Saturday night and just got really depressed.

Leader: Can anybody help Elijah out here? What do you think he was saying to himself when he got so depressed Saturday night?

Su Lee: Well, one thing was probably a statement that everybody else is out having a good time and I should be, too.

Leader: Do you think this included anything negative about this situation?

Su Lee: Yes, he was probably telling himself that nobody really wants to go out with him.

Leader: OK, before we ask Elijah how true this is, are there other ideas?

This dialogue comes after the group members have learned about cognitive therapy. This might be the third session. The leader is trying to facilitate the group so that other group members will help Elijah take a look at his irrational beliefs. After they identify his irrational beliefs and thinking, the leader can facilitate a discussion of rational statements and help Elijah work on challenging his negative automatic thoughts. The group may even be able to help identify some of Elijah's schemas about not being very likable and having nothing to offer socially. The power of a group, in this instance, is the peers' ability to challenge the schema from their own experience with Elijah in the group.

Rose (1998) described what he calls cognitive-behavioral interactive group therapy (CBIGT) for use with troubled youth. This includes a systematic set of different cognitive and behavioral techniques, but one of the cognitive techniques illustrates the value of such techniques in a group therapy of this sort. In this exercise, participants are asked to write down what they think someone might say to himself as a result of encountering a situation. They provide some examples:

1. (Situation—On seeing a massive guy pushing the other guys around, he thinks), "Hey, that guy's big, I'd better get out of here."
2. (Situation—On seeing a policeman when driving over the speed limit, he thinks), "I'd better slow down or I'll get a ticket." (p. 103)

Participants share their responses and give each other feedback. The object of the exercise is to teach participants to identify their thinking in various situations. You can see from the topics that a discussion of the different interpretations in a delinquency setting could lead to a discussion of consequences and the impact of what one thinks.

Cognitive therapies have great potential for use with groups. Groups can be time limited; they can focus on a particular topic—say, depression or stress; and if the leader can develop the necessary group culture, the members can all become powerful therapists for each other.

BRIEF THERAPY/MANAGED CARE EFFECTIVENESS: REBT AND COGNITIVE THERAPY

In general, cognitive therapies have adapted well to a managed care environment, where cost effectiveness is a driving force. By focusing on irrational and dysfunctional thoughts, a counselor can address disturbing emotions and situations rather quickly. However, Beck's concept of schemas as life-long dysfunctional ways of thinking seems to imply something more than just a few sessions. Of course, as with all therapies, much depends on the client. We think that for clients with deeply imbedded negative schemas, brief therapy will be much more difficult. We note that this is based on the perspective of Beck's theory, not of Ellis's theory. As you have seen, REBT pays no attention to the past or to past schemas, and its present focus makes it quite adaptable to managed care environments.

These cognitive therapies can work well in conjunction with drug treatment and may well decrease treatment time considerably. For example, a person who is depressed tends to cling to his very negative beliefs about himself and the world around him. These are accompanied by a kind of emotional darkness, an apathetic, hopeless feeling that robs life of any joy or satisfaction. A therapist may find it much easier to help the client give up these negative beliefs and distortions, often related to life-long negative schemas and beliefs, if the client's mood can be lifted by an antidepressant. There is some controversy among nonmedical therapists about using medication as an adjunct to therapy, but as we argue in Chapter 14, medications and their use for psychological problems have become a part of our culture, a fact that cannot be ignored by nonmedical therapists.

INTEGRATING THE THEORY WITH OTHER APPROACHES

Cognitive therapy fits well with a number of other approaches. Cognitive and behavior therapies have already been integrated by many therapists into cognitive-behavioral therapy (CBT). As you saw in the previous chapter on behavioral approaches, the early behavior therapies have incorporated a stronger emphasis on cognitive process, while at the same time cognitive therapists have added more behavioral techniques to their approaches. One might say this is a marriage made in heaven, since the CBT approach allows a strong focus on two very important elements of human functioning—thinking and behaving.

Cognitive therapy also fits well with both Adlerian and some more traditional analytic approaches. In Adlerian therapy, you will recall that a person's lifestyle consists of his beliefs about himself and the world, a concept not too distant from Beck's notion of a schema or schema modes. Both are a description of the glasses through which a person views the world. In Adlerian therapy, considerably more time is spent in analyzing how the client developed his lifestyle, although Beck certainly talks about discussing the client's life experiences as part of changing the client's schemas. Insight into the past and into the lifestyle probably plays a larger role in Adlerian therapy, but for both lifestyle and schemas, an understanding of material of which the client was not really aware is seen as helpful. One might integrate these approaches by spending more time on the development of lifestyle—through early recollections, dream analysis, and so on—and then incorporate some of the more specific techniques of the cognitive therapies to help the client change his lifestyle beliefs in a positive direction.

Beck & Weishar discuss the interpersonal aspects of couples therapy: ". . . patients may misunderstand what the therapist says, resulting in anger, dissatisfaction, or hopelessness. When the therapist perceives such a reaction, her or she elicits the patient's thoughts, as with any other automatic thoughts" (261). It is not difficult to imagine an interpersonally based dynamic therapist (one who relies heavily on the client-counselor interaction) using this interpersonal dynamic to help persuade a client to give up certain dysfunctional thoughts. In a similar vein, Gestalt therapy might be used to help a client become more aware of her emotions and beliefs so that she can analyze and modify them. An exercise like the empty chair technique, with a client expressing anger and deep hurt to an imagined dead father, might open up emotions that could be processed in a way that would help the client become much more aware of her life schemas. She might realize how deficient and unlovable she has always felt because she could never please her father. A cognitive therapist might be able to use this process to help the client focus on irrational thinking and beliefs that she has been hanging onto for many years.

RESEARCH

In general, cognitive therapy has been shown to be effective with a wide variety of problems. Lyons and Woods (1991) reviewed 70 outcome studies of REBT, and Engels, Garnefsky, and Diekstra (1993) examined 28 studies. Both of these reviews provide support for the efficacy of REBT. Butler and Beck (2000) reviewed 14 meta-analyses of the efficacy of cognitive therapy. These involved 325 studies with over 9,000 subjects. They found that cognitive therapy was effective for a number of different psychological problems, including adult and adolescent depression, anxiety disorder, social phobia, and marital distress. Cognitive therapy has been more widely researched and is often defined as an "empirically based" treatment because a number of studies demonstrate its effectiveness. Some of these studies have been criticized for not using real-life settings. In the study described here, the researchers have set up a study in a field environment rather than in a university clinic or lab.

SAMPLE RESEARCH: Effectiveness of a Manualized Cognitive Treatment for Depression in a Community Mental Health Setting

Goals of the Research

In this study, the researchers (Merrill, Tolbert, & Wade, 2003) wanted to find out if a manualized cognitive therapy (CT) treatment for depression would be as effective in an in-the-field community mental health setting as it was in a university clinic. They noted that one of the criticisms of the research on these manualized treatments was that it had not shown such treatments would work as well outside of a university setting.

(continued)

Participants

In this study, 192 adult outpatients received the CT protocol from therapists at a community mental health center. Five master's-level and 3 doctoral therapists conducted the counseling from 1994 to 1997.

Method

The therapists were trained in the use of Beck's manualized CT protocol (Beck, Rush, Shaw, & Emery, 1979). The researchers used a "benchmark" strategy, which involves comparing therapy outcomes with those of previously completed randomized controlled studies. If the populations are similar, it is assumed that the control groups in the other studies can be used for comparison. Several measures were used, including the Beck Depression Inventory, the Hamilton Rating Scale for Depression, and the Global Assessment of Functioning. The effectiveness of the CT protocol for this study was similar to that for the two randomly controlled comparison studies.

Results

Positive outcome was associated with less severe initial depression, more therapy sessions, more years of education, and the absence of a co-morbid personality disorder. The authors concluded that this study demonstrates that this manualized CT treatment could be used effectively in a clinical setting.

Implications of the Research

This study, using a benchmarking strategy, is noteworthy for several reasons. First, use of the benchmarking strategy allows researchers to conduct studies at in-the-field mental health centers, where use of a randomized control design would probably not be feasible. Second, the study supports the idea that a structured CT treatment program can be used successfully by a number of different therapists. The study has a number of weaknesses, including the fact that treatment was terminated prematurely by 68% of the sample; 58% of them left without notice. This is not unusual for a community agency, however, and since the researchers' primary goal was to test the method in a naturalistic setting, there doesn't appear to be any way they could have avoided these terminations. The study is considerably more complex than we have been able to describe, and several other interesting results were obtained.

EVALUATION OF COGNITIVE APPROACHES

Cognitive approaches to therapy have been widely researched and are currently used by many counselors and therapists. Cognitive therapy works well in brief formats, and the models are easy for clients to understand. They are concrete in that they give clients something specific to work on almost immediately. Clients get a sense early in counseling that they can have some control over their problems and are assumed by the therapist to be capable of making changes. A great variety of techniques is available to help the therapist in his work to get clients to interpret various life events and circumstances in a more positive fashion. The cognitive methods have considerable face validity; that is, they make sense to the client. We have all heard that "positive thinking" can be very beneficial. Cognitive therapies appear to be useful with a large variety of problems, and Beck and his colleagues have expanded their therapy from a specific treatment for depression to include applications to many other problems, such as personality disorders.

Cognitive therapies are very well suited for use in workshops, with groups, and for self-help. Because the methods are clear and easy to understand, group leaders can efficiently teach the method in groups and workshops and then discuss personal applications. We mentioned some of these kinds of groups earlier. The theories and techniques of Beck and Ellis have also been used in hundreds, if not thousands, of self-help books, tapes, and computer programs.

Both Ellis and Beck have training institutes that offer extensive training in REBT and cognitive therapy, respectively (Web sites are listed in the resources section on the book's Web page). Beck has developed a detailed checklist for therapists (Competency Checklist for Cognitive Therapy), that includes a list of competencies in three sections: general interview procedures, use of specific techniques, and personal and professional characteristics (Beck & Weishar, 2005). These training institutes are a decided advantage to these cognitive therapies because they help ensure a cadre of very well trained therapists and teachers and they also focus attention of the best methods and techniques for teaching these particular approaches.

One common criticism of cognitive therapy is that the therapist imposes his values on the client. Since there is always an educational component to the cognitive and REBT approaches, the therapist in large measure decides what thinking is rational and distorted and what is not, even when using Beck's collaborative empiricism. As we have pointed out, deciding what is rational and what is distorted thinking may certainly be related to a client's culture. In our view, there is no escaping the fact that in cognitive therapies the therapist does ultimately decide what the irrational thinking or thoughts are that are related to the problem. In Beck's approach, there is a great effort to collaborate with the client and to use Socratic questions, but the direction still comes from the therapist. This does give the therapist power, and we believe that the client should be made aware of this power at the outset of counseling as part of the informed consent.

Another criticism, often made by novice counselors, is that these approaches are superficial. The argument here is that just getting a client to change what he says to himself doesn't really change the way he feels. A client can work on stopping the automatic thought that "I am worthless," but deep down that feeling doesn't go away. We have quoted Beck earlier that his therapy doesn't really work unless the client's core beliefs (schemas) are changed. These core beliefs are often very hard to change. Will seeing a client a few times in brief therapy and helping him understand the connections among thoughts, feelings, and behaviors really bring about more basic schema change? Many factors enter in here: the length of the therapy, the strength of the relationship, the depth of the client's negative life experiences, and the client's external life circumstances. Certainly, the administration of a number of the techniques advocated by both Beck and Ellis does not guarantee more basic change of core beliefs.

Cognitive therapy has also been criticized for not dealing with emotions. With the emphasis on thinking and thoughts, do emotions get left behind? Imagine a client who tends to be a very emotional person. How would she react to this focus on thoughts? We tend to believe that client characteristics play an important role in the success of various therapies, and the cognitive therapies are no exception.

One might also consider the fact that cognitive therapists must be quick thinking and persuasive in their work in order to convince clients to give up negative beliefs. This might be a disadvantage to therapists who don't have this facility. If you watch videotape of Ellis, Beck, or any cognitive therapist, you will see that in their own way they must "sell" the system and work cleverly from many different directions to challenge negative beliefs. It does take a certain kind of person to be able to do this, and this might be seen as a limitation, although in our view a therapist's personality probably plays a rather large role in determining the style and approach of therapy that he adopts.

Questions and Learning Activities

These questions and activities are designed to stimulate your thinking about this theory and to help you apply some of the ideas to your own life and experience. If possible, you should work with another person or with a small group. Getting others' points of view and sharing your own ideas and perspectives will be invaluable as a way to help you evaluate this theory and its applications.

Personal Application Questions

1. Do you believe that if you change a person's thinking, you can change the way they behave and feel?
2. Are you someone who talks to yourself a lot? Can you identify statements of beliefs that negatively affect you?
3. Do you agree with Ellis's ideas about what is irrational?
4. How well do you think the Socratic method works with clients? Can you recall a situation where someone used the Socratic method with you? How did you respond?
5. Do you think there are significant differences between Beck's theory and Ellis's theory?
6. How does the idea of EMDR strike you? Do you think it could work?
7. Have you ever used a variation of the problem-solving method? How does it work for you? When it doesn't work, what do you think might get in the way?
8. Do you use self-talk to cope with difficult situations? Does it help?
9. Do any of your friends or family members engage in dysfunctional thinking very much?

Learning Activities

Identifying your Irrational Beliefs

Look over the list of Ellis's common irrational beliefs and pick the two or three that you are most likely to believe about yourself. Can you relate these to a general theme in your life? How have the irrational beliefs that you picked affected your life? What is their effect in the present? Discuss these questions with a partner or in a small group.

Using the ABC's with your Irrational Beliefs

List two recent situations where you felt anxious, depressed, or hurt or were unhappy with the way you behaved. Determine the A (activating event) and C (consequence). Then identify B, the irrational belief that, in Ellis's terms, was responsible for the negative consequence. After that, list a more logical belief that would have helped decrease the negative feeling or behavior.

Example

A = Visiting my father and his new wife. She has been very cool to me and certainly doesn't go out of her way to be friendly.

C = I felt uncomfortable, and anxious, and I only stayed a few minutes.

B = My father's new wife has to like me a lot. I must be a perfect daughter (son) and please my father. She should give me a chance and be fair to me.

D = It would be nice if my father's new wife liked me, but she may not, and I can live with that. I will try to be a good daughter (son), but I can't control how Dad's new wife treats me. I would like to have her be friendly to me, but I don't need her approval.

E = The next time I see them I will put much less pressure on myself, and I will feel more relaxed and be able to visit longer with Dad.

Counselor Statements

Imagine that you are doing cognitive therapy with someone and he makes one of the following statements. Write out two or three different ways you might challenge the dysfunctional beliefs using the Socratic method.

Example:

We haven't had sex in over a month. I guess she no longer finds me attractive.
1. Can you think of any other explanations for her behavior?
2. Has she said anything about it to you?
3. Tell me more about what this means to you.
4. How is the rest of your relationship going?

Statements:

- *My life is totally out of control. Nothing is going right.*
- *I have always been a nerd and always will be.*
- *I know I will get so anxious, I won't be able to get an erection.*
- *This C in organic chemistry means I will never be a doctor.*
- *My best friend really got angry and told me off. I guess I screwed up that relationship.*
- *My mom is always in my face. I can't do anything right.*
- *The doctor had to send the test off to a lab in Philadelphia. I just know I have cancer. I guess it's all over for me.*
- *I am always depressed.*

Discuss your ideas for counselor responses with a partner or in a small group. If you had difficulty, try to determine what got in your way.

Explaining a Cognitive Approach to a Client

Think about how you might explain your counseling approach to a client if you were practicing either REBT or cognitive therapy. Write out some ways that might be helpful. To make things interesting, imagine that you are going to work with a teenager. *Hint:* Can you think of any metaphors that might be helpful? After you have come up with some ideas, practice with a partner who will role-play a teenage client.

Developing a Structured Depression Group

If possible, work with a partner or in a small group on this project. You have been asked by a local mental health center to develop a plan for a structured group to help clients manage their depression. The clients have been screened and none are suicidal, but many have struggled with depression several times in their lives. The group is to last 10 sessions. Develop an overall plan for the group using REBT or cognitive therapy. If you have time, suggest a structure for the 10 sessions including what homework you might give. Also, discuss what kind of group process you want to create.

Identifying Schemas

Try to identify some of your important life schemas—beliefs you have about yourself, how you interact with others, and what motivates you. Put them into one sentence.

Examples

- I have always been shy around strangers.
- I am pretty emotional in relationships.
- I have always been the person people come to for help.

Then discuss your schemas with a partner or in a small group. Try to determine how you learned these schemas and how they affect the way you think, feel, and behave.

Stress Inoculation Self-Statements

Think of a situation in which you feel anxious. Develop three or four positive coping statements for yourself, using the four stress inoculation anxiety stages: (1) preparing for a stressor, (2) confronting a stressor, (3) coping with feelings of being overwhelmed, and (4) evaluating efforts and providing self-rewards. Try these statements out the next time you find yourself in that anxiety-producing situation. Combine the use of these statements with cue-controlled muscle relaxation by using "Relax, and take a deep breath" as both a statement and a cue to relax.

Problem Solving

With a partner or in a small group, apply the problem-solving method to a problem situation that you have encountered recently. Use the following guidelines:

1. Define the problem.
   - Try to see the problem as something that has potential, if not perfect, solutions.
   - Try for a one- or two-sentence definition.
   - Identify the feelings and thoughts related to the problem.
   - Talk with a classmate if you have trouble sorting out the problem.
   - Take one problem area at a time.
   - Use the 5 W's (who, what, where, when, why) to define the problem.
2. Generate some alternative solutions.
   - Brainstorm as many ideas as possible (without initially rejecting any).
   - Try to be creative and entertain new and unusual alternatives.
   - Work with a classmate or group to get help on generating ideas.
   - Put aside past failures, lack of skill, and practicality of solutions.

3. Evaluate and decide on the best alternative.
   - Remember it doesn't have to be perfect; be willing to compromise.
   - Identify new skills you might need to carry out the solution.
   - Identify people in your life who might help or hinder this solution.
   - Identify obstacles and ways to overcome them.
   - Identify how you will feel.
   - Can you tolerate setbacks in this plan?
4. Plan for implementation of the solution alternative.
   - Make a step-by-step plan.
   - Identify how you will acquire any new skills needed.
   - Identify how you will get help from others involved.
   - Develop a timeline.
   - Plan how you will overcome obstacles and setbacks.

Companion Website

Now go to the Companion Website at www.prenhall.com/archer, to assess your understanding of chapter content with multiple-choice and essay questions, and broaden your knowledge with related Web resources and additional print resources.

CHAPTER 10

Feminist Therapy

NATALIE ARCE INDELICATO AND SHAUNA H. SPRINGER

VOICES FROM THE FIELD: COUNSELOR AND CLIENT REACTIONS

Yes, it works for me

Client: At first, I thought that counseling would be a mysterious experience, but my counselor explained a lot about what the process would be like. She made me feel very involved in setting the rules for how our relationship would work. It felt like she was on my side. It felt good to be treated as an equal and to have my counselor recognize how tough it is to be a mom, be a wife, and work full-time. I really felt supported, and I liked the fact that the counselor told me something about herself. I guess I was a little afraid that a counselor would start right off telling me what to do.

Counselor Trainee: It's wonderful to discover a way of doing therapy that allows me to be a real person when I work with clients. I was relieved that I didn't need to feel guilty about this. I really like feminist therapy because it empowers clients, builds on their natural strengths, and explores the social and cultural context of problems. I also identify with the social action part of feminist theory. I'm committed to helping women and men break out of the traditional gender roles often forced on them, and I want to help women fight against the oppression that still exists in many parts of our society.

No, it doesn't work for me

Client: I just wasn't comfortable with this counselor—she kept telling me that she wasn't the expert and that we were going to have a relationship based on equality. That sounds fine, but I wanted some answers out of counseling. She kept avoiding giving me any advice. She seemed to focus a lot on sex role issues and how society forces us into roles. I think that there are different roles for men and women, and I don't see how being a woman has anything to do with my problems.

Counselor Trainee: This theory feels outdated, since women are no longer oppressed the way they used to be. My parents always told me I could do anything I wanted, and my teachers encouraged me, too. Nobody really told me I had a lot of limitations because I am female. And I don't really buy this idea that counselors and clients are equal. If we're not experts, why do we have to go to graduate school? Also, what does social action have to do with counseling? Am I supposed to tell my clients to go out and get political? Isn't that telling them what to do? It always sounds like women are victims in feminist therapy. Don't we all have to work to overcome our problems, even if we are victims in some way?

Sharon, an African-American, 40-year-old, female business executive, came to counseling with concerns related to body dissatisfaction. She grew up in a middle-class family and attended a predominately white, prestigious university. In the past 4 years, as she has moved up the executive ladder, she has felt increasingly alienated from her colleagues, who have joined a gym together and seem to connect with each other through discussions of their latest diet or exercise regimen. Recently, Sharon began to restrict her calories and has initiated a rigorous exercise routine with the hope that she will be able to get back down to her "college size."

> **Counselor:** When was the first time you remember feeling dissatisfied about the way you look?
>
> **Sharon:** I noticed it in college when I felt different from my girlfriends. They would talk about the makeup and hair products they used, and I remember feeling very self-conscious and different.
>
> **Counselor:** Sharon, what messages have you gotten about how you measure up to the standards of beauty held by your colleagues?
>
> **Sharon:** It's not like anyone has ever said anything explicitly to me, but I never feel like I measure up to the models on TV and in fashion magazines. I don't look like any of the other executives that I associate with, and . . . .
>
> **Counselor:** I can imagine those experiences make most women feel inadequate. The ideal of beauty in our society is incredibly unrealistic and narrow. As a woman of color, I have struggled with those feelings at times, too, especially when I don't see women who look like me as models of what is beautiful in society.
>
> **Sharon:** Yes, that's *exactly* how I feel.
>
> **Counselor:** How can we go about challenging those messages together? Can you tell me what you think makes a woman beautiful?

Feminist therapy places a great deal of emphasis on the ways in which gender roles, socialization, and women's minority status affect how people make meaning of their lives and the psychological distress they experience. In addition, categories such as age, race, ability, sexual orientation, and class inform the process of therapy. Many clients come to counseling without ever questioning the cultural messages they have received, which may contribute to their distress. Like Sharon, they often internalize their difference rather than looking at how disempowering social, cultural, and political processes interact with their development. The counselor will work to challenge cultural norms and empower Sharon based on her strengths.

HISTORICAL BACKGROUND

Historical Context

Feminist therapy is rooted in the modern women's movement and places a high value on the experiences and empowerment of women and the analysis of gender. Living in the twenty-first century, it is often hard to imagine that women just four generations ago did not have the right to vote, own property, run their own businesses, or have equal access to education. The women's movement has a rich history dating back to the late eighteenth century, and over time, women have bravely paved the way for the major social, economic, and political changes of the modern women's movement.

In the 1960s, events such as the marketing of the first birth control pill (1960), the publishing of Betty Friedan's *The Feminine Mystique* (1963), the passage of the Equal Pay Act of 1963 and the Civil Rights Act of 1964 and the formation of the National Organization for Women (NOW) (1966) began to expand possibilities for women and other marginalized groups. In the 1970s, women began entering the workforce in increasing numbers, discrimination on the basis of sex was legally prohibited in the United States (1972), some of the first domestic violence shelters began to open in the United States and around the world (1972), the U.S. Supreme Court's *Roe v. Wade* decision legalized abortion (1973), the American Psychological Association established Division 35 to address the psychology of women (1973), the first United Nations convention on women was held (1975), and the first marital rape law was enacted (1976).

It was a time of political and social change for women as they began to raise their voices against traditional female roles, which were seen as limiting and oppressive. Women were speaking out about their invisibility and the lack of information based on women's lives. One of the significant effects of this environment on the fields of counseling and psychology was the emergence of feminist theory. Women began to voice their opinion that traditional psychotherapies were nonsupportive of women and potentially damaging (Enns, 1993; Sturdivant, 1980). Many female psychotherapists became critical of traditional views of mental health, since the evaluation of the social and cultural sources of mental distress was lacking. There was a call for approaches that would empower women living in a patriarchal society (one dominated by men) and support a positive model of women's mental health (Dutton-Douglas & Walker, 1988). Approaches that are recognized as key to feminist therapy, such as consciousness-raising groups, social and gender-role analysis, resocialization, and social activism, were developed to address these issues.

Consciousness-raising (CR) groups were formed in part to give women a place to come together to voice their concerns and talk about how they could collectively take action to achieve social, economic, and political equality (Dutton-Douglas & Walker, 1988; Enns, 1993; Sturdivant, 1980). In the beginning, CR groups were typically leaderless groups in which women would discuss shared experiences such as sexual harassment, multiple-role strain, workplace issues, and sources of depression in women. During the mid-1970s, the focus of the CR groups shifted from social and political change to personal empowerment. The phrase "the personal is political" was coined during this time as women came to recognize the interrelationship between political, social, and economic concerns and personal concerns. Feminist therapy evolved as a result of these conversations and the emergence of resources centered on the needs of women.

It is important to note that some of the most critical changes in feminism during the past 20 years have grown out of criticism about the limitations of examining gender without an integrated analysis of oppression and about who has been defining and continues to define the needs and experiences of women. A majority of the conversations within the mainstream women's movement were limited by the fact that they included mainly White, middle- or upper-class women. Black, Latina, Asian-American, and Native American women often supported women's rights but felt that White-dominated feminism did not address their primary concerns, including poverty and discrimination. Some women of color also were concerned about dividing men and women struggling for racial equality. Because of these concerns feminism has not developed as a monolithic theory; rather, it incorporates many voices and viewpoints, with the unified aim of challenging the status quo that keeps certain groups in power over others. Women-of-color feminists have played a critical role in the history of feminist counseling and continue to shape feminist theories and therapies (see Adleman & Enguídanos, 1995; Collins, 2000; Comas-Díaz & Greene, 1994; Davis, 1981; Enns, 2004; hooks, 1984; Jackson & Greene, 2002).

Feminist therapy has evolved not only because of the progress women have made but also because of the resistance and backlash they have faced along the way, the lack of change in many areas, and the remaining inequalities and marginalization of women. For example, even at the beginning of the twenty-first century, women are still working toward an Equal Rights Amendment;

equal pay and equal opportunity in the workforce; equal political and civil rights and representation; reproductive rights progress; access to affordable health care, child care, and housing; and freedom from sexual and domestic violence. Feminist therapy has developed considerably since the 1960s and continues to encompass a diverse body of theoretical and therapeutic elements that help clients address oppression based on gender and how the intersections of factors such as race, ability, class, sexual orientation, age, and religion impact their daily lives, as well as their positions within the social context.

These ideas continue to impact the way that counselors, psychologists, and other mental health providers think about how to work with women and girls. Professional organizations continue to examine the practice of counseling and psychotherapy with women and girls. For example, the American Psychological Association has proposed guidelines of practice with women and girls. A summary can be found in the appendix of Kopala and Keitel's *Handbook of Counseling Women* (2003).

Development of the Theory

The development of feminist therapy grew out of the application of feminist political principles to counseling. Feminist counselors do not view the individual, couple, or family as the root of the issue; rather, it is cultural patriarchy, that hierarchy of value and power—based on gender, race, class, sexual orientation, ability, and age—that pervades inner life and interpersonal relationships (Brown, 1994). Feminist practitioners view their work as a part of achieving the overarching feminist goal of social justice.

Feminist therapy is not a specific set of techniques but a philosophical and political perspective from which the counselor practices; therefore, feminist therapy is about how the counselor thinks about what is being done in therapy. It is a way of observing and understanding clients and the psychological distress they are experiencing. The range of problems treated using feminist therapy is as wide as the client population.

Unlike most psychological theories, feminist theory cannot be attributed to any one founder. The theory represents the work of many women from a variety of academic backgrounds, such as counseling and psychology, sociology, psychiatry, and anthropology, who were working for social change and applied this work to psychology. In fact, some contend that there is no one feminist theory but rather a variety of feminist theories (Dutton-Douglas & Walker, 1988; Osmond & Thorne, 1993).

Phyllis Chesler (1972, 1997), one of the critics of the mental health system, was the catalyst for its reexamination. In particular, she was critical of the idea of counselor as expert, which she saw as part of the patriarchal structure of psychotherapy. In her book *Women and Madness* (1972), Chesler described examples of sexism in psychotherapy and counseling and proposed radical changes within the mental health system. Chesler pointed out that many women were being pathologized because they were not conforming to gender-role stereotypes that society and their counselors prescribed.

Gender-schema theory (Bem, 1981, 1983) also had a strong impact on the psychology of women. Bem proposed that children are exposed to and learn from society's view of gender and apply it to themselves. The theory attempts to account for children's socialization into gender-specific roles. The child encodes and organizes incoming information according to society's definitions of what is masculine and feminine. For example, children learn that girls play with dolls and boys play with trucks; girls play dress-up and boys play football. It is important as a feminist counselor to be aware of the "gendered lenses" through which we see clients and their presenting problems.

Nancy Chodorow (1989) also spoke about the constraints socialization places on men and women. She proposed that psychological differences between men and women are largely a result of the fact that women are often children's primary caretakers. Young girls internalize the messages their mothers send about what it means to be a woman, while at the same time young boys form their identity contrary to their interactions with their mothers. In essence, boys learn to give up their identification with their mothers and identify with the masculine characteristics of their fathers or the masculine characteristics portrayed in the culture. Chodorow (1978) described this in her book *The Reproduction of Mothering* as a "division of psychological capacities" between girls and boys, given that mothers tend to connect more with their daughters and separate more from their sons. It is through these interactions that girls tend to be socialized to be affiliative, nurturing, and self-sacrificing and boys tend to be socialized to be aggressive, individualistic, and power-seeking.

In the 1980s, after the experiences of women were observed more closely, there was a paradigm shift toward the use of relational theories to explain human development (Belenky, Clinchy, Goldberger, & Tarule, 1986; Chodorow, 1978; Gilligan, 1982; Jack, 1987; Jordan, Kaplan, Miller, Stiver, & Surrey, 1991; Josselson, 1996; Miller, 1976). Relational theories attempted to provide alternative ways of thinking about human identity development and challenged the traditional emphasis placed on separation and individuation, focusing instead on the basic human need for connection and interdependence (Chodorow, 1978; Jordan et al., 1991; Miller, 1976; Surrey, 1985). Carol Gilligan's *In a Different Voice* (1982) specifically addressed women's and girls' experiences related to moral development. Gilligan recognized that women often utilize a relational perspective and take contextual factors into account when making choices or dealing with situations of conflict. Gilligan's research on a group of adolescent girls showed that their sense of identity developed through and because of their relationships. These girls defined themselves in relational terms such as "giving," "helping," "caring," and "being kind to others." It is within these types of relationships, which are based on facilitating connections, that girls begin to develop a sense of self-competence.

Belenky and colleagues (1986) added to the relational paradigm shift by describing women's "ways of knowing." They believed that women tend to construct and develop knowledge through "connected knowing," which is contextual and experiential, as opposed to "separate knowing," which is objective and uses logical analysis. Another relational theory is the relational-cultural theory (RCT), which was developed by feminist scholars and researchers at the Stone Center at Wellesley College and which has evolved over the past 25 years from the ideas set out in Jean Baker Miller's *Toward a New Psychology of Women* (1976). The theory focuses on the idea that identity development, because it is intimately tied to relationships, develops through differentiation rather than through disengagement and separation (Jordan et al., 1991). Jordan (1997) wrote, "We are suggesting that the deepest sense of one's being is continuously formed in connection with others and is inextricably tied to relational movement" (p. 15). The basic tenets of RCT include the idea that all interpersonal growth occurs in connection, that all people yearn for connection, and that mutual empathy and mutual empowerment are at the root of growth-fostering relationships (Jordan et al., 1991).

The feminist frameworks that converged with relational models of development in the 1980s and 1990s were applied to specific "women's issues" in counseling such as depression, eating disorders, sexual assault, and abusive relationships (Enns, 2004), and this gave rise to multiple and diverse forms of feminist therapy (Dutton-Douglas & Walker, 1988). Among these feminist therapeutic approaches, Enns (1993, 2004) discussed four underlying feminist philosophies: radical, liberal, cultural, and socialist feminism. These approaches, as well as an approach called *womanism*, will be discussed in more detail later.

Multiple definitions of feminism continue to influence the integration of feminist principles into counseling practice, including hooks' (2000) definition of feminism as "a movement to end sexism, sexist exploitation, and oppression" (p. 1) and the more general definition of feminism as the principle that women should have political, economic, and social rights equal to those of men. Brown (1994) defined feminist therapy as "the practice of therapy informed by feminist political philosophies and analysis, grounded in the multicultural feminist scholarship on the psychology of women and gender, which leads both counselor and client toward strategies and solutions advancing feminist resistance, transformation and social change in daily personal life, and in relationships with the social, emotional, and political environments" (p. 22). Despite the variation in the use of words, these definitions as applied to feminist counseling include the concept that counseling is a political, action-oriented process, which embraces diversity of thought and experience. Feminist counselors strive to represent multiple voices, rather than repeating dominant discourses, and emphasize collaboration between counselor and client leading to individual and social change.

ASSUMPTIONS AND CORE CONCEPTS

View of Human Nature

There is a fundamental paradox underlying the feminist view of human nature. On one hand, feminist counselors highly value positive relationships with others. Social support networks are perceived to be critical in the development of a healthy self. In the therapeutic setting, feminist counselors extend positive regard as they actively seek to identify clients' natural strengths and competencies. Yet despite valuing close relationships and having a positive perspective with regard to individual clients, feminist counselors view society as a whole from a critical perspective. The feminist approach assumes that human development is shaped by political, social, economic, and historical forces as much as or more than by physical, mental, and familial components (Feminist Therapy Institute, 2004).

Feminist therapy is not simply about accomplishing personal change or decreasing specific psychological distress; it also examines the cultural, historical, and social roots of distress in order to work toward deconstruction and change of the status quo. There is a clear assumption that clients' status in society affects psychological functioning (Atkinson & Hackett, 1988). For example, women from various minority groups may be at greater risk for developing difficulties as they are frequently stigmatized and blamed for their problems (Comas-Díaz, 1987, 1988; Worell & Remer, 2003). Feminists are critical of a society that stigmatizes individuals based on their gender, race, ethnicity, and sexual orientation and blames oppressed groups for their problems. This is the fundamental paradox of the feminist view of human nature. At the individual level, feminist counselors hold a very favorable view of human nature. However, at the broader societal level, they critically view the numerous forms of oppression and prevailing norms created by those in power.

Core Concepts

As stated previously in this chapter, there are multiple theoretical perspectives from which feminist counselors practice. However, there are core concepts that are addressed by feminist counselors regardless of the specific interventions used. Enns (1993, 2004) discussed four underlying feminist philosophies: radical, liberal, cultural, and socialist feminism. Radical, liberal, cultural, and socialist feminists all believe in activism and social change but differ in their beliefs on sources of oppression and on the most effective methods for social change.

Radical feminists focus on ending the oppression of women rooted in a patriarchal society and changing society through activism. Liberal feminists examine and challenge socialization patterns that work to limit women as well as men, who are often constrained by rigidly defined roles such as main "breadwinner." Cultural feminists focus on the belief that oppression is rooted in the devaluation of women's strengths in society. Socialist feminists focus on multiple oppressions such as race, class, sexual orientation, and ability.

Radical and liberal feminist therapies focus on the political nature of the individual, the importance of working to change social institutions, the use of anger as an appropriate response to social conventions, the view that psychological distress is due to the interplay between individual development and societal oppression, and the examination of power differences between the counselor and the client. Enns (2004) pointed out that the differences between radical and liberal feminist therapy lie in the level of counselor involvement with social change, the level of counselor self-disclosure, and the belief that men can be feminist counselors. Radical feminist counselors believe that it is essential to become involved in working to change social issues and to self-disclose in therapy in order to reduce power differentials. Typically, radical feminist counselors believe that men cannot be feminist counselors because they cannot fully validate women's experiences, although they can be pro-feminist. Liberal feminist counselors may or may not choose to participate in activities related to social change, may use self-disclosure less in therapy, and believe that men can be trained as feminist counselors. Aside from their particularities, all feminist counselors hold gender at the center of analysis and of therapeutic practice.

It is also important to address nonsexist and womanist approaches. Nonsexist therapy is defined as therapy that is free of gender bias and stereotypes. There is a greater equality of power between the counselor and the client, and clients are expected to be active in the course of therapy. Additionally, it focuses on the counselor's awareness of her values but does not focus on social change, anger, or power issues. Its emphasis still is on bringing about individual change.

Alice Walker (1983) defined a womanist as "a black feminist or feminist of color" (p. xi). Enns (2004) described the term *womanist* as referring to "women who love other women, appreciate women's culture, women's strength, and women's emotional flexibility" (p. 204). Womanism is the belief that multiple forms of oppression pose unique concerns to women of color and should be given distinctive attention. Womanism has evolved into a version of feminism that encompasses race and class. Womanism arose from important critiques from women of color who felt that feminism had not adequately addressed issues of diversity and the intersections of factors such as class, race, gender, ability, and sexual orientation. Helms (in Ossana, Helms, & Leonard, 1992) continued this work and developed the womanist identity model, which is characterized by multiple definitions of womanhood. From a womanist perspective, therapy focuses on encouraging women to value themselves as women in whatever roles they choose for themselves.

Since multiple persons have contributed to feminist counseling theory and there are several underlying philosophies from which feminist counselors practice, the development of a distinct theory has been difficult. Yet a number of feminist theorists and practitioners have put forth core concepts that make up the foundation of feminist therapy:

1. **The personal is political.** Feminists believe that there is an interrelationship between the social and political context and individual experiences. The goal of therapy is to produce social as well as individual change. External sources are identified as major contributors to individual distress.
2. **Therapy is based on multiple categories of analysis, including gender, race, class, ability, and sexual orientation.** Feminist counselors perceive therapy as a political action that has meaning in the larger social context and has the ability to produce change, whether acknowledged or not. The meanings that are derived from feminist theory and enacted in practice allow for the encouragement of individual, collective, cultural, and invisible acts of resistance and connections between individual experience and the shared realities of others shaped by sociopolitical influences (Brown, 1994).
3. **Therapy is centered on the experiences of women.** Women's experiences are valued and viewed as central in informing practice. This translates into helping clients come to value their own needs, while respecting the importance of multiple roles and relationships in their lives.
4. **Mental health and disorders are reframed.** Clients are conceptualized based on their strengths, and the disease model of mental illness is rejected. Feminist counseling theory calls for a reframing of treatment models so that clients are seen from a resources perspective rather than a deficit or pathology perspective. Feminist counselors emphasize the clients' strengths and believe in their abilities, facilitating client empowerment.
5. **The therapeutic relationship is egalitarian.** Feminist counselors place their clients in the role of expert and engage in a relationship of shared power. They foster clients' awareness regarding their own power to influence their lives.

In addition to the general core concepts in feminist therapy, Lerman (1986) described eight meta-assumptions essential to feminist therapy theory:

1. The theory is clinically useful, it is applicable to clients' lives, and it grows out of practice.
2. It reflects the diversity and complexity of women and their lives, and there is no norm against which one gets defined.
3. It views the "other" (e.g., women, marginalized groups) centrally and positively.
4. It arises from the experience of the "other."
5. It remains close to the data of people's real-world experiences.
6. It theorizes that behavior arises from an interplay of internal and external worlds.
7. It avoids mystifying language.
8. It supports feminist modes of practice, leading toward egalitarian and empowering strategies for practice.

Since Lerman's articulation of the basic principles of feminist therapy theory, others, such as Brown (1994) and Brabeck and Brown (1997), have identified core components of feminist therapy theory. Brown offered the following proposed assumptions of feminist therapy theory:

> An understanding of the relationship of feminist political philosophies to therapeutic notions of change; an analysis and critique of the patriarchal notions of gender, power, and authority in mainstream approaches to therapy; a feminist vision of the nature and meaning of psychotherapy as a phenomenon in the larger social context; concepts of normal growth and development, distress, diagnosis, boundaries and relationships in therapy that are grounded in feminist political analysis and feminist scholarship; an ethics of practice tied to feminist policies of social change and interpersonal relatedness; and a multicultural and conceptually diverse base of scholarship and knowledge informing this theorizing. (p. 23)

In addition, Brabeck and Brown emphasized the importance of the movement and adaptability of feminist theory in order to reflect new and changing knowledge arising from feminist scholarship and practice. The final assumption of feminist theory that Brabeck and Brown identified is important because it acknowledges the history of feminist thought and openness to the future of feminist counseling theory. The commonalities of the basic assumptions that inform feminist counseling theory all affect the meaning and practice of counseling men and women independently and collectively.

THERAPEUTIC RELATIONSHIP

Counselor's Role

Regardless of theoretical orientation, all counselors are involved in a therapeutic relationship to some degree. However, because of the focus on power arrangements within feminist counseling theory, the meaning of the therapeutic relationship becomes a source of analysis and an opportunity to create an egalitarian, empowering relationship. Feminist counselors address power in therapy openly and try to create an egalitarian relationship with their clients. This is not the same as an equal relationship because power differentials inevitably exist between the counselor and the client. However, feminist counseling recognizes the inequalities of power, while at the same time making a commitment to decreasing the barriers to equality (Brown, 1994). Inequality of power is acknowledged, and counselors consciously work to empower clients. Clients are encouraged to regain and establish power within their relationships outside of counseling and use counseling as a model for practice.

One of the ways the counselor tries to redistribute some of the power within the relationship is by using empathy and by clearly delineating the client as an expert or authority in her life (Robinson & Howard-Hamilton, 2000). There is a focus on the figurative nature of the relationship, examining the ways that social categorization and discrimination play out in the therapeutic relationship, as well as on the real-world nature of the therapeutic relationship, examining issues such as fees, time, diagnosis, and conditions of sessions.

Feminist counselors must have an understanding of each client's culture and should practice from a culturally competent framework. Feminist theorists and practitioners should treat clients as unique individuals rather than assuming that all individuals share the same perspective based on gender. The counselor should have the ability to model her own cultural competence, as well as be willing to acknowledge a lack of knowledge about others' cultural backgrounds.

Counselor-Client Relationship

From a feminist perspective, the therapeutic relationship should include collaboration, clear therapeutic goals, and attention to the power of language. Language use in counseling is intentional, its purpose being to promote change and empowerment in the client's life. Externalizing the problem, using language that leads the client to believe a more positive future is possible, matching language, demystifying language, reframing, using nonblaming language, and allowing the client to tell her story are all ways that language can be used intentionally in counseling. By understanding the role that language has in all aspects of intrapersonal and interpersonal functioning, clients can begin to assess the benefits and limitations of language in their own lives and make changes if they feel that it is necessary. For example, take the case of Jana, a woman in her mid-twenties, married for 5 years, and working as a legal assistant. She comes to counseling because she has been feeling depressed.

See DVD

Chap. 10
Clip 1

Jana: I've been depressed now for several months, and I even had thoughts about suicide. I must be really going nuts.

Counselor: Jana, things must be pretty bad for you to be so depressed, and I don't mean to minimize what you are telling me, but having suicidal thoughts doesn't mean that you are really "going nuts." I think it means that you are in a lot of pain.

Jana: Well, I am really unhappy, but it feels like I'm going crazy sometimes.

Counselor: You may be really unhappy, but you don't have to see yourself as being crazy or nuts. From what I've learned about you so far, you are a competent woman who has reached a very rough spot in her life and feels pretty disconnected to others. But I do take any talk about suicide seriously. I'd like to ask you some questions about those feelings.

Jana: That would be OK.

Counselor: Tell me a little more about the suicidal thoughts. Have you ever made a plan for how you would do it?

In this example, you can see how the counselor works to help the client stop using language that may, in itself, be harmful to her. At the same time, the counselor takes the suicide threat seriously and begins a lethality assessment (a series of questions designed to assess the degree of risk of suicide).

Rules of the relationship must be mutually created, stated, and agreed on. Many feminist counselors will probably ask the client to call them by their first name, since using the counselor's first name doesn't create the power differential implied in a doctor/client relationship. The counselor is highly present within the relationship, sharing in the change process. At the same time, the counselor allows the client to do a majority of the "work" and interpretation. The counselor acts as a facilitator of change. The goals for counseling, treatment strategies, and interventions are created collaboratively.

Feminist counselors welcome clients' inquiries about their values, interventions, and therapeutic orientation. They tend to have fewer boundaries related to disclosure than do those who have adopted most other therapeutic orientations. For example, the counselor may appropriately share her own experience to facilitate growth of the client, engage the client in making active decisions about the course of therapy, and extend choices to the client regarding the pacing of the therapy, interventions, and session content. Counselor self-disclosure used in the therapeutic process is always done in the client's interest and not the counselor's.

ASSESSMENT, GOALS, AND PROCESS OF THERAPY

Assessment

Feminist counselors have been critical of diagnosis using the fourth edition of the *Diagnostic and Statistical Manual of Mental Disorders (DSM–IV)*, as well as the earlier versions (Brown, 1994; Worell & Remer, 2003). In their view, what is perceived as being psychologically "normal" has generally been defined by men based on their experiences, from research that has historically been done by men and on men, and social factors, particularly gender oppression and discrimination, have not been considered. Feminists have challenged sexism in traditional categorization and assessment and have worked to create alternative methods for classification that are more reflective of women's experiences. From a feminist perspective, diagnosis creates a set of arbitrary behavioral norms in order to keep power within and among professionals and away from clients; furthermore, traditional diagnostic methods claim to be atheoretical, but feminists contend that they are entrenched in patriarchal and monocultural assumptions (Brown, 1994). As a result, such diagnosis selectively stigmatizes and pathologizes clients, what Lerman (1996) called "pigeonholing misery."

Although diagnosis is not practiced by feminist counselors per se, they will typically look for social factors and gender issues related to their clients' presenting problems. Feminist counselors view the initial information-gathering phase of counseling as a way to engender closeness with the client. This influences the techniques that are chosen and the way in which treatment plans are created.

Despite their critical view of traditional diagnosis and assessment, feminist counselors will utilize the standard diagnoses required by managed care in order to provide therapy to clients. However, in this situation, the counselor will explain to the client the reasons diagnoses are used; she will also explain the diagnosis she is providing the insurance company, perhaps sharing the *DSM* with the client during this process (Brown, 1994). Brown encouraged feminist counselors to "think diagnostically" (p. 128), which she defined as potentially including, but not limited to, formal diagnosis and also the counselor's intentional creation of hypotheses with the client about the "nature, origins, and meanings" of the client's distress.

Goals

Due to the egalitarian nature of the therapeutic relationship, feminist counselors and their clients co-construct specific goals for therapy. Therefore, these goals vary greatly depending on the changes desired by individual clients. However, there are a number of general goals that characterize the feminist approach.

First, feminist counselors work to *remove or alleviate the symptoms of psychological distress* that are presented by their clients as therapy begins. Often, this may involve helping clients clarify any vague or ambiguous sources of distress. As Friedan expressed in *The Feminine Mystique* (1963), it may be possible for clients to experience symptoms of distress without a full awareness of the source and nature of those negative feelings. Depression or anxiety, for example, may be described at first as feeling "overwhelmed" or "vaguely dissatisfied with my life." In working to remove or alleviate symptoms of distress, feminist counselors facilitate an unflinching evaluation of power dynamics in their clients' immediate and broader social environments.

It is important to note that while feminist counselors hope that a fuller understanding of the clients' social context will alleviate some negative symptoms, such as depression, it is possible that other negative symptoms, such as anger, may emerge in their place. In fact, Helms (in Ossana, et al., 1992) has outlined a stage model of womanist identity, in which women proceed from unawareness of their disenfranchisement, a "pre-encounter" stage, through an "encounter" stage, characterized by anger at those who hold power over them or display gender bias toward them. Feminist counselors recognize that anger has an adaptive value, since such righteous indignation can be channeled into positive social action.

The second general goal of feminist therapy is to *empower clients to take action* to work as agents of change. In becoming empowered, clients may focus their energy on changing immediate relationship contexts. Radical feminist counselors would likely advocate participation in greater social change in addition to change affecting immediate sources of distress, such as the relationship with one's romantic partner. While a more complete discussion of specific techniques will come later, focusing on clients' strengths and intentionally constructing an egalitarian therapeutic relationship are examples of methods that feminist counselors use to empower their clients.

The third goal of feminist therapy, illustrated by the analogy of "zooming out" to gain a fuller perspective of how societal factors systematically disempower females, is to *help clients gain a new understanding of themselves and increase self-esteem*. This goal relates to clients' passage through the encounter stage of awareness of gender bias. Ideally, clients will reach a stage of "integrated awareness," in which the negative emotions generated by the awareness of gender bias motivate positive changes in clients' lives rather than increasing feelings of helplessness or discontent.

The fourth general goal of feminist therapy is to *improve the quality of interpersonal relationships in clients' lives*. The feminist approach assumes that a general drive to achieve power over others is a primary cause of psychological distress. For both female and male clients, a positive goal relates to increasing the value one places on the creation and maintenance of healthy close relationships. Social support networks are critical in the development of a healthy self. Feminist counselors use the therapeutic setting to model a mutually energizing relationship with clients.

Feminist counselors do not assume that clients should have positive relationships with everyone in their lives. According to this approach, clients may need to take risks that may be perceived as threatening to others in their lives. For example, a wife may need to insist on a more equal allocation of household chores, or a working father may need to advocate for a fair paternity leave accommodation in the workplace. However, feminist counselors would encourage clients to take these interpersonal risks in the context of a network of supportive relationships.

Finally, the fifth goal of feminist therapy is to *focus on and affirm diversity* and the valuing of differences among clients. Even though many women share common experiences and can bring similar issues to counseling, feminist counselors recognize that there is variation based on cultural, class, spiritual, economic, and sexual orientation backgrounds. Counseling will work to unravel clients' experiences based on individual circumstance and the client's position within the social context.

Process of Therapy

As noted previously, feminist therapy is not a specific process or set of techniques but a philosophical and political perspective from which the counselor practices. This approach serves as one way of conceptualizing clinical problems and provides a foundation for the use of a variety of counseling methods, often from other counseling theories. It is possible, however, to identify four basic "stages" in a typical course of feminist therapy.

The initial stage of feminist therapy involves an open discussion and joint negotiation of the nature of the therapeutic relationship. From the perspective of the feminist counselor, the primary goal of the initial stage of therapy is to achieve an egalitarian construction of power in the therapeutic relationship. For instance, a feminist counselor endeavors to demystify the process of therapy by choosing to be transparent about that process. By electing to be transparent, the counselor demonstrates an intentional willingness to share some of the power that the client may confer on her as an authority figure. Another counselor behavior that differentiates the feminist approach from other approaches involves self-disclosure to the client. Furthermore, any power differences that may exist in the therapeutic relationship are openly recognized and discussed. Following is a typical interchange aimed at achieving the goal of constructing an egalitarian relationship.

Counselor: Michiko, as we begin to discuss what has been troubling you, I am wondering if you have any questions about me or about the process of therapy.

Michiko: Well, actually yes. I have never been in counseling before, so I am not sure what to expect.

Counselor: The first time I came to therapy as a client, I was also not sure what to expect, and this made me feel somewhat anxious. How does it make you feel?

Michiko: To be honest, I feel a little nervous and even a little bit ashamed to be here.

Counselor: It sounds like not knowing what to expect makes you feel a little nervous. You are also feeling some shame. If it's OK with you, I'd like to spend some time talking about these feelings during our session today. However, before we talk about the feelings, would you like me to share with you what might happen in a typical session of therapy?

The second stage of feminist therapy involves a discussion of the presenting problem or problems. As the client discusses her problem, it is possible for the feminist counselor to perceive herself as an "expert" in the process of change, while recognizing the client's "expertise" about what changes are most likely to liberate her. During this phase of therapy, an open mind and respect for the client's natural competencies are central to the feminist approach. The counselor works to uncover strengths that the client may not fully appreciate, while validating the strengths in the client's current awareness. Counselor self-disclosure is often used to normalize a presenting problem and provide the client with evidence that what she is feeling is understandable and acceptable. The following statement excerpted from the initial case vignette presented in this chapter illustrates this point.

Counselor: I can imagine those experiences make most women feel inadequate. . . . As a woman of color, I have struggled with those feelings at times, too. . . .

The third phase of feminist therapy, which entails a consideration of the broader context of the presenting problem, may occur subsequent to or in conjunction with the client's description of the issue. During this phase of therapy, the counselor may ask questions that prompt the client to consider the contextual and environmental factors that may play a part in the problem. To achieve the same goal, the counselor may assign homework that will facilitate greater reflection on contextual factors, use self-disclosure, or simply point out how the environment may be playing a role. The following homework assignment fits with a feminist perspective.

Counselor: Loretta, what messages have you gotten about the ideal of beauty in mainstream culture?

Loretta: I'm not really sure what you mean. There are so many beautiful women in the media—is that what you mean?

Counselor: Would you be willing to try an experiment after our session today, Loretta?

Loretta: OK, sure.

Counselor: On your way home, pick up the latest copy of an entertainment magazine. Then make a collage of all the pictures of females in the magazine. When your collage is assembled, take note of any patterns or similarities you see in terms of the bodies, faces, and skin and hair colors of the celebrities featured in the magazine. In fact, would you be willing to journal on some of what you observe in your collage and bring that journal entry to our next session?

The fourth phase of feminist therapy is one of active empowerment. Depending on whether the counselor has adopted a liberal or a radical feminist perspective, this empowerment phase may or may not entail client participation in feminist social action. However, feminist counselors of all persuasions seek to empower their clients with new understanding of the social context that has given rise to their problems. Although social action may not be used by every feminist counselor, all feminist counselors maximize the degree to which each client feels empowered to alter the course of her life. The client may alter patterns in her life after she learns new behaviors and more assertive ways of relating to others. The following dialogue illustrates one way in which a liberal feminist counselor might work to empower a client.

See DVD

Chap. 10
Clip 2

Vinita: Roger is really starting to get to me . . . he constantly expects me to pick up after him. He actually has a ritual of coming home every day, flopping down on the couch, taking his shoes off, and throwing his stinking socks on the living room floor. It's like he's marking his territory with those smelly socks!

Counselor: I'd feel pretty disrespected if my partner did that in our home. How have you been handling this behavior?

Vinita: In the past, I have simply overlooked it, but lately his "smelly sock routine" is just too much!

Counselor: How could you express these feelings to Roger?

Vinita: Well, I guess I could tell him that I'm feeling angry that he is creating more work for me around the house. I could tell him that since I'm his wife, and not his mother, I'm not going to continue to clean up his messes and that if he continues to leave socks and dirty dishes around the house, I'll simply pick them up and put them on the floor in his home office.

Counselor: How did you feel when you were saying that?

Vinita: I felt *great*, actually!

THERAPEUTIC TECHNIQUES

Feminist counselors may practice from a variety of theoretical orientations (cognitive-behavioral, psychodynamic, solution-focused, family systems, constructivist, and interpersonal), and they may use a variety of treatment modalities (individual, couples, family, and group therapy). Some of the specific techniques that feminist counselors may use are described below.

Gender-Role Analysis

The aim of gender-role analysis is to explore the impact that gender-role expectations may have on clients (Worell & Remer, 2003). To facilitate this exploration, a feminist counselor may ask a client to reflect on any messages that she has received about appropriate behavior for each gender. For example, the notions that "women should keep the house clean" and "husbands should make more money than their wives" represent gender-based expectations. After gender-role expectations have been identified, the counselor helps the client reflect on the positive and negative consequences of adhering to or rejecting those messages. Finally, the counselor aids the client in formulating a plan to challenge some of the detrimental gender-role expectations.

A full and careful exploration of the possible outcomes of change is very important in facilitating gender-role analysis. In some cases, change within a system—for example, within a marriage—may increase one partner's marital satisfaction while decreasing the satisfaction of the other. For example, an at-home mother who wishes to return to work may gain fulfillment from her new role while at the same time her husband may lament the loss of a domestic caretaker. In many cases, however, a change that frees one partner from blindly following prescribed gender expectations results in positive changes in the relationship. Using the same example, a husband may have difficulty adjusting to a dual-earner relationship at first but may come to appreciate changes such as the higher family income and the positive effects of being married to a happier partner.

Power Analysis

Power analysis has some conceptual overlap with gender-role analysis. For example, both are strategies geared toward helping clients become more aware of underlying reinforcers of their behaviors. The purpose of power analysis is to explore how power is held and used in clients' lives. Gender-role messages may partly determine the extent to which clients wield legal, financial, physical, and psychological power in their relationships. Income disparities in the workplace highlight power differences that may be based in gender bias. On the domestic front, unequal allocation of chores or disproportionate access to financial resources may bring power analysis to the forefront of therapy.

Consciousness-Raising Groups

Consciousness-raising groups may be used as a place where clients can increase their awareness of the oppression of women and other marginalized groups, as well as clarifying the social and personal changes that they want to make in their lives. As a therapeutic technique, consciousness-raising groups may help women realize that they are not the cause of their distress and that others share their problems. Additionally, the aim of consciousness-raising groups is to empower women to take action against oppression through the mutual support of members of the group and the counselor. A criticism of traditional psychotherapy also arose out of these groups, as group discussions were focused on various power differences and the ways in which power hierarchies are maintained. This criticism of traditional psychoanalysis occurred as those in the women's movement were voicing their concerns about their personal and political rights.

Assertiveness Training

Nonassertive behavior involves deferring to others and refusing to express one's honest thoughts, feelings, and beliefs. A client who admits to being a "doormat" with her colleagues at work and a client who "just can't say no" to frequent requests for personal favors are both engaging in nonassertive behavior. A feminist counselor would argue that engaging in nonassertive behavior creates a sense of helplessness in the client's life. In direct contrast to nonassertiveness, aggressiveness entails a violation of others' rights in order to pursue one's own goals.

Assertiveness, however, involves being honest and forthright about your own thoughts and feelings without violating someone else's rights. Assertiveness training is illustrated in the following example of part of a counseling session with Marie, a 38-year-old woman who has lived with her partner for several years.

> **Marie:** My partner and I decided that I would cook dinner in the evening and she would clean the dishes and load the dishwasher, but lately she has been leaving the dishes in the sink and I end up putting them in the dishwasher.
>
> **Counselor:** Have you told her how that makes you feel?
>
> **Marie:** No, most of the time it is not worth even bringing up. I just deal with it—do the dishes and go on with the evening. I wish I could tell her that it makes me feel unappreciated and irritated.
>
> **Counselor:** What do you think stops you from telling her?
>
> **Marie:** I don't know . . . afraid, I guess.
>
> **Counselor:** Yet you say you want to be more assertive and tell her how you feel.
>
> **Marie:** That's true.
>
> **Counselor:** Do you think you deserve to express your feelings and get a fair shake?
>
> **Marie:** Yes, I do.
>
> **Counselor:** Well, would you be willing to work on learning how to be more assertive?
>
> **Marie:** Yes, I think I would!

In this example, you see how the counselor moves toward assertiveness training by checking to see if the client feels that she deserves to be assertive. Sometimes the first step is talking with the client about her own sense of worth and power. Once she sees that she deserves to express her feelings, the actual training can begin. Assertiveness training is described in more detail in Chapter 8, covering behavioral approaches to therapy.

Feminist counselors may use assertiveness training to expand the range of options for clients who feel helpless in certain interpersonal situations. For clients unwilling to try such a new behavior, "empathic" assertion may be taught as a less threatening option. Empathic assertion specifically includes an element of putting oneself in another's shoes before making a request. For example, when an upstairs neighbor is playing loud music late into the night, an empathically assertive response might be "You probably don't realize this, but I can hear your music through the ceiling and it is keeping me awake. Can you turn it down please? My workday starts early so I need to get good sleep."

Reframing and Relabeling

Reframing and relabeling are closely tied to "zooming out" to take in a more global view of how society may contribute to clients' issues. As noted previously, a core goal for feminist counselors is to help clients come to understand and appreciate how societal context reinforces various types of gender-based bias. When a problem is successfully reframed, it is common for clients to transfer the weight of blame from themselves to the larger social context. For instance, consider the example of a woman who states, "Right after reading [women's beauty magazines] I feel like throwing out all my clothes and everything in the refrigerator and telling my boyfriend never to call me again and blowtorching my whole life" (Wolf, 1991, p. 62). A feminist take on this woman's experience would be "Do you know that the women in those magazines are airbrushed to look that way? The women in those magazines are made to look a certain way so that women will never be satisfied with themselves, thereby encouraging consumerism." Anger, rather than self-blame, would be the likely consequence of this client's process of relabeling her self-loathing as the understandable result of these magazines' intentional ploy to hurt women's self-images.

Demystification of Therapy

Demystification of the therapeutic process is another common technique used by feminist counselors. Traditional forms of therapy that give much more power to the counselor than the client are seen as conforming with the prevailing social order, which puts men in positions of power over women (Dutton-Douglas & Walker, 1988; Marecek & Hare-Mustin, 1991). As mentioned previously in this chapter, the power inherent in a doctor-patient relationship and the power demonstrated by keeping private case notes and diagnosing clients with disorders are central points of contention for feminist counselors. Feminist counselors are uniquely motivated to combat the power differences that exist in society at large.

Thus, the process of therapy is demystified in several ways. Within the first few sessions, a set of mutually created goals and treatment strategies is formed, which allows the client and the counselor to share the power within the relationship. By externalizing the problem and focusing on individual resources, problems are no longer viewed as inherent to the client, and she can now identify strengths that assist in the change process. Educating the client about the process of therapy and jointly negotiating the rules for the therapeutic relationship are also power-sharing techniques. Finally, counselor self-disclosure is another way of leveling the playing field between clients and counselors in order to set up a therapeutic relationship that does not mirror the differences between those who have power and those who do not in the larger society.

Imparting useful information in therapy to be applied outside of the therapy sessions and also to be generalized to other problems that occur in the client's life is an important part of empowering the client. Techniques used to assess the contexts that contribute to the client's presenting issue vary depending on the individual. Some of the techniques used in this approach include examining the client's social and familial network, providing education related to communication styles, and focusing on what has worked for the client. In addition, role-playing, using the empty chair technique, providing social skills training, learning to identify inner voice or "gut instinct," becoming aware of physical responses and connections to emotions, normalizing the client's experience, and using counselor self-disclosure when appropriate are techniques the counselor would use. Note that these techniques come from several different theories that you have studied, which shows how feminist approaches utilize many different kinds of techniques. Art therapy, bibliotherapy, journaling, and homework assignments might also be an integral part of the counselor's repertoire. The specific techniques used in the therapeutic session are not as important as the way that the counselor and the client relate to one another. In general, techniques implemented must be usable with a diverse range of clients and conform to the theoretical principles associated with the approach.

MULTICULTURAL AND DIVERSITY EFFECTIVENESS

Because of the focus it places on analyzing oppressive societal circumstances, feminist therapy is uniquely sensitive to diversity and the social contexts that may limit a clients' life satisfaction. Since feminist counselors are particularly attuned to sources of oppression, they are committed to understanding clients' experiences and the obstacles to life satisfaction that they have encountered based on race, ethnicity, and culture in addition to gender. In the following example, a school counselor gives attention to multiple forms of bias.

> **Counselor:** What I'm hearing, Eloisa, is that you really feel you have to fight to get what you want. You've got strong interest and talent for engineering, but it's hard to be the only female and the only minority member in your class. And, the pressure you are feeling from your family to marry and start a family also seems like it is making you doubt this career path.
>
> **Eloisa:** Yeah . . . it is so confusing and frustrating, and when I talk to my friends about it, they all say, "Just do whatever makes you happiest." But they don't understand that in my family it is not just about me and what makes me happy, but more about the family being happy as a whole.
>
> **Counselor:** That's a lot to be dealing with, especially when you are getting two separate messages. Is there any way to feel empowered in your field without distancing yourself from your family?

In order to be more effective in clinical settings, many counselors, including feminist counselors, feel that it is important to acknowledge the ways in which they themselves may transmit biases in their attitudes toward clients (Howard, 1990; Kupers, 1981). An awareness of one's biases requires an understanding of aspects of one's own background and core values (Sue, Arredondo, & McDavis, 1992). There are at least three advantages associated with engaging in this type of honest self-examination. First, counselors who reflect on their own experience of bias will have a deeper foundation for empathizing with and normalizing the concerns of their clients. Second, counselors who pursue an awareness of their own biases may be better able to model a process of critical thinking about forms of oppression. Finally, critical self-examination is important because counselors cannot create effective therapeutic relationships if they avoid, or are embarrassed by, the ways in which they are privileged (McIntosh, 1988).

Self-reflection may also lead to self-disclosure in therapy that normalizes the negative feelings that come from dealing with unfair biases.

> **Sarah:** My fiancé's family is putting a lot of pressure on me to change my last name, and I am not sure what I want to do. My name feels so much a part of who I am.
>
> **Counselor:** I had that same dilemma when I got married . . . it was a very tough decision.
>
> **Sarah:** Did you feel a lot of pressure to change it?
>
> **Counselor:** I think my pressure was more internal, but I did get a lot of opinions from people. How are you dealing with the pressure you are feeling?

Feminist therapy and multicultural therapy are similar in that they both aim to create change at the individual and social levels. Neither approach operates from a neutral perspective: Multicultural and feminist counselors are not willing to settle for adjustment to the status quo;

instead, they encourage clients to understand the interaction between their personal lives and the larger social context in which they live them. Feminist therapy, because it advocates exploring social barriers and oppression, is a useful framework for working with diverse clients.

PRIMARY APPLICATIONS

Couples and Families

Feminist theory can be used with couples and families to address power and division of labor issues, to enhance the sense of connection within the family, and to recognize social constraints that may have an effect on the interactions between members of the family. In feminist therapy, the definition of family is very diverse, and it can be an affirming theory to use with same-sex couples, blended families, families dealing with adoption issues, and unmarried, cohabitating couples. Feminist counselors tend to challenge traditional notions for how a family "should" be and roles that individual members "should" play.

The Power Equity Guide (Haddock, Zimmerman, & MacPhee, 2000) was created to incorporate gender as an organizing factor in family therapy theory, practice, and training. It is often used to evaluate the practice of gender-informed family therapy. It promotes both feminist conceptualizations of families and interventions that are personalized for families' specific situations. It also allows counselors and clients to address gender in a goal-directed way. For example, regarding division of household labor, the counselor would ask clients to do a homework assignment in which they answer specific questions about the way housework is divided and negotiate a contract for an equitable distribution of labor.

Similarly, counselors can use the Feminist Family Therapy Behavioral Checklist (FFTBC) (Chaney & Piercy, 1988) to assess whether their counseling includes components critical to feminist theory. The FFTBC can be used to analyze not only family sessions but also individual, couples, and group sessions. The checklist is broken up into five categories: sex-role analysis, shifts balance of power between male and female clients, therapist empowers female clients, skill training, and therapist minimizes hierarchy between therapist and client. For example, one item on the checklist assesses whether the counselor educates clients regarding the inequality of status and power between the sexes. The checklist also includes items that challenge clients to develop more egalitarian relationships, emphasize female clients' competence, use role-playing to help clients integrate new sex-role behaviors, and assume a collaborative role with the family. The checklist is available in Chaney and Piercy's (1988) article in the *American Journal of Family Therapy*.

Men

Almost all traditional therapies that are used to work with women were developed by men, thereby imparting male assumptions about women's psychological development. Feminist therapy has provided a paradigm shift in that it attempts to center women's psychological development on the experiences of women. Additionally, feminism has shed light on the negative effects that traditional gender roles have on men. Often males are impeded by cultural messages such as "Be physically strong, be in control, financially support the family, and don't show your emotions," which can be just as limiting as the constraints placed on women. Levant and Pollack (1995) recognized domestic violence, homophobia, objectification of women, neglect of health needs, and emotionally distant fathering as negative consequences of male socialization.

Work with male clients may include power analysis, but it may be different from the power analysis used with female clients in that it may focus on an assessment of the drawbacks of pursuing power over others or of maintaining a consistent persona of strength. Counseling may also address the role strain that men feel between family and work domains, as well as helping them recognize ways that they can work for social change. Applications of feminist therapy with men have included working with abusive men in battering groups, modeling how to express emotions and self-disclosure, and working to balance achievement and relational needs. McGregor, Tutty, Babins-Wagner, and Marlyn (2002) evaluated Responsible Choices for Men, a feminist-based, 14-week group therapy program for abusive men using narrative interventions. They assessed participants before and after the program for their levels of physical and nonphysical abuse, self-esteem, perceived stress, family relations, depression, assertiveness, and sex-role beliefs. The participants improved in all categories. The program's goal was to educate men on how to express their concerns in nonabusive ways that respect the rights and feelings of others.

Children and Adolescents

Many practitioners, researchers, and educators have pursued sex equity in education over the years, since education is critical to gaining gender equality in society. School counselors and other practitioners working with children and adolescents have played and continue to play an important role in this effort. They can facilitate the challenging of sex roles, provide exposure to a wide variety of traditional and nontraditional career choices for male and female students, and educate teachers on ways to limit gender bias in classrooms. Additionally, they can have a significant impact on school policy by consulting with school administrators.

Some researchers have encouraged practitioners working with young men and women to use techniques similar to those used in other settings with adults, including bibliotherapy, group therapy, and assertiveness training. These techniques offer children and adolescents practical strategies for developing resilience. Relevant books that examine and challenge traditional gender roles, such as *Reviving Ophelia: Saving the Selves of Adolescent Girls* (Pipher, 1995), *Urban Girls: Resisting Stereotypes, Creating Identities* (Leadbeater & Way, 1996), and *Women, Girls, and Psychotherapy: Reframing Resistance* (Gilligan, Rogers, & Tolman, 1991), can inform the interventions that practitioners use and help them contextualize the difficulties young women face related to their identity development and gender roles. In *Reviving Ophelia,* Pipher described what has become a common crisis: Adolescent girls are particularly susceptible to becoming depressed in their teenage years. She contended that maintaining self-confidence is very difficult when young women are bombarded with media images of extremely thin, airbrushed models and actresses.

At all ages and grade levels, having students read biographies can expose them to new ways of thinking and looking at the world around them and to a variety of philosophical views of life. For adolescent students, groups can address problems involving racism, sexism, and/or classism as catalysts for discussions. During these discussions, feminist counselors act as "nonexperts" and allow discussion to be based on students' lived experiences. Since many female students and students of color experience rejection, disapproval, and/or prejudice inside and outside the school setting, they may feel a great deal of anxiety and apprehension about turning to a counselor. School counselors can use feminist therapy techniques to establish an egalitarian therapeutic relationship and to demystify the counseling process. School counselors and other practitioners working with children and adolescents can empower their clients by helping them manage the impact of others' negative perceptions, by giving them a voice, and by encouraging social action.

Feminist Groups

Group therapy has been at the core of feminist therapy. Since the 1960s, women have used a group format to address women's roles and experiences in a patriarchal culture. Feminist groups began informally, often in women's homes, and became more organized as the years progressed, focusing more on personal and social change rather than just social change. Women's groups have also developed for subgroups of women such as women of color, adolescent females, women in prisons, sexual assault survivors, lesbians, and single mothers. The topics of feminist group therapy range widely but often include eating disorders, relationships, role strain, sexual assault, and interpersonal violence, to name a few. Feminist therapy group members validate and affirm other members' experiences, gain a sense of strength from their support, and feel less isolated in their distress. Counselors work to encourage personal and political empowerment and action.

To date, many articles have addressed group interventions for women. Weiland-Bolwing, Schindler-Zimmerman, and Carlson-Daniels (2000) introduced a feminist group for female adolescents that included the following topics: self-knowledge, self-esteem, assertive communication, relationship violence, body image, sexual decision making, career exploration, and self-care. These authors suggested a need for feminist interventions in order to empower adolescent females, making them aware of and enabling them to reject unhealthy societal messages. Kessell (1994) discussed an experiential group for women consisting of several yoga sessions, a dance therapy session, a challenge course in the woods, and a rock-climbing experience. The women in this group had been diagnosed with major depression, post-traumatic stress disorder, anxiety, and adjustment disorder. Postgroup follow-up indicated that the group was successful in sparking changes in the lifestyles and attitudes of many of the participants. Maass has published a book called *Women's Group Therapy: Creative Challenges and Options* (2002), which highlights many case studies using feminist strategies in group work with women.

Feminist Supervision

Feminist theory crosses over into more than just counseling practice and is used to inform other areas related to counseling such as research, teaching, and supervision. The principles, objectives, and purposes of feminist supervision are derived from the basic assumptions of feminist therapy. Like counseling from a feminist perspective, feminist supervision does not concentrate as much on the techniques used in supervision as on how the supervisor conceptualizes the process of supervision. The supervisory relationship is central to the supervision process (Prouty, 2001).

Feminist supervision also examines supervisees' struggles in the broader sociopolitical context and works toward social change. For example, if a supervisee is feeling that her practicum or internship site treats counseling interns who are women of color differently than male counseling interns, the supervisor will not just work through the supervisee's feelings regarding the discrimination but also will work toward ways of resolving the inequality from an institutional, social perspective.

Prouty, Thomas, Johnson, & Long (2001) found that in feminist supervision there are three methods that are used to organize supervision: the supervision contract, collaborative methods, and hierarchy and the use of power. Dutton-Douglas and Rave (1990) stated that because feminist therapy is not limited to working with women clients, "what is considered adequate in supervision should enable trainees to work effectively with all clients within a framework that both recognizes and challenges the social and economic oppression of women in society" (p. 145).

BRIEF THERAPY/MANAGED CARE EFFECTIVENESS

Feminist therapy generally functions as a rather short-term therapy focused on individual and social change. Because feminism is not so much a set of integrated theoretical propositions as it is a way of seeing the world and conceptualizing clinical issues, specific time-limited interventions can be used in combination with the feminist approach. Feminist therapy meets three of the four core characteristics of brief therapy: it establishes a rapid and effective therapeutic alliance, assumes that the client is resilient and can make significant progress relatively quickly, and encourages the client to do work outside of the counseling office (Cooper, Archer, & Whitaker, 2002). The one brief-therapy characteristic that does not fit as well within the feminist therapy frame is the quick development of a specific focus for counseling, which is typically led and structured by the counselor. In contrast, feminist counseling gives more control to the client when it comes to pacing sessions and choosing content to be discussed. Nevertheless, feminist therapy blends well with brief therapy in that its goal is to empower the client and create a situation where the client can function and thrive without a reliance on her counselor. However, there are certain issues such as sexual abuse, post-traumatic stress disorder, domestic violence, and eating disorders that may require longer-term treatment.

Feminist theorists have been critical of managed health care and traditional mental health diagnostic classification systems. Managed care systems are, for the most part, theoretically incompatible with feminist therapy; however, feminist counselors do not refuse to use diagnoses and insurance companies to receive payments, given the constraints that they impose in order for clients to receive services. Rather than limiting the information that clients receive about how managed care systems operate and the types of information they must receive in order to allow services, feminist counselors attempt to disclose as much information as possible, thereby demystifying the managed care process and identifying and making clear its potential benefits and drawbacks.

Feminists have called for a feminist-empowered informed consent, which includes sharing information so a client can make decisions about therapy, including describing the diagnosis and what it means to other mental health and medical providers, offering a copy of the DSM to the client so that she is informed about the diagnosis being given, offering to discuss alternatives that the client may suggest, and disclosing the risks involved in using an insurance company to obtain counseling services (Brown, 1994). Giving clients this type of information allows them to make an informed choice about whether to use their health insurance to pay for services.

INTEGRATING THE THEORY WITH OTHER APPROACHES

Feminist and humanistic-existential theories have a number of commonalities such as the importance of the therapeutic relationship, the fact that they do not rely on specific techniques, their emphasis on the client's frame of reference, a belief in the basic positive potential of humans, and a deep respect for every person's right to make life choices. Both theories emphasize the authentic expression of the counselor and the creation of a safe environment in which the client's natural strengths can emerge.

Feminist therapy can be integrated with narrative and solution-focused approaches as well. Both feminist therapy and narrative therapy attempt to facilitate a deeper consideration of contextual influences on the problem. In narrative therapy, the client begins with a "thin," "problem-saturated" story (White & Epston, 1990) that is "thickened" in part through a consideration of contributing contextual factors. In parallel fashion, the client in feminist therapy becomes a critical thinker who is able to evaluate how societal and contextual factors give life to and sustain the presenting problem.

In narrative therapy and in solution-focused therapy, the client's plot is also "thickened" by the consideration of "unique outcomes," evidence of past resilience or strengths outside of the client's current awareness. In like manner, feminist counselors actively draw out the client's strengths as the basis for greater empowerment. This focus on the client's naturally emergent strengths evidences a positive view of humanity that cuts across the feminist, humanistic, narrative, and solution-focused traditions. Interestingly, while a feminist counselor typically has positive regard and empathy at the level of individual clients, the feminist view of society at large, characterized by sexism and other forms of discrimination, suggests a less positive view of humanity as a whole.

Another parallel between these modes of therapy and feminist therapy is the respect given to the client's perspective. Feminist counselors, like narrative and solution-focused counselors, are likely to adopt an attitude of curiosity in order to enter the client's frame of reference. However, feminist counselors then actively work to challenge the client's frame of reference by "zooming out" until the effects of gender-based oppression have been clarified.

Despite the historical gender bias of Freudian psychoanalytic theory, feminist therapy has notable similarities to recent psychodynamic approaches (e.g., time-limited dynamic psychotherapy (TLDP), Strupp & Binder, 1984). One broad parallel between the two approaches lies in the use of self. In TLDP, the counselor uses herself in the generation of an emotionally corrective experience designed to facilitate new self-understanding on the part of the client. In like manner, a feminist counselor might use here-and-now reflections and self-disclosures designed to increase the client's awareness of her unappreciated strengths or to increase her understanding of the self within society. For instance, consider the following therapeutic exchange.

> **Aimee:** Lately, my job has really been stressing me out. I'd really like to quit this job, but I feel like I should keep pitching in to help my family.
>
> **Counselor:** Aimee, it seems like you are always trying to take care of everyone. I even notice that in our counseling. If we come to a place where neither of us knows what to say, you seem to always break right in and try to help me do the counseling.

Finally, feminist therapy is such a broad philosophy that parallels might even be observed with a behavioral approach. As mentioned in Chapter 8, on behavioral therapy, behaviors are seen as a method for allowing the client to have greater control over her life circumstances. In feminist therapy, the counselor uses behavioral interventions such as assertiveness training (e.g., standing up to the "smelly sock ritual") and encourages social action to empower clients.

To summarize, even though feminist therapy shares many common themes with other prominent therapies, such as humanistic-existential, narrative, solution-focused, psychodynamic, and behavioral theories, its chief distinction lies in the central emphasis that the feminist approach places on the concept of power differentials, the influences of class and culture on the understanding of individual experience, and social change. As noted above, a feminist theoretical orientation invites the use of multiple theories of change and a diverse set of techniques.

RESEARCH

The study of gender and the impact of gender on counseling process and effectiveness are at the core of feminist counseling theory research and scholarship. Feminists are committed to embracing multiple viewpoints and methodologies. Rather than focusing on one methodology, feminist theory is concerned with how oppressive views and meanings of gender may be reinforced in research. Fox and Murry (2000) identified four elements often present in and critical to feminist scholarship: reflexivity, the centrality of practice, a focus on social processes, and a critical attitude toward traditional paradigms and theories.

SAMPLE RESEARCH: Does "feminist" plus "therapist" equal "feminist therapist"?

Goals of the Research

Moradi, Fischer, Hill, Jome, and Blum (2000) examined links between self-reported feminist orientation and various therapeutic behaviors thought to characterize the feminist approach.

Participants

The research sample was 101 practicing therapists, 70% of whom were women. The sample was diverse in terms of age and sexual orientation but not as diverse in terms of racial background, with 78% being White, 8% African American, 2% Latino/a, 3% multiracial, and 8% self-identifying as other. The mean number of years in practice was 13. Overall, the participants indicated slight to moderate feminist orientations.

Methods

Therapists were asked to complete two measures.
1. The first questionnaire asked therapists to rate the frequency with which they perform 64 behaviors on a Likert-type scale ranging from 1 (0%–20% of the time) to 5 (80%–100% of the time). Therapist participants were also asked to rank the 5 most important behaviors in conducting therapy with women clients from the first 64 items mentioned above.
2. Four items were used to assess feminist self-labeling. Three were rated on a Likert-type scale (1 = strongly disagree to 5 = strongly agree). Those items were "I am a feminist,"

(continued)

"I am a feminist therapist," and "I practice feminist therapy." The fourth item required participants to rank, out of nine choices, up to three descriptors that best identified their theoretical orientation.

Results

Three themes characterized the therapy behaviors of the more feminist counselors. The authors refer to those three themes as "Personal Is Political" (e.g., "Raising sex-role issues whether or not clients bring them up"), "Empowerment" (e.g., "Teaching clients to negotiate a balance between their own needs and the needs of their significant other"), and "Assertiveness/Autonomy" (e.g., "Educating clients about assertive and functional ways of expressing anger").

Feminist self-labeling by therapists predicted therapy behaviors. Those therapists who most strongly self-identified as feminist counselors could be distinguished by the attention they paid to issues of oppression (e.g., sexism, racism) and socialization. Also, therapists reported equally engaging male and female clients in these behaviors.

Implications of the Research

There appears to be evidence from this study that a structure and set of concepts can be identified for feminist therapy as practiced by self-labeled feminist therapists.

Reflexivity refers to the active role that the researcher plays in the research process. Rather than being an objective observer, collecting, analyzing, and reporting data from a distance, the researcher is engaged in the generation of knowledge. Thus, the researcher must be willing to self-reflect and acknowledge her orientation as a part of the research process. The centrality of practice implies that knowledge gained through the research process should be applied to social change. The focus on the social process of research means that the emphasis is on the process rather than the product of research. Finally, taking a critical stance includes questioning both prevailing epistemologies and the appropriateness of things like models, instruments, and participant populations in research.

Thompson (1992) described the fundamental aspects of feminist research methodology as agenda, epistemology, and ethics. Other issues often represented in feminist research are the notion that objectivity is not objective, the need for greater sensitivity to the inclusion of diverse participants, the importance of attending to power processes in research, and the distinction between sex and gender (Allen, 2000; Fox & Murry, 2000; Osmond & Thorne, 1993).

EVALUATION OF FEMINIST THERAPY

In their critique of feminist theories and therapies, some have said that they place too much blame on society, creating a victim mentality for clients. Looking at contextual factors that contribute to clients' problems is a large part of feminist counseling, making some question whether this stance contributes to clients' not taking personal responsibility to create change in their lives. Feminist counselors are given the task of educating clients on the oppressive environments in which their problems are situated, while at the same time offering empowerment strategies to help clients work to change regardless of whether the society changes.

Another potential limitation of the feminist orientation is that a counselor's radical or militant beliefs may be imposed on a client's values. Feminist counselors do not take a neutral stance related to advocating for social change. However, the purpose of therapy is not to persuade clients to take on the specific beliefs or activist stance of the counselor. One way of advocating feminist beliefs is for feminist counselors to be very explicit about their theoretical stance and discuss their values with the client before beginning therapy.

One of the main criticisms of the theory has been that the foundations of feminist counseling theory are primarily identified with the political feminism of White, middle-class, heterosexual women and have been considered limited in their applicability to women of color (Brown, 1994). Women-of-color feminists have challenged the assumption held by White feminists that gender is the primary category of analysis. Currently, many feminist theorists are reconceptualizing gender and culture and identifying gender as one of many factors that affect development and inform the meaning given to life experiences (Miller, Jordan, Kaplan, Stines, & Surrey, 1997; Robinson & Howard-Hamilton, 2000). Counselors should be aware of the history of feminist theory in terms of its critiques so that the more current and inclusive conceptualization of feminist counseling theory can be incorporated into practice with diverse populations of women and men.

Critics have also raised the question whether feminism polarizes male and female development. According to Knudson-Martin and Mahoney (1999), the status quo is maintained when theorists either overemphasize or ignore gender differences. They wrote, "In the rush to address gender, many therapists reinforce a false dichotomy between women and men. At the same time they fail to address how differences in gender equality may be damaging to relationships" (p. 325). One of the goals of feminist therapies and theories is to challenge the status quo related to gender roles without creating false differences or similarities between the sexes.

Despite these limitations, feminists have made major contributions to the fields of counseling and psychology. There is no other theory that places gender at the center of its analysis, creating gender-sensitive practices in therapy with couples, families, and individuals. Moreover, because of the emphasis that is placed on challenging the status quo, it is possible that feminist theory could be conceptualized as more open to multiple voices than any other counseling theory. Additionally, feminist theory has contributed to important shifts in thinking by actively challenging traditional notions of psychological development, particularly of women, in its externalization of clients' problems, its nonpathologizing stance, and its view of social action as a critical part of individual change.

Questions and Learning Activities

These questions and activities are designed to stimulate your thinking about this theory and to help you apply some of the ideas to your own life and experience. If possible, you should work with another person or with a small group. Getting others' points of view and sharing your own ideas and perspectives will be invaluable as a way to help you evaluate this theory and its applications.

Reflection Questions

1. What message do you think the author is trying to communicate in the following quote?

    > "I'm not a feminist, but . . . ." has become an infamous and numbingly overused cliché . . . . As I understand this conversational gambit, it means that the speaker probably supports some combination of equal pay for equal work; reproductive freedom for women; equal access to the same educational, professional, and financial opportunities as men; expanded child-care facilities for working parents; more humane maternity and paternity leave policies; marriages in which husbands cook dinner and empty the diaper pail; and an end to—or even a slowing of—our national epidemic of violence against women of all ages. It also means that the speaker shaves her legs, bathes regularly, does not want to be thought of as a man-hater, a ball-buster, a witch, a shrew, and maybe even wears mascara, blush, and a bra. Most of all, it means that the possibility of having, inside you, a unified, coherent self that always believes the same things at the same time is virtually zero. (Susan J. Douglas, 1995, *Where the Girls Are*, p. 272–273)

2. What does being a "feminist" mean to you?
3. Why do you think people are reluctant to identify themselves as feminists?
4. In what ways does feminism not fit with contemporary society?
5. How can feminists go about making continued progress when a conservative political climate exists?
6. Do you see any contradictions in your own life that address mixed messages targeted at women? How do you resolve these contradictions?
7. How could you help a client work through contradictions related to identifying as a feminist?
8. Do you think that the kind of egalitarian relationship that feminist counselors suggest is possible between counselors and clients?
9. Do you think that men can be feminists? Can males be feminist counselors?
10. What do you think of the social action aspect of the feminist approach?

Learning Activities

Self-Assessment: Exploring Personal Identity

This activity was adapted from one developed by Worell and Remer (2003, pp. 29–30). Some of the group identities individuals use to define themselves are listed below. In the space next to the identifier, write how you define yourself. For example, in the space next to "Educational Level," you may write "First to go to graduate school" or "1st-generation college student." Each of the categories provides an opportunity to locate yourself in a position of relative social advantage (privilege) or disadvantage (oppression). After filling in the blanks, use what you wrote to think about your position in each category and engage in a conversation about these characteristics and how they enable individuals to access social resources. Also think about how your position within these categories may impact your work with clients.

Gender   _____

Age   _____

Educational Level   _____

Nationality   _____

Sexual Orientation   _____

Ethnicity   _____

Race/Skin Color   _____

Religious/Spiritual Orientation   _____

Social Class Status   _____

Immigration/Citizenship Status   _____

Primary/Secondary Languages   _____

Physical Characteristics/Body Image   _____

Physical Ability/Disability   _____

Other   _____

(J. Worell and P. Remer, *Feminist Perspectives in Therapy: Empowering Diverse Women*, 2e, © 2003. Reprinted with permission of John Wiley & Sons, Inc.)

Client Empowerment Assessment

Client Scenario: Susie came to counseling feeling overwhelmed and unusually tired. Susie's mother has Alzheimer's disease, which requires constant care and supervision. Susie's older brothers provide moderate financial support but believe Susie should be responsible for the daily care of their mother, since she is a stay-at-home mother of two. Susie feels guilty about asking her two older brothers for help but is not sure how much longer she can continue to balance all of her responsibilities to her family.

Counselor Questions

1. How might this client's issues or problems be redefined in an empowering way?
2. What strengths and competencies does this client bring to counseling and exhibit in her life?
3. How has this client been affected by issues of gender stereotyping and discrimination?
4. How could you as a counselor address the gender-driven factors in counseling?
5. What are some counseling strategies that can be used to help empower your client?
6. What resources can the client access outside of counseling as a source of empowerment?

Making Therapy Political

1. What groups or individuals benefit from certain feelings, behaviors, and experiences being called mental illness?
2. Who benefits from the belief that people need an expert to heal or to solve their problems?
3. Who benefits from placing blame for problems on individuals rather than society?
4. What are the consequences of helping individuals to relieve their symptoms without addressing larger social issues?
5. What messages does it send when counselors use power and social influence in therapeutic relationships?

Research Corner

Broverman (1970) asked a sample of male and female mental health practitioners to rate the qualities that are most healthy for a mature, socially competent (a) adult (sex unspecified), (b) man, and (c) woman. Some of the qualities rated most desirable for females were "tactful, gentle, aware of feelings of others, religious, neat, enjoys art and literature, expresses feelings, has strong need for security." Some of the qualities rated most desirable for males were "aggressive, independent, not emotional, dominant, active, competent, competitive, decisive, adventurous, self-confident, and ambitious."

1. Based on the lists of personal qualities thought to be desirable for members of each gender, can you identify any themes in the descriptors used?
2. What do the words listed as desirable for males and females say about the culture's messages about how women and men should be or act?
3. If a client possesses qualities deemed undesirable or inappropriate for his or her gender, how might this affect the client?

Personal Inquiry

The following questions are meant to allow you to reflect on your personal beliefs about gender.

1. If men and women were socialized the same way, do you think there would still be pronounced gender differences?
2. If you could choose your gender, what would you choose? Why?
3. How has your gender constrained you in your life?
4. If you had to choose, would you rather raise a baby girl or a baby boy in our society? What makes you choose one or the other?

Developing a Women's Empowerment Group

Women's groups have played an integral part in the creation and evolution of feminist counseling. The purpose of most women's empowerment groups is to increase awareness of self and others while discussing social and personal issues as shared experiences. How would you go about creating a women's empowerment group? How would you work to create a nonjudgmental, respectful environment in which to bring out and support participants' experiences? Think about issues such as how many participants you would have in your group, what types of questions you would ask each member prior to starting the group, and what types of group norms or rules you would work to create in terms of confidentiality, group structure and content, and involvement of counselors.

Assertiveness Training Role-Play

Pair up with a partner. One person acts as the client and the other acts as the counselor. Practice the preparation stages for using an assertiveness training role-play with a client. Create a situation for the client where a role-play might be appropriate (e.g., the client is struggling with speaking up at work or telling a roommate to clean up the apartment).

Preparation for role-play:

- What is the goal of this assertive behavior? What am I trying to accomplish?
- What are the barriers to acting assertively?
- What are my personal rights in this situation?
- Remember to sit or stand in an attentive position that commands respect, take a few deep breaths, speak in a relaxed manner, and look at the person you are addressing

Evaluation of assertion:

- Did I achieve my goal and say what I wanted to get my point across assertively?
- Was I direct and honest?
- Did I stand up for my rights without violating the rights of others?
- Was my voice strong and relaxed?
- How could I improve my assertiveness?

Quotes and Miscellaneous

- When asked who was smarter, men or women, Samuel Johnson replied, "Which man? Which woman?"
- "People call me a feminist whenever I express sentiments that differentiate me from a doormat." -Rebecca West
- "When I am alone I am not aware of my race or my sex, both in need of social context for definition." -Maxine Hong Kingston
- "You must do the thing that you think you cannot do." -Eleanor Roosevelt

Companion Website

Now go to the Companion Website at www.prenhall.com/archer to assess your understanding of chapter content with multiple-choice and essay questions, and broaden your knowledge with related Web resources and additional print resources.

CHAPTER 11

Family Systems Approaches

VOICES FROM THE FIELD: COUNSELOR AND CLIENT REACTIONS

Yes, it works for me

Client: I was really impressed with my family counselor. I liked the way she viewed our son's problem as a family problem rather than just putting all the responsibility on Jared. My husband and Jared are always at each other because of Jared's low grades. I think part of the problem does involve how Jared fits into the family, even though his low grades and negative attitude always seem to be what we talk about. Jared really responded well when the counselor went around and asked each family member for thoughts about the problem. It gave Jared a chance to put in his two cents. . . . Maybe he will feel more involved and willing to help us all make some changes. I think this will be hard for my husband, though.

Counselor: The more I learn about a family systems approach, the more I like it. Looking at things from a "systems approach" really makes sense. People don't exist in a vacuum, and anyone who comes in with a problem is involved in a family system in some way or other. I don't see how you can counsel someone without understanding the system within which she operates. Whenever I see a client, I try to think in terms of her family system and how I might help her and her system work in a healthier way.

No, it doesn't work for me

Client: We took our daughter, Merideth, to counseling because she flunked out of college twice and has been sitting around doing nothing for over a year. She seems pretty depressed and can't seem to get on with her life. She didn't have many friends growing up, and we wonder if that isn't a big part of it. Anyway, when we took her in, the counselor wanted the entire family to come also, even my 10-year-old son. He seemed to be focusing on how the family communicates. It was interesting to talk about that, and like any family, we can certainly improve the way we communicate. But I don't see how this is going to help our daughter with her problems. Merideth didn't have much to say in the session. I got the impression there was a lot more going on for her that she wouldn't talk about with the whole family there. I can see that our relationship with Merideth might be important, but I think she needs to get some individual counseling to figure out what keeps her so depressed and afraid to move on in life.

Counselor: I just don't get this big emphasis on "systemic thinking." Of course, everyone has a family system, but how can you say that a person's problem is always a result of the "system"? We are all individuals with our own issues. I think that a person can best be helped by having a chance to sit down individually with a counselor and figure out just what he wants out of life and what is getting in the way of achieving that. There might be family issues involved, and it may even be smart to bring in a partner or other family member at some point in therapy, but I just don't see people's problems as always a function of their family system.

Theodore and Alexandria Jacobs have been increasingly worried about their 15-year-old son, Martin. They feel that he is becoming too distant. He spends a great deal of time in his room by himself, and he often disobeys them. He has taken to sneaking out his bedroom window very late at night. They also have a 19-year-old daughter who is away at college. She was a very successful volleyball player, had very high grades, and got an athletic scholarship to a very good university. The Jacobs report that they have come to counseling to try to get their son "back on the right track."

> **Counselor:** I learned a bit about your family situation from Mrs. Jacobs when I spoke with her on the phone, but I would like to hear what each of you thinks is going on with your family.
>
> **Theodore:** Well, the basic problem is Martin. We don't know how to handle him. He won't listen to us, and he seems to be on another planet.
>
> **Alexandria:** Now, Ted, things aren't that bad. I think. . . .
>
> **Counselor:** Pardon me, Mrs. Jacobs, but I would like to give your husband a chance to express his views about the situation before we go on.
>
> **Theodore:** That's pretty much it. I know I have lost my temper a lot, but I just don't know what to do.
>
> **Counselor:** Martin, can we get your point of view on the problem?
>
> **Alexandria:** I believe that Martin is unhappy and taking out. . .
>
> **Counselor:** Sorry to cut in again, Mrs. Jacobs, but I really do want to give each member of the family a chance to get his perspective out, and I would like to hear from Martin.

There are a number of different types of family systems counseling models. However, they are all known for their emphasis on viewing the family as a system rather than looking at the problems of individual family members. In the scenario above, which is pretty typical, a family comes in with one member identified as the "problem person," sometimes referred to as the identified patient (IP). Rather than focusing on this person and his problems (in this case, Martin's behavioral problems, as reported by his parents), the family counselor will try to assess problems in how the family operates as a system. Often this involves looking at family structure or communication patterns. You see the counselor here interrupting the mother in order to give each person a chance to express his views on the family's situation and to avoid going along with the idea that one person is necessarily the family problem. In particular, the counselor will work to get the family to see how parts of the family's structure or communication patterns might be responsible for problems. In this family, perhaps Martin needs to act out so that his mother will come to rescue him from the demands put on him by his father—we see a little evidence for this when the mother tries to interrupt and protect him from the father's comments and again when she tries to speak for him.

Although the idea of a systems approach (the theories covered in this chapter) was at the heart of the strong movement in the 1950s and 1960s toward family counseling, a number of other approaches to family work have also been developed. We have already discussed the fact that Alfred Adler developed child guidance clinics in his early career and the Adlerian movement in the United States has been heavily involved in parent and family counseling and education. We noted also that Albert Ellis has done a great deal of work with couples and marriage counseling and with related issues like sexuality. Gladding (2002), Goldenberg and Goldenberg (2005), and Nichols and Schwartz (2004) also mentioned a number of other significant family counseling applications, including psychoanalytic and cognitive-behavioral approaches, in their family counseling textbooks. And both of the postmodern theories that we cover later in this book, solution-focused therapy and narrative therapy, were developed within a family counseling framework. As you have probably guessed, family counseling and couples counseling are very significant areas of study and practice.

In this chapter, we will discuss four prominent family systems models: structural family therapy, strategic family therapy, Bowen's intergenerational family systems therapy, and Satir's humanistic existential Family Therapy. In order to cover four different theories, we have modified our general chapter outline somewhat. In the first part of the chapter, we discuss the historical context and development of the systems approach in general. Next we individually examine the four specific theories, including coverage of the basic concepts: therapeutic relationship; assessment, goals, and process; and therapeutic techniques. Then we provide a general discussion of the systems approach as a whole with regard to diversity effectiveness, applications, brief therapy and managed care, integration with other theories, research, and evaluation.

HISTORICAL BACKGROUND

Historical Context

Family therapy, as a treatment modality and as a new profession, became prominent in the 1950s and 1960s. In a sense, the field of counseling and psychology was ready for this development. Gladding (2002) cited several developments in the 1940s that seemed to lay the groundwork for family therapy, including the establishment of the American Association of Marriage Counselors in 1942. This represented the official beginning of marriage and couples counseling. Because of increasing interest in family therapy, as opposed to just marriage counseling, the name of this organization was eventually changed in 1978 to the American Association for Marriage and Family Therapy (Goldenberg & Goldenberg, 2005).

Gladding (2002) reported that Bela Mittleman published a paper in 1948 stressing the importance of object relations in couples therapy, a radical departure from classic Freudian doctrine. Other developments included the beginning of research on families and schizophrenia and the family upheaval that occurred when soldiers returned to their families after World War II. Nichols and Schwartz (2004) also mentioned the study of small-group dynamics, the child guidance movement, and early social work as influential. You will recall that both Carl Rogers and Alfred Adler were involved in early childhood guidance clinics. According to Nichols and Schwartz (2004), "These turn-of-the-century caseworkers were well aware of something it took psychiatry fifty years to discover—that families must be considered as units" (p. 20).

Another important contextual detail was the fact that individual therapy was just not working in many instances. Psychiatrists who were treating schizophrenics and other mentally ill patients began to notice that sometimes, when their patients got better, someone else in the family seemed to develop a serious problem. They also observed that patients who seemed to be much better while treated in an inpatient setting often rapidly regressed to previous problem behaviors when they were sent back to their families.

In the past several decades, the American Association for Marriage and Family Therapy (AAMFT), with a membership of over 20,000 (Kaslow, 2000), has been a leading organization in helping establish marriage and family therapy as a distinct profession. Kaslow noted that as the field of family therapy has grown and matured over the past several decades, other organizations have been established to reflect the varying professional orientations of those who practice family therapy. For example, in 1977 the American Family Therapy Association was established to promote the interests of those who practiced family counseling using a systems approach (Gladding, 2002). This organization eventually came to focus more on promoting ideas about family therapy, while the AAMFT retained its role of establishing credentials for practice. A formal division of the American Psychological Association was established in 1985 to address the professional needs of psychologists who work with families.

In retrospect, it may seem odd that the idea of working with the entire family didn't really develop in any significant way until the middle of the twentieth century. Gladding (2002) reasoned that several factors inhibited the growth of family therapy: the myth of rugged individualism and the idea that one should be able to solve one's own problems; the Puritan belief that to admit problems was to admit a failure to achieve God's favor; the tradition of taking family problems to clergy, doctors, and lawyers rather than counselors; and the strong preference for treating the individual as a result of the dominance of psychoanalysis in the first half of the century.

Development of the Theory

Perhaps the most prominent influences on the early development of family systems therapy were the studies of communication patterns in schizophrenic families by two different researchers, Gregory Bateson and Theodore Litz. Bateson approached the study of these families from a non-psychological perspective, applying cybernetic principles to the observation of communication patterns. Cybernetics is the study of communication and how systems automatically control themselves to achieve homeostasis (equilibrium/stability). He and several colleagues published a famous paper discussing *double-bind* communication in schizophrenic families (Bateson, Jackson, Haley, & Weakland, 1956). They hypothesized that schizophrenia might result when children are put in double-bind positions by their parents. They gave a now famous example of a double bind:

> Her son was glad to see her and impulsively put his arm around her shoulders, whereupon she stiffened. He withdrew his arm and she asked, "Don't you love me any more?" He then blushed, and she said, "Dear, you must not be so easily embarrassed and afraid of your feelings." The patient was able to stay with her only a few minutes more, and following her departure, he assaulted an aide and was put into the tubs. (Bateson, Jackson, Haley, & Weakland, 1976, pp. 14–15)

As you can see in this example, the mother has put her son in a classic double-bind position. His attempt at physical affection is rebuffed, but he is then told not to be afraid of his feelings. Another way to express a double bind is "damned if you do, damned if you don't."

Litz and colleagues (Litz & Litz, 1949) studied 50 families who had schizophrenic members and found that many of these families had experienced considerable marital strife. Further, many of the schizophrenics came from homes with only one parent. Although Litz was a psychoanalyst, this study challenged the psychoanalytic notions of oral fixation and maternal rejection. Instead, he noted the influence of both the mother and the father.

According to Nichols and Schwartz (2004), "The Bateson group stumbled onto family therapy more or less by accident" (p. 27). As this group, located in Palo Alto, California, moved toward applying its ideas to family therapy (the group's original interests were more theoretical), its members were joined by Virginia Satir, who was also interested in family communication patterns and the strong affect (feeling) involved in family relationships. During this same period, Murray Bowen, a psychiatrist who specialized in schizophrenia, also became interested in the role of the family. He focused on the emotional entanglements inherent in many families and in the generational influences. His own personal struggle with his family led to perhaps his most famous concept, the idea of *differentiation of self*. Many other theorists and researchers were also instrumental in the development of family systems approaches. We cannot mention them all, but in addition to Jay Haley, who is discussed in more detail later, some of the other significant contributors include Carl Whitaker, John Weakland, Don Jackson, Lynn Wynne, John Bell, and Nathan Akerman (Goldenberg & Goldenberg, 2005; Nichols & Schwartz, 2004).

In the 1970s, the most important center of family systems study and treatment was the Philadelphia Child Guidance Center. Salvidor Minuchin was the director of this center, and many other well-known theorists and practitioners in the field, including Jay Haley and Cloe Madanes, were on the staff. The focus of family therapy moved from communication patterns, as emphasized by the Palo Alto group, to the structure of the family.

The 1980s ushered in the practice of strategic family therapy, a problem-solving approach in which the therapist used unconventional methods to get families to act differently. It was based primarily on Milton Erickson's work and the idea of unconscious strengths and natural abilities (Erickson & Harley, 1985). Erickson identified the *utilization principle*, which relies on a client's own language and perceptions to break through resistance. This allows therapists to get right to an action stage in therapy and direct families to carry out activities, often indirect and unconventional, that will help them solve their problems.

By the end of the 1980s, the initial surge of energy that came with the emergence of a new model and approach to counseling began to fade. Feminists argued that the family therapy movement was male oriented (almost all the prominent theorists and practitioners were men) and tended to overvalue masculine qualities like autonomy and independence, while devaluing feminine qualities such as the emphasis on relationships and caretaking (Goldenberg & Goldenberg, 2005; Hare-Mustin, 1978, 1980). At the same time, the late twentieth century saw family therapy increase its presence and strength as a profession, as research and publications in the area increased tremendously.

At the core of family systems approaches is the assumption that families and their interaction patterns profoundly affect human beings. These patterns work as a system, so that the internal family system works to achieve stability through interaction and communication patterns and through the way the family is structured. In simpler words, whatever happens to the family or to one member of the family affects the system and therefore affects each individual family member. In the late twentieth and early twenty first centuries family therapy continued to grow, embracing new postmodern approaches like narrative therapy and solution-focused therapy. The ideas behind these approaches, and how they have been translated into individual counseling modalities, will be discussed later in the book.

STRUCTURAL FAMILY THERAPY

Salvidor Minuchin

Salvidor Minuchin grew up in rural Argentina in what he called a "shtetl", which is a "small, tightly woven Jewish enclave turning inward for protection and continuity within a majority society that was very different" (p. 6) He described living with four thousand people, many of them cousins and relatives, within six blocks. In *Family Healing* (Minuchin & Nichols, 1993), he talks about his own early life and the roles and structures in place in his family. As a young man, he was jailed for revolutionary activities in Argentina. After finishing medical school, he went to Israel and worked as a pediatrician, served in the Israeli army, came to the United States for psychiatric training, emigrated to Israel with his wife, returned to the United States for additional training in psychiatry, and eventually stayed. In many ways, Minuchin's personal family experiences and his professional experiences led him to an emphasis on the family and family structure.

Minuchin, along with a number of colleagues, began to develop structural family therapy when he worked at the Wiltwyck School for Boys in Harlem, New York. He and his colleagues soon learned that working with the boys when they were in the school had little impact on the boys when they returned to their same family environments. So, out of frustration, they began to see the boys with their families. They had little experience in doing this, and as Minuchin put it, "We had no models, and there was no literature to guide us" (Minuchin & Nichols, 1993, p.18).

ASSUMPTIONS AND CORE CONCEPTS: STRUCTURAL FAMILY THERAPY

View of Human Nature

A number of assumptions underlie structural family therapy. First is the basic assumption that humans must live in social groups to survive. The family is the basic social unit. According to Minuchin (1974), the family serves two functions: "One is internal—the psychosocial protection of its members; the other is external—the accommodation of a culture and the transmission of that culture" (p. 46).

A second assumption relates to the relationship between the individual and the family. Minuchin and Fishman (1981) borrowed the term *holon* from Arthur Koestler, to label what they argued should be the unit of intervention in counseling:

> Every holon—the individual, the nuclear family, the extended family, and the community—is both a whole and a part, not more one than the other, not one rejecting or conflicting with the other. A holon exerts competitive energy for autonomy and self-preservation as a whole. It also carries integrative energy as a part. (p. 13)

In other words, there is a separate way of looking at the connection and interaction between an individual and the family that is different from a consideration of either the part or the whole.

A third assumption is that a family is constantly in a state of change, moving from periods of stability to periods of instability. In this sense, there is no "normal" family, since families are always in a state of transition, shifting their structure and functions to deal with the present realities. Minuchin and Fishman (1981) suggested four general stages of family development: couple formation, families with young children, families with school-age or adolescent children, and families with grown children. They conceded that this is a stereotypic scheme that seems to apply only to the traditional family and that many forms of families exist; however, their main point is that families are always in a state of transition, negotiating changing conditions.

Core Concepts

Family Structure The idea of family structure is the basis for this approach to family therapy. According to Minuchin (1974), "Family structure is the invisible set of functional demands that organizes the ways in which family members interact. A family is a system that operates through transactional patterns. Repeated transactions establish patterns of how, when, and to whom, and these patterns underpin the system" (p. 51).

There are several ways to look at family structure, all related to interaction patterns. You might assess structure by looking at family roles and who takes on what roles. For example, in one family the father may be a "soft touch" and take on the role of sympathizer, while the mother might be the limit setter, always working to keep the children in line. Although these are roles, we see that they also clearly reflect interaction patterns. You can also assess family structure from the viewpoint of how the family interacts with other families. For example, the mother may take the lead in setting up social events such as parties that allow for interactions with neighbors, or the older son of a recently immigrated family may handle all outside interactions because he is the only one who speaks English. Families all also have a hierarchical structure, determining how power in the family is distributed. Often one parent is the covert head of the household, making the important decisions.

Family problems most often occur when the family structure cannot accommodate itself to change, as is the case in the following example. Jessie, a 13-year-old boy, reaches puberty and begins to challenge the authority of his mother, who is the one who sets out the rules governing his behavior. She has always insisted that he come home directly after school. As he reaches puberty, he wants the freedom to hang out at a friend's house. The family must be able to accommodate his new demands for more self-direction. This is but one demand from Jessie for more independence, and there will be many more. These demands will require the mother to give up some level of control over Jessie's behavior, perhaps even encouraging him to be more autonomous. In being more flexible, she may also want to modify her role as the sole disciplinarian, perhaps gaining her husband's help in dealing with this common but difficult situation. To gain her husband's help, some of the basic rules and perhaps communication patterns among all family members may need to be altered. In other words, some accommodation of the family structure is required to adapt to the normal developmental changes Jessie is experiencing. If the family can't manage this, serious disruptions in the family's relationships may result.

Subsystems and Boundaries Every family has a number of different subsystems. These involve alliances, and special relationships between different members. Minuchin (1974) talked about the spousal subsystem, the parental subsystem, and sibling subsystems; there may also be other subsystems across generations. Family members play different roles and have different levels of power in different subsystems; for example, a man may be a father, a brother, and a son. Subsystems are formed according to roles, skills, and functions and allow the family to carry out its various functions. For example, the parental subsystem has one function: raising the children.

Systems and subsystems have boundaries, which are the rules governing how individuals participate within each system and subsystem. Boundaries are important because they enable the subsystems to operate effectively within the overall system, allowing each family member important roles and at the same time providing for independence and individual differentiation. When boundaries are too permeable (not clear enough), the family members are *enmeshed*, and when they are too rigid, they are said to be *disengaged*. Either of these conditions can create problems for a family and interfere with its ability to function effectively. The following two dialogues illustrate these two conditions. The Perez family has come in for counseling because daughter Rachel has been kicked out of school twice for getting in trouble.

DISENGAGED BOUNDARIES

Therapist: Tell me what happened the second time Rachel was expelled.
Father: Well, we told her that if this happened again, she was going to find herself in jail. She is 16 and has to take responsibility for herself. We really don't know why the school sent us here.
Mother: I agree. I don't have to treat her like a child. It's all I can do to go to work and keep up the house.
Father: My older son doesn't have these kinds of problems.

ENMESHED BOUNDARIES

Therapist: Tell me what happened the second time Rachel was expelled.
Father: We were all really upset. My wife was really torn up. Her mother had to come down to help out. We've just been in an uproar over this. I don't know what to do.
Mother: It just broke my heart to see her get into so much trouble. And her grandparents were really worried, too. We had to cancel a vacation because of this, and I had so much trouble sleeping I had to get pills from the doctor.
Father: Things are so bad that our baby daughter, Isabel, wants to come and sleep with us every night—she hasn't done that for over a year.

In the first example, the family, particularly the parents, does not seem to have much of an emotional connection to Rachel. In some respects, it sounds like they do not want to deal with the situation and want to put all of the responsibility on her. In the second example, that of an enmeshed family, we see that everyone is very upset. There is evidence that perhaps the boundaries between parents and children are not clear and also that the boundaries may not be clear between parents and grandparents. Since this is a Hispanic family, any hypotheses about the nature of the boundaries between parents and grandparents should take into account cultural factors. In fact, the definition of boundaries might be very different for different cultures.

According to Minuchin (1974), in disengaged families the rigid boundaries may interfere with the family's supportive systems, while enmeshed families may discourage autonomy and differentiation. So in the Perez family, with its disengaged boundaries, the parents seem disengaged from their daughter. Their boundaries are too rigid, and they don't seem to have an emotional connection or a sense of responsibility regarding their daughter. In the enmeshed example, the daughter may be deprived of taking some responsibility for her actions because her parents are so involved in her life and will have trouble allowing her to experience the consequences of her actions. This kind of enmeshment will probably keep her from developing a sense of independence and identity, part of which is learning to deal with the consequences of one's actions.

THERAPEUTIC RELATIONSHIP: STRUCTURAL FAMILY THERAPY

The nature of the relationship the therapist has with the family is somewhat complex in structural family therapy. In the early stages, the therapist must join the family and accommodate to its patterns and norms (Minuchin, 1974). Yet from the very beginning, the therapist must assume a leadership role (Minuchin & Fishman, 1981). In simple terms, he joins the system in order to take a leadership role in changing the structure. According to Minuchin and Fishman, "Like every leader, he will have to accommodate, seduce, submit, support, direct, suggest, and follow in order to lead" (p. 29). It takes considerable training for the structural family therapist to be able to join and accommodate the family and at the same time lead and direct the family.

Minuchin's style is often confused with the general role of the therapist. As with any therapy, the therapist's style is the way in which he applies the theory and is strongly affected by his personality. Minuchin was a charismatic man and could be quite directive and authoritative. You can get an idea of his style from a story he uses in one of his books to illustrate the concept of intensity (a technique to increase emotion and get the attention of the family). It seems that a farmer owned a donkey that was very well trained. When the farmer told him to eat, he ate; when the farmer told him to move, he moved. He sold the donkey to another man, who returned complaining that the donkey would not obey him. The farmer picked up a board and whacked the donkey on his rear end, telling the purchaser that the donkey obeys, but first you must get his attention (Minuchin & Fishman, 1981). This is a rather crude story but one that Minuchin used as a not-too-subtle way of teaching therapists that they must sometimes actively intervene to get things moving.

ASSESSMENT, GOALS AND PROCESS OF THERAPY: STRUCTURAL FAMILY THERAPY

Assessment in structural family therapy consists of the therapist's hypotheses about the family structure. This assessment starts as soon as the family enters the room, or even before if the therapist talks with any family members on the phone. The way the family members enter the room, their nonverbal and verbal behaviors, and their seating arrangement preferences are all important. However, the therapist really doesn't make a diagnosis or hypothesis about family structure until he "joins" the family and is able to experience the family's transactions as a member. According to Minuchin (1974), the therapist focuses on transactions in six areas: (1) structure, transaction patterns, and available alternatives; (2) flexibility and ability to restructure; (3) sensitivity of members to each other—ranging from enmeshment to disengagement; (4) the family's life context; (5) the family's developmental stage; and (6) ways the identified patient's symptoms are used to maintain the family's transaction patterns.

The goals for each family are different; however, they always involve restructuring the family so that it can function more effectively. These structural problems are typically not pathological and involve the family's inability to adjust to transitions and different circumstances. There are some common structural goals, such as creating an effective family hierarchy with parents in charge and helping parents function more cohesively. Also, enmeshed families are encouraged to strengthen boundaries to allow for differentiation of individual members, and disengaged families are encouraged to decrease the rigidity of boundaries to allow for closer interactions.

The process of structural family therapy involves three general steps or phases. First, as we have described, the therapist must join the family and accommodate to the family. Second, he must assess the family structure and transactions, with particular attention to how they are related to the problem presented. Finally, he must intervene and help the family modify itself so that structure and transactions are more effective and the presenting symptoms are alleviated. This simple scheme creates a complex and difficult job for the therapist.

THERAPEUTIC TECHNIQUES: STRUCTURAL FAMILY THERAPY

Intensity

The therapist cannot have an impact if he is unable to communicate. To do this, he needs a certain level of intensity. Something dramatic, as you saw in the metaphor of whacking the donkey with a board, is one way, albeit a risky one, to get the family's attention. Minuchin and Fishman (1981) suggested several others: using repetition, changing the time, changing the distance, and resisting the family's pull. Repetition means repeating questions or comments until the family responds. Changing the time means getting the family members to continue to interact beyond their usual transaction limits. Changing the distance is just what it sounds like—moving closer to or farther away from members of the family. Resisting the family's pull means that the therapist resists attempts to pull him into the dysfunctional transactions.

The following dialogue illustrates the idea of changing the time. In the Sparkman family (father Herb, mother Janice, and son Andrew, 14), the mother tends to get angry quickly and withdraw from confrontations with her husband or son.

> **Janice:** I will not be involved in this kind of discussion. It makes no sense!
> **Andrew:** You never listen to me. . . then you wonder why we can't communicate!
> **Therapist:** Janice, why don't you go ahead and say what you think? Go ahead!
> **Janice:** I just don't think it's worth it.
> **Therapist:** Just humor me. Let it all out just this once.

The idea is for Janice to express herself and break through some of the transaction barriers that have prevented her from honest and direct communication. Hopefully, this will help her develop a more mature relationship with her son and also change the family structure so that all members can learn to express themselves. Of course, changing this transaction pattern will have other ramifications for the entire family. Part of the therapist's job will be to help make these changes positive in terms of family functioning.

Enactment

With enactment, the counselor simply uses the family session as a laboratory to learn things about the family members' transactions that they will not otherwise disclose. For example, by observing how the parents interact with each child, he can gain valuable information about the family structure, boundaries, and subsystems.

Unbalancing

Unbalancing occurs when the therapist deliberately sides with a less powerful member or subsystem of the family, thereby unbalancing the family. The purpose is to get the family to restructure so that one of the less powerful members gains power. This allows everyone in the family to experience expanded roles and functions (Minuchin & Fishman, 1981). The therapist might, for example, take the side of a teenager who is being treated unfairly and not allowed to grow up and gain appropriate independence. The dangers of this approach lie in the power the therapist assumes and the decisions that he makes for the family—clearly an example of the therapist as expert. With this kind of power comes the potential for ethical problems and abuse of power. The therapist may also jeopardize his relationship with the rest of the family members with this technique.

Complementarity

With this technique, the therapist attempts to help family members gain a sense of connectedness to the family and assume responsibility for improving family transactions. The idea is that members learn how they can "complement" each other and work together. One method of achieving this is with a paradoxical assignment (Minuchin & Fishman, 1981). In the family sequence below, the Hoffman family (father Maurice, mother Hilda, and sons Albert and Arthur, 12 and 10, respectively) is having a terrible time with Arthur, who is constantly having temper tantrums like a much younger child, often at very embarrassing moments.

> **Hilda:** Here we are again! I just don't know how we can control Arthur; he ruined a very nice dinner the other night by flying off the handle. It happens all the time.
>
> **Arthur:** You didn't see Albert making those faces at me—he does it all the time.
>
> **Maurice:** Don't blame your brother for everything; you need to learn self-control.
>
> **Therapist:** OK, we seem to be on the same merry-go-round again. I want to give you an assignment, but I need everyone to cooperate. Can I count on all of you? What about you guys, Arthur and Albert? Will you help? Here's what I want you to do. Every day before breakfast and before dinner, I want Albert to do something to tease Arthur, and Arthur, I want you to scream at him at the top of your lungs for 5 minutes. Mom and Dad, I want you just to watch. No hitting or throwing or anything like that.
>
> **Maurice:** I don't see the purpose in this.
>
> **Therapist:** You have to trust me. Just do the assignment for a week.

This is a classic paradox assignment, and the hope is that the family will see the problem in a different context and come together to work toward a solution. Part of this may be an alignment against the therapist for giving them something so foolish to do.

Reframing

Reframing has the same goal as a complementary technique: to get the family to see what is, usually seen as one family member's problem as a family problem. The therapist might, for example, label a behavior or symptom in a different way. A family that comes to counseling because the father can't communicate with anyone in the family, including his wife, will probably present the problem to the therapist as belonging to the father. The wife might say something like "He just never talks to anyone in the family. He comes home from work and immediately goes down to his workroom. I don't know if he is depressed or just wants to get away from all of us. He doesn't even know the kids." The therapist might try to reframe by saying something like "It sounds like the family has a problem making Dad feel welcome in the family. What do you think can be done to make him feel more welcome?" The purpose is to get the family to look at the situation from a new and more soluble perspective. From this perspective, the entire family can get involved to help Dad be more involved.

STRATEGIC FAMILY THERAPY

Jay Haley

Strategic family therapy is most closely associated with Jay Haley; however, according to Nichols and Schwartz (2004), three different variations emerged in the 1960s and 1970s. These came from the MRI group, a direct outgrowth of the work of Bateson and his colleagues on schizophrenia, in Palo Alto; the Milan group, originally organized in Italy by Mara Selvini Palazzoli; and Haley and Madanes at the Family Therapy Institute in Washington, D.C. Our discussion will focus on Haley and the development of his approach.

Haley did not start out as a professional counselor or helper. His degree was in communications, and he played an important role in Bateson's original research on schizophrenics in the 1950s. During that period, he also became interested in hypnosis and began to study with Milton Erickson. In his book about Erickson, Haley (1973) credited Erickson as the originator of the principles underlying strategic family therapy.

Erickson's approach to therapy was brief, direct, well planned, and different for each client. He was a very charismatic figure and had a great talent for developing therapy plans that helped individuals access hidden strengths and abilities. He often gave specific directives to clients, carefully designed to help them solve a particular problem.

Haley was also strongly influenced by Salvidor Minuchin. He and Minuchin were codirectors of the Philadelphia Child Guidance center for several years during the 1960s, and you will note a number of similarities between structural and strategic family therapy. In 1975, Haley and Cloe Madanes formed the Family Therapy Institute of Washington, D.C., and further developed and practiced strategic family therapy. He wrote several books describing his approach and its application and evolution (Haley, 1963, 1979, 1984) and more recently a book and videotapes describing strategic family therapy (Haley & Richaport-Haley, 2003). Madanes (1981) also wrote a widely used book, *Strategic Family Therapy* (1981).

ASSUMPTIONS AND CORE CONCEPTS: STRATEGIC FAMILY THERAPY

View of Human Nature

The general assumptions about human nature for strategic family therapy are similar to those for structural family therapy. Human behavior is seen from a social, family context, and the family is the core unit within which humans exist and develop. Gladding (2002) described several assumptions about families that are common to both strategic and structural family therapy: People operate within an interactionist context, and they influence and are influenced by others; concomitantly, symptoms are created by the system and also maintain the system. Gladding also wrote that these approaches assume that family members can change their behavior if the system is changed and that families go through developmental stages.

Perhaps the most unique assumption about human nature comes from Milton Erickson's belief that the unconscious is, in fact, a great source of strength and positive energy. Thus, many of his techniques and the techniques of strategic family therapy are designed to mobilize these positive unconscious forces. In many ways this seems to be a precursor to the constructivist solution-focused and narrative therapies, which emphasize the strengths and positive forces within each person.

Core Concepts

Therapist Responsibility One of the most striking features of strategic family therapy is the fact that the therapist assumes responsibility for developing and carrying out a therapy plan. Madanes (1981) put it this way: "The therapist sets clear goals, which always include solving the presenting problem. The emphasis is not on a method to be applied to all cases but on designing a strategy for each specific problem" (p. 19). Since symptoms are seen as attempts at adaptation and are thought to be primarily a result of family relationship patterns and power struggles, the therapist must take on the role of director or authority figure and develop strategies to intervene.

Symptoms as Attempts at Communication Since family members' problematic symptoms are seen as attempts to communicate when all else fails, they are often viewed as a kind of metaphor for the way in which the family operates. For example, if a teenager is constantly involved in battles with her father over issues of freedom and responsibility and is constantly acting out in ways that cause her parents grief, a strategic family therapist might view this acting out as an attempt to communicate with her father. On a more general level, this might be a metaphor for a kind of family interaction where communication concerns are expressed only when a problem arises. Family rules are another way of describing the often unspoken principles that govern a family.

Redefining Symptoms/Problems The idea of reframing a problem so that it can be solved is not new or unique to this approach, but what is different is the creative and innovative ways used to do this. For example, in the previous case the therapist might redefine the problem as being one of communication between the husband and wife about how best to allow their son freedom and responsibility. This moves the problem from a contentious, and perhaps seemingly insoluble, battle between father and son to one of communication. The husband and wife can work on their communication about their son, perhaps in front of the son. It might look something like this in a counseling session.

> **Therapist:** You know, I think the problem is not so much the constant conflict between you and your son, Howard. I would say it is more a problem of communication between you and Sarah about how to best to allow Jeremiah to grow up.

> **Sarah:** I suppose I can see that. It seems like Howard is always the disciplinarian. I just don't like to fight.
>
> **Howard:** It does seem like I'm always the bad guy.
>
> **Jeremiah:** Wait a minute, I don't have a hassle with Mom. . . he's the one who is always on my case.
>
> **Therapist:** I see your point, Jeremiah, but I want you to just sit back and listen for a while. I want your mom and dad to have a chance to talk to each other about their communication problems. Then you will have a turn.

In this example, the therapist has shifted the problem to one that is easier to solve, communication between parents about Jeremiah. The assumption is that one strategic way to improve the conflict between father and son might be to involve the mother and get the mother and father to talk about how they want to approach their son's need for more freedom. This might break into the cycle of conflict between father and son and at the same time give the son and his parents a chance to negotiate some more effective ways to manage freedom, discipline, and limits.

Brief Therapy Focused on the Present Strategic family therapy was a clear break with the tradition of working with a single patient and also with the idea that the therapist needs to find the cause of the problem in order to provide treatment. The focus of strategic family therapy is on solving a problem in the present, without needing to interpret causes of the problem rooted in the past. There is no assumption that understanding or insight will necessarily cause change. It is up to the therapist to create new conditions within the family that will bring about change. This certainly doesn't always happen within a few sessions. Sometimes the therapist will need to move the family along through several stages of change before the ultimate goal is reached.

Units A problem is not seen in terms of individual psychopathology or development. The strategic family therapist thinks in terms of units of two or more people. For example, depression reported by a wife might be conceptualized in terms of the dynamics between husband and wife (a unit of two) or in terms of a coalition of the husband and son that leaves out the wife (a unit of three). You can see how different the intervention would be here from interventions based on the view that the depression is a result of the wife's past experience or personal thinking patterns.

Circularity The idea of linear causality, with one event directly causing another, is replaced in strategic family therapy with the notion of circularity. A family event—say, a son running away from home—is not viewed as being "caused" by certain feelings or events. Rather, the event is part of a kind of circular causation, with multiple events interacting (moving back and forth in feedback loops) to create the event. In this case, the circularity might look like this:

1. Father expresses anger at son for getting bad grades.
2. Son feels misunderstood, tries unsuccessfully to explain his situation.
3. Father can't understand, grounds son.
4. Son feels very hurt and humiliated, lashes out at younger brother.
5. Younger brother exaggerates older brother's lashing out.

6. Mother gets incensed because younger brother reports being hit.
7. Father threatens older son and tells him he is no good.
8. Son runs away from home.
9. Father feels guilty, becomes distant from entire family.

You probably recognize the complexity of interactions that can take place in a family, as represented by this example. The idea of circularity provides the therapist with a different way to view the cause-and-effect feedback loops that often take place.

THERAPEUTIC RELATIONSHIP: STRATEGIC FAMILY THERAPY

As we have already noted, the therapist is the director and authority in the therapeutic interaction. This is particularly true at the earlier stages. Later on, the therapist's strategy might be to empower others to take control and reform the family hierarchy, but in general, the therapist plays a major overt and covert role. Murdock (2004) noted that Haley was flexible in terms of where and when he conducted family counseling. He was not bound by the traditional 50-minute hour, and he was willing to work in homes, schools, and other locations. We have also noted previously that Haley was an imposing, charismatic person, as were many of the early family therapy theorists. This undoubtedly affected his relationships with families, and probably contributed to the development of hope by troubled families as well as to their willingness to carry out his therapy directions.

ASSESSMENT, GOALS, AND PROCESS OF THERAPY: STRATEGIC FAMILY THERAPY

Assessment is important in strategic family therapy because the therapist must identify the problem and develop a strategy for its solution. Haley (1978) placed a great deal of emphasis on the first interview: "If therapy is to end properly, it must begin properly—by negotiating a solvable problem and discovering the social situation that makes the problem necessary" (p. 9). He identified five stages in the first interview, with the first stage involving social interaction with the family members in order to help put them at ease and establish rapport. The next four stages were the problem, interaction, goal-setting, and task-setting stages (Goldenberg & Goldenberg, 2005). In the problem stage, the therapist works to get the problem out. He does not interpret or give advice, and he listens in an interested fashion. Next is the interaction stage, during which the therapist tries to gather information from everyone in the family and works to get the family members to talk with each other about the problem. In the goal-setting stage, the therapist works with the family to define the problem in a solvable way. Finally, at the end of the session, the therapist sets out tasks for the family to begin the therapeutic work.

After this initial interview and goal setting, the stage for the therapy is set. The process itself is unique to the particular family and is essentially the "strategy" that the therapist uses to solve the problem. This may involve a number of strategies and steps but is typically brief and focused.

THERAPEUTIC TECHNIQUES: STRATEGIC FAMILY THERAPY

Directives

Directives are basically instructions to the family or the family members to behave in a particular way. They are primarily designed to get family members to experience new ways of interacting so that they will have different experiences and feelings and therefore behave differently. The success of directives depends a great deal on the family's perception of the therapist's power and expertise. Although direct suggestions are often not followed, they are more likely to be followed when the therapist has a strong relationship and is seen as having knowledge and expertise. For example, a family might be in constant turmoil because the husband's father is constantly calling and trying to control how the parents deal with their children. This disrupts the relationship between the husband and wife and sets up a difficult triangulation involving the grandfather, parents, and children. A directive might be for the family not to answer calls from the grandfather and perhaps to call him once a week to see how he is doing. This, of course, might be particularly difficult for the husband to do, but if he carried out the directive, it would certainly shake things up and give the therapist a chance to observe how the family reacted and perhaps empower the parents and clarify parenting responsibility.

But directives often don't work. It is likely that this obvious suggestion, not to take the grandfather's advice, has already been given to the family by friends or other relatives. If this doesn't work, a paradoxical directive might be given. For example, the therapist might tell the husband and wife that they must call the grandfather at least five times a day to report on family matters and seek his direction. The rationale behind this type of intervention will next be described.

Paradoxical Interventions

As you have already learned, these interventions typically involve directing the client to act in a way opposite to the desired behavior change. Strategic family therapists have refined this method and have practically made it into an art form. These paradoxical interventions are usually used when a more direct approach, such as a directive, will not work.

As an illustration of this kind of intervention, Madanes (1981) described a 60-year-old man who had become depressed later in life and had been neglecting his business. As his wife, who was a therapist, became more successful outside the home, he became more depressed. A summary of the counseling follows:

Session 1. The husband came in alone and was told that the proper diagnosis was not depression but irresponsibility on his part. He was told to set an alarm clock for 3:00 A.M., and to get up and worry for one half an hour but not to worry at any other time. He was also instructed to catch up on his work and told that if he didn't, he would have to do more worrying at 3:00 A.M.

Session 2. The husband and wife appeared, and the husband reported that he had complied with the 3:00 A.M., worrying routine once but that he refused to do it again because it was so ridiculous. He also reported having slept well and not having worried much during the week. His wife agreed with the diagnosis of irresponsibility, rather than depression, and was becoming impatient with him because their finances were in trouble. She was instructed to make a list of what he needed to do and to check up on him regularly to see that he was doing his work.

Session 3 (2 weeks later). Both the husband and wife came to this session, and the husband reported having improved in his work. The therapist told the wife that she had been neglecting her husband and that she should spend more time with him. They were given the assignment to discuss personal issues for half an hour each day. In their sex life, the husband was always the initiator, so the therapist told the wife to take the lead once during the week. The therapist also told the wife that the husband had been protecting her by not allowing her to initiate sex.

Session 4 (2 weeks later). The wife reported that the husband was doing much better at work and was more upbeat, but he denied it. The therapist told them that they had obvious communication problems and instructed the husband during the next week to pretend to be irresponsible and inadequate; he then instructed the wife to attempt to determine if he really was feeling that way.

Session 5. Two weeks later, the husband had not done his assignment of pretending to be irresponsible and inadequate, so the therapist told him to pretend in the session. The wife didn't find him very good at the pretense. (Typically, the husband was irresponsible and inadequate, and the wife was supportive, but in a kind of reversal, here the husband was not very good at being irresponsible and the wife complained that he wasn't very good.) Since the husband was no longer depressed or irresponsible at work, the therapist suggested that the couple go out to lunch instead of coming to the next session.

Session 6 (2 weeks later). Since the improvement continued from both spouses' perspective, the therapist suggested termination.

Follow-up (4 months later). Both husband and wife were upbeat, and the husband had caught up with 4 years of unfinished work. They supported each other through a family death and the birth of a grandchild. (C. Madanes, *Strategic Family Therapy*, © 1981, pp. 34–48. Reprinted with permission of John Wiley & Sons, Inc.)

Madanes (1981) provided a listing of each intervention and its purpose:

1. Depression was renamed irresponsibility, something that the client could change. This also affected the couple's interaction patterns.
2. The paradoxical intervention of instructing the husband to worry at 3:00 A.M. worked to stop the sleep problems related to depression.
3. The wife was put in charge of making the husband be more responsible (making a list, checking up on him). This paradoxical directive exaggerated the problem of the wife being in a superior position and motivated the couple to arrive at a more balanced relationship.
4. Another paradoxical directive to the husband to pretend to be irresponsible encouraged him to rebel and be the opposite. (C. Madanes, *Straegic Family Therapy*, © 1981, pp. 34–48. Reprinted with permission of John Wiley & Sons, Inc.)

According to Madanes, "The interaction between husband and wife was improved, so that they were spending more time together and their sex relations were more varied. As their relationship improved they no longer needed to use the system of interaction around a symptom as an analogy and solution to their difficulties" (p. 38). The complexity and creativity of these interventions provide a good example of how innovative strategic interventions work. This case also provides some clues as to how directive, creative, and authoritative the therapist must be.

Ordeal Directive

Haley (1984) borrowed this approach from Erickson. It involves assigning an unpleasant task to be carried out whenever the symptom occurs. The idea is that the "ordeal" of carrying out the directive will move the family toward giving up the problem symptom or behavior and also increase its motivation for doing so. For example, a family complains that dinner almost always results in an argument, with the daughter and son always complaining about how they are treated by each other. The therapist might give the directive that if there is any arguing or fighting at dinner, the family members must all get up at 3:00 A.M. and sit around the dinner table to discuss the activities of the previous day. This kind of therapy depends a great deal on the motivation of the family members and their willingness to follow the directive. In this case, the ordeal is designed not only to stop the fighting at the table but also to change the nature of the relationship between siblings and with their parents.

INTERGENERATIONAL FAMILY SYSTEMS THERAPY

Murray Bowen

Murray Bowen was born in 1913 and raised in Waverly, Tennessee, a rural community that had been home to his ancestors for several generations. He grew up in a family with five siblings. He attended college and medical school in Tennessee, and when he was an adult, he maintained a fairly distant relationship from his parents (Gladding, 2002). He served as a medical officer in World War II and became interested in psychiatry as a result of encountering soldiers with emotional disturbances caused by the war. In 1946, he began psychiatric training at the Menninger Clinic, which was, like most psychiatric training at that time, psychoanalytically oriented. He remained there until 1954. During this period, he began to question the basic tenets of psychoanalysis and studied evolution, biology, and the natural sciences. As he noted in an interview, it was during this period that the basic formulation of his theory began. "It seemed to me that emotional illness is a deeper phenomenon that can be explained by disturbed relationships in a single generation. I had a hunch that emotional illness is somehow related to that part of man he shares with the other forms of life, rather than a phenomenon peculiar to man" (Bowen, 1978, p. 390).

In 1954, he worked on a groundbreaking study of schizophrenic families, and in 1959, he moved to the medical school at Georgetown University. In 1975, he began the Georgetown Family Center, where he remained until his death in 1990. He also maintained a private practice. Like many of the family systems pioneers, Bowen was a gifted clinician and attracted a number of dedicated students who studied with him at the Family Center.

ASSUMPTIONS AND CORE CONCEPTS: INTERGENERATIONAL FAMILY SYSTEMS THERAPY

View of Human Nature

As did all systems theorists, Bowen saw human behavior as inextricably tied to family relationships and the systems that govern these relationships. His viewpoint came more from the natural sciences and biology than from cybernetic metaphors relying on mathematics, chemistry, and other physical sciences. At the very base of his assumptions is the notion that emotional illness is a part of existence in all life forms:

> Emotional functioning includes the force that biology defines as instinct, reproduction, the autonomic activity controlled by the autonomic nervous system, subjective emotional and feeling states, and the forces that govern relationship systems. In broad terms the emotional system governs the "dance of life" in all living things. (Bowen, 1975, p. 380)

Bowen further developed the theory that the family operates as an emotional system and that this system, which is influenced by previous generations, governs family life. Part of this idea came from his study of schizophrenic families and the transgenerational influences of a "mother-child symbiosis" in schizophrenia. The family emotional system reacts to what he considered to be a kind of innate or chronic anxiety in humans, as well as in other species. In families, this anxiety is a natural part of the struggle between individuality and togetherness, If the family moves too far in the direction of togetherness, then individuality (and differentiation, which will be discussed soon) is stifled and chronic anxiety is increased, thus causing emotional problems. Bowen's assumptions about human functioning are most easily seen in the interlocking core concepts of the theory.

Core Concepts

Bowen's theory of transgenerational systemic counseling has a more explicit set of principles than do any of the other systemic approaches. The theory involves eight interlocking theoretical concepts, which are described below. The first six concepts were formulated by 1963 and the last two (emotional cutoff and emotional process in society) were added in 1976 (Papero, 1990).

(1) *Differentiation of Self* This concept is the foundation for all the others. The process of differentiation from parents occurs in all biological species in some form. In humans, differentiation means the formation of an independent self with the ability to recognize the difference between emotion and thinking and to react well to stress and crisis situations. Undifferentiated people are overly controlled by their emotions and are typically not able to respond well or rationally in

stressful situations. A differentiated self develops as a person grows up and moves away from her family. If she is unable to develop and differentiate, she doesn't learn to operate independently. According to Bowen, this leaves the person emotionally tied to, and dependent on, the family. Consequently, she never develops the ability to recognize and control her own emotions. This does not mean that a differentiated person doesn't have or respond to feelings. A differentiated person can maintain close and loving relationships with her family of origin while still being independent.

Bowen (1966) used a theoretical scale going from 0 to 100 to illustrate the concept of differentiation. This was not a formal scale and he used it only to show the degree of differentiation in different people. Those with scores below 25 are classified as emotionally dependent on their parents and as highly reactive emotionally, with little development of intellect and self-control. People in the 25–50 range are strongly influenced by their emotional system, are not self-directed, and typically work to please others. The 50–75 range includes people who have a sense of self and are not dominated by feelings in situations causing high anxiety. People in the highest range, those from 75 to 100, have a strong sense of self, know how to separate thinki[...]ions under stress, and are able to experience intimacy in [...] Bowen (1978), those over 75 are considered to have a hig[...] a small percentage of people would actually score above 60[...]

Triangulation Triangul[...]aship becomes too stressful or conflicted and a third perso[...] the tension. This typically occurs in families, often involvin[...]artners) and one of their children. Triangulation is a negativ[...]direct expression of feelings between the members of original[...] as stress increases in a family, more than one triangle can be [...]er might be triangulated because the parents are feeling confl[...]ght feel conflict or perhaps anger at one of his parents and tr[...]ring her in the conflict. Triangles are typically used to decreas[...]several triangles are formed in a family, this may well increas[...]

The more family m[...] likely they are to triangulate. For example, a person who is [...] void being emotionally drawn into a dyadic conflict. She, may, in fact, be able to help diffuse the situation without triangulation. For example, let's say two grown sisters in a family don't get along and get into a heated argument while on a walk with their sister-in-law before a Thanksgiving dinner. Both sisters have in the past tried to triangulate her and bring her in on their side. She has steadfastly refused to take sides, and she does so again. She reminds the sisters that it is, after all, Thanksgiving and asks that they put aside their differences for the sake of their parents.

Nuclear Family Emotional System According to Bowen (1978), people with equivalent levels of differentiation are likely to choose each other as spouses. Consequently, someone with low differentiation who is still fused to his own family of origin is likely to choose someone who is also fused to her family of origin. They, in turn, are likely to become fused to each other and to raise children who are undifferentiated. This creates considerable emotional turmoil and instability in the family. According to Nichols and Schwartz (2004), one or more of four different scenarios are likely to occur. The members of the couple may maintain an emotional distance between themselves, they may have a very conflicted relationship, either of them may have physical or emotional problems, or through projection a child may become the focus of their problems.

Family Projection Process   In the family projection process, parents transmit their own lack of differentiation to their children. This typically involves parents triangulating one of their children—thus, the family or parental problems are, in essence, projected onto the child. Projection is a Freudian term and refers to the situation where what is inside the person is misunderstood as coming from the outside; in other words, thoughts and feelings that one finds unacceptable are attributed to another person. If there is more than one sibling, the projection often goes to the most immature or vulnerable child. This child will be the most undifferentiated of all the children and will have the most difficulty achieving any separation from the family. Consequently, the child will have the most difficulty adapting to various situations and is likely to develop emotional problems.

Take the example of a father and mother who have become increasingly distant from each other. Both have demanding careers, but the father has been dissatisfied with his for some time. They have three children. Their daughter is a straight-A student and a talented violinist. The family also includes two younger boys who are athletic, are sociable, and spend a lot of time away from the house. The father and daughter have always had a special bond, and as he has become more distant from his wife, the father seems to live vicariously through his daughter. They are both very interested in music, and they often attend concerts together. Every night after dinner the father and daughter discuss her school day in some detail, and he very often expresses his desire for her to get top grades and attend an Ivy League school. The mother has tried to be more involved with her daughter but feels closed out. As the daughter reaches her midteens, she doesn't seem to have many friends. She becomes depressed, and to the shock and horror of her family, the school guidance counselor calls and says that they have discovered a number of cuts on her arm and that she has admitted they are self-inflicted.

In this scenario, a Bowenian therapist might interpret the parents' emotional problems as being projected onto the daughter. She is clearly triangulated between the mother and father and is likely the least differentiated sibling. The father, in particular, has projected his anxiety and disappointment with his work and his marriage, and being undifferentiated himself, he has become too close to his daughter and stunted her emotional development and differentiation. Consequently, she doesn't develop effective coping mechanisms and the ability to form friendships, becomes depressed and eventually resorts to cutting herself.

Multigenerational Transmission Process   In this process, perhaps the most fascinating of Bowen's ideas, there can be a kind of downward dysfunctional spiral over several generations. When the least differentiated children in two families marry and this process continues through several generations, a general increase in anxiety and fusion can result across generation. In each generation, at least one of the children is the victim of projected anxiety and suffers a lower level of differentiation. Of course, this would not necessarily happen in a linear or systematic way, but the general idea is that over several generations the dysfunction may become serious enough to produce very serious emotional problems in members of the family.

Sibling Position Bowen considered functional birth order to be important. Functional birth is considered important in personality development and also in how the next generation's marital dyad and family function. Oldest children are considered to be conservative, well socialized, and adultlike, while younger siblings, particularly the youngest or middle child, are seen as more sociable, more spontaneous, and more apt to push boundaries and be creative. If two first-born children marry, they may both want to take responsibility for decisions, and they might want to have a very well behaved, structured family. This could lead to problems if they are competitive or if they have children who are not as highly socialized as they might like. On the other hand, if two later-born siblings marry, neither of them may want to take responsibility for decisions, and there might be a certain amount of chaos in the relationship and the family. There are many other factors here that can influence personality and subsequent family and couple behavior, but the point is that sibling order can influence personality, which can certainly influence marital and family relationships.

Emotional Cutoff Emotional cutoff is a reaction of family members to the conflict and anxiety inherent in undifferentiated fused families. Instead of undergoing what might be called a healthy separation from family—growing up and becoming differentiated but maintaining a loving and close relationship with parents and siblings—a person cuts herself off from the family to avoid the anxiety. Just about everyone has heard of families where one member is not talking to another. This is a form of emotional cutoff. Sometimes it is a bit difficult to see the difference between healthy differentiation from family and cutoff. For example, a son might join the army and remain out of touch with his family for very long periods of time. This could be seen as the natural process of growing up and moving away; however, it might also represent an emotional cutoff. In order to make this determination with a family in therapy, a Bowenian therapist would want to understand the reasons behind the son's decision, his role in the family system, and the impact of his decision on the rest of the family.

Societal Emotional Process Bowen (Kerr & Bowen, 1988) recognized the impact of societal factors, such as poverty, sexism, racism, and disaster, on the family. Bowen suggested that such negative social forces created chronic pressures on families that increased anxiety and decreased the likelihood of differentiation. He also felt that society's levels of functioning and differentiation were deceasing, so that in general society was operating less with intellect and less from a differentiated position (Goldenberg & Goldenberg, 2005).

THERAPEUTIC RELATIONSHIP: INTERGENERATIONAL FAMILY SYSTEM THERAPY

The therapist acts as a coach or consultant, is respectful of all members present, and helps the family and its members find ways to become more differentiated. He maintains an objective stance and avoids becoming triangulated in the interaction. In order to be helpful and objective, he must be able to avoid being drawn in by the strong emotionality and must therefore be highly differentiated himself. This requires the therapist to have worked through his own family of origin issues. For trainees, this often involves some kind of therapy to assess their own relationships with their families. As part of this, they will probably undertake a "journey home" to help reassess their connections to their own families. This technique will be described in detail later.

ASSESSMENT, GOALS, AND PROCESS OF THERAPY: INTERGENERATIONAL FAMILY SYSTEMS THERAPY

Bowen's approach to therapy begins with a careful assessment of the family and its interactions. In this initial evaluation interview, the symptoms and problems, as well as a history of the problems, are discussed. Any number of family members may be present, and each member present is asked to give his or her perception of the situation. The therapist asks questions to elicit information about the general emotional functioning of the family and the level of differentiation of its members. An exploration of the transgenerational nature of family emotional functioning completes the initial interview. This involves examining at least three generations of family members using a technique called a genogram (to be described in the "Therapeutic Techniques" section immediately following). As noted before, a crucial requirement for the therapy is the ability of the therapist to maintain his own objectivity, requiring the therapist to be well differentiated himself.

The process of therapy proceeds with the therapist working as a kind of coach to help the family learn more about its functioning. Bowen (1976) believed that the addition of another person (therapist, clergyman, even friend) could help a family modify problem relationships and interaction patterns. Bowen worked with any combination of family members that were willing to be involved in therapy, but he typically worked with parents on their relationship as a way to solve problems with the family or with individual children. Considerable time in therapy is spent on an analysis of the extended family, helping the parents understand how their connections with their own families are influencing their current behavior. Nichols and Schwartz (2004) noted that what they call "second-generation Bowenians" focus more on the nuclear family and use the family of origin only to consolidate and reinforce gains.

A major goal of Bowenian therapy is to help family members understand more about their own processes of thinking and decision making, and in particular the role emotion plays in their self-control—in other words, how well differentiated they are, particularly in stressful situations. Process questions that ask family members to explore their own behavior and motivations, often right in the therapy session, are used extensively to help them look at their roles in relationships and in relationship conflicts. Process questions can also be used to help clients understand the connection between their internal processes and their families of origin. Take the following example of Jennifer, an Anglo American, who is married to Han, a Vietnamese American.

> **Therapist:** Han, it seems clear that Jennifer feels angry and left out because you seem to contact your mother whenever you need advice.
>
> **Han:** Well, I think she is being unreasonable. I don't know why she is so jealous. It really gets to me.
>
> **Therapist:** Well, can you tell me what goes on inside your head when you feel the need for advice?

Han: Well, I don't know . . . I guess I just call Mom—I always have.

Therapist: Do you ever think about talking to Jennifer rather than your mom?

Han: Well, I do talk with her if it is a family thing.

Therapist: Yes, but why do you think you automatically call your mom for other advice? Have you always gone to her for advice—even as a kid?

You can see here that the therapist is trying to get Han to look at his internal processes regarding this situation, to learn more about what goes on when he chooses to talk with his mom rather than his wife. You are probably also wondering about cultural issues here. Since Han is an Asian man married to Jennifer, a Caucasian woman, cultural issues may be a part of this problem. Ask yourself this question: Does Bowen's theory allow for different cultural norms regarding family relationships?

THERAPEUTIC TECHNIQUES: INTERGENERATIONAL FAMILY SYSTEMS THERAPY

Genograms

Bowen is best known for the genogram technique. This is basically a way of diagramming several (typically three) generations of family relationships, indicating the nature of the relationships between members in nuclear families and in different generations. Different symbols are used to represent different kinds of relationships and characteristics. Figure 11.1, found on a Web site containing downloadable resources for family therapy, provides some of the standard symbols.

Don't be put off by the complexity of the symbols. Simpler forms of genograms, such as those in Figure 11.2, which denote interaction patterns between people, can be just as useful. The important thing is the information that the therapist can glean from pictorial representations of intergenerational relationships, which helps promote discussions about the people and relationships in the different generations.

For the previous example of Han and Jennifer, the symbols in Figure 11.2 might be used. Here we see that Han is fused with his mother and that at the moment he is distant from his wife (at least she feels this way). If we completed a genogram, we might find a number of other relationship factors explaining the situation. Han might be very distant from his father, perhaps partially explaining why he is fused with his mother. His mother might be fused with her mother, suggesting transgenerational transmission as a possible explanation for Han's fusion with his mother. Or we might find that Jennifer is cut off from both her parents and therefore is very anxious about also feeling cut off from her husband. As you can see, the genogram can be a very useful way of looking at transgenerational patterns.

Detriangulation

This involves helping the numbers of a family or couple avoid projecting their stress and emotionality onto a third party, particularly in times of crisis. Remember that triangulation occurs when people are not well differentiated and are driven primarily by their emotions. If

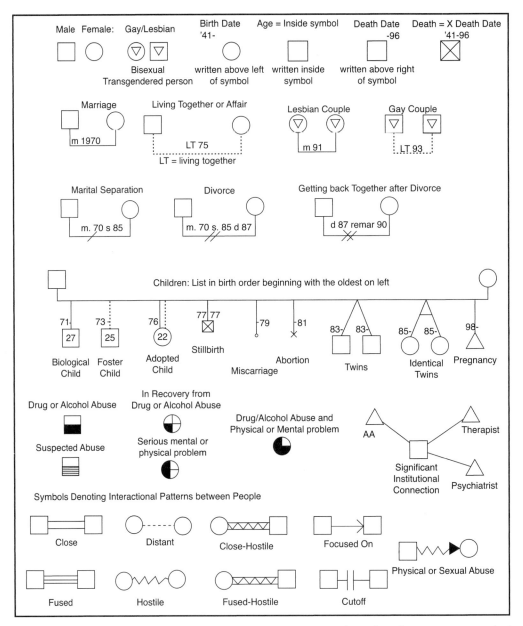

Figure 11.1 Genogram symbols. Retrieved May 16, 2005, from http://www.us.oup.com/us/companion.websites/019516606x/files/?view=usa
("Standard Symbols for Genograms" from *Psychologist's Desk Reference*, edited by G. Koocher, J. Norcross, and S. Hill, copyright © 1998 by Gerald P. Koocher, John C. Norcross, and Sam S. Hill. Used by permission of Oxford University Press, Inc.)

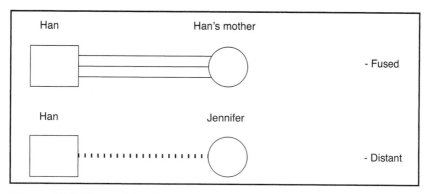

Figure 11.2 Han and Jennifer

a husband and wife learn to recognize emotional patterns that lead to triangulation by gaining more insight into how they learned these patterns through transgenerational transmission, they will be less likely to need to triangulate their son or daughter when things get tough in the family.

As an example, consider the case of Alexander and Marsha. They have two sons, and Alexander tends to form an alliance with his older son, 17-year-old Jochaim, whenever he and his wife are dealing with strong emotional issues. He inappropriately discusses his feelings with his son and puts pressure on his son to play golf every weekend when his son would rather be out with his friends. It so happens that Alexander was his mother's confidant as he grew up because he had a verbally abusive father. He was very conflicted about his relationship with his mother. On the one hand, he felt adult and strong because she relied on him; on the other hand, he felt scared and uncomfortable sharing this type of intimacy with his mother. When the therapist began to talk with him about his genogram and his relationship with his mother, Alexander began to see how he was repeating that pattern with his own son. He also began to gain a better understanding of how his emotions prevented him from better controlling his anxiety whenever his wife began to feel angry at him.

Going Home Again

This is a simple technique that can have powerful results. It involves sending a client back to visit his family of origin to better understand his relationship to the family and how this has affected his own development (i.e., how it has affected his differentiation).

Clients usually need preparation for this kind of visit. Since the client is in a kind of reflective state and perhaps open or willing to take in or admit things to himself that he has previously ignored, he needs to be able to handle the strong emotions involved. A certain amount of sensitivity and common sense is also required. There may be a great deal of "unfinished business" with his family, and the purpose of this visit is not really to work through all of the past conflicts and hurts. The Bowenian therapist usually proposes this as an observational visit to help the client better understand the family dynamics and what he has brought from these dynamics to his present life and family. He does not send the client into the family with the idea of conducting an intervention on the spot or having the client confront family members.

HUMANISTIC EXPERIENTIAL FAMILY THERAPY

Virginia Satir

Virginia Satir was one of the few female family systems pioneers. She was an enormously popular therapist and workshop presenter, and her warm, humanistic approach to therapy and to her students and colleagues was a powerful influence in the family therapy field. She was born in 1916 and grew up on a farm in Wisconsin. She was exceptionally bright, although she was a sickly child and missed many school days. Her exceptionality and the fact that she was a tall, awkward child probably led to her great sensitivity to others (Gladding, 2002). She was a teacher and social worker until 1951, when she began a private practice in Chicago. During that period, she was influenced by Don Jackson and Bowen (Gladding, 2002), and she was one of the founding members of the Mental Research Institute (MRI) group in Palo Alto in 1959. She was more interested in the practice of family systems therapy than in cybernetic research, and during that period, she developed her own approach that was more experiential and humanistic.

In 1964, Satir became the first director of the Esalen Institute, which was the center of humanistic psychology at the time, and also published her groundbreaking book, *Cojoint Family Therapy* (1964, 1967). She continued to work and present workshops around the world until her death in 1988. In her early work, she was influenced by the communications model of the MRI group, and at Esalen, she became interested in more sensory and body-mind approaches. She discussed her work as a "Human Validation Model" in her later writings. We note that Carl Whitaker, although he is not covered here, is often considered together with Satir in what is sometimes called an experiential model of family therapy.

ASSUMPTIONS AND CORE CONCEPTS: HUMANISTIC EXPERIENTIAL FAMILY THERAPY

View of Human Nature

Satir was a humanist in the truest sense of the word. She believed that every human being has innate worth and that all individuals and families have the potential to grow and flourish. She had much in common with Carl Rogers in her basic view of humankind. She also saw honest communication as an essential part of human functioning, and she valued the affective part of human beings. Perhaps the best window into her basic view of human nature is found in some of her quotations.

Quotations from Virginia Satir

Every human being is a miracle . . . The job is to make those miracles function as such. The purpose of life is to help each miracle find its own uniqueness.

Adults are just children grown up—just with bigger bodies.

The only real certainty in life is change.

Healing occurs when you can express what you knew all of the time but didn't have the words for or couldn't express.

Growth and creativity come from what "fits," not "should be."

Misery is optional.

Look at the past; don't stare at it.

Our goal is not to understand pain, but to understand what to do with it.

Feelings give us our juice.

Touching is a universal language.

All children are first-born. There is the first second child, the first third child, and so on.

Parents are teachers of human beings, not owners of human beings.

(Used with permission of AVANTA the Virginia Satir Network, 2104 SW 152nd Street, #2, Burien, WA 98166 www.avanta.net. All rights reserved.)

Core Concepts

Individual Growth and Development A cornerstone of Satir's theory is her conceptualization of individual growth and development. She saw a person's growth as a result of three factors: (1) genetic endowment, (2) learning acquired over a lifetime, and (3) the body-mind connection (Goldenberg & Goldenberg, 2005). Like Rogers, she viewed the growth of self as strongly influenced by one's early family experience. What she called the *primary triad*—mother, father, and child—was extremely important in the development of a positive or negative self-concept. She also identified a body, mind, feeling triad, and she believed that people often have negative feelings about how they look and about particular parts of their body (e.g., my nose is too big, my hips are too wide). She identified eight essential interacting parts crucial to the core of each person: physical, intellectual, emotional, sensual, interactional, contextual, nutritional, and spiritual (Goldenberg & Goldenberg, 2005). Much of her work with families involved helping each member develop individually in a holistic way.

Family Balance, Roles, Communication Styles Satir viewed any symptom or problem as blocked growth for that person and for the family at large. She was interested in what price a family had to pay in order to maintain this kind of negative balance. Satir was also interested in family structure and in family "rules." Rules can be overt or covert, and part of the therapy process is to clarify these rules and how they affect individuals and the family. Since family communication was so important, Satir (1983; Satir & Baldwin, 1984; Griffin & Shannon, 1999) identified five different communication styles: placator, blamer, super reasonable, irrelevant, and congruent.

Seed Model In this model, there are two ways of viewing the world and how humans live in it. First is the threat-and-reward model. In this model, behavior is controlled by individuals who are at the top of a heirarchy. These individuals work to maintain their status with a set of rules that determine if a person is rewarded or punished. Failure or inability to follow the rules can lead to failure and low self-esteem. Creativity and innovation are not valued in this model. In the seed model, each human being has a "seed" when she is born that has the innate potential to grow and develop into a healthy human being, with the proper love and nurturance. In this model, the seed is growing continuously throughout life.

THERAPEUTIC RELATIONSHIP: HUMANISTIC EXPERIENTIAL FAMILY THERAPY

The therapist is both a facilitator and a real person in humanistic experiential family therapy. He is also a powerful figure—but in a different way than in the previously discussed systems approaches. In this approach, his power comes from an emotional connection with the individuals and family rather than from a more direct application of structured principles of therapy. The therapist is often active and definitely gives direction to the family, but the focus is on attempts to provide emotional experiences that will enhance communication and family relationships. In other words, the therapist is a "change agent." As Satir (1983) put it, "I think the difference between whether a family grows, a family that comes asking for help, first, foremost, and primarily, has to do with the therapist and his input" (p. 37). This is not to say that the idea of the family as a system is not important but rather that the system intervention often comes through powerful therapist-client interactions or through exercises or activities that create clearer emotional communication.

ASSESSMENT, GOALS, AND PROCESS OF THERAPY: HUMANISTIC EXPERIENTIAL FAMILY THERAPY

As with the other systems approaches we have discussed, there is no formal diagnosis used in Satir's model. In fact, formal diagnosis is seen as a possible impediment to treatment because labeling individuals can interfere with their growth. The main kinds of assessment are observation of the family communication dynamics and discussion with individuals about their perceptions of family communication patterns and roles. Dialogue with the family also reveals the level of self-esteem and need for personal growth in each family member.

Satir (1972) summarized the goals of her therapy this way:

> We attempt to make three changes in the family system. First, each member of the family should be able to report congruently, completely, and honestly on what he sees and hears, feels and thinks, about himself and others. Second, each person should be addressed and related to in terms of his uniqueness, so that decisions are made in terms of exploration and negotiation rather than in terms of power. Third, differentness must be openly acknowledged and used for growth. (p. 120)

When this occurs and all members can be more themselves and can be honest in their communication with each of the other members, the family system then fosters growth, acceptance, and effective communication.

Satir and Baldwin (1984) identified three process stages: contact, chaos, and integration (Musdock, 2004). In the contact stage, the therapist establishes trust with each member of the family, observes their communication patterns, and provides them with feedback about his observations. During the chaos stage, one family member risks being honest and expresses feelings like fear, anger, or hurt. This typically has strong effects on other members of the family and can make the family feel anxious and uncertain of the outcome of therapy. Out of this chaos comes the integration stage, where the family members learn more effective ways to communicate and accept themselves and each other.

THERAPEUTIC TECHNIQUES: HUMANISTIC EXPERIENTIAL FAMILY THERAPY

Use of "I" Statements

"I" statements force family members to acknowledge and own their own feelings. When a person makes a statement about a situation or feeling in the second or third person, the therapist intervenes and asks him to restate what he has said with an "I" statement. In the following counseling dialogue, you can see "I" statements used in family counseling with partners Mark and Blaine and their teenage son Corky.

> **Mark:** It's always the same . . . yelling and conflict all the time.
> **Blaine:** It is true there is a lot of anger in this family.
> **Therapist:** Blaine, I wonder if you could restate what you just said starting with an "I" statement.
> **Blaine:** OK. . . . I am angry at Corky for skipping school and not taking his studies seriously.
> **Therapist:** Blaine, I really appreciate your being honest about your feelings. I wonder if there are any other feelings tied up with your anger. Can you try saying "I also feel . . ."?
> **Blaine:** Well, I also feel scared that Corky is going to come between Mark and me. We worked so hard to make a family . . . it hasn't been easy, you know. People still aren't very accepting of gay men having children.

You can see how powerful this technique is in encouraging honest expressions of feeling. By getting Blaine to identify his feelings and put them out there, the therapist encourages some new, and perhaps scary, dialogue with this family. From this scenario, we can also see that the therapist has the opportunity to encourage a discussion of oppression related to the couple's being gay and how this plays a part in the dynamics for this family.

Family Sculpting

Family sculpting involves placing family members in specific positions, typically to represent some aspect of how they communicate with or are involved with the other family members. The therapist may set the scene up, or he may ask one family member to arrange the family in poses and positions as she sees the family. This technique is a way of using the body-mind connection to help families see aspects of their behavior and communication that are hidden or not talked about. Gladding (2002) listed four stages of sculpting: setting the scene, choosing the role players, creating the sculpture, and processing the sculpture. One example might be a family with two children. One child behaves well and is very close to her mother; she works hard to please her parents, particularly her mother. The other child is a teenager in a rebellious stage who feels that he should be given more freedom. The father works late most evenings and weekends.

A therapist might sculpt the family this way. The mother and daughter are close together, with the daughter down on her knees holding her hands out to the mother as if she is seeking approval. The son is some ways away, with his hands in the air in an exasperated pose. The father is nearer the son but with his back turned to everyone. During the processing of this scene, we might expect the father to see how much his son and the rest of the family need him and how he is not involved with any of them. The mother might realize that she is too involved with her daughter and not with the rest of the family. The son might realize how separated he is from his father. The basic idea here is that physical representation will help people make emotional connections and have insights into their ways of relating and behaving. One variation is a family stress ballet where movement is involved in the experience.

Family Reconstruction

According to Gladding (2002), a family reconstruction has three parts: family map, family chronology, and wheel or circle of influence. The family map is similar to a genogram. The family chronology is a listing of all the important events in a person's life, including important family events (births, deaths, etc.). The wheel is perhaps the part of the reconstruction that best illustrates Satir's approach. In it, a "star," the person being focused on, puts himself in the center of the wheel and draws lines out to all of the significant people in his life. The darker the line, the more significant the relationship. "When completed, the wheel of influence displays the star's internalized strengths and weaknesses, the resources on which he or she may rely for new and, it is hoped, more effective ways of coping" (Satir, Bitter, & Krestensen, 1988, p. 205; Gladding, 2002, p. 155).

Therapist Touch and Humor

In Satir's kind of humanistic therapy, the therapist is directly and emotionally involved with the clients. Touch, empathy, and sincere involvement are hallmarks of the Satir approach. Virginia Satir might be called the mother of "touchy-feely" approaches to family counseling. Although this phrase has pejorative connotations in many quarters, we attribute it to her with great respect and admiration.

Satir and humanistic therapists really do "touch" their clients on many levels. Satir used physical touch in a variety of ways. In one case example, given by Nichols and Schwartz (2004), she was working with a family where the pregnant wife was afraid that her boys from a previous marriage, who had been exposed to physical abuse by their father, would be violent with her new baby. The boys had already acted out in this way, fighting and being violent with other children. Satir encouraged the parents to touch and hold the children as often as possible, even though the parents had been responding roughly with the children because of their anger and frustration.

Satir used touch extensively in their sessions, working to model and teach the parents how to provide touch that would nurture and also touch and holding that would help demonstrate boundaries. She noted that part of her motive was to counter the image of these children as little monsters and to show the parents that the children would respond well to touch in a loving way.

The use of humor is certainly not unique to this approach but can be viewed as another way of humanizing the therapist and the situation and helping the therapist. In addition to breaking the ice and putting a family or couple at ease, humor can allow clients to gain a little distance from their situation and thus some perspective on it.

MULTICULTURAL AND DIVERSITY EFFECTIVENESS: FAMILY SYSTEMS APPROACHES

The systems approaches in general have been criticized on many fronts for their failure to account for gender, racial, and cultural differences. Rachel Hare-Mustin (1978) was the first feminist family therapist to criticize the cybernetic communication model of family therapy. She pointed out that the focus of these approaches on communication problems within family systems doesn't take into account external social context factors, like gender oppression and discrimination. Feminists also objected to the prototypic problem family with a disengaged father and an over-involved mother, which failed to take into account the fact that women had few other options than being housewife and mother (Nichols & Schwartz, 2004). Also, as more information about family violence surfaced, the idea of "blaming" the family system, rather than inherent gender power dynamics, became hard to justify.

As with most other theories, it wasn't until the late twentieth century that practitioners became more aware of the role of culture. Since the systems approaches focus so much on the family and family interactions and for the most part put considerable power in the therapists' hands, the danger of imposing values on client families is great. Recent research and writing have focused on cultural differences in how families are defined and how they operate. Multicultural writers, for example, have noted important differences in how African-American, Native American, Asian-American, and Hispanic families typically function (Hong & Domokos-Cheng Ham, 2001; Roysircar, Singh, & Bibbins, 2003).

Nichols and Schwartz (2004) noted that Bowen did attend to the external factors affecting families and also that Minuchin was a pioneer in working with low-income minority families. Satir's humanistic approach is perhaps harder to criticize on gender or multicultural grounds because of the underlying humanistic principles that posit an intrinsic value in every human being. We don't think Satir was immune to gender roles and stereotypes, but there is a strand running through her quotes and writings recognizing that individuals must fight against being controlled by the power inherent in hierarchies.

There is a developing literature on therapy with gay and lesbian families (Laird & Green, 1996); however, we found very little written about using systems approaches in particular with gay, lesbian, and transgendered families. We know of family and couples therapists in the 1970s and 1980s who worked with gay and lesbian couples, some with children. And they were able to apply, to some extent, systems approaches to those families; however, those therapists tended to adapt the theories, understanding the powerful oppression involved in having a different sexual orientation and living as a couple or family.

PRIMARY APPLICATIONS: FAMILY SYSTEMS APPROACHES

Family systems therapy has been employed as a primary or adjunct approach with nearly every possible problem and population. Keep in mind, as we have in the entire chapter, that a family may be just a couple. Very few contemporary therapists are not willing to involve a partner or family members in some aspect of therapy—a recognition on their part that the "family system," at least as broadly defined, is important. A therapist might bring in the client's son, daughter, mother, father, sister, brother, or best friend, or anyone else involved with the client, to help treat depression, anxiety, phobias, suicide, cutting, and the like. The role that these people might play depends on the therapist and his theoretical approach. For example, a cognitive-behavioral therapist might enlist a brother to help with in vivo desensitization of his sister, or a wife might attend some sessions to help a husband deal with a severe depression. Although the "family system" per se is not being treated, family systems issues must typically be dealt with in order to carry out the therapy.

Although family systems therapy techniques might be employed to some degree in many different kinds of situations, in this section we will discuss some applications where family systems therapy has been demonstrated to be very effective. These include couples-marital, juvenile detention, domestic violence, and eating disorders. There are many other important and interesting applications, and this is but a representative sample.

Couples/Marital Counseling

Goldman and Greenberg (1992), in a study comparing integrated systemic and emotionally focused approaches, reviewed eight steps of their model for emotionally focused couples therapy (Greenberg & Johnson, 1988). These steps include defining the problem; identifying the negative interaction cycle; helping the clients realize and accept their feelings about the cycle that were previously unknown; redefining the problem, taking into account the new feelings and reactions; accepting these feelings; accepting the partner's emotions; facilitating the clients' expressing their needs and wants now that they have uncovered new emotions; helping them find new solutions; and helping them reach new levels of intimacy and ways of relating. Goldman and Greenberg called this an integrated-systemic approach, with therapy aimed at interpersonal and intrapersonal growth.

The systemic model Goldman and Greenberg (1992) used in the study had seven steps: "(1) Define the issue presented. (2) Identify the negative interactional cycle. (3) Attempt restructuring. (4) Reframe the problem using positive connotation followed by prescribing of the symptom. (5) Restrain, using 'go slow' and dangers of improvement. (6) Consolidate the frame. (7) Prescribe a relapse" (p. 964).

The models described in this study are an excellent example of the contemporary work being done in this area. Couples experiencing both approaches improved, although gains were better maintained with the systemic model. In another study, a very brief three-session approach using an MRI model with reframing (helping couples perceive different meanings of behavior) and restraining (a paradoxical intervention telling couples not to change quickly) was effective in improving marital adjustment, conflict resolution skills, and the couples' main presenting problems (Davidson & Horvath, 1997).

Juvenile Offenders and Substance Abuse

The field of adolescent substance abuse counseling has recently emerged from the shadows of adult treatment (Liddle, 2004), and there is empirical evidence that family-based counseling can improve adaptive behavior and decrease drug use in adolescents. Deas and Thomas (2001) noted that a fundamental assumption of family-based approaches to adolescent substance abuse is that the family system contributed to the development of the problem in the first place and can also play a vital role in its remediation. Kumpfer, Alvarado, and Whiteside (2003) noted that involving the family in treatment has been shown in research to be more effective than individual treatment with just the youth who is abusing substances.

A number of reviews of the literature on family-based substance abuse treatment for adolescents indicate that there is substantial support not only for the fact that this treatment is effective, but also for the fact that it is actually superior to other forms of counseling (Deas & Thomas, 2001; Williams & Chang, 2000). Liddle and Dakof (1995) reported a similar finding and even went on to note that family therapy for adolescent drug abuse is more developed than family therapy for adult drug abuse. However, they did caution that because of the relatively small number of studies in the area and their methodological weaknesses, no definitive statement can be made about the effectiveness of family therapy for adolescent substance abuse.

In the last decade, there have been significant attempts to create family treatment programs for adolescents who have problems with the law regarding substance abuse in order to prevent them from entering the criminal justice system at a later time. Henggeler, Melton, and Smith (1992) reported on a study using multisystemic therapy (MST) with juvenile offenders. MST has its roots in strategic and structural family systems therapies, but it also takes into account the multitude of systems within which a juvenile and her family live. MST includes problem-focused interventions within the family and with peers, teachers, schools, and any other relevant systems. In other words, the therapist's purview is expanded to several different systems, and he may choose to work with the offender in any of these systems, the assumption being that dysfunctional behavior can be caused and maintained in many different arenas.

Domestic Violence

The use of family therapy when violence among family members has occurred has a history of controversy. The legal system is often involved, and the safety of all family members is, of course, paramount. Offering treatment interventions where the family is the focus of treatment, rather than just the perpetrator, can lead at least to the perception that the victim is being blamed for her circumstances. However, Rivett (2001) noted that the occurrence of violence can be understood at the individual, family, and societal levels and that there is increasing interest in finding which therapeutic interventions hold the most promise for intervention.

Gelles and Maynard (1987) described how Minuchin's structural family systems approach could be used with families in which violence has occurred. Three major techniques they described are (1) creating a transaction, (2) joining, and (3) restructuring the transaction. By creating a transaction, the therapist is attempting to diagnose systemic patterns that lead to violence in the family; he could begin by asking members to describe their daily activities and perceptions of events that have occurred. Events that lead to conflict among family members can provide the therapist with insight into patterns that lead to violence. The second technique requires the therapist to "join" with the family as an intermediate step toward promoting structural change. Gelles and Maynard provided an example of joining with a family in which the father's loss of a job contributed to the occurrence of violence; they described how the therapist engaged the family in a discussion of work, values, and how money conveys acceptance of and respect for family members. The third major technique described by Gelles and Maynard is restructuring the family to reduce systems conflict and to deal with structural inefficiencies. As an example, they noted how displays of tension and aggression could be reframed as desperate attempts by family members to reach out to each other.

Gladding (2002) described three approaches to treating domestic violence: (1) couples therapy, (2) intimate justice, and (3) education. He suggested that if one believes that both parties are equally responsible for the violence, then a more traditional couples counseling approach can be taken. If one believes that one party is responsible, then the intimate justice theory is used, with a focus on power relationships and an understanding of the social and ethical contexts related to this kind of abuse. He noted that in this approach the focus is on changing beliefs about power and looking for solutions to change the violence. The third approach, education, assumes that domestic violence is a result of learning and that it is possible to "teach" people new ways to behave and think.

We note that this is a controversial area and that if a therapist agrees to treat a couple, or family, while any domestic violence is occurring, there is always the danger of harm to the victim. Certainly, it is preferable to prevent domestic violence before it begins. The issue is even more complicated with child physical or sexual abuse. Since a therapist must report any evidence of these kinds of abuses, treatment of families would occur only as part of a court-ordered treatment program—sometimes as a condition of placing a child back in the home where abuse occurred. The bottom line is that therapists are required to ensure the safety of family members who are the victims of violence, as well as to involve legal authorities according to legal and ethical guidelines, in addition to treating the family system.

Eating Disorders

Minuchin (1974) described using family therapy for anorexia several decades ago, and there is some evidence that family-based therapy is effective for anorexia and bulimia (Lemmon & Josephson, 2001; Nichols & Schwartz, 2004). A model using many of Minuchin's techniques has been under study in a London hospital and has shown effectiveness at a 5-year follow-up (Nichols & Schwartz, 2004). The model includes the use of a family meal and a later restructuring of the family, changing parental coalitions. It also includes some work with intergenerational influences (Russel, Dare, Eisler, & LeGrange, 1994).

Eisler (2005) noted that since Minuchin and his colleagues published the first family therapy follow-up study for anorexia nervosa, several other studies have largely supported its effectiveness. However, Eisler noted three main caveats: (1) The studies that have been published are relatively small and have methodological limitations, (2) there has hardly been any research comparing family therapy to other forms of treatment, and (3) most have a strong "structural" emphasis (i.e., they emphasize helping the parents take a strong instrumental role in opposing the anorexia).

Lock and LeGrange (2005) noted that both structural and strategic family therapies have been utilized when an adolescent in the family has anorexia nervosa. They noted that in structural family therapy, anorexia is viewed as a way of helping the family maintain pathologic processes such as avoidance of conflict and rigidity. Interventions such as family meals, where the therapist and family join in a meal together, which serves as a foundation for therapeutic inter-ventions, are used to enhance parental authority, block inappropriate alignments between chil-dren and parents, and encourage the development of sibling subsystem development. In contrast, Lock and LeGrange (2005) noted that strategic family therapy for anorexia is focused specifically toward the impact of its symptoms on the patient and family. They also noted that while family therapy is commonly used for anorexia, surprisingly little research evaluating its effectiveness has appeared. Finally, Lock and LeGrange noted that far fewer examples of using family therapy with bulimia have been reported, and while Michael and Willard (2003) suggested that the evidence so far is supportive, systematic empirical research on its effectiveness for this use is scarce.

With respect to how family therapy is used to treat eating disorders, Michael and Willard (2003) noted that two important components of family therapy with anorexia are assessing family dynamics and using a multidisciplinary approach in treatment. With respect to assessment, they note that the goal is to determine if the family environment played a role in the development and maintenance of the eating disorder and if so, the extent to which problems in the family that contributed to the disorder still remain. Eisler (2005) cautioned, however, that while a number of different assessments can be used to understand the family's dynamics, no consistent pattern or structure of families has been identified as causing anorexia nervosa. The multi-disciplinary approach refers to the idea that no single health care professional can provide comprehensive care for those suffering from eating disorders (Michael & Willard, 2003). Family therapy, marital counseling for the parents, and nutritional counseling, to name but a few, may all be important in treating both the individual suffering from the disorder and the family as a whole.

Eisler (2005) provided a four-stage approach to treating families in which a member has anorexia nervosa. In the first stage, the family engages in a therapeutic contract, in which the therapist makes contact with each family member and identifies the focus for the work ahead. The second stage involves helping the family challenge the symptoms of anorexia, which can be done through a family meal, as described earlier in this section. The third stage, exploring issues of individual and family development, is the least structured and predictable part of the therapy and involves exploring the consequences of symptom improvement for the whole family. For example, self-esteem, identity, and independence issues may be explored—the un-derlying idea is that once the grip of anorexia has been loosened, the family can look forward to the future and deal with normal developmental issues that have been put on hold due to the anorexia (Eisler, 2005). The final stage, ending treatment and discussing future plans, involves reflection on the gains made by the family and discussion of how the family will handle reoccurrence of the symptoms.

Asen (2002) discussed a "multiple family therapy" approach to working with families who have children with eating disorders. She described two similar programs in which up to eight fam-ilies meet as a group in an inpatient facility. In one of the models, they meet for an evening to hear from families who have already completed the program, they then meet for 8 hours a day for a week, and finally they have one or two all-day follow-ups. The rationale is that families with sim-ilar problems can help each other by recognizing patterns, gaining support, and getting specific ideas on how to change family patterns and behavior. The approach is very eclectic, with a num-ber of games, exercises, sculpts, and role-plays used. From a systems perspective, one of the most important aspects is that the families get to observe each family system and reflect on how their own family operates and, in turn, how they might want to change structural and communication patterns to help the child with eating disorder problems.

BRIEF THERAPY/MANAGED CARE EFFECTIVENESS: FAMILY SYSTEMS APPROACHES

The various family systems approaches reviewed in this chapter tend to be brief, active interventions. Kaslow (2000) noted that with the advent of managed care, the goal is rapid restoration of function, and thus shorter-term approaches to working with families are even more preferable these days compared to longer-term models such as psychodynamic family therapy. For example, in a study of the practice patterns of Nebraska marriage and family therapists, Christensen and Miller (2001) found that over half used solution-focused therapy (*A Brief Model*) as their guiding approach in conducting family therapy.

As we have suggested in this chapter, part of the appeal of many of the shorter-term approaches to family work has been the fact that they provide some practical and focused interventions to families experiencing difficulties. Family systems therapists are not afraid to intervene and to "mix things up" in order to facilitate change. You would think that this approach would fit well with the current managed care environment, with its emphasis on efficiency and limits.

This is not the case, however, because insurance companies have never really accepted the idea that the "unit" of treatment can be a couple or a family (Coffey, Olson, & Sessions, 2001). Very few insurance companies cover any kind of family or couples intervention. Family systems therapists are forced to follow a kind of single-person pathology approach and give one family member an appropriate diagnosis. For example, a couple comes in for counseling after 15 years of marriage because the wife has just had an affair. The husband has been very depressed, sleeping a lot and losing interest in activities from which he had previously gotten great satisfaction. The wife has been feeling very guilty and having a number of anxiety symptoms. A family systems therapist will most likely see this as a "systems" problem having to do with their relationship. In order to receive insurance reimbursement, however, the family systems therapist will need to use a more individualistic perspective and diagnose either the husband or the wife with depression or some kind of anxiety or depressive disorder. The potential problem in this situation is that one member of the couple gets labeled as "the problem," which has the potential to interfere with the relationship as the focus of treatment.

Coffey et al. (2001) noted that as a result of the trend toward shorter, more cost-effective interventions, family therapy has become less visible in community mental health centers and health maintenance organizations (HMOs). However, on college campuses and in institutions affiliated with universities that have to worry less about third-party reimbursement, family therapy still retains a strong presence. In our view, this is an unfortunate situation, since brief, systemic interventions may well serve a kind of preventive function and should be encouraged in the many settings in which counselors and psychologists work. Perhaps the couple discussed above would have sought out marriage counseling earlier if counseling had been covered by the couple's insurance. This is not to deny the fact that a husband, a wife, or any family member might have a legitimate individual diagnosis. The point is just that the system is not set up for "systemic" approaches.

Despite the problems we have noted with using family therapy in managed care settings, the news is not all bad. There is hope that the emphasis on creatively solving problems in a time-limited manner in families can ultimately find a home in managed care settings. For example, Sullivan and Goldschmidt (2000) described the use of a 15-hour program to teach couples communication and problem-solving skills at Kaiser Permanente in Los Angeles. According to Sullivan and Goldschmidt, the program was designed to intervene with couples in the HMO system before they experienced severe relationship difficulties. They reported data suggesting the program was well received by participants, although data were not collected to determine if the program actually reduced future problems for the couples who participated. In summarizing their intervention, Sullivan and Goldschmidt stated that prevention and innovative treatments are uniquely supported in a managed care environment, particularly those that obviate the need for long-term individual psychotherapy.

INTEGRATING THE THEORY WITH OTHER APPROACHES

The integration of the systemic approaches into a broader field of family therapy has been a natural part of the evolution of the field. The systems approaches were originally developed partly as a reaction to psychoanalysis, and all four approaches that we have described here embrace the notion that a family system must be considered and in most cases is the unit of treatment. What was once a radical notion has evolved, however, into an understanding that there are multiple approaches to working with families and couples. The strong allegiance to specific systems approaches has given way to a broader perspective that respects multiple approaches. This is in no small way a result of the postmodern movement and the emerging idea that there is no absolute truth or method for working with families.

It is possible to integrate the different systems approaches in a number of ways. This is, perhaps, a natural result of the fact that so many of the founders of different schools worked with and influenced each other. For example, Satir included a form of genograms in her therapy, and Haley and Minuchin both used very active intervention techniques to realign family communication and relationship patterns. An integration of these systems approaches with more modern approaches such as narrative or solution-focused therapy is more difficult. A major difficulty lies in the differences in the role of the therapist. Both the narrative and solution-focused approaches take the view that the therapist is not the "expert," which is certainly not the case in any of the systems approaches. However, these systems approaches have evolved, particularly in terms of the power of the therapist. Nichols and Schwartz (2004) talked about "selective borrowing" as one type of integration. They quoted Betty Carter, a feminist Bowenian therapist, to illustrate how this particular therapy evolved and was integrated into Carter's feminist approach: "I never felt I had to trash the whole theory and start over again. Though, of course, Bowen theory had the same blind spot that all the early theories had about power, so that all had to be added" (MacKune-Karrer, 1999, p. 24).

As with other theories, when you talk about integration, it is important to distinguish between an eclectic borrowing of different techniques from many different theories and a more intentional combining of basic theoretical principles and ideas. It is much easier to use different techniques developed in family systems approaches with other theories than it is to integrate them on a theoretical level. For example, an individual therapist using a variety of different theories might be able to use the genogram as a way to talk about family influences. Or a discussion of triangulation might be useful in many approaches when the counselor is talking about relationships that are problematic and involve three people. The use of "I" statements has been integrated into many approaches to group work and can also be very useful for clients who intellectualize or refuse to own or talk about their own feelings. Integration on a conceptual level is much more difficult and beyond the scope of this very brief outline of family systems theories. However, as you study the solution-focused and narrative therapies, you will at least be able to compare and contrast the systems approaches with the newer postmodern approaches to family therapy.

RESEARCH

Research in family therapy has exploded in the past two decades as more and more researchers have begun to focus on this increasingly popular therapy method. This research can be categorized as either outcome research (What was the result of the therapy?) or process research (How do different variables relate to other variables?). For example, an outcome study might compare two different types of family therapy with a third no-treatment control group on a number of outcome measures designed to assess family functioning in some way. Process research might explore how the strength of alliances relates to therapy dropout (as does the sample study in this section).

One indicator of the explosion of interest in both family therapy and family therapy research is the literally hundreds of instruments available to measure family functioning processes. Carlson (2003) summarized some of the key domains in the family context for which assessment instruments have been developed. She noted a number of measures that have been developed in recent years to assess family relationships, including sibling, multigenerational family, and family-of-origin relationships. Another domain for which assessments have been developed is parent-child relationships, including parenting style (Carlson, 2003). Family adjustment, health, and well-being is another area that has received increasing assessment interest in the past several decades. Assessment of family problems, particularly parental stress, has also been a focus recently, as has assessing marital relations. Grovtevant and Carlson (1989) created a comprehensive guide to family assessment, one of many resources providing information about this growing area.

Because there are many schools of family therapy and because trying to measure something about a family rather than an individual complicates the research task, it is difficult to generalize as to whether or not family therapy is effective. Shadish and Baldwin (2002) reviewed the literature on family therapy and found that both marital and family therapies are more effective than receiving no treatment, with clinically significant results in 40%–50% of cases. While there is some evidence that marital therapy has better outcomes, this is probably because family therapists often deal with difficult family problems such as schizophrenia. The effects of marital and family therapy interventions tend to be similar, regardless of the specific theoretical orientation used, and are also comparable to those alternative interventions such as individual counseling or psychopharmacology.

Gladding (2002) summarized a number of comprehensive reviews and came up with the following results:

1. The improvement rate in family therapy is similar to the improvement rate in individual therapy.
2. The deterioration rate in family therapy is likewise similar to the deterioration rate in individual therapy.

SAMPLE RESEARCH: Alliance and dropout in family therapy for adolescents with behavior problems: Individual and Systemic Effects

Goals of the Research

The researchers in this study (Robbins, Turner, & Gonzalo 2003) wanted to evaluate the relationship of two kinds of alliances to retention in family therapy. They compared the alliance with the therapist and alliances between family members relative to how they related to the family staying in therapy.

Participants

There were 34 families in the study. The researchers used families who had already participated in a larger study. They categorized the families as either dropouts (completing fewer than eight sessions and designated as a dropout by the previous therapist) or completers (completing more than eight sessions and designated as a successful outcome by the previous therapist). Twenty completer families and 14 dropout families were selected for the study.

Method

Therapists in this study used functional family therapy (FFT) to treat behavior problems in adolescents who ranged in age from 12 to 18. FFT is a widely used method combining systemic family therapy and behavioral family therapy approaches. Trained graduate students viewed videotapes of 20-minute segments of the first session and used the Vanderbilt Therapeutic Alliance Scale–Revised to rate the alliances between family members and the therapist and also between the family members themselves. They were consistent in their ratings 92% of the time. The researchers then statistically analyzed how well the two different kinds of ratings predicted whether the family would drop out or continue.

Results

Individual levels of alliances did not predict whether the family would drop out, but a family-level analysis of discrepancy alliance scores (parent minus adolescent) did predict dropout families. In other words, in families where there were not healthy alliances between the parents and adolescent, there was a greater chance that the family would drop out of therapy early.

Implications of the Research

In order to keep the dropout families in therapy, the therapist has to overcome or modify the negative alliance between parents and child. According to the authors, "The results of this study suggest that therapists in the dropout cases may have inadvertently validated parental negativity about adolescents without adequately responding to the adolescent's needs or concerns" (p. 541). One major implication, then, is that therapists must be especially aware of how they affect negative alliances between parents and children.

3. Deterioration may occur because
   a. The therapist has poor interpersonal skills.
   b. The therapist moves too quickly into sensitive topic areas and does not handle the situation well.
   c. The therapist allows family conflict to become exacerbated without moderating or adapting the therapeutic intervention.
   d. The therapist does not provide adequate structure in the early stages of therapy.
   e. The therapist does not support family members (Fenell & Weinhohld, 1992, p. 333).
4. Family therapy is as effective as individual counseling for personal problems or family conflict.
5. Brief therapy of 20 sessions is as effective as long-term therapy.
6. The participation of fathers in family therapy is much more likely to bring about positive results than family therapy without them.
7. The relationship skills of family therapists are crucial in producing positive outcomes.
8. Less severe forms of mental/psychological distress are more likely to be successfully treated than those that are severe.
9. Psychosomatic problems can be treated successfully with a modified version of structural family therapy.
10. The type of family, its background, and its present interactional style relate to the success or failure of family therapy. (Samuel T. Gladding, *Family Therapy: History, Theory, and Practice*, 3e, ©2002, pp. 397–398. Reprinted by permission of Pearson Education, Inc., Upper Saddle River, NJ.)

Liddle and Rowe (2004) reviewed the effectiveness of family counseling in a number of different areas. They found encouraging results regarding family-based methods in the following areas: child behavior problems, parent management training, child and adolescent emotional problems, adolescent and adult substance abuse, and marital and couples problems. They also reviewed family therapy process research and suggested that this kind of research, addressing questions of why, how, what, and which, could be very valuable to the practitioner and has the potential to help narrow the gap between research and practice. As you can tell, there is a lot going on in family therapy research, and from just this brief discussion, you can probably understand why it is so difficult for practitioners who are not researchers to keep up with the latest research findings.

EVALUATION OF FAMILY SYSTEMS APPROACHES

Each of the different approaches that we have presented has made specific and unique contributions to the field of marriage and family counseling. Bowen's genogram approach is still widely used, and Satir's family sculpting and techniques to identify unwritten family rules are also still practiced. We note, a bit sadly, that touching and hugging, used so effectively by Satir, are seldom used today because of therapists' fears that they will be accused of touching inappropriately. The directives and paradox championed by Haley are still employed today, but many therapists are theoretically opposed to using techniques that are not transparent to their clients. Minuchin's idea of family enmeshment and family structure are certainly still a part of most family therapists' language.

Perhaps the greatest legacies of the systems approaches have been the emphasis on examining family communication and relationship patterns and the understanding that a system with its subsystems and feedback loops behaves in a complex and circular way. The notion that the family system must be addressed as a kind of entity in itself has been one of the great strengths of the different systems approaches. A related strength has been the understanding that it takes special training to be able to work with this "system." A corollary to this understanding has been the development of new professions and new professional organizations. It is interesting to note that all of the mental health specialties developed "family therapy" subdivisions as they came to realize the importance of seeing the family as a system. The training programs for each of the approaches discussed in this chapter have greatly enriched our understanding of the family and of how to work with the family in therapy. Some of the most perplexing contemporary problems like substance abuse, eating disorders, and domestic violence have been addressed from a family systems perspective.

The systems approaches also fit very well with the emphasis on brief treatment. In fact, the roots of many brief therapy approaches lie in earlier work with family systems approaches. The fact that systems approaches can offer brief, strategic interventions that can have a profound impact on the family and its members is clearly a strength in our contemporary mental health system. A related strength has to do with the absence of individual pathology. It is far less stigmatizing to diagnose the system as ineffective than to label a person as pathological. The reverse of this strength, however, is the notion that individual pathology (biological depression, for example) might be missed as a result of looking for systemic causes. Of course, the system is greatly influenced when one member of the family is severely depressed, and both an individual and a family treatment might be in order.

A major weakness of the family systems approaches, especially in the early phases, has been an underlying assumption that all problems are a result of family systems problems and need to be treated in a family context. As one might expect with the development of a new and truly revolutionary approach, early advocates tended to overreach themselves in their theory and practice. A more practical weakness of these approaches in contemporary practice is the difficulty in identifying what actually constitutes a family and in getting families to come in to therapy. We have already mentioned the feminist critique of structural family therapy, in which the idea of a family hierarchy placed the father at the head of the household. Intervening in the family system is more difficult if only one or two members of the family appear. Husbands and other family members often refuse to join their families for therapy sessions. Much of the work with juvenile offenders and substance abuses involves families with only one parent. In these cases, it is very difficult for the single parent to get off work or to find a babysitter for the other children. Many creative attempts have been made to mitigate these problems, such as after-school programs and free babysitting, but they remain tough obstacles to working with a family as a system.

Another very practical consideration that we have already mentioned deserves reemphasis. Under current health insurance rules, family or marriage counseling is seldom covered, and therefore a model of individual therapy is encouraged when a family approach might be more appropriate. The "borrowing" of cybernetic language and its serendipitous application to therapy with families has been one of the great developments in the evolution of psychotherapy.

Questions and Learning Activities

These questions and activities are designed to stimulate your thinking about this theory and to help you apply some of the ideas to your own life and experience. If possible, you should work with another person or with a small group. Getting others' points of view and sharing your own ideas and perspectives will be invaluable as a way to help you evaluate this theory and its applications.

Discussion Questions

1. Do you believe that the focus in family counseling should be on interaction/communication rather than on a specific family member?
2. Do you think that the identified patient (IP) always represents a family problem?
3. How would you feel if you were given a paradoxical assignment or an ordeal assignment?
4. The therapist who uses systems approaches is typically very active. How does that fit with your personality and your idea of how a counselor should operate?
5. Do you think that family systems therapists assume too much power?
6. What is your view on working with individuals or only the family members willing to come to counseling? What about working with a husband or wife or partner when the other one refuses to come?
7. When family systems approaches were developed, they focused on the nuclear family. Can they be adapted to today's broader definition of family? To gay or lesbian partners with children, for example?
8. Do you believe that family behavior patterns are passed down from generation to generation?
9. Would you seek out family counseling or marriage counseling if you were having problems? How is your attitude toward counseling affected by your parents' attitudes?
10. Would you be comfortable using a paradoxical intervention with a couple or family? Why or why not? Do you think that paradoxical interventions are ethical?
11. How differentiated are the different members of your family?
12. Do you see differentiation as working very differently in different cultures?

Learning Activities

Family Rules
What were the overt and covert (written and unwritten, so to speak) rules in your family? How did these affect family life and communication?

Scapegoat
Do you know of any family in which one child is a continual problem? Do you think that this child was or is a kind of scapegoat for a family problem?

Boundaries and Enmeshment

Have you observed any family whose boundaries seem to be either too rigid (lack of engagement) or too permeable (enmeshment) between parents and children? What was the effect on the family and on the individuals?

Multigenerational Transmission

Are there any particular communication or behavior patterns in your family or in individuals in your family that have been passed down from previous generations (e.g., anger is not openly expressed, children do not challenge parents, men don't touch)?

Genogram

Create a genogram for your own family for three generations (yours, your parents, and your grandparents). Use the symbols in Figure 11.1, but don't get too complicated. After you are finished and have discussed your genogram with a partner or in a small group, make a list of what you have learned about your family. Did you identify any multigenerational transmissions?

Family Sculpting

If you were going to "sculpt" your family, what would it look like? Make a drawing of the positions, and describe in writing what each member's pose would be and why?

Differentiation

Examine your own personal development in terms of differentiation. Look at several life points—say, 10, 15, 20, and 25 (you can adjust these points depending on your age). Are you now differentiated from your family? Enmeshed? Cut off?

Family Structure

What was the structure of your family as you were growing up? Was your mother or your father in charge? Were there sibling alliances? Did one sibling have more power than others? Were any siblings aligned with a parent? Include yourself in these considerations.

Companion Website

Now go to the Companion Website at www.prenhall.com/archer to assess your understanding of chapter content with multiple-choice and essay questions, and broaden your knowledge with related Web resources and additional print resources.

CHAPTER 12

Solution-Focused Therapy

VOICES FROM THE FIELD: COUNSELOR AND CLIENT REACTIONS

Yes, it works for me

Client: I really didn't expect that—we started looking for ways to solve my problem right away. I thought that counseling took a lot longer and that you had to figure out what caused a problem. My counselor really helped me see some things about myself—I guess I've got more going for me than I thought. And in just a few sessions, I felt like I made real progress.

Counselor: When I go to the medical doctor, I want to get better as soon as possible, and I know my clients want the same thing from me in counseling. Solution-focused counseling fits for me because I'm good at helping people see possibilities and their strength. I guess I'm a real optimist—I think each person has the solutions to his problems inside himself. So far, it's worked for me and I really feel good about getting right to helping people do something about what's bothering them.

No, it doesn't work for me

Client: To be honest, solution-focused counseling seems kind of superficial. I mean, I realize that I have made it this far in life and must have something going for me, but in counseling, I need someone who understands how tough things have been for me. I guess I need to talk about my feelings a lot more. My solution-focused counselor seemed more interested in "fixing" me than listening to me.

Counselor: With the managed care movement taking over the counseling field, I can see why some counselors are attracted to this approach. But solution-focused counseling really does not offer much of a framework for understanding human beings or how their concerns arise—it seems more like a set of techniques that can at the time be useful in helping people work toward their goals. But something seems to be missing. I guess it just isn't satisfying for me as a counselor—I want to be able to really get into what is going on for my clients and understand the dynamics of their problems.

Since I am devoting my career to being a counselor, I want an approach that will help me understand people, not just work on goals.

María is a 35-year-old Mexican-American teacher who wants to qualify to teach bilingual elementary education. In order to do this, she must pass an oral proficiency exam in Spanish. This is causing her considerable anxiety because while she was born in Mexico, she has spent most of her life in the United States speaking English. While she is still fluent in Spanish, she is worried that she will get tripped up in the exam due to a lack of everyday practice in the language. Her anxiety has started to interfere with her ability to prepare for the exam, and she has decided to see a solution-focused therapist.

> **María:** For some reason, I just get paralyzed by the thought of having to use my Spanish in conversation. I have to take a Spanish proficiency exam in a few weeks, and if I don't pass, I can't be a bilingual educator!
>
> **Counselor:** Are there any times when you feel less anxiety?
>
> **María:** Well, when I'm studying and making some progress—at least then I think I might pass.
>
> **Counselor:** Is there any way you can do more of that?
>
> **María:** I guess I can focus more on studying, maybe also practice more speaking.
>
> **Counselor:** I'm really impressed with your study methods and ideas. It sounds like you have a lot of determination to do well on this exam.

Steve de Shazer and Insoo Kim Berg developed solution-focused therapy (SFT) from their work with families in Milwaukee, Wisconsin. Like other brief models of counseling, SFT involves helping clients make significant progress in just a few sessions. However, the brevity of this approach stems from theoretical principles about the change process rather than simply an attempt to shorten the length of counseling. For example, SFT theorists maintain that once changes are set in motion, they tend to snowball and generalize to other parts of life.

SFT is focused on helping clients utilize their strengths and be proactive in handling life demands. SFT counselors tend to be very active in sessions and utilize techniques such as looking for exceptions and capitalizing on a person's strength. The language used is important because the counselor doesn't want clients to focus on problems and always works toward finding exceptions that can help the person overcome the problem.

HISTORICAL BACKGROUND

Historical Context

SFT counselors view humans as meaning-making creatures and incorporate ideas from the social constructionist movement, a school of philosophy that maintains people attach meaning to their own experiences through their interactions with others (O'Connell, 1998). This has important implications for the practice of SFT because it suggests that we have many creative ways of understanding our lives and generating solutions to problems. SFT is a relatively new model of counseling. It was developed by Steve de Shazer and Insoo Kim Berg, who in 1978, along with several other colleagues, established the Brief Family Therapy Center in Milwaukee, Wisconsin. SFT emphasizes identifying and working toward solutions for clients rather than focusing on problems and the clients' past. The success of this approach is measured by the progress clients make toward reaching their goals rather than the amount of time clients spend in counseling (de Shazer, 1985; 1988).

Both SFT and narrative therapy, which will be described in the next chapter, developed from postmodern philosophy. Specifically, SFT is based on a postmodern philosophy called social constructivism (sometimes called just constructivism), which views truth in life not as "out there," waiting to be discovered, but as socially constructed through daily interactions and dialogue with

other people (Freedman & Combs, 1996). According to this view, we actively participate in constructing the realities of our daily lives rather than passively absorbing that which is going on
cial constructivism, Lewis (2003) wrote, "[R]eality is not out there to
inually negotiate meanings in our conversations with others. People
ig to make sense of and take action in the world" (p. 314).
re assume that no one individual has a special claim or vantage point
93). Scientists, teachers, doctors, and counselors operate in the same
ects, students, patients, and clients and are subject to the same biases
at is "real."
ides, however, a number of trends have converged to create a climate
ented, and, above all, short-term approaches such as SFT have flour-
; on briefer forms of therapy in general as part of the managed health
ed States and many other Western countries. A second, related factor
alth delivery systems on tangible goals and outcomes. While the social
of SFT does not necessarily embrace empirical research, it remains an
ch. Humanitarian concerns are a third important factor in the wide-
er approaches such as SFT. Given the pressing needs and financial
e who seek counseling, therapists have increasingly emphasized the
ething" to create change. In other words, the concern is on changing
the present rather than delving into psychological histories. Shorter-term, solution-oriented
approaches fit well with the emphasis on creating the maximum amount of change in the shortest
amount of time, trusting that good things will continue to happen in the client's life once things
begin to improve.

Development of the Theory

de Shazer and Berg were strongly influenced by Milton Erickson's ideas about the use of
metaphors and hypnosis in therapy. Erickson was a rather unorthodox psychiatrist, and in
Chapter 11, we described the impact that his ideas had on Jay Haley and the development of
strategic family therapy, a brief, problem-solving approach. de Shazer (1985) wrote that the
development of brief approaches to counseling can be traced to Erickson's article "Special
Techniques of Brief Hypnotherapy" (1954). In this paper, Erickson used case examples to demonstrate how clients could use their own abilities and strengths to make a satisfactory life for
themselves without uncovering the past. Erickson was a pioneer who challenged the dominant
medical model that emphasized diagnosing client problems and finding "the" answer for a given
problem (Lewis, 2003). Erickson emphasized divergent thinking about the problems clients bring
to counseling and the multiple ways in which clients could apply untapped strengths and
resources to overcome them.

de Shazer (1985) noted that for 10 years following the publication of Erickson's paper, little
appeared in print about brief therapy. It was not until the late 1960s and early 1970s, as family
therapy gained widespread acceptance, that attention to brief forms of counseling also increased.
Interest in working with families and doing so in a time-limited manner tended to go hand in
hand, since it was very impractical to think that all the members of a family would present themselves for counseling month after month.

Another significant influence on SFT was the work conducted at the Mental Research
Institute (MRI), which was founded in 1958 in Palo Alto by Don Jackson. Researchers at the

MRI studied communication patterns among families where one member was diagnosed with schizophrenia. One pattern noted was that family members tended to use ineffective communication patterns over and over rather than changing their patterns. The more they met with failure using a particular pattern, the more their use of that pattern intensified. Therefore, therapists at the MRI focused on interrupting the faulty attempts at communication and problem resolution in the family. The development of brief interventions for families was facilitated in the mid-1960s when Richard Fisch, a research associate at the MRI, wrote to Don Jackson about the possibility of investigating effective short-term interventions. By 1968, the Brief Therapy Center was established at the MRI, with John Weakland, Paul Watzlawick, and Art Bodin joining the project.

Lipchik (2002) described the Brief Family Therapy Center (BFTC) that de Shazer and Berg established in 1978 as the younger sibling of the Brief Therapy Center at the MRI. de Shazer and Berg's approach was more collaborative than the MRI model and was based on the idea that the family had the resources for its own solutions. de Jong and Berg (2002) noted that the ideas behind SFT as a distinct approach to counseling really took hold at the BFTC in 1982 when, during a session with parents experiencing conflict with their daughter, the suggestion was made that during the next week each family member make a list of what he or she did not want to change. Surprisingly, at the session the following week, all the members of the family were able to come up with numerous examples of things they appreciated about each other. In doing so, a number of other positive changes occurred: There was less tension in the home, the parents felt their daughter's attitude had changed, and the daughter reported that her parents were less critical of her. This suggestion was tried with several more families with repeated success. In an empirical study of this phenomenon, de Shazer (1985) found that concrete changes in clients' lives had little to do with the initial complaints they had reported, and that these initial changes could serve as the foundation for long-term solutions.

de Shazer, Berg, and their colleagues continued to work with families and individuals by collaborating on their goals, focusing on exceptions to problems rather than the problems themselves, and concentrating on what "worked" in therapy (Hawkes, Marsh, & Wilgosh, 1998). de Shazer published a model for the practice of SFT in books such as *Patterns of Brief Therapy* (1982), *Keys to Solutions in Brief Therapy* (1985), and *Clues: Investigating Solutions in Brief Therapy* (1988).

Over the past 15 years, a number of similar approaches have been developed based on working toward solutions with clients in a time-limited manner. For example, O'Hanlon and Weiner-Davis (1989) developed what they called solution-oriented brief therapy, which is focused on helping clients work toward future goals. It could be said that Talmon carried the brief counseling movement to its logical extreme with his publication of *Single Session Therapy* (1990). Talmon was not seriously proposing that effective counseling could routinely take place in a single session, although a sizable proportion of clients seeking services comes for only one session. Single-session therapy was really developed to suggest how counselors could begin intervening with clients from their very first contact.

A number of terms, such as *solution-oriented, problem-focused*, and *brief therapy* have all been applied to de Shazer and Berg's SFT as well as to some of the other brief models of counseling that have been developed. However, SFT is the focus of this chapter because it has been important to the development of brief models of counseling and because it is representative of other solution-oriented approaches. Keep in mind that while our focus is SFT, many of the ideas and techniques reviewed are used in many forms of brief counseling.

ASSUMPTIONS AND CORE CONCEPTS

View of Human Nature

While SFT is not based on a well-developed theory of human personality development, several assumptions about human nature are central to the approach. First is the observation that every human being is unique (Lipchik, 2002). Each of us has a different genetic makeup, history of social development, and pattern of meaning that we have attached to our experiences. This has important implications for the practice of SFT because potential solutions to client problems will also be unique to the individual. What has worked for one person in a given situation will not necessarily work for another. Therefore, SFT counselors must draw from their past experience but also must be open to the creative possibilities for solutions with each new client.

SFT counselors are very optimistic about the potential of human beings to work toward solutions (de Shazer, 1985; 1988). Clients are viewed as possessing most of the skills, capabilities, and resources necessary to work toward creative solutions to their difficulties. According to Lipchik (2002), this assumption is at the heart of SFT and is sometimes the most difficult for counselors to remember. When a client presents for counseling in a state of crisis or disrepair, there is a natural temptation to want to "fix" him. It is also easy to overlook the many resources he has already used to get this far and to bring himself to counseling. When a counselor is overwhelmed with the travails a client shares at the outset of counseling, Lipchik recommended asking the client how he has been coping with the problem thus far, which shifts the focus away from problems toward strengths the client has for coping.

Core Concepts

Solutions are Not Necessarily Related to Problems The social constructivism at the foundation of SFT is a postmodernist philosophy. Perhaps most important for the practice of SFT is the idea that solutions can be unrelated to problems. It is not necessary to know what a problem is in order to solve it (Fish, 1996). In fact, de Shazer (1988) believed it is only by thinking about solutions that one can fully understand a problem.

Recall that de Shazer and his colleagues first developed SFT by asking family members to focus on what they did not want to change rather than on what they did want to change. By asking family members why they did not want to change certain things about their lives, both the counselors and the families they worked with were able to change how they understood their lives and the options they had for change. In order to do this, according to SFT, it is not necessary to understand all the ins and outs of a problem and how it developed: Such an orientation can actually be counterproductive because it tends to put the focus on the problem rather than the solution (Hawkes et al., 1998).

Maintain a Future Orientation SFT counselors spend little time hypothesizing about the factors that have led to their clients' current circumstances; they keep their focus on future possibilities for clients' ways of thinking, acting, feeling, and relating to other people (de Shazer, 1985). SFT counselors will rarely ask many questions about the history of a particular problem, although they will listen carefully when clients choose to volunteer this information on their own. However, when clients are recounting their history, SFT counselors are not listening as much to the details of that history with a problem as they are to what clients have learned as a result of the experience, what issues and concerns they need to leave behind, what they wish had happened differently in the past, and what difference it would make now in their lives had that actually happened (O'Connell, 1998).

Lipchik (2002) noted that a future orientation in counseling is also a good reminder that the past cannot be changed, a self-evident truth that often gets in the way of client change. SFT counselors believe that clients can often get stuck looking for insight into the causes of their problems, and even looking for a "why" answer after they have already resolved a situation. According to Lipchik, this past orientation can be particularly problematic for couples who want to stay together but who have become mired in dwelling on how they have hurt each other in the past. While such experiences might not ever be forgotten, a focus on the future can allow clients to move beyond their histories and focus on future change.

Focus on Strengths In SFT, only the client, not the counselor, has the power to effect change (de Shazer, 1985; 1988). Fortunately, SFT counselors believe very strongly in the ability of clients to find solutions to their own problems in creative and resourceful ways. No matter how difficult a situation a client is facing, the SFT counselor will keep the focus on what has enabled the client to make it this far in life and the strength it has taken for him to ask for help. The SFT counselor believes that the client is the expert on his own life and very often has useful ideas about how to help himself. This can be of vital assistance in helping the client take stock of his abilities and skills and frame life situations in a way that allows him to utilize his resources most effectively.

Change is Inevitable de Shazer (1988) wrote that successes and failures are an inevitable part of one's life journey, particularly given the complex nature of modern life. At any point in our lives, we are involved in change in some way. This change may be generated within us, our family, or our friends, or it may come from outside our immediate world, including our neighborhoods, our nation, and even the global community. In many cases, we have little direct control over these events, and it is therefore inevitable that at least some of it will impact us negatively. The key, SFT counselors believe, is to never stop looking for creative ways to resolve the difficulties that beset us and to accept that even small changes can have tremendous benefits for us in the long term.

Nothing is All Negative Readers who are familiar with Aaron Beck's cognitive-behavioral therapy will be aware of what he described as some clients' tendency to think about experiences in a dichotomous way (i.e., by viewing a situation as entirely negative or entirely positive). Once something negative has happened, it is often difficult to look past its negative features and see opportunities for growth or change. In SFT, events are not accepted as entirely negative (or entirely positive, for that matter). Even the gravest of situations offers opportunities for creativity, growth, and change. Therefore, SFT counselors are constantly looking for exceptions to problems and signs of client strengths in negative circumstances, and they are constantly asking themselves what has helped the client keep going in the past and how can that be built on for future change.

There is No Such Thing as Resistance The notion of resistance was originally a Freudian concept, describing how various defense mechanisms are used to protect the ego by "resisting" interpretations made by the analyst. When a counselor today refers to client resistance, he is usually talking about a situation where the client is not being compliant with the counselor's suggestions for change. SFT counselors reject such notions completely: The client is viewed as an adaptive, capable individual who is always seeking growth. If the client is stuck or unable to act on a counselor's suggestions, it is because of a misunderstanding on the part of the counselor about the client's goals or the best way to reach them. Lipchik (2002) recommended that if a counselor feels frustrated with a client's lack of progress or the direction counseling has taken, it is time to ask the client, "What do you think should be done at this time to make your situation better?"

Simplicity is the Key Hawkes et al. (1998) noted that de Shazer was fond of saying that "complex problems do not always need complex solutions." SFT counselors disagree with relying on thick case notes, complicated diagnostic systems, and batteries of assessment measures to work with clients. While such practices may be useful at times, the SFT counselor considers it presumptuous to make assumptions about the difficulty of a problem without first understanding the clients' perspective, how he would like the situation to change, and his ideas about potential solutions. The SFT counselor would not hesitate to endorse simple steps toward solutions such as taking a walk, keeping a journal, or taking a short vacation if they offer the opportunity for improving a client's life.

THERAPEUTIC RELATIONSHIP

Counselor's Role

The counselor's role in SFT is that of a consultant whom the client has hired in order to reach his goals, even though at the outset of counseling the client may not know exactly what those goals are (de Shazer, 1988). The client is viewed as the expert in establishing goals for counseling, while the SFT counselor's expertise lies in helping the client examine his resources and develop goals for change. In other words, the role of the SFT counselor is to work with his clients to create an environment in which change is identified and amplified (O'Hanlon & Weiner-Davis, 1989).

The focus on solutions, rather than problems, necessitates a very different role for the counselor than in counseling theories that take a problem-focused approach, in which the counselor diagnoses the client's difficulties and recommends treatments. Figure 12.1 sets out O'Connell's (1998) summary of these role differences.

Counselor-Client Relationship

Berg and Miller (1992) distinguished among three different types of counseling relationships: (1) the complainant, (2) the visitor, and (3) the customer. The complainant relationship exists when a goal is identified, but the client does not see that he is part of the change process. In other words, he wants the counselor to be the primary change agent, as in "Tell me how to make my life better." In the visitor relationship, both a clearly defined goal and the client's participation in the change process are lacking—this often occurs when a client is ambivalent about seeking help or committing to change. In a customer relationship, a clear goal has been established, and the client has the view that he is part of the change process.

As you might suspect, SFT counselors strive to establish a counseling relationship in which the client is a customer. When this happens, the client and counselor form a collaborative relationship

Figure 12.1 A Comparison Between Problem-Focused and Solution-Focused Approaches

Problem-Focused	Solution-Focused
How can I help you?	How will you know when therapy has been helpful?
Could you tell me about the problem?	What would you like to change?
Is the problem a symptom of something deeper?	Have we clarified the central issue on which you want to concentrate?
Can you tell me more about the problem?	Can we discover exceptions to the problem?
How are we to understand the problem in light of the past?	What will the future look like without the problem?
What defense mechanisms are operating?	How can we use the skills and qualities of the client?
In which ways is the relationship between the therapist and the client a replay of past relationships (psychodynamic models)?	How can the therapist collaborate with the client?
How many sessions will be needed?	Have we achieved enough to end?

(Reproduced with permission from B. O'Connell, *Solution-Focused Therapy*, © Bill O'Connell, 1998, by permission of Sage Publications Ltd.)

that is based on continuing change and a mutual understanding of the client's goals (de Shazer, 1988). It is expected that at times the client might still behave as a complainant or a visitor, but the SFT counselor is encouraged to view such frustrations as temporary side effects and to strive to find the client's "inner customer" (Berg & Miller, 1992).

The collaborative aspect of the relationship flows from the complementary nature of the roles of the client and the counselor: The former is seeking a solution to a problem, and the latter is dedicated to helping him reach those goals. Lipchik (2002) described the counselor-client relationship as a mutual journey toward solutions that will work for each individual client. The knowledge and expectations of each establish the unique nature of each relationship. The client is the person who decides which solutions will work best for him, and it is the counselor who is ultimately responsible for guiding the relationship in a direction that will serve the client's goals. According to Lipchik, the client takes the lead in the relationship by deciding where to go, how he will cooperate with the counselor, and what his expectations and readiness for change are. The counselor functions as a guide by choosing questions and answers that help the client clarify his goals for change.

Empowerment of the client is an important aspect of the counseling relationship in SFT, which de Jong and Miller (1995) described as establishing a context in which clients can discover their own power and abilities. For example, SFT counselors seek to have clients define their own worlds, problems, and aspirations to create more satisfying lives as a way to honor the meaning they attach to their experiences. A client who is concerned about harmful levels of stress in his life would be asked to describe exactly what he means by stress and to be as specific as possible about where the stress comes from. The counselor would not seek to minimize the stress or argue with the client about what should or should not be regarded as stressful. The client is in charge of his life and is perfectly capable of deciding when stress is harmful.

ASSESSMENT, GOALS, AND PROCESS OF THERAPY

Assessment

Pichot and Dolan (2003) defined the goal of assessment in SFT as finding out what needs to happen in the client's life in order for treatment to be useful. de Shazer (1982, 1985) rejected the problem-focused orientation of traditional methods of assessment and suggested that it is more important to interview the client for strengths. Formal means of assessment, such as psychological tests or inventories, are therefore not typically used because SFT counselors believe there are usually no clear signs as to whether a given person will be able to benefit from counseling (O'Connell, 1998). de Jong and Miller (1995) believed that instead of completing assessment instruments each client should be interviewed at the outset of counseling for strengths and for well-formed goals, which go hand in hand to increase the likelihood of uncovering strengths most appropriate for the client's goals.

Hawkes et al. (1998) noted two questions that can be useful to SFT counselors in assessing a client's needs at the outset of counseling: "What brought you here today?" and "How can I help?" With regard to the first question, the counselor is attempting to understand what will need to happen in order for the first counseling session to be a success. Hawkes et al. noted that the client might be expected to respond to this question with a description of his immediate concerns, which could include a sudden crisis, an ongoing source of stress, or a life transition such as taking a new job. As the client describes his concerns, the SFT counselor listens empathically but does not necessarily ask the client to elaborate on his concerns or provide further detail. In other words, the SFT counselor demonstrates a willingness to listen but not to dwell on past problems.

SFT counselors seek to clarify the clients' goals as soon as possible. Therefore, Hawkes et al. (1998) noted that adding the question "How can I help?" serves to both clarify the client's expectations for change and invite the client to take some initial responsibility at the outset of counseling. The assessment process is therefore not one of classification, but rather one of helping the client define goals and uncover the resources to attain them.

Consider the example of Philipe, a high school senior who seeks out his counselor because of his anxiety about graduating. At the outset of the session, he has described how most of his friends have plans for college, vocational training, or employment, but he has been unable to motivate himself so far. His parents are upset with him, and he has started to withdraw from his friends. After a few minutes of this type of discussion, he asks his counselor if his disengagement from postgraduation plans means he is "crazy."

> **Counselor:** How would it help for me to tell you whether you are crazy or not?
> **Philipe:** I guess I need to know if it's normal to go through this sort of thing. I mean, why can't I get off my butt?
> **Counselor:** So you want to find ways to get yourself working toward a plan after high school?

In this short example, the "How can I help?" question transforms the process of self-exploration into goal setting (Hawkes et al., 1998). An SFT counselor would not be as interested in diagnosing a mental disorder as on helping Philipe first establish goals and then decide the best way to accomplish them. It is important to note here that SFT counselors are not Pollyannas or cheerleaders: Ignoring clients' concerns or conspiring to form unrealistic goals does not promote clients' welfare. Instead, SFT counselors listen to their clients' concerns while looking for clues about the clients' goals and resources. In summary, SFT counselors conduct assessments but not in the traditional role of an expert who objectively gathers information in order to make a diagnosis. Rather, SFT assessment is interwoven with goal setting and the entire counseling process, as both clients and counselors collaborate to define the goals that would best serve the clients and the resources they have to attain them. Goal setting and the process of counseling will be described in more detail in the following sections.

Goals

O'Hanlon and Weiner-Davis's (1989) observation that the client, not the counselor, defines the goals in SFT should come as no surprise at this point in the chapter. At the outset of counseling, the focus will be on the client's concerns and problems, and while it is important for the counselor to listen carefully at this point and make sure the client's safety is not at risk (for example, that he is not suicidal or engaging in otherwise dangerous behaviors), the conversation should be turned toward developing well-formed goals (de Jong & Miller, 1995).

Berg and Miller (1992) noted the following characteristics of well-formed goals in SFT:

1. The goals are important to the client. In other words, the goals should belong to the client and be expressed in the client's words. The SFT counselor is very careful not to impose his own values and solutions on the client, and to make sure he understands exactly what it is that the client hopes to accomplish.
2. Attainable goals are usually small. Berg and Miller noted that it is easier to fill out a single job application than to do something as hefty as "getting a job."
3. Goals are concrete, specific, and tied to specific behaviors. Making an appointment to talk to one's high school counselor in the next week to discuss three options for attending local colleges is better than something more ambiguous like "finding the right college."
4. Goals are typically defined in terms of the presence of some behavior, not its absence. A client who finds it difficult to be assertive is helped to communicate his needs clearly, for example–not to simply stop being unassertive.
5. Goals in SFT focus on beginnings more than endings. Berg and Miller noted that many clients focus on the ultimate outcome, such as becoming a straight-A student, rather than on the beginning, such as planning an effective way to study for the next test.
6. Goals need to be realistic in the context of a client's life. For example, the SFT counselor would not endorse educational goals that seem unrealistic for a client, such as making immediate plans to attend medical school when the client has failed his college science classes.
7. Goals are acknowledged to involve hard work. Berg and Miller noted that this technique protects the client's dignity. Change is presumed to be difficult, and if the client reaches his goals, this makes the achievement noteworthy, and if he does not, it underscores that more work needs to be done.

Process of Therapy

As was noted in the "Counselor's Role" section of this chapter, the primary task at the beginning of SFT is to transform the client's perceptions of his problems and concerns into attainable goals on which immediate progress can be made. The counselor will utilize a range of questions to uncover client strengths and resources and to help the client decide how best to use them in order to meet his goals.

O'Connell (1998) noted that in the first meeting with the client the process between counselor and client occurs at three levels. One of the counselor's primary responsibilities at the outset of counseling is to establish what O'Connell labeled a *discourse on change*, in which he communicates to the client that change is expected, is constant, and should be part of the therapeutic dialogue. In addition to the change discourse, the counselor engages in a *solution discourse*, which involves the formation of a collaborative relationship with the client and the use of techniques that will help the client reach his goals. The third type of discourse is the *strategy discourse*, which consists of identifying strategies the client can use to reach his goals. It is important to note that O'Connell did not believe these three discourses happen in a linear sequence, with one followed by the other. Instead, the counselor and the client may move in and out of each type of discourse or use combinations of two or more types simultaneously as the process of counseling unfolds.

We will next describe each type of discourse in more detail, with a particular emphasis on the change discourse, which is at the heart of the process of SFT. The discussion here of the solution and strategy discourses will be brief because they are conducted through the use of specific techniques that will be described in the "Therapeutic Techniques" section of the chapter.

Change Discourse   SFT counselors express at the outset of counseling a belief that change is already taking place in counseling and even ask questions about what has changed in the client's life between the time he made the appointment with the counselor and the time of the very first session. If a counselor feels overwhelmed by the enormity of a client's problems at the outset of counseling, the first step is to realize that change is inevitable, and the second step is to engage the client in talking about how to do something, no matter how small, that will make a difference in the client's life (Lipchik, 2002).

How exactly does a counselor develop a discourse on change? O'Connell (1998) noted several elements of such a dialogue; we describe them below and then provide examples from the case of María, the 35-year-old teacher who wants to be a bilingual elementary school teacher. Recall that she is experiencing anxiety about preparing for an oral exam in Spanish to receive this certification.

Exception talk occurs when the client is asked to examine situations where his current problems have not arisen or he has dealt with similar circumstances more effectively. In the case of María, the counselor might attempt to help her uncover exceptions to the situation she is describing, that of being overwhelmed with anxiety about being able to communicate fluently with an examiner in Spanish.

> **Counselor:** María, this oral exam in Spanish sounds very important to your career. How can I help?
>
> **María:** Well, you can help me not be so nervous!
>
> **Counselor:** Well, that's what we're working toward. I wonder if there are times in your life where you've been able to battle this type of feeling—I think you called it a "scared and anxious feeling"—and overcome it?
>
> **María:** I've always had this anxiety in pressure situations.
>
> **Counselor:** Have there been times when you've been able to charge ahead and do something in front of people, even though you felt anxious?

María: [*Pauses for a moment*] I guess I had to do a presentation earlier this year with some other teachers, and I don't think we did too bad.

Counselor: What helped you that time?

María: The other people, mainly—I wasn't the only one talking! When I take this Spanish exam, I'll be all alone.

Counselor: I'm guessing though that even in a group you had to put some work into getting ready for that presentation, and you had to do something to get yourself prepared to talk.

María: Yes, I guess I did—I made a bunch of note cards, and we practiced as a group.

In this exchange, the counselor used a series of questions to help María focus on a time in her life that was an exception—that is, when she was successful in talking in front of other people. At first, María is focused mainly on how her previous success was *unlike* her current situation, but by keeping the focus on what went well, the counselor was able to elicit some discussion of how she was able to succeed. In doing so, María was able to reveal some of her capabilities—that is, that she did certain things to prepare herself for the presentation beyond the group effort. In order to elicit more discussion along these lines, the counselor might use competence talk, which is described next.

Competence talk refers to the counselor's effort to focus attention on the resources that the client has for dealing with life circumstances. At the end of the last example, María described how she used note cards and group practice to prepare successfully for a previous oral presentation, and an SFT counselor might use competence talk to have her elaborate on this.

Counselor: María, could we talk some more about your preparation for that presentation you did with the other teachers—about how you prepared by using note cards and practicing with your group?

María: Well, I just hate being put on the spot, and I hate feeling unprepared. By doing a few run-throughs with the other teachers, the ones who were presenting with me, we were able to kind of get ourselves organized, you know, work the kinks out. I realized in our first run-through how nervous I was getting, so I made up note cards with just a few words about the areas I was supposed to cover.

Counselor: And that was helpful to you?

María: Yes, it was, but I don't see how that helps my current problem. To take this test, you have to just converse with the examiner in Spanish, and they grade you on everything—grammar, fluency in conversation, all that stuff—and you either know it or you don't! And I can't use any note cards.

At this point in the dialogue, we can see that the counselor focused María, however briefly, on some of the competencies she has already exhibited in making presentations and speaking in front of others. While she quickly returned to her concerns about preparing for her upcoming test, the counselor was at least able to discuss some of the specifics of how working with other people and preparing note cards worked in the past. However, María is still concerned with what is different about this exam. In the next segment, we see how the counselor might use the skill of deconstructing the problem to accomplish continued discourse on change.

Deconstruction of the problem is accomplished through descriptive language as the counselor attempts to use the client's words to clarify changes that need to be made to meet the client's goals. This discussion attempts to take more abstract notions, such as "being stressed out," and turn them into detailed descriptions of the client's everyday behavior in order to provide a more concrete foundation for solutions. At this point in our case example of María, we can see that she recognizes situations in which she has coped successfully and the skills she has used previously to do this, but she still feels anxious about her upcoming proficiency exam in Spanish. The counselor attempts to deconstruct the problem by getting María to be as specific as possible about the feelings, thoughts, and behaviors involved in her situation.

> **Counselor:** María, we've talked about your feeling anxious about this test, and I wonder if you could talk a little more about that?
>
> **María:** Well, I don't know what else to say—just thinking about it now makes my stomach tighten up. All I can think about is getting tripped up on the exam—you know, just freezing and not being able to think of some phrase in Spanish.
>
> **Counselor:** And those feelings are also interfering with your preparation for the exam?
>
> **María:** Yes, what I think would help me most would be to practice a little, but I get so anxious about the whole situation that I just put it off.
>
> **Counselor:** Is there anything else that seems to be causing you anxiety about this situation?
>
> **María:** Well, I didn't want to tell you this at first, but, well, I'm also a little ashamed to be so worried about speaking Spanish. It's like I've sold out in some way by being too American—I can't even remember the language I was raised in.

In deconstructing the problem, the counselor is not attempting to have María dwell on her difficulties or figure out what is "causing" her anxiety. The point of this kind of exchange is to have María specify in concrete terms exactly what is happening so that the counselor can move toward a solution with her. Therefore, it is necessary to gain some specificity about what exactly is interfering with her attempts at preparing. From the exchange above, we can see that one of María's goals is to prepare for the exam by practicing her conversational Spanish with others, but her anxiety about the test is blocking that goal right now. There is an important diversity consideration demonstrated here as well: Part of María's anxiety may have to do with her identity as a Mexican American. She is particularly concerned about "tripping up" on the exam in Spanish because this might signal to her that she has lost touch with her Mexican cultural roots. In helping her move to prepare for this exam, it will be important for the counselor to be sensitive to these issues. Next, context-changing talk is described as a way to help clients move toward their goals.

Context-changing talk is what the counselor uses to help a client frame a situation or experience differently than he has about it before. This type of talk incorporates both the social constructionist philosophy, which is a part of SFT, and the notion that the way we behave and the problems we encounter all occur within the context of the people and situations that surround us. In other words, a problem with "lack of motivation" that a client experiences in an academic environment may look completely different in the context of sports participation. By inviting this comparison, the counselor engages the client in a discussion of what makes the two contexts different and how resources that are helpful in one arena can be transferred or adapted to another. In our final segment of dialogue in this section, the counselor's attempt to change the context with María is demonstrated.

> **Counselor:** María, I wonder if we could talk a little about the impact this exam has on your career. What will you continue to be able to do if you don't pass it?

María: Well, if I do pass, I think I'll have more job opportunities as a bilingual educator, and I think I can also get paid more. Plus it would allow me to help kids with backgrounds similar to mine.

Counselor: So being able to pass this test would really be a boost to your career, but it wouldn't be make-or-break in terms of your being able to work as a teacher.

María: I suppose not, but it would certainly close down some options, at least until I can pass this test.

Counselor: It sounds like being able to help other students adjust to life in the United States is also very important to you.

María: It sure was a struggle for me at first, and I'd like to make it easier for others.

In this brief example, we can see that the counselor is attempting to help María examine the context in which she views this upcoming exam. While certainly important to her, the counselor is helping her discuss whether the exam is really "make-or-break" for her career, and thus worthy of her attaching such overwhelming importance to it. In addition to the career opportunities presented, we can see the personal importance María attaches to helping students who are Spanish-speaking succeed in U.S. schools.

As we can see from these examples, the discourse on change, which occurs from the very first moment of counseling, helps establish the therapeutic alliance and sets the stage for a discourse on solutions and strategies for change, which are discussed next.

Solution Discourse O'Connell (1998) has suggested that in addition to the change discourse, the counselor should engage in a solution discourse. It builds on the collaborative relationship by adding techniques that orient the client toward solutions. As part of the solution discourse, at some point in the first interview, the therapist will ask the client a miracle question about how his life would suddenly be changed if his problems were removed (de Shazer & Berg, 1997). For example, in the case of María, she could be asked, "What would be different if a miracle occurred and tomorrow you had no more anxiety about your proficiency exam?" We will describe this technique in more detail in the "Therapeutic Techniques" section of this chapter, but for now it is enough to know that it is an important technique in SFT (de Shazer and Berg, 1997) and is used to focus clients on future possibilities and ideal solutions.

Also, at least once during the first interview and subsequent ones, the client will be asked to rate his current concerns using a scaling question; that is, he will be asked to rate a problem or potential solution on a scale from 1 to 10. As an example, the counselor might ask María, "On a scale of 1 to 10, with 1 being the problem at its very worst, and with 10 meaning the problem has gone away completely, how would you rate the past week?" Such questions can be extremely useful, particularly since most clients will not give a problem the lowest rating of 1. This allows for the fact that the problem is not hopeless, and the counselor may ask the client what would need to happen in order for his rating of the problem to improve one or two notches. Scaling questions will also be described in detail in the "Therapeutic Techniques" section of this chapter.

A final component of the solution discourse noted by O'Connell (1998) is the use of reframing, in which the counselor helps the client find another way of looking at his problem. For example, María's anxiety about her proficiency exam could be reframed as something that will motivate her to prepare for the exam, once she has learned to modulate it a bit so that she is not overwhelmed by her feelings.

Strategy Discourse The SFT counselor will close the first session with the strategy discourse (O'Connell, 1998), which consists of identifying strategies the client can use to accomplish some type of change before the next session. The client takes the lead in establishing goals for SFT, and the specific type of change desired here develops out of a mutual agreement between the counselor and the client, based on the work that was done in the first session. Recall that SFT counselors do not believe in the idea of client resistance, and no matter how difficult it is for a client to come up with steps for improvement, they will work with the client to find a suggestion that he feels he could accomplish before the next session.

As counseling progresses, SFT counselors follow up on any suggestions that were made in previous sessions, but the client would never be called to task for not following through on a suggestion. Instead, the counselor will usually ask the client what has improved in their life since the last meeting. Such improvements, even if they occurred only for a short amount of time, will be thoroughly explored and additional steps for improvement would be identified with the client and developed into future goals. This process would continue until the client is able to achieve what she or he deems to be an acceptable level of progress. In the case of María, we might expect that the counselor would continue to work with her on to prepare for her exam by identifying what strategies are most helpful to her to lessen her anxiety and get ready for her exam.

THERAPEUTIC TECHNIQUES

Techniques are an integral part of SFT and were mentioned briefly in the previous section. Questions are a vital part of the therapists' arsenal in SFT and are used in a very specific ways. SFT counselors also seek to be as creative as possible when working with clients to decide what types of activities or behaviors will be most useful to them between sessions. Following are descriptions of some of the most widely used SFT techniques.

✦ Miracle Question

The miracle question is an integral part of SFT. Alfred Adler, one of the pioneers of this type of question, asked clients how their lives would be different if their symptoms disappeared (Mosak & Maniacci, 1999).

de Shazer (1988) described the use of the miracle question in SFT as asking a client to imagine that, after sleeping, he woke up and whatever problem he brought to counseling miraculously disappeared. Because the individual was asleep, he wouldn't know how or when it happened, so de Shazer asked the client to describe how he would know the problem had disappeared: What would be different in his life? What would he do differently now that the problem was gone? Miracle questions reflect the basic philosophy of SFT: Be optimistic, look to the future, and recognize that you have the strength to make your own miracles.

Rita (1998) noted that the miracle question helps the client and the counselor agree on the description of what a solution looks like and helps the client establish small, concrete behaviors that will signal that the problem is being solved. It is anticipated that many clients will first focus on the fact that their symptoms have disappeared, but in SFT, the client is encouraged to focus on the future in positive behavioral terms rather than on the absence of symptoms. According to Rita, a client's initial response may be too broad and unrealistic. Therefore, he recommended helping the client focus on the smallest piece of the miracle that is achievable and will signal that progress in the right direction is being made.

In the example below, a counselor uses the miracle question with Benjamin, a client who grew up in Germany. He has been transferred by his company to the United States, and he has struggled tremendously with feelings of isolation and loneliness. He is having trouble sleeping, has few friends, and is considering quitting his job so he can return home. Benjamin has visited the employee assistance counselor provided by his company.

See DVD

Benjamin: I'm just so upset—I can't possibly function at work. If I don't stop feeling depressed soon, I'll have to quit and go back to Germany.

Counselor: Benjamin, could we try a little experiment? Could you imagine what it would be like if you woke up tomorrow and suddenly by some miracle all those ;s were gone?

I'd wouldn't be dreading getting out of bed. I wouldn't have this heavy on me all the time, this feeling of loneliness.

: And what would be *different*? How would you notice that the problem ne?

I think I'd be able to concentrate better. I'd be able to sleep better, that's for And I'd be able to make some friends at work.

: That's great! I think you've really painted a wonderful picture of what it will : when those feelings are gone. I wonder if there's some small piece of that pic- e could start working on immediately—for example, making some friends.

I would like that. I had a lot of friends at home, and I guess I should stop ing so much about my accent and just try to talk to people more often.

r: That sounds like a good start. Can we talk more about the best ways to tt?

ijamin's cultural background is an important aspect of his experience in coun- 'e example, the counselor might be encouraged by the vision Benjamin has for v," but it might also be important for the counselor to discuss further what it means to "stop worrying so much about my accent." In understanding Benjamin's answer, the counselor may want to consider whether it would be important to discuss further the reaction Benjamin is having to living in this country before deciding whether this is reasonable or even desirable. In asking the miracle question, the counselor will want to be as sensitive as possible to cultural factors that may be at play in this situation.

Exception-Finding Questions

SFT counselors believe that no situation or problem is ever "all bad," and de Shazer and Berg were particularly interested in finding exceptions: in other words, times in a client's life when problems were lessened or even nonexistent. Following is an example in the case of Benjamin.

See DVD

Chap. 12
Clip 2

Counselor: Benjamin, are there ever times or situations where you feel less lonely or isolated?

Benjamin: I guess so.

Counselor: Could you give me an example?

Benjamin: I'm usually the most lonely at home in the evenings. At work, it's less . . . especially when people take an interest and ask me about myself and my life in Germany.

Counselor: So you are not so lonely at work? And you notice you don't feel as awkward talking to people there?

Benjamin: Yes, I feel a lot less self-conscious.

Counselor: Is there any way we can use those experiences to make it easier to socialize with people outside of work?

Scaling Questions

Scaling questions are used very frequently in SFT to help clients assess their current problems, their willingness to do something different to achieve their goals, and their confidence about being able to change (de Shazer, 1988; Hawkes et al., 1998). The client is usually asked to provide a rating using a scale from 0 to 10. Clients might be asked, for example, to rate the severity of a problem from 0, representing the worst it has ever been, to 10, meaning the problem has gone away completely. Consider again the case of Benjamin.

Counselor: Benjamin, on a scale from 0 to 10, can you rate how lonely you feel today? 0 means it is as bad as it has ever been, and 10 means you are not lonely at all.

Benjamin: Well, today wasn't great—I feel a lot of pressure at work, and there's no one to talk to me about it. But it has been worse at times, so I'd say about a 4.

This use of a scaling question does a number of important things in SFT. First, clients are rather unlikely to give their problem a "worst ever" rating, which establishes at the outset that things are not hopeless. Second, the counselor can then ask the client in a more concrete way what it would take for him to raise his rating even a notch or two, which can be suggested as homework between sessions. As we noted, scaling questions about the client's motivation for change and confidence in his ability to solve his problems can also be used.

Coping Questions

Coping questions recognize that while the client has very real concerns and difficulties, he has also managed to survive to this point in life and at the very least was able to seek out help (Berg & Miller, 1992; Ozeki, 2002). The basic structure of such questions is quite simple: Since [the problem] started, how do you [the solution]? (Ozeki, 2002). For example, in the case of Benjamin, he might be asked, "Since your feelings of loneliness became troublesome, how have you managed to complete your work and survive on your own in a foreign country?"

Coping questions reframe the client's reactions to problems as resources for future solutions. Ozeki (2002) pointed out that in order to make this question effective, it is necessary to carefully attend to the client's concerns and to acknowledge the pain they have caused. Coping questions are then used to focus on what has kept the client going so far because this can be a key resource for future solutions.

Breaks

de Shazer and Berg (1997) noted that along with miracle and scaling questions the counselor's use of breaks, or short time-outs, in a session is a hallmark of the practice of SFT. de Shazer (1988) noted that in SFT before a recommendation is made to the client, an "intervention break" is first taken in which the counselor leaves the room to collect his thoughts and gather ideas about what would work best. Sharry, Madden, Darmody, and Miller (2001) noted that these breaks may last only a few minutes but allow time for the therapist to consult with colleagues and to prepare constructive feedback and helpful therapeutic tasks for the client. Although this technique is typically used for consultation with others, the SFT counselor can also use this time by himself to reflect on how best to assist the client.

Hawkes et al. (1998) noted that "physically removing yourself from the session helps you to get your thoughts together and develop the intervention" (p. 28). It also has a dramatic effect on the client, who is also given a chance to collect his thoughts. Upon returning, the SFT counselor usually offers a compliment to the client about his ability to cope so far. The counselor then makes what is called a bridging statement, which demonstrates to the client that his concerns have been heard and were incorporated into the suggested intervention (Hawkes et al., 1998). For example, in the case of Benjamin, the counselor could start with a postbreak statement such as "Because I know you want to do as well as possible in your job and adjust as much as possible to life in a different country, ..."

Following this bridging statement, the counselor will suggest an activity or task that will help the client work toward his goal. Hawkes et al. (1998) noted that the type of activity suggested will depend on the client's levels of motivation and readiness for change: If these appear to be low, the client might be given a suggestion to notice something in his life that he would like to keep happening. If, on the other hand, the client is able to give very specific responses to the miracle question and appears highly motivated, he might be given a very specific task to do, such as "Talk to three friends who you might enjoy spending time with outside of work."

Compliments

Positive reinforcement and validation are important methods of empowering clients and establishing trust in the counseling relationship. Pichot and Dolan (2003) suggested that SFT counselors do this by (1) expressing surprise at one of the client's accomplishments and (2) asking the client to describe how this was accomplished. This should be done in a genuine manner, and it suggested that this happen during the first session (de Shazer & Berg, 1997). Hawkes et al. (1998) noted that compliments should be genuine and low-key and that the counselor should not attempt to insincerely flatter the client. Instead, genuine admiration should be expressed for the client's resourcefulness in managing difficulties thus far (Hawkes et al., 1998). In the case of Benjamin, after asking a miracle question and a few scaling questions about the severity of his problems, the counselor might offer a compliment.

> **Counselor:** Benjamin, I know that you're having a hard time, but I am really impressed with the progress you have made. Working in a foreign country and having to use a different language are really hard. Truthfully, I don't think I could do as well as you're doing.

Tasks

This is a general term describing something that the counselor would like the client to do between sessions—essentially, tasks are a type of "homework," which can be tailored to the specific needs of the client to help him reach his goals (de Shazer, 1988). Rita (1998) noted that tasks can be particularly helpful when used to follow up on a client's answer to the miracle question. The counselor and the client can construct a plan based on something that is already happening in the client's life that she would like to happen more often, for example.

Rita (1998) noted the following steps for developing tasks based on the client's response to a miracle question:

1. Upon completion of the problem description by the client, the miracle question is posed by the counselor.
2. The counselor compliments the client for his response to the miracle question and for the strength he has demonstrated in coping so far with his situation and in seeking help.
3. Miracle questions often have several components and can be quite broad and ambitious. At this point, the counselor asks the client to simplify his response to the miracle question. The client may be given a short break to decide on the smallest piece of the miracle that is achievable and would signal progress in a direction he finds desirable.
4. The session usually ends with a task for the client based on his smallest-piece-of-the-miracle response.

Molnar and de Shazer (1987) noted that depending on the client's motivation, the task could be something very simple, such as keeping track of things he did that made him feel more on top of his concerns. These are sometimes called *generic tasks* (O'Hanlon & Weiner-Davis, 1989) and help the client focus on exceptions to his current concerns.

SFT counselors are extremely flexible when designing tasks. For example, one type of task is to "do something different," which is often utilized when a client feels very stuck in his current problems (de Shazer, 1985). Or prediction tasks can be used in which the client is asked to predict at a certain point in the day whether his problems will continue the next day (de Shazer, 1988). This type of task is useful when problems seem to occur randomly for a client: The prediction task can help him eventually feel more in control of its occurrence.

MULTICULTURAL AND DIVERSITY EFFECTIVENESS

SFT emphasizes understanding the client's subjective frame of reference in terms of both the problems he is experiencing and the solutions he sees as desirable. This has the potential to help the SFT counselor keep from imposing his own culturally laden values on the client. Further, the fact that SFT emphasizes strengths and resources could be empowering for the client who has encountered systematic discrimination or racism in his life.

Echoing these themes, Corcoran (2000) reviewed the appropriateness of a number of the key assumptions of solution-focused family therapy for working with African-American and Latino families and found much to recommend it. While noting the caveat that the congruence of any theory with a particular group's norms and attitudes is based mainly on generalizations, she identified several ways in which SFT might be appropriate for working with African Americans and Latinos. These include the assumptions that individual behavior is shaped by its context (for example, one's family and social relationships), that the counselor must collaborate with the client in establishing goals that are meaningful to the client, and that it is important to change behaviors and perceptions, not just feelings.

A number of authors have also evaluated the potential utility of SFT with Asian and Asian-American clients with positive results. For example, Cheung (2001) noted that some Asian cultures place a particular emphasis on finding pragmatic solutions to problems and are less comfortable focusing on emotions. Hung-Hsiu, Chang and Ng (2000) noted that an emphasis on change as a continual and natural process is consistent with the prevailing belief of many Asian cultures. However, Chueng noted that the egalitarian nature of the SFT relationship may run counter to cultural expectations in some Asian cultures that there should be a hierarchical relationship between counselor and client. Further, Yeung (1999) noted that linguistic considerations must be taken into account when using SFT with Chinese-speaking clients. While the specific points of departure between the Chinese and English languages are beyond the scope of this chapter, it is important to recognize that solutions between counselors and clients can be deeply embedded in notions of culture and language and that caution is warranted in making sure the counselor and the client have come to agreement about future goals.

Dermer, Hemesath, and Russell (1998) wrote about the consistency of SFT with feminist approaches to counseling. They noted a number of areas where these approaches are consistent, including the idea that the relationship should be egalitarian, the focus on collaborating and finding client strengths, and the ideas that each person in the counselor-client relationship has something to offer and that this cooperation can create a model for other relationships in a client's life.

However, Dermer et al. noted the limitations of SFT when working from a feminist perspective. Specifically, SFT does not provide a mechanism for challenging societal stereotypes including notions about male dominance and the abuses of power and professional privilege associated with some institutions. While feminist approaches maintain that the counselor must deal with these issues directly in counseling, SFT does not take a specific stand on such topics. Many feminist counselors would expect that unless explicit attention is drawn to prevailing cultural stereotypes—for example, the patriarchal status quo or the role of women in society—they could be carried out unintentionally in the counseling relationship.

Ivey, D'Andrea, Ivey, and Simek-Morgan (2002) noted some general limitations of using brief counseling approaches with clients who are concerned with the meaning of life and who want to examine their life histories. This could extend to some cultural and ethnic groups who take great pride in family connections and histories and who might see attention to such matters as an important component of counseling. Ivey et al. also noted that the time-limited nature of approaches such as SFT may be problematic when used with clients whose views about the nature of time are different than those of European Americans. For example, they noted the example of Native Americans, whose values and cultural norms are not consistent with the traditional boundaries of the "therapy hour" and the emphasis on getting as much accomplished in a short amount of time as possible. In support, they cited LaFromboise's (1996) contention that in Native American culture time is more elongated and subtle—it is more important to be where you are needed rather than keeping appointments to be in a certain place at a certain time.

PRIMARY APPLICATIONS

Groups

Hawkes et al. (1998) reported that de Shazer was initially unsure if it was possible to apply SFT to group work, since SFT traditionally centered on individual conversations and the negotiation of goals with clients. Hawkes et al. argued that it was important to use SFT in group counseling, particularly since they found that many of their clients in psychiatric settings expressed frustration with group work that lasted a year or more, focused mainly on their relationships and causes of their problems, and seemed to get them no closer to solutions for their problems.

Pichot and Dolan (2003) noted that SFT groups depart in significant ways from many of the traditional assumptions of group therapy. For example, pioneers in group therapy such as Irvin Yalom (1995) suggested that groups act as a social microcosm, with members' patterns of relating to other people in the outside world being re-created in the group. The group leader's role is to observe how these patterns have been re-created in order for other members to provide feedback about them. Many traditional forms of group counseling also have fairly structured topics that are covered in the group in a sequential way.

In contrast, Pichot and Dolan (2003) suggested that in SFT each client is viewed as having meaningful and unique goals. The SFT group leader makes no assumptions about the types of information a member may need and is committed to the idea that what happens outside the group is more important than what happens inside the group. Rather than creating a social microcosm, the leader helps members use the group as a safe environment for exploring how they would like their outside lives to change. Therefore, the group leader's primary tasks are to maintain a safe environment in the group for this exploration, to ask questions that assist members in identifying what life will be without the problem, and to help group members explore what steps they need to take to get there.

Many of the same techniques used in individual SFT are used in group work. Hawkes et al. (1998) described the application of SFT to groups as a type of workshop approach, in which clients in the group are first taught SFT techniques and then use them to interview each other. In this format, the group leader then acts as a sort of moderator, keeping track of time and providing assistance as needed to individual members.

Pichot and Dolan (2003) described a somewhat different approach to SFT groups, in which the group leader organizes the group around themes common to all members. First off, the group leader asks questions that focus the group on themes for change: What is one thing that you have done between this and the last meeting that helped you get closer to your goals? What would your family members tell me your most important quality is? The group leader's task is then to identify overarching themes for the whole group from the answers to these questions. Such themes could include overcoming the loss of an important person in one's life and dealing with unexpected setbacks such as the loss of a job or the breakup of a romantic relationship. Traditional SFT techniques such as the miracle question, scaling questions, and homework are all then used to help members work toward their goals.

Several authors have suggested that when using SFT groups with certain types of clients, it is necessary for the leader to structure the group around the presentation of specific topics. For example, Banks (1999) described the use of SFT in groups of adolescents who bully other students and suggested certain topics such as "Is bullying behavior okay?" And Nelson and Kelley (2001) described how SFT couples groups could use a mixed education and discussion format for relationship enhancement. SFT interventions with couples and in school settings are described in more detail next.

Couples

Lipchik (2002) noted that solution-focused work with couples is similar to that with individuals, but it is more difficult in that the solution has to work for the relationship, which consists of two I individuals with different points of view. According to Lipchik, SFT couples work will not be successful unless both partners are committed to improving the relationship; if one or both partners are ambivalent about this goal, individual work might be necessary in order to help that individual decide if he or she wants to commit to working on the relationship. While we noted earlier in this chapter that assessment does not typically play a prominent role in SFT, Lipchik did suggest that an initial assessment session with both partners is important to establish that both have committed to working on the relationship. During this initial session, both partners are instructed that their contract for therapy is with their relationship, not with them as individuals, and that the goal is to bridge their differences in order to find a solution that will improve their relationship (Lipchik, 2002).

Hoyt and Berg (1998) noted that at the outset of counseling it is important to engage the couple in a solution-oriented discourse. Recall from the "Process of Therapy" section in this chapter that O'Connell (1998) suggested that the solution discourse revolve around exception talk, competence talk, deconstruction of the problem, and context-changing talk. In the case of couples counseling, the SFT counselor therefore orients the couple's initial description of the problems toward what would generally constitute a favorable outcome from both of their perspectives (Hoyt & Berg, 1998).

According to Hoyt and Berg (1998), what must happen next is that each member of the couple must describe specific behaviors of his partner that would indicate to both of them that the relationship is improving. This is demonstrated in the following excerpt from a couples session with Roger and Franco, two men involved in a romantic relationship for over two years. They recently decided that they would like to pursue adopting a child but had no idea about whether they would legally be permitted to do this in their state or what obstacles they might encounter.

Both of them acknowledged that Roger immediately devoted enormous amounts of time to researching the adoption process for same-sex couples in their state, but Franco soon became disinterested. This caused considerable conflict in their relationship, as Roger concluded Franco was only in the relationship for "fun" and not a serious commitment. For his part, Franco reported feeling pressured by Roger to immediately jump into an adoption that would change their lives forever, a step he wanted to take more slowly. Both expressed being committed to working on their relationship, and during their initial counseling session, they expressed a mutual desire to communicate better with each other. In the example below, their SFT counselor attempts to have both partners be as specific as possible about the behaviors each would need to see to conclude they are communicating better.

> **Counselor:** Roger, what would Franco have to be doing to let you know that he is open to your perspective and what you have to say?
>
> **Roger:** I want him to be interested in the kinds of things I find out about the adoption process. Right now, he just doesn't seem to give a darn one way or the other.

Counselor: So if he did give a darn, what would he be doing or saying?

Roger: He might be helping me research things or at least letting me know that he has thought about the information I give him.

Counselor: So after you give him some information, you'd like him to let you know that he has been thinking about it and possibly that he would follow up on that with some research of his own?

Roger: That *would* be a miracle!

Counselor: Franco, how about you? What kinds of behaviors from Roger would let you know that your communication is better?

Franco: Giving me some space now and then, not forcing us to talk about adoption *all* the time.

Counselor: What would he be doing instead?

Franco: I don't know. He's so gung-ho on this adoption, it's like we have nothing else to talk about.

Counselor: So talking about things other than the adoption would be a sign of better communication for you?

Franco: That would show me there are other things going on in our relationship.

This example demonstrates how early in SFT couples counseling both members in the relationship are asked to describe in positive behavioral terms what the other person needs to be doing to improve the relationship. After getting specifics, the counselor might ask a miracle question about what would signal to each partner that the problem they brought to counseling had disappeared (Hoyt & Berg, 1998). Procedures similar to those used in individual counseling might then be used to identify specific parts of the miracle that the couple could begin working on to improve the relationship. For example, exception questions could be used to identify times when the relationship is problem-free. Hoyt and Berg noted that a unique aspect of couples work in SFT, as opposed to individual work, is that the counselor must work to bridge the ideas of change and the solutions offered by both members of the relationship. For example, they might be asked to talk about solutions from different perspectives, including those of their children if they are parents or caregivers. Scaling questions can still be used to evaluate the severity of the problem and their confidence about change, and the therapist might still take a break in the session before offering feedback and suggestions for homework between sessions, as well as complimenting both partners on the strengths they have demonstrated in working on their problems.

We note here that the SFT therapist makes no mention of what might be behind Franco's hesitation to discuss adoption. For example, he might be very nervous about being a gay parent in a society that discriminates against same-sex parents. A discussion of this aspect of the situation is not strictly a solution-focused technique, but it could come up as part of a solutions discourse, for example. However, the SFT counselor could perhaps frame it in terms of the strength and courage it takes for gay men to consider adoption when so many in our culture are opposed to this idea.

School Counseling

The application of SFT to schools was first suggested by Rhodes and Ajmal (1995), so it is therefore relatively new in educational settings. The school counselor is faced with meeting the counseling needs of several hundred students, as well as interacting with parents, teachers, and administrators. Williams (2000) wrote that many teachers and administrators refer students to helping professionals in the hope that they will somehow "cure" the student or at least provide a psychological explanation for why the student cannot be helped and must therefore be sent elsewhere.

Williams (2000) pointed out that not only does SFT offer solutions and hope to students but also "the model, and its underlying assumptions, is often as energizing for our staff as it is for our clients" (p. 76). School counselors usually cannot count on seeing students individually for extended amounts of time and thus will often refer students with serious mental health concerns to another professional in the school (for example, a school psychologist or social worker) or in the community. Therefore, the limited-time format of SFT and its focus on client strengths as well as concrete indicators of progress are well suited to the work of school counselors.

Davis and Osborn (2000) suggested that many of the techniques described earlier in this chapter are appropriate for use with younger persons with a few modifications. For example, adults may be asked scaling questions, which require them to rate the severity of a problem or the prospects for change on a 10-point scale. For younger elementary school students, this might be a bit too abstract, so instead of using numeric ratings, a counselor may ask a student to pick from a series of caricatured faces (i.e., from a very happy face to a very unhappy face) to indicate how things are going that day. Or the student could be asked to choose a point on a line that describes how they are doing that day, with one end representing "very good" and the other end representing "not good."

Davis and Osborn (2000) also cited Chang's (1998, p. 63) suggestion that when using the miracle question, children could be asked to draw the miracle rather than describing it, which might allow more opportunity for them to be self-expressive. Counselors using the miracle question with students may also need to make sure the students know what a miracle is and to encourage them to be as creative as possible. As an example, let us consider the case of Vincent, a fourth grader whose best friend, Pete, has recently moved away. Since then, Vincent has been very despondent at school and unwilling to interact with other students. His teacher has sent him to the school counselor to talk about his concerns. After exploring the problem with Vincent, the counselor decides to use the miracle question.

> **Counselor:** Hi, Vincent. Your teacher told me you've been looking sad lately. And your mom called and told me that you are pretty sad because your best friend, Pete, moved away.
>
> **Vincent:** Yeah, I guess so.
>
> **Counselor:** Would you be willing to try an experiment with me?
>
> **Vincent:** OK.
>
> **Counselor:** Imagine that you go to sleep one night, and a miracle happens. Do you know what a miracle is?
>
> **Vincent:** Yeah, it's when something really great happens. Like you win a million dollars or something like that.
>
> **Counselor:** You've got the idea. Anyway, say you go to sleep and a miracle happens and you wake up and you aren't sad anymore and everything is just the way you want it to be. What would you notice?
>
> **Vincent:** OK, let me think . . . . Well, first of all, school would be over, and my friend Pete and I would be playing down by the creek because Pete would move

back here. And my dad would win the lottery and we would go on a vacation to Florida.

Counselor: Good job, Vincent. That's a miracle with a lot of parts. Can we talk about the part where Pete moves back?

Not surprisingly, Vincent's initial description of the miracle was quite grandiose, so the counselor attempted to have him downscale it a bit. Maybe Vincent and his counselor would eventually focus on a part of the miracle that Vincent might work on—say, a visit with Pete or a way to find a friend with whom to play.

The use of SFT with groups was described earlier in this section, but it should be pointed out here that SFT groups can be particularly useful in school settings because counselors are often unable to meet with students individually due to time limitations. Such groups can be developed around themes that all members of the group have in common. For example, Young and Holdorf (2003) described the use of an SFT group for students who were the victims of bullies, while Banks (1999) described how a group could be used to explore alternative behaviors for students who themselves had bullied other students. In the former case, Young and Holdorf described how the group time could be used to help students talk about instances when they had successfully avoided bullies or coped with them. In the latter case, Banks described the use of unique interventions such as the "older wiser self" to help students focus on the benefits of nonbullying interactions with peers. The activity was used to encourage students to give themselves some advice: They were asked to imagine themselves several years in the future as an older and wiser person and to describe the advice they might give to someone in the same position they are now. This activity served as a way to imagine more prosocial behaviors than bullying.

Involuntary Clients

Counselors frequently work with involuntary clients or clients who are referred by someone else; typical examples include children brought to counseling by their parents, patients sent by doctors, older parents brought by their children, and individuals mandated to come to counseling by employers or the judicial system (Lipchik, 2002). Tohn and Oshlag (1996) noted that SFT counselors work with involuntary clients the same way they do with voluntary clients: by cooperating with them in reaching their goals. The authors maintained that in order to do so the counselor must follow de Shazer's suggestion that "resistance is dead." Tohn and Oshlag advised that involuntary clients should be viewed not as resistant or in denial about their problems, but as having multiple goals. A student referred to counseling by a teacher for talking in class, for example, may have several goals, which might include (a) getting the teacher off his back, (b) having a good time in school, and (c) not looking "dumb" in class by being unable to answer a teacher's questions. A counselor who takes the view that it is only the referral source's goals that matter—in this case, the teacher's—is not cooperating with his client.

While many aspects of SFT are appropriate to use with involuntary clients, some modification of the techniques may be necessary. For example, Rosenberg (2000) noted that use of the traditional miracle question may be inappropriate for involuntary clients. Mandated clients are already being treated as if the referring source knows more about what they should be doing than the clients, and the traditional miracle question fails to address the disparity in power between mandated clients and the referral source. Rosenberg suggested that this variation of the miracle question is appropriate for many mandated clients:

> Suppose that one night, while the [insert person or agency mandating the client's attendance in counseling] was asleep, a miracle happened and [referring person or agency] recognized that you never had to go back to see them again. The next day this person says that he or she could not believe it, but you never have to come back again. The case was closed. What would that person notice that is different in your lives that would allow [him or her] to say that? (p. 94)

According to Rosenberg, this rephrasing of the miracle question allows the client to feel a measure of control over the outcome of their work in counseling. The client can view the development of goals as a way to get the referring agency off his back rather than simply giving in to the agency's demands.

BRIEF THERAPY/MANAGED CARE EFFECTIVENESS

As we noted at the beginning of this chapter, SFT is but one of many counseling models appropriate for short-term, solution-oriented work with clients. These approaches continue to be very popular today, and on this count at least, SFT is well positioned for managed care environments that stress brevity in working with clients. Despite current interest in such approaches, there are a number of factors, mainly having to do with de Shazer and Berg's rejection of the traditional medical model, that mitigate against the acceptance of SFT in managed care settings. For example, SFT counselors do not believe in the role of formal assessment in assigning a "diagnosis" to a client. In fact, SFT counselors reject a problem-focused orientation altogether and focus instead on client strengths and possibilities for growth. However, in many managed care settings, a formal psychiatric diagnosis and a treatment plan are required for reimbursement. Since SFT counselors usually work by developing tasks for clients that come out of conversations with these clients, SFT counselors may find it hard to follow a diagnosis with a prescribed treatment plan for reimbursement purposes. While the spirit of SFT is very much in line with managed care settings, its rejection of some of the central tenets of the medical model in treatment may make its use difficult in such settings.

INTEGRATING THE THEORY WITH OTHER APPROACHES

SFT provides specific techniques for working with clients that make it an attractive candidate for integration with other theories. Techniques such as the miracle question, scaling questions, and tasks such as "do something different" can seem quite compelling, particularly for counselors who favor using structured techniques and being active in sessions. It might therefore be tempting for a client-centered counselor, for example, who mainly relies on listening actively and developing empathy with clients, to throw the occasional miracle question into a session to keep things moving.

In discussing the integration of SFT with other counseling approaches, Beyebach and Morejon (1999) noted that this can be done at the level of theory or at the level of technique. In other words, one can seek to integrate the theoretical propositions of SFT with those of other approaches, or seek to simply integrate the techniques (technical integration), or do both.

However, Beyebach and Morejon noted that the research base for SFT is still quite thin. This leaves open the question of whether SFT is effective at all, an important question that must be answered before one attempts to integrate it on a theoretical level with another counseling model.

Another potential problem for integrating SFT with other approaches is that its theoretical framework is not as well developed at this point as those of many of the theories covered in this book. de Shazer and Berg (1997) defined the hallmarks of SFT mainly in terms of its technical characteristics, such as the use of the miracle question, the use of scaling questions, the break taken by counselor and client, and the like. However, it is problematic to define SFT only in terms of the techniques used because one could well be practicing in the spirit of SFT without using one of these techniques.

Beyebach and Morejon (1999) therefore thought that at this point it is more appropriate to consider integrating SFT on a technical level. The main advantages of doing so would be the following features of SFT:

1. Its simplicity, which reduces the likelihood of its conflicting with other theoretical models of counseling.
2. Its pragmatism, which focuses on what works, not why it works.
3. Its respect for diversity in technique, which gives the counselor greater latitude in using techniques that have contrasting theoretical assumptions.
4. Its emphasis on listening to clients and tailoring interventions to their needs, increasing the likelihood that a given technique will be useful to a client.

In evaluating the potential for integrating SFT with other prominent models of counseling, it makes sense to begin with family therapy approaches such as those developed by Minuchin and Bowen, which view family members as interconnected and mutually dependent (see Chapter 11 for more description of these approaches). Since SFT developed out of such models, many of its techniques share the assumption that change directed at one part of a system (for example, a parent or child) has the potential to influence the rest of the system.

With respect to counseling models aimed at working with individuals, William Glasser's reality therapy may be the most congruent with SFT. In both approaches, the client's past history is not the focus, and the counselor mainly attempts to help the client make positive changes in his life, focusing mainly on what works. The major point of difference between the two approaches is that reality therapy is built on the philosophy of choice theory, a model of how various personality functions (thoughts, feelings, behaviors, and physiology) work in an integrated fashion to help us meet our needs in the outside world. Glasser's emphasis on teaching clients choice theory is not consistent with SFT's emphasis on working toward solutions constructed from conversations with clients.

The behavioral and cognitive-behavioral counseling approaches also emphasize making changes in clients' current behaviors and modes of thinking rather than uncovering historical reasons for these patterns. It is assumed that if clients can effect such changes in the present, they will be able to apply the new skills they have learned to other areas of their lives without ongoing assistance from the counselor. Behavioral and cognitive-behavioral practitioners use a wide range of techniques and interventions to help clients change, and they urge clients to practice these new skills as much as possible, both in the counselor's office and in the outside world, through homework assignments. Like those used in SFT, these methods are quite transparent in the sense that the counselor tries to explain the reasons for the interventions so that client can continue to use them once the client has left counseling.

SFT therefore has the potential to be integrated on a technical level with the behavioral and cognitive-behavioral approaches, which emphasize helping clients make tangible changes in their lives with respect to their thoughts and cognitions. For example, a cognitive-behavioral counselor might be able to use scaling questions to gauge the persistence or severity of a client's irrational thoughts. Or a behavioral counselor could use a miracle question to uncover future behaviors that a client would like to move toward in counseling. However, it should be pointed out that the theoretical premises of both approaches are not entirely consistent with SFT. For example, the central notion of clients having "irrational thoughts" is not consistent with the practice of SFT, in which clients' resources, not their pathological thinking, are emphasized. And it is worth noting that behaviorists assume it is the environment that determines our behaviors, while SFT counselors again focus on the strengths and resources that clients have for meeting their goals.

It would seem more difficult to attempt to use SFT with counseling theories that emphasize exploration of a client's psychological history, such as psychodynamic or Adlerian counseling. Further, the emphasis on a search for meaning that does not necessarily entail changes in behavior represented by existential counseling would seem to be difficult to integrate with SFT.

RESEARCH

There is little research on the effectiveness of SFT. It is therefore difficult to know whether the overall approach is effective or whether specific techniques like the miracle question actually end up being useful for clients. Much to their credit, de Shazer and his colleagues conducted exploratory studies on the effectiveness of their procedures early in the development of SFT. *Keys to Solutions in Brief Therapy* (de Shazer, 1985) presented the results of an exploratory study in which 28 clients were contacted between 6 months and 1 year after completing counseling. Graduate students at the BFTC conducted telephone surveys using a six-item questionnaire, which asked clients about whether the problems they brought to counseling were worse, the same, or better, and 82% reported they were better. In the following year, de Shazer et al. (1986) followed up on 25% of the 1,000 clients they had seen between 1978 and 1983. Again, clients were surveyed by telephone about their progress since completing counseling: 72% had made enough improvement that they thought further therapy was not necessary.

Similar investigations of client progress have been reported by other researchers. de Jong and Hopwood (1996) found that 45% of clients seen at the BFTC between 1992 and 1993 reported the goals they developed had been achieved, with another 32% reporting some progress. And other researchers have had comparable success rates in other settings. Lee (1997), for example, reported on a 6-month follow-up on the use of SFT in a children's mental health facility: 59 children aged 4–17 were included in the study, with a 64.9% success rate after an average of 5.5 sessions over an average of 3.9 months. And Beyebach et al. (2000) reported on 83 cases seen at the Universidad Pontificia de Salamanca in Spain between 1992 and 1996: 82% of those seen reported their problems were solved during therapy.

While such descriptive information about clients' progress following SFT is useful, such research does not possess the scientific rigor necessary to really evaluate the model. And in more recent work, de Shazer (1991) has tended to rely more on case examples to offer evidence for the effectiveness of the approach rather than empirical studies.

Research has suggested the potential utility of SFT for behavior problems in school-aged children. For example, two studies using versions of the Conners' Rating Scale, a checklist with which a teacher or parent rates the frequency of behavior problems exhibited by a child, have shown improved behavior after SFT was used with the child (Corcoran & Stephenson, 2000; Franklin, Biever, Moore, Clemons, & Scamardo, 2001). Other authors seeking to comment on the overall utility of SFT (Hawkes et al., 1998; McKeel, 1996) have relied to a certain extent on general therapy outcome studies of brief interventions, since few studies aimed exclusively at SFT exist.

In order to address this gap in the SFT research literature, Gingerich and Eisengart (2000) conducted a review of all of the controlled-outcome studies on SFT (i.e., those in which SFT was actually compared to a group not receiving counseling or receiving some alternative form of

---

SAMPLE RESEARCH: Solution-Focused Parenting Groups

Goals of the Research

Zimmerman, Jacobsen, Macintyre, and Watson (1996) investigated the benefits of a 6-week solution-focused parenting (SFP) group for parents who were having trouble with their adolescents. The authors of the study noted that most of the previous evidence for the effectiveness of SFT had been based on case studies or theoretical papers, not empirical research.

Participants

In order to conduct the study, Zimmerman et al. advertised in a local newspaper for parents who were currently undergoing difficulties with their adolescents' behavior. As parents responded to the advertisement, they were randomly placed in the control group, which received no treatment, or the SFP group, which received 6 weeks of half-hour sessions on solution-focused parenting. A total of 30 parents were placed in the experimental group and 12 parents in the control group.

Methods

In order to gauge the effectiveness of the intervention, all study participants completed two measures. The first measure was the Parenting Skills Inventory (PSI), an 86-item true/false questionnaire designed to measure parenting skills such as setting appropriate expectations, using communications skills, and establishing rapport. The second measure was the Family Strengths Assessment (FSA), a 12-item scale measuring what are theorized to be important components of family happiness, including love, religion, respect, communication, and individuality.

The SFP groups formed for the study consisted of six to eight parents each, met in a clinic on the campus at Colorado State University, and were led by graduate students working toward a degree in marriage and family therapy. The primary focus of each group was to instruct parents on the assumptions of SFP and have them apply these ideas to interactions with their adolescent. The topics covered in the groups included instruction in the inevitability of change, how to focus on their children's positive behaviors, and other aspects of SFT. After the 6-week SFP intervention was over, the PSI and the FSA were readministered to participants in both the control and the treatment conditions.

Results

The study authors performed two sets of statistical analyses: (1) comparing whether members in each group (experimental and control) improved on the measures from pre-test to post-test and (2) comparing whether, as hypothesized, members of the treatment group showed more improvement on these measures than those in the control group. With regard to whether members of the treatment group and the control group each improved on the two study measures from pre-test to post-test, it was found that the experimental group improved from pre-test to post-test on six of the nine subscales of the PSI, while the control group improved on only one of the subscales. The experimental group also scored significantly higher on the FSA at the end of the study, while the control group did not.

The authors next analyzed whether members of the treatment group improved more on the measures than members of the control group. It was found that the experimental group was significantly higher than the control group on five of the nine PSI scales at the end of the study, but there was not a statistically significant difference between the experimental and control groups on the FSA at the end of the study. In other words, the study authors found that members of the experimental group improved on the PSI compared both to their own pre-test scores and to the scores of the control group. However, while members of the treatment group improved on the FSA compared to their own pre-test scores, they did not show a statistically significant difference at post-test compared to the control group.

Implications of the Research

Zimmerman et al. concluded that their study provided empirical support for the application of SFT principles to parenting groups, at least insofar as members of the treatment group showed improvement on specific parenting skills measured by the PSI. The study authors were not surprised, given this finding, that members of the treatment group also reported a stronger sense of family strength, which was measured by the FSA. The authors were surprised that members of the treatment group did not show a significant difference on the FSA compared to the control group, and they speculated that members of the control group may have begun engaging in problem-solving discussions as a result of calling the researchers and agreeing to be in the study.

It should also be noted that the sample used in this study was relatively small and that many of the people who were assigned to be in the control condition dropped out of the study by not completing the study questionnaires during the follow-up. Another significant limitation of the study is that it did not use a no-treatment group—in other words, a third group of participants in which members got together to talk but did not receive the SFT treatment. This would have allowed the authors to make a stronger conclusion that the differences they found were due to the effects of SFT and not just to the benefits of meeting with other parents who shared similar concerns, for example.

counseling). They found a total of 15 studies, 5 of which were rated as being well controlled according to standards developed by the American Psychological Association's Task Force on Promotion and Dissemination of Psychological Procedures. All five of these studies showed positive outcomes for SFT: In four of the studies, SFT was found to be more effective for clients than no treatment or standard institutional services, and in one study, SFT was found to be comparable to a well-known intervention, interpersonal psychotherapy for depression. The remaining 10 studies reviewed by Gingerich and Eisengart, which were rated as moderately or poorly controlled studies, showed at least some evidence for the effectiveness of SFT. Overall, the authors concluded that this review of the literature provided preliminary support for SFT but was far from conclusive about its effectiveness. The sample study below is one of the five studies rated by Gingerich and Eisengart as well controlled (i.e., possessing more scientific rigor).

EVALUATION OF SOLUTION-FOCUSED THERAPY

Solution-focused therapy is the one of the most prominent brief counseling approaches practiced today, focusing on identifying client strengths and helping clients reach their own goals in the shortest amount of time possible. SFT represents a rather unique approach that is particularly useful to counselors who philosophically focus on human potential rather than psychopathology. Since many of the counseling models reviewed in this book emphasize human dysfunction to one degree or another, it can be refreshing to learn about an approach that views humans as capable and growth oriented.

Much of the appeal of SFT, in our view, also stems from the practical approach of its developers, Steve de Shazer and Kim Insook Berg, who focused mainly on "what works." While developing specific guidelines for the use of interventions such as the miracle question, SFT counselors are not dogmatic and stress that counselors must adapt their approach to what will work for each individual client and his particular goals. Thus, the approach has some particular advantages for working with clients from diverse backgrounds, as each intervention should be unique and tailored to the client.

In our experience teaching and supervising graduate students, the emphasis on practical techniques in SFT also increases its acceptance by practitioners. When learning about SFT, counseling students at first have a hard time focusing on client strengths and possibilities, since so much of their training is focused on client deficits and exploration of psychological histories. But once students become familiar with the approach, they tend to view the well-delineated techniques as useful and worthy of at least integrating with other approaches, even if they do not devote their practice entirely to SFT.

It is also worth pointing out one more time that SFT is in step with the times in its practical, time-limited approach to counseling. For better or worse, the days of unlimited counseling sessions are over. de Shazer (1991) reported that the average length of SFT is approximately five sessions, which is about the same as the averages for clients in other forms of counseling (Garfield, 1994). In other words, most counseling interventions are "brief" whether or not the counselor defines them as such, and it makes sense for the field of counseling to develop interventions with an emphasis on working toward clients' goals in the shortest amount of time possible.

The issues that stand out to us as the major limitations of the approach at this time are the lack of a theoretical framework for how humans change and the dearth of research as to the effectiveness of SFT. Doing what works is well and good, but we must first be able to show that what we are doing does, in fact, work. Additionally, for SFT to fulfill its promise of helping clients make changes in the shortest amount of time possible, it seems important to develop a theoretical framework for how this change occurs. Hopefully, in the near future, research will be forthcoming on the effectiveness of various SFT techniques, and when it does, a theoretical explanation for why certain techniques work or do not work will be necessary.

Finally, it seems clear to us that at least some clients seek out counseling to explain or understand their lives and to attach meaning to their experiences. Particularly in the case of clients who have suffered trauma or abuse, it may be important to talk about their experiences and the impact these have had on their lives. While SFT does not necessarily recommend against this type of exploration, it also does not offer much assistance or guidance for this process, either.

Questions and Learning Activities

These questions and activities are designed to stimulate your thinking about this theory and to help you apply some of the ideas to your own life and experience. If possible, you should work with another person or with a small group. Getting others' points of view and sharing your own ideas and perspectives will be invaluable as a way to help you evaluate this theory and its applications.

Personal Application Questions

1. A key assumption of SFT is that solutions are always possible and that clients have the resources and capacities to change their lives. Do you agree with this basic assumption about human beings? Can you think of certain situations where this might not be true?

2. Another key assumption of SFT is that small changes lead to larger changes—in other words, if you get the ball rolling in clients' lives, change will inevitably occur. Can you think of examples in your own life where this has been true? On the other hand, can you think of times when small changes were insufficient to effect larger changes?

3. SFT counselors assume that the counseling relationship is important but that it need not be extended for more than a few sessions. In your own experience, is it necessary for a relationship to be long-lasting for it to have a powerful impact on your life?

4. The practice of taking a break during the session, when the counselor leaves the room for a few minutes to think about the session and then returns with a compliment for the client, is a bit unorthodox. In your view, will clients find such activities to be helpful? If you are working with a client, will you feel comfortable doing this?

5. When using the miracle question, SFT counselors are attempting to help clients generate a positive vision for the future that they can build toward. Would you be confident that every client in counseling could come up with such a vision?

6. SFT counselors give their clients tasks, or homework activities, between sessions based on their goals. Do you think in general that it is more effective to generate such unique assignments following every counseling session, or would SFT counselors be better off giving their clients "time-tested" homework assignments that they have used before?
7. Language is a crucial part of SFT. Do you think that using "solution-focused" language is a key to being helpful? In your everyday life, do you tend to use solution- or problem-focused language?
8. What do you think of the idea of finding solutions without necessarily identifying problems?
9. How do you think you would react to SFT as a client? Would you feel cut off if the counselor wanted to move right into solutions?

Learning Activities

Miracle Question
In pairs, take turns describing a problem or situation that you are currently dealing with. Make sure that you select a situation that is not serious and you do not mind sharing with other people. Then, take turns asking the miracle question of each other, working until you have developed a positive vision or goal that you would like to work toward. Did you find the discussion helpful? Did it provide you with alternate ways of viewing your current concerns?

Scaling
Use scaling, as described earlier in this chapter, to evaluate the severity of a problem you are currently experiencing. Track this problem for several weeks and attempt to notice when the problem gets worse or better. What were the exceptions to the problem (i.e., times when it got better) and what were you doing at the time?

Uncovering Strengths
In a group of three to four people, take turns describing a situation that has caused you difficulty in the past few weeks. The other members of the group should then attempt to formulate a compliment that focuses on the strengths you used to cope with the problem. Did this activity uncover strengths you hadn't realized you were using?

Solution Language
Role-play the beginning of a counseling session using a solution-focused approach. Have one or two observers stop you whenever you use problem- rather than solution-focused language.

Personal Strengths
Make a list of your strengths and then share them with your small group. Explain how each strength has helped you grow and develop. After everyone has completed the activity, discuss what it felt like to complete this exercise.

Exceptions
Work with a partner who is willing to discuss a problem that seems insurmountable. Make sure that you select a situation that is not serious and you do not mind sharing with other people. As the counselor, practice looking for exceptions, even when the client seems to have given up hope for resolving the problem. You and your partner can take turns in the role of the counselor.

Companion Website

Now go to the Companion Website at www.prenhall.com/archer to assess your understanding of chapter content with multiple-choice and essay questions, and broaden your knowledge with related Web resources and additional print resources.

CHAPTER 13

Narrative Therapy

VOICES FROM THE FIELD: COUNSELOR AND CLIENT REACTIONS

Yes, it works for me

Client: I really liked the idea of writing a new story for my life. I certainly needed to get a new start. My counselor helped me see parts of my life history in a new light. And I was able to understand how much my story has been affected by what other people expected of me. I also like the way my counselor respects my opinion about things and asks me really helpful questions.

Counselor: I think that everyone has a unique story to tell about her life. People often don't see how strong they have been during their lives, and I think it really helps them to be able to rewrite their stories from different perspectives to acknowledge this. Helping people understand the ways in which they have been oppressed can also really open up new story lines for their life.

No, it doesn't work for me

Client: At first, I was really intrigued by the idea that I could develop a new story for myself. But while this approach works for me on an intellectual level, pretending that my situation is better than it is really doesn't help. I still get anxious at work, and I just can't help how I feel, no matter how differently I "write" my life story. I always felt charged up about changing my life after talking to my narrative therapist, but when I got back to my real life, I just felt stuck again. I think I need a more concrete approach.

Counselor: I can see using narrative therapy in some settings, but I think it won't work with many clients. The philosophy behind the approach is interesting, but my clients want concrete solutions to their problems. I cannot see trying to get some of them to simply "rewrite" their life stories when they have been victims of child abuse or neglect.

Shin was born in Korea and moved with his family to the United States when he was very young. He did very well academically in high school but decided to help his parents run the family dry cleaning business rather than attending college. Both he and his parents are very proud of their Korean heritage, and this decision was consistent with his parents' expectations that he contribute to the economic well-being of his family.

Eventually, Shin became dissatisfied, however, and got a job with a friend who does landscaping. He enjoys this work but feels conflicted about leaving his parents to run the business alone. A friend suggested he seek out a local narrative therapist.

> **Shin:** I am actually enjoying this landscaping work quite a bit—if I could only stop worrying about my parents.
> **Counselor:** So compared to the last 2 years working at your parents' dry cleaning place, this job really feels satisfying.

Shin: Yes, but I can't shake the feeling that I'm leaving something behind—namely, my parents and their expectations.

Counselor: Tell me more about that—I'm very interested in what you mean by leaving something behind.

Shin: Well, it's like I'm leaving behind the part of me that did what his parents expected, and never thought much about it.

Counselor: So in that story of your life, you pretty much stuck to your parents' expectations. And now it sounds like you are changing this story.

Shin: Yes, but I still feel pretty shaky about it. It's like my parents are always looking over my shoulder.

In narrative therapy, a client's life is seen as a story in progress, which can be authored according to many different viewpoints. Narrative therapists first attempt to understand the client's perspective on her life and the problems she confronts, which is sometimes termed the *dominant plot*. Change comes from "thickening the plot" by finding new subplots and alternative plots. This consists of helping the client consider new possibilities about her life and the way she relates to others. It also hopefully gives her a wider array of choices in dealing with the situations she brings to counseling.

In the scenario above, Shin is struggling with reauthoring the dominant plot of following his parents' expectations. At this early point in counseling, the narrative therapist is attempting to understand both the dominant plot Shin previously constructed ("I do what my parents expect") and a newer plot ("I also want to do what interests me"). The narrative therapist will help Shin examine several different alternate plots, perhaps including one such as "I can honor my parents while still choosing a career that will make me happy." Narrative therapists rely on their relationship with the client and the use of appropriately worded questions to bring out narratives and to help the client decide what alternative story lines she wishes to create for herself.

HISTORICAL BACKGROUND

Historical Context

Once upon a time everything was understood through stories—examples include Aesop's fables, Shakespearean literature, and the many stories found in the Bible, Torah, Koran, and other holy books (Parry & Doan, 1994). This way of knowing was increasingly overshadowed in the previous century with the rise of the scientific method in Western cultures, which is often equated with modernity and the development of industrial societies. Modernity emphasizes that the truth is not passed on through stories or fables but must be sought through impartial analysis of objective facts. While credited with most of the technological developments of the twentieth century, many scholars, philosophers, artists, and concerned citizens increasingly became convinced over the past few decades that "scientific" methods of understanding are not the only, or even the best, route to obtaining knowledge and understanding.

Foremost among the critiques of empiricism is the idea that seekers of truth can never be separate from, or objective about, that which they study (Weingarten, 1998). Consider this African proverb: "Until the lions have their own historians, tales of hunting will always glorify the hunter." The scientists who frame and conduct empirical research reflect the biases and assumptions of their own culture as much as their "subjects," and a failure to recognize this means that many of society's prejudices and inequities can be perpetuated under the guise of science.

Narrative therapy, as well as the solution-focused approach discussed in the preceding chapter, was strongly emphasized by the philosophical movement known as postmodernism. Doan (1997) noted that a similar philosophical approach, social constructionism, is closely related to postmodernism and is concerned with how ideas and attitudes have developed over time within a social, community context. Both approaches offered not just an alternative to the modern tradition of empiricism but also a powerful critique of its impact on human welfare.

One philosopher who had a strong influence on the ideas that informed narrative therapy was Foucault (1965), a French intellectual who studied the various ways in which societies classify people as "normal" or "abnormal." According to Foucault, those in authority control the discourse of its citizenry. Foucault therefore believed that knowledge and power are intertwined. Similar to the existentialists introduced in chapter 5, such as Thomas Szasz, Foucault believed politicians, doctors, lawyers, and other members of the professional class can determine who has a say in the direction of a society by labeling, and thus determining, what is healthy or unhealthy, who are criminals or upstanding citizens, and that constitutes sane or insane behavior. These labels also determine who gets a say in the affairs of society and who does not. Felons, for example, are not allowed to vote in many elections in the United States, and those labeled "insane" may not have the legal right to make decisions about their own welfare.

Gergen (1992) was another important influence on the philosophical foundation of narrative therapy, and he also saw danger associated with the assumption that only an objective analysis by experts can ascertain the truth. The notion that there is an objective viewpoint from which to observe the nature of truth and reality, he believed, leads to an overreliance on generalized rules and principles about human activity that ignore specific, localized meanings that people attach to their everyday experiences. In other words, we can come to place more faith in very general, simplified, and abstract notions about how the world works at the expense of our everyday experience of what we know to be true and meaningful in our own corners of the world. Postmodernists would rather we acknowledge our biases, selective memories, and need to impose meaning on our experiences than attempt to create a myth that there is an objective truth "out there" waiting to be discovered.

Narrative therapists therefore operate from a philosophical assumption that no one person has a better vantage point for seeing the "truth" than anyone else. Clients' stories, or narratives, about their experiences, problems, and concerns are ultimately more important than determining whether objective facts support their beliefs. In order to effect change, clients must be able to see things from a variety of perspectives and author an alternate narrative about their lives and their futures. Narrative therapists are careful to avoid being the "expert" in the helping process. While clients may attempt to place the counselor in this role, narrative therapists are unwilling to reduce their clients to being the passive recipients of the judgments of experts. According to this approach, subjecting ourselves to experts can strip us of our potential to construe meaning based on our own unique vantage point on our lives and the world around us.

Development of the Theory

Narrative therapy is based on the work of Michael White, codirector of the Dulwich Center in Adelaide, South Australia, and David Epston, codirector of the Family Therapy Center in Auckland, New Zealand. Their book *Narrative Means to Therapeutic Ends* (White & Epston, 1990) was a landmark publication and drew on sources such as family therapy, postmodern philosophy, social psychology, feminist theory, and literary theory (White, 1995). Simply put, they sought to develop an approach to therapy that recognized that each person's life is a story in progress, which can be viewed from a variety of perspectives and can have any number of outcomes.

Many of the pioneers of narrative therapy started in the 1970s and 1980s as family therapists (Swan, 1998). In its beginnings, family therapy shifted the focus of counseling from *intra*psychic factors and historical causes of problems found in individual counseling to the *inter*personal factors and current behaviors of family members (Kelley, 1998). However, a number of its practitioners, including Michael White and David Epston, found prevailing approaches to family therapy to be too mechanistic by presupposing that therapists are separate from, and able to control, families (Freedman & Combs, 1996). In other words, while traditional family therapies shifted attention to interpersonal processes and current behaviors, families were still treated as "machinery" that could be fixed by an outside expert. There was little recognition that the observer and the observed affect one another.

Developing narrative therapy using a postmodern foundation meant that its practitioners viewed clients' stories as the mechanism through which the clients communicated their lives and future possibilities to a therapist who is just as influenced by the process as the clients are. Further, because narratives are crafted from only one possible interpretation of events, based on a very selective editing of these experiences, narrative counselors see their task as helping clients construct new narratives based on possibilities for future change and growth. The research evidence for the effectiveness of narrative therapy is scarce at this point, but in recent years, numerous books and articles developing the approach have appeared. There are indications that narrative therapy will continue to develop and establish itself among the major approaches to counseling.

ASSUMPTIONS AND CORE CONCEPTS

View of Human Nature

Narrative therapy offers an essentially optimistic view of human nature based on the idea that we have the ability to construct meaning in our lives and to reauthor the meaning we attach to our experiences. Doan (1997) did note some "realities" that come with the postmodern philosophy that there is no objective reality. On the plus side, the ability to create one's own life narrative offers freedom and flexibility in facing life and challenges the undisputed authority of experts. However, just as existentialists noted that embracing the finite nature of life could lead to hopelessness and despair, fully embracing a social constructionist philosophy can lead to a psychological free fall, once the comfortable, socially accepted pillars of modern life are removed (Doan, 1997). It means that we are responsible collectively for everything we know to be true about the world—we cannot accept anything as a given and have to accept ownership of the realities we create.

Bruner (2004) made a similar point in noting that in narrative approaches to counseling, there is no such thing as a "fixed" sense of one's personhood, waiting to be discovered. According to Bruner, "[W]e constantly construct and reconstruct our selves to meet the needs of the situations we encounter, and we do so with the guidance of our memories of the past and our hopes and fears for the future" (p. 4). Narrative therapists note that the self must always be understood in the context of the larger society and that this is important to pay attention to in the process of counseling. Some of society's narratives—for example, about the role of men and women in relationships—can be recreated in therapy, and there exists the possibility that repressive aspects of these narratives will be reenacted between the client and the counselor. For example, a male therapist might have "bought into" the narrative that females are less able than males to take control of their lives or function independently. In counseling relationships with women, this therapist could subtly convey the attitude that women need to be taken care of in the interventions he uses with women.

On a more optimistic note, however, narrative therapists are careful to separate people from the problems they encounter (Epstein, 1994). In other words, we are not defined by our careers, our relationships, or our psychological difficulties; these are outside of us and always subject to interpretation. As Monk (1997) wrote, the person is not the problem—the problem is the problem. No matter what obstacles and difficulties one is encountering, it always possible to separate oneself from current circumstances and reauthor a new narrative that allows for more possibilities and creative attempts to cope with life.

Core Concepts

Two aspects of the term *narrative* are important to understanding this counseling approach (Payne, 2000). First, a dictionary definition of the word *narrative* refers to an account of an event, such as might be constructed in a story or newspaper article, in which a selected sequence of events is recounted and brought into existence through the act of being told. In therapy, therefore, a person might tell a therapist a narrative of her life circumstances and problems, filled with her own remembrances of events and people that have shaped her life history.

While clients are encouraged to tell their stories in therapy, it is the second, philosophical sense of the word *narrative* that is most important to understanding how White and Epston (1990) viewed narrative therapy. They believed that the narratives we construct about ourselves and our worlds are highly selective, influenced by a range of social factors, and in fact, they shape the realities of our lives. This narration exists not only in our interactions with other people but also in our inner lives, as we constantly revisit our experiences psychologically and "re-edit" our life stories (Payne, 2000). Our narratives not only occur in the present but also are projected into the future as we anticipate how our life story will unfold. For example, a person with a history of academic achievement might construct a future narrative of herself as a noted scientist or teacher, while an individual who views herself as making poor choices in romantic relationships might envision a future of loneliness and isolation. We tend to act based on whatever narratives we have constructed and therefore create our own realities. A person who views herself as a strong student may be more likely to study hard for an exam or seek out a teacher after school, while a self-described "romantic failure" may be more likely to settle for dating partners with little to offer.

Two sets of concepts will be introduced next that are important to understanding narrative therapy. First are the philosophical assumptions of postmodern philosophy, and second are several key concepts about the practice of narrative therapy.

Philosophical Assumptions The basic philosophical assumptions of narrative therapy were summarized by Freedman and Combs (1996) in their book *Narrative Therapy: The Social Construction of Preferred Realities*. They noted that understanding the postmodern, narrative, social constructionist worldview is more important to the practice of narrative therapy than any specific technique. This attitude toward and outlook on the search for meaning and truth are essential to utilizing this approach. Freedman and Combs noted four ideas that are essential in this regard.

REALITIES ARE SOCIALLY CONSTRUCTED A central tenet of the postmodern worldview is that all of the things that make up the psychological fabric of reality arise through social interactions over time. Our beliefs, customs, laws, manner of dress, and food choices arise because of social constructions over time. In an everyday sense, it may seem self-evident to people living in a culture that one should eat in a certain way (i.e., sit down at a table with others), organize work in a particular manner (for example, everyone shows up at 9 A.M. and leaves at 5 P.M.), and interact with those around us in certain established patterns (for example, with greetings such as "How are you doing?"). However, the emergence of such patterns of behavior is the result of an ongoing and extremely complicated process of social interactions. Over time, certain patterns become established in a culture through necessity or custom and then are institutionalized in the form of religious practices, government laws, regional customs, and the like.

REALITIES ARE CONSTITUTED THROUGH LANGUAGE Freedman and Combs noted that in the modernist worldview, language corresponds in a one-to-one way with the external world: There is a clear distinction between the external objective world and our internal, subjective experiences. Modernists view language as a way to link the two: In our language, we can accurately represent external realities so that our internal experience of them accurately mirrors what is happening in the outside world. For example, on the nightly television news broadcasts, a reporter uses language to describe events that occur in a community (for example, a building fire or crime wave) to a television audience, which is then presumed to have an accurate, internal understanding of what is "really" happening in the outside world.

Postmodernists view the function of language differently: They focus on how language is used to constitute our world and beliefs. Accordingly, language is not seen as neutral or passive but is viewed as bringing forth a reality in collaboration with others. Gergen (1992) contended that knowledge is not something people possess in their heads but rather something they do in collaboration with other people. Such things as race, sexual identity, and freedom are legitimized as concepts once they become an established part of the dialogue among a group of people. We can share a consensus as to what reality is, but this understanding is constantly developing and shifting over time as new voices, practices, and people are brought into the dialogue. The television broadcaster who reports on a fire is not a neutral conduit of information but is actively choosing what events will be reported on and how they will be described.

The emphasis on language in the construction of reality is an important component of the practice of narrative therapy. Through their dialogue, counselors and clients are viewed as constantly negotiating new meanings for problematic beliefs, feelings, and behaviors (Freedman & Combs, 1996). In doing so, therapists attempt to offer their clients new possibilities for construing their lives and choosing future courses of action.

REALITIES ARE ORGANIZED AND MAINTAINED THROUGH STORIES Constructionists maintain that language is the mechanism by which truth is constructed and that stories, or narratives, maintain these truths over time. Through all of the dialogue, discussion, and interaction that members of a society have, only certain "truths" are enshrined in stories and thus maintained through time. For example, in the United States one dominant narrative that might be introduced to children very early in school is that Christopher Columbus traveled from Spain to "discover" America. Another is that the first president, George Washington, could not tell his father a lie about chopping down a cherry tree. Each of these stories is a rather simple skeleton around which to hang larger societal beliefs and customs—in this case that the United States was founded by brave European explorers and that presidents (particularly the first) should be seen as basically trustworthy and honest. Over time, of course, students learn that there is much more to such stories, but it could be argued that the original narratives do not change fundamentally. We may still want to view our country as founded by brave people searching for freedom and our leaders as honest and trustworthy. This chapter could be considered a narrative about narrative therapy—we have attempted to distill a considerable amount of information into a concise "story" about how this therapy works.

It is important to note that all stories leave out far more information that they include. Freedman and Combs noted that "in any life there are always more events that don't get 'storied' than there are ones that do—even the longest and most complex autobiography leaves out more than it includes" (p. 32). In narrative therapy, then, counselors are intensely interested in how clients have selected certain elements of their lives to construct a narrative. They focus on individuals with "stories that have gone awry or outlived their usefulness" (Doan, 1997, p. 131). If a client wants to construct a different narrative for her life, it is inevitable that she will have considerable material to re-edit into her narrative that had previously been excluded. For example, a client who considers herself a failure in her career may have many examples of successes in previous jobs or careers, successes that she had previously chosen to ignore but that could be included in a new narrative.

THERE ARE NO ESSENTIAL TRUTHS. Freedman and Combs pointed out that in the narrative/social constructionist worldview, we cannot know reality, only interpret experience. They urged narrative counselors to think more like novelists and less like "technocrats." Every client's life can be told from many different perspectives: While no self is truer than any other, particular people within particular cultures may have very definite ideas about preferred selves. The work of narrative therapy is to help bring forth various experiences of the client's self, determine which are preferred in different contexts, and then support the growth and development of these new narratives.

Key Concepts While the above assumptions are important to understanding postmodern philosophy, McKenzie and Monk (1997) described several other concepts that are essential to understanding narrative therapy as it is actually practiced.

DISCOURSE This refers to a cluster of ideas produced within the wider culture and communicated through a variety of media, including children's stories, books, songs, television programs, and movies. While the discourse on topics such as sexuality, sex roles, civic duty, and education, for example, can be undertaken from a variety of perspectives, societies often coalesce around a favored or accepted view on such matters, which is referred to by postmodernists as a *dominant discourse*. For example, a dominant discourse about females throughout most of the twentieth century is that they should be concerned with keeping their man happy and taking care of the household. While this dominant discourse has been challenged over the past several decades, its effects can still be seen in the unequal levels of pay for women and in the workplace and the lack of women in charge of Fortune 500 companies.

Once established, a dominant discourse in society or a dominant plot authored by an individual can be very powerful. A clear example occurs in political advertising, where competing candidates use television commercials and speaking appearances to cast their opponents in a certain light. Once established, narratives such as "tax-and-spend liberal" and "heartless conservative" tend to be powerful and difficult to argue against, no matter what facts are presented.

While a dominant discourse refers to a taken-for-granted assumption about an event or circumstance, *alternative discourses* and stories are present in every situation. No matter how strong the dominant discourse in a society on a given topic, there are always those who see the situation differently. Most people living in the United States see the progress of technology as positive, for example, although there are many who choose lives of voluntary simplicity. This underscores the fact that we are always picking and choosing which facts we incorporate into our narratives and which we exclude.

DOMINANT PLOTS AND COUNTERPLOTS   Just as a society can construct a dominant discourse around a given topic, a client can develop a highly particular narrative about her own life that is sometimes referred to by the narrative therapist as a dominant plot. The dominant plot is the story the client tells about her life in which she takes a certain perspective on events and projects how events will turn out in the future. The plot that the client brings to counseling often revolves around problems in her life and involves limited possibilities for success in the future. However, just as alternative discourses can be established in groups and communities, the counselor and the client working together can develop a "counterplot" based on a different interpretation of the details of a client's life and her future possibilities for coping.

DECONSTRUCTION   During the process of deconstruction, the taken-for-granted assumptions that are made about an event or circumstance are systematically "re-examined in detail" (Payne, 2000). As was noted previously, once established, a dominant discourse or dominant plot tends to take on a life of its own and is often not even questioned. In counseling, therefore, a primary task of counselors is to help clients deconstruct narratives and plots that have caused them difficulty. Clients are then encouraged to develop alternative stories about their lives that will allow for creative resolutions to their problems. We describe how this happens in the following sections.

THERAPEUTIC RELATIONSHIP

Counselor's Role

Biever and McKenzie (1995) noted that the primary task of narrative therapists is to become skilled at facilitating therapeutic conversations. Narrative therapists must first embrace a postmodern, constructionist worldview and accept that ultimate truth is found not "out there" in the world but rather in the realities we create. Narrative therapists must be fully cognizant of the fact that realities are constructed in the dialogue between the counselor and the client as well.

Biever and McKenzie (1995) suggested a number of ways in which narrative therapists can facilitate this dialogue. First, they cited Andersen's (1991) contention that the therapist should assume a "not knowing stance" by not assuming she knows what is best for the client—the client is the expert on this. Another phrase used in this regard is that the therapist should be "slow to know." Each of these ideas conveys the importance of a counselor not assuming the expert role with respect to a client's life. In order to demonstrate this idea, we will return to the case of Shin, the individual introduced at the beginning of this chapter who had recently started a new job in landscaping. Near the beginning of their first session, the counselor is assuming a "not knowing" position while attempting to explore Shin's current experiences.

See DVD

Chap. 13
Clip 1

Shin: Like I said, this job has been going much better—it feels very rewarding.
Counselor: Rewarding. What do you mean by that?
Shin: Well . . . I look forward to each day, and I like the people I work with.
Counselor: What's it like, looking forward to each day?
Shin: It's great. I really like having people around who are friendly.
Counselor: Friendly people do make a job much better. What is it about having these people around that feels so good?

You can see here how the narrative counselor is very inquisitive, always looking for new information and meanings. These new "stories" and "subplots" can be used to infer possibilities about what is happening in a client's life, but it is up to the client to determine exactly what her own stories mean for her.

In listening to Shin's story, the counselor will be open to Shin's description of what seems to be working for him now and how this is different from the frustrations he experienced in the past. However, the counselor will avoid drawing any firm conclusions about how events will turn out in the future—for example, by assuming that Shin can only succeed in this new career or that because he has established these friendships, he will never encounter difficulties again. Because Shin comes from a Korean family, it is also important to consider how cultural narratives are affecting his experience. How do his parents feel about his career choice? What are their expectations for his level of involvement in the family business if they are unable to continue to work there? How does Shin's view of himself as a Korean American influence the career choices he has made or the type of social relationships he has developed? These are but a few of the considerations the counselor might entertain in working with Shin.

Such human diversity considerations lead to a second important attribute of the therapist's role, according to Biever and McKenzie (1995): Counselors must be open to, and help generate, alternatives. They noted Andersen's (1991) assertion that two questions must be kept in mind: (1) "How else can a situation be described?" and (2) "How else can this situation be explained?" In other words, even when a client presents a compelling rationale for the events in her life, the counselor does not assume this is the only possible way of looking at the situation or explaining what is happening. A given narrative is always a selective editing of the facts, and alternative viewpoints are always possible and likely to be just as valid.

In Shin's case, he seems to be connecting his work happiness with his increased access to social support. However, it is likely that in further dialogue other factors contributing to his success at work may become apparent—perhaps he feels a sense of freedom in charting his own course, and he simply is more suited to landscaping work than dry cleaning work, for example. However, in future dialogue, Shin may want to further explore his relationship with his parents, their cultural framework, and how such influences have shaped his current experiences. Such possibilities do not undermine the narrative that Shin has constructed but would be important for a counselor to keep in mind as they continue to work together.

Biever and McKenzie (1995) noted that a third function of the counselor is to help a client think of "both/and" rather than "either/or." As was suggested earlier, the client may tend to favor only one way of viewing problem or situation as a part of narrative, and thus can restrict choices and limit possibilities. A student may see herself as either failing or succeeding in school or as being popular or unpopular. However, the narrative therapist sees many shades of gray in the world, and part of her role is to continually underscore the notions that coming up with creative resolutions to problems is always possible and that no particular path is always better than another in doing so.

Fourth, narrative therapists share a belief with other theorists introduced in this book, such as person-centered and solution-focused therapists, that clients have strengths and resources. The dominant narratives that clients bring to counseling may be constructed around themes of helplessness and ineptitude, but narrative therapists will always look for evidence of strengths and abilities in their clients.

Finally, narrative therapy requires that a counselor be open to her own biases, values, and beliefs. These are powerful influences on the way we construct our realities, and it would be impossible for counselors to help clients understand their own life stories without acknowledging that counselors construct their own realities as well. This, of course, does not mean that counselors seek to impose their own values on clients, but it does underscore that both counselors and clients are involved in the construction of new narratives.

Counselor-Client Relationship

The relationship between counselor and client in narrative therapy is based on shared authority for shaping and directing the nature of the counseling relationship (Winslade, Crocket, & Monk, 1997). In fact, Winslade et al. suggested that the client should be viewed as a senior partner in the relationship, checking in with and bouncing ideas off the counselor. However, there are no hard and fast rules for how this is done: Every relationship is treated as unique in narrative therapy, and no attempt is made to categorize or describe what is to be expected as the relationship unfolds.

Narrative therapists reject the notion that the counselor is an expert or authority, and therefore every opportunity is given to the client to determine the exact nature of the dialogue that must take place in order to tell her story and uncover the alternative perspectives necessary for establishing useful counterplots. Narrative therapists use the term *coauthoring* to describe how this happens (Winslade et al., 1997). This term implies a shared responsibility for the conversation that needs to happen in narrative therapy. The counselor should not assume the role of expert, but should also not be overly cautious about injecting her ideas and impressions into the dialogue with a client. As Winslade et al. noted, "[T]o co-author a conversation, counselor and client will achieve shared meanings and coordinate their relationship according to their mutual meaning-making" (p. 55).

Both counselor and client are viewed as vibrant, living beings who are operating in a social context and struggling to understand each other and the world around them. What comes out of this relationship will be highly unique and particular to the dialogue they establish, and it is ultimately up to the client to determine what meaning this relationship has for the story she is seeking to author about her life.

ASSESSMENT, GOALS, AND PROCESS OF THERAPY

Assessment

At this point, it will probably not surprise you to learn that narrative therapists are unlikely to be caught pulling out a copy of the *Diagnostic and Statistical Manual of Mental Disorders (DSM)* or attempting to conduct formal assessments of their clients' presenting difficulties. Tools such as the *DSM* and formal assessment inventories are seen as part of the modernist paradigm of problem diagnosis and treatment, which is at odds with the constructionist approach of narrative therapy. Narrative therapists do not reject the importance of assessment with clients; however, they differ in how this should be accomplished.

First, White and Epston (1990) noted that at the outset of counseling it is important to understand the client's original construction of the problem she has brought to counseling. The client is encouraged to explain in her own words her understanding of the situation, the people involved in it, and the impact it has had on her life. The narrative therapist is also concerned with what this construction of events holds for the client: In other words, what will happen in the future if this story line continues?

Another important component of assessment in narrative therapy is to separate the description of the problem from the person telling the story (Monk, 1997). As we noted in the "View of Human Nature" section of this chapter, the narrative therapist is careful to separate the person from the situations she describes. Even psychological problems such as depression and anxiety are viewed not as innate characteristics of the person but as part of the context in which a person's story about her life is written. Therefore, at the outset of the relationship, the narrative therapist uses a certain type of dialogue, called *externalizing language*, to reinforce the notion that the person is not the problem. We will describe externalizing language in more detail in the "Therapeutic Techniques" section of this chapter.

Finally, the narrative therapist encourages the client to talk about her family history, cultural experiences, and other details from past experiences that might have informed the stories she has brought to counseling. As we have noted, the context in which people shape their realities must be understood if new narratives are to be constructed; therefore, it is essential that the counselor explore this part of the client's life.

Goals

White and Epston (1990) provided a rather elegant description of the goals of narrative therapy: (1) Clients are asked to describe the problems they have brought to counseling (i.e., dominant plots), (2) they are encouraged to embrace alternate perspectives through deconstruction of their narratives, and (3) they are then helped to create new narratives (i.e., counterplots) that will be more useful and satisfying to them. Throughout counseling, the client is in charge of deciding which details about her life hold significance for her current problems and determining which counterplot will be embraced as offering up creative possibilities for the future.

Thus, the goals of narrative therapy are dictated by the client. These goals are not unlike the goals clients have in other forms of therapy: For example, the client might want to feel less anxious, to have better relationships, or to have more self-confidence. Such goals would be respected by the therapist and be seen as part of the ongoing narrative of that person's life. The assumption being made is that the client can re-author her life to achieve these goals. Of course, the actual practice of counseling using this approach has much more nuance and complexity than this broad generalization suggests, and we now turn to a description of the process of counseling in narrative therapy.

Process of Therapy

White and Epston's (1990) three goals of narrative therapy give some structure to the process of this approach, but since narrative therapy is based on postmodern philosophy, the process cannot be formulaic or prescriptive. As we have noted earlier in this chapter, narrative therapy begins with the counselor's embrace of social constructionist principles, not a set of techniques or a formula for its practice (Weingarten, 1998). However, most of the major theorists in narrative therapy do acknowledge that the process of counseling unfolds in the following manner.

Describing the Problem   At the outset, the narrative therapist encourages the client to describe the concerns that have brought her to counseling. In doing so, the counselor must display what McKenzie and Monk (1997) described as a persistent and genuine curiosity about the client's life, while at the same time realizing that any life story will necessarily be incomplete and told from a certain perspective—that is, the client will be presenting a narrative, not a complete description of all the facts. Payne (2000) noted that no autobiography is ever complete and described an activity he used to train counselors in this idea. In workshops, Payne asked counselors to spend 10 minutes writing their own autobiographies, which inevitably led to complaints that 10 minutes is simply not enough time to complete such a task. Payne used this opportunity to ask the participants how much time would be sufficient: One hour? One day? One week? The point here is that we could never possibly describe all of the events and details that make up our lives—to do so would consume much of the rest of our lives.

Former President Bill Clinton spent months writing his autobiography, *My Life*, which in hardcover was over 1,000 pages, and he doubtless left out many, many details. If you find humorous examples of what former President Clinton might have left out of his autobiography popping into your mind, consider whether those are part of the dominant discourse that was constructed about Clinton's presidency. The point here is that no such life story can ever be completely described, and what the counselor is looking for is a sense of the narrative a client has constructed, not a complete accounting of everything that has happened.

Oftentimes a client will spend considerable time during the initial counseling session describing what brought her to counseling—something McKenzie and Monk (1997) labeled the client's "preferred story." Some narrative therapists also refer to this as the dominant plot. The client may exhibit considerable energy in telling this "story," but the therapist expects that at some point in the session there will be a pause or break in the action after she has gotten it "off her chest."

It is at this point in the session that a narrative counselor will swing into action with a range of questions designed to encourage a more complete account of the problem and a discussion of the whole range of effects that the problem has on the person (McKenzie & Monk, 1997). Payne (2000) noted that the purpose here is not to make the client feel diagnosed or interrogated but rather to make her feel understood and cared about. Questions are designed to gain a fuller understanding of the manifestations of the problem and also to ascertain its limits—in other words, to reveal that the problem is finite in nature and does not necessarily touch every part of a client's life all the time. The client's acknowledging that the problem is not all-encompassing, and that other ways of looking at the problem are possible, opens up the door for the construction of alternative narratives, or counterplots, later in counseling.

We will provide more details about the types of questions used by narrative therapists in the "Therapeutic Techniques" section of this chapter, but we present the following example to give a more complete picture of how a counselor might use questions to gain a better understanding of the problems a client perceives in her life. Kevin is a 66-year-old man who has recently retired. He has fantasized about retiring for years but now feels depressed and unsettled. He is having conflicts with his wife, who tells him to get out of the house more and do something productive.

> **Kevin:** Like I told you, I just don't know what to do with myself.
> **Counselor:** What do you mean, do with yourself?
> **Kevin:** I don't know . . . I just sit around the house all day. I guess I miss seeing all the people I used to work with and having some structure to my life.
> **Counselor:** Can you tell me more about what you got out of work that you aren't getting now?
> **Kevin:** Well, I felt like I was doing something useful. I've just about fixed everything that can be fixed around the house. What now?
> **Counselor:** And you said earlier you had a picture of what retirement would be like?

The questions that a narrative therapist uses, shown in this example, are not all that different from those used in other counseling approaches. The counselor is attempting to understand the scope of Kevin's worries and the impact they are having on his life. As we can see from this example, there may be many different subplots to this story—for example, his feelings of uselessness and lack of structure and his wife's attitudes and feelings. The narrative therapist, in her questioning, is careful not just to attend to the details of a situation but also to understand the context as fully as possible. Included in this context are human diversity factors, which can impact a client's understanding of her life and her world. In this case, the context is related to Kevin's age and stage in life. The narrative therapist will try to get as much information as possible regarding these contextual issues.

We can also see from this example that the problem does not touch every aspect of his life. For example, it sounds as if Kevin had devoted himself for awhile to fixing up his house, which may have been a source of satisfaction. This sets the stage for something else that must happen at the outset of counseling: naming the problem and evaluating its effect on the client. When the client describes the problem that brought her to counseling and the counselor uses questions to uncover the impact, extent, and limits of the problem, what they are doing is *naming the problem* (White & Epston, 1990). In other words, the counselor encourages the client to identify the problem in order to have more control over it.

White and Epston (1990) believed that clients begin counseling using *problem-saturated language*; that is, they describe problems as intractable and interwoven with their lives. As the process of counseling progresses, narrative therapists attempt to *externalize* the problem by (1) freeing clients from problem-saturated descriptions of their lives, (2) encouraging more rewarding narratives, and (3) assisting clients in developing a new relationship with the problem. We will discuss techniques for doing this in the next section of this chapter, but at this point, it is important to note that as the client talks, the counselor looks for further descriptions of the problem that reinforce the idea that the problem is "out there" and is not intrinsic to the client.

Giving the problem a name or label is also useful in this regard, since it reinforces the notion that the problem is separate from the person. For example, a narrative therapist would not want to label a client a "procrastinator" but could acknowledge the person has a "procrastination problem." The client can also be encouraged to think about metaphors that represent her problems. A person who describes herself as anxious around other people might be encouraged to describe the "walls" that separate her from other people (Legowski & Brownlee, 2001).

At this point, we think it is important to note that the emphasis on externalizing problems in narrative therapy is a philosophical departure from counseling theories that situate responsibility for problems with the clients. For example, Freud thought clients needed insight into their own psychic conflict and seemed to place the blame for problems squarely on the clients' shoulders. Other theories, including Rogers's person-centered approach, also seem to suggest that clients should start by looking inward to resolve their problems. The narrative therapist begins by placing the problem outside the client. This is not to suggest that narrative therapists want to blame others for clients' problems or give this responsibility to other people—on the contrary, they think that by separating people from their problems, clients will be better able to take responsibility for constructing narratives that will lead to problem resolution.

As a client tells her story to a counselor, usually using problem-saturated language, the counselor explores the problem with the client, using appropriate questions, with the aim of placing the problem outside the client. The counselor is also alert to the details of the client's life that can form the basis of new narratives (Payne, 2000), such as unique events in the client's life when the problems she is describing did not have an adverse impact. This sets the stage for the next element of the process of narrative therapy, encouraging a wider perspective.

Encouraging a Wider Perspective Payne (2000) noted that at the heart of narrative therapy is the assumption that clients' lives incorporate many potential stories waiting to be told. Freedman and Combs (1996) noted that there are always more events that don't get included in client stories than those that do; therefore, there are always opportunities to look for alternative subplots in the narratives clients have constructed.

Once a client has told her initial story in counseling, full of problem-saturated talk, the process of counseling then turns to "re-storying" her life. The focus moves from exploring the impact of problems on the client's life to finding new subplots based on times when the problem did not occur or did not have the same impact on the client's life. This is done by identifying unique events outside the narrative during which the problem was not as severe or did not even adversely affect the client (McKenzie & Monk, 1997). Payne (2000) described this as looking for clues in the client's life that might suggest exceptions to her problems, which, if confirmed, could be thought of as "unique outcomes" useful in constructing new narratives.

Freedman and Combs (1996) noted that therapists uncover these unique outcomes by using deconstructive listening "to open spaces for aspects of people's life narratives that haven't yet been storied" (p. 46). Earlier in this chapter, it was suggested that deconstruction is the process of disassembling the taken-for-granted assumptions that are made about a circumstance or event, thus exposing discourses and revealing people's positions within them (McKenzie & Monk, 1997). As part of this process, it must be acknowledged that our identities have been constructed in a socio-cultural environment and that therapists must be mindful of how discourses associated with ethnicity, gender, and sexual orientation, for example, can impact clients. Clients' original narratives are not to be invalidated; rather, they are to be supplemented. In the following example, using the case of Kevin again, the narrative counselor attempts to look for exceptions to Kevin's initial narrative about how difficult his retirement seems to be.

> **Kevin:** It just seems like this whole retirement thing is not working out.
> **Counselor:** Have you been able to do anything in retirement that you feel good about?
> **Kevin:** Well . . . we have gotten to travel some, and like I said, I've worked around the house. But now when I'm at home, I get depressed and bored.
> **Counselor:** What is it about traveling that gives you so much pleasure?
> **Kevin:** I'm a real history buff. I love to see historic places.

Kevin's comment that he is a real history buff may open up some new options and creative solutions that can be constructed by the client and the therapist. For example, he might consider taking a history course or volunteering to work in a museum. However, any concrete plans such as these would be left up to the client: The counselor's main job is to help the client open up alternate stories of her life in order to give her more possibilities for creative living.

Forming New Narratives Typically, the dominant plot that a client brings to counseling focuses on her problems, has limited options, and has a predictably negative ending. As new subplots are explored between the counselor and the client, new narratives can be constructed that allow for new possibilities and creative solutions to problems. The process of narrative therapy continues until the client is satisfied with the new stories, or counterplots, that have been created. In the following section, we turn to some of the techniques used to accomplish these ends. But first, we use Doan's (1997) summary of narrative therapy assumptions, and the practices they inform, as a way of transitioning from the process of narrative counseling to the techniques used in this approach. See Figure 13.1.

Figure 13.1 Narrative Assumptions and the Therapeutic Practices They Inform

Assumption	Therapy Implications
1. People live their lives by the stories they tell themselves or allow others to tell them. Stories are constructed of events as well as the application of meaning to events.	The therapist is interested in liberating the client's voice and perceptions and in understanding how individuals were recruited into their current stories and meanings.
2. The stories that people tell themselves are not representations of the world; they are the world. The map is the territory.	It is the client's voice, not the therapist's, that informs and constructs his or her world. Therapy seeks to liberate alternative voices from the client rather than from the therapist.
3. The narratives we tell ourselves are not neutral in their effects. Neither are their effects imagined. Stories have formative and creative effects, and some stories are more useful than others. All accounts are not created equal.	Therapists challenge and critique stories, but not from a knowing stance. Rather, curiosity guides the therapist in a collaborative exploration of story lines, authors, and meanings. Together they search for the story that would match the preferred intentions of the client.
4. Most clients are unwittingly cooperating with a singular account, one that leaves little optionality or choice. They are being lived by a story rather than being the author of multiple accounts.	Therapists seek to provide space for alternate accounts from clients. Therapy is a comparison of at least two stories (problem story versus preferred story). Choice creates options.
5. Stories are negotiated between people and the institutions of their culture. Most accounts are the result of an interaction between individuals and their families and their cultures; that is, stories are socially constructed and informed.	The therapist actively explores the familial and cultural history/herstory of clients. Authors other than the client are identified and held up for inspection. Past events may not be changeable, but it is possible to alter the meaning attached to events. (For example, "I'm bad versus Bad things were done to me.")
6. It is useful to speak of problems as problems rather than of people as problems. This reframes the socially constructed story concerning labeling and locating problems inside of persons.	Therapists engage in externalizing dialogues with clients rather than internalizing ones. People are far more than the problems that visit them on occasion. Problems are objectified rather than people. The therapy allows the client to analyze the problem separately from his or her identity.

(Reproduced with permission from R.A. Doan, Narrative Therapy, Postmodernism, Social Constructivism, and Constructivism: Discussion and Distinctions, *Transactional Analysis Journal* 27, 128–133, © 1997 by International Transactional Analysis Association.)

THERAPEUTIC TECHNIQUES

Narrative therapy is based on a postmodern, constructionist view of the world that informs the way a therapist interacts with her clients, and it does not rely heavily on specific methods and techniques. However, narrative counselors frequently use a number of practices. These are reviewed below.

Questions

Questions are used to probe clients' stories, look for missing information, and bring new facts to light that will eventually help clients reauthor new narratives. Narrative therapists rely on the use of questions as much as any of the counseling approaches reviewed in this book. Payne (2000) pointed out that many counseling theorists, including Carl Rogers, discouraged the use of questions. Rogers suggested that counselors should reflect the thoughts and feelings that clients express rather than using questions to direct clients toward certain types of information. He worried that an overreliance on using questions put the counselor, rather than the client, in charge of the session and put the counselor in the role of expert.

In contrast, Payne (2000) pointed out that narrative therapy is mainly carried forward by the use of the therapists' questions. Freedman and Combs (1996) suggested that questions are used in narrative therapy mainly to generate *experiences*, not information. In other words, properly worded questions allow clients to consider their lives from different vantage points. The mental search involved in answering counselors' questions allows clients to experience a different way of being that will hopefully translate to other parts of their lives (Freedman & Combs, 1996, p. 115).

Questions can be used to accomplish a wide range of objectives in narrative therapy. One of the most important types of questioning was labeled *relative influence questioning* by White and Epston (1990). It is usually used at the outset of the first interview with a client to immediately separate her life and relationships from the problems that brought her to counseling. There are actually two sets of relative influence questions: one set that encourages the client to "map" the influence of a problem in her life, and a second set that asks the client to "map" her own influence on the problem. Both sets of questions are designed to establish that "rather than *being* the problem, the person has a relationship with the problem" (Freedman & Combs, 1996, p. 66).

First, let us consider how clients are asked to map the influence of a problem in their lives. With this type of questioning, counselors seek to identify the sphere of influence of the problems in all aspects of the clients' lives: their behaviors, emotions, thoughts, attitudes, and relationships (White & Epson, 1990). In other words, counselors are asking clients to "deconstruct" their experiences (Freedman & Combs, 1996) by providing details about the dominant narratives they have constructed. Typically, this type of questioning elicits "problem-saturated" talk from clients, in which they describe few opportunities for change.

In this type of questioning, the therapist's aim is not to uncover the entire narrative a client has constructed but to identify specific parts of the story that help the client maintain the overall narrative or dominant plot. In doing so, she asks questions that underscore her belief that the problem itself—and the belief, practices, and attitudes that go along with it—is separate from the client. In order to provide an example, let us consider how such questions could be used with Robert, a middle-aged man from Latin America who moved to the United States to seek better employment prospects. He is married and has children, and he has a long history of alcohol abuse. He was recently arrested for the second time for driving under the influence, and the court has mandated that he attend counseling as a condition of his probation. His counselor uses a narrative approach and begins the session by using questions to map the influence of the problem (Roberto's drinking) on his life.

> **Roberto:** The arrest wasn't my fault—I just had a few beers. But that other driver runs into my car, and here come the police! Once they showed up, and heard my accent, it was all over. They thought because I was Latino I must be drunk. They give me this breathalyzer, and then I'm off to jail.

Counselor: Can you tell me about the impact this arrest has had on your life?

Roberto: Well, my wife is so upset. I might lose my job. I need my license to work, and if I lose my license because of this, I can't do my job.

Counselor: So your wife is very upset and you're worried you'll lose your job. The drinking has really put you in a spot.

Roberto: Yes, my wife thinks it's my fault—I should not drink and drive, I know. But I work construction, and after work we usually have a few beers to unwind. It's never been a problem, except for that other time I got arrested. But that was after a party—it was different.

Counselor: What was different about that time?

Roberto: Well, that was a party for a friend who was moving away, and I had much more than I ever should have. But that doesn't happen much.

Counselor: And was there anything different about what you drank before this most recent arrest?

Roberto: Well, it was an especially long week, and I did have a few more than I usually do.

In this example, we can see the counselor using a variety of questions to map the influence of Roberto's drinking on his life. While the counselor asks about his wife's reaction to his recent arrest and the circumstances surrounding his other arrest, we can see that each question is externally focused and that the counselor does not try to directly tie the events to Roberto. As an example, the counselor follows a question with the statement "The drinking has really put you in a spot" to situate the problem outside of Roberto. As Freedman and Combs (1996) put it, such questions presuppose "that the belief, practice, feeling, or attitude is separate from the person" (p. 121). This approach might be particularly effective in establishing a therapeutic relationship with Roberto, as he seems convinced the police arrested him mainly because of his accent. Roberto would likely dismiss as culturally insensitive any counselor who rejected this explanation, and the "slow to know" approach would be useful in helping establish trust with him at the outset.

We can also see from this exchange that Roberto's end of the dialogue is full of problem-saturated talk—he is describing events mainly in terms of the problems that beset him, and there is as yet little indication that he sees possibilities for a different way of behaving.

The second component of relative influence questioning, mapping the influence of the person on her problems (White & Epson, 1990), was also called *opening space questioning* by Freedman and Combs (1996). These questions can follow the externalizing questions described previously and invite a search for exceptions to the problematic story line a client has described. The counselor searches for "unique outcomes": examples in which the problem did not have its usual deleterious effect on the client. Hypothetical questions can be asked soliciting different points of view and a future orientation to accomplish this end. The point here is that once the client has presented her dominant discourse, full of problem-saturated talk and limited possibilities, the counselor looks for ways to focus the client on exceptions to the problem and future possibilities for alternate outcomes.

Let us now return to the case of Roberto, who has described his two arrests for driving under the influence to his counselor. They have talked about the impact his drinking has had on his work life, his marriage, and his social life, while the counselor has been careful to externalize the drinking problem. Eventually, Roberto has begun to describe how he drinks more when he is under pressure, and he has suggested this is one area of his life he would like to change. His counselor then uses opening space questions to expand on the possibilities for an alternate story, or plot, in his use of alcohol.

> **Counselor:** Roberto, can you describe a time when you were able to deal with stress without drinking?
>
> **Roberto:** Maybe. [*Pauses*] My son was very sick and in the hospital for a month. I was miserable and scared. I knew that if I started drinking too much then, I might never stop.
>
> **Counselor:** And what happened?
>
> **Roberto:** I pretty much didn't drink at all. I drank a couple of times when I went out with friends, but when I was feeling really bad about my son, I didn't.
>
> **Counselor:** So it seemed that when you made the decision to stop drinking that time, you did it.
>
> **Roberto:** Yeah, I just knew it would be bad to drink in that situation.

In this short segment, we can see that the counselor is focusing on a unique outcome in Roberto's life—a time when the problem (drinking) did not have its usual effect. Freedman and Combs (1996, p. 125) noted that unique outcomes do not have to involve a triumph over the problem a client is describing. Any thoughts at odds with the problem story or preparation to have a different relationship with the problem can be considered a unique outcome.

Freedman and Combs (1996) described other types of questioning, which we will mention only briefly here. *Preference questions* can be used to explore with clients their own preferred outcomes to stories. For example, in Roberto's case, he could be asked if it is in his best interest to continue his current pattern of alcohol use or if some modification might be preferred. These types of questions are often used after some preferred alternate story has begun to emerge in the process of counseling—in Roberto's case, he might have begun to seriously examine a life in which he didn't consume alcohol when socializing with his friends.

As Freedman and Combs put it, "Since we co-construct alternative stories a bit at a time from experiences that do not fit with dominant, problematic stories, it is important that therapists check frequently to be sure that the direction or meaning of these experiences is preferred to that of the problematic stories" (p. 129). If you have ever been fitted for eyeglasses, you might think of such questions as similar to those you get when looking at an eye chart with different sets of lenses: The doctor asks you to look at the chart and asks which is better, this one (you look through one set of lenses) or this one (you look through another set of lenses). Such questions allow the client to assert out loud her preferred story and also underscore that ultimately it is the client, not the counselor, who is in charge of authoring the new story.

Other important types of questions identified by Freedman and Combs are *story development* questions and *meaning* questions. Once unique outcomes and preferred stories begin to emerge in counseling, story development questions are used to focus the client on events that led up to desired behaviors: What did you do differently this time? When did you do it? How did you do it? Meaning questions invite the client to reflect on different aspects of herself, the stories she has developed, and the relationships she has with other people. For example, in Roberto's case, the counselor might ask the following: What would it mean to you to stop drinking around your friends? What significance would it have to your family members, especially your wife? What did it mean to you that you were able to stop drinking for the most part when your son had health problems? What cultural beliefs about the use of alcohol did you learn in your native country and how do those fit with the attitudes you have encountered in the United States?

Freedman and Combs (1996) noted that there is no particular order in which these questions must be asked, although relative influence questions (deconstruction and opening space questions) tend to be asked near the beginning of counseling, while story development and meaning questions tend to be asked as soon as preferred outcomes are identified by the client. Preference questions can be used at any point in the counseling process when a client is considering possibilities for reauthoring stories.

Metaphors

Payne (2000) noted that all language is metaphorical, and Legowski and Brownlee (2001) suggested that the metaphor implicit in narrative therapy is the notion of narrative itself: It is through language and stories that our understanding and experience of the world are constructed. Narrative therapists believe strongly in the power of metaphors to symbolize clients' experiences and use metaphors in the service of constructing new narratives (Pearce, 1996).

Payne (2000) noted that many metaphors in other systems of counseling locate problems *within* the person: ego, id, repression, and denial in Freud's psychoanalysis, for example. Payne suggested that narrative therapists use metaphors that place problems outside the person. For example, White and Epston (1990) described the use of metaphor for a young boy with encopresis (a disorder in which the child defecates somewhere other than the bathroom, such as in his clothing), who had taken to "playing" with his feces by hiding them in various places in his house and taking them into the bath with him. The tension created by this behavior had a devastating effect on the entire family, and in treatment, a metaphor was developed for the feces to externalize the problem. The metaphor was that of the "Sneaky Poo," which sometimes tricked the young boy into playing with it, but which he sometimes managed to resist. This allowed for a concrete way to represent the problem that was external to the child and around which alternate stories could be constructed: for example, that the "Poo" was a trickster the child could creatively find ways to combat.

Therapeutic Documents

White and Epston (1990) wrote extensively about the use of therapeutic documents, which are written to summarize the discoveries and progress a client has made in counseling. They point out that in Western society in particular, documents of every sort are used to record transactions, signify status, and proclaim achievement. In narrative therapy, the client, the counselor, or both in collaboration can develop the document.

White and Epston (1990) provided many examples of documents that could be used in counseling, including one that reinforces a new narrative a client has developed and an end-of-counseling certificate to be awarded when a client finishes counseling. Other types of documents can be developed to meet the unique needs of certain clients. For example, younger children might benefit from creative expression through painting. Figure 13.2 is an example of a therapeutic document that might be developed for a business professional who worked with a counselor to overcome a fear of public speaking.

Therapeutic Writing

Therapeutic documents derive their utility from the symbolic value of what they represent, but the act of writing itself is thought to be therapeutic by narrative therapists. Therefore, therapeutic writing can be thought of as a technique separate from therapeutic documents. This approach

Figure 13.2 Therapeutic document for an adult

Certificate of Progress

This is to certify that Thomas Rivers has developed the following strategies to overcome stressful speaking situations:

- Overpreparing in order to feel more relaxed
- Reviewing mental pictures of past successful speeches
- Using deep breathing to relax just prior to giving a speech

By signing below, Thomas has indicated confidence that he will be able to employ these strategies effectively in the future. His counselor has also signed as a witness to his progress.

Signed,

Thomas Rivers

Mary Smith, Counselor

---

has received support from researchers who are not narrative therapists but who attest to the benefits of writing in therapy. For example, L'Abate (1991) noted that writing can be used to increase therapeutic efficiency and effectiveness in many ways. Both counselors and clients can use writing as a means to comment on various aspects of the counseling experience and as homework to further explore topics developed in counseling.

James Pennebaker developed a writing paradigm that has shown powerful health benefits. In a series of studies, Pennebaker (1990) was able to demonstrate that simply asking participants to write about their deepest thoughts and feelings about topics of importance to them could have important health benefits. For example, college students who participated in his research were asked to write about their deepest thoughts and feelings; in subsequent months, they were shown to visit their college student health center less often than students in non-experimental groups (who were, for example, asked to simply describe events in their lives rather than their deepest thoughts and feelings). While his research has not shown definitively the exact mechanism by which writing has such therapeutic benefits, Pennebaker has speculated that writing about our thoughts and feelings allows us to make sense of our experiences and spend less energy trying to inhibit painful feelings. Interested readers are directed to Pennebaker's book *Opening Up* (1990) for a very readable summary of this research.

With respect to the use of writing in narrative therapy, White and Epston (1990) used letters of invitation to clients, for example, as a way to engage persons in therapy who are reluctant to attend. Writing can also be used for a variety of other therapeutic ends, as when letters are written to clients to "relieve" them of certain obligations, such as always having to be a caretaker for an irresponsible sibling, or to predict positive outcomes for new narratives they have constructed.

MULTICULTURAL AND DIVERSITY EFFECTIVENESS

Narrative therapists view their approach as particularly well suited to working with clients from diverse backgrounds (Semmler & Williams, 2000). White and Epston (1990) wrote about the importance of understanding how social constructs such as ethnicity, gender, and socioeconomic status affect an individual client's narratives, and much of the early stages of counseling is spent "deconstructing" these factors. Kelley (1995) noted that narrative therapists avoid labels, are accepting of individual differences, and stress the importance of an egalitarian counseling relationship. Therefore, clients who have faced discrimination may find this approach to be one that validates their experience.

Further, within a narrative therapy framework, clients can explore family dynamics and cultural practices that have been marginalized by the dominant culture. Ivey, D'Andrea, Ivey, and Simek-Morgan (2002) noted that many cultural and ethnic groups take great pride in family connections and histories, and they view attention to such matters as an important component of counseling. Swan (1998) discussed the potential utility of narrative therapy for women who feel constrained by cultural stereotypes about the roles of women and men. She noted that the goal of narrative therapy is to bring to awareness the taken-for-granted stories of the larger culture, as well as the ideas and beliefs that support them. Many cultures endorse the idea of women as nurturers who strive mightily to meet all the needs of those around them. If not identified and deconstructed, these dominant narratives can be powerful, and women can feel trapped, with no other options for constructing alternative lifestyles based on more egalitarian notions about the roles of men and women. The reexamination and critique of such dominant discourses in narrative therapy can therefore be very empowering.

While these applications of narrative therapy hold great promise for working with clients from diverse backgrounds, several limitations should also be noted. First, the assumption of an egalitarian relationship between the counselor and the client may not conform to some clients' expectations. For example, clients from some Asian cultures assume that helpers are a source of wisdom and advice, and they may be confused by a counselor who does not assume such a role (Ivey et al., 2002). In addition, some clients may be more interested in a problem-solving orientation and may find that narrative approaches offer little in this respect, at least at the outset. Finally, it should be noted that there is at present little research suggesting the effectiveness of narrative therapy with clients from diverse backgrounds.

PRIMARY APPLICATIONS

Family Therapy

Narrative therapy was developed by Michael White and David Epston as an approach to family therapy; therefore, the principles, techniques, and ideas contained in this chapter apply to both individual and family work. However, the actual practice of narrative therapy with families is necessarily different from individual work because each member of a family has a different perspective on the problems brought to therapy. In *Narrative Means to Therapeutic Ends* (1990), White and Epston noted that while the more traditional systems-oriented approaches to family therapy assume that some underlying structure or dysfunction in the family determines the members' behavior, in the narrative approach it is the meaning that members attribute to events that determines the problem.

Just as in individual therapy, therapeutic conversations are used with family members to help them construct an alternative view of their problem that emphasizes solutions that were already available but were underutilized (O'Connor, Meakes, Pickering, & Schuman, 1997). Early in the therapy process, families are encouraged to externalize problems; alternate stories are then explored through the search for unique occurrences in which the dominant problem did not have its usual effect on the family (White & Epston, 1990).

White and Epston (1990) noted that externalizing and developing a mutually acceptable definition of a family's problem are particularly important in working with caregivers who have concerns about their adolescents. In the following example, Frank and Ellen are devout Baptists and the parents of a 16-year-old boy who in their view has become increasingly rebellious. He has stopped participating in his church youth group and has even started skipping Sunday services. While his grades in school have been consistently good, his parents are also worried that he has started hanging out with friends from his public school more often than the friends he used to have from church. They have decided to seek out the services of a narrative family therapist, and Zack has reluctantly agreed to attend to "get them off his back." In this example, the therapist is attempting to develop a mutually acceptable definition of an external problem the family can work on.

> **Therapist:** Ellen and Frank, what do you fear might happen if Zack does not attend church with you?
>
> **Ellen:** That he'll lose his way—he already seems to hang around with kids who are troublemakers.
>
> **Zack:** They are not! You don't even know my friends.
>
> **Frank:** How are we supposed to know them when you don't even bring them home? If you had more friends from the church youth group, we might at least know who they are!
>
> **Therapist:** I wonder if we could all agree that the anxiety produced by your concern, Ellen and Frank, is a problem for everyone? Zack, does it seem this anxiety interferes with your life?
>
> **Zack:** Every day. They always seem concerned about where I'm going. It's always nag, nag, nag.
>
> **Frank:** Well, what are we supposed to do, Zack? We don't even know where you're going half the time!
>
> **Therapist:** The anxiety seems like a burden for you and Ellen, too. Am I correct?
>
> **Frank:** A big burden.
>
> **Ellen:** Yes, it has been quite difficult.
>
> **Therapist:** I wonder if we could all talk a bit more about this anxiety: What has it done to your family life? What has it done to your relationships? Could we all agree to look at the problem in this way for a while?

In this example, the therapist is attempting to enlist the cooperation of all the family members in a mutually agreed upon external definition of the problem—in this case, the impact of the anxiety that Ellen and Frank are experiencing on the entire family. Each of the family members can then be called on to explore its effects, and Zack can be asked to join with his parents in an attempt to undermine the influence of this anxiety on the family (White & Epston, 1990). The religious values of each of the family members will be important to address in this example as well, since Ellen and Frank's expectations for Zack in this area seem to be a primary source of this anxiety. While the therapist will avoid taking sides in the matter, the story of each family member's religious faith will be viewed as an important narrative to explore.

All of the techniques previously reviewed in this chapter, including the use of questions, metaphors, and therapeutic documents, can be brought in to work with families as well. While each member of the family has a unique perspective on the problems brought to therapy, White and Epston (1990) noted that these problems can also be seen as trends that seem to take on a life of their own. The family members' lives can become increasingly organized around these problem-saturated narratives, and alternative courses of behavior can become less apparent. One of the primary tasks of the therapist therefore is to help family members externalize and name the problem in an effort to enlist their cooperation in identifying alternate discourses. The family therapist then helps each family member author counterplots that offer creative ways to address the family members' concerns, just as is done in individual counseling.

Couples Therapy

Brimhall, Gardner, and Henline (2003) pointed out that just as in individual and family therapy, when working with couples, a narrative therapist elicits the partners' stories regarding their difficulties, strengths, and solutions. The couple is recognized as the expert on its own relationships, and in the process of the therapy, the counselor strives to use language and interaction styles that are familiar to the couple. While a behavior therapist might attempt to teach a couple new skills for communicating, the narrative therapist would attempt to understand and use the couple's own language in deconstructing the partners' stories. Metaphors and examples would come from the couple, for example, not the therapist.

Keskinen (2004) wrote that with couples in which one partner is female, cultural discourses about the role of women in relationships can be particularly important to address in therapy. For example, Keskinen described how in countries such as Finland, where women's participation in the labor market is extensive, females often have enough economic independence to divorce violent husbands. However, expectations about women's role in maintaining family relations and close emotional bonds with family members persist. Women confronting violence in relationships therefore can experience conflict between societal expectations that females maintain close emotional bonds in the family and public policies based on individual autonomy.

In order to provide an example of how such narratives might be addressed in couples therapy, let us consider the case of JoAnne and Brad, two married heterosexual advertising executives living in the southeastern United States. They have sought out a narrative couples counselor for communications problems in their relationship. As their first session progressed, it became clear to their counselor that JoAnne was quite concerned about occasional bursts of anger from Brad, especially when he worked long hours at his job. While he was never violent with her, this behavior upset JoAnne greatly. It also contrasted with her notion of herself as a tough businessperson who does not put up with garbage from anyone. Even though narrative counselors strive to be egalitarian, this counselor decided this issue in their relationship had to take center stage.

See DVD

Chap. 13
Clip 2

Counselor: JoAnne, could you tell me a little bit more about the effect Brad's anger has on you?

JoAnne: Well, usually it isn't even anything that starts between us. I can just tell when he comes home from work sometimes that he's upset, and I know the littlest thing will set him off. I'm afraid to talk to him.

Counselor: So you know right away, and you start walking on eggshells to avoid setting Brad off?

JoAnne: Yes, which upsets me even more, because at work I'm this tough, no-nonsense person, and I go home to a place where I have to be this meek little woman.

Brad: Come on, JoAnne, you have bad days, too. You can't blame this all on me.

Counselor: Brad, before we talk about JoAnne's bad days, I'm wondering what these bad days are like for you.

Brad: Well, she's right that I get stressed out at work sometimes, and I do take it home with me. But I feel a great deal of pressure at work, and I can't wave a magic wand and make it all go away.

Counselor: So it sounds like being tense and upset is a problem for you as well.

In this example, we can see the counselor is making an initial attempt to externalize Brad's anger and to explore how it might have negative effects on both members of the relationship. The role of societal attitudes about gender are also demonstrated, as part of JoAnne's concern comes from the fact that at work she feels able to deal with conflict but in her marriage less so. We might suspect that Brad's method of handling his emotions could stem from gender stereotypes as well about men not showing vulnerable feelings to others, even a spouse.

The counselor in this example is also appropriately concerned about the nature of Brad's anger and whether it represents a threat to JoAnne's safety. We can see that the counselor does not allow Brad to shift the focus of attention onto JoAnne and her expressions of anger. Concerns about the welfare of both clients are paramount, of course, and if the counselor suspects any physical violence in the relationship, he needs to take appropriate steps to protect both partners.

Counseling Children and Adolescents

Thomas (2002) noted that the same factors that are important in narrative therapy with adults apply to work with adolescents and children, particularly in the provision of an atmosphere of validation and safety that encourages children to explore problematic stories about their lives. In particular, children can find relief in the emphasis in narrative therapy on placing problems outside the individual, since they may often feel blamed by the adults in their world.

The use of stories with children, either those in the published literature or those created by the children themselves, can be powerful therapeutic tools (Gardner, 1993), particularly for children who have experienced trauma and abuse (Lawton & Edwards, 1997). Therefore, when eliciting stories about adolescents' children's lives, narrative therapists can be creative in using a variety of media that allow them to express themselves.

Winslade and Chesire (1997) noted the usefulness of narrative therapy for school counseling settings. Narrative therapy developed from work with families, and students often seek out counselors because of family concerns. Further, students' narratives can be profoundly influenced by their school community. Earlier in this chapter, we described the use of therapeutic documents as a technique for narrative therapy. Figure 13.3 is an example of a therapeutic document a high school counselor might use during counseling with a student who suffered from extreme anxiety about testing.

Group Work

Groups are another modality in which narrative therapy can be used to help members share problematic narratives about their lives in order to author counterplots. As opposed to families, where members have a history with each other and may share a similar problem that has brought them to therapy, group members may not know each other but could be called upon to help the other members explore the problems that brought them to the group. While family members may have a shared history, groups can be constructed around common areas of concern for members, such as substance abuse or grief.

Silvester (1997) pointed out that narrative therapy groups differ from traditional groups in terms of some of the assumptions made about the group. For example, in the traditional approach to groups, the leader is assumed to have good interpersonal and didactic skills that will be transmitted to members. Silvester noted that this assumption places the group members in a less

Figure 13.3 Therapeutic document for a high school student

Smalltown High School
Certificate of Achievement
This is to certify that Marshall Schmidt, a junior, has taken the following steps necessary to combat anxiety during test time:
• Studied the effects of stress on concentration and memory • Practiced relaxation strategies • Learned how to use "self talk" to calm himself down during exam time
By signing below, his school counselor expresses confidence that Marshall will be able to use these skills and knowledge in upcoming exams.
Signed,
Mary Smith, School Counselor

powerful position. Silvester also noted that by placing the leader in the expert role, it is more likely that dominant cultural stories will be reenacted, since the members' experiences may not be given the same weight as the leader's. In contrast, a narrative group leader assumes that members have the resources to make changes in their lives, even though at the outset of the group these resources may be obscured by problem-saturated stories. In group work, as in individual work, members are encouraged to share their stories, externalize problems, and call on the group members for alternate perspectives.

BRIEF THERAPY/MANAGED CARE EFFECTIVENESS

Narrative therapy does not share the core philosophical assumptions of managed health care systems. The latter emphasizes empiricism and traditional aspects of the medical model such as an expert health care provider who makes a diagnosis that serves as the basis for treatment. However, Kelley (1998) noted that narrative therapy is still compatible with the managed health care environment in many respects. First, although the narrative approach does not share the modernist assumptions of managed care systems, it can be conducted in just a few sessions, which in many cases can be scattered across weeks or months. Further, White and Epston (1990) did not reject the notion that clients could try out new behaviors or carry out homework activities between sessions, a well-accepted practice of other brief approaches. Also, White and Epston may not have placed a great deal of faith in standardized means of assessment such as the *DSM*, but they also did not reject their use or overlook the need to explore, discuss, and label clients' problems (Kelley, 1998).

Narrative therapists might argue that these factors position the approach to potentially flourish in the current climate of managed mental health care, while at the same time offering creative possibilities for understanding clients' lives in a postmodern world. However, a potential limitation of this approach in managed care settings is the paucity of empirical research demonstrating the effectiveness of the approach. This will be described further in the "Research" section of this chapter.

INTEGRATING THE THEORY WITH OTHER APPROACHES

Given that narrative therapy is a relative newcomer to the counseling scene and has yet to establish a substantial body of research attesting to its effectiveness, some have suggested that at the current time it represents more of a philosophical stance than a comprehensive theory of counseling. According to Amundson, Webber, and Stewart (2000), "[N]arrative ideas need not be a theoretical system unto itself with all the attendant pronouncements and specifications of theory. Instead, it might be simply a means to conjoin theory from a variety of perspectives into ideas that are useful to people" (p. 21). It could be argued that a narrative perspective could enrich some of the models of counseling already discussed in this book.

Since they are both based on postmodern philosophy, it would seem natural to combine narrative therapy with solution-focused therapy (SFT). However, Prochaska and Norcross (2003) noted that in SFT, counselors help clients construct their future by choosing goals in the present, while narrative therapists help clients construct their past through the stories they tell in the present. Therefore, the goals of the two therapies are different and might be difficult to integrate in practice. An SFT counselor would be constantly encouraging clients to develop goals for the future, while a narrative therapist would focus on stories from the past and present.

Psychodynamically oriented models of counseling offer some potential for integration with narrative therapy. While Freud clearly situated psychological problems inside the individual, which is not consistent with the narrative approach to externalizing clients' problems, he did believe in the powerful influence of culture in contributing to intrapsychic conflict. Society's rigid standards, he believed, are incorporated into the superego, and the ego must balance these demands, as well as the more primitive desires of the id. And while Freud was not a postmodern philosopher, most of psychoanalytic thought and research is conducted by analyzing case studies. As Trad (1992) put it, "[T]he patient's narrative is viewed as the centerpiece of psychotherapeutic work" in psychoanalysis" (p. 159). Understanding clients' stories and using them to promote insight into clients' behaviors could therefore be seen as an area of overlap between the two approaches.

Cognitive therapy is another counseling modality that might be considered as a candidate for integration with narrative therapy. According to cognitive therapy theorists such as Aaron Beck and Albert Ellis, it is clients' perceptions of their experiences that ultimately cause dysfunction, not the reality of a situation. There is therefore overlap with the postmodern philosophy of narrative therapy that we create our own realities through the way that we construe our experiences. However, the types of interventions that cognitive therapy therapists use may be harder to integrate with narrative therapy. The "collaborative empiricism" of Beck, in which irrational beliefs are disputed through a careful analysis of the facts of a situation, is one such example. Narrative therapists would disagree that there are ever "facts" that will help clients decide whether beliefs are accurate or not. Instead, narrative therapists would suggest to clients that there will always be facts that support a variety of different ways of looking at themselves and the world, and it is up to the clients to decide which story line they want to pursue.

Humanistic theories of counseling would also seem to be potential candidates for integration with narrative therapy. For example, in developing person-centered counseling, Carl Rogers described the central importance of establishing a warm therapeutic relationship and helping clients discover, and value, their internal experiences. Narrative therapists also strive to establish an egalitarian relationship with clients and help them value their internal frame of reference. Another humanistic approach, existential counseling, would also seem to have the potential for successful integration with narrative therapy. Existential counselors embrace a philosophical outlook on life and suggest that clients need to create their own realities in order to find meaning in the world. However, these two systems have somewhat different emphases: Postmodernists focus on the subjective nature of reality, while some existentialists emphasize undeniable truths about life that we need to embrace.

It would seem problematic to attempt to integrate narrative therapy with some counseling theories that endorse a modern, as opposed to a postmodern, view of the world. The more radical behaviorist approaches would be one such example: It is the external world, and its power to shape our behavior, that is the prime therapeutic ingredient in such approaches, and there would seem to be little room to incorporate narrative therapy. Approaches such as Glasser's reality therapy represent more of a mixed bag in our opinion in terms of their potential for integration with narrative therapy. On the one hand, Glasser did maintain that the external world only provides us information (it does not *make* us feel a certain way or dictate a certain course of action) and that it is through our interpretation of this information that we either move toward or away from getting our needs met. This position is consistent with a postmodern emphasis on deconstructing reality. However, Glasser's model of counseling more or less assumes that there is a real world out there and that it is in this world that we can satisfy our needs (thus the term *Reality therapy*). This emphasis on the external world as the ultimate arbiter of our satisfaction of needs is less consistent with narrative therapy and its postmodern emphasis.

RESEARCH

Research evidence for the effectiveness of narrative therapy is sparse. Etchison and Kleist (2000) cited Hevern's (1999) contention that few actual studies are represented among the more than 2,000 articles, books, book chapters, and doctoral dissertations on narrative therapy. In their review of the literature, Etchison and Kleist found only a handful of empirical studies, mainly having to do with family counseling. These few studies did provide some support for narrative approaches.

Neimeyer (1993) commented that one explanation for the lack of research is the relative newness of social constructionism as a philosophy and narrative therapy as a counseling application. Etchison and Kleist (2000) further noted that quantitative research, involving the use of experimental and control groups and rigorous methodology, for example, is lacking because social constructionists do not embrace empirical research. Many social constructionists are not trained in such methods.

What appears more promising for future research is qualitative research methods that allow the researcher to focus in depth on the experiences of individual participants in research. This is particularly consistent with the views of postmodern researchers, who tend to see study participants as coresearchers, not subjects to be analyzed. In light of this, the sample research study below describes a case study that allowed the investigators to explore in depth the experience of the research participant.

SAMPLE RESEARCH: Narrative therapy in rehabilitation after brain injury: A case study

Goals of the Research

Hogan (1999) reported a case study of the use of narrative therapy with a client 18 years after a brain injury to help him "claim an identity as an author not only of a book telling his story of life after brain injury but also of his life from which he has felt alienated since his injury" (p. 21).

Participant

The patient in this case study was Jeff, who at age 20 sustained a severe brain injury in a motor vehicle accident. His symptoms included motor and balance difficulties, mood instability, and decreased cognitive function.

Methods

Hogan reported that the first few times she met with Jeff, he refused to say more than a few words or to let her say anything. Instead, he wanted her to listen to a sample of his music collection, including a song by Steely Dan ("Doctor Wu") about the limitations and pretensions of doctors. Hogan reported that after sessions with Jeff, she wrote down everything she could remember, no matter how trivial it seemed at the time. Eventually, she began reading Jeff's words back to him at their next session, and she reported that this let him know she had been listening and helped him separate the meaning of his words from the emotions he was experiencing at the time.

Results

Hogan reported that Jeff's dominant story at the time he began therapy was "I'm too slow. I'm a screw-up. I don't do anything, and I'm not going to change" (p. 23). But after working in therapy with Hogan, he came to believe that he had something important to say to the world, especially in helping others understand his brain injury. She even reported that Jeff began working with a new psychotherapist, who was also a musician, and they started to coauthor music; one of their first compositions was "The Brain."

Implications of the Research

This study is, of course, not a research study in the traditional sense. However, it does suggest alternative methods of investigation that can be used to better document what happens in narrative therapy and the types of outcomes that can be expected.

EVALUATION OF NARRATIVE THERAPY

Our experience is that graduate counseling students often know quickly when first reading about narrative therapy whether this approach appeals to them. First used as an approach for working with families, it has developed into an approach for working with individuals, couples, families, and groups. In order to use the approach, one must be aware of the postmodern worldview, which puts narrative therapy at odds with the prevailing zeitgeist of empirically validated treatments. While it shares a philosophical approach with solution-focused counseling, the approach is not nearly as practical. It may therefore seem fuzzy or vague to some clients and counselors.

However, we do not believe it is possible to deny the powerful influence of narratives on human culture. Humans today still tend to organize their experience in terms of stories; whether from sacred texts that reveal religious truth or from news media that report the deeds of great political leaders, humans tend to gravitate to stories. It therefore makes sense to incorporate this powerful aspect of human experience into the work that counselors do.

It also seems that there is room to incorporate narrative models into other systems of counseling, including the psychoanalytical, cognitive therapy, and existential approaches.

However, there is no denying that the lack of research on the effectiveness of this approach is a problem. While it may seem unfair to use empirical investigation as a yardstick to measure this approach, Trad (1992) pointed out that no satisfying alternative method of evaluation has been used extensively by narrative researchers. Given that those who pay for therapeutic services usually want some evidence that what they are paying for is effective, it seems that narrative therapists will continue to be challenged to evaluate the effectiveness of this approach and counselors may still feel compelled to combine it with other approaches that have more research support.

Questions and Learning Activities

These questions and activities are designed to stimulate your thinking about this theory and to help you apply some of the ideas to your own life and experience. If possible, you should work with another person or with a small group. Getting others' points of view and sharing your own ideas and perspectives will be invaluable as a way to help you evaluate this theory and its applications.

Personal Application Questions

1. To what extent do you believe that reality is not "out there" in the world but rather socially constructed through language and dialogue? Can you think of examples of things that you consider to be "the truth" that are not subject to interpretation?
2. Postmodernists believe that our dialogue and language have a powerful impact on how we see reality: In effect, we do not use language; it uses us. Think, for example, of the way politicians frame debates about taxes by describing them as payroll deductions or levies or the way companies describe mass firings as "downsizing." Can you think of examples of language use that affects perceptions of everyday reality?
3. There has been a movement to use nonsexist language in many Western cultures. What do you think of this idea of using nonsexist language in all aspects of life?
4. How important to our self-perceptions are the stories that we tell about ourselves? Is there a story about some event in your life that is particularly meaningful or important to you?
5. Do you believe that a client who has authored highly problematic narratives about herself can find "alternate plots" through dialogue with a counselor, or do you believe that the counselor needs to intervene in some concrete way to improve the client's life circumstances? To what extent is it important for a counselor to teach a client skills or to offer advice or interpretations, as opposed to helping her understand her narratives?
6. If you had to describe a dominant plot for your life, what would it be?
7. Think about someone you know who has authored a dominant plot that is unsatisfying to her. What alternate plots are available to that person? Can you imagine being able to help her see these alternate plots?
8. How do you feel about a therapist using documents, letters, and even artwork in the practice of narrative therapy? Do you see it as a legitimate way to practice counseling? Can you see any potential problem with this type of intervention?
9. Are there some types of client concerns that you think would not be appropriate for narrative therapy?
10. What type of person do you think would be attracted to the practice of narrative therapy? In your opinion, could a person use this approach without extensive knowledge of the philosophy behind it?

11. In your opinion, should narrative therapy be acceptable to a cost-conscious health maintenance organization? In your opinion, should every approach to counseling be subject to empirical evaluation?

Learning Activities

Therapeutic Documents

As a group, develop two or three examples of therapeutic documents that could be used with different clients. For example, what kind of certificate could you create for an adolescent male who has worked on being more assertive in counseling? For a substance abuser who has managed to avoid alcohol for one month? For a chronic smoker who has worked on other ways of coping with stress than using nicotine?

Expanding Narratives

In a small group of three to four people, have one person describe a situation that is mildly distressing to her and involves other people. This should be a safe topic that does not invoke strong emotion and is not too personal. The person should take several minutes to describe everything about the situation that she thinks is important. The other members of the group should be assigned to the roles of other people involved in the situation and listen to the story from their perspectives. For example, if one person is having a conflict with a supervisor at work, each member of the group would take a role: One would be the worker, one would be the supervisor, and perhaps the others might be fellow workers involved in the situation. After the first group member finishes telling his story, other members of the group describe their reactions to the situation from the viewpoint of the person they are playing. Following this activity, the group can discuss the various perspectives that arose through this exercise and how each person involved has a different perspective on it.

Externalizing Problems and Finding Exceptions

Have each member of your group identify a problem in her life that she does not mind sharing in a group. This should be a safe topic that does not invoke strong emotion and is not too personal— such as difficulties with a roommate or concerns about declaring a major. Through group discussion of that problem, attempt to help that individual "externalize" the problem, perhaps by coming up with a name or metaphor for the problem. How successful was your group in doing this for each member?

After each member has shared a problematic narrative, the other members of the group should take turns asking questions about exceptions to this narrative: for example, about times when the problem did not occur for the person, situations in which the problem did not arise, and so on. Then, as a group, discuss your ability to find such alternative plots for each member of the group.

Have each member of your group describe an ideal job. For each member of the group, attempt to "deconstruct" the values or assumptions that lie beneath this career choice. For example, ask that member to label the values this career choice embodies. How did she develop those values? What role models did she have in selecting this ideal career? Where did she get information about the career?

Companion Website

Now go to the companion Website at www.prenhall.com/archer to access your understanding of chapter content with multiple-choice and essay questions, and broaden your knowledge with related Web resources and additional print resources.

CHAPTER 14

Psychopharmacological (Biological) Approaches

STEPHANIE SARKIS AND JAMES ARCHER, JR.

VOICES FROM THE FIELD: COUNSELOR AND CLIENT REACTIONS

Yes, it works for me

Client: I was really skeptical about taking drugs for my depression. I just don't like the idea of relying on medicine to feel better, but since I couldn't seem to get better with counseling alone, I decided to ask my family doctor about an antidepressant. When he learned that I was already in counseling, he suggested that I try an antidepressant and continue with counseling. I have been taking it now for several weeks, and I do believe that I am less depressed and anxious. It's not a dramatic change, but I do feel better. I am also finding that the counseling has helped me, and I am now able to try some of the things that my counselor and I have been discussing.

Counselor: Well, I know that prescription medications are sometimes abused, but I also know that a number of my clients need them and are using them successfully. I have two aunts who have been taking an antidepressant for a long time, and it seems to work for them. I think it is a good idea to learn something about what medications are out there and how they are used. Plus I have a good relationship with the consulting psychiatrist where I work. She does not fit the drug-pusher image that some people have of psychiatrists, and she really knows what medicines are good for what problems. She also knows the value of counseling and almost always recommends it in addition to prescribing medicine.

No, it doesn't work for me

Client: No way that I will ever take mind-altering drugs. I just don't believe in them. I want to feel my real emotions and deal with my problems myself. I was really offended when my counselor suggested that I get an evaluation for medication. I just think everyone in our society is looking for a quick fix, and I hate all those advertisements on TV for antidepressants. I'll take my chances with counseling and try to improve myself without using the pills.

Counselor: I just don't see it. It seems like the answer to every problem in our society is medication. Sometimes it seems like everyone is on some kind of antidepressant, and there is so much advertising! I can see drugs for people who are psychotic or maybe for people who have really severe anxiety problems, but for the people I am working with, I think psychotherapy is a better answer. Anyway, I don't know enough about these medications to give advice about them. I'm just going to stay away from clients who use them.

Mark is a 26-year-old man who has recently gone back to college for an A.A. degree. He was strongly motivated to become a nuclear medicine technician but sought out counseling because he was having great difficulty with the academic work.

> **Mark:** I was talking with my aunt about how difficult it is for me to focus and concentrate, and she mentioned that she thought I might have ADHD. Do you think I should get some medication?
>
> **Counselor:** Well, that is something that you can certainly investigate. We've only worked together for a few weeks, and you have made some progress in keeping more on task at school, but it has been pretty difficult for you. How do you feel about taking medication?
>
> **Mark:** Well, when I was younger, one of my teachers told my mom I needed to get evaluated for ADHD, but she thought I was just a normal, active little boy.
>
> **Counselor:** Yes, but how do you feel about the whole idea?
>
> **Mark:** I don't know . . . I guess, at this point, I would be willing to try whatever might work. What are the risks, do you know?
>
> **Counselor:** That's a good question, but I don't feel qualified to answer it. Let's talk about finding a referral for someone who can evaluate you for ADHD and, if appropriate, prescribe some medication. He would be the one to tell you about the risks.
>
> **Mark:** OK. Can I still come in and see you?
>
> **Counselor:** Well, I would want a release to be able to talk with the person who works with you on the medication. I do think it is a good idea for you to continue counseling whether or not you wind up with medication.

The situation portrayed in the dialogue above is one that is commonly faced by counselors in just about any setting. Mark has presented with a particular concern—in this case, academic problems—and he has heard, read about, or seen something on television that makes him wonder if medication would be helpful. The counselor, who is a nonmedical therapist, must deal with this request and decide how to explore the option with the client. Although we have titled this chapter "Pharmacological (Biological) Approaches," counselors typically deal with this approach as part of an overall therapy plan, and there is research evidence that a combined counseling/medication approach, in many instances, is the most desirable treatment mode. In this case, we see that the counselor is open to the possibility of medication and will discuss a referral with the client. The counselor is staying within her area of expertise but is not excluding the possibility of medication. This is the stance that we see most counselors taking today. Since this is a new and difficult area for counselors, in this chapter we focus considerable attention on the role of nonmedical therapists regarding the use of psychoactive medications.

HISTORICAL BACKGROUND

Historical Context

Psychopharmacological approaches to helping people manage behavior and emotion are not new, but the use of psychoactive drugs has dramatically increased in the last few years. The movement toward increased use of psychotropic medications and acceptance of a more biological approach in treating psychological problems has been driven by a number of factors in contemporary society: an increase in our understanding of the brain and brain chemistry; knowledge about how specific drugs affect specific emotions and behavior; managed care and the need for briefer and more efficient treatments; the availability of safer and better-tolerated medications; personal referrals and testimonials; and a greatly increased public awareness of psychopharmacology from television, the Internet, and books. Some counselors and other therapists see this increase in knowledge about medications and medical intervention as a positive development that can enhance therapy and provide quicker and more thorough relief for many clients/patients who are suffering from various psychological complaints. Others feel that the use of psychotropic medications has spiraled out of control and that they are overprescribed.

In counseling practice, a therapist's perspective regarding the use of medications is often shaped by the point of view she takes on the role of biological influences on emotions and behavior. Many therapists consider recommending psychotropic medications only if they believe that there is evidence that a particular disorder has a biological component. For example, they might consider the use of medications for certain classes of disorders that have been shown to have biological components, such as schizophrenia and attention deficit disorder, and that typically do not respond to the use of counseling alone. Or they might consider the use of medication when there is strong evidence of a family history of that disorder. For example, if there is a history of depression in a client's family, antidepressants might be considered. On the other hand, some therapists, physicians, and other health care providers recommend and/or use antidepressants or antianxiety medications just for symptom relief, without necessarily believing that these conditions are primarily caused by a genetically based chemical imbalance in the brain. The degree of chemical imbalance and the cause of the imbalance (genes, experience, or an interaction) remain to be discovered.

The issue of managed care and cost containment is another important part of the contextual background when considering biological approaches to counseling. The U.S. Congress in 2003 passed an attempt to reform Medicare by including a prescription drug benefit because pharmaceuticals have become far more prevalent and costly in medical treatment in recent decades. However, in the mental health field, psychotropic drug treatment can be less expensive than counseling, psychotherapy, or hospitalization. If a client can take a course of antidepressants to deal with depression, it may require only a visit to the family doctor and a prescription. However, in an article on common factors in the use of psychotropic drugs, Greenberg (1999) argued that the patient-doctor relationship, expectancy (what the client thinks will happen), and client circumstances are likely to be stronger curative agents than the drugs themselves. He has taken the stance that these factors are more important in terms of curative effect than are the medications.

Another related issue for counselors and other mental health therapists has to do with the public demand for and the widespread use of psychotropic medications. As noted in our initial example of counseling with Mark, counselors very frequently encounter clients who are on psychotropic medications or who have heard about them and want to consider using them. We believe that it is important for counselors to learn about medications as a part of mental health treatment. In a study by Scovel, Christensen, and England (2002), 90% of mental health counselors surveyed felt that psychopharmacological training was needed in their coursework. Even though some counselors and nonmedical therapists are strongly opposed to the idea of medications to deal with issues like anxiety and depression, there is no escaping the fact that medications for various emotional and behavioral problems have become a part of our culture and appear to be helpful to large numbers of people.

Development of Psychopharmacological Approaches

Psychoactive drugs have been used for thousands of years. Alcohol, coca leaves, tobacco, tea, valerian root, and coffee are examples of substances that have been used in many different cultures. Although these and other substances have been part of healing practices for centuries, their specific use in modern medicine to treat psychiatric disorders began in the late nineteenth century. In 1869, chloral hydrate was introduced as a treatment for melancholia and mania. In 1917, Julius Wagner-Jauregg, a psychiatrist, won the Nobel Prize for discovering the use of a malaria toxin to treat the mental and neurological symptoms of syphilis. In 1948, the Australian psychiatrist John F. Cade discovered the use of lithium for mania. Henri Laborit, a French anesthesiologist, tried to find a medication that reduced swelling of the brain (edema) in patients after surgery. While the medication Thorazine did not help edema, Laborit discovered that his patients felt calmer for a few days after surgery. Thorazine was approved in the United States in 1954 for the treatment of schizophrenia.

By 1960, there were medications for most major classes of mental disorders. The use of Haldol, Thorazine, and other antipsychotics contributed to the closing of many mental hospitals worldwide because this allowed many to function outside institutions. In 1963, Valium, a medication that helped alleviate anxiety, was introduced. This medication was the most widely prescribed drug from 1969 to 1982. The fact that 90% of Valium prescriptions were written by nonpsychiatric physicians seems to indicate the use of psychoactive medications was expanding into general practice (Beardsley, Gardocki, Larsen, & Hidalgo, 1988).

In the 1950s, a class of antidepressants called tricyclics was developed, but they were difficult to prescribe well. They had many side effects and were lethal in overdoses. Patients sometimes needed electrocardiograms to evaluate any damage the medicine might be causing to the heart, and blood work was sometimes required to make sure medication in the body was at a therapeutic level. In 1987, the "Prozac Revolution" started when Prozac, a selective serotonin reuptake inhibitor (SSRI) became available for the treatment of depression. Prozac was a great improvement over the previously used antidepressants because it was much safer. Prozac demonstrated efficacy with both depression and anxiety. After the development of Prozac, other SSRIs were developed, and this class of drugs became widely used, being advertised first to physicians and later to the general public.

The advent of SSRIs increased physicians' comfort in prescribing antidepressants and patients' demand for psychotropic medication. The efficacy and safety of these new medications and referrals from friends and relatives also increased demand considerably. With a limited number of psychiatrists, more tolerable medications, and limited insurance payments for counseling and mental health services, other clinicians, such as primary care physicians, nurse practitioners, and physician assistants, began to prescribe psychotropic medication more frequently. In recent years, psychologists have begun to lobby for limited prescription privileges. The evidence for an increasing acceptance and use of psychoactive medications seems clear.

ASSUMPTIONS AND CORE CONCEPTS

View of Human Nature

The use of psychoactive medications is based on the assumption that many psychiatric and psychological problems are, at least partially, a result of chemical imbalances in the brain. There is an underlying assumption that human behavior and emotions can be explained and eventually understood in scientific terms. Despite its great complexity, the human brain is essentially seen as an organ that eventually will be mapped and understood. Theoretically, then, drugs will be used to alter brain chemical imbalances and improve any behavior, emotions, and cognitions. As you have no doubt observed, these assumptions lead to a number of ethical, social, and political concerns.

In a more practical sense, another underlying assumption is that the "medical model" is preferred in treating psychiatric problems. Using this model, a problem is typically defined as a kind of disease and requires a diagnosis before it can be treated. However, with psychoactive medications, symptoms are often treated without a definitive diagnosis due to the fact that, unlike with many other medical disorders, there are no specific tests for mental disorders. Like the other branches of medicine, psychiatry is a mixture of art and science. Many of the drugs used for psychiatric and psychological problems work quite differently with different people, and side effects and dosages vary. These drugs may also interact with other medications, sometimes in idiosyncratic ways. In reality, those who prescribe medications for psychiatric problems often need to prescribe different medications and dosages before they can find the most effective treatment with the fewest side effects.

Core Concepts

It is important for counselors to have a basic understanding of the biochemistry of the brain with regard to psychoactive medications. An understanding of the basic action of neurons and neurotransmitters makes it easier to understand the benefits and side effects of a particular class of medication.

Neurons (nerve cells) (see Figure 14.1) communicate with each other by using chemicals called neurotransmitters. Neurotransmitters are the messengers of the neurons. When neurotransmitters leave the axon (an extension of the neuron that moves neurotransmitters out of the neuron), they go out into the synapse, the space between the neuron releaser and the neuron receiver (see Figure 14.2).

There are hundreds of neurotransmitters, but scientists have focused on four that are involved in mood and emotion regulation and are central to psychiatric and psychological disorders: dopamine, norepinephrine, serotonin, and GABA. So how does this process affect psychiatric disorders and medication? In some disorders, the neurons do not make enough neurotransmitters, not enough neurotransmitters are released, or too many neurotransmitters are destroyed while in the synapse. This can affect mood and perception, causing depression or anxiety, hallucinations, or other psychotic symptoms.

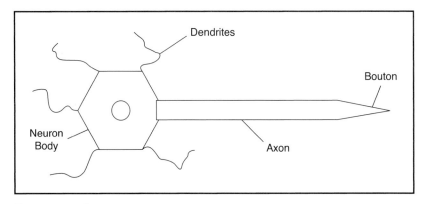

Figure 14.1 Neuron

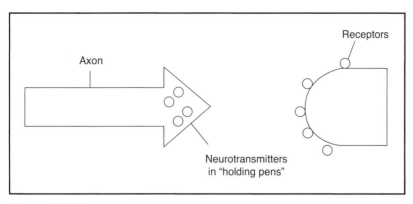

Figure 14.2 Synapse

Some medications block the path back to the original neuron, so the neurotransmitters remain longer in the synapse. The class of antidepressants named selective serotonin reuptake inhibitors (SSRIs) (e.g., Prozac) blocks the neurotransmitter serotonin from being reabsorbed into its transmitting neuron. This increases serotonin in the synapse, along with other complex reactions, and eventually leads to improved mood and fewer depressive symptoms. Some medications, such as antipsychotics, stop the receiving neuron from accepting so much of the neurotransmitter dopamine. By blocking the receiving neuron from taking up too much dopamine, hallucinations are decreased.

Major Classes of Medications

Counselors are most likely to encounter a number of different classes of medications, including antidepressants, antianxiety medications, antipsychotics, mood stabilizers, and stimulants. A brief discussion of each of these classes follows.

Antidepressants There are five classes of antidepressants: tricyclic antidepressants (TCAs), monoamine oxidase inhibitors (MAOIs), selective serotonin reuptake inhibitors (SSRIs), sedating serotonin and norepinephrine reuptake inhibitors (SNRIs), and norepinephrine reuptake inhibitors (NRIs). These classes of antidepressants differ based on the chemical they target in the brain.

The TCAs (Pamelor—nortriptyline, Elavil—amitriptyline, and Tofranil—imipramine) are used to treat pain, nocturnal enuresis (bed wetting), obsessive-compulsive disorder, and ADHD, as well as depression. In addition to targeting the norepinephrine and serotonin systems, TCAs have an impact on many other neuroreceptors. TCAs take several weeks to become effective in treating depression. However, they appear to be quicker in treating nocturnal enuresis (Dulcan, 1999). Side effects include dry mouth, dizziness, weight gain, and on rare occasions sudden death. Tricyclic antidepressants are an older class of antidepressants and are not prescribed as often as the newer antidepressants, which have fewer side effects.

MAOIs are rarely used. They are prescribed only when other antidepressants have failed to reduce symptoms. MAOIs are the oldest class of antidepressants. They were originally used to treat tuberculosis but were found to have the beneficial effect of improving mood (Preston, O'Neal, & Talaga, 2002). Patients who take MAOIs must follow a very strict diet, eliminating all foods that contain the chemical tyramine. Foods that have tyramine include meats, cheeses, wine, beer, and some fruits and fish. Eating these foods while taking MAOIs may cause a sudden elevation in blood pressure. For these reasons, MAOIs are not used widely in the treatment of depression.

SSRIs are selective because they increase only serotonin in the brain. Prozac, Celexa, Lexapro, Zoloft, Paxil, and Luvox are all SSRIs. SSNRIs work on both the serotonin receptors and the norepinephrine receptors. These medications include Desyrel (trazodone) and Remeron. NRIs such as Wellbutrin block norepinephrine reuptake. Due to its different mechanism of action, Wellbutrin has a different side-effect profile than the SSRIs. On rare occasions, Wellbutrin will precipitate seizures in susceptible individuals. It does not cause weight gain or sexual dysfunction, and it has less of a sedating effect. Wellbutrin has demonstrated efficacy and has been approved for smoking cessation under the name Zyban. Another medical treatment for depression is electroconvulsive therapy. Although historically there has been considerable controversy about this treatment, it is being used more often when medication is not effective.

These medications all have different therapeutic and side-effect profiles. Some are more sedating, while others are more activating. They may also have differing effects on different people. Counselors can be very helpful to prescribers by observing side effects and urging clients to report them to their physician. One particular side effect, sexual dysfunction, is worth noting specifically. Clients may be least willing to discuss this side effect with their doctor or therapist. Recent findings indicate that the prevalence of this side effect is greater than was originally known, probably because of this patient reluctance to mention it. In our view, this is a side effect that clients may need to be specifically asked about.

Antianxiety Medications   Antianxiety medications or anxiolytics, commonly called tranquilizers, are prescribed for all anxiety disorders and panic attacks. These medications work quickly but can be addictive, cause sedation, and impair reflexes. Benzodiazepines, one class of anxiolytics, help with anxiety, depression, and muscle relaxation. They include Valium, Xanax, Ativan, and Klonopin. People usually are prescribed anxiolytics for only a few weeks, due to the addictive potential of these drugs (Dulcan, 1999); however, there are patients who are successfully put on longer-term courses of these medications. Immediate discontinuation of this class of medications can lead to anxiety, restlessness, and on rare occasions seizure (Dulcan, 1999). These effects are more likely to occur if there has been longer-term use of these medications.

Antipsychotics   Antipsychotics are used to decrease symptoms such as auditory hallucinations, paranoia, extreme agitation, and aggression. There are two general categories of antipsychotics: first generation and second generation. The older (first-generation) antipsychotics are divided into high potency—Haldol (haloperidol) and Prolixin (fluphenazine), with more movement disorder side effects—and low potency—Thorazine (chlorpromazine) and Mellaril (thioridazine), with more anticholinergic side effects. Some of the side effects of these antipsychotics are sedation, movement disorders, inner restlessness (akathesia), and decreased cognitive ability (Pliszka, 2003). Antipsychotics may also cause involuntary movements of the body (Dulcan, 1999). The new (second-generation) antipsychotics, or Atypicals, are Zyprexa and Clozaril. In addition to improving the positive symptoms of psychosis, these antipsychotics reduce the negative symptoms of psychosis, including social withdrawal and apathy.

There are also even newer antipsychotics, including Risperdal, Seroquel, Geodon, and Abilify. They are much better tolerated than the older antipsychotics, as they do not cause movement disorders. The most common serious side effects of these medications are weight gain, diabetes, and sedation, and they may also have cardiac side effects.

Figure 14.3 Side Effects by Drug Class

This is not a complete list of side effects.

Antidepressants

TCAs	SSRIs	SSNRIs
Dry mouth	Sexual dysfunction	Dizziness
Dizziness	Nausea	Dry mouth
Weight gain	Dizziness	Headache

Antianxiety Medications

Benzodiazepines

Addiction
Sedation
Impaired reflexes

Antipsychotics

First-Generation	Second-Generation
Movement disorders	Weight gain
Sedation	Diabetes
Decreased cognitive ability	Sedation
Involuntary movements	

Mood Stabilizers

Lithium	Lithium toxicity	Anticonvulsants
Nausea	Slurred speech	Weight gain
Vomiting	Confusion	Drowsiness
Headaches	Stupor	Harm to fetus
Rash	Worsening tremors	
Tremors	Seizures, coma, death	
Weight gain		

Stimulants

Methylphenidate/Dextroamphetamine

Decreased appetite
Headaches
Difficulty sleeping
Possible tics

Mood Stabilizers Mood stabilizers are used for bipolar disorder, also known as manic-depressive disorder, which is characterized by mood swings from euphoria to deep depression. There are two classes of mood stabilizers: lithium and anticonvulsants. Lithium, a naturally occurring salt, was found in 1948 to be an effective treatment for mania. Lithium has a narrow therapeutic window, meaning that the amount of lithium that is therapeutic, or helpful, is close to the amount that is toxic to the body. For this reason, a patient's blood must be tested to make sure the dose of lithium is not at a harmful level. Side effects of lithium include nausea, vomiting, headache, rash, tremors, and weight gain. Signs of lithium toxicity include slurred speech, confusion, stupor, and worsening tremors. Lithium toxicity can lead to seizures, coma, and death (Preston et al., 2002).

The other mood stabilizers are called anticonvulsants. These medications help stabilize the neuron membranes and increase the amount of the neurotransmitter GABA in the brain. Depakote, Tegretol, Trileptal, and Lamictal are all anticonvulsants used by psychiatrists. Side effects of mood stabilizers include weight gain, drowsiness, and harmful effects to fetuses.

Stimulants Stimulants increase attention, decrease hyperactivity, and decrease impulsivity by stimulating the frontal lobes of the brain. Methylphenidate and amphetamines are the most commonly used stimulants. The most noticeable side effects of stimulants are headaches and decreased appetite. In some cases, a client may develop tics (involuntary movements) after taking stimulants. However, an increase in the dose of the stimulant does not seem to increase the tics (Varley, Vincent, Varley, & Calderon, 2001). In general psychiatric practice, stimulants have been thought to decrease appetite and make it difficult for growing children to gain weight; however, a recent study by Sund and Zeiner (2002) provides contrary evidence. Extended-release stimulants, such as Concerta, Adderall XR, and Dexedrine spansules, last from 8 to 12 hours, improving the convenience of taking these medications. Extended-release stimulants can allow a child to take his medication before school and not during class time. Immediate-release stimulants, such as Ritalin, Focalin, and Dexedrine, last 3 to 4 hours.

THERAPEUTIC RELATIONSHIP

Counselor's Role

In general, the counselor's role is one of consultant and referral agent regarding medication for her clients. Counselors do not prescribe medications, and they must be aware of boundaries and ethics regarding the advice they give to clients. They do, however, play a very significant role. As we have noted before, counselors are frequently confronted with clients who are on medications or who want advice about medications. Also they may need to consider medications for their own clients. And it is not just a question of making a referral. Counselors are often in a position to observe side effects and to talk with clients about the effects of their medications. Because of the importance of the counselor's role, we have included an extensive discussion of the referral process and also the methods of communication between counselors and medical prescribers later, in the "Therapeutic Techniques" section.

Counselor-Client-Physician Relationships

Greenberg (1999) and Fisher and Greenberg (1997) have reported there is evidence that the doctor-patient relationship and placebo effects play a significant role in the curative power of psychoactive medications. In fact, one study indicates that at least 75% of drug effectiveness is the result of placebo effects (Kirsch & Sapperstein, 1998). An effective doctor-patient alliance may be as important in a medical context as it is in a counseling situation. For family physicians and nonpsychiatric medical personnel, however, establishing an effective alliance may be difficult because of the limited amount of time available for each patient. In some cases, the medication may decrease the impairing symptoms to the point where the patient is able to live successfully without professional counseling. Or the patient may prefer to use medication without counseling, even if counseling is recommended. However, we tend to agree with research findings that concurrent counseling or therapy is most effective.

When both counselors and medical personnel are working with a client, a kind of triangular relationship, counselor-client-prescriber, is formed. This can raise new therapy issues, as the client might show "splitting" behavior, playing the counselor against the prescriber or vice versa. For example, the client might tell the counselor that she has been attending therapy for a year with no results, while the prescriber whom she has been seeing for only a month has helped so much more. Or the client might tell the counselor that while the counselor is a wonderful therapist and has helped a great deal, the prescriber did not listen appropriately, only spent 15 minutes with her, and just prescribed some medication without explaining it. Splitting behavior occurs often with borderline clients. These clients can change rapidly from very positive to very negative feelings about specific relationships. The counselor may see this behavior in other clients as well (Kaplan & Sadock, 1998).

A solution to the splitting phenomenon is to obtain a release from the client at the beginning of treatment, allowing the counselor to stay in touch with the prescriber. The splitting can also be used as a topic in therapy sessions. It is up to the counselor, who has the time to focus on the dynamics of the splitting behavior, which may be directly related to important psychological issues (Kaplan & Sadock, 1998).

ASSESSMENT, GOALS, AND PROCESS OF THERAPY

The counselor's role in assessment, diagnosis, and goal setting with regard to medication is primarily related to the referral process. In this section, we talk primarily about the counselor's decision making about referral, the process she uses, and her goals for referral. Part of this discussion involves the counselor's attitudes toward the role of medication and the medical model of treatment. As you have seen while studying the different theories, many of them do not include a formal diagnosis or extensive assessment. However, even in counseling approaches where assessment and diagnosis are not particularly relevant, we believe that it is useful to do an initial intake to gather basic information about a client's physical health and current and previous medications.

Even counselors who reject a medical-diagnostic model should consider an initial assessment to see if psychotropic medications are already being taken or if the client has symptoms for which she might want to consider medication. Appropriate informed consent would require a therapist who does not want to work with clients on medications to be clear about this at the beginning of counseling. Take the case of Francine.

> **Counselor:** What brings you in?
> **Francine:** I've just been feeling very down. I even have trouble getting out of bed sometimes. My dad suggested I get help.
> **Counselor:** It sounds like things have been pretty tough for you lately. Do you have any kind of physical problems that might be involved here?
> **Francine:** No, I don't think so. I saw my family doctor, and she gave me a complete physical and said that there is nothing physically wrong with me. She suggested that I try some Lexapro to help with the depression.
> **Counselor:** Well, it was a good idea to rule out any medical issues that might cause you to feel apathetic and to have low energy.

> **Francine:** I suppose, but I am still depressed. The doctor said it might take several weeks for the antidepressant to work.
>
> **Counselor:** Why did you decide to also seek counseling?
>
> **Francine:** My doctor thought it would be a good idea.
>
> **Counselor:** Well, let me go over my approach to counseling. Do you remember reading the informed consent that I sent you?
>
> **Francine:** Well, not exactly, but I do remember signing something.
>
> **Counselor:** The informed consent was a letter telling you about my counseling approach. It is called existential counseling, and I work with clients from the standpoint of the meaning and choices in their life. I find that medication is not helpful in dealing with these kinds of issues. I think counseling is a good idea for you, but with a therapist who has an approach that can work along with medications. I can refer you to some other therapists.

This is perhaps an extreme example. Most counselors would probably agree to work with a client who was taking Lexapro as long as the use of the medication was under medical supervision.

Therapists who do believe in using psychotropic medications must often make judgments about when to refer a client for evaluation. This may require the counselor to be able to use the *Diagnostic and Statistical Manual of Mental Disorders* (*DSM*). The *DSM* IV is particularly useful in making referrals and discussing referrals with medical practitioners. The referral process and judgments about when to refer are complicated, and both diagnostic and philosophical questions are involved. As we have noted earlier, a counselor's view of medication clearly affects how and when she refers. We suggest that a medical referral should be considered in the following situations:

- If there are problems that may be health related. Many psychological problems can have physical causes or components. Stress, depression, apathy, eating disorders, sleeping problems, and many other issues that clients may present to a therapist might have a physical component. For example, a deficiency in folic acid may cause depression (Morris, Fava, Jacques, Selhub, & Rosenberg, 2003). Children who have difficulty listening or paying attention may have an auditory processing disorder or chronic ear infections, instead of ADHD (Adesman, Altshuler, Lipkin, & Walco, 1990; Chermak, Tucker, & Seikel, 2002).
- If the problem and symptoms are severe enough to require immediate relief. Examples might include a client who is psychotic or who clearly has a thought disorder; a client who is in a manic phase and appears to have symptoms of a manic-depressive disorder, such as not sleeping for days; and a client who has severe panic attacks or who is exhibiting symptoms of obsessive-compulsive disorder (OCD) that are very seriously interfering with his life. These disorders can also be treated with behavioral and other methods, but we list them here as considerations for possible medication.
- If a client's family has a history of specific disorders and the client is exhibiting some of the same symptoms. A number of problems have been shown to have some genetic component. These disorders include bipolar disorder, affective disorder, ADHD, OCD, and psychotic disorders.
- If there is any evidence of an organic problem (a physical injury or problem usually associated with the brain). For example, if the client states that only after a car accident did she begin to have angry outbursts, there was most likely some form of brain trauma. In a study

by Brewer, Metzger, and Therrien (2002), 20% of study participants who had a traumatic brain injury 30 days earlier still had symptoms of distractibility, impulsivity, and irritability.

- If a client is so anxious, depressed, or inattentive that he is not processing the events of the session or benefiting from therapy. As with all of these referral considerations, the availability of medical services and the client's economic status may be considerations.
- If the client requests a referral. When a client presents to a nonmedical therapist and is convinced that medication may be helpful, the therapist should consider the expectancy effect.

If a referral is made, it is advisable to educate and empower the client regarding her visit with her physician. She can be encouraged to write out her questions and keep a log of symptoms and their frequency, intensity, and duration. Contact with the physician via a telephone call or letter (with the client's permission, of course) can be very helpful.

THERAPEUTIC TECHNIQUES

In the previous section on assessment, goals, and process, we discussed the decision-making process for the counselor regarding referrals for medication and the use of medication in counseling. In this section on methods and techniques, we cover what we consider to be important issues involved in working with clients who are on psychotropic medications. When medication is introduced as part of a treatment program, two of the counselor's primary responsibilities will likely be to help the client use the medication effectively and to assist the client in providing good feedback to the doctor who is prescribing the medication. To fulfill these, the counselor may help the client comply with the medication requirements (i.e., learn how to take the medication appropriately) or consult with the doctor regarding the client's reactions to the medication.

Obviously, the counselor and the physician should not work at cross-purposes. Communication is essential, and if the client is experiencing side effects or if the medication is not working, it is important for the counselor to get this information to the physician. As we have mentioned, prescribing medications for psychological problems is not an exact science. Many times the dosage or the type of medication must be changed until a positive result is obtained. Clients often expect a quick and magical solution to their problems when they take some form of psychoactive medication. There may be an immediate effect, as in the case of antianxiety medications, or the medication may take some time to work.

Referrals for Medication

We have already discussed in some detail when a referral might be appropriate and have provided basic information about current psychoactive drugs. But what about the referral process itself? How should referrals be made? The first requirement is that the counselor be familiar with community mental health resources and medical referral possibilities. Many clients do not have health insurance and may not be able to go to a private physician. In this case, other community resources must be utilized.

Decisions regarding the appropriate referral professional are important. If a client is hallucinating and having psychotic episodes, he would clearly need to see a psychiatrist and not another kind of physician. However, if a client is experiencing disabling situational anxiety (e.g., because a loved one has been critically injured) as a result of some temporary life circumstance (a short-term issue), referral to a family physician may be appropriate. The complexity of the situation, possible side effects, and availability are all factors that enter into the referral decision.

A variety of specialized clinics can often be found in larger metropolitan areas. These are frequently multidisciplinary and include a physician who can provide medication. Some examples of these include pain clinics, fear and anxiety clinics, eating disorder clinics, post-traumatic stress clinics, and ADHD clinics. There are also some population-defined clinics that provide a broad range of health care for specific groups such as geriatric clinics.

Should the counselor suggest an evaluation for psychotropic medications to a client? Bringing up medication to the client depends on the counselor's comfort level with not only the client but also psychotropic medication and possible referral sources. The counselor should be able to discuss the pros and cons of medication with the client and provide some understanding of potential benefits. Of course, the counselor herself must be comfortable with the use of medication if she is to make effective referrals. This does not mean that a counselor communicates that medication will provide a "cure." What needs to be communicated is that the counselor believes that it is worth the client's effort to seek a medical evaluation and opinion about medication. It is also quite important to assure the client that she ultimately has the choice about using a medication. This is illustrated in the following case.

> **Counselor:** Jackie, you know we have talked about your family and the history of depression, and also the fact that both your mother and your uncle have had very good responses with antidepressants. Since you have a long history of depression, do you think it might make sense for you to consider medication?
>
> **Jackie:** Oh, I really don't like the idea of antidepressants. I think I should be able to solve my own problems.
>
> **Counselor:** Well, it is certainly your choice, Jackie, but have you considered that there might be some biochemical components to your depression?
>
> **Jackie:** Well, I know it runs in the family, . . . but I was hoping when I changed jobs things would get better.
>
> **Counselor:** Well, we can continue our work, Jackie, but you've had a number of sessions of counseling on three different occasions and it is still hard for you to fight depression.
>
> **Jackie:** Well, can I think about it?
>
> **Counselor:** Sure, like I said, it is really up to you. Have you talked with your mom or your uncle about how they have dealt with their depression?
>
> **Jackie:** Yes, I did talk to my mom—she's had a lot of counseling and she thinks that antidepressants have helped some. I don't know . . .
>
> **Counselor:** Well, give this some more thought. Remember, too, that if you go to see a psychiatrist for an evaluation, she can tell you a lot more about how helpful medication might be, and also about the side effects. And remember also that it is always your choice.
>
> **Jackie:** OK, I'll definitely think about it.

There are a number of questions or comments that are common when medication is suggested to clients. Clients may believe that this means that they are crazy, that they will be on medication forever, that some terrible side effect might occur, that they will no longer be able to come for counseling, or that they will be forced into something they don't want to do.

As illustrated in the above example, the best approach is to reinforce the fact that the client always has a choice and that she needs to discuss all of her concerns in detail with the prescribing doctor.

There are also additional points to keep in mind. Counselors may find that the client's resistance to medication (and possibly therapy) may be a subconscious ambivalence about personal change (Kaplan & Sadock, 1998). Also, we believe that the client should be told that the therapist will make every effort to continue to see him. As we noted previously, communication with the physician or other prescriber is important. If at all possible, a counselor can consider writing a short letter outlining the patient and family dynamics and identifying troublesome symptoms. In addition, she may want to briefly discuss the counseling treatment plan. Phone conversations are also desirable throughout therapy. Some physicians and counselors use e-mail with appropriate firewalls and permission of the client. One advantage of this method is a written record of the communication. Although this kind of communication will increase in the future, confidentiality cannot yet be guaranteed. Similarly, although faxes are also used to transmit referral letters, a wrong number could result in the letter going to another fax machine.

Educating Patients About Their Medication

Although it is the primary responsibility of the physician or other medical personnel to educate patients about side effects, a discussion of these side effects may come up during sessions. Knowledge about potential side effects can be very helpful to counselors. Figure 14.3 summarized some of the more common side effects of the different classes of medications. This does not mean that the counselor is responsible for giving out medical information, but if she sees a possible side effect, a discussion and possible referral back to the prescriber may be in order. As we mentioned earlier, it may even be desirable for counselors to take a more active stance and ask clients direct questions to elicit information about side effects.

Sexual Side Effects Although we discussed some major side effects of the different classes of medications, sexual side effects deserve special attention. Symptoms occur in both males and females and include decreased libido, inorgasmia (inability to reach orgasm), and delayed ejaculation. Up to 67% of patients will have sexual dysfunction from antidepressants, and approximately 50% of patients who take psychotropic medications will have sexual dysfunction (Feiger, 1996; Hirschfeld, 1999). By addressing sexual dysfunction directly in counseling sessions, other related issues can be addressed. Patients are more likely to talk about sexual dysfunction when asked directly. In a study of 344 patients, 14.2% spontaneously reported sexual dysfunction to their doctors, while 58.14% disclosed sexual dysfunction in a written questionnaire (Montejo-Gonzalez et al., 1997). The solutions to the problem of medication-induced sexual dysfunction are to stop the medication temporarily, decrease the medication dose, switch medications, or add another medication (Hirschfeld, 1999). Again, close communication with a prescriber is necessary.

Psychotropic Medications and Pregnancy The counselor's role here is to encourage women to inform their physician if they become pregnant. There are no controlled studies on the effect of psychotropic medication during pregnancy because of the risk the medication will affect the fetus. In a study by Hendrick et al. (2003), babies whose mothers took Prozac during their pregnancies had the same rate of congenital abnormalities as the average population. However, many anticonvulsants, used for bipolar disorder, pose risks of congenital abnormalities to the fetus (Arnon, Shechtman, & Ornoy, 2000). Psychotropic drugs can be excreted in breast milk and may pose a danger to the baby; however, Burt et al. (2001) point out that in some cases the risks of not taking the medication may outweigh the risk to the baby. These issues are clearly beyond the expertise of nonmedical therapists, but an understanding of the risks can help counselors make appropriate referrals.

MULTICULTURAL APPLICATIONS

Studies regarding the use of psychopharmacological medications with minorities are scarce. Those that have been conducted have methodology and design flaws (Strickland et al., 1991); however, cultural issues can be an important influence on the use of medication. One very significant factor is the reality that many people just cannot afford medications. Approximately 43 million people in the United States are without health insurance, and persons from minority groups are overrepresented among the ranks of the uninsured. It is clear that psychopharmacological medications and psychotherapy may not be available to large numbers of poor and minority clients.

There may also be a bias among prescribers. In a study by Zito, Safer, dosReis, and Riddle (1998), African-American children 5 to 14 years old with Medicaid insurance were less likely to be prescribed psychotropic medications than Caucasian children of the same age with Medicaid at a rate of 39% to 52%. In the same study, stimulants were prescribed more frequently to Caucasian children than African-American children, at a rate of 2.5 to 1. A study by Cuffe, Waller, Cuccaro, Pumariega, and Garrison (1995) showed that African-American children spent less time in medication treatment than Caucasian children. This might also be explained by the fact that physicians know that these clients cannot afford medications and therefore do not prescribe them as readily.

As with all approaches to therapy, racial, ethnic, class, and even gender differences play into the relationship between the patient and the prescriber and between the client and the counselor referring for a medical evaluation. Studies have shown that African Americans are less likely to receive medication for mental disorders due to unfamiliarity with and distrust of the mental health care system and cultural beliefs against seeking mental health treatment (Johnson, 1996; Sussman, Robins, & Earls, 1987).

For example, an African-American client who feels uncertain about going to a Caucasian counselor because she feels she may not be understood may react negatively to a suggestion for a medication referral. She might interpret it as a brush-off from a therapist who sees her as inferior or crazy. This scenario can occur in any client-counselor situation but is more likely when there are cultural differences present. Another example might be a woman who is a strong feminist who believes that woman are overmedicated for depression when the problems are actually sociocultural and caused by gender-role restrictions. She might react negatively to a suggestion for evaluation for depression. This kind of response could also occur with a minority client who believes that medication is being suggested to help him "adjust" to an oppressive culture. The inclusion of medication as a possible treatment can complicate already complex multicultural dynamics.

As Sue and Sue (2003) pointed out, in some other cultures, such as the Native American culture, the body, mind, and spirit are considered holistically and are seen as connected to all things in the universe. Prescribing a specific medication for depression may not make sense to a person from this culture for whom specific symptom relief would not make sense without focusing on the relationships in a more holistic context. Similarly, for a person with a traditional Chinese view of medicine, stressing health and the strengthening of different energy systems in the body, a specific remedy for depression would make little sense unless it had an effect on the energy systems related to mood. If a substance was to be used, it would more likely be some form of a naturally occurring plant that would have an effect on the energy systems.

PRIMARY APPLICATIONS

Psychotropic medications are used in many different ways and in many settings. Substance abuse programs, schools, and criminal justice settings are of particular interest to us here because so many counselors are employed in these areas.

Substance Abuse

Patients with a history of substance abuse are more likely to abuse prescription medications. For example, a person who is prone to addiction might have a difficult time controlling benzodiazepine drugs—which can themselves be addicting. On the other hand, having patients take certain antidepressants while in substance abuse treatment can help increase the period of abstinence. By increasing the period of abstinence, the patient is better able to benefit from treatment. This extended period of abstinence also gives the clinician more time to help the patient emotionally and behaviorally, thereby leading to a greater chance at sobriety (Zweben, 2001).

A history of substance abuse can affect the decision to use medication and the type of drug a patient is prescribed. For example, a patient with a history of cocaine abuse would most likely not be prescribed a stimulant for ADHD. This is due to the possible addictive potential of the stimulant if it is taken in an overdose or crushed and snorted. Since many additional problems are a result of a person attempting to medicate herself for depression or stress, behavioral and other counseling methods are often more appropriate.

Schools

A larger number of psychotropic medications are now available in extended-release formulation. This means that a client can take the medication before school, eliminating the need to take a dose of medication during school hours. While the use of extended-release medication reduces the issue of administering psychotropic medication in schools, the counselor in the school setting will still interact with students who are taking medication. School counselors may also be called on by teachers and parents for opinions about the desirability and appropriateness of medication treatment for school-aged children, particularly for ADHD and conduct disorders. As noted before, this will require a school counselor to form some opinions about the use of these medications.

Also, school counselors and psychologists who are willing to recommend evaluation for medication need to develop a close working relationship with local psychiatrists, family practice physicians, and pediatricians. In fact, an ongoing medical consultant is desirable for a school system's guidance and counseling programs. Given the funding level of our schools, a paid consultant is probably not realistic, but school counselors might be able to obtain periodic voluntary consultations or make connections with psychiatrists or physicians who work in local community mental health agencies.

Criminal Justice

The typical patient in mental health treatment in a correctional facility has a history of substance abuse and has abused multiple drugs. Most have mood, adjustment, or psychotic disorders (Kemph, Braley, & Ciotola, 1997). In 1998, there were 283,800 mentally ill offenders in U.S. federal and state prisons, and approximately 547,800 mentally ill offenders were living in the community and were on probation (Bureau of Justice Statistics, 1999). According to a report by the U.S. Department of Justice, 1 out of 8 inmates in state prisons receives mental health counseling, and 1 out of 10 inmates in state prisons receives psychotropic medications.

The availability of psychoactive medication and of referral resources varies in different criminal justice systems. Many ethical questions arise for counselors working within a prison, including the use of drugs as a control method and also the potential abuse by prisoners. In juvenile facilities and in prevention programs, counseling is typically more available, as are referral resources. A counselor in one of these settings is quite likely to be working with parents and family as part of the treatment, so medication issues must often be discussed with both the parents and the child or adolescent. The most frequently encountered medication questions involve ADHD and oppositional defiant disorder (ODD). Children with these conditions are more likely to act out and encounter the juvenile justice system. In a study by Teplin, Abram, McClelland, Duncan, and Mericle (2002), more than 40% of the youth in a juvenile detention center met the criteria for a disruptive behavior disorder. This category includes ADHD and ODD. The counselor working in a juvenile justice setting may be faced with parents or school officials who want medication to control behavior. Since many families of troubled youth are fragmented, it becomes quite difficult to sort out behavior and its causes. Caution is advised; however, for some youngsters, the proper diagnosis and treatment of ADHD or ODD can have a very positive effect on them and their family.

BRIEF THERAPY/MANAGED CARE EFFECTIVENESS

The effectiveness of psychotropic medications in managed care is somewhat paradoxical. On the one hand, as we have already noted, medications are often sought out and used to help clients deal with emotional problems, sometimes in a relatively short period of time. For example, antianxiety medication might be used to help a client cope with a severe crisis by alleviating some or most of his symptoms in a very brief period of time. Or antidepressants might help a chronically depressed person gain enough momentum to make some changes in her life, sometimes in a matter of a few weeks. On the other hand, if managed care companies rely too much on medications and greatly decrease the coverage for counseling, we believe that in the long run this will not be cost effective. As noted in the "Research" section, there is evidence that a combination of counseling and medication works best, and this appears to be the way in which psychotropic medications can be used most effectively in managed care.

INTEGRATING PSYCHOTROPIC MEDICATION
WITH COUNSELING THEORIES

Most of the counseling theories covered in this book do not include specific recommendations about the use of medication. One reason for this lack of coverage is the fact that many of the theories were developed before effective medications for psychological problems were developed.

In contemporary practice, most counselors from many different theoretical perspectives find a way to integrate the use of psychotropic medication into their theoretical approach. Aaron Beck (1996) indicated that antidepressant medications may have an effect similar to cognitive therapy in terms of biochemical changes in the brain. Cognitive-behavioral approaches lend themselves to integration with psychopharmacological approaches because they focus on particular symptoms or problems.

The key for many counselors is the notion that the psychotropic treatment is "integrated" with counseling. The American Psychological Association's Division of Humanistic Psychology took a strong position on this issue:

> As a general rule, humanistic psychologists do not believe that such medications (or any other invasive procedures) should ordinarily be prescribed without an ongoing weekly therapeutic relationship with a primary therapist. Absent such a relationship, medication only can provide a chemical controlling of behaviors without potential for a transformation of suffering into a growth experience and may negatively affect the prospects for future success should such a relationship become available. (American Psychological Association Division of Humanistic Psychology, 1997.)

There are also voices opposing psychotropic medication altogether. Peter Breggin, a staunch critic of psychopharmacological medication, wrote in *The Humanistic Psychologist* (1997) that psychotherapeutic medication is "disempowering" to the client and clinician, even in times of crisis. Clearly, psychotropic medications cannot be integrated into treatment approaches from this anti-medication perspective.

In our view, most contemporary counselors probably take a much less negative view of medication; however, a number of theories, like the existential, narrative, and gestalt theories, are difficult to reconcile with the use of psychoactive medication. In existential therapy, the focus is on meaning and personal responsibility, and one might interpret the use of medication as an abdication of responsibility. In narrative therapy, the client and the counselor work to reconstruct harmful narratives and to create new life stories. The assumption is made that the person has the power to reshape his own narrative, and the use of medication might be seen as a form of control or oppression. In gestalt therapy, medication might be seen as interfering with the person living fully in the present. As we have mentioned earlier, we think that practitioners of any theory will have to deal with psychopharmacology just because of the widespread use of these medications by many of their clients; however, the use of medication does fit better with some theories than with others.

RESEARCH

It is not possible here to review the medical research on the large number of psychotropic medications available; however, we will review several studies that examine the effectiveness of medication and psychological/behavioral treatment together. These studies have shown that, for certain disorders, medication and therapy work better together than either treatment alone.

In a study by Keller et al. (2000), 519 adults with major depressive disorder were randomly assigned to 12 weeks of outpatient treatment with medication, cognitive-behavioral psychotherapy, or both. The overall rate of remission of symptoms was 55% in the medication-only group and 52% in the psychotherapy-only group, as compared with 85% in the combined-treatment group. In a study by Biondi and Picardi (2003), patients were treated for panic disorder with agoraphobia with either a combination of cognitive-behavioral therapy and medication or medication alone. At follow-up, 14.3% of the combination therapy-and-medication group relapsed, compared to 78.1% of the medication-only group. In a study by Burnand, Andreoli, Kolatte, Venturini, and Rosset (2002), patients with major depression were treated with either a combination of therapy and medication or medication alone. The combined-treatment group had lower rates of treatment failure and hospitalization compared to the medication-only group, and the cost per patient was $2,311 lower when compared to the medication-only group. This was due to fewer hospitalizations and less absenteeism from work.

Feldman and Rivas-Vazques (2003) reported that a meta-analysis of studies of social anxiety disorder over a 20-year period indicated that psychotropic medication and psychological treatment are comparably positive in their effectiveness. They also reported that limited data suggest that a combination treatment is more effective over the long run. Root II and Resnick (2003) reviewed a large, multisite study of ADHD treatments and reported that a combined medical and behavioral psychosocial treatment (COMB) group showed higher gains on core ADHD symptoms.

This area of research, examining combined medical and psychological/behavioral treatment, has received considerable attention in recent years. There appears to be evidence that a combined approach is most effective. Hopefully, as the research progresses, more definitive information on combined treatments will be forthcoming.

EVALUATION OF PSYCHOPHARMACOLOGICAL APPROACHES

A number of criticisms have been leveled against the use of psychotropic medications. Some critics feel that these medications alter people's personalities. The book *Listening to Prozac* helped raise this issue in the popular press. Many negative satirical cartoons, jokes, and references to people on psychotropic medications have been published. In response to one such nationally sydicated cartoon published in the (2003) *Morrow County Sentinel*, Dr. Brian Bachelder wrote the following letter to the editor:

> The January 22nd, 2003 edition of the Morrow County Sentinel printed an editorial cartoon, which depicted a figure representing the American public and a caption stating "One Nation under Prozac, with Antidepressants and Euphoria for All." In this age of enlightened understanding of depression, I find this cartoon both offensive and totally insensitive. Several times a month I struggle in the office to explain to patients that depression is just not a weakness that you can pull yourself out of, but rather a physical chemical imbalance in the brain that can lead to serious consequences if not appropriately treated. Your depiction of a "street drug type high" with an artificial euphoria is not only inappropriate, but totally wrong. Antidepressants do not create an artificial high, but rather bring people back from the depths of depression to a normal level of functioning. I have personally seen lives transformed and potential suicides prevented when these treatments have been started. This cartoon does a great disservice to the community by promoting a backwards way of thinking about these truly amazing medications. In the future I would encourage newspapers to think about the harm that may be caused before printing these satirical pieces. (Reprinted with permission of Hirt Media.)

Whether or not you believe in a biological explanation of depression, this letter raises two important points: that psychotropic medications are a serious part of medicine and that public attitudes play an important role in how the public views the use of these medications. The increased advertising regarding psychoactive medications in recent years has forced the general public to confront the issue. Unfortunately, a very simplistic view of medications as a panacea to cure all that ails one poses a difficult dilemma for therapists who want to give clients a reasoned and objective view.

Some critics have argued that there is a link between psychotropic medication and suicide. Teicher, Glod, and Cole (1990) noted an increased rate of suicide for patients taking Prozac. They studied six patients who had recurring suicidal thoughts after taking Prozac. However, these six patients had been diagnosed with severe depression before taking Prozac, and none attempted suicide after treatment with Prozac. Other studies have refuted the correlation between Prozac and suicide. In a study by Beasley, Dornseif, Bosomworth, and Sayler (1992), patients who took either imipramine or a placebo had a higher rate of suicidal ideation than those who took Prozac. The rate of suicide while taking Prozac is very low compared to the rate of suicide from untreated depression (Preston et al., 2002). Recently, the danger of suicide by children and adolescents using some antidepressants is under study.

The rate of outpatient treatment for ADHD rose from 0.9 per 100 children in 1987 to 3.4 per 100 children in 1997 (Olfson, Gameroff, Marcus, & Jensen, 2003). Depending on your point of view, this is an encouraging or alarming statistic. There has been criticism of the use of psychoactive medications for children. Some critics contend that treating children with psychotropic medication increases their chances of becoming substance abusers. However, the use of stimulant medication was found to actually decrease the rate of substance abuse in ADHD children (Biederman, Wilens, Mick, Spencer, & Faraone, 1999).

Some argue that the rights of children are not considered when stimulants are prescribed. Critics state that sometimes children are given medication for ADHD when they do not want the treatment and that prescribers are not listening to the child and taking her decisions into account (Cohen et al., 2002). There has also been concern about the use of antidepressants with children, since none of them has been officially cleared by the U.S. Food and Drug Administration for use with children, and the studies confirming their safety were with adult populations.

Clearly, the use of psychotropic medications is here to stay, and newer and more targeted medications are likely for the future. Controversy regarding the ethics, utility, and economics of this phenomenon is also sure to continue. Counselors and other nonmedical therapists are strongly affected by this "theory" or approach to treating emotional problems and are called on to learn as much as possible in order to decide how to approach the issue with their clients, and provide the best client care.

Questions and Learning Activities

These questions and activities are designed to stimulate your thinking about this theory and to help you apply some of the ideas to your own life and experience. If possible, you should work with another person or with a small group. Getting others' points of view and sharing your own ideas and perspectives will be invaluable as a way to help you evaluate this theory and its applications.

Discussion Questions

1. Have you seen a client for counseling who was taking psychotropic medication? How did you feel about that? Did you feel that it helped therapy, hindered therapy, or had no impact?

2. Your client comes in and says she has been having flu-like symptoms for the past few days. You ask whether she has been taking her antidepressant medication. She tells you, "I didn't think it was doing any good," so she stopped it last week. As her therapist, what would you do?

3. Your client, a 14-year-old African-American male with a history of aggression and oppositional behavior, tells you that his parents took him to see a psychiatrist who gave him medication for acting out. He tells you that he doesn't want his friends to know he is taking medication. "Besides," he says, "there's nothing wrong with me anyway. Mom and Dad just want me to take it so they can control me." As his therapist, what would you do?

4. How would you address medication noncompliance with a client?

5. A client you see for therapy takes Concerta, a stimulant, for ADHD and Luvox, an antidepressant, for OCD. She tells you she thinks she forgot to take her birth control pills, and she thinks she is pregnant. What should you advise her to do?

6. A mother brings her 7-year-old son in for therapy. She says he has compulsively washed his hands since he was 4 years old. You notice that her son's hands look red and raw. He is getting into trouble at school for leaving his seat and going to the bathroom several times during the class. What would you recommend to the mother? Do you feel an evaluation for medication is appropriate at this time?

7. Do you feel therapy works better than psychotropic medication? Or vice versa? Do you feel both work together better than either treatment alone? What experiences have you had as a therapist that lead you to believe this? As a client?

Learning Activity

Discussing Medications with Clients

In a small group, role-play the following client situations, and exchange feedback. In particular, discuss your knowledge and comfort level in these situations.

1. A client is currently on Wellbutrin, prescribed by his family doctor, and has come to counseling because he is still depressed.

2. A mother brings her son in because she thinks he has ADHD and wants your recommendation about medication.

3. A client with whom you have worked for several weeks continues to be depressed. She has reported a family history of depression, and you need to discuss the possibility of medication with her.

4. A client with whom you have worked for several weeks continues to be depressed and plans to discontinue counseling and go to her family doctor to get Prozac. As the counselor, you believe that she is ignoring self-destructive thinking and behavior and that medication will not really solve her problem.

5. A student comes in and reports that he is having a lot of trouble studying and concentrating. He wants your opinion on taking Ritalin.

6. A Hispanic-American woman who has just moved to the area comes in for counseling because she is feeling very lonely and depressed. She misses her friends and family and has no relatives or friends here. She raises the issue of antidepressant medication with you.

7. An Asian-American man who is currently under psychiatric treatment for a bipolar disorder has just been referred to you, as the employee assistance counselor. His fellow workers find him just too high strung, and he can't seem to get his work done. He is very upset that he has been forced to come in for counseling and does not want anyone to know that he is taking drugs for his disorder.

Companion Website

Now go to the Companion Website at www.prenhall.com/archer to assess your understanding of chapter content with multiple-choice and essay questions, and broaden your knowledge with related Web resources and additional print resources.

CHAPTER 15

Review and Current Trends

Quon: Wow, we studied a lot of theories! It's really confusing to a new counseling student. I liked something about them all. But I don't feel competent to use many of the techniques.

Andrea: I know—there are so many theories and techniques to choose from. I like the idea of trying to use different techniques and different approaches, but I don't know if I can integrate them into one coherent "Andrea approach."

Marge: I really liked the cognitive-behavioral approaches; they fit perfectly for me, and they have good research support. I'm pretty sure I'm going to go in that direction.

Ed: I don't know . . . they all seem to be saying the same thing with different language.

Quon: I wish I had a strong preference like you do, Marge. And the research is confusing. How can you really control all of the variables in counseling?

Andrea: Another problem I'm having . . . how these theories work in real life. It's one thing to read about them, but another to know how they work on real clients.

Marge: That's true. I am really anxious to try out the cognitive-behavioral approach with clients.

Andrea: You know, cognitive-behavioral therapy really does fit your personality, Marge. I remember from some of the role-plays that you like to be active and focus right in on problem solving.

Marge: I don't see it as just a personality thing. After all, cognitive-behavioral therapy has the best research behind it.

Quon: I agree that it has a good research base, but it also really fits your personality, Marge. What about the underlying assumptions? Marge, do you really think that you can change a person's thoughts without taking the time to find what they believe is meaningful in life?

Marge: Quon, I don't see the relevance of having a deep existential discussion with a client just to help her deal with social anxiety. And I know that managed care won't pay for that!

This is a discussion that we have heard, in different forms, many times among students studying counseling theories. You have probably raised many of these questions yourself. How do I put it all together? Aren't the theories all saying basically the same thing? What fits my personality, my basic view of human nature? What does the research evidence really mean? How will the approach work in our current managed care environment? As you probably know by now, there are no definitive answers to these questions. In this chapter, we will discuss a number of topics that should help you in your journey toward developing a counseling approach that works for you—and hopefully your clients.

First, we provide a brief review of most of the theories covered. Since we used the same structure for each chapter, this gives you a chance to clarify and to compare and contrast the theories on many different dimensions. Next we review the common factors theory: Do the theories all say the same thing? Finally, we discuss a number of trends and issues that we think will be important in the next few decades.

REVIEW

Figure 15.1 is intended to help you compare and contrast the theories that have been presented in this book. We have outlined the major concepts in very brief phrases. We do this with some trepidation, however, since many of these concepts are complex and are not easy to distill into brief phrases. We trust that you will use these as a kind of stimulus-reminder and that you will be encouraged to compare, reflect on, and review the concepts, while still appreciating the incredible contributions that each of the theorists has made to the field of counseling and psychotherapy.

THE COMMON FACTORS AND EMPIRICALLY SUPPORTED TREATMENT APPROACHES

In Chapter 1 of this book, we described the two seemingly opposing forces at work in the field of counseling and psychotherapy: the common factors approach, which basically views most counseling approaches as effective because they share certain core therapeutic ingredients, and the empirically supported treatment approach, which does not assume all approaches are equally effective and calls for rigorous scientific research to determine effectiveness.

This topic is important to revisit. You will recall that the common factors researchers contend that the particular theory or approach accounts for only 15% of the curative factors, with the rest being related to ingredients common to all counseling situations (40% client factors, 30% relationship, 15% hope/expectancy). The empirically supported treatment researchers argue that only scientifically demonstrated methods should be used. Since you have now studied a number of theories of counseling and psychotherapy, you are in a better position to evaluate these positions. You have probably also come to understand the complexities of this issue, such as the pressure from managed care for empirically validated treatments and the constructionist theorists' admonition to consider the fact that since we construct our realities, the traditional scientific method doesn't necessarily apply to fields like counseling. Multicultural theorists seem to support the constructionist view in some ways because of its strong emphasis on the importance of considering culture and context and of understanding very different worldviews. For example, the Native American idea of a spiritual connection between all humans and their environment appears to defy a scientific explanation or examination.

Wampold (2001) called the two forces (empirical and common factors) the medical model and the contextual model, respectively. He discussed them as separate "cultures" of psychology and suggested the contextual (common factors) model is the minority culture. He hypothesized that this "minority" has three alternatives. One is to assimilate into the dominant culture

Figure 15.1 A Comparison of Counseling Approaches

	Psychoanalytic	Adlerian	Person-centered
Historical background	• Initially developed in late nineteenth/early twentieth centuries, Victorian era • Freud influenced by Breuer's work on hypnosis • Neo-Freudians further developed theory • Psychoanalysis dominant in United States in early twentieth century • Briefer psychodynamic approaches developed in late twentieth century	• Adler was colleague of Freud • Rejected many Freudian concepts • Early family clinics; social and educational emphasis • Influenced by childhood sickness • Overshadowed early in twentieth century by psychoanalysis • Dreikurs revived interest through Chicago Institute	• Rogers saw importance of empathy in working with children and families • Revolutionary ideas about a client-centered therapy • Evolution from nondirective to focus on experiencing • Rogers's influence spanned several decades, starting in 1930s • In 1960s and 1970s, influential in encounter groups, international work with groups for peace
Human nature	• Deterministic; humans driven by instincts, sex, aggression • Humans strive to control instincts, conform to societal stands • Personality formed in first 5 years of life	• Humans construct own reality, strive for superiority • Person must be viewed holistically • Behavior is goal oriented (teleological) • Social interest in healthy personality • Personality formed early in life	• People have a natural tendency toward positive growth • Phenomenological approach—each person's perception is reality
Basic concepts	• Unconscious • Id, ego, superego • Transference, countertransference • Defense mechanisms used to ward off anxiety • Freud's psychosexual stages • Erikson's psychosocial stages	• Lifestyle, convictions about self, world • Early influence of family constellation, atmosphere • Mistaken beliefs— mistaken goals • Therapy modifies mistaken beliefs • Life tasks	• Conditions of worth block self-actualizing tendency • Necessary and sufficient facilitative conditions: empathy, genuineness, unconditional positive regard • Counselor must "experience" each client, not parrot back responses
Relationship	• Analyst is expert; passive early on encourages transference • Analyst keenly aware of dynamics; requires personal analysis • In brief approaches, analyst is more active, focused	• Therapist balances rapport with educator role • Mutual goals required • Therapist works to understand private logic	• Facilitative relationship is the curative force • Rogers argued that this was sufficient for client growth • Counselor not in an expert role

Existential	Gestalt	Reality
• Philosophic roots—Heidegger, Kierkegaard, Nietzsche, Sartre • Peaked after WWII; search for meaning in a modern, changing world • Frankl a founder of existential counseling—found meaning in Nazi concentration camp	• German psychology; humans have innate capacity to impose patterns, meaning on perceptions • Fritz and Laura Perls developed Gestalt therapy in mid-1900s • Associated with encounter, humanistic psychology movement, Esalen in 1960s and 1970s	• Glasser developed in 1960s to help juvenile offenders cope with the outside world • Adopted by a variety of institutions looking for better, more concrete ways to help members • Evolved into what is now called choice theory • Wubbolding developed systematic approach
• Yalom—four givens of existence: realization of death, freedom, isolation, and meaninglessness • Four ways of being in the world: Umwelt—natural world; Mitwelt—with others; Eigenwelt—personal world, perceptions; Uberwelt—spiritual being	• Holistic view of human functioning, focus on internal perceptions of meaning and connection with outside influences • Personal responsibility for decisions, living creatively • Humans more than just a combination of individual perceptions	• Humans strive to meet basic needs of belonging, power, freedom/independence, fun/enjoyment • Humans are capable of choosing and are responsible • Mental illness is what occurs when people cannot meet their basic needs
• Existential anxiety is natural response to being in the world • Counseling helps clients confront existential anxiety, meaninglessness	• Figure/ground demonstration of how gestalts change • Unfinished business (unmet needs) interfere with ability to function well • Polarization, top dog/underdog • Present awareness stressed • Layers of neurosis—peeling the onion	• Choice theory versus External control psychology • Four elements of human activity: actions, thinking, feeling, physiology • Car metaphor: front wheels (behavior and thoughts) guide the car; rear wheels, (feelings and physiology) follow along
• I-thou authentic relationship • Counselor is mentor, guide; doesn't have answers	• Counselor focuses on the obvious (body language) • Focus on patterns • Language—questions to raise awareness • Sometimes strong affect; counselor is "real" and encourages expression of feeling	• Friendly relationship, with the counselor as a good listener • Counselor works to get information and frame problems in solvable terms • Helps client identify how he or she can take responsibility and satisfy needs

(continued)

	Psychoanalytic	Adlerian	Person-centered
Assessment	• Classic analysis does not use formal assessment • Early development analyzed; focus is on unconscious processes • Free association • Projective tests • Briefer forms use test analysis and assess client's ability to form therapeutic alliance	• Lifestyle assessment, which is also a process of insight/change • Counselor's experience of client important • Early recollections	• Not important, since clients determine content for counseling • No formal diagnosis
Goals	• Insight into unconscious, understanding of inner conflicts and unhealthy use of defense mechanisms • Focus is on character change and healthier use of defense mechanisms • Briefer forms focus on problems, core conflicts	• Insight into mistaken beliefs • Develop social interest, healthier beliefs, socially useful behavior	• Client comes to accept his/her personal worth • Self and ideal self are closer together—conditions of worth no longer have power
Process	• Psychoanalytic situation • Working through transference • Briefer forms use anger, anxiety to break through defenses • Unconscious becomes conscious • Triangle of conflict • Triangle of person	• Establish relationship • Assessment of lifestyle • Ongoing insight • Reorientation and change	• Counselor very aware of personal reactions, self-disclosure • Nonverbal communication important • Counselor's empathy leads to deeper understanding by client
Techniques	• Not technique oriented • Free association, dream analysis, projective assessment • Analysis of transference relationship and patterns of client resistance • Briefer forms use confrontation, speeding up transference	• Encouragement • Task setting • Antisuggestion • Acting as if • Catching onself • Push-button technique • Creating images • Spitting in the soup • Avoid the tar baby	• Not technique oriented • Rote "listening skills training" not a valid representation of Rogers

Existential	Gestalt	Reality
• No formal assessment; seen as interfering with I-thou relationship • Counselor may help client focus on basic existential issues, meaning, death, anxiety • May use four ways of being as structure	• No formal assessment • Counselor tracks patterns	• Diagnostic labels used only for insurance purposes • No formal assessment • May use checklists, Need-Strength Profile
• Authenticity, awareness • Frankl's logotherapy helps clients accept personal responsibility	• Increase awareness in order to create change and fulfillment	• Defining needs, how effectively they are being met • Taking responsibility for choosing new, more effective ways to meet needs
• Socratic dialogue to explore themes • Importance of I-thou relationship • Translate understanding of meaning and purpose in life decisions	• Contact, process, experimentation • Peel back layers of neurosis to reveal the authentic self	• WDEP systems: W—explore needs, wants, commitment; D—explore behavior, what is the client doing; E—help client evaluate his or her behavior; P—plan for change
• Generally no techniques • Frankl—paradoxical intention, dereflection	• Experiments, suggested by counselor, are spontaneous and anchored in relationship • Staying with feeling • Dialogue between parts of self • Playing the projection • Top dog/underdog	• Questions help clients evaluate life directions • Do the unexpected • Bibliotherapy • Allow/impose consequences • Physical activity, humor, meditation • Listen for and use metaphors

(*continued*)

	Psychoanalytic	Adlerian	Person-centered
Multicultural	• Neglects culture, social factors • Not affordable • Psychosexual stages negative to women	• Each individual is seen as unique • Emphasizes understanding each person's frame of reference • Emphasis on nuclear family, not extended cultural influences	• Not specifically covered • Deep respect for and understanding of each individual perspective by therapist • Indirect understanding of oppression (conditions of worth) • Individual focus rather than cultural focus
Brief/ Managed Care	• Classic analysis takes years • Briefer forms typically take months, not weeks • Briefer forms can be problem focused	• Lifestyle analysis can be shortened • Active techniques like task setting, acting as if • Insight leads to behavior change	• Not a good fit because of client-centered focus, no time limits • Motivational interviewing fits with briefer, involuntary counseling

	Behavioral	Cognitive	Feminist
Historical background	• Roots in early experimental psychology, Pavlov, Watson, Thorndike, Wolpe • Behavior therapy emerged in 1950s as an alternative to psychoanalysis • Influence of Bandura and social learning • In late 1900s, evolved into CBT; influence of Meichenbaum and others	• Mid–twentieth century • Both Ellis and Beck dissatisfied with psychoanalysis	• Developed out of the women's liberation movement—1960s, 1970s • Consciousness-raising groups • Chesler: Female clients pathologized because of gender oppression • Research, human development theories based on male gender
Human nature	• Human behavior governed by learning principles • Humans not inherently good or bad; they are shaped by environment • Human behavior capable of change under the right conditions	• Ellis—humans are both rational and irrational; biological tendency toward irrationality • Beck—individuals construct reality; cognition mediates affect and is knowable; cognitive change central to human change	• Oppressive social/political influences on women and others • Need for social justice for gender and other oppressed groups • Women/all people have strengths, potential that need to be allowed to develop

Existential	Gestalt	Reality
• Some argue that existential themes are universal • Philosophy is based on Western values; questionable applicability to other cultures • Does not provide concrete solutions • Does not consider specific cultural contexts	• Emphasis on understanding each individual's experience • Focus on personal responsibility may not reflect cultural factors like oppression • Emphasis on emotional expression may be particularly difficult for males and members of some cultures	• Belief in choice means that limitations are not imposed on minority clients • Belief in individual responsibility may not allow for consideration of oppression and its consequences • Counselor works to understand each individual's "quality world," including culture
• Limited applicability, not designed for brief formats • Hard to grapple with issues of meaning in time-limited format Doesn't provide concrete, empirically supported treatments	• Powerful techniques can move clients quickly • Each session can be seen as a "whole" • Adaptable to brief interventions for appropriate clients	• Focus on responsibility, results • Well-developed plan for change • Useful in institutional settings with time-limited treatment programs

Solution-focused	Narrative
• Developed by de Shazer and Berg from their work with families • Influenced by Erickson's work • Based on postmodern philosophy that truth is socially constructed; solutions are not necessarily linked to problems • Among the most influential of short-term counseling models	• Influenced by intellectuals such as Foucault and Gergen who saw knowledge, culture, and power as intertwined • Embraces the postmodern view that reality is socially constructed • Developed by White and Epston, family therapists in Australia and New Zealand, respectively
• Humans possess the capacity to overcome obstacles • Solutions to problems are unique to each individual • It is not necessary to understand problem to arrive at solution	• Humans socially construct meaning and are able to reauthor narratives about their lives • The self must always be understood in the context of the larger society • We are not defined by life's problems; the person is not the problem—the problem is the problem

(continued)

	Behavioral	Cognitive	Feminist
Basic concepts	• Classical conditioning—pairing UCS with UCR to produce CR • Operant conditioning—reinforcement, shaping, token economies, stimulus control • Social learning—modeling, self-efficacy	• Ellis—ABC theory; irrational beliefs create problems for people; counseling involves helping people give up irrational beliefs • Beck—schemas > automatic thoughts > • Beck—thinking distortions (e.g., dichotomous thinking, overgeneralization)	• Personal is political • Mental disorders reframed • Oppression, including gender, race, class, ability, and sexual orientation, important in therapy • The therapeutic relationship is egalitarian
Relationship	• Working relationship; therapist applies behavioral principles • Mutually decided goals • Therapist can be powerful reinforcer	• Ellis—most effective relationship is one that solves people's problems; therapist is an active persuader • Beck—collaborative empiricism, using Socratic dialogue	• Egalitarian, empowering • Therapist self-disclosure • Openness, informed consent
Assessment	• Behavioral interview, ratings, inventories, charting • Counselor observation of in-session behavior	• Ellis—clients taught to identify their irrational beliefs; therapy begins with this assessment • Beck—automatic thoughts chart, automatic thought > emotion > behavior • Beck—identify schemas • Beck—Beck Depression Inventory	• Diagnostic categories harmful • Assessment research based on male research/experiences • When diagnosis necessary, shared with client
Goals	• Modify behaviors • Teach new behaviors	• Ellis—teach clients to assess and challenge irrational beliefs, live rational lifestyle • Beck—modify dysfunctional thinking and related schemas	• Symptom removal • Empowerment • Understanding, increase self-esteem • Improve quality of interpersonal relationships • Focus on an affirmation of diversity

Solution-focused

- SFT focuses on the
  future, not the past,
  and on client strengths,
  not weaknesses
- Simplicity is the key
  to successful interventions
- Change is inevitable:
  all situations
  have positives
  and negatives

- Counseling relationship
  is collaborative; counselor
  is a consultant
- Clients are encouraged
  to describe problems
  using their own language
- Empowerment of the client
  is key: Counselor looks
  for signs of strength in client's
  description of problems

- Focuses on what needs
  to happen in client's life
  in order for counseling
  to be effective
- Formal assessment and
  diagnosis not emphasized

- Goals are determined
  by the clients in
  their own words
- Goals are specific,
  attainable, and usually
  spelled out in
  terms of concrete,
  positive behaviors
- Goals need to be realistic
  in the context of a client's
  life and are seen
  as beginnings, not endings

Narrative

- Realities are socially constructed
  through language and
  maintained through stories
- There are no essential truths:
  We cannot know reality,
  only interpret experience
- Dominant plots and counter plots
- Deconstruction is a process
  in which taken-for-granted
  assumptions are reexamined

- Counselor assumes a "not
  knowing" stance and
  shares authority and power
- Counselor actively questions
  to probe client's understanding
  of problems, search for
  alternative interpretations
- Clients encouraged to see
  the world as "both/and"
  rather than "either/or"
- Counselor always looks for
  evidence of strengths and
  abilities in clients

- Formal assessment and
  diagnosis not used
- Counselor seeks to
  understand the client's
  original construction
  of the problem
- Separates description of the
  problem from the person
  telling the story
- History is important to
  understand how narratives are
  constructed

- Help clients describe the
  problems they have brought to
  counseling (i.e., dominant plots)
- Encourage clients to
  embrace alternate
  perspectives through
  deconstruction of
  their narratives
- Help clients form new
  narratives (i.e., counterplots)
  that will be more useful
  and satisfying to the clients

(continued)

	Behavioral	Cognitive	Feminist
Process	• Counselor uses empirically demonstrated methods • Treatment manuals, clearly specified approaches • Token economies involve the systemic use of reinforcements	• Ellis—initially negotiate problem identification; help client see connection between irrational thoughts and negative feelings/ behaviors; then teach client how to challenge irrational beliefs • Beck—three stages: build relationship; focus on client' thinking and homework; client takes more responsibility for analyzing thinking, developing homework	• 4 stages: Open discussion and joint negotiation; discussion of presenting problem; consideration of broader social context, (i.e., gender, oppression); client empowerment, which may include political action
Techniques	• Relaxation methods • Systematic desensitization • In vivo desensitization • Assertiveness training • Self-management • Problem solving • Integrative—stress inoculation, EMDR, multimodal treatment protocols	• Ellis—rational, emotive, and behavioral methods to dispute irrational beliefs • Beck—rational ways to challenge dysfunctional thinking (i.e., reattribution, identify automatic thoughts) • Beck—homework is to help challenge dysfunctional thoughts	• Feminist approach can be used with many theories, techniques • Gender-role analysis • Power analysis • Consciousness-raising groups • Assertiveness training • Reframing and relabeling • Demystification of therapy
Multicultural	• Concreteness often a positive • Separation of behavior, feelings doesn't fit with holistic cultural norms • Potential danger of control • Behavioral interventions must fit cultural norms	• Criticized for ignoring context; too much emphasis on "blaming" clients' thinking • Life schemas affected by oppression • Ellis was early crusader against sexual orientation oppression	• Strong focus on culture, oppression • Diversity highly valued
Brief/ Managed Care	• Brief, specific focus fits well • Manualized treatments can be empirically validated • Effective symptom removal	• Generally works well in brief formats • Beck's work on schemas may be longer term • Can work well with psychopharmacological treatment	• Feminist approach often brief • Exceptions: abuse issues, rape, violence • Incompatible with diagnosis, medical model of managed care

Solution-focused	Narrative
• Discourse on change: Counselor communicates that change is expected • Solution discourse: Involves the formation of a collaborative relationship • Strategy discourse: Identifying strategies clients can use to reach their goals	• Clients describe their concerns • Counselors encourage a wider perspective by helping identify potential stories waiting to be told • New narratives are constructed that allow for new possibilities and creative solutions to problems
• Miracle question: What would it look like if problem went away? • Exception-finding questions: When has the problem not occurred or been less severe? • Scaling questions: Client rates severity • Using breaks • Using compliments • Tasks assigned to client on the basis of preferred solutions	• Externalizing problems to separate problem from client • Extensive use of questions to explore client narratives • Metaphors • Therapeutic documents • Therapeutic writing
• Individual behavior is shaped by the context of a client's life • Counselor must collaborate with the client in establishing goals that are meaningful to the client • Importance of changing behaviors and perceptions, not just feelings • Lack of emphasis on historical factors and view of counselor as consultant, not expert, may limit applicability to some groups	• Emphasizes understanding how social constructs such as ethnicity, gender, socioeconomic status affect a client's narrative • Early stages of counseling spent "deconstructing" the effect of oppressive discourses • Attention is paid to client's personal, family, and cultural history • Egalitarian relationship and lack of concrete solutions to problems may limit applicability to some groups
• Short-term focus and emphasis strengths • Lack of adherence to medical model in terms of diagnosis and understanding history of problem are limitations	• Does not share core philosophical assumptions of managed health care systems • Therapists do explore, discuss, and label clients' problems • Can be practiced with limited sessions

(medical model). If this occurs, he predicts, as we discuss later in this chapter, that psychotherapy will be restricted to brief, medically necessary treatments. His next alternative, separation of counseling and psychotherapy from medicine, would involve a choice for clients: Some clients would opt for medically oriented treatment, while "Other clients may wish to achieve benefits through confronting their core issues, changing their sense of the world, grieving for the dissolution of their marriages, facing the changes in their lives that accompany aging, or learning how to interact honestly and intimately with others" (p. 229). He noted that this strategy would be dangerous because separating counseling and psychotherapy from medicine would probably lead to few resources for counseling (i.e., no insurance or HMO coverage). His third alternative is for the two cultures (medicine and psychotherapy) to become separate but equal. He contended that at this time this alternative doesn't seem realistic.

As we noted in Chapter 1, theoretically we see some coming together of these two theories. We don't see theories as insignificant, as the common factors model seems to imply. We see many interactions between the factors and different theories. From a practical standpoint, the identification of common factors provides another lens through which one can view the different theories. We think the question "How does this particular theory interact with the therapist, with the context, and with the client in order to enhance counseling outcome?" is a very significant one.

TRENDS AND ISSUES

We see a number of changes in store for the helping professions in the next decade or two. We've already alluded to many of these throughout the book, but we hope that a review here, now that you have studied the different theories, will add further perspective.

Multiculturalism

During the later part of the twentieth century, there was an increasing understanding of the importance of minority cultures in terms of both their contributions and their minority status. In the United States, significant increases in minority populations, particularly the Hispanic and Asian populations, have been predicted. Adding to this mix is the increasing visibility of other minorities, such as people with different sexual or gender orientations and people with disabilities. As we noted in Chapter 1, a strong movement toward increasing counselors' competence levels in dealing with minority and oppressed populations has emerged. Although different, in some respects, this movement has paralleled the feminist movement and an increased understanding of gender issues and oppression. Although many multicultural and feminist scholars are very unsatisfied with the speed with which the profession is moving toward cultural competence, we see considerable progress and predict further growth in this area for the helping professions.

One potential problem that we see is the increasing emphasis by some segments of society on what are called "traditional values." Traditional in this context often means the desire to return to oppressive gender roles; homophobic treatment of gay, lesbian, bisexual, and transgendered people; and the expectation that people from all cultural backgrounds should adhere to basic White, European values. We see a divergence here, with the helping professions moving in one direction and many members of society moving in a different one. We're not sure what the implications of this are for counselors, but if counselors become more involved in the overall social and political process, as advocated by multicultural and feminist scholars, there may be some conflict between a counselor's role as advocate and his role as counselor to people who advocate strongly for "traditional values."

Integration

There is clearly a trend toward integration of counseling theories and approaches. This is at least partly influenced by a growing understanding of the common factors in psychotherapy. Although research has consistently found that counseling is generally helpful, attempts to differentiate which theories work best have met with only limited success. We think the trend toward integration is also fueled by the need for practical, tangible results. Related to this is the fact that many specific approaches, particularly cognitive-behavioral techniques, offer these tangible, practical results.

The most common integration of theories that we have observed is a marriage of insight/relationship-oriented approaches with cognitive-behavioral techniques. For example, it seems logical to many therapists to use a Rogerian approach to "get out the story" and provide some insight and then to try some cognitive or behavioral technique to facilitate behavior change. Psychodynamic therapists have also often included some focused behavioral or problem-solving technique in addition to insight and more interpersonal awareness. Feminist and multicultural theorists generally conceptualize their approaches as different ways of viewing clients and their context. They have integrated these different paradigms with various counseling theories.

We see two kinds of integration. The first is when a particular counselor develops an approach that integrates what he has learned about counseling and client change into a personal way of operating. Typically, the individual counselor is not that concerned about the theoretical connections of his approach. In fact, it would be fair to describe this level of integration as eclecticism. We call it integration because we believe that individual therapists do integrate their different methods and techniques with their own personalities, settings, and experiences. Lazarus's technical eclecticism (1997) using the BASIC ID, which we described in Chapter 9 as an integrated behavioral approach, is a creative way to assess and use an eclectic method. It provides a model that can be used as a guide in deciding on different approaches.

The second kind of integration occurs when the theorist attempts to formulate an integrated theory with some kind of theoretically consistent model. The most well known of these is the transtheoretical model described by Prochaska and Norcross (2003). There are three dimensions to this model. The first dimension is the stages of change (precontemplation, contemplation, preparation, action, and maintenance) which we discussed in Chapter 1. The second dimension includes the processes of change.

Early in counseling a client is likely to increase his understanding of his situation and problem and then to experience some dramatic relief as he becomes aware of feelings about the problem and his situation as a result of an empathic counselor. Finally, self-reevaluation occurs as the client begins to take a hard look at his life and his problems. As he prepares to confront his problems directly, he begins to believe that he can do something about his problem, and this is a liberating experience. Finally, as he moves into action and maintenance, he and his counselor use various behavioral methods to help him change behavior.

Figure 15.2 Integration of Psychotherapy Systems Within the Transtheoretical Model

	Stages of Change				
Levels	**Precontemplation**	**Contemplation**	**Preparation**	**Action**	**Maintenance**
Symptom/situational	Motivational interviewing			Behavior therapy EMDR and exposure	
Maladaptive cognitions		Adlerian therapy		Rational-emotive behavior therapy Cognitive therapy	
Interpersonal conflicts	Sullivanian therapy	Transactional analysis	Interpersonal therapy (IPT)		
Family systems/conflicts	Strategic therapy	Bowenian therapy		Structural therapy	
Intrapersonal conflicts	Psychoanalytic therapy	Existential therapy	Gestalt therapy		

From *Systems of Psychotherapy: A Transtheoretical Analysis*, 5th edition by Prochaska/Norcross. © 2003. Reprinted with permission of Wadsworth, a division of Thomson Learning: www.thomsonrights.com. Fax 800 730–2215.

The third part of their model is levels of change. "The *levels of change* represent a hierarchical organization of five distinct but interrelated levels of psychological problems that can be addressed in psychotherapy" (p. 528). These levels, which occur in order, are (1) symptom/situational problems, (2) maladaptive cognitions, (3) current interpersonal problems, (4) family/systems conflicts, and (5) intrapersonal conflicts (p. 528).

Prochaska and Norcross (2003) used their model as a way to examine how different theories might be used in the process of change at different stages and levels (see Figure 15.2). Although we cannot discuss this theory of integration in more detail, one example will provide an idea of how the theory might be related to integrating different counseling theories. Take the case of Manfred, a man in his forties who has struggled with anxiety problems his entire life. His wife urged him to see a counselor, and although skeptical, he began counseling. In his first few sessions, he began to think more about the idea of change and making a commitment to make a real effort in that direction. In terms of the process of change, he is somewhere between contemplation and preparation, probably closer to preparation.

All five levels of change might be addressed in his counseling. Although the levels of change are hypothesized to occur in order, they are certainly not discrete. Manfred might want some immediate relief from his symptoms (perhaps some physical manifestations of the anxiety like stomach problems), so that might be an initial focus. However, working with maladaptive cognitions could be a part of this symptom removal. Since this anxiety has probably affected his relationships with others, including his family, those levels of the problem might become important rather quickly. Perhaps least urgent would be a more in-depth look at his intrapersonal conflicts and their role in his anxiety.

Should he seek out additional counseling, several theories might be useful in addressing the different levels of change. Adlerian therapy could be used to help him understand and focus on how his anxiety is created by mistaken lifestyle beliefs (maladaptive cognitions). Psychodynamic interpersonal therapy might be used to deal with anxiety generated in interpersonal situations (interpersonal conflicts). Some kind of family therapy would be appropriate to work on the stress he feels regarding his family life (family systems/conflicts), and existential therapy might be appropriate in helping him deal with intrapersonal conflicts related to his anxiety. As he moves through the counseling readiness process, cognitive-behavioral approaches might be appropriate to help him deal specifically with his anxiety.

Brief Therapy

It seems clear to us that briefer methods of counseling are here to stay. As you saw throughout the book, a number of theorists and practitioners have developed briefer forms of therapy during the last several decades. The development of much briefer psychodynamic approaches is an excellent example. Bloom (1997) in his book on planned short-term therapy reported on the *dose response* literature, which shows that the gain from counseling is greatest at the beginning and then deceases with the number of sessions. In other words, in general, the most value for a client comes in the first few sessions. Bloom also cited studies indicating that brief therapy is generally as effective as longer-term therapy. Actually, for practical reasons, almost all of the research done on counseling and psychotherapy has involved time-limited counseling.

Although managed care and the necessity for briefer treatments have often been cited as the reasons for the shift from time-unlimited to time-limited counseling, it is important to understand that the emphasis on briefer therapies has been building for several decades. An argument for the briefer forms of counseling can be made without referring to managed care.

Managed Care

We included a section in each chapter evaluating the efficacy of the theory under study in terms of how well it fits into a brief counseling/managed care model. Although we have noted that brief counseling can be justified from an efficacy standpoint only, there is also no question regarding the fact that managed care is having a profound effect on the counseling profession. As we see it, this will only continue. Because of the rapidly rising costs of health care, we believe that counselors and therapists will have to fight for their share of the health care dollar. This is a survival issue for all of the counseling professions, and as we have already seen, in many ways they are being forced to embrace a medical model of counseling and psychotherapy. This is trend that continues despite the fact that many of the theories of counseling and psychotherapy we have covered reject this kind of model.

Historically, counselors and counseling psychologists, as opposed to psychiatrists, clinical psychologists, and psychiatric social workers, have used a "growth-oriented" model, which viewed human growth as a continuous process. Counselors helped their clients grow into happier and more effective human beings. They typically worked with the broad range of clients who were not considered to be mentally ill. You can see how a number of the theories we included in the book (Rogerian, existential, Gestalt, etc.) worked well with this model. Problems were typically viewed not as psychopathological, but as normal developmental blocks. In recent years, primarily because of managed care and the need to "medicalize" their treatments, counselors have become "mental health" counselors, and counseling psychologists have expanded their work to include clients with severe pathology. Paradoxically, other, more clinically oriented professions have expanded their work into more growth-oriented arenas. The relatively new profession of marriage and family counseling was developed to focus on couples and family counseling. Marriage and family counselors have largely been left out of the managed care system, so that their work typically cannot be paid for unless a diagnosis is provided for one member of the family.

If all this seems confusing, it is, but we don't see it clearing up any time soon. We think that a two-tiered system is developing, with most counseling being brief and focused on medically oriented diagnoses of problems (types of depression, anxiety, etc.). This counseling will be reimbursable under insurance and managed care systems. More growth-oriented and unlimited counseling will be available outside the health care system and will be paid for by the consumer without reimbursement. Marriage and family counseling will probably be in this category, too. However, we also predict that therapists will continue to diagnose problems using medical terminology, even though many of them work in therapeutic models that are inconsistent with specific diagnosis of mental disorders.

In some ways, this future is similar to Wampold's idea of two separate cultures, one medically oriented and one contextually oriented; however, there is not a clear dividing line. Medically oriented counseling can still involve growth and isn't necessarily a separate kind of reality. For example, a person who manages her depression with brief psychotherapy and medication will most likely lead a more fulfilled life and be able to develop in new and productive ways of living. And growth-oriented counseling outside a medical context will certainly have positive health benefits for many clients. A client who solidifies his identity and improves his relationships is less likely to become depressed and suffer the associated medical symptoms.

This last example might be called preventive counseling. The idea that counseling can prevent more serious psychological and physical problems is not new. For example, many proponents of counseling services in colleges and universities suggest that counseling during this formative stage in life can prevent future problems related to substance abuse, depression, anxiety, and many other disorders (Archer & Cooper, 1998; Cooper, Archer, & Whitaker, 2001). Since we now have evidence that many physical problems are related to stress, depression, and other psychological problems, there seems to be a strong argument for this kind of preventive counseling. Unfortunately, medical managed care systems have largely ignored this argument.

Psychopharmacology

In Chapter 14, we predicted a continued increase in the use of medication in the field of counseling and psychotherapy. We see this as a mixed blessing. On one hand, we have observed first-hand how effective medications can be with certain psychological problems and conditions. However, like many other mental health professionals, we are concerned about the overuse and inappropriate use of medications. We don't see medications as a substitute for the healing power of counseling and psychotherapy. We are particularly concerned about the use of medication without some kind of follow-up or adjunctive counseling. It may well be that the mysteries of the brain will unfold in the future and that psychoactive medications will be used for an even broader range of human problems and concerns. And we don't think that it is too close to science fiction to imagine that medication will be used not only to solve problems but also to enhance human functioning.

We're not certain of the outcomes of this particular trend. Certainly more and better medications are on the way; however, because of the high cost, many people will be unable to afford them. We hope that one aspect of this trend will be a better understanding of the need for counseling, when appropriate, as part of any treatment program using medications. We envision better cooperation between counselors of all types and medical personnel, particularly as understanding of the holistic nature of healing increases. We would like to see a counseling professional as a part of any family practice. In fact, why not provide a psychological checkup with every annual physical?

Computer Applications

According to Cook and Doyle (2002) and Rochlen, Zack, and Speyer (2004), the practice of online counseling continues to grow. There are also literally thousands of chat rooms available on subjects ranging from depression to pet loss. There has been limited research on the effectiveness of online counseling, and even less on the usefulness of chat room participation. Although one basic criticism of online counseling has been the lack of nonverbal communication, and therefore of an effective therapeutic relationship, there is some evidence that these relationships can be formed online (Cook & Doyle, 2002).

We wonder how this increasing use of the Internet for counseling might affect the evolution of counseling theories and also how well the different theories might be adapted for Internet use. For example, how might Gestalt counseling, which relies heavily on nonverbal communication, be adapted? Would manualized cognitive-behavioral treatments lend themselves to a kind of structured counseling lesson, with minimal contact with a therapist? Marks, Kenwright, McDonough, Whittaker, and Mataix-Cois (2004), for example, described the use of computer-assisted technology in the treatment of phobias.

Another area of interest is how counselors doing face-to-face counseling might use the Internet as a supplement to their practice. Will better encryption of e-mail communication lead to widespread use of the Internet for counselor-client contacts? Would this enable a counselor to check up on a client between sessions and reinforce whatever behavior or dysfunction they are trying to change? Could some kind of automated system be used to have clients check in periodically or chart their behavior change plans on a counselor's Web site? Would a narrative therapist be able to use e-mail for the letters typically written to clients between sessions? Could a personalized video message in which the Adlerian counselor encourages the client be available to the client whenever she needs a boost? Clearly, there are many possibilities; however, there are also many ethical and legal questions regarding confidentiality, crisis management, and so on.

A final area to consider is the use of counseling-oriented software. While computer programs have been used for several decades in career counseling and in psychological assessment, few have been available for personal counseling. Favelle (1994) reported on an interesting application of commercially available programs to counseling. He described the use of fantasy role-play games in simulating real-life situations that may be faced by adolescents.

We suspect that increasing work in artificial intelligence will lead to software that can respond to clients' personal concerns. A computer program that can replace a therapist seems a long way off to us, but with the rate of technological advance, one never knows. One thing does seem certain: Applications of computer technology to counseling are increasing rapidly. Cabaniss (2001) found, in a Delphi study (a survey of the opinions of experts in a particular field), that respondents predicted that by 2008, 90% of professional counselors will be using some form of computer technology in work-related tasks.

WHAT NEXT?

Now that you are at the end of your journey through some of the major theories of counseling and psychotherapy, what next? Are you totally confused, like Quon in the opening dialogue, or have you really been drawn to a particular approach? From our experience, we would say that either position or somewhere in between is fine at this point in your career. Hopefully, you at least have some ideas about which theoretical approaches you want to learn more about. We have included many resources on the book's Web page, and we're certain that you can find many more. One of the best ways to learn about particular approaches is to attend workshops and conventions where you can see and hear experts on the different theories. Students can often get a considerable reduction in the fee for these events. And don't forget to learn more about the research related to different theories. Why not do an in-depth study of the research in a particular theoretical area, perhaps as part of one of your classes?

When you begin your practicum and internship work, we urge you to explore how to apply some of the different theories, under supervision, of course. Take the initiative to ask your supervisor about theory applications and how your work fits in. Even if you agree with the common factors researchers, who say that it all boils down to a few factors, remember that your approach and theory make a difference in how you see your work and in how your clients see you and what you do. Find an approach that fits you and that gives you confidence. We are continually impressed by the quality and compassion of students who want to be counselors. You are entering a profession where you will truly make a difference.

References

A biography of Aaron Beck, MD. (2003). Retrieved February 7, 2003, from mail.med.up.upenn.edu/~abeck/biography.html

Adesman, A., Altshuler, L., Lipkin, P., & Walco, G. (1990). Otitis media in children with learning disabilities and in children with attention deficit disorder with hyperactivity. *Pediatrics, 85*(3), 442–446.

Adler, A. (1927). *Understanding human nature.* New York: Garden City.

Adler, A. (1938). *Social interest: A challenge to mankind.* Oxford, England: Farber & Farber.

Adler, A. (1947). How I chose my career. *Individual Psychology Bulletin, 6,* 9–11.

Adler, A. (1956). *The individual psychology of Alfred Adler.* New York: Basic Books.

Ainslie in Texas. Austin, TX: University of Texas Press.

Ainslie, R. (2004). *Long, dark road: Bill King and murder in Texas.* Austin: University of Texas Press.

Ainsworth, M. D. S. (1991). Attachment and other affectional bonds across the life cycle. In C. M. Parkes, J. Stevenson-Hinde, & P. Marris (Eds.), *Attachment across the life cycle* (pp. 33–51). New York: Routledge.

Alberti, R. E., & Emmons, M. L. (1990). *Your perfect right: A guide to assertive living* (6th ed.). San Luis Obispo, CA: Impact.

Alexandria, VA: Association for Multicultural Counseling and Development.

Allen, K. R. (2000). A conscious and inclusive family studies. *Journal of Marriage & the Family, 62,* 4–17.

Alpert, M. C. (1992). Accelerated empathic therapy: A new short-term dynamic psychotherapy. *International Journal of Short-Term Therapy, 7,* 133–156.

American Psychiatric Association. (1996). *American Psychiatric Association Practice Guidelines.* Washington, DC: American Psychiatric Association.

American Psychological Association Division of Humanistic Psychology. (1997). *Training and ethics: Guidelines for humanistic practice.* Retrieved March 21, 2003, from http://www.apa.org/divisions/div32/training.html

Amundson, J. K., Webber, Z., & Stewart, K. (2000). How narrative therapy might avoid the same damn thing over and over. *Journal of Systemic Therapies, 19,* 20–31.

Andersen, T. (1991). *The reflecting team: Dialogues and dialogues about the dialogues.* New York: Norton.

Ansbacher, H. L. A. R. R. (1964). *The individual psychology of Alfred Adler* (2nd ed.). New York: Harper Torchbooks.

Arbuckle, D. S. (1975). *Counseling and psychotherapy: An existential-humanistic view.* Boston: Allyn & Bacon.

Archer, J., & Cooper, S. (1998). *Counseling and mental health services on campus: A handbook of contemporary practices and challenges.* San Francisco: Jossey-Bass.

Archer, J. (1991). *Managing anxiety and stress* (2nd ed.). Muncie, IN: Accelerated Development.

Arlow, J. A. (2005). Psychoanalysis. In R. J. Corsini & D. Wedding (Eds.), *Current psychotherapies* (7th ed.) (pp. 15–51). Pacific Grove, CA: Thomson/Brooks Cole.

Arnon, J., Shechtman, S., & Ornoy, A. (2000). The use of psychiatric drugs in pregnancy and lactation. *Israel Journal of Psychiatry & Related Sciences, 37*(3), 205–222.

Ascher, L. M., & Turner, R. M. (1979). Controlled comparison of progressive relaxation, stimulus control, and paradoxical intention therapies for insomnia. *Journal of Consulting & Clinical Psychology, 47,* 500–508.

Asen, E. (2002). Multiple family therapy: An overview. *Journal of Family Therapy, 24*(1), 3–16.

Atkinson, D. (2004). *Counseling American minorities.* Boston: McGraw Hill.

Atkinson, D. R., & Hackett, G. (Eds.). (1988). *Counseling non-ethnic American minorities.* Springfield, IL: Charles C. Thomas.

Atkinson, D., & Hackett, G. (2004). *Counseling diverse populations.* Boston: McGraw Hill.

Austad, C. S. (1996). *Is long term therapy unethical?: Toward a social ethic in an era of managed care.* San Francisco: Jossey-Bass.

Austad, C. S. (1997). *Is long term therapy ethical?* San Francisco: Jossey-Bass.

Axline, V. M. (1947). *Play therapy: The inner dynamics of childhood.* Boston: Houghton Mifflin.

Bachelder, B. (2003, January 27). OAFP president responds to recent editorial cartoon on depression [Letter to the editor]. *Morrow County Sentinel.* Retrieved March 21, 2003, from http://www.ohioafp.org/LTE_Editorial_Reply_Depression_Cartoon_To pic.htm

Balint, M., Hunt, J., Joyce, D., Marinker, M., & Woodcock, J. (1970). *Treatment or diagnosis: A study of repeat prescriptions in general practice.* Philadelphia: Lippincott.

Bandura, A. (1969). *Principles of behavior modification.* New York: Holt, Rinehart & Winston.

Bandura, A. (1977). *Social learning theory.* Englewood Cliffs, NJ: Prentice Hall.

Bandura, A. (1986). *Social foundations of thought and action: A social cognitive theory.* Englewood Cliffs, NJ: Prentice Hall.

Bandura, A. (1997). *Self-efficacy: The exercise of control.* San Francisco: W. H. Freeman.

Banks, V. (1999). A solution-focused approach to adolescent groupwork. *Australian & New Zealand Journal of Family Therapy, 20,* 78–82.

Barrett-Lennard, G. T. (1998). *Carl Rogers' helping system.* London: Sage.

Bateson, G., Jackson, D. D., Haley, J., & Weakland, J. (1956). Towards a theory of schizophrenia. *Behavioral Science, 1,* 251–264.

Bauer, G. P., & Kobos, J. C. (1995). *Brief therapy: Short-term psychodynamic intervention.* Northvale, NJ: Aronson.

Beardsley, R. S., Gardocki, G. J., Larsen, D. B., & Hidalgo, J. (1988). Prescribing of psychotropic medication by primary care physicians and psychiatrists. *Archives of General Psychiatry, 45*(12), 1117–1119.

Beasley, C. M., Dornseif, B. E., Bosomworth, J. C., & Sayler, M. E. (1992). Fluoxetine and suicide: A meta-analysis of controlled trials of treatment for depression. *International Clinical Psychopharmacology, 6* (Suppl. 6). 35–57.

Bechtoldt, H., Norcross, J. C., Wycoff, L. A., Pokrywa, M. L., & Campbell, L. F. (2001). Theoretical orientations and employment settings of clinical and counseling psychologists: A comparative study. *Clinical Psychologist, 54*(1), 3–6.

Beck, A. (1996). Beyond belief. In P. M. Salkovskis (Ed.), *Frontiers of cognitive therapy* (pp. 1–25). New York: Guilford Press.

Beck, A. T. (1967). *Depression: Clinical, experimental, and theoretical aspects.* New York: Hoeber.

Beck, A. T. (1967). *Depression: Clinical, experimental, and theoretical aspects.* New York: Hoeber. (Republished as *Depression: Causes and treatment.* Philadelphia: University of Pennsylvania Press, 1972.)

Beck, A. T. (1976). *Cognitive therapy and the emotional disorders.* New York: International Universities Press.

Beck, A. T. (1985). *Anxiety disorders and phobias: A cognitive perspective.* New York: Basic Books.

Beck, A. T., Emery, G. T., & Greenberg, R. L. (1985). *Anxiety disorders and phobias.* New York: Basic Books.

Beck, A. T., Rush, A. J., Shaw, B. F., & Emery, G. (1979). *Cognitive therapy of depression.* New York: Guilford Press.

Beck, A. T., Steer, R. A., & Brown, G. K. (1996). *BDI–II manual.* San Antonio, TX: Psychological Corporation.

Beck, A., & Weishar, M. (2005). Cognitive therapy. In R. Corsini & D. Wedding (Eds.), *Current psychotherapies* (7th ed.). Belmont, CA: Brooks/Cole.

Beck, J. (1995). *Cognitive therapy: Basics and beyond.* New York: Guilford Press.

Beck, M. A. (1997). Managing the unmanageable student: A choice theory/reality therapy approach to understanding behavior. *International Journal of Reality Therapy, 17,* 37–41.

Belenky, M., Clinchy, B., Goldberger, N., & Tarule, J. (1986). *Women's ways of knowing.* New York: Basic Books.

Bem, S. L. (1981). Gender schema theory: A cognitive account of sex typing. *Psychological Review, 88*(4), 354–364.

Bem, S. L. (1983). Gender schema theory and its implications for child development: Raising gender-aschematic children in a gender-schematic society. *Signs, 8*(4), 598–616.

Benson, H. (1975). *The relaxation response.* New York: Avon.

Benson, H. (1975). *The relaxation response.* New York: Morrow.

Berg, I. K., & Miller, S. D. (1992). *Working with the problem drinker: A solution-focused approach.* New York: Norton.

Beutler, L. E., Crago, M., & Arezmendi, T. G. (1986). Research on therapist variables in psychotherapy. In S. L. Garfield & A. E. Bergin (Eds.), *Handbook of psychotherapy and behavior change* (3rd ed.) (pp. 257–310). New York: Wiley.

Beyebach, M., & Morejon, A. R. (1999). Some thoughts on integration in solution-focused therapy. *Journal of Systematic Therapies, 18,* 24–42.

Beyebach, M., Rodriguez, M. S. R., De Miguel, J. A., De Vega, M. H., Hernandez, C., & Morejon, A. R. (2000). Outcome of solution-focused therapy at a university family therapy center. *Journal of Systematic Therapies, 19,* 116–125.

Bibbins, V. E. (Ed.). *Multicultural competencies: A guidebook of practices.* Alexandria, VA: Association for Multicultural Counseling and Development.

Biederman, J., Wilens, T., Mick, E., Spencer, T., & Faraone, S. V. (1999). Pharmacotherapy of attention-deficit/hyperactivity disorder reduces risk for substance use disorder. *Pediatrics, 104*(2), 20.

Biever, J. L., & McKenzie, K. (1995). Stories and solutions in psychotherapy with adolescents. *Adolescence, 30,* 491–500.

Binswager, L. (1975). *Being-in-the-world: Selected papers of Ludwig Binswager.* London: Souvenir Press.

Biondi, M., & Picardi, A. (2003). Increased probability of remaining in remission from panic disorder with agoraphobia after drug treatment in patients who received concurrent cognitive-behavioural therapy: A follow-up study. *Psychotherapy & Psychosomatics, 72*(1), 34–42.

Bitter, J. R., & Nicoll, W. G. (2000). Adlerian brief therapy with individuals: Process and practice. *Journal of Individual Psychology, 56,* 31–44.

Blankenship, M. L. (1984). *Adolescent and adult women's perceptions of social rules based on gender.* Paper presented to the Midwestern Society for Research in Lifespan Development, Akron, OH.

Blankstein, K. R., & Zindel, S. V. (2001). Cognitive assessment. In K. S. Dobson (Ed.), *Handbook of cognitive-behavioral therapies* (pp. 40–85). New York: Guilford Press.

Bloom, B. (1997). *Planned short-term psychotherapy.* Boston: Allyn & Bacon.

Boss, M. (1963). *Psychoanalysis and Daseinsanalysis.* New York: Basic Books.

Boss, M. (1983). *Existential foundations of medicine and psychology.* New York: Jason Aronson.

Bowen, M. (1966). The use of family therapy in clinical practice. *Comprehensive Psychiatry, 7,* 345–374.

Bowen, M. (1975). Family therapy after twenty years. In S. Arieti (Ed.), *American handbook of psychiatry: Vol. 5. Treatment.* New York: Basic Books.

Bowen, M. (1978). *Family therapy in clinical practice.* New York: Jason Aronson.

Bowlby, J. (1969). *Attachment and loss* (Vol. 1). New York: Basic Books.

Bowlby, J. (1988). *A secure base: Clinical applications of attachment theory.* London: Routledge.

Brabeck, M., & Brown, L. S. (1997). Feminist theory and psychological practice. In J. Worell & N. Johnson (Eds.), *Shaping the future of feminist psychology: Education, research, and practice* (pp. 15–36). Washington, DC: American Psychological Association.

Breggin, P. R. (1997). Psychotherapy in emotional crises without resort to psychiatric medications. *Humanistic Psychologist, 25*(1), 2–14.

Breggin, P. R. (2003). Psychopharmacology and human values. *Humanistic Psychologist, 43*(2), 34–49.

Brenner, C. (1974). *An elementary textbook of psychoanalysis.* New York: Doubleday.

Bretz-Joachim, H., Heekerens, H. P., & Schmitz, B. (1994). A meta-analysis of the effectiveness of Gestalt therapy. *Zeitschrift fur Klinische Psychologie, Psychopathologie und Psychotherapie, 42*(3), 241–260.

Brewer, T. L., Metzger, B. L., & Therrien, B. (2002). Trajectories of cognitive recovery following a minor brain injury. *Research in Nursing & Health, 25*(4), 269–281.

Brickman, P. (1982). Models of helping and coping. *American Psychologist, 37,* 368–384.

Brimhall, A. S., Gardner, B. C., & Henline, B. (2003). Enhancing narrative couple therapy process with an enactment scaffolding. *Contemporary Family Therapy, 25,* 391–414.

Brody, C. M. (1999). Existential issues of hope and meaning in late life therapy. In M. D. Duffy (Ed.), *Handbook of counseling and psychotherapy with older adults* (pp. 91–106). New York: Wiley.

Bromfield, R. (1999). *Doing child and adolescent psychotherapy: The ways and whys.* Northvale, NJ: Aronson.

Brooks, P., & Woloch, A. (2000). *Freud? The place of psychoanalysis in contemporary culture.* New Haven, CT: Yale University Press.

Broverman, I. K. (1970). Sex role stereotypes and clinical judgments in mental health. *Journal of Consulting & Clinical Psychology, 34*(1), 1–7.

Brown, L. S. (1991). Antiracism as an ethical imperative: An example from feminist therapy. *Ethical & Behavior, 1*(2), 113–127.

Brown, L. S. (1994). *Subversive dialogues: Theory in feminist therapy.* New York: Basic Books.

Bruner, J. (2004). The narrative creation of the self. In L. E. Angus & J. McLeond (Eds.), *The handbook of narrative and psychotherapy: Practice, theory, and research* (pp. 3–14). Thousand Oaks, CA: Sage.

Buber, M. (1958). *I and thou* (2nd ed.). New York: Charles Scribner's Sons.

Buber, M. (1958). *I and thou* (2nd ed.). New York: Scribner.

Bugental, J. F. T. (1981). *The search for authenticity: An existential-analytic approach to psychotherapy.* New York: Holt, Rinehart, & Winston.

Bugental, J. F. T. (1990). Existential-humanistic psychotherapy. In J. K. Zeig & W. M. Munion (Eds.), *What is psychotherapy? Contemporary perspectives* (pp. 189–193). San Francisco: Jossey-Bass.

Bureau of Justice Statistics (1999, July 11). More than a quarter million prison and jail inmates are identified as mentally ill. Retrieved December 1, 2003, from http://www.ojp.usdoj.gov/bjs/pub/press/mhtip/pr

Burnand, Y., Andreoli, A., Kolatte, E., Venturini, A., & Rosset, N. (2002). Psychodynamic psychotherapy and clomipramine in the treatment of major depression. *Psychiatric Services, 53*(5), 585–590.

Burns, D. (1999). *The feeling good handbook*. New York: Plume.

Burns, R. K., Kaufman, S. (1970). *Kinetic family drawing (KFD): An introduction to understanding children through kinetic drawings*. New York: Brunner/Mazel.

Burt, V., Suri, R., Altshuler, L., Stowe, Z., Hendrick, V., & Muntean, E. (2001). The use of psychotropic medications during breast feeding. *American Journal of Psychiatry, 158*(7), 1001–1009.

Butler, A. C., & Beck, A. T. (2000). Cognitive therapy outcomes: A review of meta-analyses. *Journal of the Norwegian Psychological Association, 37*, 1–9.

Cabaniss, K. (2001). Counseling and computer technology in the new millenium: An Internet Delphi study. *Dissertation Abstracts International, 62*(01), 87A.

Campbell, L. F. (2003). Student success training: An Adlerian approach. *Journal of Individual Psychology, 59*, 327–333.

Campbell, L. F., White, J., & Stewart, A. E. (1991). The relationship of psychological birth order to actual birth order. *Journal of Individual Psychology, 47*, 380–391.

Cangelosi, D. M. (1993). Internal and external wars: Psychodynamic play therapy. In T. Kottman & C. S. Schaefer (Eds.), *Play therapy in action: A casebook for practitioners*. Northvale, NJ: Aronson.

Carkhuff, R. R. (1993). *The art of helping* (7th ed.). Amherst, MA: Human Resource Development Press.

Carkhuff, R. R. (2000). *The art of helping in the 21st century* (8th ed.). Amherst, MA: HRD Press.

Carlson, C. I. (2003). Assessing the family context. In C. Reynolds & R. Kamphaus (Eds.), *Handbook of psychological and emotional assessment of children* (pp. 163–182). New York: Guilford Press.

Carlson, J., & Dinkmeyer, D. (2002). *Time for a better marriage: Training in marriage enrichment*. Atascadero, CA: Impact Publishing.

Cartledge, G., & Milburn, J. F. (1986). *Teaching social skills to children*. New York: Regano Press.

Cashdan, S. (1988). *Object relations therapy*. New York: Norton.

Chambless, D. L. (1993). *Task force on the promotion and dissemination of psychological procedures: A report by the Division 12 board*. Washington, DC: American Psychological Association.

Chaney, S. E., & Piercy, F. P. (1988). A feminist family therapy behavior checklist. *American Journal of Family Therapy, 16*, 305–318.

Chang, J. (1998). Children's stories, children's solutions: Social constructionism therapy for children and their families. In M. F. Hoyt (Ed.), *The handbook of constructive therapies: Innovative approaches from leading practitioners* (pp. 251–275). San Francisco: Jossey-Bass.

Cheong, E. S. (2001). A theoretical study on the application of choice theory and reality therapy in Korea. *International Journal of Reality Therapy, 20*, 8–11.

Chermak, G. D., Tucker, E., & Seikel, J. A. (2002). Behavioral characteristics of auditory processing disorder and attention-deficit hyperactivity disorder: Predominately inattentive type. *Journal of the American Academy of Audiology, 13*(6), 332–338.

Chesler, P. (1972). *Women and madness*. Garden City, NY: Doubleday.

Chesler, P. (1997). *Letters to a young feminist*. New York: Four Walls Eight Windows.

Cheston, S. E. (2000). A new paradigm for teaching counseling theory and practice. *Counselor Education & Supervision, 39*, 254–269.

Cheung, S. (2001). Problem-solving and solution-focused therapy for Chinese: Recent developments. *Asian Journal of Counseling, 8*, 111–128.

Chodorow, N. (1978). *The reproduction of mothering: Psychoanalysis and the sociology of gender*. Berkeley: University of California Press.

Chodorow, N. (1989). *Feminism and psychoanalytic theory*. New Haven, CT: Yale University Press.

Christensen, L. L., & Miller, R. B. (2001). The practice of marriage and family therapists with managed care clients. *Contemporary Family Therapy, 23*, 169–180.

Clark, D. A., & Steer, R. A. (1996). Empirical status of the cognitive model of anxiety and depression. In P. M. Salkovskis (Ed.), *Frontiers of cognitive therapy* (pp. 75–96). New York: Guilford Press.

Clarke, K. M., & Greenberg, L. S. (1986). Differential effects of the Gestalt two-chair intervention and problem solving in resolving decisional conflict. *Journal of Counseling Psychology, 33*, 11–15.

Coffey, E. P., Olson, M. E., & Sessions, P. (2001). The heart of the matter: An essay about the effects of managed care on family therapy with children. *Family Process, 40*, 385–399.

Cohen, D., Leo, J., Stanton, T., Smith, D., McCready, K., Laing, M. S., et al. (2002). A boy stops taking stimulants for "ADHD": Commentaries on a pediatrics case study. *Ethical Human Sciences & Services, 4*(3), 189–209.

Cohn, H. W. (1997). *Existential thought and therapeutic practice: An introduction to existential psychotherapy*. Thousand Oaks, CA: Sage.

Collins, P. H. (2000). *Black feminist thought: Knowledge, consciousness, and the politics of empowerment* (2nd ed.). New York: Routledge.

Collins, P. L. (1997). The historical development of reality therapy. *TCA Journal 25*, 50–57.

Comas-Díaz, L. (1987). Feminist therapy with Hispanic/Latina women: Myth or reality. *Women & Therapy, 6*(4), 39–61.

Comas-Díaz, L. (1988). Cross-cultural mental health treatment. In L. Comas-Díaz & E. E. H. Griffith (Eds.), *Clinical guidelines in cross-cultural mental health* (pp. 337–361). Oxford, England: Wiley.

Comas-Díaz, L., & Greene, B. (Eds.). (1994). *Women of color: Integrating ethnic and gender identities in psychotherapy*. New York: Guilford Press.

Comas-Díaz., L. (1992). The future of psychotherapy with ethnic minorities. *Theory, Research, Practice, & Training, 29*, 88–94.

Cook, J., & Doyle, C. (2002). Working alliance in online therapy compared to face to face therapy: Preliminary results. *Cyberpsychology & Behavior, 15*, 95–105.

Cooper, S. E., Archer, J., & Whitaker, L. C. (Eds.). (2002). *Case book of brief psychotherapy with college students*. New York: Haworth Press.

Cooper, S., Archer, J., & Whitaker, L. (2001). *Case book of brief psychotherapy with college students*. New York: Hayworth Press.

Corcoran, J. (2000). Solution-focused family therapy with ethnic minority clients. *Crisis Intervention, 6*, 5–12.

Corcoran, J., & Stephenson, M. (2000). The effectiveness of solution-focused therapy with child behavior problems: A preliminary report. *Families in Society: The Journal of Contemporary Human Services, 81*, 468–474.

Corey, G. (2004). *Theory and practice of group counseling*. Belmont, CA: Brooks/Cole–Thomson Learning.

Corey, G., Corey, M. S., & Callanan, P. (2003). *Issues and ethics in the helping professions* (6th ed.). Pacific Grove, CA: Brooks/Cole.

Craig, P. E. (2000). Sanctuary and presence: An existential view of the therapist's contribution. *Humanistic Psychologist, 28*, 267–274.

Crits-Christoph, P., Cooper, A., & Luborsky, L. (1998). The measurement of accuracy of interpretations. In L. Luborsky & P. Crits-Christoph (Eds.), *Understanding transference*. Washington, DC: American Psychological Association.

Crowne, D. P., & Marlowe, D. (1960). A new scale of social desirability independent of psychopathology. *Journal of Consulting Psychology, 24*, 349–354.

Crumbaugh, J. C., & Henrion, R. (1988). PIL Test: Administration, interpretation, uses, theory, and critique. *International Forum for Logotherapy, 11*, 76–88.

Cuffe, S. P., Waller, J. L., Cuccaro, M. L., Pumariega, A. J., & Garrison, C. Z. (1995). Race and gender differences in the treatment of psychiatric disorders in young adolescents. *Journal of the American Academy of Child & Adolescent Psychiatry, 34* (11), 1536–1543.

Curtis, F. (1994). Gestalt couples therapy with lesbian couples: Applying theory and practice to the lesbian experience. In G. Wheeler & S. Backman (Eds.), *On intimate ground: A Gestalt approach to working with couples* (pp. 188–209). San Francisco: Jossey-Bass.

Cushman, P. (1990). Why the self is empty: Toward a historically situated psychology. *American Psychologist, 45*, 599–611.

D'Andrea, M. D. (2000). Postmodernism, social constructionism, and multicultural counseling. *Journal of Mental Health Counseling, 22*, 1–16.

Dattilio, F. M. (1998). *Case studies in couple and family therapy: Systemic and cognitive perspectives*. New York: Guilford Press.

Davanloo, H. (1978). *Principles and techniques of short-term dynamic psychotherapy*. New York: Spectrum.

Davanloo, H. (Ed.). (1980). *Short-term dynamic psychotherapy*. New York: Aronson.

Davidson, G. N. S., & Horvath, A. O. (1997). Three sessions of brief couples therapy. *Journal of Family Psychology, 11*(4), 422–435.

Davidson, K. W., MacGregor, M. W., Johnson, E. A., & Chaplin, W. F. (2004). The relation between defense and adaptive behavior. *Journal of Personality Research, 38*(2), 105–129.

Davis, A. Y. (1981). *Women, race, and class*. New York: Vintage Books.

Davis, T. E., & Osborn, C. J. (2000). *The solution-focused school counselor: Shaping professional practice*. Ann Arbor, MI: Accelerated Development.

de Jong, P., & Berg, I. K. (2002). *Interviewing for solutions* (Vol. 2). Pacific Grove, CA: Brooks/Cole.

de Jong, P., & Hopwood, L. E. (1996). Outcome research on treatment conducted at the Brief Family Therapy Center, 1992–1993. In S. D. Miller, M. A. Hubble, & B. L. Duncan (Eds.), *Handbook of solution-focused brief therapy* (pp. 272–298). San Francisco: Jossey-Bass.

de Jong, P., & Miller, S. D. (1995). How to interview for client strengths. *Social Work, 40*, 729–736.

de Shazer, S. (1982). *Patterns of brief therapy*. New York: Guilford Press.

de Shazer, S. (1985). *Keys to solutions in brief therapy*. New York: Norton.

de Shazer, S. (1988). *Clues: Investigating solutions in brief therapy*. New York: Norton.

de Shazer, S. (1991). *Putting differences to work*. New York: Norton.

de Shazer, S., & Berg, I. K. (1997). "What works?" Remarks on research aspects of solution-focused brief therapy. *Journal of Family Therapy, 19*, 121–124.

de Shazer, S., Berg, I. K., Lipchik, E., Nunnally, E., Molnar, A., Gingerich, W., et al. (1986). Brief therapy: Focused solution development. *Family Process, 25*, 207–221.

Deas, D., & Thomas, S. E. (2001). An overview of controlled studies of adolescent substance abuse treatment. *American Journal of Addictions, 10*, 178–189.

Della Selva, P. (1996). *Intensive short-term dynamic psychotherapy: Theory and technique*. Oxford, England: Wiley.

Dermer, S. B., Hemesath, C. W., & Russell, C. S. (1998). A feminist critique of solution-focused therapy. *American Journal of Family Therapy, 26*, 239–250.

Derogatis, L. R., & Lazarus, L. (1994). SCL-90-R, Brief Symptom Inventory, and matching clinical rating scales. In M. E. Maruish (Ed.), *The use of psychological testing for treatment planning and outcome assessment* (pp. 217–248). Hillsdale, NJ: Erlbaum.

Dettrick, C. (2004). Reality therapy and Christian belief—Can they be reconciled? *International Journal of Reality Therapy, 23*, 23–25.

Dialessi, F. (1999). Choice theory applications to creating assessment instruments for schools. *International Journal of Reality Therapy, 19*, 42–43.

DiClemente, C. C. (1991). Motivational interviewing and stages of change. In W. R. Miller & S. Rollnick (Eds.), *Motivation interviewing: Preparing people for change*. New York: Guilford.

DiClemente, C. C. (1990). Stages of change in outpatient alcoholism treatment. *Journal of Substance Abuse, 2*, 217–235.

Dierks, J. M. (1996). Listening within: A brief therapy model for use with Gestalt theory. *Gestalt Journal, 19*(2), 51–99.

Dinkmeyer, D. C., Dinkmeyer, D., & McKay, G. D. (1997). *Systematic training for effective parenting*. Circle Pines, MN: American Guidance Services.

Dinkmeyer, D. C., McKay, G. D., Dinkmeyer, D., & McKay, J. L. (1998). *Parenting teenagers*. New York: Random House.

Dinkmeyer, D., & McKay, G. D. (1996). *Raising a responsible child: How to prepare your child for today's complex world*. New York: Fireside.

Dinkmeyer, D., & Sperry, L. (2000). *Counseling and psychotherapy: An integrated, individual psychology approach*. Upper Saddle River, NJ: Prentice Hall.

Doan, R. E. (1997). Narrative therapy, postmodernism, social constructivism, and constructivism: Discussion and distinctions. *Transactional Analysis Journal, 27*, 128–133.

Dobson, K. S. (2001). *Handbook of cognitive-behavioral therapies*. New York: Springer.

Downing, N. E., & Roush, K. L. (1985). From passive acceptance to active commitment: A model of feminist identity development for women. *Counseling Psychologist, 13*, 695–709.

Dreikurs, R. (1964). Children: The challenge. New York: Hawthorne.

Dreikurs, R. (1973). Psychodynamics, psychotherapy, and counseling: Collected papers. Chicago: Alfred Adler Institute.

Dreikurs, R., & Cassel, P. (1972). Discipline without tears. New York: Hawthorne.

Dreikurs, R., & Cassel, P. (1991). *Discipline without tears* (2nd ed.). New York: Penguin.

Dreikurs, R., & Dinkmeyer, D. (2000). *Encouraging children to learn*. Dallas, TX: Behavioral Science.

Dreikurs, R., & Stolz, V. (1990). *Children: The challenge*. New York: Plume Books.

Dryden, W. (1984). Rational-emotive therapy. In W. Dryden (Ed.), *Individual psychotherapy in Britain* (pp. 347–372). London: Harper & Row.

Dryden, W. (1998). *Rational emotive behavioural counseling*. London: Sage.

Dulcan, M. K. (1999). *Helping parents, youth, and teachers understand medications for behavioral and emotional problems: A resource book of medication information handouts*. Washington, DC: American Psychiatric Press.

Dunn, R. L., & Shwebel, A. I. (1995). Meta-analytic review of marital therapy outcome research. *Journal of Family Psychology, 9*, 58–68.

Dutton-Douglas, M. A., & Rave, E. J. (1990). Ethics of feminist supervision of psychotherapy. In H. Lerman & N. Porter (Eds.), *Feminist ethics in psychotherapy* (pp. 137–146). New York: Springer.

Dutton-Douglas, M. A., & Walker, L. (1988). *Feminist psychotherapies: Integration of therapeutic and feminist systems*. Westport, CT: Ablex.

D'Zurilla, T. J., & Nezu, A. M. (2001). Problem solving therapy. In K. Dobson (Ed.), *Handbook of cognitive-behavioral therapies* (2nd ed.) (pp. 211–246). New York: Guildford Press.

D'Zurilla, T. J., & Nezu, A. M. (2002). *Problem-solving therapy: A social competence approach to clinical intervention* (2nd ed.). New York: Springer.

Eckstein, D. (2000). Empirical studies indicating significant birth-order-related personality differences. *Journal of Individual Psychology, 56*, 482–494.

Eckstein, D., Baruth, L., & Mahrer, D. (1992). *An introduction to life style.* Dubuque, IA: Kendall/Hunt Publishing.

Eisler, I. (2005). The empirical and theoretical base of family therapy and multiple family day therapy for adolescent anorexia nervosa. *Journal of Family Therapy, 27,* 104–131.

Eleftheriadou, Z. (1997). The cross-cultural experience— Integration or isolation? In S. du Plock (Ed.), *Case studies in existential psychotherapy and counseling* (pp. 59–67). New York: Wiley.

Ellerman, C. P. (1999). Pragmatic existential therapy. *Journal of Contemporary Psychotherapy, 29,* 49–64.

Ellis, A. (1965). *Sex without guilt.* North Hollywood, CA: Wilshire Books. (Original publication 1958.)

Ellis, A. (1988). *How to stubbornly refuse to make yourself miserable about anything, yes anything!* New York: Lyle Stuart.

Ellis, A. (1994). Reason and emotion in psychotherapy. New York: Carol Publishing.

Ellis, A. (1994). *Reason and emotion in psychotherapy.* New York: Kensington.

Ellis, A. (1995). *Better, deeper, and more enduring brief therapy.* New York: Brunner/Mazel.

Ellis, A. (1999). *How to make yourself happy and remarkably less disturbable.* Atascadero, CA: Impact.

Ellis, A. (2001a). *Feeling better, getting better, staying better.* Atascadero, CA: Impact.

Ellis, A. (2001b). *Overcoming destructive beliefs, feelings, and behaviors.* Amherst, NY: Prometheus Books.

Ellis, A. (2005). Rational emotive behavior therapy. In R. Corsini & D. Wedding (Eds.), *Current psychotherapies* (pp. 166–201). Itasca, IL: Peacock.

Ellis, A., & Abrams, M. (1994). *How to cope with a fatal disease.* New York: Baricade Books.

Ellis, A., & Dryden, W. (1997). *The practice of rational emotive behavior therapy.* New York: Springer.

Ellis, A., & Harper, R. A. (1997). *A guide to rational living.* Hollywood, CA: Wilshire.

Ellis, A., & Velten, E. (1992). *When AA doesn't work for you: Rational steps for quitting alcohol.* Fort Lee, NJ: Barricade Books.

Ellman, S. J. (1991). *Freud's technique papers.* New York: Other Press.

Ellman, S. J., & Antrobus, J. S. (1991). *The mind in sleep.* New York: Wiley.

Ely, A. L., Guerney, B. G., & Stover, L. (1973). Efficacy of the training phase of conjugal therapy. *Psychotherapy: Theory, Research and Practice, 10,* 201–207.

Engles, G. I., Garnefsky, N., & Diekstra, F. W. (1993). Efficacy of rational-emotive therapy: A quantitative analysis. *Journal of Consulting & Clinical Psychology, 6,* 1083–1090.

Enns, C. Z. (1992). Toward integrating feminist psychotherapy and feminist philosophy. *Professional Psychology: Research & Practice, 23,* 453–466.

Enns, C. Z. (1993). Twenty years of feminist counseling and therapy: From naming biases to implementing multifaceted practice. *Counseling Psychologist, 21*(1), 3–87.

Enns, C. Z. (2004). *Feminist theories and feminist psychotherapies: Origins, themes, and diversity* (2nd ed.). New York: Haworth Press.

Enright, J. B. (1975). An introduction to Gestalt therapy. In F. D. Stephenson (Ed.), *Gestalt therapy primer.* Springfield, IL: Charles C. Thomas.

Epstein, D. (1994). Extending the conversation. *Family Therapy Networker, 18,* 31–63.

Epstein, N. (2002). *Enhanced cognitive-behavioral therapy for couples: A contextual approach.* Washington, DC: American Psychological Association.

Epstein, N., Schlesinger, S., & Dryden, W. (1998). *Cognitive-behavioral therapy with families.* New York: Brunner/Mazel.

Erdman, P., Lampe, R., & Lampe, R. (1996). Adapting basic skills to counsel children. *Journal of Counseling & Development, 74,* 374–377.

Erickson, M. H. (1954). Special techniques of brief hypnotherapy. *Journal of Clinical & Experimental Hypnosis, 2,* 109–129.

Erickson, M., & Haley, J. (Eds.). (1985). *Conversations with Milton Erickson, M.D.* New York: Triangle Press.

Erikson, E. H. (1950). *Childhood and society.* New York: Norton.

Erikson, E. H. (1968). *Identity: Youth in crisis.* New York: Norton.

Erikson, E. H. (1982). *The life cycle completed.* New York: Norton.

Erikson, E. H., & Erikson, J. M. (1997). *The life cycle completed* (Extended version). New York: Norton.

Esman, A. (1994). Psychoanalytic play therapy. In K. J. O'Connor & C. E. Schaefer (Eds.), *Handbook of play therapy* (pp. 11–20). New York: Wiley.

Espin, O. M., & Gawelek, M. A. (1992). Women's diversity: Ethnicity, race, class, and gender in theories of feminist psychology. In L. S. Brown & M. Ballou (Eds.), *Personality and psychopathology: Feminist reappraisals* (pp. 88–107). New York: Guilford Press.

Esser, U., & Schneider, I. (1990). Client-centered partnership therapy as relationship therapy. In J. R. G. Lietaer & R. Van Balen (Eds.), *Client-centered and experiential psychotherapy in the nineties* (pp. 829–846). Leuven, Belgium: Leuven University Press.

Etchison, M., & Kleist, D. M. (2000). Review of narrative therapy: Research and utility. *Family Journal: Counseling & Therapy for Couples and Families, 8*, 61–66.

Fairbairn, W. R. D. (1952). *Psychoanalytic studies of personality*. London: Tavistock Publications and Kegan Paul, Trench, & Trubner.

Fairbairn, W. R. D. (1954). *An object relations theory of personality*. New York: Basic Books.

Faust, J. (2000). Integration of family and cognitive behavioral therapy for treating sexually abused children. *Cognitive & Behavioral Practice, 7*(3), 361–368.

Favelle, G. K. (1994). Therapeutic applications of commercially available computer software. *Computers in Human Services, 11*(1–2), 151–158.

Feder, B., & Ronall, R. (Eds.). (1980). *Beyond the hot seat: Gestalt approaches to group*. New York: Brunner/Mazel.

Feiger, A. (1996). A double-blind comparison of gepirone extended release, imipramine, and placebo in the treatment of outpatient major depression. *Psychopharmacology Bulletin, 32*(4), 659–665.

Feldman, L. B. (2003). Assessment and treatment of social anxiety disorder. *Professional Psychology: Research and Practice, 34*(4), 396–405.

Feminist Therapy Institute. (2004). *What we strive for*. Retrieved October 1, 2004, from www.feministtherapyinstitute.org

Ferguson, R., & O'Neil, C. (2001). Late adolescence: A Gestalt model of development, crisis, and brief psychotherapy. In M. McConville & G. Wheeler (Eds.), *The heart of adolescence: Gestalt approaches to working with children, adolescents, and their worlds* (vol. 2). Cambridge, MA: Gestalt Press Books.

Fischer, C. T., McElwain, B., & DuBoise, J. T. (2000). Existential approaches to psychotherapy. In C. R. Snyder & R. E. Ingram (Eds.), *Handbook of psychological change: Psychotherapy processes and practices for the 21st century* (pp. 243–257). New York: Wiley.

Fish, J. M. (1996). Prevention, solution-focused therapy, and the illusion of mental disorders. *Applied & Preventive Psychology, 5*, 37–40.

Fisher, D. B. (2003). People are more important than pills in recovery from mental disorder. *Journal of Humanistic Psychology, 43*(2), 65–68.

Fisher, S., & Greenberg, R. P. (Eds.). (1997). *From placebo to panacea: Drugs to the test*. New York: Wiley.

Foucault, M. (1965). *Madness and civilization: A history of insanity in the age of reason*. New York: Random House.

Fox, G. L., & Murry, V. M. (2000). Gender and families: Feminist perspectives and family research. *Journal of Marriage & the Family, 62*, 1160–1172.

Frank, J. D., & Frank, J. (1991). *Persuasion and healing*. Baltimore: Johns Hopkins University Press.

Frankl, V. (1963). *Man's search for meaning*. Boston: Beacon Press.

Frankl, V. (1965). *The doctor and the soul*. New York: Bantam Books.

Frankl, V. (1967). *Psychotherapy and existentialism: Selected papers on logotherapy*. New York: Clarion.

Frankl, V. (1978). *The unheard cry for meaning*. New York: Simon & Schuster.

Frankl, V. (1985). Logos, paradox, and the search for meaning. In M. J. Mahoney & A. Freeman (Eds.), *Cognition and psychotherapy* (pp. 259–275). New York: Plenum Press.

Frankl, V. (1988). *The will to meaning: Foundations and applications of logotherapy*. New York: Meridian Printing.

Franklin, C., Biever, J., Moore, K., Clemons, D., & Scamardo, M. (2001). The effectiveness of solution-focused therapy with children in a school setting. *Research on Social Work Practice, 11*, 411–434.

Franklin, M. E., Abramowitz, J. S., Kozak, M. J., Levitt, J. T., & Foa, E. (2000). Effectiveness of exposure and ritual prevention for obsessive-compulsive disorder: Randomized compared with nonrandomized samples. *Journal of Consulting & Clinical Psychology, 68*, 594–602.

Freedman, J., & Combs, G. (1996). *Narrative therapy*. New York: Norton.

Frew, J. (1988). The practice of Gestalt therapy in groups. *Gestalt Journal, 11*(1), 77–96.

Frey, D. H., & Heslet, F. E. (1975). Existential theory for counselors. In S. C. Stone & B. Shertzer (Eds.), *Guidance monograph series* (vol. 8). Palo Alto, CA: Houghton Mifflin.

Frey, L. L. (2003). Use of narratives, metaphor, and relationship in the assessment and treatment of sexually reactive Native American youth. In G. Roysircar, D. S. Sandhu, & V. E. Bibbins (Eds.), *Multicultural competencies: A guidebook of practices*. Alexandria, VA: Association for Multicultural Counseling and Development.

Friedan, B. (1963). *The feminine mystique*. New York: Norton Books.

Fromm, R. (1941). *Escape from freedom*. New York: Aaron Books.

Fromm, R. (1976). *To have or to be?* New York: Harper & Row.

Fukuyama, M., & Sevig, T. (1999). *Integrating spirituality into multicultural counseling*. Thousand Oaks, CA: Sage.

Galatzer-Levy, R. M., Bachrach, H., Skolnikoff, A., & Waldron, W. (2000). *Does psychoanalysis work?* New Haven, CT: Yale University Press.

Gardner, R. A. (1993). *Storytelling in psychotherapy with children*. Northvale, NJ: Jason Aronson.

Garfield, S. L. (1994). Research on client variables in psychotherapy. In S. L. Garfield & A. E. Bergin (Eds.), *Handbook of psychotherapy and behavior change* (pp. 213–256). New York: Wiley.

Gaston, L. (1990). The concept of the alliance and its role in psychotherapy: Theoretical and empirical considerations. *Psychotherapy, 27,* 143–153.

Gay, P. (1988). *Freud: A life for our time.* New York: Anchor Books.

Geertjens, L., & Waaldijik, O. (1998). Client-centred therapy for adolescents: An interactional point of view. In E. L. B. Thorne (Ed.), *Person-centred therapy: A European perspective* (pp. 159–175). London: Sage.

Gelles, R. J., & Maynard, P. E. (1987). A structural family systems approach to intervention in cases of family violence. *Family Relations, 36,* 270–275.

Gergen, K. (1992). The postmodern adventure. *Family Therapy Networker, 52,* 56–57.

Gfroerer, K., Gfroerer, C., Curlette, W. L., & William, L. (2003). Psychological birth order and the BASIS-A Inventory. *Journal of Individual Psychology, 59,* 30–41.

Gilligan, C. (1982). *In a different voice.* Cambridge, MA: Harvard University Press.

Gilligan, C., Rogers, A. G., & Tolman, D. L. (Eds.). (1991). *Women, girls, and psychotherapy: Reframing resistance.* New York: Harrington Park Press.

Gingerich, W., & Eisengart, S. (2000). Solution-focused brief therapy: A review of the outcome research. *Family Process, 39,* 477–498.

Gladding, S. T. (2002). *Family therapy: History, theory, and practice* (3rd ed.). Upper Saddle River, NJ: Prentice Hall.

Glasser, W. (1961). *Mental health or mental illness?* New York: Harper & Row.

Glasser, W. (1965). *Reality therapy.* New York: Harper & Row.

Glasser, W. (1968). *Schools without failure.* New York: Harper & Row.

Glasser, W. (1972). *The identity society.* New York: Harper & Row.

Glasser, W. (1976). *Positive addiction.* New York: Harper & Row.

Glasser, W. (1980). *What are you doing?* New York: Harper & Row.

Glasser, W. (1984). *Control theory.* New York: Harper & Row.

Glasser, W. (1986). *Control theory in the classroom.* New York: Harper & Row.

Glasser, W. (1989). Control theory. In N. Glasser (Ed.), *Control theory in the practice of reality therapy* (pp. 1–15). New York: Harper & Row.

Glasser, W. (1995). *Staying together: The control theory guide to a lasting marriage.* New York: HarperCollins.

Glasser, W. (1998). *Choice theory: A new psychology of personal freedom.* New York: HarperCollins.

Glasser, W. (2000a). *Counseling with choice theory: The new reality therapy.* New York: HarperCollins.

Glasser, W. (2000b). *Reality therapy in action.* New York: HarperCollins.

Glasser, W. (2002). *Unhappy teenagers: A way for parents and teachers to reach them.* New York: HarperCollins.

Glasser, W., & Glasser, C. (2000). *Getting together and staying together: Solving the mystery of marriage.* New York: HarperCollins.

Glauser, A. S., & Bozarth, J. D. (2001). Person-centered counseling: The culture within. *Journal of Counseling & Development, 79,* 142–147.

Glenn, S., & Nelsen, J. (2000). *Raising self-reliant children in a self-indulgent world: Seven building blocks for developing capable young people.* Roseville, CA: Prima Lifestyles.

Goldenberg, H. (1997). Who am I, if I am not a mother? In S. du Plock (Ed.), *Case studies in existential psychotherapy and counseling* (pp. 96–106). New York: Wiley.

Goldenberg, I., & Goldenberg, H. (2004). *Family therapy: An overview* (6th ed.). Belmont, CA: Brooks/Cole.

Goldenberg, I., & Goldenberg, H. (2005). Family therapy. In R. J. Corsini & D. Wedding (Eds.), *Current psychotherapies.* Belmont, CA.: Brooks/Cole.

Goldfried, M., & Davison, G. (1994). *Clinical behavior therapy.* New York: Wiley.

Goldman, A., & Greenberg, I. (1992). Comparison of integrated systemic and emotionally focused approaches to couples therapy. *Journal of Consulting & Clinical Psychology, 60*(6), 962–969.

Goldstein, K. (1939). *The organism.* New York: American Book.

Goode, E. (2000). *A pragmatic man and his no-nonsense therapy.* Retrieved February 7, 2003, from www.cognitivetherapy.com/beck_times.html

Graham, P. (1998). *Cognitive-behavior therapy for children and families.* New York: Cambridge Press.

Grawe, K., Donati, R., & Bernauer, F. (1998). *Psychotherapy in transition.* Seattle, WA: Hogrefe & Huber.

Greenberg, L., & Johnson, S. (1988). *Emotionally focused therapy for couples.* New York: Guilford Press.

Greenberg, L. S., Rice, L. N., & Elliott, R. (1993). *Facilitating emotional change: The moment-by-moment process*. New York: Guilford Press.

Greenberg, R. (1999). Common psychosocial factors in psychiatric drug therapy. In M. Hubble, B. Duncan, & S. Miller (Eds.), *The heart and soul of change: What works in therapy* (pp. 297–328). Washington, DC: American Psychological Association.

Greenberger, D., & Padesky, C. A. (1995). *Mind over mood: Change how you feel by changing the way you think*. New York: Guilford Press.

Greene, B. (1994). Diversity and difference: The issue of race in feminist therapy. In M. Mirkin (Ed.), *Women in context: Toward a feminist reconstruction of psychotherapy* (pp. 333–351). New York: Guilford Press.

Gregg, G. (2003). *A sketch of Albert Ellis*. Retrieved February 7, 2003, from www.rebt.org/dr/biography.asp

Griffin, W. A., & Shannon, M. G. (1999). *Models of family therapy*. Philadelphia: Taylor & Francis.

Grotevant, H. D., & Carlson, C. I. (1989). *Family assessment*. New York: Guilford Press.

Haddock, S. A., Zimmerman, T. S., & MacPhee, D. (2000). The Power Equity Guide: Attending to gender in family therapy. *Journal of Marital & Family Therapy, 26*, 153–170.

Haley, J. (1963). *Strategies of psychotherapy*. New York: Grune & Stratton.

Haley, J. (1973). *Uncommon therapy: The psychiatric techniques of Milton Erickson*. New York: Norton.

Haley, J. (1978). *Problem-solving therapy*. San Francisco: Jossey-Bass.

Haley, J. (1979). *Leaving home: Therapy with disturbed young people*. New York: McGraw-Hill.

Haley, J. (1984). *Ordeal therapy: Unusual ways to change behavior*. San Francisco: Jossey-Bass.

Haley, J., & Richeport-Haley, M. (2003). *The art of strategic therapy*. New York: Brunner-Routledge.

Hall, C. (1999). *A primer of Freudian psychology*. New York: Plume Books.

Hansen, L. S., Gamma, E. M. P., & Harkins, A. K. (2002). Revisiting gender issues in multicultural counseling. In P. B. Pedersen, J. G. Draguns, W. J. Lonner, & J. E. Trimble (Eds.), *Counseling across cultures* (5th ed.) (pp. 163–184). Thousand Oaks, CA: Sage.

Hare-Mustin, R. (1978). A feminist approach to family therapy. *Family Process, 17*, 15–27.

Hare-Mustin, R. (1980). Family therapy can be dangerous to your health. *Professional Psychology, 11*, 935–938.

Harman, B. (1995). Gestalt therapy as brief therapy. *Gestalt Journal, 18*(2), 77–85.

Harman, R. (1984b). Gestalt therapy research. *Gestalt Journal, 7*(2), 61–69.

Harman, R. L. (1984a). Recent developments in Gestalt group therapy. *International Journal of Group Psychotherapy, 34*(3), 473–483.

Harman, R. L. (1989). *Gestalt therapy with groups, couples, sexually dysfunctional men, and dreams*. Springfield, IL: Charles C. Thomas.

Hawkes, D., Marsh, T. I., & Wilgosh, R. (1998). *Solution-focused therapy*. Boston: Butterworth Heinemann.

Hawlin, S., & Moore, J. (1998). Empowerment or collusion? The social context of person-centred therapy. In E. L. B. Thorne (Ed.), *Person-centred therapy: A European perspective* (pp. 91–105). London: Sage.

Hayes, S. C. (1981). Single case experimental design and empirical clinical practice. *Journal of Consulting & Clinical Psychology, 49*, 193–211.

Heidegger, M. (1962). *Being and time* (J. Macquarrie & E. Robinson, Trans.). New York: Harper & Row.

Helms, J. E., & Cook, D. A. (1999). *Using race and culture in counseling and psychotherapy: Theory and process*. Needham, MA: Allyn & Bacon.

Helms, J. E., & Cook, D. A. (1999). *Using race and culture in counseling and psychotherapy*. New York: Allyn & Bacon.

Hendrick, V., Smith, L. M., Suri, R., Hwang, S., Haynes, D., & Altshuler, L. (2003). Birth outcomes after prenatal exposure to antidepressant medication. *American Journal of Obstetrics & Gynecology, 188*(3), 812–815.

Henggeler, S. W., Melton, G. B., & Smith, L. A. (1992). Family preservation using multisystemic therapy: An effective alternative to incarcerating serious juvenile offenders. *Journal of Consulting & Clinical Psychology, 60*(6), 953–961.

Hersen, M. (2002). *Clinical behavior therapy*. New York: Wiley.

Hevern, V. W. (1999). *Narrative psychology: Internet and resource guide*. http://maple.lemoyne/narpsych.html

Hill, C. E., & O'Brien, K. M. (1999). *Helping skills*. Washington, DC: American Psychological Association.

Hillman, M. (2004). Viktor E. Frankl's existential analysis and logotherapy. In W. M. Cox & E. Klinger (Eds.), *Handbook of motivational counseling* (pp. 357–372). Hoboken, NJ: Wiley.

Hirschfield, R. M. (1999). Management of sexual side effects of antidepressant therapy. *Journal of Clinical Psychiatry, 60*(14), 27–35.

Hogan, B. A. (1999). Narrative therapy in rehabilitation after brain injury: A case study. *NeuroRehabilitation, 13*, 21–25.

Hong, G. K., & Domokos-Cheng Ham, M. A. (2001). *Psychotherapy and counseling with Asian American clients*. Thousand Oaks, CA: Sage.

hooks, b. (1984). *Feminist theory: From margin to center*. Boston: South End Press.

hooks, b. (2000). *Feminism is for everybody: Passionate politics*. Cambridge, MA: South End Press.

Horney, K. (1942). *Self-analysis*. New York: Norton.

Houston, G. (2003). *Brief Gestalt therapy*. London: Sage.

Howard, D. (1990). Competence and professional self-evaluation. In H. Lerman & N. Porter (Eds.), *Feminist ethics in psychotherapy* (pp. 131–136). New York: Springer.

Howatt, W. A. (2001). The evolution of reality therapy to choice theory. *International Journal of Reality Therapy, 21*, 7–12.

Hoyt, M. F., & Berg, I. K. (1998). Solution-focused couple therapy: Helping clients construct self-fulfilling realities. In M. F. Hoyt (Ed.), *The handbook of constructive therapies: Innovative approaches from leading practitioners* (pp. 314–341). San Francisco: Jossey-Bass.

Hubble, M. A., Duncan, B. L., & Miller, S. D. (1999). *The heart and soul of change*. Washington, DC: American Psychological Association.

Huffstetler, B. C., Mims, S. H., & Thompson, C. L. (2004). Getting together and staying together: Testing the compatibility of the Needs-Strength Profile and the Basic Needs Inventory. *International Journal of Reality Therapy, 23*, 4–8.

Hung-Hsiu Chang, T., & Ng, K. S. (2000). I Ching, solution-focused therapy and change: A clinical integrative framework. *Family Therapy, 27*, 47–57.

Ivey, A. E., D'Andrea, M. D., Bradford, M. B., & Simek-Morgan, L. (2002). *Theories of counseling and psychotherapy: A multicultural perspective*. Boston: Allyn & Bacon.

Ivey, A. E., D'Andrea, M. D., Ivey, M. B., & Simek-Morgan, L. (2002). *Theories of counseling and psychotherapy: A multicultural perspective* (5th ed.). Boston: Allyn & Bacon.

Jack, D. C. (1987). Self-in-relation theory. In R. Fromanek & A. Gurian (Eds.), *Women and depression: A lifespan perspective* (pp. 41–45). New York: Springer.

Jackson, L. C., & Greene, B. (Eds.). (2002). *Psychotherapy with African American women: Innovations in psychodynamic perspectives and practice*. New York: Guilford Press.

Jacobson, E. (1938). *Progressive relaxation*. Chicago: University of Chicago Press.

Jacobson, N. S., Christensen, A., Prince, S. E., Cordova, J., & Eldridge, K. (2000). Integrative behavioral couple therapy: An acceptance-based, promising new treatment for couple discord. *Journal of Consulting & Clinical Psychology, 68*, 351–355.

James, A. K., & Guilliland, B.E. (2003). *Theories and strategies in counseling and psychotherapy*. Boston: Allyn & Bacon.

Jeffers, S. (1992). *Feel the fear and do it anyway*. New York: Fawcett.

Jensen, J. P., Bergin, A. E., & Greaves, D. W. (1990). The meaning of eclecticism: New Survey and analysis of components. *Professional Psychology: Research and Practice, 21*, 124–130.

Johnathan, A. L. (1997). Unhappy success—A mid-life crisis: The case of Janet M. In S. du. Plock (Ed.), *Case studies in existential psychotherapy and counseling* (pp. 126–140). New York: Wiley.

Johnson, B. (1996). The service use of African-American and white adolescent girls prior to psychiatric hospitalizations and attitudes of their social network (abstract). *Psychopharmacology Bulletin 32*, 460.

Jones, A. C. (1985). Psychological functioning in Black Americans: A conceptual guide for use in psychotherapy. *Psychotherapy, 22*, 363–369.

Jones, E. (1961). *The life and work of Sigmund Freud*. Edited and abridged by L. Trilling & S. Marcus. New York: Basic Books.

Jones, E. (Ed.). (1953, 1955, 1957). *The life and works of Sigmund Freud* (3 vols.). New York: Basic Books.

Jordan, J. V. (Ed.). (1997). *Women's growth in diversity*. New York: Guilford Press.

Jordan, J. V., Kaplan, A. G., Miller, J. B., Stiver, I. P., & Surrey, J. L. (1991). *Women's growth in connection: Writings from the Stone Center*. New York: Guilford Press.

Josselson, R. (1996). *Revising herself: The story of women's identity from college to midlife*. New York: Oxford University Press.

Kaplan, H. I., & Sadock, B. J. (1998). *Synopsis of psychiatry: Behavioral sciences/clinical psychiatry* (8th ed). Baltimore: Williams & Wilkins.

Kaslow, F. W. (2000). Continued evolution of family therapy: The last twenty years. *Contemporary Family Therapy, 22*, 357–386.

Kaufman, W. (1989). *Existentialism: From Dostoevsky to Sartre* (2nd ed.). New York: Penguin Books.

Kazdin, A. (1994). *Behavior modification in applied settings*. Pacific Grove, CA: Brooks/Cole.

Keith-Spiegel, P., & Koocher, G. P. (1998). *Ethics in psychology: Professional standards and cases* (2nd ed.). Oxford: Oxford University Press.

Keller, M. B., McCullough, J. P., Klein, D. N., Arnow, B., Dunner, D. L., Gelenberg, A. J., et al. (2000). A comparison of nefazadone, the cognitive behavioral-analysis system of psychotherapy, and their combination for the treatment of chronic depression. *New England Journal of Medicine, 342*(20), 1462–1470.

Kelley, P. (1998). Narrative therapy in a managed care world. *Crisis Intervention, 4*, 113–123.

Kelly, P. (1995). Integrating narrative approaches into clinical curricula: Addressing diversity through understanding. *Journal of Social Work Education, 31*, 347–358.

Kelsch, D. M. (2002). Multiple sclerosis and choice theory: It is a disease and choice theory works! *International Journal of Reality Therapy, 22*, 24–29.

Kemph, J. P., Braley, R. O., & Ciotola, P. V. (1997). Description of an outpatient psychiatric population in a youthful offender's prison. *Journal of the American Academy of Psychiatry & the Law, 25*(2), 149–160.

Kern, R., Edwards, D., Flowers, C., Lambert, R., & Belangee, S. (1999). Teachers' lifestyles and their perceptions of students' behavior. *Journal of Individual Psychology, 55*, 422–436.

Kern, R., Wheeler, M. S., & Curlette, W. L. (1994). *BASIS–A Inventory interpretive manual*. Highlands, NC: TRT Associates.

Kerr, M., & Bowen, M. (1988). *Family evaluation*. New York: Norton.

Keskinen, S. (2004). Between abstract individualism and gendered lives: Negotiating abused women's agency and identity in therapy. In A. Lieblich, D. P. McAdams, & R. Josselson (Eds.), *Healing plots: The narrative basis of psychotherapy* (pp. 67–87). Washington, DC: American Psychological Association.

Kessell, M. J. (1994). Women's adventure group: Experiential therapy in an HMO setting. *Women & Therapy, 15*(3–4), 185–203.

Kim, K. (2002). The effect of a reality therapy program on the responsibility for elementary school children in Korea. *International Journal of Reality Therapy, 22*, 30–33.

Kirsch, I. & Sapperstein, G. (1998). Listening to Prozac but hearing placebo? A meta-analysis of antidepressant medication. *Prevention and Treatment, 1*(1), 2.

Kirschenbaum, H., & Henderson, V. L. (1989). *The Carl Rogers reader*. Boston: Houghton Mifflin.

Klein, M. (1975/1984). *The psychoanalysis of children*. Authorized translation by A. Strachey; revised in collaboration with A. Strachey by H. A. Thomer. London: Hogarth Press. (Originally published in 1932.)

Klerman, G. L., & Weissman, M. M. (1995). Interpersonal psychotherapy for depression. *Journal of Psychotherapy Practice & Research, 4*(4), 342–351.

Klerman, G. L., Weissman, M. M., Rounsville, B. J., & Cheveron, E. S. (1984). *Interpersonal psychotherapy for depression: A brief, focused, specific strategy*. New York: Basic Books.

Knudson-Martin, C., & Mahoney, A. R. (1999). Beyond different worlds: A post-gender approach to relational development. *Family Process, 38*(3), 325–340.

Koocher, G. P., & Norcross, J. C. (2005). *Psychologist desk reference: Downloadable resources*. Retrieved May 13, 2005, from http://www.us.oup.com/us/companion.websites/019516606X/files/?view=usa

Kopala, M., & Keitel, M. A. (Eds.) (2003). *Handbook of counseling women*. Thousand Oaks, CA: Sage Publications.

Kopp, R., & Lasky, A. (1999). Brief therapy using Kopp's typology: A case example. *Journal of Individual Psychology, 55*, 51–61.

Korb, M. P., Gorrell, J. J., & Van De Riet, V. (1989). *Gestalt therapy: Practice and theory*. New York: Pergamon Press.

Kottman, T. (1995). *Partners in play: An Adlerian approach to play therapy*. Alexandria, VA: American Counseling Association.

Kottman, T. (1999). Play therapy. In R. Watts & J. Carlson (Eds.), *Interventions and strategies in counseling and psychotherapy* (161–179). Philadelphia: Taylor & Francis.

Krumboltz, J. D. (1994). Improving career development theory from a social learning perspective. In M. L. Savickas & R. W. Lent (Eds.), *Convergence in career development theories* (pp. 9–32). Palo Alto, CA: Consulting Psychologists Press.

Kumpfer, K. L., Alvarado, R., & Whiteside, H. O. (2003). Family-based interventions for substance use and misuse prevention. *Substance Abuse & Misuse, 38*, 1759–1787.

Kupers, T. A. (1981). *Public therapy: The practice of psychotherapy in the public mental health clinic*. London: Free Press.

L'Abate, L. (1991). The use of writing in psychotherapy. *American Journal of Psychotherapy, 55*, 87–98.

LaFromboise, T. (1996). On multicultural issues. *Microtraining Newsletter, 5*.

Laine, C., & Davidoff, F. (1996). Patient-centered medicine: A professional evolution. *Journal of the American Medical Association, 275*, 152–156.

Laird, J. G., Green, R. J. (1996). *Lesbians and gays in couples and families: A handbook for therapists*. San Francisco: Jossey-Bass.

Lang, R. D. (1959). *The divided self*. Baltimore: Penguin.

Lantz, J. (2000). *Meaning centered marital and family therapy: Learning to bear the beams of love*. Springfield, IL: Charles C. Thomas.

Lantz, J. (2004). Research and evaluation issues in existential psychotherapy. *Journal of Contemporary Psychotherapy, 34*, 331–340.

Lantz, J., & Gregoire, T. (2000). Existential psychotherapy with Vietnam veteran couples: A twenty-five year report. *Contemporary Family Therapy, 22*, 19–37.

Lantz, J., & Kondrat, M. E. (1997). Evaluation research problems in existential psychotherapy with couples and families. *Journal of Family Psychotherapy, 8*, 55–71.

Lapid, G. (1980). Exploring sex roles in Gestalt workshops. In B. Feder & B. Ronall (Eds.), *Beyond the hot seat: Gestalt approaches to group* (pp. 212–219). New York: Brunner/Mazel.

Latner, J. (1973). *The Gestalt therapy book.* New York: Julian Press.

Latner, J. (1992). The theory of Gestalt therapy. In E. C. Nevis (Ed.), *Gestalt therapy: Perspectives and applications* (pp. 13–56). New York: Gestalt Institute of Cleveland Press.

Lawton, S., & Edwards, S. (1997). The use of stories to help children who have been abused. In K. N. Dwivedi (Ed.), *The therapeutic use of stories* (pp. 185–197). New York: Routledge.

Lazarus, A. A. (1982). Multimodal group therapy. In G. M. Gazda (Ed.), *Basic approaches to group psychotherapy and group counseling* (3rd ed.) (pp. 116–135). Springfield, IL: Charles C. Thomas.

Lazarus, A. A. (1989). *The practice of multimodal therapy: Systematic, comprehensive, and effective psychotherapy.* Baltimore: Johns Hopkins University Press.

Lazarus, A. A. (1997). *Brief but comprehensive psychotherapy: The multimodal way.* New York: Springer.

Lazarus, A. A. (Ed.) (1976). *Multimodal behavior therapy.* New York: Springer.

Leadbeater, B. J. R., & Way, N. (Eds.). (1996). *Urban girls: Resisting stereotypes, creating identities.* New York: New York University Press.

Lee, M. Y. (1997). A study of solution-focused brief family therapy: Outcome and issues. *American Journal of Family Therapy, 25*, 3–17.

Leeper, R. (Ed.) (1967). *Humanizing education: The person in the process.* Alexandria, VA: Association for Supervision and Curriculum Development.

Legowski, T., & Brownlee, K. (2001). Working with metaphor in narrative therapy. *Journal of Family Psychotherapy, 12*, 19–28.

Lemmon, C. R., & Josephson, A. M. (2001). Family therapy for eating disorders. *Child & Adolescent Clinics of North America, 10*(3), 519–545.

Lennon, B. (2000). From "reality therapy" to "reality therapy in action." *International Journal of Reality Therapy, 20*(1), 41–46.

Lerman, H. (1986). *A mote in Freud's eye: From psychoanalysis to the psychology of women.* New York: Springer.

Lerman, H. (1996). *Pigeonholing women's misery: A history and critical analysis of the psychodiagnosis of women in the twentieth century.* New York: Basic Books.

Lerner, H. (1992). The limits of phenomenology: A feminist critique of the humanistic personality theories. In M. B. L. Brown (Ed.), *Theories of personality and psychopathology* (pp. 8–19). New York: Guilford.

Levant, R. F. (1983). Client-centered skills-training programs for the family: A review of the literature. *Counseling Psychologist, 11*, 29–46.

Levant, R. F., & Pollack, W. S. (1995). *A new psychology of men.* New York: Basic Books.

Levant, R. F., & Shlien, J. M. (1984). *Client-centered therapy and the person-centered approach.* New York: Praeger.

Levenson, H. (1995). *Time-limited dynamic psychotherapy.* New York: Basic Books.

Lewinsohn, P., Munoz, R., Youngren, A., & Zeiss, A. (1996). *Control your depression.* Englewood Cliffs, NJ: Prentice-Hall.

Lewis, M. (1974). Interpretation of child analysis: Developmental considerations. *Journal of the American Academy of Child Psychiatry, 13*, 32–53.

Lewis, R. E. (2003). Brief theories. In D. Capuzzi & D. R. Gross (Eds.), *Counseling and psychotherapy: Theories and interventions* (3rd ed., pp. 307–331). Upper Saddle River, NJ: Merrill–Prentice Hall.

Liddle, H. A. (2004). Family-based therapies for adolescent alcohol and drug use: Research contributions and future research needs. *Addiction, 99*, 76–92.

Liddle, H. A., & Dakof, G. A. (1995). Efficacy of family therapy for drug abuse: Promising but not definitive. *Journal of Marital & Family Therapy, 21*, 511–543.

Liddle, H. A., & Rowe, C. L. (2004). Advances in family therapy research. In M. P. Nichols & R. C. Schwartz (Eds.), *Family therapy: Concepts and methods.* New York: Pearson.

Lieberman, M. A., & Yalom, I. (1992). Brief group psychotherapy for the spousally bereaved: A controlled study. *International Journal of Group Psychotherapy, 42*, 117–132.

Lieberman, M., Yalom, I., & Miles, M. (1973). *Encounter groups: First facts.* New York: Basic Books.

Lin, K. M., Smith, M. W., & Ortiz, V. (2001). Culture and psychopharmacology. *Psychiatric Clinics of North America, 24*(3), 523–538.

Linnenberg, D. M. (1997). Religion, spirituality, and the counseling process. *International Journal of Reality Therapy, 17,* 55–59.

Lipchik, E. (2002). *Beyond technique in solution-focused therapy.* New York: Guilford Press.

Litz, R. W., & Litz, T. (1949). The family environment of schizophrenic patients. *American Journal of Psychiatry, 106,* 332–345.

Lock, J., & le Grange, D. (2005). Family-based treatment of eating disorders. *International Journal of Eating Disorders, 37,* 564–567.

Luborsky, L., & Crits-Christoph, P. (1998). *Understanding transference* (2nd ed.). Washington, DC: American Psychological Association.

Luborsky, L., Crits-Christoph, P., Mintz, J., & Aurbach, A. (1988). *Who will benefit from psychotherapy? Predicting therapeutic outcomes.* New York: Basic Books.

Luborsky, L., Singer, B., & Luborsky, L. (1975). Comparative studies of psychotherapy. *Archives of General Psychiatry, 32,* 995–1008.

Lyons, L. C., & Woods, P. (1991). The efficacy of rational-emotive therapy: A quantitative review of the outcome research. *Clinical Psychology Review, 11,* 357–369.

Maass, V. (2002). *Women's group therapy: Creative challenges and options.* New York: Springer.

Mackewn, J. (1997). *Developing Gestalt Counseling.* London: Sage.

MacKune-Karrer, B. (1999, Winter). A conversation with Betty Carter. *American Family Therapy Academy Newsletter,* p. 24.

Madanes, C. (1981). *Strategic family therapy.* San Francisco: Jossey-Bass.

Mahler, M. S. (1968). *On human symbiosis and the vicissitudes of individuation: Infantile psychosis.* New York: International Universities Press.

Malan, D. (1963). *A study of brief psychotherapy.* New York: Plenum.

Malan, D. (1976). *Frontier of brief psychotherapy.* New York: Plenum.

Malan, D. (1979). *Individual psychotherapy and the science of psychodynamics.* London: Butterworth.

Malan, D. (1980). The most important development in psychotherapy since the discovery of the unconscious. In H. Davanloo (Ed.), *Short-term dynamic psychotherapy* (pp. 13–23). Northvale, NJ: Aronson.

Malan, D. (2000). Beyond interpretation: Initial evaluation and technique in short-term dynamic psychotherapy: Parts I and II. *International Journal of Intensive Short-Term Dynamic Psychotherapy, 14,* 59–82.

Mann, J. (1973). *Time-limited psychotherapy.* Cambridge: Harvard University Press.

Marcus, E. H. (1979). Gestalt therapy and beyond. In E. H. Marcus (Ed.), *Gestalt therapy and beyond* (pp. 3–95). Cupertino, CA: META Publications.

Marecek, J., & Hare-Mustin, R. T. (1991). A short history of the future: Feminism and clinical psychology. *Psychology of Women Quarterly, 15,* 521–536.

Marks, I., Kenwright, M., McDonough, M., (2004). Cois, D. (2004). Saving clinicians' time by delegating routine aspects of therapy to a computer: A randomized controlled trial in phobia/panic. *Psychological Medicine, 34*(1), 9–17.

Martin, J. C., Carkhuff, R. R., & Berenson, B. G. (1966). Process variables in counseling and psychotherapy: A study of counseling and friendship. *Journal of Counseling Psychology, 13,* 356–359.

Maslow, A. (1970). *Motivation and personality* (2nd ed.). New York: Harper & Row.

Masters, W. H., & Johnson, V. E. (1970). *Human sexual inadequacy.* Boston: Little, Brown.

Mattis, S. G., & Ollendick, T. H. (2002). School refusal and separation anxiety. In M. Hersen (Ed.), *Clinical behavior therapy: Adults and children* (pp. 304–325). New York: Wiley.

May, R., & Yalom, I. (1984). Existential psychotherapy. In R. J. Corsini & D. Wedding (Eds.), *Current psychotherapies* (pp. 354–391). Itasca, IL: Peacock Publishers.

May, R. (1953). *Man's search for himself.* New York: Delta.

May, R. (1958). Contributions of existential psychotherapy. In R. May, E. Angel, & H. E. Ellenberger (Eds.), *Existence: A new dimension in psychiatry and psychology* (pp. 37–92). New York: Basic Books.

May, R. (1961). The emergence of existential psychology. In R. May (Ed.), *Existential psychology* (pp. 11–51). New York: Random House.

May, R. (1977). *The meaning of anxiety.* New York: Norton.

May, R. (1981). *Freedom and destiny.* New York: Norton.

May, R. (1983). *The discovery of being.* New York: Norton.

May, R., Angel, E., & Ellenberger, H. E. (1958). *Existence: A new dimension in psychiatry and psychology.* New York: Basic Books.

Mays, V., & Comas-Díaz, L. (1988). Feminist therapy with ethnic minority populations: A closer look at Blacks and Hispanics. In M. A. Dutton-Douglas & L. E. A. Walker (Eds.), *Feminist psychotherapies: Integration of therapeutic and feminist systems* (pp. 228–251). Westport, CT: Ablex.

McGregor, M., Tutty, L. M., Babins-Wagner, R., & Marlyn, G. (2002). The long term impacts of group treatment for partner abuse. *Canadian Journal of Community Mental Health, 21*(1), 67–84.

McIntosh, P. (1988). White privilege: Unpacking the invisible knapsack. In M. McGoldrick (Ed.), *Re-visioning family therapy: Race, culture, and gender in clinical practice* (pp. 147–152). New York: Guilford Press.

McKay, G. D., & Dinkmeyer, D. (2002). *How you feel is up to you.* Atascadero, CA: Impact Publishing.

McKeel, A. J. (1996). A clinician's guide to research on solution-focused brief therapy. In S. D. Miller, M. A. Hubble, & B. L. Duncan (Eds.), *Handbook of solution-focused brief therapy* (pp. 251–271). San Francisco: Jossey-Bass.

McKenzie, W., & Monk, G. (1997). Learning and teaching narrative ideas. In G. Monk, J. Winslade, K. Crocket, & D. Epston (Eds.), *Narrative therapy in practice: The archaeology of hope* (pp. 82–120). San Francisco: Jossey-Bass.

McKnight, J. (1996). *The carless society: Community and its counterfeits.* New York: Basic Books.

McWilliams, N. (1994). *Psychoanalytic diagnosis: Understanding personality structure in the clinical process.* New York: Guildford.

Meador, B. D., & Rogers, C. R. (1984). Person-centered therapy. In R. J. Corsini (Ed.), *Current psychotherapies* (3rd ed., pp. 142–195). Itasca, IL: Peacock.

Meichenbaum, D. (1974). Self-instructional training: A cognitive prosthesis for the aged. *Human Development, 17,* 273–230.

Meichenbaum, D. (1985). *Stress inoculation training.* New York: Pergamon.

Meichenbaum, D. (1993). Changing conceptions of cognitive behavior modification: Retrospect and prospect. *Journal of Consulting & Clinical Psychology, 61,* 202–204.

Meichenbaum, D. (1996). *Mixed anxiety and depression: A cognitive-behavioral approach: A viewer's manual.* New York: Newbridge Communications.

Meichenbaum, D. (1997). The evolution of a cognitive-behavior therapist. In J. Zieg (Ed.), *The evolution of psychotherapy.* Philadelphia: Brunner/Mazel.

Meichenbaum, D., & Goodman, J. (1971). Training impulsive children to talk to themselves: A means of developing self-control. *Journal of Abnormal Psychology, 77,* 115–126.

Merrill, K. A., Tolbert, V. E., & Wade, W. A. (2003). Effectiveness of cognitive therapy for depression in a community mental health center: A benchmarking study. *Journal of Consulting & Clinical Psychology, 71,* 404–409.

Michel, D. M., & Willard, S. G. (2003). Family treatment of eating disorders. *Primary Psychiatry, 10,* 59–61.

Miller, J. B. (1976). *Toward a new psychology of women.* Boston: Beacon Press.

Miller, J. B., Jordan, J. V., Kaplan, A. G., Stiver, I. P., & Surrey, J. L. (1997). Some misconceptions and reconceptions of a relational approach. In J. Jordan (Ed.), *Women's growth in diversity* (pp. 25–49). New York: Guilford Press.

Miller, S. D., Hubble, M. A., & Duncan, B. L. (1996). *Psychotherapy is dead, long live psychotherapy.* Paper presented at the 19th annual family therapy network symposium, Washington, DC.

Miller, W. R., & Rollnick, S. (2002). *Motivational interviewing: Preparing people for change* (2nd ed.). New York: Guilford.

Miller, W. R., Taylor, C. A., & West, J. C. (1980). Focused versus broad-spectrum behavior therapy for problem drinkers. *Journal of Consulting & Clinical Psychology, 48,* 590–601.

Minuchin, S. (1974). *Families and family therapy.* Cambridge, MA: Harvard Press.

Minuchin, S., & Fishman, C. H. (1981). *Family therapy techniques.* Cambridge, MA: Harvard University Press.

Minuchin, S., & Nichols, M. P. (1993). *Family healing.* New York: Free Press.

Mitchell, L. K., & Krumboltz, J. D. (1996). Krumboltz's social learning theory of career choice and counseling. In D. Brown, L. Brooks (Eds.), *Career choice and development* (3rd ed., pp. 233–280). San Francisco: Jossey-Bass.

Molnar, A., & de Shazer, S. (1987). Solution-focused therapy: Toward the identification of therapeutic tasks. *Journal of Marital & Family Therapy, 13,* 349–358.

Monk, G. (1997). How narrative therapy works. In G. Monk, J. Winslade, K. Crocket, & D. Epston (Eds.), *Narrative therapy in practice: The archaeology of hope* (pp. 3–31). San Francisco, CA: Jossey-Bass.

Monte, C. F. (1987). Beneath the mask (3rd ed.). New York: Holt, Rinehart, & Winston.

Monte, C. F. (1987). *Beneath the mask: An introduction to theories of personality* (3rd ed.). New York: Holt, Rinehart, & Winston.

Montejo-Gonzalez, A. L., Llorca, G., Izquierdo, J. A., Ledesma, A., Bousono, M., Calcedo, A., et al. (1997). SSRI-induced sexual dysfunction: Fluoxetine, paroxetine, sertraline, and fluvoxamine in a prospective, multicenter, and descriptive clinical study of 344 patients. *Journal of Sex & Marital Therapy, 23*(3), 176–194.

Moore, S. E. (2001). Substance abuse treatment with adolescent African American males: Reality therapy with an Afrocentric approach. *Journal of Social Work Practice in the Addictions, 1,* 21–32.

Moradi, B., Fischer, A. R., Hill, M. S., Jome, L. M., & Blum, S. A. (2000). Does "feminist" plus "therapist" equal "feminist therapist"? An empirical investigation of the link between self-labeling and behaviors. *Psychology of Women Quarterly, 24*, 285–296.

Morano, C. L. (2002). A cognitive approach to intergenerational family therapy. *Family Therapy, 29*(2), 63–76.

Morris, M. S., Fava, M., Jacques, P. F., Selhub, J., & Rosenberg, I. H. (2003). Depression and folate status in the US population. *Psychotherapy & Psychosomatics, 72*(2), 80–89.

Mosak, H. (2000). Adlerian psychotherapy. In R. J. Corsini & D. Wedding (Eds.), *Current psychotherapies* (6th ed.) (pp. 52–95). Itasca, IL: Peacock.

Mosak, H. H. (1954). The psychological attitude in rehabilitation. *American Archives of Rehabilitation, 2*, 9–10.

Mosak, H. H. (1959). The getting type, a parsimonious social interpretation of oral character. *Journal of Individual Psychology, 21*, 71–81.

Mosak, H. H. (1973). *Alfred Adler: His influence upon psychology today.* Park Ridge, NJ: Noyes Press.

Mosak, H. H. (1979). Mosak's typology: An update. *Journal of Individual Psychology, 35*, 192–195.

Mosak, H. H., & Maniacci, M. (1998). *Tactics in counseling and psychotherapy.* Itasca, IL: Peacock.

Mosak, H. H., & Maniacci, M. P. (1999). *A primer of Adlerian psychology: The analytic-behavioral-cognitive psychology of Alfred Adler.* London: Taylor & Francis.

Mosak, H., & Maniacci, M. (1999). *A primer of Adlerian psychology: The analytic-behavioral-cognitive theory of Alfred Adler.* Philadelphia: Brunner/Mazel.

MTA Cooperative Group (1999). A 14-month randomized clinical trial of treatment strategies for attention-deficit/hyperactivity disorder. *Archives of General Psychiatry, 56*(12), 1073–1086.

Mullan, H. (1992). "Existential" therapists and their group therapy practices. *International Journal of Group Psychotherapy, 42*, 453–468.

Murdock, N. L. (2004). *Theories of counseling and psychotherapy.* Upper Saddle River, NJ: Pearson.

Murphy, L. (1997). Efficacy of reality therapy in the schools: A review of the research from 1980–1995. *International Journal of Reality Therapy, 16*, 12–20.

Neimeyer, R. A. (1993). An appraisal of constructivist psychotherapies. *Journal of Consulting & Clinical Psychology, 61*, 221–234.

Nelsen, J. (1996). *Positive discipline.* New York: Ballantine.

Nelsen, J. (1999). *Positive discipline A–Z* (2nd ed.). Roseville, CA: Prima Lifestyles.

Nelson, T. S., & Kelley, L. (2001). Solution-focused couples group. *Journal of Systematic Therapies, 20*, 47–66.

New Harbinger Publications. (2002). *Practice protocols.* Retrieved October 16, 2002, from www.newharbinger.com/cgi-local/SofaCart.exe/online-store/scstore/c-Practice Protocols.html?E+scstore

Nichols, M. P., & Schwartz, R. C. (2004). *Family therapy: Concepts and methods* (6th ed.). Boston: Pearson.

Nicoll, W. G. (1999). Brief therapy strategies and techniques. In R. Watts & J. Carlson (Eds.), *Interventions and strategies in counseling and psychotherapy* (pp. 15–30). Philadelphia: Taylor & Francis.

Nicoll, W. G., & Hawes, E. (1985). Family lifestyle assessment: The role of family myths, values in the client's presenting issues. *Individual Psychology: Journal of Adlerian Theory, Research, & Practice, 41*(2), 147–160.

Niemeyer, R. A. (1993). An appraisal of constructivist psychotherapies. *Journal of Consulting and Clinical Psychology, 61*(2), 221–234.

Nystul, M. (1999). Problem-solving counseling: Integrating Adler's and Glasser's theories. In R. Watts & J. Carlson (Eds.), *Interventions and strategies in counseling and psychotherapy* (pp. 31–42). Philadelphia: Taylor & Francis.

O'Connell, B. (1998). Solution-focused therapy. Thousand Oaks, CA: Sage.

O'Connell, W. E. (1972). Adlerian action therapy techniques. *Journal of Individual Psychology, 28*, 184–191.

O'Connell, W. E. (1975). *Action therapy and Adlerian theory.* Chicago: Alfred Adler Institute.

O'Connor, T. S. J., Meakes, E., Pickering, M. R., & Schuman, M. (1997). On the right track: Client experience of narrative therapy. *Contemporary Family Therapy, 19*, 479–495.

O'Hanlon, B., & Weiner-Davis, M. (1989). *In search of solutions: A new direction in psychotherapy.* New York: Norton.

Oaklander, V. (2002). The therapeutic process with children and adolescents: A Gestalt therapy perspective. In G. Wheeler & M. McConville (Eds.), *The heart of development: Gestalt approaches to working with children, adolescents, and their world* (vol. 1, pp. 85–112). Hillsdale, NJ: Analytic Press.

Olfson, M., Gameroff, M. J., Marcus, S. C., & Jensen, P. S. (2003). National trends in the treatment of attention deficit hyperactivity disorder. *American Journal of Psychiatry, 160*(6), 1071–1077.

Orgler, H. (1963). *Alfred Adler: The man and his work.* New York: Mentor Books.

Orlinsky, D. E., & Howard, K. I. (1986). Process and outcome in psychotherapy. In S. L. Garfield & A. E. Bergin

(Eds.), *Handbook of psychotherapy and behavior change* (3rd ed.) (pp. 311–381). New York: Wiley.

Osmond, M. W., & Thorne, B. (1993). Feminist theories: The social construction of gender in families and society. In P. G. Boss, W. J. Doherty, R. LaRossa, W. R. Schumm, & S. K. Steinmetz (Eds.), *Sourcebook of family theories and methods: A contextual approach* (pp. 591–625). New York: Plenum Press.

Ossana, S. M., Helms, J. E., & Leonard, M. M. (1992). Do "womanist" identity attitudes influence college women's self-esteem and perceptions of environmental bias? *Journal of Counseling & Development, 70*, 402–408.

Ozeki, T. (2002). "Problems" as resources: A practical guide to addressing clients' description of their problems in solution-focused therapy. *Journal of Systematic Therapies, 21*, 35–47.

Padesky, C. A., & Greenberger, D. (1995). *Clinician's guide to Mind over mood*. New York: Guilford Press.

Paivio, S., & Greenberg, L. S. (1995). Resolving "unfinished business": Efficacy of experiential therapy using empty-chair dialogue. *Journal of Consulting & Clinical Psychology, 73*, 419–425.

Papero, D. V. (1990). *Bowen family systems theory*. Boston: Allyn & Bacon.

Parker, W. M. (1998). *Consciousness-raising: A primer for multicultural counseling*. Springfield, IL: Thomas.

Parry, A., & Doan, R. E. (1994). *Story re-visions: Narrative therapy in a postmodern world*. New York: Guilford Press.

Patterson, C. H. (1958). The place of values in counseling and psychotherapy. *Journal of Counseling Psychology, 5*, 216–223.

Patterson, C. H. (1985). *The therapeutic relationship*. Monterey, CA: Brooks/Cole.

Patterson, C. H., & Watkins, C. E. (1982). Some essentials of a client-centered approach to assessment. *Measurement & Evaluation in Guidance, 15*, 103–106.

Patton, M. J., & Meara, N. M. (1992). *Psychoanalytic counseling*. Chicester, England: Wiley.

Patton, M. J., Kivlighan, D. M., & Multon, K. D. (1997). The Missouri Psychoanalytic Counseling Research Project: Relation of changes in counseling process to client outcomes. *Journal of Counseling Psychology, 44*(2), 189–208.

Payne, M. (2000). *Narrative therapy: An introduction for counselors*. Thousand Oaks, CA: Sage.

Pearce, S. S. (1996). *Flash of insight*. Needham Heights, MA: Allyn & Bacon.

Pedersen, P. B., Draguns, J. G., Lonner, W. J., & Trimble, J. E. (2002). *Counseling across cultures*. Thousand Oaks, CA: Sage.

Pennebaker, J. W. (1990). *Opening up*. New York: Guilford Press.

Perls, F. (1947). *Ego, hunger, and aggression*. London: Allen & Unwin.

Perls, F. (1969a). *In and out of the garbage pail*. Lafayette, CA: Real People Press.

Perls, F. (1969b). *Gestalt therapy verbatim*. Lafayette, CA: Real People Press.

Perls, F. (1973). *The Gestalt approach and eyewitness to therapy*. New York: Science and Behavior Books.

Perls, F., Hefferline, R. F., & Goodman, P. (1951). *Gestalt therapy: Excitement and growth in human personality*. New York: Dell.

Persons, J. B., & Davidson, J. (2001). Cognitive-behavioral case formulation. In K. S. Dobson (Ed.), *Handbook of cognitive-behavioral therapies* (pp. 86–110). New York: Guilford Press.

Peters, M. F., & Massey, G. (1983). Mundane extreme environmental stress in family stress theories: The case of Black families in White America. *Marriage & Family Review, 6*(1–2), 193–218.

Phelan, T. W. (1996). *1–2–3 magic: Effective discipline for children 1–12*. Glen Ellyn, IL: Child Management.

Physicians' Desk Reference. (2002). *PDR drug guide for mental health professionals*. Montvale, NJ: Thomson Medical Economics.

Pichot, T., & Dolan, Y. M. (2003). *Solution-focused brief therapy: Its effective use in agency settings*. New York: Hawthorn Press.

Pinkerton, R. S., & Rockwell, W. J. (1994). Brief psychotherapy with college students. *Journal of American College Health, 42*, 156–162.

Pipher, M. (1995). *Reviving Ophelia: Saving the selves of adolescent girls*. New York: Ballantine Books.

Platts, J. W., & Williamson, Y. (2000). The use of cognitive-behavioral therapy for counseling in the schools. In N. Barwick (Ed.), *Clinical counseling in context* (pp. 96–107). Philadelphia: Routledge.

Pliszka, S. R. (2003). *Neuroscience for the mental health clinician*. New York: Guilford Press.

Polster, E., & Polster, M. (1973). *Gestalt therapy integrated*. New York: Brunner/Mazel.

Powers, M. D. (Ed.) (1988). *Expanding systems of service delivery for persons with developmental disabilities*. Baltimore: Paul H Brookes.

Powers, W. (1973). Feedback: Beyond Behaviorism. *Science, 179*, 351–356.

Preston, J., & Johnson, J. (2000). *Clinical psychopharmacology made ridiculously simple*. Miami: MedMaster.

Preston, J., O'Neal, J. H., & Talaga, M. C. (2002). *Handbook of clinical psychopharmacology for therapists* (3rd ed.). Oakland, CA: New Harbinger Publications.

Prochaska, J. O., & Norcross, J. C. (2003). *Systems of psychotherapy: A transtheoretical analysis* (5th ed.). Pacific Grove, CA: Brooks/Cole.

Prochaska, J. O., & DiClemente, C. C. (1992). Stages of change in the modification of problem behaviors. In M. Hersen, R. M. Eisler, & P. M. Miller (Eds.), *Progress in behaviors modification*. Sycamore, IL: Sycamore.

Prochaska, J. O., & Norcross, J. C. (2003). *Systems of psychotherapy: A transtheoretical approach* (5th ed.). Pacific Grove, CA: Brooks/Cole.

Prochaska, J. O., DiClemente, C. C., & Norcross, J. C. (1992). In search of how people change: Applications to the addictive behaviors. *American Psychologist, 47*, 1102–1114.

Prouty, A. (2001). Experiencing feminist family therapy supervision. *Journal of Feminist Family Therapy, 12*(4), 171–203.

Prouty, A. M., Thomas, V., Johnson, S., & Long, J. K. (2001). Methods of feminist family therapy supervision. *Journal of Marital & Family Therapy, 27*, 85–97.

Rachman, S. (1996). *Frontiers of cognitive therapy*. New York: Guilford Press.

Radtke, L., Sapp, M., & Farrell, W. C., Jr. (1997). Reality therapy: A meta-analysis. *International Journal of Reality Therapy, 17*, 4–9.

Rank, O. (1929). *The trauma of birth*. New York: Harper & Row.

Reker, G. T. (1994). Logotheory and logotherapy: Challenge, opportunities, and some empirical findings. *International Forum for Logotherapy, 17*, 44–55.

Rhodes, J., & Ajmal, Y. (1995). *Solution focused thinking in schools*. London: BT Press.

Richardson, B. G., & Wubbolding, R. E. (2001). Five interrelated challenges for using reality therapy with challenging students. *International Journal of Reality Therapy, 20*, 35–39.

Richardson, F. C., Fowers, B. J., & Guignon, C. B. (1999). *Re-envisioning psychology: Moral dimensions of theory and practice*. San Francisco: Jossey-Bass.

Rigazio-DiGilio, S. A., Ivey, A. E., & Locke, D. C. (1997). Continuing the postmodern dialogue: Enhancing and contextualizing multiple voices. *Journal of Mental Health Counseling, 19*, 233–255.

Rita, E. S., Jr. (1998). What do you do after asking the miracle question in solution-focused therapy? *Family Therapy, 25*, 189–195.

Rivett, M. (2001). Comments—Working systematically with family violence: Controversy, context, and accountability. *Journal of Family Therapy, 23*, 397–404.

Robbins, M. S., Turner, C. W., & Perez, G. A. (2003). Alliance and dropout in family therapy for adolescents with behavior problems: Individual and systemic effects. *Journal of Family Psychology, 17*(4), 534–544.

Roberts, A. (Ed.). (1999). *From the radial center: The heart of Gestalt therapy*. Cambridge, MA: GIC Press.

Robinson, T. L., & Howard-Hamilton, M. F. (2000). *The convergence of race, ethnicity, and gender: Multiple identities in counseling*. Upper Saddle River, NJ: Prentice Hall.

Rochlen, A., Zack, J., & Speyer, C. (2004). Online therapy: Review of relevant definitions, debates, and current empirical support. *Journal of Criminal Psychology, 60*(3), 269–283.

Rogers, C. R. (1939). *The clinical treatment of the problem child*. New York: Houghton Mifflin.

Rogers, C. R. (1942). *Counseling and psychotherapy: Newer concepts in practice*. Boston: Houghton Mifflin.

Rogers, C. R. (1951). *Client-centered therapy: Its current practice, implications, and theory*. Boston: Houghton Mifflin.

Rogers, C. R. (1957). The necessary and sufficient conditions of therapeutic personality change. *Journal of Consulting Psychology, 21*, 95–103.

Rogers, C. R. (1959). A theory of therapy, personality and individual relationships as developed in the client-centered framework. In S. Koch (Ed.), *Psychology: A study of a science* (pp. 184–256). New York: McGraw-Hill.

Rogers, C. R. (1961). *On becoming a person*. Boston: Houghton Mifflin.

Rogers, C. R. (1969). *Freedom to learn*. Columbus, Ohio: Merrill.

Rogers, C. R. (1970). *Carl Rogers on encounter groups*. New York: Harper & Row.

Rogers, C. R. (1972). *Becoming partners: Marriage and its alternatives*. New York: Delacorte Press.

Rogers, C. R. (1977). *Carl Rogers on personal power*. New York: Delacorte Press.

Rogers, C. R. (1980). *A way of being*. Boston: Houghton Mifflin.

Rogers, C. R. (1989). Resolving intercultural tensions. In H. Kirschenbaum & V. L. Henderson (Eds.), *The Carl Rogers reader* (pp. 438–445). Boston: Houghton Mifflin.

Root, M. P. P. (2001). Future considerations in research on eating disorders. *Counseling Psychologist, 29*(5), 754–762.

Rose, S. D. (1989). *Working with adults in groups*. San Francisco: Jossey-Bass.

Rose, S. D. (1998). *Group therapy with troubled youth*. Thousand Oaks, CA: Sage.

Rosenberg, B. (2000). Mandated clients and solution-focused therapy: "It's not my miracle." *Journal of Systematic Therapies, 19*, 90–99.

Rowen, T. (1997). *Cognitive developmental therapy with children*. New York: Wiley.

Roysircar, G., Sandhu, D. S., & Bibbins, V. E. (Eds.). (2003). *Multicultural competencies: A guidebook of practices*. Alexandria, VA: Association for Multicultural Counseling and Development.

Roysircar, G., Singh, D. S., & Bibbins, V. E. (2003). *Multicultural competencies: A guidebook of practices*. Alexandria, VA: Association for Multicultural Counseling and Development.

Rubin, L. R., Fitts, M. L., & Becker, A. E. (2003). Whatever feels good in my soul: Body ethics and aesthetics among African American and Latina women. *Culture, Medicine, & Psychiatry, 27*(1), 49–75.

Russel, G. F. M., Dare, C., Eisler, I., & LeGrange, P. D. F. (1994). Controlled trials of family treatments in anorexia nervosa. In K. A. Halmi (Ed.), *Psychobiology and the treatment of anorexia nervosa and bulimia nervosa* (pp. 237–261). Washington, DC: American Psychiatric Press.

Sanau-Beckler, P. A, Devall, E., & de la Rosa, I. A. (2002). Strengthening family resilience: Prevention and treatment for high risk substance-affected families. *Journal of Individual Psychology, 58*, 305–329.

Sanchez, W. (1998). Quality world and culture. *International Journal of Reality Therapy, 17*, 12–16.

Sanchez, W., & Thomas, D. (1998). The Americans with Disabilities Act: Meeting basic needs and quality world enhancement for people with disabilities. *International Journal of Reality Therapy, 18*, 12–17.

Saner, R. (1989). Culture bias of Gestalt therapy: Made-in-U.S.A. *Gestalt Journal, 12*(2), 57–71.

Sansone, D. (1998). Research, internal control, and choice theory: Where's the beef? *International Journal of Reality Therapy, 17*, 39–43.

Sapp, M. (1997). *Counseling and psychotherapy: Theories, associated research, and issues*. New York: University Press of American.

Sartre, J.-P. (1956). *Being and nothingness* (H. E. Barnes, Trans.). New York: Philosophical Library.

Satir, V. (1964). *Cojoint family therapy*. Palo Alto, CA: Science & Behavior Books.

Satir, V. (1964/1967). *Cojoint family therapy* (Rev. ed.). Palo Alto, CA: Science & Behavior Books.

Satir, V. (1972). *Peoplemaking*. Palo Alto, CA: Science & Behavior Books.

Satir, V. (1983a). *Helping families change*. New York: Aronson.

Satir, V. (2004). *Just a few sayings I made up*. Burien, WA: Avanta.

Satir, V., & Baldwin, M. (1984). *Satir step by step: A guide to creating change in families*. Palo Alto, CA: Science & Behavior Books.

Satir, V., & Bitter, J. R. (1991). The therapist and family therapy: Satir's human validation model. In A. M. Horne & J. L. Passmore (Ed.), *Family counseling and therapy*. Itasca, IL: Peacock.

Satir, V., Bitter, J. R., & Krestensen, K. K. (1988). Family reconstruction: The family within—A group experience. *Journal of Specialists in Group Work, 13*, 200–208.

Schwartz, B. (2004). *The paradox of choice*. New York: Ecco.

Scovel, K. A., Christensen, O. J., & England, J. T. (2002). Mental health counselors' perceptions regarding psychopharmacological prospective rights. *Journal of Mental Health Counseling, 24*(1), 36–50.

Seligman, L. (2001). *Systems, strategies, and skills in counseling and psychotherapy*. Upper Saddle River, NJ: Prentice-Hall.

Seligman, L. (2001). *Systems, strategies, and skills of counseling and psychotherapy*. Upper Saddle River, NJ: Merrill Prentice Hall.

Semmler, P. L., & Williams, C. B. (2000). Narrative therapy: A storied context for multicultural counseling. *Journal of Multicultural Counseling & Development, 28*, 51–61.

Shadish, W. R., & Baldwin, S. A. (2002). Meta-analysis of MFT interventions. In D. H. Sprenkle (Ed.), *Effectiveness research in marriage and family therapy* (pp. 339–370). Alexandria, VA: American Association for Marriage and Family Therapy.

Shapiro, F. (2001). *Eye movement desensitization and reprocessing* (2nd ed.). New York: Guilford Press.

Shaps, E. (2000). Community in school: A key to violence prevention. *Character Educator, 8*(2), 14–156.

Share, T. L., & Mintz, L. B. (2002). Differences between lesbians and heterosexual women in disordered eating and related attitudes. *Journal of Homosexuality, 42*(4), 89–106.

Sharf, R. S. (Ed.). (2004). *Theories of psychotherapy and counseling: Concepts and cases*. Pacific Grove, CA: Brooks/Cole.

Sharry, J., Madden, B., Darmody, M., & Miller, S. D. (2001). Giving our client the break: Applications of client-directed, outcome-informed clinical work. *Journal of Systematic Therapies, 20*, 68–76.

Shaver, P. R., & Mikulincer, M. (2005). Attachment theory and research: Resurrection of the psychodynamic approach to personality. *Journal of Research in Personality,* 22, 22–45.

Sherman, R. (1999). Family therapy: The art of integration. In R. Watts & J. Carlson (Eds.), *Interventions and strategies in counseling and psychotherapy* (pp. 101–134). Philadelphia: Taylor & Francis.

Shlien, J. M., Mosak, H. H., & Dreikurs, R. (1962). Effect of time limits: A comparison of two psychotherapies. *Journal of Counseling Psychology, 9,* 31–34.

Shore, K. (1998). Managed care and managed competition: A question of morality. In R. Small & L. Barnhill (Eds.), *Practicing in the new mental health marketplace: Ethical, legal, and moral issues.* Washington, DC: American Psychological Association.

Sichel, J., & Ellis, A. (1984). *RET self-help form.* New York: Institute for Rational-Emotive Therapy.

Siegel, D. J. (1999). *The developing mind: How relationships and the brain interact to shape who we are.* New York: Guilford.

Sifneos, P. (1972). *Short term psychotherapy and emotional crisis.* Cambridge: Harvard University Press.

Sifneos, P. (1979). *Short-term dynamic psychotherapy.* New York: Plenum.

Silvester, G. (1997). Appreciating indigenous knowledge in groups. In G. Monk, J. Winslade, K. Crocket, & D. Epston (Eds.), *Narrative therapy in practice: The archaeology of hope* (pp. 233–251). San Francisco: Jossey-Bass.

Simkin, J. S., & Yontef, G. M. (1984). Gestalt therapy. In R. J. Corsini & D. Wedding (Eds.), *Current psychotherapies* (3rd ed., pp. 279–319). Itasca, IL: Peacock.

Skeen, J. W. (1998). Choice theory balance and the values-based, mean approach to living well. *International Journal of Reality Therapy, 18,* 48–53.

Skinner, B. F. (1971). *Beyond freedom and dignity.* New York: Knopf.

Skinner, B. F. (1948, 1976). *Walden II.* New York: Macmillan.

Smith, E. W. L. (1976). The roots of Gestalt therapy. In E. W. L. Smith (Ed.), *The growing edge of Gestalt therapy* (pp. 3–36). New York: Brunner/Mazel.

Smith, M. L., & Glass, G. V. (1977). Meta-analysis of psychotherapy outcome studies. *American Psychologist, 32,* 752–760.

Smith, M. L., Glass, G. V., & Miller, T. I. (1980). *The benefits of psychotherapy.* Baltimore: Johns Hopkins University Press.

Solyom, L., Garza-Perez, J., Ledwidge, B. L., & Solyom, C. (1972). Paradoxical intention in the treatment of obsessive thoughts: A pilot study. *Comprehensive psychiatry, 13,* 291–297.

Sommers-Flanagan, J., & Sommers-Flanagan, R. (2004). *Counseling and psychotherapy theories in context and practice.* New York: Wiley.

Spear, J. (2003). *A pragmatic approach.* Retrieved February 7, 2003, from www.findarticles.com/cf_dls/g2699/0000/2699000035/ print.jtml

Sperry, L. (1999). Biopsychosocial therapy. *Journal of Individual Psychology, 55,* 535–563.

Sperry, L. (2003). Integrating spiritual direction functions in the practice of psychotherapy. *Journal of Psychology & Theology, 31*(1), 3–13.

Spiegler, M. D., & Guevremont, D. C. (1998). *Contemporary behavior therapy.* (3rd ed.). Pacific Grove, CA: Brooks/Cole.

Spielberger, C. D. (1988). *State-Trait Anger Expression Inventory.* Orlando, FL: Psychological Assessment Resources.

Spinelli, E. (1989). *The interpreted world.* London: Sage.

Spira, J. L. (1997). Existential group psychotherapy for advanced breast cancer and other life-threatening ilnesses. In J. L. Spira (Ed.), *Group therapy for medically ill patients* (pp. 165–222). New York: Guilford Press.

St. Clair, M. (2000). *Object relations and self psychology: An introduction* (3rd ed.). Belmont, WA: Wadsworth.

Stein, H. (2003). A questionnaire to save interview time in Adlerian brief therapy. Retrieved July 18, 2003, from our world.compuserve.com/homepages/ listein/ questbr.htm

Steinar, K. (2003). The psychoanalytical interview as inspiration for qualitative research. In P. Camic, J. Rhodes & L. Yaroley (Eds.), *Qualitative research in psychology: Expanding perspectives in methodology and design.* Washington, DC: American Psychological Association.

Stephenson, F. D. (Ed.). (1975). *Gestalt therapy primer.* Springfield, IL: Charles C. Thomas.

Stephenson, W. (1953). *The study of behavior: Q-technique and its methodology.* Chicago: University of Chicago Press.

Stewart, A. E., & Campbell, L. F. (1998). Validity and reliability of the White-Campbell Psychological Birth Order Inventory. *Journal of Individual Psychology, 54,* 41–61.

Stewart, A. E., Stewart, E. A., & Campbell, L. F. (2001). The relationship of psychological birth order to the family atmosphere and to personality. *Journal of Individual Psychology, 57*(4), 363–387.

Stewart, M., Brown, J. B., Weston, W. W., McWhinney, I. R., McWilliam, C. L., & Freeman, T. R. (1995). *Patient-centered medicine*. Thousand Oaks, CA: Sage.

Strasser, F., & Strasser, A. (1997). *Existential time-limited therapy*. New York: Wiley.

Strickland, T. L., Ranganath, V., Lin, K. M., Poland, R. E., Mendoza, R., & Smith, M.W. (1991). Psychopharmacologic considerations in the treatment of Black American populations. *Psychopharmacological Bulletin, 27*(4), 441–448.

Strupp, H. H. (1992). The future of psychodynamic psychotherapy. *Psychotherapy, 29*(1), 21–27.

Strupp, H. H., & Binder, J. L. (1984). *Psychotherapy in a new key*. New York: Basic Books.

Strupp, H. H., & Binder, J. L. (1984). *Psychotherapy in a new key: A guide to time-limited dynamic psychotherapy*. New York: Basic Books.

Stuart, R. B., Jayaratne, S., & Tripodi, T. (1976). Changing adolescent behaviour through reprogramming the behaviour of parents and teachers: An experimental evaluation. *Canadian Journal of Behavioral Science, 8*, 132–144.

Sturdivant, S. (1980). *Therapy with women: A feminist philosophy of treatment*. New York: Springer.

Sue, D. W., & Sue, D. (2003). *Counseling the culturally diverse: Theory and practice*. New York: Wiley.

Sue, D. W., Arredondo, P., & McDavis, R. J. (1992). Multicultural counseling competencies and standards: A call to the profession. *Journal of Multicultural Counseling & Development, 20*, 64–88.

Sue, D. W., Arrendondo, P., & McDavis, R. J. (1992). Multicultural competencies/standards: A call to the profession. *Journal of Counseling and Development, 70*(4), 477–486.

Sullivan, H. S. (1953). *The interpersonal theory of psychiatry*. New York: Norton.

Sullivan, H. S. (1962). *Schizophrenia as a human process*. New York: Norton.

Sullivan, K. T., & Goldschmidt, D. (2000). Implementation of empirically validated interventions in managed-care settings: The prevention and relationship enhancement program. *Professional Psychology: Research & Practice, 31*, 216–220.

Sulloway, F. J. (1996). *Born to rebel*. New York: Random House.

Sund, A. M., & Zeiner, P. (2002). Does extended medication with amphetamine or methylphenidate reduce growth in hyperactive children? *Nordic Journal of Psychiatry, 56*(1), 53–57.

Surrey, J. (1985). *Self-in-relation: A theory of women's development*. Work in Progress No. 13. Wellesley, MA: Stone Center for Developmental Services and Studies.

Sussman, L. K., Robins, L. N., & Earls, F. (1987). Treatment-seeking for depression by Black and White Americans. *Social Science & Medicine 24*(3), 187–196.

Swan, V. (1998). Narrative therapy, feminism, and race. In I. B. Seu & M. C. Heenan (Eds.), *Feminism and psychotherapy* (pp. 30–42). Thousand Oaks, CA: Sage.

Sweeney, T. J. (1998). *Adlerian counseling: A practitioner's approach* (4th ed.). Philadelphia: Accelerated Development.

Szasz, T. (2000). A plea for the cessation of the longest war of the twentieth century—The war on drugs. *Humanistic Psychologist, 28*(1), 67–78.

Szasz, T. S. (1960). The myth of mental illness. *American Psychologist, 15*, 113–118.

Talmon, M. (1990). *Single session therapy*. San Francisco: Jossey-Bass.

Tan, S.-Y. (2003). Integrating spiritual direction into psychotherapy. *Journal of Psychology and Theology, 31*(1), 14–23.

Task Force for the Development of Guidelines for the Provision of Humanistic Psychosocial Services. (1997). Training and ethics: Guidelines for humanistic practice. *Humanistic Psychologist, 25*(3), 309–317.

Taylor, J. (1992). *Where people fly and water runs uphill: Using dreams to tap the wisdom of the unconscious*. New York: Warner Books.

Teicher, M. H., Glod, C., & Cole, J. O. (1990). Emergence of intense preoccupation during fluoxetine treatment. *American Journal of Psychiatry, 147*(2), 207–210.

Teplin, L. A., Abram, K. M., McClelland, G. M., Dulcan, M. K., & Mericle, A. A. (2002). Psychiatric disorders in youth in juvenile detention. *Archives of General Psychiatry, 59*(12), 1133–1143.

Tervo, D. (2002). Physical process work with children and adolescents. In G. Wheeler & M. McConville (Eds.), *The heart of development: Gestalt approaches to working with children, adolescents, and their world* (vol. 1, pp. 113–146). Hillsdale, NJ: Analytic Press.

Thomas, V. (2002). Existential/experiential approaches to child and family psychotherapy. In R. Massey & S. D. Massey (Eds.), *Comprehensive handbook of psychotherapy* (vol. 3, pp. 83–107). New York: Wiley.

Thompson, L. (1992). Feminist methodology for family studies. *Journal of Marriage & the Family, 54*, 3–18.

Thorne, B. (1992). *Carl Rogers*. London: Sage.

Tohn, S. L., & Oshlag, J. A. (1996). Solution-focused therapy with mandated clients. In S. D. Miller, M. A. Hubble, & B. L. Duncan (Eds.), *Handbook of solution-focused brief therapy* (pp. 152–183). San Francisco: Jossey-Bass.

Trad, P. V. (1992). Editorial: Is the narrative a reliable method for conducting psychotherapy? *American Journal of Psychotherapy, 66*, 159–161.

Van Bilsen, H. P. (1991). Integrated treatment of social skill deficits in children from special education. *Kind en Adolescent, 12*(2), 78–86.

van Deurzen, E. (1997). *Everyday mysteries: Existential dimensions of psychotherapy*. London: Routledge.

van Deurzen, E. (2002). *Existential counseling and psychotherapy in practice* (2nd ed.). Thousand Oaks, CA: Sage.

Van Kalmthout, M. (1998). Person-centered theory as a system of meaning. In E. L. B. Thorne (Ed.), *Person-centered therapy: A European perspective* (pp. 11–22). London: Sage.

Varley, C. K., Vincent, J., Varley, P., & Calderon, R. (2001). Emergence of tics in children with attention deficit hyperactivity disorder treated with stimulant medications. *Comprehensive Psychiatry, 42*(3), 228–233.

Walker, A. (1983). *In search of our mother's gardens: Womanist prose*. New York: Harcourt, Brace, Jovanovich.

Walsh, F. (1998). *Strengthening family resistence*. New York: Guilford Press.

Wampold, B. F. (2001). *The great psychotherapy debate: Models, methods, and findings*. Mahwah, NJ: Erlbaum.

Watchtel, P. L., & Stanley, B. M. (Eds.) (1997). *Theories of psychotherapy: Origins and evolution*. Washington, DC: American Psychological Association.

Watkins, C. E., & Guarnaccia, C. A. (1999). The study of scientific Adlerian theory. In R. Watts & J. Carlson (Eds.), *Interventions and strategies in counseling and psychotherapy* (pp. 207–231). Philadelphia: Taylor & Francis.

Watson, M. E., & Buja, W. L. (1997). The application of reality therapy and choice theory in health care. *International Journal of Reality Therapy, 17*, 29–33.

Watts, R., & Carlson, J. (Eds.). (1999). *Interventions and strategies in counseling and psychotherapy*. Philadelphia: Taylor & Francis.

Weiland-Bolwing, S., Schindler-Zimmerman, T., & Carlson-Daniels, K. (2000). "Empower": A feminist consciousness-raising curriculum for adolescent women. *Journal of Child & Adolescent Group Therapy, 10*(1), 3–28.

Weingarten, K. (1998). The small and the ordinary: The daily practice of a postmodern narrative therapy. *Family Process, 37*, 2–15.

Weisz, J. R., Weiss, B., Han, S. S., Granger, D. A., & Morton, T. (1995). Effectiveness of psychotherapy with children and adolescents: A meta-analysis for clinicians. *Psychological Bulletin, 117*, 450–468.

Wessler, R. A., & Wessler, R. L. (1980). *The principles and practices of rational-emotive therapy*. San Francisco: Jossey-Bass.

Westen, D. (1998). The scientific legacy of Sigmund Freud: Toward a psychodynamically informed psychological science. *Psychological Bulletin, 124*, 333–371.

Wheeler, G. (1991). *Gestalt reconsidered: A new approach to contact and resistance*. New York: Gestalt Institute of Cleveland Press.

Wheeler, G., & Backman, S. (Eds.). (1994). *On intimate ground: A Gestalt approach to working with couples*. San Francisco: Jossey-Bass.

Whiston, S. C., & Sexton, T. L. (1993). An overview of psychotherapy outcome research: Implications for practice. *Professional Psychology: Research & Practice, 24*, 43–51.

White, J. (1999). *Overcoming generalized anxiety disorder: Therapist protocol*. Oakland, CA: New Harbinger.

White, M. (1995). *Re-authoring lives: Interviews and essays*. Adelaide, Australia: Dulwich Centre Publications.

White, M., & Epston, D. (1990). *Narrative means to therapeutic ends*. New York: Norton Press.

Wilens, T. E. (1999). *Straight talk about psychiatric medications for kids*. New York: Guilford Press.

Williams, G. R. (2000). The application of solution-focused brief therapy in a public school setting. *Family Journal: Counseling & Therapy for Couples & Families, 8*, 76–78.

Williams, R. J., & Chang, S. Y. (2000). A comprehensive and comparative review of adolescent substance abuse treatment outcome. *Clinical Psychology Science Practice, 7*, 138–166.

Wilson, S. A., Becker, L. A., & Tinker, R. H. (1995). Eye movement desensitization and reprocessing (EMDR) treatment for psychologically traumatized individuals. *Journal of Consulting & Clinical Psychology, 63*(6), 928–937.

Winnicott, D. W. (1965). *The maturational processes and facilitating environment*. New York: Basic Books.

Winnicott, D. W. (1971). *Playing and reality*. London: Tavistock.

Winnicott, D. W. (1975). Fear of breakdown. *International Review of Psychoanalysis, 1*, 103–107.

Winslade, J., & Chesire, A. (1997). School counseling in a narrative mode. In G. Monk, J. Winslade, K. Crocket, & D. Epston (Eds.), *Narrative therapy in practice: The archaeology of hope* (pp. 215–232). San Francisco: Jossey-Bass.

Winslade, J., Crocket, K., & Monk, G. (1997). The therapeutic relationship. In G. Monk, J. Winslade, K. Crocket, & D. Epston (Eds.), *Narrative therapy in practice: The archaeology of hope* (pp. 53–81). San Francisco: Jossey-Bass.

Wolf, D. (2000). *What is self psychology?*. Retrieved June 24, 2004, from www.selfpsychology.com/whatis/gossmannwolf.htm

Wolf, N. (1991). *The beauty myth*. New York: Doubleday Books.

Wolpe, J. (1958). *Psychotherapy by reciprocal inhibition*. Stanford CA: Stanford University Press.

Wolpe, J. (1990). *The practice of behavior therapy* (4th ed.). New York: Pergamon.

Worell, J., & Remer, P. (2003). *Feminist perspectives in therapy: Empowering diverse women* (2nd ed.). New York: Wiley.

Wubbolding, R. E. (1988). *Using reality therapy*. New York: Harper & Row.

Wubbolding, R. E. (1989). Radio station WDEP and other metaphors used in teaching reality therapy. *International Journal of Reality Therapy, 8*, 74–79.

Wubbolding, R. E. (1991). *Understanding reality therapy: A metaphorical approach*. New York: HarperPerennial.

Wubbolding, R. E. (2000). *Reality therapy for the 21st century*. Philadelphia: Brunner-Routledge.

Wubbolding, R. E. (2003). Reality therapy theory. In D. Capuzzi & D. R. Gross (Eds.), *Counseling and psychotherapy: Theories and interventions* (3rd ed., pp. 255–282). Upper Saddle River, NJ: Merrill Prentice Hall.

Wubbolding, R. E., & Brickell, J. (1998). Qualities of the reality therapist. *International Journal of Reality Therapy, 17*, 47–49.

Wubbolding, R. E., & Brickell, J. (2000). Misconceptions about reality therapy. *International Journal of Reality Therapy, 19*, 64–65.

Wubbolding, R. E., Brickell, J., Kakitani, M., Kim, R. I., Lennon, B., Lojk, L., et al. (1998). Multicultural awareness: Implications for reality therapy and choice theory. *International Journal of Reality Therapy, 17*, 4–6.

Wulf, R. (1998). The historical roots of Gestalt therapy theory. *Gestalt Journal, 21*(1), 81–92.

Yalom, I. (1980). *Existential psychotherapy*. New York: Basic Books.

Yalom, I. (1995). *The theory and practice of group psychotherapy* (4th ed.). New York: Basic Books.

Yalom, I. (1999). *Momma and the meaning of life: Tales of psychotherapy*. New York: Basic Books.

Yalom, I. D. (1989). *Love's executioner and other tales of psychotherapy*. New York: Basic Books.

Yalom, I. D. (1995). *The theory and practice of group psychotherapy*. New York: Basic Books.

Yalom, I. D. (1995). *Theory and practice of group psychotherapy* (3rd ed.). New York: Basic Books.

Yeung, F. K. C. (1999). The adaptation of solution-focused therapy in Chinese culture: A linguistic perspective. *Transcultural Psychiatry, 36*, 477–489.

Young, J. (2003). *Schema therapy*. Retrieved June 19, 2005, from www.schematherapy.com

Young, J. E. (1999). *Cognitive therapy for personality disorders: A schema-focused approach*. Sarasota, FL: Professional Resources Press.

Young, J. E., & Beck, A. T. (1980). *Development of an instrument for rating cognitive therapy: The Cognitive Therapy Rating Scale*. Philadelphia: University of Pennsylvania.

Young, M. E., & Long, L. L. (1998). *Counseling and therapy for couples*. Pacific Grove, CA: Brooks/Cole.

Young, S., & Holddorf, G. (2003). Using solution focused brief therapy in individual referrals for bullying. *Educational Psychology in Practice, 19*, 271–282.

Zarb, J. M. (1992). *Cognitive-behavioral assessment and therapy with adolescents*. New York: Brunner/Mazel.

Zimmerman, T. S., Jacobsen, R. B., Macintyre, M., & Watson, C. (1996). Solution-focused parenting groups: An empirical study. *Journal of Systematic Therapies, 15*, 12–25.

Zimring, F. M., & Raskin, N. J. (1992). Carl Rogers and client/person-centered therapy. In D. K. Freedheim (Ed.), *History of psychotherapy: A century of change* (pp. 629–656). Washington, DC: American Psychological Association.

Zinker, J. (1977). *Creative process in Gestalt therapy*. New York: Brunner/Mazel.

Zito, J. M., Safer, D. J., dosReis, S., & Riddle, M. A. (1998). Racial disparity in psychotropic medications prescribed for youths with Medicaid insurance in Maryland. *Journal of the American Academy of Child & Adolescent Psychiatry, 37*(2), 179–184.

Zweben, A. (2001). Integrating pharmacotherapy and psychosocial interventions in the treatment of individuals with alcohol problems. *Journal of Social Work Practice in the Addictions, 1*(3), 65–80.

Index

AA. See Alcoholics Anonymous
ABC theory, 271–72, 306–7
  see also Rational emotive
      behavior therapy (REBT)
Abilify, 454
Abortion, legalization of, 312
Abram, K.M., 464
Abuse, 229
  abusive men, 329
ACA. See American Counseling
  Association
Acting, 198, 206
Action stage, 7
Activating events, 271–72
  internal, 272
Activity scheduling, 290
ADA. See Americans with
  Disabilities Act
Adderall XR, 456
Addictions
  negative, 202
  positive, 203
Adesman, A., 458
ADHD. See Attention
  deficit/hyperactivity disorder
Adleman, J., 312
Adler, Alfred, 23, 23–24, 24, 64–95,
  65–67, 120, 342, 398
  see also Adlerian counseling
Adlerian counseling, 64–95, 225,
  258–59, 302, 341, 411, 472,
  474, 476
  acting as if, 81–82
  Adlerian systems theory, 86
  antisuggestion/paradoxical
      intention, 81
  assessment, 74–79
  avoiding the tar baby, 83
  brief therapy/managed care
      effectiveness, 118–19
  catching one's self, 82
  children/adolescents, 87
  counselor-client relationship, 74
  counselor's role, 74
  creating images, 83
  development of the theory, 66–67

encouragement, 80–81
evaluation of, 92–93
family constellation and
    atmosphere (birth order),
    69–70
family counseling/parenting,
    85–87
goals, 79
group work, 87–88
historical context, 65–66
integrating with other theories,
    89–90
life tasks, 72–74
lifestyle, 68–69, 76–78
mistaken beliefs, 72–73
multiculturalism and diversity
    effectiveness, 84–85
process of therapy, 79–80
psychology of use, 70–72
push buttons, 82–83
research, 90–91
setting tasks, 81
spitting in the client's soup,
    83–84
view of human nature, 67–68
see also Adler, Alfred
Adolescents, 39, 40, 115–16, 392
Adlerian counseling and, 87
behavior therapy and, 253–55
cognitive therapy, 299–300
family systems approaches, 379
feminist therapy and, 329–30
Gestalt therapy and, 187
narrative therapy and, 439,
    441–42
person-centered counseling and,
    104, 115–16
rational emotive behavior
    therapy (REBT) and, 299–300
reality therapy and, 194–95,
    213, 219
Adult development, 39
African Americans, 10, 14, 15, 78–79,
    84–85, 162–63, 228, 252, 402–3
communication and, 13
feminist therapy and, 310–11

person-centered counseling and,
    109–11
psychopharmacological
    (biological) approaches, 462
reality therapy and, 216
Afrocentric psychologists, 85
Aggression, 37
Aggressive responses, 249
Ainslie, R., 61
Ainsworth, Mary, 28
Ainsworth, M.D.S., 28
Ajmal, Y., 406
Akathesia (inner restlessness), 454
Alberti, R.E., 248, 256
Alcohol abuse, 112–14, 123, 182,
    228, 257, 433–35
Alcoholics Anonymous (AA), 7, 257
Allen, K.R., 334
Alpert, M.C., 46
Alternative discourse, 424
Alternative plots, 419
Altshuler, L., 458
Alzheimer's disease, 153
AMCD. See American Multicultural
    Counseling Division
American Association for Marriage
    and Family Therapy, 342–43
American Association of Marriage
    Counselors, 342
American Counseling Association
    (ACA), 14
American Family Therapy
    Association, 343
American Journal of Family Therapy,
    328
American Multicultural Counseling
    Division (AMCD), 14
American Psychological Association
    Division of Humanistic
        Psychology, 465
    Task Force on Promotion and
        Dissemination of Psychological
        Procedures, 414
Americans with Disabilities Act
    (ADA), 217
Amitriptyline (Elavil), 453

Amphetamines, 456
Amundson, J.K., 443
Anal-aggressive, 38
Anal phase, 38
Anal-retentive, 38
Analytical psychotherapy, 24
Andersen, T., 425, 426
Andreoli, A., 466
Angel, E., 149
Anorexia nervosa, 374
Antianxiety medications, 454–55
Anticonvulsants, 455–56, 461
Antipsychiatry movement, 132
Antipsychotics, 451, 453,
    454–55
Antisuggestion, 81
Antrobus, J.S., 52
Anxiety, 32, 34, 451
    existentialism and, 131, 136–37,
    149–50
Anxiety disorder, 296–97
Anxiolytics. See Antianxiety
    medications
Apperzeptionshema (schema
    of appreciation), 37
Arbitrary inference, 280
Arbuckle, D.S., 156
Archer, J., 52, 86, 245, 249, 331,
    448–69, 486
Archer, Jr., James, 448–69
Arezmendi, T.G., 121
Arlow, J.A., 44, 45, 46, 50, 59
Arnon, J., 461
Arrendondo, P., 14, 327
As if acting, 81–82
Ascher, L.M., 157
Asen, E., 375
Asian Americans, 14, 81–82, 84–85,
    228, 403
Assertiveness training, 248–49, 264
    feminist therapy, 325, 338–39
    see also Behavior therapy;
        Counterconditioning
Assessment
    Adlerian counseling, 74–79, 474
    behavior therapy, 240–43, 478
    cognitive therapy, 283–85, 478
    existential counseling, 141–145,
        475
    feminist therapy, 320, 478

Gestalt therapy, 176–78, 475
    humanistic experiential family
        therapy, 368–69
    intergenerational family systems
        therapy, 362
    narrative therapy, 427–28, 479
    person-centered counseling,
        107, 474
    psychoanalytic and psycho-
        dynamic theories, 43–44, 474
    psychopharmacological (bio-
        logical) approaches, 457–59
    rational emotive behavior
        therapy (REBT), 273
    reality therapy, 204–6, 475
    solution-focused therapy,
        392–93, 479
    strategic family therapy, 354
    structural family therapy, 348
Association for Multicultural Coun-
    seling and Development, 216
Atheistic existentialism, 131, 134
Ativan, 454
Atkinson, D., 12, 15, 16, 54, 315
Attachment theory, 27–28
Attention deficit/hyperactivity disorder
    (ADHD), 463–64, 466, 467
Atypical antipsychotics, 454
Austad, C.S., 8, 56, 57
Authentic living, 136
Automatic thoughts, 279–80, 283–84
    identifying, 288
Awareness journal, 193
Awfulising, 274
Axline, V.M., 115

Babins-Wagner, R., 329
Bachelder, B., 466
Bachrach, H., 58
Backman, S., 166, 186
Baldwin, M., 368, 369
Baldwin, S.A., 378
Balint, M., 119
Bandura, Albert, 234, 238–39
Banks, V., 404
Barrett-Lennard, G.T., 107, 108, 109
Baruth, L., 74
Basic Adlerian Scales for
    Interpersonal Success—Adult
    Form (BASIS-A), 90–91

BASIC ID (behavior, affect,
    sensations, images, cognitions,
    interpersonal relationships,
    drugs), 251–52
Basic needs, 101
BASIS-A. See Basic Adlerian Scales
    for Interpersonal Success—
    Adult Form
Bateson, Gregory, 132, 343
Bauer, G.P., 42, 43, 47, 57
BDI-II. See Beck Depression
    Inventory
Beardsley, R.S., 451
Beasely, C.M., 467
Bechtoldt, H., 5
Beck, Aaron, 89, 278–306, 389,
    443, 465
    see also Cognitive therapy
Beck, A.T., 89, 219, 225, 240, 241,
    267, 268, 278–306, 389,
    443, 465
Beck Depression Inventory (BDI-II),
    285
Beck Depression Inventory (BDI-III),
    240, 241
Beck Institute for Cognitive Therapy
    and Research, 278
Beck, Judith, 278
Becoming Partners: Marriage and Its
    Alternatives (Rogers), 115
Behavior, total, 200–201
Behavior medicine, 257
Behavior therapy, 5, 57, 120,
    232–65, 332–33, 410–11,
    444, 476, 478, 480
    Albert Bandura and social
        learning, 238–39
    assertiveness training, 248–49
    assessment, 240–43
    behavioral medicine, 257
    B.F. Skinner and operant
        (instrumental) conditioning,
        236–38
    brief therapy/managed care
        effectiveness, 258
    career counseling, 255–56
    children and adolescents, 253–55
    counselor-client relationship, 240
    counselor's role, 239–40
    couples and families, 258

in criminal justice systems,
    257–58
development of the theory, 234
evaluation of, 262–63
goals, 243
group work, 256
historical context, 233
integrating with other theories,
    258–59
Joseph Wolpe and classical
    conditioning, 235–36
multicultural and diversity
    effectiveness, 252–53
multimodal therapy, 250–52
prevention programs, 257
process of therapy, 243–44
research, 259–61
self-management, 249–50
stages of development, 234
for substance abuse, 357
systematic desensitization and
    relaxation methods, 244–47
view of human nature, 234–35
virtual reality exposure therapy,
    248
in vivo desensitization, 247–48
see also Cognitive therapy;
    Rational emotive behavior
    therapy (REBT)
Behavioral interview, 240–41
Behaviorists, 22
Behaviors, evaluation of, 210
Being and Nothingness (Sartre), 131
Being and Time (Heidegger), 130
Being-in-the-world (Dasein), 130, 135
Being mode, 25
Belangee, S., 91
Belenky, M., 314
Belief, 87
Bell curve, 220
Belonging need, 199–200, 220
Bem, S.L., 313
Benson, H., 244
Benzodiazepines, 454
Berenson, B.G., 122
Berg, I.K., 385, 387, 390, 391,
    393, 397, 399, 400, 401,
    405, 406, 410, 414
Berg, Insoo Kim, 385–417
    see also Solution-focused therapy

Bergin, A.E., 5
Bernauer, F., 121, 260
Beutler, L.E., 121
Beyebach, M., 409, 411
Beyond Freedom and Dignity
    (Skinner), 237
Bias, 327
    see also Diversity effectiveness;
        Multiculturalism
Bibbins, V.E., 10, 371
Bibliotherapy, 214
Biederman, J., 467
Biever, J., 412, 425, 426
Binder, J.L., 29, 42, 332
Binswager, L., 132, 135
Biochemistry of the brain,
    psychoactive medications and,
    450, 452–53
Biological causation, 228, 270
Biondi, M., 465
Bipolar disorder, 455–56, 461
    see also Manic-depressive disorder
Birth control pill, 311
Birth order, 69–70, 90, 94
Bitter, J.R., 88, 89, 370
Black-and-white thinking, 281
Blankstein, K.R., 285
Bloom, B., 44, 45, 46, 47, 485
Blum, S.A., 333
Bodin, Art, 387
Boeree, G., 65, 66
Borderline personality disorder, 27
Bosomworth, J.C., 467
Boss, M., 132, 135, 153
Boss management, 223
Boss, Medard, 132
Boundaries, families and, 346–47,
    383
Bowen, M., 344, 357–66, 358,
    359, 361, 363, 366, 410
    see also Intergenerational family
        systems therapy
Bowlby, J., 27, 28
Bozarth, J.D., 115
Brabeck, M., 318
Bradford, M.B., 11, 252
Brain chemistry, 450, 452–53
Brain injury, narrative therapy and,
    444–45
Braley, R.O., 464

Breaks, intervention, 401
Breggin, Peter, 465
Brenner, C., 40, 41, 51
Breuer, Josef, 23, 50
Brewer, T.L., 459
Brickell, J., 198, 203, 204
Brickman, P., 216
Brief dynamic theory, 43–45
Brief Family Therapy Center, 385,
    387, 411
Brief therapy, 8–9, 22, 485
    Adlerian counseling, 88–89, 476
    behavior, 244, 258, 480
    cognitive therapy, 302, 480
    existential counseling, 155–56,
        477
    family systems approaches, 376–77
    feminist, 331, 480
    Gestalt, 187, 477
    narrative therapy, 442, 481
    person-centered counseling,
        119–20, 476
    psychoanalytic and psycho-
        dynamic theory, 56–57, 476
    psychopharmacological
        (biological) approaches, 464
    rational emotive behavior
        therapy (REBT), 302
    reality therapy, 224–25, 477
    solution-focused therapy, 409, 481
    see also Managed care; Solution-
        focused therapy
Brief Therapy Center, 387
Brimhall, A.S., 440
Brody, C.M., 152, 153
Broverman, I.K., 337
Brown, G.K., 240
Brown, L.S., 313, 315, 317,
    318, 320, 331
Brownlee, K., 430, 436
Bruner, J., 421
Buber, M., 132, 137, 140, 165, 175
Bugental, J.F.T., 136, 137, 138, 140,
    141, 145, 146
Buja, W.L., 224
Burnand, Y., 466
Burns, R.K., 87
BURP, 88
Burt, V., 462
Butler, A.C., 303

Cabaniss, K., 487
Cade, John F., 451
Calderon, R., 456
Callanan, P., 16
Campbell, L.F., 5, 88, 90
Cangelosi, D.M., 54
Capitalism, 25
Career counseling, behavior therapy
    and, 255–56
Carkhuff, R.R., 118, 119, 120, 122,
    123, 124, 259
Carl Rogers on Encounter Groups
    (Rogers), 118
Carl Rogers on Personal Power
    (Rogers), 126
Carlson, C.I., 378, 380
Carlson-Daniels, K., 330
Carter, Betty, 377
Cartledge, G., 254
Cashdan, S., 26, 27
Castration anxiety, 38–39
Catching one's self, 82
Cats, counterconditioning, 236
Cause-and-effect approach, 71
CBIGT. See Cognitive-behavioral
    interactive group therapy
Celexa, 454
Center for the Studies of the Person,
    100
Chaney, S.E., 328
Chang, J., 403, 407
Chang, S.Y., 373
Change, stages of, 7
Change discourse, 394–97
Charcot, J., 23
Charting, 242–43
Cheong, E.S., 217
Chermak, G.D., 458
Chesire, A., 441
Chesler, P., 313
Cheston, S.E., 120
Cheung, S., 403
Children
    Adlerian counseling and, 87
    behavior therapy and, 253–55
    cognitive therapy and, 299–300
    feminist therapy and, 329–30
    Gestalt therapy and, 1873
    minority, 252–53
    narrative therapy and, 441–42

person-centered counseling and,
    115–16
rational emotive behavior
    therapy (REBT) and,
    299–300
reality therapy and, 219
socialization and gender-specific
    roles, 313–14
solution-focused therapy and,
    407–8
see also Play therapy
Children: The Challenge (Dreikus &
    Stolz), 86
Children's Depression Inventory, 254
Children's Yale-Brown Obsessive-
    Compulsive Scale, 254
Chinese, 9
    psychopharmacological
        (biological) approaches, 463
Chodorow, N., 314
Choice theory, 196
    see also Control theory; Reality
        therapy
*Choice Theory: A New Psychology
    of Personal Freedom* (Glasser),
    198, 201, 204, 214, 218
Christensen, L.L., 376
Christensen, O.J., 450
Ciotola, P.V., 464
Clark, D.A., 279
Clarke, K.M., 189, 190
Classical conditioning, 235–36
    see also Behavior therapy
Clemons, D., 412
Client, first use of term, 97
Client-centered counseling, 3,
    99, 409
    see also Person-centered
        counseling
Client-Centered Therapy (Rogers), 99
Clinchy, B., 314
*Clinical Treatment of the Problem
    Child* (Rogers), 99
Clinton, Bill, 429
Clozaril, 454
*Clues: Investigating Solutions in Brief
    Therapy* (de Shazer), 387
Coffey, E.P., 376
Cognitive-behavioral interactive
    group therapy (CBIGT), 301

Cognitive-behavioral therapy (CBT),
    6, 120, 225, 234–35, 268,
    291–97, 302, 443, 465, 466
    see also Behavior therapy;
        Cognitive therapy; Learning
        theory; Rational emotive
        behavior therapy (REBT)
Cognitive therapy, 5, 266, 278–306,
    410–11, 476, 478, 480
    assessment, 283–85
    automatic thoughts and
        schemas, 279–80, 288
    avoiding reattribution, 289
    brief therapy/managed care
        effectiveness, 302
    challenging maladaptive
        assumptions, 289–90
    children and adolescents
        counseling, 299–300
    cognitive-behavioral techniques
        (CBT)
    constructivist, 293
    eye movement desensitization
        reprocessing (EMDR), 294
    problem-solving therapy,
        294–96
    stress inoculation, 291–93
    treatment protocols, 296–97
    counselor-client relationship,
        282–83
    counselor's role, 282
    couples counseling, 298–99
    decatastrophizing, 289
    dysfunctional modes, 281
    evaluation of, 304–6
    family counseling, 299
    goals, 286–87
    group work, 300–301
    historical background,
        278–79
    integrating with other
        approaches, 302–3
    Jeffrey Young's expansion
        of schemas, 282
    modifying cognitions, 290–91
    multicultural and diversity
        effectiveness, 297
    process of therapy, 287
    research, 303–4
    thinking distortions, 280–81

using logical analysis, 288
view of human nature, 279
Cognitive triad, 280
Cohen, D., 467
Cohn, H.W., 141
Cole, J.O., 467
Collective unconscious, 24
Collectivist orientation, 13
Collins, P.H., 312
Collins, P.L., 197, 200
Comas-Díaz, L., 312, 315
Combined medical and behavioral
    psychosocial treatment, 466
Combs, G., 386, 421, 422, 423,
    424, 431, 433, 434, 435
Common factors approach, 3–4
Communication process, 87
Community involvement, 68
Compensatory model, 216
Competence talk, 395
Competency, 18
Competency Checklist for Cognitive
    Therapy, 305
Competency guidelines,
    multicultural, 14–15
Complementarity, 350
Compliments, 401
Computer applications, 487
Concerta, 456
Conditioned response (CR), 236
Conditioned stimulus (CS), 236
Conditioning, 234
    classical, 235–36
    operant (instrumental), 236–38
    see also Behavior therapy
Conditioning approaches stage, 234
Conditions of worth, 102–3
Confidentiality, 16
Confirmation, 141
Confluence, 173
Confrontation, 50
Congruence, 104, 106, 120
Conjugal therapy, 115
Conners' Rating Scale, 412
Consciousness Raising: A Primer
    for Multicultural Counseling
    (Parker), 16
Consciousness-raising groups,
    312, 324
Consequences, 214

Constructivism, 67, 89, 269–70,
    293, 388, 421–23
    see also Narrative therapy;
        Solution-focused therapy
Contact, 171–73
    avoidance of (defense
        mechanisms), 172–73
Contemplation stage, 7
Context-changing talk, 396–97
Control theory, 197–98
    see also Choice theory
Control Theory (Glasser), 197
Control Theory in the Classroom
    (Glasser), 217
Cook, J., 487
Cooper, A., 59, 60
Cooper, S., 331, 486
Coping questions, 400
Coping styles, 282
Corcoran, J., 402, 412
Corey, G., 16, 55, 56
Corey, M.S., 16
Counseling Across Cultures
    (Pederson), 16
Counseling American Minorities
    (Atkinson), 16
Counseling and Psychotherapy
    (Rogers), 99
Counseling approaches, summary
    and comparison of, 472–81
Counseling Diverse Populations
    (Atkinson & Hackett), 16
Counseling the Culturally Diverse:
    Theory and Practice (Sue &
    Sue), 16
Counseling with Choice Theory: The
    New Reality Therapy (Glasser),
    196, 199
Counselor-client-physician
    relationships, psycho-
    pharmacological (biological)
    approaches, 456
Counselor-client relationship
    Adlerian counseling, 74, 472
    behavior therapy, 240, 478
    cognitive therapy, 282–83, 478
    existentialism and, 140–41, 473
    feminist therapy, 319, 478
    Gestalt therapy, 175–76, 473
    narrative therapy, 427, 479

person-centered counseling,
    105–6, 472
psychoanalytic and psycho-
    dynamic theories, 42, 472
rational emotive behavior
    therapy (REBT), 273
reality therapy, 204, 473
solution-focused therapy,
    390–91, 479
Counselor training, person-centered,
    118–19
Counselors' roles
    Adlerian counseling, 74
    behavior therapy, 239–40
    cognitive therapy, 282
    existential counseling, 137–40
    feminist therapy, 318
    Gestalt therapy, 173–75
    narrative therapy, 425–26
    person-centered counseling,
        103–5
    psychoanalytic and psycho-
        dynamic theories, 41–42
    psychopharmacological
        (biological) approaches, 456
    rational emotive behavior
        therapy (REBT), 273
    reality therapy, 203
    solution-focused therapy, 390–91
Counterconditioning, 234, 235, 236
    see also Assertive training;
        Behavior therapy
Counterplots, 425
Countertransference, 41
Couples counseling
    behavior therapy, 258
    cognitive therapy, 298–99
    existential, 154–55
    family systems approaches, 372
    feminist therapy, 328
    Gestalt therapy, 183–84, 186–87
    narrative therapy, 440–41
    person-centered, 115
    rational emotive behavior
        therapy (REBT), 298–99
    reality therapy, 220–22
    solution-focused therapy, 405–6
CR. See Conditioned response
Crago, M., 121
Craig, P.E., 146

Criminal justice, psychopharmacological (biological) approaches, 464
Criminal justice settings, behavior therapy and, 252, 257–58
Crits-Christoph, P., 42, 59, 60
Crocket, K., 427
Crumbaugh, J.C., 141
CS. See Conditioned stimulus
Cuccaro, M.L., 462
Cuffe, S.P., 462
Cultural feminists, 316
Curlette, W.L., 91
Curtis, F., 184
Cushman, P., 129, 159
Cybernetic principles, 343

Dakof, G.A., 373
D'Andrea, M.D., 11, 13, 114, 152, 183, 252, 297, 403, 438
Dare, C., 374
Darmody, M., 401
Darwin, C., 21
Dasein (being-in-the-world), 130, 135
Dattilio, F.M., 298
Davanloo, H., 29, 42, 44, 46, 47
Davidoff, F., 119
Davidson, G.N.S., 372
Davidson, J., 285
Davis, A.Y., 312
Davis, T.E., 407
Davison, G., 263
de Jong, P., 387, 391, 393, 411
de la Rosa, I.A., 86
de Shazer, S., 385–417
    see also Solution-focused therapy
Deas, D., 373
Death, existentialism and, 131, 133–34, 136–37
Death instinct, 30
Decatastrophizing, 289
Deconstruction of the problem, 395–96
Deep muscle relaxation, 244–46, 264
Defense mechanisms, 32, 34–37, 63
    Gestalt, 172–73, 183, 192
    higher-order, 36–37
    primary, 35–36
Deflection, 172–73
Della Selva, P., 43, 45

Demystification of therapy, 326
Denial, 35
Depakote, 456
Depression, 229, 279–80, 303–4
    medication for, 451
Dereflection, 151
    see also Hyper-reflection
Dermer, S.B., 403
Desensitization, 236, 244–48, 260
    in vivo, 247–48
Desyrel (trazodone), 454
Detriangulation, 363, 365
Dettrick, C., 217
Devall, E., 86
Developmental theory, 9
Dexedrine, 456
Diagnostic and Statistical Manual of Mental Disorders (DSM), 12, 27, 141, 229, 240, 320, 427, 442
Dialessi, F., 206
Dialogue, 141
Dichotomous thinking, 281
DiClemente, C.C., 111
Diekstra, F.W., 303
Dierks, J.M., 188
Differentiation of self, 344, 358–59, 383
Dinkmeyer, D., 86, 87
Directives, 180–81
Discomfort disturbances, 270
Disconnected, 199–200
Disengaged boundaries, 347
Displacement, 36
Dissociation, 36
Diversity effectiveness, 9–16, 327–28
    Adlerian counseling, 84–85
    behavior therapy, 252–53
    cognitive therapy, 297
    existential counseling, 151–52
    family systems approaches, 371
    Gestalt therapy, 183–85
    narrative therapy, 437–38
    person-centered counseling, 114–15
    psychoanalytic and psycho-dynamic theories, 52–54
    rational emotive behavior therapy (REBT), 297
    reality therapy, 215–17
    solution-focused therapy, 402–3

Diversity issues, 9–16
    see also Multiculturalism
Division 35 (American Psychological Association), 312
Doan, R.E., 419, 420, 421, 424, 431, 432
Doctor and the Soul, The (Frankl), 132
Dogmatic demands, 274
Doing, 207, 209
    see also WDEP system
Dolan, Y.M., 392, 401, 404
Domestic violence, 373–74
Domestic violence shelters, 312
Dominant discourse, 424
Dominant plot, 419, 425
Dominant society, 15
Domokos-Cheng Ham, M., 371
Donati, R., 121, 260
Dopamine, 452, 453
Dornseif, B.E., 467
Dose response theory, 8
dosReis, S., 462
Double-bind communication, 343
Doyle, C., 487
Draguns, J.G., 15
Dream analysis, 51–52, 63
Dream workshops, 52
Dreams, 33, 142
Dreikurs, R., 67, 85, 86, 90
Dryden, W., 269, 270, 271, 273, 274, 298, 299
DSM. See Diagnostic and Statistical Manual of Mental Disorders
Dulcan, M.K., 454
Dulwich Center, 420
Duncan, B.L., 3, 5, 464
Dutton-Douglas, M.A., 312, 313, 315, 326, 331
Dynamic approach, 6
Dysfunctional modes, 281
D'Zurilla, T.J., 291, 294, 295

Earls, F., 462
Early childhood, 39
Early recollections, 77, 94
Eating disorders, 374–75
Eckstein, D., 74, 90
Eclectic/integrative therapists, 5
Edema, 451

Educational settings, person-centered counseling and, 116
Edwards, D., 91
Edwards, S., 441
Effect size, 226
Ego, 23–25, 30–33, 89
Ego disturbances, 270
Ego strength, 31
Eigenwelt (world of the self), 135, 142–45
Eisengart, S., 412, 414
Eisler, I., 374, 375
Elavil (amitriptyline), 453
Electra complex, 38, 39
Electroconvulsive therapy, 454
Eleftheriadou, Z., 152
Ellenberger, H.E., 149
Ellerman, C.P., 155
Elliott, Helen, 98
Elliott, R., 182
Ellis, Albert, 89, 225, 267–79, 298–306, 341, 443
   see also Rational emotive behavior therapy (REBT)
Ellman, S.J., 49, 50, 52
Ely, A.L., 115
EMDR. *See* Eye movement desensitization reprocessing
Emery, G.T., 280, 304
Emmons, M.L., 248, 256
Emotional cutoff, 361
Empathy, 104–5, 106, 112, 126, 174, 225, 318
Empirically validated treatments, 4
Empiricism, 419
Employee assistance programs, 223
Empowerment, 391, 401
   for women, 312, 323, 337–38
Empty chair, 181–82, 192
Enactment, 349
Encounter groups, 118
Encouragement, 80–81
Engels, G.I., 303
England, J.T., 450
Enguidanos, G., 312
Enjoyment need, 200, 220
Enmeshed boundaries, 347, 383
Enns, C.Z., 312, 314, 315, 316
Environmental adaptation, 235, 250, 253

Epstein, D., 298, 422
Epston, David, 332, 420–47
   see also Narrative therapy
Equal Pay Act (1963), 311
Equal Rights Amendment, 312
Erdman, P., 116
Erickson, M.H., 344, 351, 386
Erikson, E.H., 25, 39, 40
Erikson, J.M., 25, 39
Erikson's stages, 39–40
Esalen Institute, 165
Esman, A., 54, 55
Essential Attributes of Culturally Skilled Counselors (Association for Multicultural Counseling and Development), 216
Esser, U., 115
Etchison, M., 444, 445
Ethics, 16–18, 78
   defined, 16
   ethical codes, 16–17
   principles, 17–18
Evaluation, 207, 209–11
   Adlerian counseling, 92–93
   behavior therapy, 262–63
   cognitive therapy, 304–6
   existential counseling, 159–60
   family systems approaches, 380–81
   feminist therapy, 334–35
   Gestalt therapy, 190–91
   narrative therapy, 445–46
   person-centered counseling, 123–24
   psychoanalysis, 60–62
   rational emotive behavior therapy (REBT), 304–6
   reality therapy, 228–29
   solution-focused therapy, 414–15
   see also WDEP system
Everyday Mysteries: Existential Dimensions of Psychotherapy (van Deurzen), 133
Exception-finding questions, 399–400
Exception talk, 394–95, 416
Existence precedes essence, 129
Existentialism, 25

Existential counseling, 119, 128–61, 225–26, 411, 420, 421, 443, 458, 465, 473, 475, 477
   assessment, 141–45
   authentic living, 136
   being in the world, 135
   brief therapy and managed care effectiveness, 155–56
   counselor-client relationship, 140–41
   counselor's role, 137–40
   couples counseling, 154–55
   dereflection, 151
   development of the theory, 130–33
   evaluation of, 159–60
   existential (normal) and neurotic anxiety, 136–37
   goals, 145–46
   group counseling, 153–54, 158–59
   historical context, 129–30
   integrating with other approaches, 156
   medical patients, 153
   multicultural and diversity effectiveness, 151–52
   paradoxical intention, 149–50
   process of therapy, 146–48
   research, 157–59
   search for meaning, 137
   ultimate concerns of life, 133–34
   view of human nature, 133
Existential Counseling and Psychotherapy in Practice (van Deurzen), 133
Existential-humanistic theory, 6, 97, 100
Existential (normal) anxiety, 136–37
Existential philosophy, 130–31
Existential Psychotherapy (Yalom), 133
Expectancy effects, 3
Experiencing, 99–100
Explosive layer, 173, 185–86
External control psychology, 201, 220
Extinction, 237
Eye movement desensitization reprocessing (EMDR), 294

Fairbairn, W.R.D., 26, 27
False self, 26
Families, feminist therapy, 328
Family atmospheres (birth order), 69–70, 76–77, 94
Family counseling, 85–87
  behavior therapy, 258
  cognitive therapy, 299
  person-centered, 115
  rational emotive behavior therapy (REBT), 299
Family Healing (Minuchin & Nichols), 345
Family of origin, 365–66
Family projection process, 360
Family reconstruction, 370
Family rules, 368, 382
Family sculpting, 369–70, 383
Family Strengths Assessment (FSA), 412–13
Family structure, 346, 383
  see also Structural family therapy
Family systems approaches, 340–83, 410, 421
  brief therapy/managed care effectiveness, 376–77
  couples/marital counseling, 372
  development of the theory, 343–44
  domestic violence, 373–74
  eating disorders, 374–75
  evaluation of, 380–81
  historical context, 342–43
  integrating with other approaches, 377–78
  juvenile offenders and substance abuse, 373
  multicultural and diversity effectiveness, 371
  research, 378–80
  see also Humanistic experiential family therapy; Intergenerational family systems therapy; Strategic family therapy; Structural family therapy
Family systems therapist, 4, 6
Family therapy, narrative therapy, 438–40
Family Therapy Center, 420

Family Therapy Institute, 351
Faraone, S.V., 467
Farrell, W.C., Jr., 226
Fatal Attraction (film), 27
Faust, J., 298
Fava, M., 458
Favelle, G.K., 487
Feder, B., 186
Feedback, 117
Feeling, 198, 206
Feeling vocabulary, 125–26
Feiger, A., 461
Feldman, L.B., 466
Feminine Mystique, The (Friedan), 311, 320
Feminism, definitions of, 315
Feminist approaches, 120, 403
Feminist Family Therapy Behavioral Checklist (Chaney & Piercy), 328
Feminist perspective, 53, 57–58
Feminist supervision, 330–31
Feminist therapy, 310–39, 476, 478, 480
  assertiveness training, 325
  assessment, 320
  brief therapy/managed care effectiveness, 331
  children and adolescents, 329–30
  consciousness-raising groups, 324
  core concepts, 316–17
  counselor-client relationship, 319
  counselor's role, 318
  couples and families, 328
  demystification of therapy, 326
  development of the theory, 313–15
  evaluation of, 334–35
  feminist groups, 330
  feminist supervision, 330–31
  gender-role analysis, 324
  goals, 320–21
  historical context, 311–13
  integrating with other approaches, 332–33
  men, 328–29
  meta-assumptions, 317
  multicultural and diversity effectiveness, 327–28
  power analysis, 324

  process of therapy, 321–23
  reframing and relabeling, 325–26
  research, 333–34, 337–38
  stages of, 321–23
  view of human nature, 315
Feminist Therapy Institute, 315
Feminists, 344
  types of, 316
Ferguson, R., 187
Figure, 168–69
Figure/ground example, 168
First-generation antipsychotics, 454
Fischer, A.R., 333
Fish, J.M., 388
Fisher, S., 456
Fishman, C.H., 345, 348, 349, 350
Fixation, 37
Flowers, C., 91
Fluphenazine (Prolixin), 454
Focalin, 456
Folic acid, 458
Foucault, M., 420
Fowers, B.J., 130
Fox, G.L., 333, 334
Frank, J., 120
Frankl, V., 130, 132, 133, 137, 145, 146, 149, 150, 151, 152, 153, 156, 159
Franklin, C., 412
Franklin, M.E., 260–61
Free association, 23, 33, 63
Freedman, J., 386, 421, 422, 423, 424, 431, 433, 434, 435
Freedom, existentialism and, 134
Freedom need, 200, 220, 221
Freud, Anna, 24, 25, 34, 51, 54
Freud, Sigmund, 20–24, 29, 30, 31, 34, 38, 39, 61, 62, 66, 129–30, 133, 142, 159, 443
  Freud's stages, 38–39
  see also Psychoanalytic and psychodynamic theories
Freudian slips, 23, 30, 33
Frey, D.H., 149
Frey, L.L., 13
Friedan, Betty, 311, 320
Fromm, E., 24, 25
Frustration tolerance, 274

FSA. *See* Family Strengths
    Assessment
Fukuyama, M., 73
Fun need, 200, 220, 221
Future orientation, 388–89

GABA, 452, 456
Gains, maintaining and
    consolidating, 250
Galatzer-Levy, R.M., 58
Gameroff, M.J., 467
Ganas (survival need), 199
Gardner, B.C., 440, 441
Gardocki, G.J., 451
Garfield, S.L., 414
Garnefsky, N., 303
Garrison, C.Z., 462
Garza-Perez, J., 157
Gaston, L., 3
Gays, 13–14, 184, 299, 405–6
Geertjens, L., 116
Gelles, R.J., 373, 374
Gemeinschaftsgefuhl (part
    of the whole), 68
Gender-role analysis, 324
Gender-schema theory, 313
Gender-specific socialization,
    313–14
Genograms, 363–65, 377, 383
Genital phase, 39
Geodon, 454
Gergen, K., 420, 423
Germans, 399–402
Gerotranscendance, 39
*Gestalt Approach and Eye Witness
    to Therapy* (Perls), 166
Gestalt number four, 167–68
Gestalt prayer, 167, 184
Gestalt therapy, 120, 162–93, 224,
    303, 465, 473, 475, 477
    assessment, 176–78
    avoidance of contact (resistance),
        172–73
    brief therapy/managed care
        effectiveness, 187
    child and adolescent counseling,
        187
    clients talking to parts
        of themselves, 183
    contact, 171–72

counselor-client relationship,
    175–76
counselor's role, 173–75
couples work, 186–87
defense mechanisms, 172–73, 192
development of the theory,
    164–66
evaluation of, 190–91
figure and ground, 168–69
Gestalt defined, 164
Gestalt formation, 167–69
Gestalt number four, 167–68
Gestalt prayer, 167
giving directives, 180–81
goals, 178
group work, 185–86
historical context, 163–64
integrating with other
    approaches, 188–89
layers of neurosis, 173
multicultural and diversity
    effectiveness, 183–85
needs and unfinished business,
    169
playing the projection, 183
polarization, 170–71
present awareness, 171
process of therapy, 178–79
research, 189–90
staying with the feeling, 181
therapeutic techniques, 179–83
top dog and underdog, 170–71,
    177
using the empty chair, 181–82,
    192
view of human nature, 166–67
see also Perls, Fritz
*Gestalt Therapy: Excitement and
    Growth in Human Personality*
    (Perls, Hefferline, & Goodman),
    165
Gestalt Therapy Verbatim (Perls),
    166, 185
*Getting Together and Staying Together:
    Solving the Mystery of Marriage*
    (Glasser & Glasser), 214, 220
Gilligan, C., 314, 329
Gingerich, W., 412, 414
Gladding, S.T., 341, 342, 343, 351,
    352, 357, 366, 370, 374, 380

Glass, G.V., 121, 189, 260
Glasser, C., 206, 214, 220, 221
Glasser, William, 120, 195–229,
    410, 444
    see also Reality therapy
Glauser, A.S., 115
Glod, C., 467
Goals, 13–14
    Adlerian counseling, 79, 474
    behavior therapy, 243, 250,
        253, 478
    cognitive therapy, 286–87, 478
    existential counseling and,
        145–46, 475
    feminist therapy, 320–21, 478
    Gestalt therapy, 178, 475
    humanistic experiential family
        therapy, 368–69
    intergenerational family systems
        therapy, 362–63
    narrative therapy, 428, 479
    person-centered counseling,
        107–8, 474
    psychoanalytic and
        psychodynamic theories,
        43–44, 44–45, 474
    psychopharmacological (bio-
        logical) approaches, 457–59
    rational emotive behavior
        therapy (REBT), 273
    reality therapy, 206–7, 475
    solution-focused therapy, 393, 479
    strategic family therapy, 354
    structural family therapy,
        348–49
Goldberger, N., 314
Goldenberg, H., 341, 342, 344,
    354, 361, 367
Goldenberg, I., 153, 341, 342, 344,
    354, 361, 367
Goldfried, M., 2, 258, 259, 263
Goldman, A., 372
Goldschmidt, D., 376, 377
Goldstein, K., 101, 164
Goode, E., 278
Goodman, P., 163, 165
Gorrell, J.J., 171
Graham, P., 298
Granger, D.A., 121
Grawe, K., 121, 260

Greaves, D.W., 5
Green, R.J., 371
Greenberg, I., 372
Greenberg, L.S., 182, 188, 189, 190, 372
Greenberg, R., 450, 456
Greenberger, D., 288
Greene, B., 312
Gregg, G., 269
Gregoire, T., 154, 157
Grief counseling, 158–59
Griffin, W.A., 368
Grotevant, H.D., 378
Ground, 168–69
Group work
    Adlerian counseling, 87–88
    behavior therapy, 256
    cognitive therapy, 300
    existential counseling, 153–54
    feminist therapy, 330
    Gestalt therapy, 185–86
    narrative therapy, 442
    person-centered counseling, 116–17
    psychoanalytical and psychodynamic theory, 55–56
    rational emotive behavior therapy (REBT), 300
    reality therapy, 222–23
    solution-focused therapy, 404–5, 412–13
Guarnaccia, C.A., 91
Guerney, B.G., 115
Guevremont, D.C., 244
Guignon, C.B., 130
Guilliland, B.E., 249

Hackett, G., 15, 16, 54, 315
Haddock, S.A., 328
Haldol (haloperidol), 451, 454
Haley, Jay, 343, 344, 351–57, 377, 386
    see also Strategic family therapy
Haloperidol (Haldol), 454
Han, S.S., 121
Handbook of Counseling Women (Kopala and Keitel), 313
Hardwired response, 235
Hare-Mustin, R., 326, 344
Harman, B., 163

Harman, R., 185, 186, 189
Having mode, 25
Hawes, E., 69
Hawkes, D., 387, 388, 390, 400, 401, 404, 412
Health maintenance organizations (HMOs), 6
    see also Managed care
Healthy cultural paranoia, 216
Healthy culture paranoia, 216
Hefferline, R.F., 165
Heidegger, M., 130, 131
Helms, J.E., 316, 321
Hemesath, C.W., 403
Henderson, V.L., 97, 117
Hendrick, V., 461
Henggeler, S.W., 373
Henline, B., 440
Henrion, R., 141
Hersen, M., 254
Heslet, F.E., 149
Heterosexual married couples, 221–22, 440–41
Hevern, V.W., 444
Hidalgo, J., 451
High-low context communication, 13
Higher-order needs, 101
Hill, C.E., 259
Hill, M.S., 333
Hill, S., 364
Hillman, M., 149
Hirschfield, R.M., 461
Hispanic males, 241–43
Historical background of theories
    Adlerian counseling, 65–67, 472
    behavior therapy, 476
    cognitive therapy, 476
    existential counseling, 129–33, 473
    family systems approaches, 342–44
    feminist therapy, 311–15, 476
    Gestalt therapy, 163–66, 473
    narrative therapy, 419–21, 477
    person-centered counseling, 97–100, 472
    psychoanalytical and psychodynamic theory, 65–67, 472

psychopharmacological (biologic) approaches, 449–51
rational emotive behavior therapy (REBT), 268
reality therapy, 195–98, 473
solution-focused therapy, 385–87, 477
HMOs. See Health maintenance organizations
Human nature, behavior therapy view, 234–35
Hogan, B.A., 444
Holddorf, G., 408
Holism, 166
Holistic perspective, 67
Homeostasis, 343
Homework, 232, 245, 278, 290, 402
    see also Tasks
Hong, G.H., 371
hooks, b., 312, 315
Hopwood, L.E., 411
Horney, Karen, 24–25, 164
Horvath, A.O., 372
Hot seat, 185–86
Houston, G., 176, 177, 178, 183
Howard, D., 121, 327
Howard-Hamilton, M.F., 318, 335
Howatt, W.A., 196
Hoyt, M.F., 405, 406
Hubble, M.A., 3, 4, 5
Huffstetler, B.C., 206
Human identity model, 10–11
Human nature
    Adlerian view, 67–68, 472
    behavioral view, 476
    cognitive therapy view, 279, 476
    existential view, 133, 473
    feminist therapy view, 315, 476
    Gestalt view, 166–67, 473
    humanistic experiential family therapy view, 366
    intergenerational family systems therapy view, 358
    narrative therapy view, 421–22, 477
    person-centered approach view, 100–101, 472
    psychoanalytic and psychodynamic view, 29–31, 472

psychopharmacological
    (biologic) approaches view,
    451–52
rational emotive behavior
    therapy (REBT) view, 269–70
reality therapy view, 198–99,
    473
solution-focused therapy view,
    388, 477
strategic family therapy view,
    351–52
structural family therapy view,
    345
Humanism, 130
Humanist counseling, 97
Humanistic-existential theory, 268
Humanistic experiential family
    therapy, 366–71, 443
    assessment, goals, process
        of therapy, 368–69
    family balance, roles, communi-
        cation styles, 367–68
    family reconstruction, 370
    family sculpting, 369–70
    individual growth and
        development, 367
    seed model, 368
    therapeutic relationship, 368
    therapist touch and humor,
        370–71
    use of "I" statements, 369
    view of human nature, 366
Humanistic Psychologist, The
    (Breggin), 465
Humanistic therapists, 22
Humor, 215, 370–71
Hung-Hsiu Chiang, T., 403
Hunt, J., 119
Husserl, E., 130, 165
Hyper-reflection, 151
    see also Dereflection
Hypnosis, 23, 33, 386
Hypnotic induction, 245
Hypothesis testing, 290
Hysterics, 29

I-It mode, 140, 176
"I" statements, 369, 377
I-Thou relationship, 140–41
Id, 24, 30–32

Ideal self, 102
Identification, 33
Identified patient, 341
Identity crisis, 25
Identity Society, The (Glasser), 197, 199
Image creation, 83
Imipramine (Tofranil), 453
Impasse layer, 173, 185
Implosive layer, 185
In a Different Voice (Gilligan), 314
In vivo desensitization, 247–48
Incongruence (Rogers), 102, 103, 106
Indelicato, Natalie Arce, 310–39
Independence need, 200
Individual psychology, 66
    see also Adlerian counseling
Individuation, 46
Industrial Revolution, 129
Infancy, 39
Infant Strange Situation, 28
Inferiority, 68
Informed consent, 17–18
Inner restlessness (akathesia), 454
Instincts, 29–30
Instrumental (operant)
    conditioning, 236–38
Integration, of counseling theories,
    483–85
Integration stage, 234
Intellectualization, 37
Intensity, of therapists, 349
Intergenerational family systems
    therapy, 357–66
    assessment, goals, process
        of therapy, 362–63
    detriangulation, 363, 365
    differentiation of self, 358–59
    emotional cutoff, 361
    family projection process, 360
    genograms, 363–65
    multigenerational transmission
        process, 360
    nuclear family emotional system,
        359–60
    sibling position, 361
    societal emotional process, 361
    therapeutic relationship, 361–62
    triangulation, 359
    view of human nature, 358
    visiting family of origin, 365–66

Internal activating events, 272
International Journal
    of Psychoanalysis, 24
International Journal of Reality
    Therapy, 227
Interpersonal factors, 421
Interpersonal therapists, 5
Interpersonally based models, 42
Interpretation, 49–50
Interpretation of Dreams (Freud), 23
Intervention breaks, 401
Interventions, 374–75
    paradoxical, 355–57
Intrapsychic factors, 421
Introjection, 171, 172
Inventories, 241–42
    for children, 254
Involuntary clients, solution-
    focused therapy, 408–9
Irish, 83–84
Irrational behavior, 269–70,
    274–75, 306–7
    list of, 270, 275
Isolation, existentialism and, 134
Italians, 78–79
Ivey, A.E., 11, 16, 53, 114, 152,
    183, 185, 252, 297,
    403, 438
Ivey, M.B., 114, 403, 438

Jack, D.C., 314
Jackson, D., 314, 343, 386, 387
Jackson, L.C., 312
Jacobsen, R.B., 412
Jacobson, E., 244, 245
Jacques, P.F., 458
James, A.K., 249
Jaspers, Karl, 131, 132, 141
Jensen, J.P., 5, 6
Jensen, P.S., 467
Johnathan, A.L., 134, 135
Johnson, B., 462
Johnson, S., 331, 372
Johnson, Virginia Eshelman, 151
Jome, L.M., 333
Jones, A.C., 85
Jones, E., 23
Jordan, J.V., 314, 335
Josephson, A.M., 374
Josselson, R., 314

Journal of Counseling and Development, 14
Journal of Individual Psychology, 90
Joyce, D., 119
Jung, Carl, 23–24
Juvenile offenders, substance abuse and, 373

Kaiser Permanente, 376
Kaplan, A.G., 314, 335
Kaplan, H.I., 457, 461
Kaslow, F.W., 342, 343, 376
Kaufman, S., 87
Kaufman, W., 131
Kazdin, A., 244
Keitel, M.A., 313
Keith-Spiegel, P., 16
Keller, M.B., 465
Kelley, L., 404
Kelley, P., 421, 438, 442
Kelsch, D.M., 224
Kemph, J.P., 464
Kinetic family drawing, 87
Kenwright, M., 487
Kern, R., 91
Kerr, M., 361
Keskinen, S., 440
Kessell, M.J., 330
Keys to Solutions in Brief Therapy (de Shazer), 387, 411
Kierkegaard, Soren, 131, 133
Kim, K., 227
Kinesis, 13
Kirsch, I., 456
Kirschenbaum, H., 97, 117
Kivlighan, D.M., 59
Klein, Melanie, 26, 54
Kleist, D.M., 444, 445
Klerman, G.L., 25, 26, 42
Klonopin, 454
Knudson-Martin, C., 335
Kobos, J.C., 42, 43, 47, 57
Koestler, Arthur, 345
Koffka, Kurt, 163–64, 167
Kohler, Wolfgang, 164, 167
Kohut, H., 28
Kolatte, E., 466
Kondrat, M.E., 157
Koocher, G.P., 16, 364
Kopala, M., 313

Kopp, R., 88
Korb, M.P., 171, 173, 174, 175, 177, 178
Korean culture
    narrative therapy and, 418–19, 425–26
    reality therapy and, 217, 227
Kottman, T., 87
Krestensen, K.K., 370
Krumboltz, J.D., 255
Kupers, T.A., 327

L'Abate, L., 437
Laborit, Henri, 451
LaFromboise, T., 403
Laine, C., 119
Laing, P.D., 132
Laing, R.D., 132, 141
Laird, J.G., 371
Lamb, C., 2
Lambert, R., 91
Lamictal, 456
Lampe, R., 116
Lang, R.D., 100, 101
Language
    narrative therapy and, 423
    problem-saturated, 430
Lantz, J., 154, 155, 157, 160
Lapid, G., 184
Larsen, D.B., 451
Lasky, A., 88
Latent phase, 39
Later life, 40
Latin Americans, 14, 96–97, 228, 402–3, 433–35
Latner, J., 163, 166, 171, 172
Lawton, S., 441
Lazarus, A.A., 235, 250, 251, 252, 483
le Grange, D., 374, 375
Leadbeater, B.J.R., 329
Learning theory, 234–35, 244
    see also Behavioral therapy
Ledwidge, B.L., 157
Lee, M.Y., 411
Legowski, T., 430, 436
LeGrange, P.D.F., 374
Lemmon, C.R., 374
Lennon, B., 197, 198
Leonard, M.M., 316

Lerman, H., 317, 318, 320
Lerner, H., 114
Lesbians, 82, 147–48, 184, 299, 325
Levant, R.F., 115, 121, 329
Levenson, H., 42
Lewis, M., 386
Lexapro, 454, 457–58
Liberal feminists, 316
Libido, 37
Liddle, H.A., 373, 380
Lieberman, M.A., 118, 154, 158, 189
Life-affirmation, 131
Life Attitudes Profile-Revised (Reker), 141
Life Cycle Completed (Erikson & Erikson), 39
Life instinct, 30
Life tasks, 72–74
Lifestyle (Adlerian counseling), 68–69, 76–78, 95
Linnenberg, D.M., 217
Lipchik, E., 387, 388, 389, 390, 391, 394, 405
Lipkin, P., 458
Lithium, 451, 455–56
Little Albert studies, 236
Litz, R.W., 343
Litz, T., 343
Lock, J., 374, 375
Locke, D.C., 297
Locke, John, 164
Logic analysis, 288
Logical fallacy, 280
Logotherapy, 130, 132, 149, 152
Long Dark Road (Ainslie), 61
Long, J.K., 331
Long, L.L., 258
Long-term therapy, 8–9
Lonner, W.J., 15
Love need, 220
Love's Executioner and Other Tales of Psychotherapy (Yalom), 133
Luborsky, L., 42, 59, 60, 259
Luvox, 454
Lyons, L.C., 303

Maass, V., 330
Macintyre, M., 412
Mackewn, J., 166, 167, 183, 184
MacKune-Karrer, B., 377

MacPhee, D., 328
Madanes, C., 344, 351, 352, 355, 356, 357
Madden, B., 401
Magical thinking, 35
Magnification, 281
Mahler, M.S., 27, 102
Mahoney, A.R., 335
Mahrer, D., 74
Maintenance stage, 7
Maladaptive assumptions, 289–90
Maladaptive schemas, 282
Malan, D., 29, 42, 43, 45, 47
Malaria toxin, 451
Managed care effectiveness, 8–9, 22, 187, 485–86
    Adlerian counseling, 88–89
    behavior therapy, 258
    cognitive therapy, 302
    existential counseling, 155–56
    family systems approaches, 376–77
    feminist therapy, 331
    narrative therapy, 442
    person-centered counseling, 119–20
    psychoanalytic and psycho-dynamic theories, 56–57
    psychopharmacological (bio-logical) approaches, 450, 464
    rational emotive behavior therapy (REBT), 302
    reality therapy, 224–25
    solution-focused therapy, 409
    see also Brief therapy; Health maintenance organizations
Mania, 451
Maniacci, M., 66, 67, 68, 72, 73, 398
Manic-depressive disorder, 455–56
Mann, J., 29
Man's Search for Meaning (Frankl), 132, 137
MAOIs. See Monoamine oxidase inhibitors
Marcus, E.H., 178
Marcus, S.C., 467
Marecek, J., 326
Marinker, M., 119
Marital counseling, family systems approaches, 372

Marital rape laws, 312
Marks, I., 487
Marlyn, G., 329
Marsh, T.I., 387
Martin, J.C., 122
Marx, Karl, 25
Maslow, A., 101, 164, 165, 199
Maslow's hierarchy of needs, 100–101, 199
Masters, V.E., 151
Masters, W.H., 151
Masturbation, 38
Mataix-Cois, D., 487
Mattis, S.G., 255
May, R., 100, 129, 132, 135, 136, 137, 140, 142, 145, 146, 147, 149, 156, 165
Maynard, P.E., 373, 374
McClelland, G.M., 464
McDavis, R.J., 14, 327
McDonough, M., 487
McGregor, M., 329
McKay, G.D., 86
McKeel, A.J., 412
McKenzie, K., 425, 426
McKenzie, W., 424, 428, 429, 431
McKnight, J., 130, 159
McWilliams, N., 34, 35, 36, 37
Meador, B.D., 101, 105
Meakes, E., 438
Meaning, search for, 137
Meaninglessness, existentialism and, 134
Meara, N.M., 59
Mechanistic drive theory, 28
Medicaid, 462
Medical-diagnostic model, 457–61
Medical patients, existential counseling and, 153
Medical referrals, 458–61
Medicare, 450
Medications, 281
    classes of, 453–56
    see also Psychopharmacological (biological) approaches
Meditation, 203, 214–15, 244
Meichenbaum, D., 291, 293
Mellaril (thioridazine), 454
Melton, G.B., 373
Men, feminist therapy and, 328–29

Mental Health or Mental Illness? (Glasser), 197
Mental health stages, 202–3
    positive stages (positive addictions), 203
    regressive stages (negative addictions), 202
Mental Research Institute, 386–87
Mericle, A.A., 464
Merrill, K.A., 303
Meta-analysis, 121, 226, 260, 466
Meta-Cognitions Questionnaire, 285
Metaphors, 386, 436
    listening for, 215
Methylphenidate, 456
Metzger, B.L., 459
Mexican Americans, 72–73, 138–40, 205–6, 208–12, 384–85, 394–97
Mexican immigrants, 104–5
MI. See Motivational interviewing
Michel, D.M., 375
Mick, E., 467
Micro-skills training, 118
Middle age, 40
Middle child, 70
Mikulincer, M., 28
Milan group, 351
Milburn, J.F., 254
Miles, M., 118, 189
Miller, J.B., 314, 335
Miller, R.B., 376
Miller, S.D., 5, 390, 391, 392, 393, 400, 401
Miller, T.I., 121, 189, 260
Miller, W.R., 111, 112, 114
Mims, S.H., 206
Minimization, 281
Minority identity model, 15
Minuchin, S., 344–51, 373, 374, 377, 410
    see also Structural family therapy
Miracle questions, 398–99, 402, 407–9, 416
Missouri Psychoanalytic Counseling Research Project, 59
Mistaken beliefs, 72–73, 78
Mitchell, L.K., 255
Mittleman, Bela, 342
Mitwelt (social world), 135, 142

Model minority (Asian Americans), 228
Molnar, A., 402
Momma and the Meaning of Life: Tales of Psychotherapy (Yalom), 133
Monk, G., 422, 424, 427, 428, 429, 431
Monoamine oxidase inhibitors (MAOIs), 153–54
Monte, C.F., 97, 100
Montejo-Gonzalez, A.L., 461
Mood stabilizers, 455–56
Moore, K., 412
Moore, S.E., 216
Moradi, B., 333
Moral anxiety, 34
Morano, C.L., 298
Morejon, A.R., 409
Moreno, Jacob, 164
Morris, M.S., 458
Morrow County Sentinel, 466
Morton, T., 121
Mosak, H.H., 66, 67, 68, 72, 73, 83, 84, 90, 398
Motivation, 254–55
Motivational interviewing (MI), 7, 111–14
Moving away, 25
Moving towards, 25
Mullan, H., 154
Multicultural Competencies: A guide-book of Practices (Roysicar), 16
Multiculturalism, 6, 9–16, 482–83
  Adlerian counseling, 84–85, 474
  assessment, 12
  behavior therapy and, 252–53, 480
  cognitive therapy, 297, 480
  competency guidelines, 14–15
  counseling relationship, 14
  counseling with specific populations, 15–16
  existential counseling, 151–52, 475, 477
  family system approaches, 371
  feminist therapy, 327–28, 480
  Gestalt therapy, 183–85, 475, 477
  goals, 13–14
  models of, 10–12

narrative therapy and, 437–38, 481
  person-centered counseling, 114–15, 474
  process, 12–13
  psychoanalytic and psycho-dynamic theories, 52–54, 474
  psychopharmacological (biological) approaches, 462–63
  rational emotive behavior therapy (REBT), 297
  reality therapy, 215–17, 475, 477
  resources for counseling, 16
  solution-focused therapy, 402–3, 481
  see also Diversity issues
Multigenerational transmission process, 360, 383
Multimodal therapy, 250–52
Multiple family therapy, 375
Multisystemic therapy, 373
Multon, K.D., 59
Murdock, N.L., 354
Murphy, L., 226
Murry, V. M., 333, 334
"Musturbating", 298
My Life (Clinton), 429

Narcissism, 28
Narrative assumptions, 432
Narrative Means to Therapeutic Ends (White & Epston), 420, 438
Narrative therapy, 120, 332, 377, 418–47, 465, 477, 479, 481
  assessment, 427–28
  assumptions, 431–32
  brief therapy/managed care effectiveness, 442
  children and adolescents, 441–42
  counselor-client relationship, 427
  counselor's role, 425–26
  couples therapy, 440–41
  deconstruction, 425
  describing the problem, 428–30
  development of the theory, 420–21
  discourse, 424
  dominant plots and counterplots, 425

encouraging a wider perspective, 431
  evaluation of, 445–46
  family therapy, 438–40
  forming new narratives, 431–32
  goals, 428
  group work, 442
  historical context, 419–20
  integrating with other approaches, 443–44
  language and, 423
  metaphors, 436
  multicultural and diversity effectiveness, 437–38
  questions, 433–36
  realities are constituted through language, 423
  realities are organized and maintained through stories, 423–24
  realities are socially constructed, 422–23
  research, 444–45
  therapeutic documents, 436–37, 441–42, 447
  therapeutic writing, 436–37
  there are no essential truths, 424
  view of human nature, 421–22
Narrative Therapy: The Social Construction of Preferred Realities (Freedman & Combs), 422
National Institute of Mental Health (NIMH), 12
National Organization for Women (NOW), 311
Native Americans, 13, 83–85, 403
  psychopharmacological (biological) approaches, 462
Natural world (*Umwelt*), 135, 142–43, 145
Need-Strength Profile, 206, 220
Needs, 100–101
  basic needs, 199–200
  unfinished business and, 169
  see also Reality therapy
Negative addictions, 202
Negative reinforcement, 237
Neimeyer, R.A., 386, 445
Nelson, T.S., 404
Neo-Freudians, 24–26, 28

Neurologizing, 28
Neurons, 452
Neurotic anxiety, 34, 136–37
Neurotic layers, 173, 185–86
Neurotransmitters, 452–53
New Harbinger, 4
New School of Psychotherapy
     and Counseling, 133
Nezu, A.M., 291, 294, 295
Ng, K.S., 403
Nichols, M.P., 341, 342, 343, 344,
     345, 351, 360, 362, 370,
     374, 377
Nicoll, W.G., 69, 88
Nietzsche, Friedrich, 131
NIMH. See National Institute
     of Mental Health
Nonassertive (passive) responses, 249
Nondirective counseling, 98,
     109–11, 120
Nonsexist therapy, 316
Nontherapy factors, 3
Nonverbal communication, 193
Nonverbal cues, 13
Norcross, J.C., 5, 7, 111, 157, 158,
     364, 443, 483, 484
Norepinephrine, 452
Norepinephrine reuptake inhibitors
     (NRIs), 453–54
Nortriptyline (Pamelor), 453
NOW. See National Organization
     for Women
NRIs. See Norepinephrine reuptake
     inhibitors
Nuclear family emotional system,
     359–60
Nystul, M., 90

Oaklander, V., 187
Obsessive-compulsive disorder
     (OCD), 458
Object relations theory, 26–27
O'Brien, K.M., 259
Observational learning/modeling,
     238
Obsessive-compulsive disorder,
     treating with exposure/ritual
     prevention, 260–61
OCD. See Obsessive-compulsive
     disorder

O'Connell, B., 385, 389, 390–91,
     392, 394, 397, 398, 405
O'Connell, W.E., 88
O'Connor, T.S.J., 438
ODD. See Oppositional defiant
     disorder
Oedipus complex, 23, 26, 38,
     39, 47, 61
O'Hanlon, B., 387, 390, 393, 402
Oldest child, 70
Olfson, M., 467
Ollendick, T.H., 255
On Becoming a Person (Rogers),
     98–99
O'Neal, J.H., 453
O'Neill, C., 187
Opening space questioning, 434–35
Opening Up (Pennebaker), 437
Operant (instrumental) conditioning,
     234, 236–38, 249
     see also Behavior therapy
Oppositional defiant disorder
     (ODD), 464
Oral phase, 38
Ordeal directive, 357
Organismic valuing process
     (Rogers), 101
Organizational patterns, 87
Origin of Species (Darwin), 21
Orlinsky, D.E., 121
Ornoy, A., 461
Osborn, C.J., 407
Oshlag, J.A., 408
Osmond, M.W., 313, 334
Ossana, S.M., 316, 321
Outcome variance, 3
Overcoming Generalized Anxiety
     Disorder (White), 296
Overgeneralization, 280–81
Ozeki, T., 400

Padesky, C.A., 288
Paivio, S., 189
Pakistanis, 128–29
Palazzoli, Mara Selvini, 351
Palo Alto group, 344
Pamelor (nortriptyline), 453
Panic Appraisal Inventory and the
     Automatic Thoughts
     Questionnaire, 285

Panic attacks, 458
Papero, D.V., 358
Paradoxical intention, 81, 149–50
Paradoxical interventions, 355–57
Paralanguage, 13
Paranoia, healthy cultural, 216
Parenting, 85–87
Parenting and family task, 73
Parenting groups, solution-focused,
     412–13
Parenting Skills Inventory (PSI),
     412–13
Parker, W.M., 11, 16
Parry, A., 419
Part of the whole
     (gemeinschaftsgefuhl), 68
Passive-aggressive, 171
Passive responses, 249
Patient, use of term, 97
Patriarchal society, 312, 313
Patterns of Brief Therapy (de Shazer),
     387
Patterson, C.H., 107, 121
Patton, M.J., 59
Pavlov, Ivan, 234, 235–36, 259
Paxil, 454
Payne, M., 422, 425, 428, 429,
     430, 431, 433, 436
PBOI. See Psychological Birth Order
     Inventory
Pearce, S.S., 436
Pederson, P.B., 15, 16
Penis envy, 39, 61, 84
Penn State Worry Questionnaire, 285
Pennebaker, J.W., 437
Perls, Fritz, 120, 163–91
     see also Gestalt therapy
Perls, Laura Posner, 163–66
Person-centered counseling,
     96–126, 225, 258–59,
     472, 474, 476
     assessment, 107
     brief therapy/managed care
          effectiveness, 119–20
     children and adolescents, 115–16
     conditions of worth, 102–3
     counselor-client relationship,
          105–6
     counselor training, 118–19
     counselor's role, 103–5

Person-centered counseling (cont.)
  couples and family counseling,
    115
  development of the theory,
    98–100
  educational settings, 117
  evaluation of, 123–24
  goals, 107–8
  group work, 117–18
  historical context, 97–98
  integrating with other
    approaches, 120
  multicultural and diversity
    effectiveness, 114–15
  organismic valuing process, 101
  process of theory, 108–11
  research, 121–23
  self-actualizing tendency, 101
  self and ideal self, 102
  therapeutic techniques, 111–14
  view of human nature, 100–101
  see also Rogers, Carl
Personal anxiety hierarchy, 264
Personal behavior recording,
    242–43
Personal defense mechanisms, 63
Personal identity model, 10–11
"Personal is political", 312
Personal responsibility,
    184–85
Personalization, 281
Persons, J.B., 285
Phallic phase, 38–39
Phenomenological world, 174
Philadelphia Child Guidance center,
    351
Phobic layer, 173, 185
Phony layer, 173, 185
Physical abuse, 104
Physiology, 198, 206
Piaget, Jean, 25
Picardi, A., 465
Pichot, T., 392, 393, 401, 404
Pickering, M.R., 438
Picture of the world (Weltbild), 69,
    77–78
Piercy, F.P., 328
"Pigeonholing misery", 320
Pipher, M., 329
Placebo effects, 3

Plans, 207, 210, 211–12
  see also WDEP system
Platts, J.W., 299
Play therapy, 26, 54–55
Play Therapy (Axline), 115–16
Pleasure principle, 31–32
Pliszka, S.R., 454
Plots, 419–25
  see also Narrative therapy
Pokrywa, M.L., 5
Polarization, 170–71
Pollack, W.S., 329
Pollster, Irving, 166
Pollster, Miram, 166
Polster, E., 172, 179, 190
Polster, M., 172, 179, 190
Positive addictions, 203,
    214–15
Positive reinforcement, 237, 401
Positive stages, 203
Positivism, 269
Post-traumatic stress disorder, 294
Postmodern approaches, 120, 420,
    421, 423, 424, 444
  see also Narrative therapy;
    Solution-focused therapy
Postmodern-constructivist theory, 6
Postmodern philosophy, 385, 388
Power analysis, 324
Power Equity Guide (Haddock,
    Zimmerman, & MacPhee), 328
Power need, 200, 220, 221
Powers, W., 197
Practice of Behavior Therapy, The
    (Wolpe), 235
Precontemplation stage, 7
Preference questions, 435
"Preferred story", 429
Pregnancy, psychopharmacological
    (biological) approaches and,
    461–62
Preparation stage, 7
Preschool age, 40
Present awareness, 171
Present moment, 166
Preston, J., 453, 456, 467
Prevention programs, 257
Primary defenses, 35–36
Primary triad, 367
Private logic, 69

Problem-focused therapy, 387
  compared to solution-focused
    therapy, 390, 391
Problem-saturated language, 430
Problem-solving therapy, 294–96
Process variables, 122–23
Process of therapy, psychoanalytic
    and psychodynamic theories,
    43–49
Prochaska, J.O., 7, 111, 157, 158,
    443, 483, 484
Projection, 35, 172, 183, 360
Projective tests, 33
Prolixin (fluphenazine), 454
Prouty, A., 330, 331
Proxemics, 13
Prozac, 451, 454, 461
"Prozac Revolution", 451
PSI. See Parenting Skills Inventory
Psychoanalytic and psychodynamic
    theories, 20–63, 120, 225, 258,
    411, 443, 472, 474, 476
  anxiety, 34
  assessment, 43–44
  attachment theory, 27–28
  brief therapy and managed care
    effectiveness, 56–57
  counselor and client reactions,
    20–21
  counselor-client relationship, 42
  counselor's role, 41
  development of the theory,
    22–29
  dream analysis, 51–52, 63
  evaluation of, 60–62
  free association, 50–51, 63
  goals, 44–45
  group work, 55–56
  higher-order defenses,
    36–37, 63
    displacement, 36
    intellectualization, 37
    reaction formation, 37
    regression, 36–37
    repression, 36
    sublimation, 36
  historical context, 21–22
  integrating with other theories,
    57–58
  interpretation, 49–50

multiculturalism and diversity
effectiveness, 52–54
Neo-Freudians, 24–26
object relations theory, 26–27
personality structure, 31–33
play therapy, 54–55
primary defense mechanisms,
34–37, 63
denial, 35
dissociation, 36
projection, 35
process of therapy, 45–49
psychosexual stages, 37–40
research, 58–60
self psychology, 28
summary of, 28–29
summary of core concepts,
40–41
triangle of conflict, 47–48
triangle of person, 47–48
the unconscious, 33–34
the Vienna Psychoanalytical
Society, 23–24
view of human nature, 29–31
see also Freud, Sigmund
Psychodynamic theories, 6
defined, 23
see also Psychoanalytic and
psychodynamic theories
Psychodynamic therapists, 5
Psychological Birth Order Inventory
(PBOI), 90
Psychology of use, 70–72, 94
Psychopathology of Everyday Life
(Freud), 23
Psychopharmacological (biological)
approaches, 448–69, 486–87
antianxiety medications, 454
antidepressants, 453–54
antipsychotics, 454
assessment, goals, and process
of therapy, 457–59
biochemistry and psychoactive
medications, 452–53
brief therapy/managed care
effectiveness, 464
counselor-client-physician
relationships, 456–57
counselor's role, 456
criminal justice and, 464

development of, 451
evaluation of, 466–67
historical context, 449–50
integrating with counseling
theories, 464–65
medical referrals, 458–61
mood stabilizers, 455–56
multicultural applications,
462–63
pregnancy and, 461–62
research, 465–66
schools and, 463
sexual side effects, 461
side effects by drug class, 455
stimulants, 456
substance abuse and, 463
view of human nature, 451–52
Psychosexual stages, 37–40
Erikson's, 39–40
Freud's, 38–39
Psychotherapy by Reciprocal Inhibition
(Wolpe), 235
Psychotropic medications. See
Psychopharmacological
(biological) approaches
Puberty, 39
Public speaking phobia, 149–50
Pumariega, A.J., 462
Punishment, 237
Purpose in Life Test (Crumbaugh
and Henrion), 141
Push buttons, 82–83

Q-sort, 102
Quality schools, 218–19
Quality world, 200
Questions
coping, 400
exception-finding, 399–400
miracle, 398–99, 402, 407–9, 416
opening space questioning,
434–35
preference, 435
scaling, 400, 416
using, 212–13

Radical feminists, 316
Radtke, L., 226
Rank, O., 23, 24, 34
Rape, marital rape law, 312

Raskin, N.J., 98
Rating scales, 3
Ratings, 241–42
Rational behavior, 269
Rational Emotive Behavior Couples
Therapy (REBCT), 298–99
Rational emotive behavior therapy
(REBT), 266–79
ABC theory, 271–72, 275–77
assessment, 273–75
counselor-client relationship, 273
counselor's role, 273
development of, 268–69
goals, 275
historical context, 268
irrationalities (list of), 270, 275
process of therapy, 275
therapeutic techniques, 276–78
view of human nature, 269–70
see also Behavior therapy;
Cognitive therapy
Rational emotive therapy (RET), 269
Rave, E.J., 331
RBCP. See Responsible Behavior
Choice Programs
RCT. See Relational-cultural theory
Reaction formation, 37
Reality anxiety, 34
Reality principle, 32–33
Reality therapy, 57, 120, 194–231,
259, 410, 444, 473, 475, 477
assessment, 204–6
basic needs
belonging need, 199–200
freedom or independence, 200
fun or enjoyment need, 200
power need, 200
survival need, 199
brief therapy/managed care
effectiveness, 224–25
counselor-client relationship, 204
counselor's role, 203
couples counseling, 220–22
development of the theory,
196–98
evaluation of, 228–29
external control psychology, 201
goals, 206–7
group counseling, 222–23
historical context, 195–96

Reality therapy (cont.)
  integrating with other
      approaches, 225–26
  multicultural and diversity
      effectiveness, 215–17
  negative addictions, 202
  positive addictions, 203, 214–15
  process of therapy, 207
  quality world, 200
  research, 226–27
  school settings, 217–19
  therapeutic techniques, 212–15
  total behavior, 200–201
  view of human nature, 198–99
  WDEP system
      D (doing), 207, 209
      E (evaluation), 207, 209–11
      P (plans), 207, 211–12
      W (wants), 207–8
  work settings, 223–24
  see also Choice theory
Reality Therapy for the 21st Century
    (Wubbolding), 226
Reality Therapy (Glasser), 197
Reality Therapy in Action (Glasser),
    220
Reattribution, 289
REBCT. See Rational Emotive
    Behavior Couples Therapy
REBT. See Rational emotive behavior
    therapy
Reciprocal inhibition, 244
Referrals for medication, 458–61
Reframing, 325–26, 350–51
Regression, 36–37
Regressive stages, 202
Reich, W., 164, 165
Reinforcement, 234
    generating, 250
    negative, 237
    positive, 237
    schedules for, 237
    see also Behavior therapy
Reker, G.T., 141
Relabeling, 325–26
Relapse prevention, 287
Relational-cultural theory (RCT), 314
Relational theories, feminist therapy
    and, 314–15
Relationship factors, 3

Relative influence questioning, 433
Relaxation methods, 236, 244–47
Remer, P., 315, 320, 324, 336, 337
Remeron, 454
Repression, 32, 36
Reproduction of Mothering, The
    (Chodorow), 314
Research, 6–7
    Adlerian counseling, 90–91
    behavior therapy, 259–61
    cognitive therapy, 303–4
    existential counseling, 157–59
    family systems approaches,
        378–80
    feminist therapy, 333–34
    Gestalt therapy, 189–90
    person-centered counseling,
        121–23
    psychoanalytic and psycho-
        dynamic theories, 58–60
    psychopharmacological (bio-
        logical) approaches, 465–66
    rational emotive behavior
        therapy (REBT), 303–4
    reality therapy, 226–27
    solution-focused therapy, 411–14
Resistance, 172–73, 389–90
    see also Defense mechanisms
Resnick, R. J., 466
Resources, 16
RESPECTFUL model, 11
Responsible Behavior Choice
    Programs (RBCP), 227
Responsible Choices for Men, 329
RET Self-Help Form (Sichel and Ellis),
    275
Retroflection, 172
Reviving Ophelia: Saving the Selves of
    Adolescent Girls (Pipher), 329
Rhodes, J., 406
Rice, L.N., 182
Richardson, B.G., 219
Richardson, F.C., 130, 159
Richeport-Haley, M., 351
Riddle, M.A., 462
Rigazio-DiGilio, S.A., 297
Risk-taking exercises, 277
Risperdal, 454
Rita, E.S., Jr., 399, 402
Ritalin, 456

Rivett, M., 373
Robbins, M.S., 379
Robins, L.N., 462
Robinson, T.L., 318, 335
Rochlen, A., 487
Roe v. Wade, 312
Rogers, A.G., 329
Rogers, Carl, 3, 97–127, 174, 176,
    225, 263, 269, 342, 367, 433
    see also Person-centered
    counseling
Role-modeling, 234
Role-playing, 238–39, 290–91
Role-reversal, 277
Rollnick, S., 111, 112, 114
Ronall, R., 186
Root, M.P.P., 466
Rorschach inkblot, 33
Rose, S.D., 256, 301
Rosenberg, B., 408
Rosenberg, I.H., 458
Rosset, N., 466
Rounsville, B.J., 26, 42
Rowe, C.L., 380
Rowen, T., 300
Roysircar, G., 10, 16, 371
Running addiction, 203,
    214–15
Rush, A.J., 280, 304
Russel, G.F.M., 374
Russell, Bertrand, 236
Russell, C.S., 403

Sadock, B.J., 457, 461
Safer, D.J., 462
SAMI²C³ (simple, attainable,
    measurable, immediate,
    involved, controlled,
    committed, consistent),
    211–12
Sanau-Beckler, P. A., 86
Sanchez, W., 216, 217
Sandhu, D.S., 10
Saner, R., 184
Sansone, D., 227
Sapp, M., 164, 166, 172, 173, 184,
    185, 189, 226
Sapperstein, G., 456
Sarkis, Stephanie, 448–69
Sartre, J.P., 131

Satir, Virginia, 343, 366–71
    quotations from, 367
    see also Humanistic experiential
        family therapy
Sayler, M.E., 467
Scaling questions, 400, 416
Scamardo, M., 412
Schaps, E., 87
Schema domains, 282
Schema of appreciation
        (*apperzeptionshema*), 37
Schema therapy, 282
Schemas, 57, 279–80, 308
    Jeffrey Young's expansion of, 282
Schemas modes, 282
Schindler-Zimmerman, T., 330
Schizophrenia, 25, 228, 387, 451
Schizophrenic families, 343–44,
        351, 357
Schneider, I., 115
School age, 40
School counseling
    person-centered, 117
    solution-focused therapy, 406–8
School phobia, 255
School settings, reality therapy and,
        217–19
Schooling, 217–18
Schools
    psychopharmacological (bio-
        logical) approaches and, 463
    quality, 218–19
Schools Without Failure (Glasser), 217
Schuman, M., 438
Schwartz, B., 134
Schwartz, R.C., 341, 342, 343,
        344, 351, 360, 362, 370,
        374, 377
Scientific method, 419
Scovel, K.A., 450
Search for meaning, 137
Second child, 70
Second-generation antipsychotics,
        454
Sedating serotonin and
    norepinephrine reuptake
    inhibitors (SNRIs), 453–55
Seed model, 368
Seikel, J.A., 458
Selective abstraction, 280

Selective serotonin reuptake
    inhibitors (SSRIs), 451,
    453–55
Self, 102
Self-actualizing tendency, 101,
        111, 164
    limits to, 101–2
Self-assessment, 336–37
Self-concept, 69, 77
Self-disclosure, 14, 319, 327, 332
Self-efficacy, 239
Self-Efficacy (Bandura), 238
Self-help forms, 277
Self-ideal, 69, 77
Self-management, 249–50
Self-management approaches stage,
        234
Self/other downing, 274
Self psychology, 28
Self-reflection, 327
Self-statements, 308–9
Self task, 73
Selhub, J., 458
Seligman, L., 66, 269
Seniors, 429–30
Sensate focus, 151
Seroquel, 454
Serotonin, 452–53
Sevig, T., 73
Sex instinct, 29–30
Sex therapy, 299, 341
Sexism, in psychotherapy, 313
Sexual orientation, 15, 47–49
Sexual side effects (medication), 461
Shadish, W.R., 378
Shame-attacking, 277–78
Shannon, M.G., 368
Shaping, 237
Shapiro, F., 294
Sharf, R.S., 83
Sharry, J., 401
Shaver, P.R., 28
Shaw, B.F., 280, 304
Shechtman, S., 461
Sherman, R., 86
Shlien, J.M., 90, 121
Shore, K., 8
Short-term psychodynamic theory,
        41–42
Sibling position, 361

Sibling relationships, 69–70
Sichel, J., 275
Side effects
    of psychotropic drugs, 453–55
    sexual from medication, 461
Siegel, D.J., 27
Sifneos, P., 29
Silvester, G., 442
Simek-Morgan, L., 11, 114, 152,
        183, 252, 297, 403, 438
Simkin, J.S., 176
Simplicity, 390
Singer, B., 259
Singh, D. S., 371
Single-session approaches, 4
Single Session Therapy (Talmon), 387
Situation, 283–84
Situation, Automatic Thought,
        Emotion, Behavior assessment
        chart, 283–84
Skeen, J.W., 198
Skill development, 253
Skills acquisition, 292–93
Skinner, B.F., 234, 236–38, 249, 259
Skinner box, 236
Skolnikoff, A., 58
Smith, E.W.L., 165
Smith, L.A., 373
Smith, M.L., 121, 189, 260
SNRIs. *See* Sedating serotonin and
        norepinephrine reuptake
        inhibitors
Social anxiety disorder, 466
Social constructivism. *See*
        Constructivism; Solution-
        focused therapy
*Social Foundations of Thought and
        Action: A Social Cognitive Theory*
        (Bandura), 238
Social learning theory, 234, 238–39
    observational learning/modeling,
        238
    role playing, 238–39
    self-efficacy, 239
    see also Behavior therapy
Social Learning Theory (Bandura),
        238
Social skills training, 254
Social task, 73
Social world (*Mitwelt*), 135, 142

Socialist feminists, 316
Societal emotional process, 361
Society for Existential Analysis, 133
Socratic dialogue, 267, 282–83
Socratic method, 147–48
Soft determinism, 67
Solution discourse, 397
Solution-focused therapy, 120, 226,
    332, 376, 377, 384–417, 443,
    477, 479, 481
  assessment, 392–93
  brief therapy/managed care
    effectiveness, 409
  change discourse, 394–97
  change is inevitable, 389
  compared to problem-focused
    therapy, 390, 391
  compliments, 401
  coping questions, 400
  counselor-client relationship,
    390–91
  counselor's role, 390
  couples, 405–6
  development of the theory,
    386–87
  evaluation of, 414–15
  exception-finding questions,
    399–400, 416
  focusing on strengths, 389
  future orientation of, 388–89
  goals, 393
  groups, 404–5, 412–13
  historical context, 385–86
  integrating with other
    approaches, 409–11
  intervention breaks, 401
  involuntary clients, 408–9
  miracle questions, 398–99, 402,
    407–9, 416
  multicultural and diversity
    effectiveness, 402–3
  nothing is all negative, 389
  research, 411–14
  scaling questions, 400, 416
  school counseling, 406–8
  simplicity and, 390
  solution discourse, 397
  solutions are not necessarily
    related to the problem, 388
  strategy discourse, 398

  strengths, 416
  tasks (homework), 402
  there is no such thing as
    resistance, 389–90
  view of human nature, 388
Solution language, 416
Solyom, C., 157
Solyom, L., 157
Sommers-Flanagan, J., 202
Sommers-Flanagan, R., 202
"Special Techniques of Brief
    Hypnotherapy" (Erikson), 386
Spencer, T., 467
Sperry, L., 73, 87, 93
Speyer, C., 487
Spiegler, M.D., 244
Spinelli, E., 135
Spira, J.L., 153, 154
Spiritual dimension (Uberwelt), 135,
    142, 144–45
Spiritual task, 73
Spitting in the client's soup, 83
Spitzer, R.S., 166
Splitting, 26–27
Splitting behavior, 457
Springer, Shauna H., 310–39
SSRIs. See Selective serotonin
    reuptake inhibitors
Staying Together: The Control Theory
    Guide to a Lasting Marriage
    (Glasser), 220
Steer, R.A., 240, 279
Stein. H., 75
STEP. See Systematic Training
    and Effective Parenting
Stephenson, F.D., 173, 175
Stephenson, M., 412
Stephenson, W., 102
Stewart, A.E., 90
Stewart, K., 443
Stewart, M., 119
Stimulants, 455–56
Stimulus control, 237–38
Stiver, I.P., 314, 335
Stolz, V., 86
Stories
  development of, 435
  narrative therapy and, 423–24
  see also Narrative therapy
Story problems, 218

Stover, L., 115
Strasser, A., 140, 146, 155
Strasser, F., 140, 146, 155
Strategic family therapy, 351–57
  assessment, goals, process
    of therapy, 354
  brief therapy focused on the
    present, 353
  circularity, 353–54
  directives, 355
  ordeal directive, 357
  paradoxical interventions, 355–57
  redefining symptoms/problems,
    352–53
  symptoms as attempts at
    communication, 352
  therapeutic relationship, 354
  therapist responsibility, 352
  units, 353
  view of human nature, 351–52
Strategic Family Therapy (Madanes),
    351, 356
Strategic goal, 44–45
Strategy discourse, 398
Strengths, focusing on, 389, 416
Stress inoculation, 291–93
  self-statements, 308–9
Stress management, 244–48
Strickland, T.L., 462
Structural family therapy, 344–51
  assessment, 348
  complementarity, 350
  enactment, 349
  family structure, 346
  goals, 348–49
  intensity, 349
  process of therapy, 349
  reframing, 350–51
  subsystems and boundaries,
    346–47
  therapeutic relationship, 348
  unbalancing, 350
  view of human nature, 345
Structured reality therapy, 220
Strupp, H.H., 29, 42, 56,
    332
Sturdivant, S., 312
Subjective units of stress, 246
Sublimation, 36
Subplots, 419

Substance abuse, 216
    behavior therapy and, 257
    juvenile offenders and, 373
    psychopharmacological
        (biological) approaches and,
        463–64
    see also Alcohol abuse
Subsystems, of families, 346–47
Sue, D., 9, 10, 12, 13, 15, 16, 52,
    53, 84, 85, 462
Sue, D.W., 9, 10, 12, 13, 14, 15, 16,
    52, 53, 84, 85, 327, 462
Suicide, medications and, 467
Sullivan, H.S., 24, 25
Sullivan, K.T., 376, 377
Sund, A.M., 456
Superego, 24, 30, 31
Superiority, 68
Surrey, J., 314, 335
Survival need, 199, 220, 221
Sussman, L.K., 462
Swan, V., 421
Synapses, 452–53
Syphilis, 451
Systematic Training and Effective
    Parenting (STEP), 86
Systemic desensitization, 236, 260
Systemic model, 372
Systems approaches. See Family
    systems approaches
Szasz, T.S., 132, 141, 420

Tactical goal, 44–45
Talaga, M.C., 453
Talmon, M., 387
Tan, S.Y., 73
Tar baby (avoiding), 83
Tarule, J., 314
Task setting, 81
Tasks, 72–74, 402
    see also Homework
Taylor, J., 52
TCAs. See Tricyclic antidepressants
Tegretol, 456
Teicher, M.H., 467
Teleological orientation, 67
Teplin, L.A., 464
Tervo, D., 187
Theistic existentialism, 131
Thematic Apperception Test, 142

Theories
    defined, 2
    number of, 5
    types of, 5
Theories of Counseling and
    Psychotherapy: A Multicultural
    Approach (Ivey et al.), 16
Therapeutic alliance, 3
Therapeutic documents, 436–37,
    441–42, 447
Therapeutic process
    Adlerian counseling, 79–80, 474
    behavior therapy, 243–44, 478
    cognitive therapy, 287, 478
    existential counseling, 146–48,
        475
    feminist therapy, 321–23, 478
    Gestalt therapy, 178–79, 475
    humanistic experiential family
        therapy, 368–69
    intergenerational family systems
        therapy, 362–63
    narrative therapy, 428–32, 479
    person-centered counseling,
        107–10, 474
    psychoanalytic and psycho-
        dynamic theories, 45–49, 474
    psychopharmacological (bio-
        logical) approaches,
        457–59
    rational emotive behavior
        therapy (REBT), 273
    reality therapy, 207–12, 475
    solution-focused therapy,
        393–98, 479
    strategic family therapy, 354
    structural family therapy, 349
Therapeutic techniques
    Adlerian counseling, 80–84, 474
    behavior therapy, 480
    cognitive therapy, 287–97, 480
    existential counseling,
        149–51
    feminist therapy, 323–26, 480
    Gestalt therapy, 179–83
    intergenerational family systems
        therapy, 363–66
    narrative therapy, 432–37, 481
    person-centered counseling,
        110–13, 474

psychoanalytic and
        psychodynamic theories,
        49–52, 474
    psychopharmacological (bio-
        logical) approaches, 459–62
    rational emotive behavior
        therapy (REBT), 273
    reality therapy, 212–15
    solution-focused therapy,
        398–402, 481
    strategic family therapy, 355–57
    structural family therapy, 349–51
Therapeutic writing, 436–37
Therapist touch and humor, 370–71
Therrien, B., 459
Thinking, 198–99, 206
Thinking distortions, 280–81
Thioridazine (Mellaril), 454
Third force movement, 130
Thomas, D., 217
Thomas, S.E., 373
Thomas, V., 331, 441
Thompson, C.L., 206
Thompson, L., 334
Thorazine, 451
Thorndike, E.L., 234
Thorne, B., 123, 313, 334
Three Essays on the Theory
    of Sexuality (Freud), 21
Tillich, Paul, 132
Time-limited dynamic
    psychotherapy, 42, 332
TLC. See Total Learning Competency
Tofranil (imipramine), 453
Tohn, S.L., 408
Toilet training, 38
Token economies, 237, 252, 257–58
Tolbert, V.E., 303
Tolman, D.L., 329
Top dog, 170–71, 177
Total behavior, 200–201
Total Learning Competency (TLC),
    218
Touching, 370–71
Toward a New Psychology of Women
    (Miller), 314
Trad, P.V., 443, 446
Tranquilizers, 454–55
Transference, 41–42, 46
Transtheoretical model, 7

Trauma, 229
Trazodone (Desyrel), 454
Treatment protocols, 296–97
Tree branch analogy, 28
Triangle of conflict, 47–48
Triangle of person, 47–48
Triangulation, 359
Tricyclic antidepressants (TCAs), 451, 453, 455
Trileptal, 456
Trimble, J.E., 15
True self, 26
Trust, 180–81
Truths, 424
Tucker, E., 458
Turner, C.W., 379
Turner, R.M., 157
Tutty, L.M., 329
Tyranny of the trivial, 130

Uberwelt (spiritual dimension), 135, 142, 144–45
UCR. See Unconditioned response
UCS. See Unconditioned stimulus
Umwelt (natural world), 135, 142–43, 145
Unbalancing, family therapy and, 350
Unconditional positive regard, 103–4, 106, 120, 125
Unconditioned response (UCR), 236
Unconditioned stimulus (UCS), 235–36
Unconscious, 30, 33–34
Underdog, 170–71, 177
Unfinished business, 169, 193
Unhappy Teenagers: A Way for Parents and Teachers to Reach Them (Glasser), 214
Urban Girls: Resisting Stereotypes, Creating Identities (Leadbeater & Way), 329
Using Reality Therapy (Wubbolding), 220
Utilization principle, 344

Validation, 401
Valium, 451, 454
Values, 16–18
    defined, 16

Van Bilsen, H.P., 254
Van De Riet, V., 171
van Deurzen, E., 130, 132, 133, 135, 136, 137, 138, 142, 143, 146, 147, 156
Van Kalmthout, M., 114
Varley, C.K., 456
Varley, P., 456
Venturini, A., 466
Vienna Psychoanalytical Society, 23–24, 66
Vietnamese, 14, 136–37
Vincent, J., 456
Virtual reality exposure therapy, 248

Waaldijik, O., 116
Wachtel, P.L., 25
Wade, W.A., 303
Wagner-Jauregg, Julius, 451
WAIS. See Weschler Adult Intelligence Scales
Walco, G., 458
Walden II (Skinner), 237
Waldron, W., 58
Walker, Alice, 316
Walker, L., 312, 313, 315, 326
Waller, J.L., 462
Walsh, F., 86
Wampold, B.F., 471, 482, 486
Wants, 207–8, 210
    see also WDEP system
Watkins, C., 90, 107
Watson, C., 412
Watson, John, 234, 236
Watson, M.E., 224
Watzlawick, Paul, 387
Way, N., 329
WDEP system (wants, doing, evaluation, plans), 198, 208–12, 222
    see also Reality therapy
Weakland, J., 343, 387
Webber, Z., 443
Weiland-Bolwing, S., 330
Weiner-Davis, M., 387, 390, 393, 402
Weingarten, K., 419, 428
Weishar, M., 279, 280, 281, 282, 283, 285, 287, 288, 290, 291, 303, 305

Weiss, B., 121
Weissman, M.M., 25, 26, 42
Weisz, J.R., 121
Wellbutrin, 454
Weltbild (picture of the world), 69, 77–78
Wertheimer, Max, 163, 167
Weschler Adult Intelligence Scales (WAIS), 43
Westen, D., 28, 30, 33, 61, 62
Wheeler, G., 166, 171, 186
Wheeler, M.S., 91
Whitaker, L., 331, 486
White, J., 90
White, Michael, 332, 420–47
    see also Narrative therapy
Whites, 75–76, 180–82, 205–6, 208–12
    communication and, 13
Whittaker, M., 487
Whole person, 66
Wholeness, 169, 182
Wilens, T., 467
Wilgosh, R., 387
Willard, S.G., 375
William Glasser Institute, 196
Williams, G.R., 407
Williams, R.J., 373
Williamson, Y., 299
Winnicott, D.W., 26
Winslade, J., 427, 441
Wolf, D., 28
Wolf, N., 326
Wolpe, J., 234, 235, 236, 244, 245
Womanism, 315, 316
Women
    in 21st century, 312–13
    of color, 312, 316
    women's issues, 315
    see also Feminist therapy
Women and Madness (Chesler), 313
Women, Girls, and Psychotherapy: Reframing Resistance (Gilligan, Rogers, & Tolman), 329
Women's Group Therapy: Creative Challenges and Options (Maass), 330
Women's liberation movement, 248
Woodcock, J., 119

Woods, P., 303
Worell, J., 315, 320, 324, 336, 337
Work settings, reality therapy and, 223–24
Working Hypothesis (Schemata, Precipitants/Activating Situations, and Origins), 285
Working models, 27
Working through character change, 45–46
Works tasks, 72
World of the self (*Eigenwelt*), 135, 142–45
Wubbolding, Robert, 195–229

Wulf, R., 163, 164, 165
Wycoff, L.A., 5

Xanax, 454

Yalom, I.D., 56, 118, 129, 132, 133, 134, 135, 136, 137, 145, 147, 149, 153, 154, 156, 158, 189
Yontef, G.M., 166, 176
Young adulthood, 40
Young, Jeffrey, 282
Young, M.E., 258
Young, S., 408
Youngest child, 70

Zack, J., 487
Zarb, J.M., 300
Zeiner, P., 456
Zimmerman, T.S., 328, 412
Zimring, F.M., 98
Zindel, S.V., 285
Zinker, J., 174, 176, 180, 182, 184, 190
Zito, J.M., 462
Zoloft, 454
"Zooming out", 321, 325
Zweben, A., 463
Zyban, 454
Zyprexa, 454